The
Psychoanalytic
Vision

Also by Reuben Fine

The Personality of the Asthmatic Child (1948)

Freud: A Critical Reevaluation of His Theories (1962)

The Psychology of the Chess Player (1967)

The Healing of the Mind (1971)

Psychotherapy and the Social Order (editor) (1974)

Psychoanalytic Psychology (1975)

A History of Psychoanalysis (1979)

The Intimate Hour (1979)

The Psychoanalytic Vision

Reuben Fine

THE FREE PRESS
A Division of Macmillan Publishing Co., Inc.
NEW YORK

Collier Macmillan Publishers
LONDON

Copyright © 1981 by The Free Press
A Division of Macmillan Publishing Co., Inc.

The Free Press
A Division of Macmillan Publishing Co., Inc.
866 Third Avenue, New York, N. Y. 10022

Collier Macmillan Canada, Ltd.

Library of Congress Catalog Card Number: 80-2154

Printed in the United States of America

printing number

1 2 3 4 5 6 7 8 9 10

Library of Congress Cataloging in Publication Data

Fine, Reuben
     The psychoanalytic vision.

     Bibliography: p.
     Includes index.
     1. Psychoanalysis. 2. Psychoanalysis—Social aspects.
I. Title. [DNLM: 1. Psychoanalysis. 2. Social sciences.
WM 460 F495pa]
RC506.F424   150.19'52   80-2154
ISBN 0-02-910270-7

For Marcia
who helped me realize my vision of love

A conscience darkened

Either with its own or another's shame
Will find thy speaking to be very harsh.
Nevertheless, all falsehood put aside and
Make thy vision wholly manifest.
And let them scratch indeed where they itch.
For if the words thou sayest shall be unpleasant
At the first taste, life-giving nourishment
They shall become when they have been digested.

Dante: *Paradiso XVII*

The voice of the intellect is a soft one
but it does not rest until it has gained a hearing.

Freud: *The Future of an Illusion* (1927)

Contents

Preface   *xi*

Part I.   Introductory

Chapter 1.   The Central Argument   3
Chapter 2.   The Expansion of Horizons   9
Chapter 3.   Mainstream Psychoanalysis: A Statement of the Essentials   32

Part II.   The Social Sciences

Chapter 4.   The Vision of Experimental Psychology   75
Chapter 5.   The Vision of Organic Psychiatry   118
Chapter 6.   Toward Clarification in the Social Sciences   164
Chapter 7.   The Dilemmas of History   185
Chapter 8.   Society Versus the Individual: Sociology and Anthropology   213
Chapter 9.   The Myth of "Economic Man"   241
Chapter 10.   Believers and Skeptics: Religion and Philosophy   256
Chapter 11.   Creativity and Communication: Art and Language   273
Chapter 12.   The Complexities of Causation   291

Part III.   Psychotherapy

Chapter 13.   The Emergence of a New Profession   305
Chapter 14.   Vision Versus Technique: Psychotherapy and Social Reform   338

Chapter 15. The Half-trained Professions: Diplomas Instead of
Analysis   352

Chapter 16. The Meaning of Love in Human Experience   386

Chapter 17. Toward an Integrative Theory of Love   443

Part IV.   A Summing-up

Chapter 18. A Program for Progress and Reform   499

Notes   523
Bibliography   538
Index   565

Preface

MY MAIN PURPOSE in this book has been to spell out the revolutionary implications of psychoanalysis for man's welfare. This is what I call the psychoanalytic vision. Engrossed in the bitter internal battles under way on the contemporary mental health scene, even some leading practitioners and theoreticians tend to lose sight of the fundamental vision at the root of the extraordinary interest in the field expressed all over the world. My motto has always been that it is better to light a candle than to curse the darkness.

In a cynical world, which in so many ways seems to be coming closer to Orwell's grim prophecy in *1984*, a note of optimism and a message of cheer may seem Pollyannish or out of place. Yet the optimism is born of solid achievement. It is essential to highlight the positive side of the advance of psychoanalysis and to see how it can be used constructively as a guide for the future.

In my previous work *A History of Psychoanalysis* (Columbia University Press, 1979) I traced the growth of psychoanalysis in its first hundred years. Cool reflection on history can provide a much-needed perspective, which is frequently absent in the struggles of the moment. Somehow, in spite of everything, psychoanalysis has forged ahead to become one of the dominant intellectual forces of the twentieth century—in the field of man the most important of all. If it has survived excommunication, book-burning, and murder, surely we can expect that it will move on to much greater heights in the future.

In spite of its successes psychoanalysis has established itself most firmly only in relation to the three major mental health professions, psychiatry, psychology, and social work. Even though it lies at the heart of all of them, it still experiences the bitterest opposition from the leaders of these professions. Further, in the area of scientific understanding in the social sciences, its enormous contributions have scarcely begun to make themselves felt. These are paradoxes that call for some resolution.

After an introductory chapter that sums up the central argument, the book is divided into four sections. The first is historical, recapitulating the way in which the psychoanalytic vision grew in the minds of Freud and his followers. As I tried to show in my earlier historical book, the differences between Freudian and neo-Freudian psychoanalysis have been and are primarily of political importance; from a scientific point of view they fade into insignificance, so that we can talk of one basic discipline, mainstream psychoanalysis. But because of the numerous misunderstandings to which it has been subjected, mainstream psychoanalysis still requires some careful exposition, and this is the subject matter of Chapter 3.

A careful review of the past shows that psychoanalysis represents a quantum jump in the sciences of man. For apart from all the technical innovations, what Freud gave us was a new and different image of man. All previous thinkers, but especially the leading ones of the nineteenth century, had seen man as rational, conscious, and subject to the control of powerful external forces. The business of science then is to pinpoint these external forces, and in its applications to show how they can be used for man's betterment. Without denying that these external forces exist, what psychoanalysis adds is a different image as well: that man is irrational, unconscious, and subject to internal forces that can be brought to light through psychotherapy and transformed from neurotic drives for destruction and power into healthy ways of creating a freer, more conscious humanity, in Thomas Mann's memorable phrase. It follows that there is really only one science of man, based on psychoanalytic psychology, and one basic form of psychotherapy, with many variations. It is our job to clarify how this science of man can look and how psychotherapy can be made more effective.

In the succeeding sections the underlying visions of the various social sciences and forms of psychotherapy are brought into the light and carefully scrutinized. In the second part, psychology and psychiatry are examined. The vision of experimental psychology has been methodological experimentation; the vision of organic psychiatry has been that some day all of psychology will be reduced to more basic physiological explanations. In spite of the vociferous claims of its proponents, neither of these visions has prevailed. Less than 10 percent of psychologists today list themselves as experimentalists.

Organic psychiatry still remains powerful, yet its leaders freely admit that they have only a vague idea of what they are doing, and in their despair, as one man recently put it, console themselves with acts of private altruism. In the meantime there has been a strong revulsion against the widespread drug addiction that many physicians seem to wish to foist on their patients. Even Congressional committees have been appointed to investigate the complaint that we are turning into a nation of drug addicts.

The third section turns to the relationship between psychoanalysis and the social sciences. Here psychoanalysis has made the fewest inroads, even though its potential for making sense of these sciences is enormous. Furthermore, all of the social sciences (and humanities) have come under severe criticism from many quarters. Economists are faulted for their inability to stop stagflation; history becomes dull and uninteresting to college students unless the psychological factors are brought in, as in psychohistory; sociology seems to most people to be an abstract series of propositions of little import for the community; and so on. My thesis is that the inadequacy of the social sciences derives from adhering to a nineteenth-century image of man, which has prevented them from even grasping the implications of the Freudian twentieth-century image.

The fourth section takes up psychotherapy. It is shown first of all that psychotherapy could scarcely be said to have existed in any meaningful form before Freud. The need for psychotherapy has always been great, but before World War II, with its unspeakable horrors, that need was scarcely recognized. As a result the whole mental health profession, now numbering perhaps 200,000 in the United States, may be said to have been born after World War II. Freud's dream that he would turn over psychoanalysis to a new profession of lay curers of souls, who need not be doctors but should not be priests, has in a sense been realized, but not in the manner for which he had hoped. For of these 200,000 mental health professionals scarcely 10 percent may be said to be adequately trained; the rest acquire degrees that are largely irrelevant to the practice of psychotherapy and then do what they can.

To clarify what has happened in psychotherapy, I show how the older professions were suddenly called upon to minister to the emotional needs of a large part of the population. Since they were not prepared for this task in 1945 and did not accept psychoanalysis, they had to devise entirely new methods of training. The result has been highly unsatisfactory. I characterize this situation as one in which the half-trained professions competed (and compete) in a struggle for power.

At the same time the official psychoanalytic establishment, enmeshed in its own struggles for power, all too often has lost sight of the basic psychoanalytic vision. Briefly, this vision may be described as one in which a hate culture is transformed into a love culture. The central value of psychoanalysis is and always has been love. In order to make this clear several chapters provide an extensive discussion of the meaning of love in human experience and of how psychotherapy first helps the patient to see that what he or she has called love generally derives from unhappy infantile experiences, then goes on to help to build to a mature, gratifying kind of love.

A final chapter offers a summing up and proposals for progress and reform.

In a work of this magnitude, it seems inevitable that errors of fact and interpretation will creep in occasionally; if any such have been overlooked I beg forgiveness. But minor errors should not be allowed to detract attention from the main argument, which is consistently pursued throughout the entire book, that psychoanalysis represents the heart of psychology, that through psychology it leads to a sensible reorganization of all the social sciences, which should be combined into one science of man, and that it is the essential ingredient not only in classical psychoanalysis but also in all forms of psychotherapy.

In a sense this book represents my intellectual Odyssey. My earliest interest and training were in mathematics and philosophy. Among my teachers and inspirers were Morris Raphael Cohen, Ernest Nagel, and John Herman Randall. But it was not until I came to Freud and psychoanalysis during World War II that I could see a way out of the intellectual morass. While the bulk of my time since then has been spent as a practicing analyst, I have always retained my interest in the history of ideas and in the theoretical structure of the sciences of man. I have tried to keep up with the latest developments in all of them.

My particular thanks go to Gladys Topkis of The Free Press for her invaluable editorial encouragement and expertise.

REUBEN FINE
New York

Part I

Introductory

Chapter 1

The Central Argument

FOR SEVERAL DECADES psychoanalysis has been in the vanguard of Western intellectual thought. Yet, paradoxically, psychoanalysis as such does not have any status. Grafted onto the major professions of psychiatry, psychology, and social work, it has led an independent and conflict-ridden existence since its inception.

My purpose in this book is to place psychoanalysis in its proper historical and philosophical perspective. In a previous work, *A History of Psychoanalysis* (1979), I attempted to trace its history; here my concern is with its destiny.

Historically, psychoanalysis began as a narrowly specialized medical approach to the treatment of a peculiar malady known—and misnamed—since the time of the Greeks as hysteria.* Gradually it broadened to the point where Freud could say that he had all of mankind as his patient. Others have had similar ideas; what has to be considered is how the approaches have differed and what the special contribution of psychoanalysis has been.

The term "psychoanalysis" has become confusing. Originally it was adopted by Freud to differentiate his system from Janet's, who used the term "psychological analysis." By psychoanalysis Freud meant no more than that: psychological analysis in accordance with his assumptions and findings. Many first-class minds outside the field have a completely mistaken view of psychoanalysis,[1] and even many professional analysts are hard put to define the field correctly. One calls it a psychology of conflict, another a drive-reduction theory, a third attacks it as antifeminist, a fourth sees it as a highly eso-

---

*The term "hysteria" derives from the Greek word for uterus. Until Freud came along, it was widely and erroneously believed that the emotional and bodily manifestations described by the diagnosis of hysteria were literally due to some defect in the woman's womb. This has been shown to be a complete myth.

teric device practiced by a few select physicians. Few realize that psychoanalysis is essentially dynamic psychology. It is a systematic approach to psychology, the most scientific and the most systematic available on the present scene.

Central to psychoanalysis are a vision of what man is, a vision of what man might become, and a technique for transforming what man is into what he might become. Psychoanalysis, in Thomas Mann's memorable phrase, is a scientific system that carries with it the promise of a freer, more conscious humanity.

Because Freud played such a central role in the history of the field, it is first necessary to trace the development of the vision in his own mind. It was a slow growth, full of incredible insights and occasional unbelievable blunders (such as the death instinct). Throughout his writings ambivalences abound to such an extent that he may be called an ambivalent revolutionary. Still, the emergence of the central vision can be discerned in the total course of his writings.

During Freud's lifetime and after his death bitter struggles erupted that have played havoc with the vision. Psychoanalysis represents an intellectual revolution. As in other revolutions, the struggle against internal enemies has at times been as sanguinary as the struggle against external foes. In fact, at present the strongest opposition to the spread of psychoanalysis may be said to come from the official mental health professions. Thus Jacob Arlow, a leader in the field, has recently said:

> I have often said that [psychoanalysts] are like the hysterical patients. They suffer from reminiscences and they are in a large sense the captives of their own history . . . which really has been institutionalized in the training procedures. That is one of the great difficulties in the field, and it has led from, shall we say, a political point of view to the American Psychoanalytic Association making, I think, the wrong decision each time in regard to medicine, the community, the broadening of its approach, and so forth.[2]

Because of all the bitter battles the real nature of psychoanalysis has often been distorted beyond recognition. Freud himself never wrote a clear account of the field. Accordingly it is necessary to state the essentials. Because the notion of "schools" has been so highly misleading, I prefer to call this "mainstream psychoanalysis," deriving from Freud but varying from him in a number of ways. A chapter is devoted to an exposition of the core of mainstream psychoanalysis.

Psychoanalysis began in the 1890s, when the other social sciences also started their existence. From our present-day point of view psychology at that time was little more than sensory physiology. Accordingly, all the founders of the social sciences adopted the view of man prevalent in the nineteenth century. This is the common-sense position that man is rational, conscious, and subject to the control of powerful external forces. In conformity with this image, the task of the social sciences was seen as discovering what these external forces are and learning how to manage them.

In sharp contrast to this nineteenth century image is the discovery of psychoanalysis that in many cases man is unconscious, irrational, and subject to internal forces over which he can gain control by the process of psychotherapy. It is the clash of these two images that explains much of the intellectual history of the twentieth century. This clash will be traced in detail.

Closest to psychology is psychiatry, with its vision that the mentally ill are suffering from organic brain damage. Even though this organic assumption rests on quicksand, it retains a powerful hold on men's minds. In the hands of the organic psychiatrist the treatment of the mentally ill remains, as many of its leaders today continue to assert, a "national disgrace."

The vision of psychology in Freud's day was based on a methodological change—experimentation. Allied to the experimental method was the theory of behaviorism. Though this is still the dominant official position in most universities, a gradual rebellion against it has taken place, until today the American Psychological Association has more clinical-dynamic psychologists than experimental. A careful examination of behaviorism also reveals that it is a serious scientific blunder and has done untold damage to the advance of psychology.

Our attention next is to the other social sciences and the humanities. Successively, history, anthropology, sociology, economics, literature, and art are examined in the light of their underlying assumptions, findings, and overall achievements in the past century.

The first but not the last surprising discovery is that the very definition of these various fields is in serious dispute. The examination of the different fields shows that the controversies and difficulties of each stem in large part from the unwitting assumption of the nineteenth-century image of man. Where significant progress has been made, it is in the application of the findings of psychoanalytic psychology.

Thus the study of current patterns reveals that psychoanalysis is a dynamic psychology indispensable for the functioning of all the social sciences. Its proper application leads to a new synthesis, far more rewarding and fruitful than anything ever seen before.

Next we turn to questions of philosophy and religion, embodied in the question: How shall man live? It comes as no surprise to find that philosophers are agreed on virtually nothing. In part they have tackled problems that have been resolved by modern science, such as the nature of the outer world. In part they have offered a therapeutic approach, such as that of the Stoics, the Epicureans, or the modern existentialists. But it is shown that all of these therapeutic approaches lack an adequate psychological basis.

While religion has lost the hold it once had, it still remains important. The history of Christianity reveals many dark and sinister episodes. Even though they have largely been outgrown, the effects remain. One thesis offered is that Christian psychiatry, which persecuted helpless women ("witches") for several centuries, was a system of delusion, paranoia, and torture that continues in modified form in the Kraepelinian system and in contemporary organic psychiatry. The hold of religion seems to be due more to its psychotherapeutic aspect than to anything else.

From these theoretical considerations I turn to psychotherapy, the discovery of Freud and psychoanalysis. Few people realize that scientific psychotherapy scarcely existed before Freud. The recognition that psychotherapy, capable of making people happier, does exist had a significant impact on society. Yet the discovery was not accepted wholesale; in large sections of society and the world it was not accepted at all. The United States took the lead in the therapeutic revolution.

After World War II the patient population shifted. Instead of the traditional psychotics and severe neurotics, the entire country woke up to realize that everybody needed help. The essential difference was that between the maladjustment neurosis and the adjustment neurosis; the older distinction between "normality" and "neurosis" receded into the background. Instead of a few thousand helpless creatures, psychiatrists and other mental health professionals were confronted with millions of functioning human beings who demanded more out of life and who turned to psychotherapy in its many different forms to find it.

For the influx of such a large number of "patients" the professions were almost totally unprepared. An entirely new profession had to be created, that of mental health. While its practitioners still come primarily from the older, more established professions of psychiatry, psychology, and social work, an entirely new kind of wine has been poured into the old bottles. What is done today by the mental health professional has almost no relation to what was done fifty years ago. Patients by the millions, therapists numbering perhaps 200,000—this is the therapeutic scene today.

And what about training? Psychoanalytic training has been reasonably uniform since it started in Berlin in 1920. Above all it has emphasized the need of the therapist to achieve an inner change in his or her own life through personal analysis. The alternative model for training rests on the academic tradition, stressing the degree rather than the person. It was inevitable that with two such entirely different underlying philosophies, serious clashes would erupt. They still abound.

Since psychoanalytic training is long and costly, and was—for internal reasons—denied to many, the other professions as a rule came to oppose it. Once a person had a degree, he was free to practice as he pleased. This led to a phenomenon I call the "half-trained professions." They oppose psychoanalysis not because they have tried it and found it wanting but because they have never wanted to take the trouble to learn it.

However, in the meantime the power struggles in the field have also had their effect on psychoanalysis and psychoanalytic therapy. A long-term study by the American Psychoanalytic Association was unable to reach any meaningful conclusions about what analysts were doing with their patients (Hamburg, 1967).

Thus it is also necessary to clarify the essentials of psychotherapy. I propose that it centers on love as the major life experience of all human beings. An examination of the social sciences shows that ours is a hate culture and has been largely that from the time of the Greeks. The major interpersonal relationships are dominated by hatred rather than by love. However, while there is a preponderance of hatred, there are some outlets for love. Consequently most people have some love relationships before they come to therapy.

The problem is that by and large these love relationships have an infantile quality to them. Hence in psychotherapy the first inevitable step is to help the patient to see that previous love encounters have to be given up because they have been so unsatisfactory. But the next and equally important step is to help the patient reconstruct his or her life so that real love may enter the picture. Sometimes this occurs with the same partner, sometimes with another partner. But in all cases that go beyond the superficial, psychotherapy of the analytic variety strives toward the attainment of mature love.

With so vast a realm of data to assimilate, it is inevitable that errors of detail may have crept in here and there. For these I can only apologize and assure the reader that utmost care has been taken to check every fact. But any error should not be seized upon to obscure the main thesis: that the proper pursuit of the psychoanalytic vision can lead to one unified science of man, one main therapy with many offshoots, and the creation of a freer, happier humanity.

Chapter 2

The Expansion of Horizons

IN 1980 PSYCHOANALYSIS celebrated its hundredth birthday. Its birth is usually dated to 1880, when Anna O., the first psychoanalytic patient, was treated by Josef Breuer. In its first century it has provided a firm psychological grounding for the understanding of the mentally ill, has constructed an imposing dynamic approach to psychology, has created a new form of therapy, has established a new profession, has supplied a new and highly significant basis for all the sciences concerned with man, and has offered a scientifically based vision of how human happiness is attainable. How this has come about, in spite of the pitifully small numbers of fully trained analysts (fewer than ten thousand in the whole world) and the unconcealed hostility of the established professions of psychiatry, psychology, and social work, is certainly worthy of careful scrutiny.

Even today few people grasp the revolutionary changes brought about by Freud and his followers. So much heat is engendered by the warring camps that little light is allowed to shine through. It is essential to place psychoanalysis in its proper historical and philosophical perspective.

The Drama of Freud's Intellectual Development

Few sciences owe as much to a single individual as psychology does to Freud. He established the basic theory, created a novel form of therapy, established a wholly new profession, and expanded his findings in numerous directions. In evaluating psychoanalysis one must begin with a proper grasp of Freud's teachings. Unfortunately, the power struggles that have dominated much of the scene since his time have obscured both his fundamental strengths and his real weaknesses.

For in spite of his greatness Freud remained an ambivalent revolutionary. Instead of formulating the psychoanalytic vision clearly he allowed himself to be diverted for most of his last five years by a study of Moses. Instead of going on to social reform he lost himself in metapsychological jargon, which even his adherents could scarcely understand. Instead of seeing himself as a founder of psychology he retreated to physiology and biology, the "solid foundations" of his academic years. Instead of recognizing the awful depths to which sexual repression could drive the human being, he postulated a preposterous death instinct. And so it goes. Always great, always ambivalent—such is the saga of Freud's life and work. It is up to us, his heirs, to describe more plainly the extraordinary promise for the future that psychoanalysis offers.

The 1890s—Continuation of Nineteenth-Century Psychiatry

One reason the far-reaching implications of Freud's thought have so often been overlooked is that all the stages of his development have been lumped together. In part Freud himself is responsible for this misunderstanding, as he found it hard to admit that he had given up any position he once held. Furthermore, the most momentous aspect of the early period, his self-analysis, which went on from about 1895 to 1902, was never described by him at all. His official autobiography, published in 1925, is a cold, impersonal document, completely silent on the enormous struggles he went through to found psychoanalysis.

Freud's practice as a neurologist started in 1886, shortly after he was married. Up to about 1895, he did what the other neurologists of his day were doing—hypnotism, electrotherapy (weak faradic shocks, unlike the electroconvulsive therapy of today), suggestion, reassurance, massage, drugs, and the like. He published only a few papers and only one book, *Studies in Hysteria* (1895), in collaboration with his older mentor Josef Breuer, who was not even a psychiatrist. While the central ideas of psychoanalysis were mostly there—

repression, the unconscious, blocking of affect, abreaction, and the like—there were only two respects in which Freud's work differed from that of his contemporaries.

One was in his insistence on the basic significance of sexuality, still seen as genital sexuality at that time. "No neurosis with a normal sex life" became his slogan. Here he was going against the prevailing trend of his times, though there were many others who were also arguing for sexual freedom—Havelock Ellis in England and Iwan Bloch in Germany, for example, and even many feminists like Victoria Woodhull, who lived completely free sex lives out of rebellion against a warped society. The chief difference between Freud and the other sexual reformers was that Freud as a physician was able to show that sexual repression led to illness, while the others merely exhorted the world to have more sense.

Paradoxically, in the following decade, Freud modified and in some respects abandoned his extreme insistence on sexuality, while other aspects of his thought have been repudiated by later analysts. For example Freud in this period held to a theory, which he called "actual neurosis," that "faulty" sexual practices, such as complete abstinence, masturbation, or coitus interruptus, led to a transformation of sexuality into anxiety by some unexplained biochemical process. This theory has since been discarded, though what the effects of complete sexual abstinence are remains an open question.

The second difference between Freud and his colleagues was in his concept of defense. In the most significant paper of this period, "The Neuropsychoses of Defense" (1894), he put forth the novel theory that neurosis arose from the need to block out unbearable ideas from consciousness. This idea did contain the germ of later psychoanalytic theory, but it was not fully developed by him at that time.

Despite these advances, it must be remembered that in the 1890s no one seriously believed that psychology was of any value. Under the influence of the enormous advances in the physical and biochemical sciences, there was a general conviction that all mental and emotional disturbances were due to some biochemical or genetic abnormality, which science would sooner or later reveal. Freud was no different. It was a long time before he freed himself from the shackles of the assumptions of organic etiology, and even then such freeing occurred only gradually. Thus as late as 1908 he still referred to a possible organic factor in impotence,[1] while as late as 1911, long after he had discarded the diagnosis of neurasthenia, he spoke of separating the psychic and toxic factors in the illness.[2] In 1910 he still saw masturbation as harmful[3] and in general was prepared to assume "that psychic processes are added on to purely physiological ones."[4]

It is not surprising that the founder of psychology, like any child of his time, should have been obsessed with physiology. Besides, the body–mind problem is one that has concerned thoughtful men ever since they began to reflect on the human condition. But it is important to remember that what Freud gave us was essentially psychology, which he developed much more fully in his next period (1900–1914), and that his physiology, which was no different from that of anyone else of his day, in many respects has been superseded. What is usually forgotten is that there is no essential connection between his psychology and his physiology.

In fact, if Freud's own personality structure is examined, it becomes clear that on the one hand he was a great innovator, a *conquistador*, as he himself once put it, and that on the other he was fearful about going too far. Thus in most cases, whenever he proposed a new psychological approach, he would buttress it with some dubious physiological or biological reasoning. While psychology has remained, his physiology has been scrapped.

Self-Analysis (1895–1902): The Real Revolution

Had Freud stopped working in 1895, or continued to work in the same vein, he would have gone down in history as another of the many competent explorers in psychiatry of that day, along with Janet, Kraepelin, Bleuler, Bernheim, Beard, James, and many others. Instead, he pushed forward and embarked on the first successful self-analysis ever conducted.

That his self-analysis was the real turning point in the development of psychoanalysis has only gradually become apparent. For this there are a number of reasons. As I have noted, Freud never described it in detail; it has had to be reconstructed posthumously from his letters to Fliess and his other books and writings of that time. Second, because of an excess of modesty, he held to the illusion for quite a while that anybody could do what he had done; only after several decades did he conclude that no one else could conduct a self-analysis and that the attempt must be replaced by a personal analysis conducted by a more experienced analyst. Third, the arguments in favor of personal analysis often sound like arguments *ad hominem*, yet it is all too true that those who have not had any personal analysis still find it quite difficult to grasp the analytic hypotheses, much less discuss them intelligently. And, finally, psychoanalysis is an extraordinary experience carried out for the relief of suffering. Freud's jump from this relief to the formation of a science of psychology is hard to fathom, yet this is the jump that was made. And it was a quantum leap, a real turn in man's understanding of himself, far more important than anything Freud (or anyone else, for that matter) had done up to that point.

THE COURSE OF FREUD'S SELF-ANALYSIS

The monumental job of clarifying Freud's self-analysis has been accomplished by the French analyst Didier Anzieu, who pieced all the available scraps of information together to form a coherent account of Freud's internal growth. Anzieu's book, in two volumes, and running to some 853 pages, was published in French in 1975.[5] His account is followed here.

When Freud began his self-analysis he was thirty-nine years old, in the best of health, father of five children with a sixth (Anna, who later became his favorite) on the way, a practicing physician, and a member of the faculty of the University of Vienna, then probably the most prestigious medical school in the world. Why then should he have bothered to analyze himself? Primarily, one could say, because of dissatisfaction with himself: The favorite son of a young mother and older father, he was always intensely ambitious; yet fame and fortune had eluded him. That is certainly true, but the same could be said of thousands of gifted men throughout the centuries. The self-analysis was a stroke of genius, really defying further explanation. Once done, it opened a whole new world for mankind.

Freud began with a dream about a patient, Irma. He kept a record of the date, July 24, 1895, when the secret of the dream was suddenly revealed to him at the Bellevue, a section of Vienna. (His hope that some day a tablet would be erected at this spot, recording the fact that it was here that the secret of the dream was revealed to him, has since been realized by the recently formed Sigmund Freud Gesellschaft.)

The most important contribution of this dream was Freud's demonstration that a dream is intelligible in terms of the associations of the dreamer. As Freud once put it, poets and writers had always known about the unconscious but it remained for him to devise a method that would allow scientists to penetrate into the unconscious. In this way the analysis of a dream, later extended to any fantasy production, became the basis for an entirely novel approach to psychology. Freud also showed that the relationship between the patient and the doctor, later to be called transference and countertransference, is of prime importance in all psychotherapy. Eventually he made it clear that the exploration of this relationship is the core of every therapeutic encounter.

After the discovery that dreams have meaning which can be deciphered by a systematic approach to the material, he came upon his Oedipus complex, the wish to kill his father and marry his mother. This was followed by his recognition of the significance of the primal scene, the first time the child observes or imagines parental intercourse.

After the primal scene came the awareness of the importance of castration anxiety. There ensued the elaboration of other aspects of what he came to call infantile sexuality, or psychosexual development in the first five years of life. With these discoveries he was able to break the transference to Fliess, the Berlin ear, nose, and throat specialist from whom he expected the gift of fundamental biological knowledge on which to base his psychological theories.

Set down in cold print, all this seems trivial, especially since it is so familiar to us nowadays. But the seven years it took Freud to reach these conclusions can by no means be considered excessive for such a pioneer labor. Unknown thousands had tried before him and had failed. The self-analysis was the acorn; now the oak could grow.

Naturally Freud's self-analysis had many omissions as well. The social milieu was ignored. Discussion of group behavior was absent. He said nothing about his feelings about his children and scarcely considered his current situation. The role of sexuality loomed much larger than the role of aggression, a one-sidedness he was later to correct, in 1920. Nevertheless, once the initial step was taken, showing that analysis was possible by means of dreams, childhood memories, and free associations, the various refinements could be introduced.

Freud's last published dream is of particular interest because of the light it sheds on his attitude toward action, an attitude that was later to have serious repercussions in the analytic organizations. The dream, which he had in 1900,[6] was published in the popular work *On Dreams*, a short book that Freud wrote subsequent to his major

publication on *The Interpretation of Dreams* (1900). He described
the dream as follows:

> Company at table or *table d'hôte*. . . . Frau E. L. was sitting beside me.
> She turns her whole attention to me and lays her hand on my knee in
> an intimate manner. I removed her hand defensively. She then said:
> "But you've always had such beautiful eyes." . . . I then had an indis-
> tinct picture of two eyes, as though it were a drawing or the outline of
> a pair of spectacles.[7]

The dream shows that with Freud, as with other men, action became equated with sexual activity. Freud wished to attract the woman and then push her away, replacing her with a picture or (later) a
book. Erikson has made the point that Freud replaced the woman
with the dream.[8] That is certainly true. Yet more broadly Freud revealed here his fear of action. The analytic situation then became the
scene in which he acted out the conflicts inherent in this dream. In a
later paper, "Observations on Transference Love" (1915), Freud provided a glimpse into some of the deep conflicts he must have experienced in this regard:

> Sexual love is undoubtedly one of the chief things in life, and the union
> of mental and bodily satisfaction in the enjoyment of love is one of its
> culminating peaks. Apart from a few queer fanatics, all the world
> knows this and conducts its life accordingly; science alone is too deli-
> cate to admit it. Again, when a woman sues for love, to reject and re-
> fuse is a distressing part for a man to play; and, in spite of neurosis and
> resistance, there is an incomparable fascination in a woman of high
> principles who confesses her passion. [These] bring with them the dan-
> ger of making a man forget his technique and his medical task for the
> sake of a beautiful experience.[9]

THE INTERPRETATION OF DREAMS AS AUTOBIOGRAPHY

The self-analysis culminated in the publication of *The Interpretation of Dreams* in 1900. Anzieu has even been able to trace the formation of two different versions through examination of the extant
material.

The final version is one of the greatest books ever written, a
landmark in intellectual history. Freud did his work so thoroughly
that no essentials have been added since. New physiological data
have of course appeared, but they do not alter the basic psychology
offered in Freud's book.

A most striking feature of the book is that a considerable percentage of the dreams cited are Freud's own. As the reason for this he states that he wanted to present the dreams of a normal individual in order to avoid the objection that the reported dreams reflected his patients' neuroses and were not characteristic of "normal" people. This objection has long since been discarded with the accumulation of dreams from hundreds of thousands of all kinds of individuals, of all ages and from many different cultures. But Freud could not know that in 1900.

However, as Anzieu has shown, a more significant reason for the inclusion of so many of his own dreams was that he was writing his autobiography. It has been pointed out[10] that the autobiographical outpourings of the nineteenth century were a reflection of the upsurge of individualism that began in the Renaissance and assumed increasing momentum with the French Revolution and the abandonment of the theory of inborn superiority of certain classes or types of human beings. However, before Freud, autobiography fell into one of four categories (Burr, 1909): boasting of exploits (Caesar's "I came, I saw, I conquered"); objective self-observation (Cardano); confessions of guilt (St. Augustine); and lurid self-revelations (Rousseau's *Confessions*). The same four categories could be said to exist for biography.

Freud introduced a fifth category, which changed the nature of biographical (including autobiographical) writing once and for all. The inner psychic development of the individual must now be considered, in as much detail as can be mustered. Since the data with which to reconstruct this inner psychic development are as a rule unavailable, the depth of the ordinary kind of biography is open to serious question. In fact, the paradox has arisen that the man whose inner life has been most clearly revealed to the world is none other than Freud himself.

If, as a result of this advance in understanding, the validity of much biographical (and later, on a larger scale, much historical) writing has come to be questioned, that need not be a surprise. It is but one of the many ways in which Freud created what Auden later referred to as a "wholly new climate of opinion."

The Transition to Normal Psychology

Freud's self-analysis is as vitally significant in the history of ideas as the microscope and the telescope. Like them, it had a number of fateful consequences. Foremost among them is the transition to normal psychology.

In the 1890s psychology in the modern sense scarcely existed. Apart from armchair speculation about a variety of matters, the prime concern of those who identified themselves as psychologists was the intensive study of the sensory apparatus, certainly a worthy subject but not one that penetrates into the soul of the human being. Instead of armchair speculation, sensory physiology, and experimental methods, Freud had discovered a technique that could be applied to anybody. While it took many decades before the full import of his discoveries dawned on the astonished world (and many still deny it today), the first giant step was taken in the 1890s.

The term "normal" has come to have several meanings. One is the statistical average, the sense in which it is most often used. The other is an ideal image of health, a norm or standard, an important though less common usage. In the statistical sense, Freud was in every respect a normal man of his times. Thus his intensive study of himself exposed the tremendous inner storms and emotional conflicts that raged in the psyche of every man. It also showed that these inner storms could be calmed down by the new technique, so that people did not have to resign themselves to lives of "quiet desperation."

The elaboration of the concept of normality led to an expansion of understanding in a number of directions. Nowadays, when the terms "normal" and "neurotic" are bandied about, this expansion is taken for granted. Few realize how long it took for these ideas to gain acceptance.

First of all Freud saw the child in himself. He was burdened by illicit desires, particularly infantile sexuality, that are characteristic of the child but denied by the adult. Second, in the irrationality and bizarreness of his dreams he could see the irrationality and bizarreness of the psychotic. It must again be recalled that at that time no professional had any idea that the ravings of the psychotic could be made intelligible; almost all assumed, with the German psychiatrist Griesinger, that "mind diseases are brain diseases." For Freud to show that the dream is a normal psychosis, or that in his nightly dreams every man is psychotic, was a momentous advance. Third, he was later to show that the same psychic mechanisms operating in civilized Western man were also operative in primitive peoples, or "savages," as they were then still called. Thus the formula arose: There is a parallelism in the psychic productions of the child, the dreamer, the psychotic, and the primitive. Further, the same psychic mechanisms exist in all persons; the differences among the normal, the neurotic, and the psychotic are only matters of degree.

PSYCHOLOGY: THE CLUE TO MENTAL AND EMOTIONAL DISTURBANCE

While many theories existed in the 1890s, no one had any real inkling of what ailed emotionally troubled individuals. Conventional psychiatry, under the banner of Emil Kraepelin, who was almost contemporary with Freud, assumed sharp differences among normality, neurosis, and psychosis, stigmatized the psychotic as organically impaired and therapeutically hopeless, played a hit-and-miss game with the neurotic, and left the "normal" strictly alone. Its main etiological theory was heredity (the "tainted" family of that day has since disappeared); its major therapeutic tools were suggestion for the neurotic and custodial hospitalization for the psychotic. Basically, all of this derived from the futile search for organic causation, which had dominated psychiatry since the French Revolution.

Again, because of the atmosphere in which he was educated, many references to heredity, constitution, biology, and physiological causation are to be found in Freud's early writings. As time went on, they became less and less frequent, although they never disappeared entirely. Freud was a stubborn man; as late as 1938, for example, when biologists had universally rejected the Lamarckian theory of the inheritance of acquired characteristics, Freud still clung to it, true to his early biological teachers.

The World and the Psychoanalytic Vision in 1900

By 1900 three important elements of the psychoanalytic vision had emerged from Freud's work. First of all he had founded a science of psychology, with a methodology and a content that were to prove extremely fruitful for the future. Second, he had for the first time in history discovered a viable method of self-analysis that could be and was later applied to other people, thus creating a wholly different kind of experience in human history. And, third, he had for the first time proposed a clue to the mystery of mental illness in terms of its psychological bases that made sense.

On several occasions Freud referred to his "ten years of splendid isolation." Exactly what he was referring to was never entirely clear.

But it is clear that his insights were so far ahead of their time, and so inappropriate to the sick world in which he lived, that they were virtually ignored until the horrors of World War I had made man's irrationality and cruelty only too apparent.[11]

Freud once said that it was his fate in history to discover the obvious: that dreams embody wishes and that children have sexual feelings. Yet these obvious truths were bitterly fought for more than fifty years. Even today psychoanalytic psychology is completely banned in all the totalitarian countries.

To many reflective men the world in 1900 seemed to have made remarkable progress. No major European war had erupted since the Napoleonic conflicts. Science was advancing on all fronts. European nations were dominant in all parts of the world, boasting that they carried the blessings of civilization to the "inferior" races elsewhere on the globe. The sun never set on British soil, while America could quietly pursue its "manifest destiny."

In such an atmosphere psychiatry had to confine itself to the aberrant. To psychiatrists at that time the "normal" man was strong, powerful, and progressive, so he needed no help. The result was that psychiatry, when Freud began, had neither any rational explanation of mental illness nor any therapeutic tools with which to combat it. The psychiatrist was in fact little more than a janitor in a mental hospital. In a world governed by madmen, the psychoanalyst was an unwanted intruder.

In retrospect, this appears to be pure rationalization. The historian Peter Gay has commented that the early years of the twentieth century were dominated by a kind of moral schizophrenia.[12] Owen Hale titles his history of this period (1900–1914) *The Great Illusion*.[13] The outbreak of two disastrous world wars and the wholesale massacres of innocent peoples that have marked the twentieth century have shattered all illusions of the "normality" of the average man.

The introspection involved in careful self-analysis was not congenial to men who could make fortunes by ruthlessly exploiting or murdering their fellow men. Scientists who dared to comment on the rapacity or cruelty of rulers would immediately lose their university jobs or be sent to prison for defamation. A few revolutionaries agitated against the reigning order, but, as Hale comments, no one before 1914 really anticipated the approaching chaos of our times.[14] Even Freud accepted the outbreak of the war in 1914 light-heartedly, with no real understanding of what lay ahead.[15]

The nineteenth century, as a result of its vast scientific and technological progress, relied on a highly intellectual image of man. According to the major thinkers of the century, man was rational, aware of his motives, and subject to powerful forces beyond his individual control. It was the task of science, therefore, to discover the powerful external forces that move man, to bring these under his control and thus to extend the range of human happiness. John Stuart Mill, and later Bertrand Russell, might be seen as the leading exponents of such a point of view. Whether verbalized or not it was shared by most.

As a child of his time, Freud began with this image of man. He even was fascinated for a while by Fliess's number theory, according to which the universe is regulated by the two numbers 23 and 28 in various combinations (28 being the number of the menstrual cycle and 23 for some reason the male number). As late as 1898, when Fliess tried to extend these numbers to a law of the cosmos, Freud hailed him as the "Kepler of biology."[16]

It is to this image of man that we owe some of Freud's most serious errors, which his more slavish followers have still been unable to overcome: the death instinct, the libido theory, the theory of psychic energy, and the great "forces" that control man's destiny, such as passivity and activity, pleasure versus reality, and the like. Whenever he felt uncertain about a new psychological theory, Freud was apt to fall back upon some basic physiological theory or universal law, as in the days of his youth.

When Freud began, everybody was struggling to find an adequate system of psychology. Peter Roche de Coppens, from the framework of the sociology of knowledge (1976), has tried to tease out of the writings of four great sociologists—Comte, Durkheim, Pareto, and Weber—their image of the ideal man.[17] He contends, and rightly so, that within the infrastructure of social theory lies hidden not only the ideal of a good society but also the ideal of a good man. Each of the thinkers he considers had such an image of an ideal man. Roche de Coppens neglects to say, however, that since no adequate psychology was available to these social theorists, the images they proposed have not stood the test of time.

Thus Durkheim, in the first two chapters of his classic work on suicide (1897), argued that "the psychopathic states . . . can give no clue to the collective tendency to suicide."[18] In 1897 Durkheim could not use psychological explanations, because no adequate psychology was available. By 1930 his own student, Maurice Halbwachs, attempted to combine psychological and sociological explanations of suicide, as most would do today, because in the meantime sufficient psychology had been established.[19]

Max Weber was even more explicit about the need for psychology and the absence of an adequate science. In *The Protestant Ethic and The Spirit of Capitalism* (1905) he wrote:

> The firmly established results of psychology, including psychiatry, do not at present go far enough to make them of use for the purposes of the historical investigation of our problems without prejudicing historical judgments.[20]

As a result of his theoretical and clinical work, Freud emerged by 1900 with a radically different image of man. He stressed the notion that man is irrational, unconscious of his motives, and moved by internal forces that can be brought under his control by the process of psychoanalysis. Further, as he noted the similarities among the dreamer, the psychotic, the child, and the primitive, the further study of these four types of individuals took first place among psychoanalytically oriented workers.

Two Contrasting Approaches to the Study of Man

Gradually it became apparent that there are two entirely different ways of approaching human problems, even though they may be complementary to one another. One, the clinical, stemming from Freud, begins with a careful self-analysis and moves on to observe other people. The other, historically older, ignores the psychology of the investigator and concentrates on an allegedly objective evaluation of other people and social facts. Although unverbalized, these two contrasting approaches account for the later twentieth-century development of the social sciences in two different directions, currently often referred to as the psychodynamic (psychoanalytic) and the behavioristic.

Since the psychoanalytic makes a more determined demand on the individual, it is not surprising that the behavioristic has been infinitely more popular among researchers, especially those attached to universities. Thus arose the bifurcation into clinical and experimental social science, which has been characteristic of the social sciences every since. It is only since the popularization of clinical psychology after World War II and the increase in the number of analysts that the situation has shown some signs of change. The parallel development of these two lines of approach helps to explain the numerous conflicts and contradictions in modern social science.

Id Psychology—The First Psychological System: 1900–1914

Two other works besides *The Interpretation of Dreams* came out of Freud's self-analysis. One was *Three Essays on Sex* (1905), a major work, the other, *The Psychopathology of Everyday Life* (1901), of minor theoretical importance but major practical consequences. Later (1910–1915) came a series of somewhat unsystematic papers on technique. With these and related works, particularly *Totem and Taboo* (1913), Freud's first psychological system, often called id psychology, was complete.

Because Freud was a practicing therapist, not a professor with an academic chair (he was a professor of neurology at the University of Vienna, but that no longer had anything to do with his current work), it was not realized that he had put forth a radically new approach to psychology. Also, he used the same terms he had been using before, such as unconscious, repression, sexual and the like. He now gave them entirely new meanings, however, and he rarely made it explicit that he had formulated a new approach to scientific psychology, so that neither the professional nor the lay public fully grasped what he had done. And finally, many of the theories he put forth were so horrifying to "normal" men of his day that without analysis they could not discuss them intelligently. Even when the Vienna Psychoanalytic Society was formed in 1902, many of Freud's followers, as the minutes show, had only a dim view of what he was talking about.

The Key Concepts

Three key conceptual frameworks stem from Freud's thinking in the period from 1900 to 1914: the unconscious, psychosexual development, and transference–resistance as the core of therapy. The interrelationship of these three concepts constitutes a quantum leap over everything that went before.

The "unconscious" of *The Interpretation of Dreams* is far different from the unconscious of the 1890s. Whereas before it was simply a matter of withholding one or two ideas from consciousness because they were unbearable, now it had become a whole structure of partially organized, partially not organized ideas and feelings that are held back, or repressed, because they arouse anxiety. Further, the unconscious is not limited to neurotic or psychotic behavior; it plays a role in everyday mistakes, in jokes, in hypnosis, in suggestion, in religion, in art—in fact, in all human activities. Thus not merely the neurotic but every human being is dominated by conflicts about unconscious motives. In this way the continuum from normal to neurotic to psychotic is clarified.

A technique was provided for determining what the unconscious motives are in any given mental event. This technique rests upon, but is not limited to, free association. In other words, the unconscious manifestations present a surface façade from which the underlying structures must be inferred. There is a primary process that seeks immediate release and is largely unconscious, and a secondary process regulating the release, which may be partly conscious, partly unconscious.

It is Freud's delineation of the details of the unconscious and his clarification of the techniques for eliciting what unconscious motives are that distinguish his thought from that of previous scholars, especially philosophers (such as Hartmann, whose book *The Philosophy of the Unconscious* (1870), had gone through many editions). Psychologists who had written about the unconscious (like the Frenchman Janet) did so in a much more superficial way, often maintaining that the unconscious was simply the manifestation of organic impairment.

Psychosexual development, which has also been referred to (incorrectly) as the libido theory, or infantile sexuality, completely replaced the 1890s emphasis on direct adult genital sexuality. A sequence of stages was now posited (oral, anal, phallic, and genital), and later a sequence of choice of persons (object choice) was described, culminating in the Oedipus complex around ages three to five and its rearousal in puberty.

Again, as has frequently been observed, there is nothing novel in these ideas considered individually, but the whole structure is entirely new and revolutionary in its implications. The key to mental and emotional illness lies in inadequate development; with one bold stroke the basic etiological problem of psychiatry was thus virtually resolved, except for those conditions which rest upon actual brain damage.

Transference and resistance form the heart of therapy; in fact, Freud once defined psychoanalysis as any system that starts from these two observations, "even though it arrives at results different from my own."[21] Transference refers to the emotional relationship between analyst and patient. It derived from the old French term *transfert*, which was used by the hypnotists from Mesmer on to explain what went on in the hypnotic situation. Something was "transferred" from hypnotist to subject; whether this transfer occurred on physical or psychological grounds could not be determined. The same confusion, embodied in the term "psychic energy," persisted in Freud.

"Resistance" came from the hypnotist's observation of "counter-will," the theory being that subjects who submitted to the hypnotic trance bent their will to that of the hypnotist while subjects who did not exerted a "counter-will."

Not until 1914, in the classic paper "Remembering, Repeating and Working Through," did Freud make explicit that the working through of transferences and resistances is the heart of therapy. Because his explanation came so late, and because they had never been analyzed themselves, two of his leading disciples in the early period, Adler and Jung, failed to grasp the essence of the therapeutic process as it had been described by Freud.

There were very few analysts in the world before 1914, and of these none had received any serious personal analysis, as would be the case today. Hence it is scarcely surprising that Freud's ideas were almost completely misunderstood by his generation. Kuhn has commented, in his famous work on scientific revolutions, that very often when a scientific revolution occurs, the older generation has to die out and a new one has to come in before it is understood. That was the case with psychoanalysis. It was not until the 1920s and 1930s that a number of serious workers could be found who grasped the essence of Freud's psychology.

There is no unanimity on anything in the mental health professions. But there are large numbers of professionals today, whether they call themselves analysts or not, whether what they practice could be called analysis or not, who have accepted the Freudian psychological scheme as the true basis of their thinking.

THE PSYCHOANALYTIC VISION IN 1914

The period from 1900 to 1914, one of the most fruitful of Freud's life, saw a further expansion and deepening of the vision. By 1912, at the suggestion of Ernest Jones, a committee had even been formed to carry on Freud's work after his death.[22] All of its members (Jones,

Abraham, Ferenczi, Sachs, Rank, and Eitingon) were to become men of distinction in their own right.

Scientifically, Freud's thought moved ahead in a number of directions in this period. First of all there was the consolidation of his psychological system, which came with the *Three Essays* in 1905 and the papers on technique in 1910–1915. Second came the recognition that neurosis was not merely confined to a few peculiar individuals but that he had "all mankind" as his patient. Third came the formation of an International Psychoanalytic Association in 1910, by which time he had enough followers to hold international meetings. Fourth came the expansion of psychoanalytic thought to art, literature, religion, and the entire gamut of human experience. Finally, in 1912–13 came the second masterpiece of this time, *Totem and Taboo*, in which Freud was able to show for the first time that the peculiar customs of other peoples made sense in terms of the conceptual framework he had developed.

It is surprising how strongly anthropologists rejected Freud's work, concentrating on the unessential theory of the primal horde and ignoring the main contribution, the idea that all men are moved by similar psychological forces. What Freud gave anthropology was a method to make field observations meaningful in human terms. His work can be contrasted with that of Boas, the "father" of modern anthropology, who published more than 10,000 pages on the Northwest Coast of North America alone, most of it without commentary or other information that would render it intelligible to the reader.[23] In *The Mind of Primitive Man* (1911), published about the same time as Freud's *Totem and Taboo*, Boas employed a commonsense rational psychology and therefore reached no conclusions of any consequence.

Meyer Fortes, the British anthropologist, has recently paid tribute to the unification of thought that eventually resulted from *Totem and Taboo*, a unification that was previously impossible. He writes:

> The central role of filio-parental relationship in social structure and in the transmission and maintenance of customary norms and values was well appreciated by anthropologists of the prefunctionalist period . . . but what was not realized before the confrontation with psychoanalysis . . . was the crucial importance of the element of parental authority in the structure of these relationships.[24]

Another major contribution of the psychoanalytic vision in this period was the stimulation of a vast amount of empirical research.

This seems all the more paradoxical because it is precisely on this score that psychoanalysis has been faulted most. Accordingly some clarification is in order.

The self-analysis had shown Freud that intensive examination of a person's dreams, memories, fantasies, associations, and childhood experiences, later crystallized in the analytic method, yields results and insights not obtainable by any other approach. Because of that, the accumulation of personal analyses of all types of individuals in all parts of the world provided a gold mine of information.

Originally it was argued that the conclusions of an analyst were limited because only "neurotic" persons had been studied. This is refuted by the discovery that there is only a quantitative, not a qualitative, difference among the categories normal, neurotic, and psychotic. As Sullivan put it pithily several decades later, we are all more human than otherwise. By now it is generally recognized that the notion that the average person in our culture, or any known culture, is analytically normal is a fiction. All men have conflicts centering on their psychosexual development, unconscious motivations, and transferences. Hence the intensive analytic study of individuals, often going on for many years, is a significant form of research, providing basic insights into human behavior.

Ego Psychology (1914–1939): Freud's Final Period

The period of ego psychology should be seen as one in which Freud's vision deepened and was increasingly passed on to and developed by others.

Technically it was highly uneven, quite different from the sustained brilliance of 1900 to 1914. The tripartite structure (id, ego and superego) was formulated in 1923. Id and ego are new terms for old ideas; the essential basis is found in Freud's first analytic paper, in 1894, stating that neurosis is a defense against unbearable ideas. An important elaboration came with the enumeration of the various defense mechanisms, a task completed by his daughter Anna in *The Ego and the Mechanisms of Defense*, published in 1936, after Freud had done the initial job in *The Problem of Anxiety* (1926). Henceforth the core of the personality was to be sought in anxiety and the means of defending against it, a conceptualization accepted by virtually all theoreticians today, even though they may prefer a different language.

The most novel departure and the most brilliant, in the ego-psychological period, was that of the superego. The superego is the internalized image of the parents, or the unconscious conscience, as it has been called. With the superego Freud could now combine individual and social psychology, since the mores of the tribe were passed on from the parents to the children and internalized through the superego. The harsh superego also formed the basis of all psychopathology, again a reflection of the fact that if parents mistreat their children in early childhood, the consequences can be disastrous.

The Deepening of The Vision

Some of the technical advances introduced by Freud in the postwar period, like the superego, were brilliant; some, like the second theory of anxiety, pointed in new directions; some, like the death instinct, made no particular sense and did serious damage to the advance of the science. But by far the most important aspect of the postwar period was the deepening of the psychoanalytic vision.

Freud himself was characteristically modest and ambivalent about the significance of his discoveries. In his official autobiography, written in 1925, he said, "I have made many beginnings and thrown out many suggestions. Something will come of them in the future, though I cannot tell myself whether it will be much or little."[25]

Others were quicker than Freud to point out the extraordinary importance of psychoanalysis, though he was obviously aware of it. In 1929 the International Psychoanalytisher Verlag, official publisher for the International Psychoanalytic Association, started a journal called The Psychoanalytic Movement (Die Psychoanalytische Bewegung). In the lead article, Thomas Mann wrote:

> And no less firmly do I hold that we shall one day recognize in Freud's life-work the cornerstone for the building of a new anthropology and therewith of a new structure, to which many stones are being brought today, which shall be the future dwelling of a wiser and freer humanity. . . . Call this, if you choose, a poet's utopia, but it is after all not unthinkable [that its realization] may one day be due to the healing effect of this very science.[26]

In 1929, when Mann wrote, there was little reason to be sanguine about man's future. The Spirit of Locarno, which had lifted men's spirits for a while after the carnage of World War I, was gone. In its stead had come militarism, depression, endlessly bloody revolutions, and (as we know now) mental illness. Nevertheless, the psychoanalytic vision had been forged and had found its place in the minds of some men. To trace the development of this vision since then and to speculate on the possibilities for its future are the tasks of this book.

In the field of therapy, Freud's second major contribution to the science of man, an equally dramatic change occurred. As has been mentioned, once he had completed his self-analysis, Freud began to expand the theater of his operations. Gradually he came to realize that neurosis was not limited to neurotic Viennese Jews or inhibited Victorian ladies. All men and women seemed to be neurotic in greater or lesser degree.

Eventually Freud defined normality as the ability to achieve and enjoy (*Leistung und Genuss*), more often translated as "to love and work." This image of normality has been expanded in various directions and has become the accepted image of mental health.

As Freud saw him, the neurotic is one who is immature (too childish), lost in his dreams, bizarre or irrational, and culturally primitive in his attitude toward life (for example, relies on meaningless obsessional rituals, as in religion). Yet it was precisely this combination that characterized most men of his time. When he came to discuss in 1915 the atrocities of World War I, he said that we need not be horrified by the low level to which men had sunk, because the notion that they had achieved a high level of civilization was nothing but an illusion. Looked at analytically, neurosis is universal and always has been.

With this discovery of the universal neurosis Freud began to recognize that psychoanalysis was not simply a science but also a philosophy of living that points the way to happiness for man. At first he stressed the role of sexuality and the need for sexual enlightenment.[27] Eventually (1930) he reached the position that whole civilizations can become neurotic and that psychoanalysis can provide a corrective to such a universal neurosis.

Here, however, his ambivalence entered the picture. Because of his training in the exact sciences and his personal conflicts about action, Freud generally tended to underplay the realization that psychoanalysis represented a new philosophy of living. Thus, when von Ehrenfels in 1908 stressed the need for reform of existing marriage relationships because of the widespread incidence of sexual neurosis in and out of marriage, Freud agreed with him privately but insisted publicly that it was not the business of the physician to press for social reform. Why not, indeed? If a physician discovers that swamps lead to malaria, is he not justified in being active in an organization to eliminate swamps? But even though he himself was on the whole cool on the subject, others after him have stressed the profound philosophical implications of psychoanalysis as pointing to a radically new and healthy way of living for mankind.

Another expansion was in the direction of creating an entirely new profession, that of psychotherapist. Freud was well aware of this when he wrote to the Swiss minister–lay analyst Pfister in 1928:

> I do not know if you have detected the secret link between the *Lay Analysis* and the *Illusion.* In the former I wish to protect analysis from the doctors and in the latter from the priests. I should like to hand it over to a profession which does not yet exist, a profession of *lay* curers of souls who need not be doctors and should not be priests.[28]

It sounds surprising that as late as 1928 Freud could be speaking of a new "profession which does not yet exist." Psychiatry had existed for centuries; psychology and social work were just coming into existence. The new profession that Freud had in mind was to be trained *analytically*; the academic degree did not matter. In fact, in *The Question of Lay Analysis* (1926), he had insisted that if a quack is defined as one who undertakes to administer treatment without the necessary knowledge and capacities, doctors form a preponderating contingent of quacks in analysis[29] in that they very frequently practice analytic treatment without having learned it and without understanding it.

In considerable measure, the process of creating a new profession has gone along the lines indicated by Freud—that is, by pursuing the analytic curriculum. But almost all who have pursued this training have come from one of the three major mental health professions: medicine (psychiatry), psychology, and social work. The fact that the title of the psychotherapist has remained unchanged has obscured the recognition that he is an entirely new kind of practitioner. The analytically trained professional has about as much similarity to the conventionally trained psychiatrist as the surgeon of today has to the barber-surgeons of the eighteenth century. The non–analytically trained professional frequently lacks the credentials to do what he is doing and, in Freud's terms, must still be considered a quack. Nevertheless, since the general public is familiar with the degree system but not with the nature of analytic training, considerable confusion reigns, and all professional therapists are called "shrinks," regardless of their training and academic discipline.

The degree to which Freud's notion of a new profession has conquered the older fields, while substantial, is hard to estimate. From an extensive survey of four thousand psychotherapists of all backgrounds, William Henry (1971) did indeed conclude that a fifth profession had emerged as distinct from psychiatry, psychology, social work, and lay analysis, and that this fifth profession did indeed have a coherence based upon the underlying doctrines of psychoanalysis. He wrote:

> Although it offered some of its own mysteries, psychoanalysis nonetheless provided a set of terms and a logic concerning the development of disturbed behavior that had a certain plausibility and that were vastly superior to the intimations of moral transgressions and mysterious medical afflictions that characterized the preceding period.[30]

Throughout the centuries philosophers had attempted to define happiness. While at times they had some following, on the whole their efforts remained sterile, because they did not have a psychology on which to base their aspirations and further because they could not establish a profession with a good training system to show people how to actualize their ideals. Both of these gaps have been filled in by psychoanalysis (McGill, 1967). In that sense psychoanalysis represents a quantum jump again, a philosophy that supersedes all previous philosophies. The psychoanalytic vision is an integral part of this philosophy.

The Psychoanalytic Vision in 1939

Freud died on September 23, 1939. The most brutal war in history had already begun. Hitler, Stalin, Tojo, and Mussolini had made a secret pact to divide the world among themselves; had it not been for a variety of accidents, they might well have succeeded.

In spite of murder and chaos the psychoanalytic vision had been formed. These were its principal features:

1. The basis of a science of psychology had been established.
2. A philosophy of living that could lead mankind to a freer, more conscious state had been forged.
3. For the first time in history a successful system of personal analysis had been devised.

All of this came about in the 1890s. From 1900 to 1914:

4. The science of psychology was put on a systematic basis (id psychology).

5. An international organization of practicing psychoanalysts had been formed (1910).

6. It had been shown that psychoanalytic psychology could be expanded to shed significant light on all the sciences of man.

Finally, in the period from 1919 to 1939:

7. With the advent of ego psychology, a sharp critique of Western culture had come into being.

8. A new profession had been created, even though the titles remained the same as the old.

9. It had become apparent that neurosis was by no means a trivial illness but a way of life. Psychoanalysts had all mankind as their patient.

What would become of the psychoanalytic vision was wholly uncertain in 1939. With the world at war, the situation did indeed look grim. It will now be our task to examine and evaluate the subsequent developments.

Chapter 3

Mainstream Psychoanalysis: A Statement of the Essentials

BECAUSE OF THE BITTER RIVALRIES among psychoanalysts, the nature of the field at times becomes almost totally obscured. Some, to bolster their professional pride, wish to see psychoanalysis as an independent discipline. Others, because of their background, insist that it is a subspeciality of psychiatry. Hartmann maintained that it was a general psychology but did not spell out how such a psychology looked. Still others resurrect old views and parade them as something new. It has often been noted that differences in theory frequently become part of a political struggle, which leads to a wholesale distortion of theory.

As I have noted, central to psychoanalysis are (1) an imaginative view of what man is, (2) an imaginative view of what man might become, and (3) an original conceptual framework with which to understand and order the data of human experience and behavior.

The view of what man is can best be described in terms of ego psychology, or the total personality structure. However, the notion that there is a special "school" of ego psychology, of which Hartmann was the chief exponent, must be rejected. All psychoanalysts since 1923, when Freud published *The Ego and the Id*, have been ego psychologists. In that work, the present terminology and concepts were firmly established.

Most useful is the expansion of Freud's metapsychological scheme, more properly called a "holopsychological" scheme, in that it relates to the whole of psychology and does not go beyond psychology. In this holopsychology, a mental act can be considered to be completely understood if it is approached from eight points of view: (1) topographic, (2) genetic, (3) dynamic, (4) economic (or quantitative), (5) structural, (6) cultural, (7) interpersonal, and (8) adaptive. Handling the manifold human responses with this approach has proved extremely fruitful. But this is to be understood as a method of analysis, not as a series of models.

The view of what man might be derives from psychotherapeutic practice and leads toward the image of the analytic ideal. This states that man can find the greatest degree of happiness if he (1) loves, (2) has pleasure, (3) allows himself sexual gratification, (4) has a wide range of feelings, yet (5) is guided by reason, (6) has a role in a family, (7) has a sense of identity, (8) can communicate with his fellow men, (9) is creative, (10) can work, (11) has a role in the social order, and (12) is free from psychiatric symptomatology. It is this image of the human estate (cf. Thomas Mann) that has been the most powerful lodestar attracting people from all cultures to Freud and psychoanalysis.

Another way of looking at it is this: Man seeks happiness, yet for the most part he finds unhappiness. Conflict results, even though some areas of functioning—how many and which ones vary from case to case—are conflict-free. The determination of what is conflicted and what is conflict-free is an empirical problem that cannot be solved by any general theory. The fact that one of man's devices for handling conflict is to conceal it from himself or his fellow men or both increases enormously the problems associated with research and empirical observation. But it should not be held to alter the theory.

The structure of psychological theory, as it evolves from these considerations, is as follows. Each component of the analytic ideal has to be understood from both a psychological and a philosophical point of view. What man does or has done must be compared with what he might do. No bit of behavior or experience, even the simplest, can be considered apart from the setting in which it occurs. Because the human being is always striving for happiness, which in practice means that he is always struggling with certain conflicts, the relevance of any action to these conflicts must always be borne in mind.

Out of these analyses more general laws could crystallize. Such a result is desirable but not absolutely necessary. It would appear that psychology is preeminently a field where generalizations are decidedly hazardous. This does not disqualify the science, it merely characterizes the field.

After a hundred years of intensive work by thousands of gifted investigators, the number of available laws in psychology is pitifully small; one may question whether there are any at all, except as guides to research. Such a result only points to the flexibility of the human being, indicating that physiological needs are more imperative than psychological, or rather that they permit fewer modes of gratification.

The Conceptual Framework

As noted, the conceptual framework is embodied in the holo-psychological (traditionally, metapsychological) scheme. Some further comments are in order.

Topography refers to the conscious, preconscious, and unconscious. The unconscious can further be subdivided into the dynamic unconscious and the descriptive unconscious. Psychoanalysis has much to say about the dynamic unconscious, which results from the repression of ego-alien wishes. Cognitive psychology specializes in the descriptive unconscious (even though as a rule it does not use that term).

The concept of the preconscious is cumbersome and unnecessary. It represents a reformulation in psychological terms of Freud's 1895 theory of three types of neurons. It refers to material that is less deeply repressed, and such terminology could just as well be used in lieu of "preconscious" (cf. Arlow and Brenner, 1964).

Genetic refers to the developmental patterns. Anna Freud's (1965) refinement into normal developmental lines provides the best basis available for comprehending both normal and pathological development.

Dynamic refers to the interplay of psychic forces. No mental act or event stands alone. For example, a fear is often an unconscious expression of a wish.

Economic refers to the quantitative factor, and the term "quantitative" might be used more efficaciously, since the more traditional term "economic" arouses much confusion. Freud tied this in with the concepts of libido and psychic energy, both of which can be dropped as needless reifications of psychological forces.

Structural refers to the tripartite structure—id, ego, and super-ego—first presented by Freud in 1923. Both the id and the ego should be regarded as loci of psychic forces, while the superego is a psychic entity in its own right, the internalization of the parents.

The ego can be divided into the defensive and the autonomous (following Hartmann). The defensive ego includes the variety of defense mechanisms first described by Freud in 1926 in *The Problem of Anxiety* and later more clearly by Anna Freud in *The Ego and the Mechanisms of Defense* (1936). The defense mechanisms have been most intensively studied by psychoanalysis.

The autonomous ego refers to those portions of the ego which are relatively conflict-free, including both primary autonomy (thinking, learning, memory, physiological functioning) and secondary (Hartmann, 1939). The autonomous ego functions have been studied most intensively by all the social sciences. Hence, a fruitful union of all the material on the autonomous ego and the defensive ego leads to the most complete psychology and social science.

Cultural refers to the influence of the culture on the individual. This is undoubtedly the most important single addition to total psychoanalytic theory since Freud. However, reification of culture as an entity in its own right, as some anthropologists have tried to do, is unwarranted.

Interpersonal refers to the interaction between people. It is both conscious and unconscious. Its development can be traced from parents to the outside world. The term "object relations" has the identical meaning, inasmuch as the significant objects in a child's life are people, primarily the parents. The concept of an "object-relations school" represents a historical distortion. Psychoanalysis has always been an interpersonal theory, but it couched its interest in people in different terms.*

Adaptive refers to the biological adaptation of the human being. Even in biology the meaning of the term is unclear (Dobzhansky, 1973). Inasmuch as the principal adaptations of the human being are to other people or to internal drives, this concept is of limited usefulness in practical work.

*Confusion in this area has arisen because of terminological differences. Lichtenberg (1979) points out that all psychoanalytic theories have been object-relations theories. And Freud, in his *Three Essays* (1905), defined the sexual object (later abbreviated merely to object) as "the person from whom sexual attraction proceeds" (SE, VII, p. 135).

The Components of the Analytic Ideal

The twelve components of the analytic ideal have all been studied from many different angles, and there is much to be said about each one. The discipline of psychology should be pursued by the systematic consideration, from both a psychological and philosophical point of view, of each of these components.

LOVE

Although love is the central experience of every human being's life, most people confess that they do not know what it really is. Even psychoanalysis, after Freud's early explorations, has tended to say very little about it, in spite of the fact that one of its cardinal tenets is that maturity implies love, while immaturity involves hatred. Much material on love is available from clinical, anthropological, historical, experimental, and ethological sources. A full theory requires integration of all of this material.

Clinical Observations

The psychoanalyst is in an especially good position to study the unconscious meanings of love. Freud and others have described a variety of clinical manifestations of love that are neurotic in character. After a brief initial euphoria, they result in a considerable amount of unhappiness. The study of these experiences occupies a major portion of every analytic treatment.

Inherent in this situation is a complex paradox. The person comes into analysis attached to some neurotic image of love. This must first be dissolved by tracing it to its childhood origins, and then the individual may be helped to a mature form of love.

Various neurotic or immature forms of love have been depicted. All of them derive from unhappy childhood experiences to which the person becomes overattached. Many of them are connected with sexual inhibitions, others with a reaction formation against rage.

In the *rescue fantasy*, a man (usually) wishes to rescue a woman from her unhappy lot. So he picks women who are realistically unhappy or social deviants, such as prostitutes. (Somerset Maugham's novel *Of Human Bondage* is a classic literary portrayal of this kind of love.) These women are mother substitutes; in the family, the mother is seen as an unhappy woman, made miserable by the brutal father, who forces sex on her, using her as a "spittoon." Obviously here the problem lies in the debased position assigned to sexuality. Love is "clean"; sex is "dirty."

Such attitudes also lead to *love of the pure woman*, who is idealized and put on a pedestal. The boy cannot believe that his mother would willingly engage in any such "dirty" activity as sex; hence he splits off the object into the good and the bad: the good woman, who is the virginal mother, forced into sex by the sadistic father, and the bad woman, the "tramp," who is at the opposite pole from mother. One is for love, the other is for sex, and never the twain shall meet. Such an outlook makes the prophecy self-fulfilling: The twain never do meet. Our culture, like many others is still rooted in this division of women into "good" and "bad," although under the impact of psychoanalytic criticism this is rapidly changing.

Much idealized love serves as a *defense against homosexuality*. An unconscious homosexual wish lies at the basis of one form of Don Juanism or its counterpart, nymphomania. Excessive sexual activity without real pleasure is engaged in to prove that the man (or woman) is not a homosexual. Clinically, in a number of these cases the homosexuality becomes overt.

Homosexual love has been brought into prominence by the gay rights movement. Analytically, exclusive homosexuality is never found among persons who have had gratifying love experiences with their parents for it involves a total denial of the opposite sex, which can only come out of a background of severe childhood frustration. When the homosexual pair is examined more closely, an enormous amount of hatred becomes manifest; one unconscious aim in the homosexuality is to deprive the partner of normal outlets for heterosexual pleasure. In many cases the two are acting out a fantasized mother–child relationship (Socarides, 1978).

All the foregoing instances of neurotic love show that it is a *transference love*. Much as a patient blindly attaches himself to an analyst because of his overwhelming need for a good parent, many people "fall in love" for the same reason. There is an almost endless variety of these transferences, all of which can be understood in terms of the idiosyncrasies of each person's background.

Historical Data

There is by now much information available about the historical development of the modern concepts of love, including romantic love, especially in Western society. Morton Hunt's *Natural History of Love* (1959) has an excellent summary, discussed more fully in Chapter 16.

As Hunt recounts it, every period in history has struggled with the problem of reconciling the tender and the sexual feelings. Some have stressed one, some the other. None has ever succeeded in reaching that union of tender and sexual feelings for the opposite sex which Freud recognized as the truly mature kind of love.

Witchcraft persecution died out in the eighteenth century, a period of free sexuality. Perhaps in reaction to that, the nineteenth century saw an attempt to restore married life. There ensued the Victorian period, when the free enjoyment of sexuality was viewed as the surest way to the destruction of the home.

Here Freud entered the picture. The twentieth century, dominated by his thought, has been characterized by a frantic search for true love, a search that is still going on. Thus the problem of combining sexual and tender feelings for the opposite sex remains.

Anthropological Data

Studies of other cultures, carried out since World War I, have demonstrated the wide variety of solutions to the problems of sex and love that can be found in human societies. A broad division into love and hate cultures becomes feasible. The love culture is one where the predominant relationships are guided by love; a hate culture is one where they are guided by hatred. Ours must be considered a hate culture. Ashley Montagu has detailed the many cultures in which love may be said to predominate (discussed later).

Ethological Data

Animal investigations have by now established the fact that affectionate needs exist in a wide variety of mammals. Schaller (1965) states his impression that gorilla couples stay together because they know and like one another. Harlow's (1974) well-known study of rhesus monkeys has shown the importance of the affectional system in monkeys and its relationship to the early contact with the mother.

Child Psychology

Direct investigation of children, first systematically initiated by Spitz in the 1930s, has shown beyond any doubt the importance of love for the well-being of the child. Loss or withdrawal of an important person is just about the most devastating experience a child can have, and its sequelae are disastrous to later well-being. The expression TLC (for "tender, loving care") has become current as a result of research by Spitz and others. In animals as well as humans, tender, loving care in childhood is the sine qua non for a happy adulthood.

An *integrative theory of love* can be set up on the basis of all of these data. Mature love reaches a conscious stage where the individual has control over his feelings. He is not carried away by love; he loves. Love is an active force, which matures through having been loved in childhood. "Falling in love" is a neurotic fantasy.

Developmentally, love may be said to go through six stages: organic affection, attachment, admiration, mutual enjoyment, intimacy, and devotion. A happy mother–child pair lays the basis for all future love relationships; an unhappy mother–child pair lays the basis for a later neurotic development. It is possible for the individual to move through life from one loving relationship to another. Such a life history, though rare in our culture, is sometimes found. A family in which the emotional climate is dominated by love is one that will produce happy adults; contrariwise, a family in which the emotional climate is dominated by hatred will produce unhappy adults (Beavers, 1977).

PLEASURE

That man seeks pleasure and avoids pain is one of the oldest and most universal of observations. Yet in the light of analytic experience it requires considerable refinement.

Two analytic observations show that the conventional image of pleasure is an oversimplification. First of all, the persistent pleasure-seeker often finds himself bored and searches for ever new forms of pleasure from which he derives little or no gratification. At a deeper level this frantic kind of pleasure-seeking is found to cover up a profound sense of depression and emptiness. Second, much of what is called the search for pleasure, such as drinking or drugs, is really an attempt to alter consciousness. In the ordinary state of consciousness nothing feels right; in the altered state of consciousness everything feels right. Since the analytic ideal involves a free, conscious humanity, the deliberate attempt to alter consciousness points to an overwhelming sense of inner frustration and dissatisfaction.

In the traditional image of pleasure, which Freud took over somewhat uncritically, gratification leads to a sense of total well-being in a state of constant equilibrium, somewhat like the Christian image of heaven. Instead, a more satisfactory model is a cycle of need-gratification-rest-need. In the older, homeostatic view, a need serves as a disrupter, a disturber of the peace, which has to be "reduced" and expelled as soon as possible. Hence the image of psychoanalysis as a need-reduction theory.

In fact, this image of need-reduction as the ideal derives historically from the religious image of calm and contentment, in which the ideal man is something like a Buddha perennially looking at his navel, and happy with what he sees. Such a position ignores the harmful effects of understimulation.

By contrast, in the cyclical image of pleasure, needs are just as important as a state of rest. Relaxation without the intrusion of needs has been upheld as a "saintly" way to live in many cultures. It is notorious that most men are unable to comply with such an ideal, the simplest explanation being that it is too foreign to human nature. Living organisms have needs; they can be manipulated, transformed, sublimated, repressed, and handled in many other different ways, but sooner or later they make themselves manifest.

Historically and currently, our society, chiefly through the family as intermediary, exerts a strong pressure to suppress many pleasurable activities. The degree of such suppression has varied through the course of human history from extreme permissiveness to tyrannical prohibition. From a theoretical point of view two comments are in order: First of all, it is possible to suppress a considerable part of the pleasurable activities of men (though not without harmful effects), and second, the greater the suppression the greater the force, both physical and ideological, needed to maintain it. In mental illness there is always a harsh superego that compels the individual to abandon a great many pleasures.

The problems associated with pleasure can be best conceptualized in terms of deviations from the model of need-gratification-rest-need. An imbalance occurs, which can take one of four forms:

1. *Disturbances in need.* The person can experience too much need or too little need. Traditionally only the individual who experienced too much need was seen as "sick." Today we know that experiencing too little need is just as harmful, in fact, often more harmful, than the reverse. For example, today a lack of sexual desire is seen as

pathological and is classified as a psychiatric disorder. Some balance must be found.

2. *Disturbances in gratification.* Some individuals have intense "peak" experiences; others feel little when their desires are gratified. Sometimes there is no gratification at all; these are the "anesthetic" individuals, the "zombies." Localized anesthesias may also occur in many people; this was one of the first symptoms to draw Freud's attention (Freud, 1895). Optimally gratification must range between certain limits; both too much and too little imply that the picture is complicated by internalized psychic factors.

3. *Disturbances in rest.* A period of quiescence is an essential part of the model. The human being, like any other animal, is not made to endure constant stimulation. Most often, the rest period involves sleep, as in infancy, following feedings. Later on there may be either hypersomnia (too much sleep) or insomnia (disturbed sleep). Sleep difficulties at all ages are extraordinarily widespread. In one sense all neurosis involves some interruption of the normal sleep pattern.

4. *Disturbances in recurrence of the cycle.* Biological clocks or biorhythms appear to govern many of the basic human activities, in spite of all individual differences. There is not too much variation from one individual to another. Hence after rest the need will reassert itself after a reasonable period of time. If it recurs too quickly, the rest is disturbed; if too slowly, the rest is too prolonged.

In addition to the basic model, *pleasure gain* can be singled out as of fundamental importance. Once the basic needs are satisfied, the human being has a wide variety of choices. One is to increase the range of his pleasures, on the basis of pleasure-gain rather than need-reduction. In *The Importance of Living* (1937), the Chinese scholar Lin Yutang has provided an eloquent description of some of the many ways in which life happiness can be expanded. Clearly, the Chinese culture for many centuries gave serious thought to these problems and came up with many profound insights.

INSTINCT AND FEELING

A fundamental question for all of psychology is: What is human nature? Historically, psychoanalysis initially stressed instinctual behavior. In this it was opposed by behaviorism, which placed the main emphasis on environmental influences. Both positions represent oversimplification. By now there is enough evidence available from many sources to integrate a coherent theory. Freud's own views kept changing throughout his life, and no one theory can be taken as typical of him.

Research indicates that an instinct may be defined as an unlearned drive, with a conative-affective core, based on preformed neurophysiological structures, which has both somatic and psychic components, as well as individual and social. Following this definition, three basic instincts can be described in the human being: sexuality, anxiety, and hostility, or, in more popular language, love, fear and hate.

"Instinct," however, is a theoretical concept (Sandler and Joffe, 1969). More crucial is what the person actually feels. These instinctual drives are experienced as *feelings*, and these feelings are part of the fundamental motivation in human existence. Every culture has to come to grips with them, and every individual has to learn how to handle them.

Love, fear, and hate can be, have been, and are handled in many ways by different cultures. The fact that the drives are always the same accounts for the unity of man; that they may be handled differently accounts for the diversity. Both the unity and the diversity must be given adequate weight in a comprehensive theory.

Some General Observations on Instinctual Feelings

Apart from data on specific feelings, some general conclusions about all instincts emerge.

1. *The need for discharge.* The instincts take priority; something has to be done about them. This "something" is usually expressed as discharge.

Freud introduced a number of subtleties into this observation, which originally goes back at least to Darwin. For Freud, the discharge may be psychic or it may be somatic, it may be conscious or it may be unconscious, it may be fairly directly observable or it may be woven into the personality structure in such subtle and devious ways that only a detailed unraveling of all the associations can lead to the awareness of some instinctual impulse at the end of the chain. The interplay between the primary and secondary processes, in which the immediate instinctual demands are held in check by ego apparatuses, accounts for a good deal of personality functioning. It is in this area that the somatic correlates of the instinctual feelings are to be sought. However, the James–Lange theory of emotion, which states that the physiological reaction *is* the feeling, is rejected; both psychic and somatic discharges are part of a broader process.

2. *Mentalization.* Since the instinct represents one linkage between the somatic and the psychic, it readily lends itself to a process of mentalization. By this is meant that from a very early stage the instincts become inextricably intertwined with the mental apparatus. As the person grows older this mentalization becomes more and more prominent because of increasing control (ego strength) and because of the increasing capacity for mental activity. For example, the adult can fantasize about eating, but the infant must eat when it feels hunger or suffer serious consequences. From a fairly early stage physiology releases the impulse, but psychology determines what happens to it. This is why it is so difficult to see the id in pure form; it is rather an inference from a variety of observations.

3. *Socialization.* Because the instinct has both individual and social components, it necessarily plays a vital role in the process of socialization, which is at the heart of all cultures. However, the exact nature of the interaction between instinct and culture remains to be clarified.

How much variability is possible in the regulation of the instinctual feelings? A great deal, but not limitless. The theory of complete cultural relativism goes too far; biology still plays a role in human affairs.

4. *Capacity for frustration.* In spite of the priority exerted by instinctual drives, the human being's capacity to frustrate them is enormous. In fact, it is precisely because of this capacity for frustration, and the consequent variability among cultures, that the instincts play such an important role. By contrast, if certain vital foods are not provided, the individual and the culture simply die.

5. *Nature of instinctual gratification.* Here the various instinctual feelings have to be evaluated differently. Sexuality readily lends itself to the paradigm for the pleasure principle: need-gratification-rest-need. Persistent lack of gratification is a neurotic symptom rather than something inherent in sexuality per se.

However, this is not true for the other two instincts. Neither hostility nor anxiety can be made to conform to this model. Rather, they obey a kind of unpleasure principle, where the person is impelled to get rid of the danger by fight (hostility) or flight (anxiety); nor is it any accident that these two are so close together that theoreticians have long spoken of the fight–flight syndrome. Further, the simple release of hostility is not pleasurable, contrary to what many allege; what is true rather is that many people find it hard to control angry feelings.

6. *Interchangeability or displacement.* One of the most significant aspects of the psychology of the instincts is their interchangeability or displaceability. Thus hostility may express sexuality or vice versa (fears and wishes are interchangeable). Fusions of the various instincts are also found all the time.

7. *Nature of drive strength.* What is it that determines the strength of any particular drive, and how is such strength to be evaluated or measured? These are both thorny questions that admit of no easy answers. Three factors seem to be at play: unconscious push, instinctual force, and historical antecedents (or pressures). It is not possible to generalize about which is more powerful. Different situations lend themselves to different resolutions. The "tyranny of the drives" can be underrated, as it was before Freud, or overrated, as it has been by many extremists such as Reich and Szondi. The lack of clarity in Freud's conception of the id has led to some of the confusion in this area.

8. *Psychic energy.* The notion that the instincts dominate the whole of mental life by providing some "energy" that is deployed in many different directions was common to all the early instinct theorists and was taken over by Freud from them. This concept is anachronistic and can just as well be dropped from psychoanalytic theory.

9. *Acting-out.* A distinction must be drawn between real satisfaction and acting-out. As a rule, the acting-out is carried on without regard for the reality of the consequences, thus giving rise to many of the most disturbing personal and social problems. Much of what was called instinctual gratification or drive in Freud's day is now regarded as acting out.

Anxiety

Among the most important analytic contributions to the theory of anxiety are the distinction between conscious and unconscious anxiety, separation as the most basic fear, the disastrous consequences of an early loss, the need to erect defenses against anxiety, the far-reaching somatic consequences, and the clarification of schizophrenic panic.

Unconscious anxiety. Inasmuch as anxiety is so uncomfortable subjectively, many persons push it back into the unconscious. This unconscious anxiety is far more damaging to the personality than conscious, paradoxically. To have conscious anxiety, there must be some ego formation; when it is completely unconscious, the ego may be reduced to helplessness.

Separation anxiety as the basic model. Freud's second theory of anxiety, first published in 1926, has been almost universally accepted. According to this theory, anxiety is a signal emitted by the ego to indicate some impending danger. The basic danger at the earliest stage of life is separation from the mother. Later anxieties transform the fear of separation. Thus depressive anxiety, which appears somewhat later in infancy, is fear of loss of the parent's love, or emotional separation. Paranoid anxiety is a fear of destruction by some external source, or, again, separation from the loving mother.

The extraordinary significance of early object loss. Because of the infant's undeveloped ego, it has little capacity to tolerate the loss of an important object, particularly the mother. As a result early object loss is one of the most traumatic of all human experiences.

Bowlby, who had extensive experience with mother–child separation during World War II in England, formulated the theory of the early mourning experience. The infant goes through three stages: protest, despair, and detachment. The detached person becomes virtually untreatable, for any new relationship would revive the trauma of the earlier loss. The detached individual is a prime example of the pathological character of unconscious anxiety.

Defense. Because anxiety is so uncomfortable, the individual erects defenses against it. These defense mechanisms have been studied and described in detail; the basic work was done by Freud.

Somatic consequences. Although anxiety is accompanied by the release of adrenalin, the injection of this hormone does not cause anxiety. Rather, anxiety has far-reaching somatic consequences, many of which have been clarified, while many remain obscure. It would appear that anxiety can alter the homeostatic balance of the body to such an extent that virtually any organ system can be affected.

Developmental considerations. Anxiety is greatest in infancy, when the ego is weakest. At first diffuse in reaction to any loss, around eight months of age the infant displays a specific reaction to the loss of the mother (eight-month anxiety). As the ego grows stronger, the person becomes better able to master anxiety.

Schizophrenic panic. The panic states displayed by many schizophrenics (catatonic episodes) represent overwhelming experiences of anxiety, often in reaction to some sudden loss or fear of loss. Inasmuch as the panic of the schizophrenic and the anxiety of the neurotic differ merely in degree, the existence of a continuum in personality functioning from normal to neurotic to psychotic is again established. Thus anxiety and the defenses against it form an essential part of every human being's personality structure.

Later object loss. Although object loss is most traumatic in infancy, it always poses a serious threat to the integrity of the organism. The capacity to mourn is an essential aspect of maturity.

Hostility

There is less agreement on the theory of hostility than on that of either anxiety or sexuality (Brenner, 1971). It is often discussed in terms of *aggression.* However, aggression must be separated into assertiveness and hostility, both of which meanings it has assumed. Assertiveness is a normal characteristic of the healthy ego; hostility remains the problem.

Physiology. There is no known physiological basis for hostility, so that it is essentially a psychological state. While there are some physiological factors that increase hostility in animals, such as an increase of male hormone or brain damage, this is highly variable, and it is striking that so many animal species have developed devices to curb the most destructive effects of hostility. In one sense, and a very important one, man is the most hostile animal known.

However, as with anxiety, while hostility has no known physiological cause, it has far-reaching somatic consequences. These consequences are much the same as those of anxiety, with which it is so closely allied that it can be assumed that the two are always paired. Why hostility is nearer the surface with one person and anxiety with another can only be explained from the life history.

Psychopathology. Excess hostility characterizes all psychopathological conditions. The reduction of hostility is thus an essential goal in all psychotherapy. This also explains the greater reluctance of the more disturbed patient to accept therapy; he anticipates a fight rather than a pleasant collaboration.

Developmental. The development of hostility, in all its forms, such as rage, anger, resentment, violence, and so forth, has been extensively studied. It is more easily aroused in the infant (as is true of anxiety) because of the weakness of the ego. The socialization process requires that this hostility be "tamed" in the course of growth. When there is too much hostility in infancy and early childhood, it becomes part of the superego, either by learning or by projection, which accounts for the central significance of hostility in all the major psychopathological disorders.

Internalization and release. From an early age (perhaps as early as three months) there is an internalization of important people (the internalized object). Soon the hostility is directed at these internal objects rather than at the external world. As a result, after a certain point hostility never finds real gratification, for the internal objects remain "immortal" (Schafer, 1968). The release of hostility cannot be said to have any intrinsic value per se; it may bring temporary relief, but not more. It may also cause severe harm, setting off strokes (the old "apoplexy"), or at times epileptic seizures.

Roots of hostility. The chief cause of hostility is frustration. However, the child may also learn various forms of hostility as part of his upbringing (for example, the American white's hatred of blacks). Thus, psychoanalysis is fully compatible with a social learning theory, except that it allows for various forms of internalization, as social learning theory does not.

Hostility and happiness. A surplus of hostility and/or violence makes for unhappiness, while an atmosphere of security and nonviolence makes for happiness. This conclusion is borne out not only by therapeutic work but also by the study of other cultures, as well as much experimental work with animals.

Sexuality

In the main, the essential points made by Freud in his writings of 1900–1914 have been upheld by subsequent research. There are some exceptions, particularly in the area of cultural influences on sexual behavior.

Freud's Psychosexual Theory. Briefly, Freud distinguished three periods of sexuality: infantile, from birth to age five; latency, from age five to puberty, and adult, from puberty on. Sexuality broadly includes both love and physical gratification, both tender and sexual feelings toward a person of the opposite sex.

Various zones of the body become successively predominant as the child grows: There is a progression from oral to anal to phallic to genital primacy. It should be borne in mind that the more direct sexual theories of the 1890s were abandoned by Freud and that the addition of the quantitative libido theory in 1914 was totally unnecessary.

Love, as noted, involves a union of tender and sexual feelings toward a person of the opposite sex and matures at puberty after a long history. Problems in the love life, which are legion, go back to disturbances in the early relationships with the parents. In general, sex and love make people happy; hatred and fear make them unhappy.

The principal changes that have taken place in the theory since the 1930s are: (1) the significance of the early mother–infant relationship for subsequent sexual behavior; (2) the internalization of the mother and other early figures; (3) the awareness that sex can be a defensive procedure and can be used for acting-out as well as for real gratification; (4) the diminished importance placed on sexuality by some theoreticians, who put it on a par with hostility and other drives; and (5) the connection between sexuality and the self-image and ego structure.

Mother–infant relationship. What happens between mother and infant has a decisive effect on the child's later behavior. (Harlow even found this to be true for monkeys.) Mahler (1975) has formulated the process of separation-individuation, distinguishing four stages in the process of separation from the mother: (1) hatching or differentiation (six months); (2) practicing (nine months); (3) rapprochement with its attendant crisis (fifteen months) and, finally, (4) object constancy (originally put at three years). This process of separation-individuation is repeated at various periods throughout the entire life cycle.

Internalization of mother and other early figures. Highly significant for the future sex life is the internalization of the mother and other early figures (objects). Originally, the mother is seen as either all good or all bad; later, different gradations are added. Gradually these internal representations come to occupy an increasingly important role in the psychic economy.

Sex as acting-out. Since the 1950s (Spiegel, 1954) it has become increasingly clear that sexuality may be used for defensive purposes. It thus becomes an acting-out, leading to conflicts rather than real gratification.

Changed emphasis on sexuality. Many theoreticians today (Heinz Kohut and Otto Kernberg, for example) place less emphasis on sexuality than did Freud. However, this is mainly a culturally determined reaction. In general, cultural factors play a preponderant role in the ways in which sexuality is molded for each individual.

Connection with self-image and ego structure. Following Freud's 1923 book *The Ego and the Id*, the emphasis in theory shifted to the ego structure, including interpersonal relationships, the self-image, healthy and pathological narcissism, and ego strength and weakness. Sexual expression in the adult thus becomes a complex affair, the dynamics of which cannot be fully understood without reference to the internal life, especially the internalized images derived from childhood. Nevertheless, this should not obscure the fact that, as Freud once put it, sexual love makes people happy; everybody knows this, except some fanatics and some scientists.

REASON

The role of reason in human affairs was underestimated by the early analysts, who were overwhelmed by their new discoveries of emotions, conflicts, and unconscious forces. At the same time, it was overestimated by nonanalytic scholars, who for that reason repudiated much of psychodynamic theory. In more recent years, more of a balance has come into both. Thus some papers now have shown that cognitive factors can explain some of the phenomena of dreams (Wolpert, 1972), although the basic dream mechanism remains the wish and its punishment or deprivation.

Piaget and Psychoanalysis

For many people today, Piaget seems to serve as a kind of bridge between conventional cognitive theory and psychoanalysis. Piaget, who was for many years (from about 1920 to 1940) a member of the Swiss Society of psychoanalysis and who went through a didactic analysis in his early years, has himself drawn a meaningful parallel between his concept of the cognitive unconscious and the psychoanalytic concept of a dynamic unconscious, showing how each plays a significant role, but in a different sphere of the mind.

Ego Autonomy

The theoretical concept that allows the incorporation of conflict-free rational material into psychoanalytic theory is Hartmann's notion of *ego autonomy*, both primary and secondary. Through these concepts, psychoanalysis can readily be expanded to become a general psychology (Hartmann, 1964).

Reason and Rationalization

Man seems to have a universal tendency to rationalize his actions, no matter how bizarre they may appear to others. The worst crimes, including murder and suicide, have been and are rationalized, as the whole course of history shows. Even in the allegedly civilized twentieth century the most horrendous kinds of behavior have been given a rationalized cast by various apologists. This need to appear rational is an important aspect of human functioning.

Reason and the Prevalence of Psychopathology

The degree to which reason prevails, rather than rationalization, which is universal, depends on the extent of the psychopathology in any given culture. Intensive studies of individuals, such as the Rennie study of New York (1962) and the Leighton study of the Maritime Provinces of Canada (1963), reveal a much higher incidence of psychopathology than had been suspected (see pp. 88–89).

It now seems quite clear that entire cultures can be seriously disturbed. For example, a number of cultures have been described in which natural causes of death are denied with the assertion that every death results from sorcery or murder. Such deaths must then be avenged. This leads to a round of murder and revenge, which can, and sometimes does, go on for centuries (for example, Fortune, *The Sorcerers of Dobu* [1932], or the common beliefs in witchcraft in many cultures).

With the present trend toward release of patients from mental hospitals, it has been noted that a considerably higher percentage of released schizophrenics than of the normal population engage in criminal or illegal activity. Hitler and Stalin in an earlier generation and Nixon and his cohorts in this generation all have suffered from or suffer from serious psychopathology. This is one reason why psychiatry and psychology have become such popular subjects.

Reason as a Goal of Psychoanalysis

Paradoxically, psychoanalysis, which has concentrated heavily on the seemingly irrational in human behavior, holds up rational behavior as one of its goals. Progress toward a freer humanity depends on making the unconscious conscious, in society as well as in the individual.

Other Disciplines

In the main rational behavior has been examined more intensively by nonpsychoanalytic disciplines. For a fuller theory, however, rational factors must be combined with dynamic ones to provide a rounded picture of the human being.

FAMILY STRUCTURE

From the very beginning psychoanalysis was family-oriented, in that the Oedipus situation is essentially the family conflict and the family romance. However, because the issue was not central at that time, Freud phrased his theory in terms of instinct rather than in terms of family.

Originally the theory postulated, or seemed to postulate, that merely lifting instinctual repressions would lead to happiness. From this standpoint the family is the enemy of mental health, for it can exist only by instituting repressions. The task in the 1920s, then, was to mitigate the severity of family restrictions, or abolish the family altogether. This attitude was most clearly formulated in Flugel's *The Psychoanalytic Study of the Family* (1921). A. S. Neill's Scottish school at Summerhill, where he abolished all restrictions on children, including the sexual ones, is a product of this thinking as well.

In the meantime anthropologists discovered that the nuclear family was indeed universal (Murdock, 1949), from which it followed that it must serve some basic need in human nature. (Even among some animal species family-like situations were found to prevail.) Further theoretical work led to the concept and importance of the superego, while further clinical work led to the realization that a good family was the best guarantee of later mental health.

After World War II psychoanalytic theory shifted to the recognition that the family is essential to the child as a source of security. It has been noted that the human is born in a more helpless state than many other animals, so that its need for care and protection are much greater. The family offers such care and protection, which probably explains why it is universal. A book that epitomizes this revised image of the family is Nathan Ackerman's *The Psychodynam-ics of Family Life* (1958).

Thus the family serves many positive functions. Parsons and Bales (1955) list six: It provides (1) the matrix within which child-hood development proceeds, (2) the socialization of instinct, (3) se-curity, (4) human models for behavior, (5) a link with the wider soci-ety, and (6) the internalization of culture. With the recognition of the central significance of the *superego*, which represents the internaliza-tion of the parents, the link between the family and the wider society is secured (Parsons, 1953).

The Family and Transference

A further fateful effect of the family lies in the phenomenon of transference. The human being, like all animals, generalizes from his childhood experiences. Thus later human relationships are based on, and derive from, early ones. Transferences are not confined to the therapeutic situation but operate in all of life. It is because of these transferences that the early objects (or people) acquire such over-whelming importance. As Freud once put it, every human being has the task of liberating himself from his mother.

The significance of the *mother* has loomed ever larger in theory as time has gone on. Where Freud often assumed that everything proceeded smoothly until the Oedipal crisis, after him a voluminous literature grew up on pregenital conflicts, including the first year of life. Spitz, the first analyst to write extensively about the first year, enumerated three phases in the development of the object (1965): (1) the preobjectal or objectless stage (birth to three months), (2) the stage of the precursor of the object (three to eight months), and (3) the stage of the libidinal object proper (eight months on).

The first year has by now been extensively studied from almost every point of view. Its centrality lies not merely in the actual experi-ences but also in the fact that the mother is internalized, so that the person carries her with him as an introject for the rest of life. If she is cruel and sadistic, a bad introject is formed; if she is good and kind, a good one. Either way her behavior becomes decisive for the child.

In the most elaborate empirical study conducted along psycho-dynamic lines, Brody and Axelrad (1978) were able to specify in more detail what constitutes adequate mothering and to show that emotional experiences in the first year are related to emotional sta-bility and to social and intellectual competency in the first years of the latency period. (Their study did not go beyond that age.)

The growth away from mother is never accomplished abruptly. The infant must find a *transitional object* of some kind (Winnicott, 1953) to which he attaches himself, sometimes for years, and through which the separation is facilitated. There are many kinds of transitional experiences. Margaret Mahler (1975) has particularly emphasized the rapprochement crisis in the period from fifteen to twenty-four months, when the toddler oscillates back and forth between mother and the outside world.

The move away from mother is first toward the father, who thus becomes the second important object in the child's life. Through tracing the vicissitudes of this move from mother to father, the individual's life history comes to make more sense. Psychoanalytic theory, like psychological theory in general, has only recently come to appreciate the importance of the father (M. E. Lamb, 1976).

Finally, a considerable literature exists on the influence of siblings. The only child, the firstborn child, the youngest child, and other variations have all been described. While generalizations are difficult, sibling rivalry is universal, and the influence of siblings remains enormous.

Social class (or socioeconomic status, SES) is one of the main determinants of family mental health. By now considerable evidence exists that there is an inverse ratio between social class and emotional disturbance. While the majority of the lower classes have maintained the intactness of the family, the emotional climate is so bad that it produces an inordinate amount of suffering and unhappiness. Lewis (1959) has described the culture of poverty (Lewis, 1966).

The core of neurosis turns out to be *family pathology*. It is no longer a question of a single traumatic incident; it is, rather, the whole emotional climate in which the child is brought up. When there is constant conflict and disharmony, these are internalized in the superego, which then bears down on the individual to create depression, schizophrenia, and many other forms of illness. The superego, in turn, is the representative and agent of the larger culture, so that it is again through the superego that the neurosis of one generation is passed on to the next.

The Self, Identity, and Narcissism

The question of identity has become one of the burning issues of our time. People come to analysis looking for a "sense of identity." National symposia are held on the subject of our identity as a nation.

Alienation, or the absence of identity, is seen everywhere as one of the root causes of emotional disturbance.

The terms "self," "identity," "identification," and "narcissism" all cover similar ground. The crucial questions to be answered are: (1) How does the individual's identity arise? (2) How does it integrate with the individual's life and happiness?

The Self-Image

Perhaps easiest to discuss is the self-image, which is closer to ordinary thinking and has a long history, especially in American philosophy. The most important analytic observations on the self-image are these:

1. Somewhere (as a rule) between two and three years of age, the child gradually develops an image of himself, which changes and grows as time goes on. To begin with, this self-image is the reflection of *parental appraisal* (Sullivan, 1940). What the child thinks of himself is what the parents think of him.

2. *The body image* is an essential part of the self. First discussed by Schilder as long ago as 1925, it has since been extensively elaborated (Lichtenberg, 1978). Inasmuch as the self-image first develops at a time when the child can scarcely distinguish the mental from the physical, the characteristics of the body become all-important. The prime fact in the child's life is *growth*, and this growth is reflected above all in his size and other bodily changes.

Recent studies on gender have shown that even when there are sexual anomalies, the gender assigned to the child is that desired by the parent, so that how the child evaluates the bodily changes taking place depends above all on how the parents evaluate them.

3. *Self-awareness.* The degree to which any person is aware of his "true" self depends on age, level of intellectual development, and degree of disturbance. In all except rare individuals the capacity is limited to some degree.

4. *Internalization.* As a result of internalization processes, the precise nature of the self-image is pushed back into the unconscious or confused with reality. The image becomes increasingly refractory to outside influences and increasingly dominated by the inner life. Surface descriptions of identifications are therefore often misleading, covering up the deep unconscious identifications that can be unraveled only by careful research.

5. *Superego regulation.* The self-image centers between two extreme poles: self-aggrandizement and self-effacement (the selflessness of the mystics). Both of these represent unworkable defensive postures. The goal of therapy becomes the person's correct awareness of the real self and appropriate efforts to change in a philosophically desirable direction.

6. *The inner self and the social order.* As a rule there is a considerable discrepancy between the inner image of the self and the outer self displayed to the culture. This discrepancy is particularly obvious to the psychotherapist, because he deals with it all the time. Anthropologists and other social scientists have paid insufficient attention to it, perhaps because the measuring tools at their disposal were inadequate.

In spite of enormous conflict, a social role can be maintained that is at a great distance from the inner self. Roheim (1932) showed that even in one of the most primitive societies ever investigated, there was some awareness of this true inner self and its difference from the social self. Every Central Australian, for example, believes that as a *ngantja* or hidden person he has never left the ancestral cave.

Conventional role theory has extensively investigated the social roles that the individual may adopt. It is striking how a social role can be adhered to, and social expectations fulfilled, in spite of tremendous inner turmoil and disturbance. The fact that disturbed, even schizophrenic individuals can nevertheless fulfill a socially meaningful role is one of the most striking contributions of psychoanalysis to social theory.

7. *The self-object: The self and the other.* For the first two years of life the child can scarcely distinguish between himself and mother; hence the self is still a self-object, or an amalgam of the inner self and the outside person (mother). As the person grows, the self becomes distinguished from the object. However, in many pathological conditions, the self-object fusion persists for a long time, sometimes indefinitely. One major consequence is that the individual is unable to see other people clearly, since he projects his own feelings onto them.

8. *Alienation* occurs when a person is frustrated with the social role imposed on him because of either excessive demands of the society or a lack of gratification of inner needs, or both. Alienation may be viewed as one measure of the stability of a social order. However, in a disordered culture alienation may actually be an advantage, as the example of the Hutterites in our own society shows (Eaton and Weill, 1955).

Identity and Identifications

As a result of the bodily changes, the growth process involves a dramatic change in the self-image at various phases of development. For these, Erikson (1950) has coined the apt term "identity crises." They are crises because the individual has to go through a total restructuring process.

Such a restructuring has many aspects. As before, it follows the symbiotic (or anaclitic) separation–identification model. If the new urges can be incorporated into the self-image, eventually the person goes on to a new stage of individuation; if not, he falls back into one or another of the many defensive postures that make up so much of human life.

The crisis aspect of identity change has been discussed most fully in connection with adolescence, where torment, conflict, despair, and rebellion are most apparent. It is in adolescence too that the child is for the first time able to choose from many alternative models provided by the culture in opposition to what his family has set out for him. Hence a new identity crisis arises for the parents, brought about by the growth of the child, and they too must go through an extensive restructuring of their world.

By their very nature, crises cannot last indefinitely. Consequently, once the crisis is resolved by the formation of a new identity, the self-image acquires considerable stability, for fear of falling back into the old turmoil. This is one of the principal factors accounting for the tenacity with which people hold on to seemingly absurd descriptions of themselves.

Because of the restructuring required, the libidinal phases pose serious threats to the equilibrium of many individuals. Not surprisingly, at every stage where there is a major libidinal change, numerous breakdowns occur.

Normal, Neurotic, and Psychotic Identifications

While the original models derive from the family, later models also serve as a basis for the child's identifications. These run from the completely normal to the psychotic. Most striking are the psychotic identifications, where there is a total denial of reality (Jesus Christ, Napoleon, and so on).

Such a psychotic identification is the last stage in a long process of successive withdrawals from human interaction; it is the expression of a deep sense of despair about ever achieving any meaningful, gratifying experiences with other human beings. The sequence that Bowlby describes in response to maternal loss in childhood—protest, despair, and detachment—is the one that leads to such a morbid result. Detachment may continue, or be defended against, by some peculiar identification. Since it arises out of deep disappointments, such an identification cannot be altered without rearousing some of the intense anxiety previously suffered. Hence it is held on to with the utmost tenacity. In therapy there is a deep distrust of the other person that can be dissolved only by a long-term process that may take years. It is only when sufficient trust has been established that the person is willing to shed his psychotic identification and see himself as he really is.

Cultural Models for Identification

The child is largely confined to the models provided by the parents. Once adolescence is reached a far wider choice is possible in more advanced cultures. Nevertheless, there are many pressures leading to a decision in favor or one or another of the models available. Certain models are strongly emphasized by each culture, for example, the warrior, the businessman, the housewife, the monk, and so forth. In each of these there are common elements, so that a basic personality structure (Kardiner, 1939) arises for each culture. This basic personality structure, though applicable to only a limited segment of the population, plays a predominant role in the psychic structure of the entire culture. Thus most Americans are not businessmen, but business plays a central role in the American psyche.

Narcissism

Narcissism is self-love. The course of life involves a balance between narcissistic gratification (pleasure in oneself) and pleasure with others (object love). Which side of this balance will prevail, as well as how intense the conflict is, depends on the vicissitudes of the relationship with the parents.

Narcissism may be healthy or pathological (Federn, 1929). Healthy narcissism arises out of a healthy sense of self-love, which in turn derives from a positive series of experiences with the parents, who explicitly or implicitly encourage the child to grow in an independent manner. Pathological narcissism is a reaction to the clinging, possessive attitudes of parents who will not allow the child to separate.

Naturally this scheme is a purely ideal one. In practice, narcissism arises on a secondary basis in response to pressures from the early milieu. Sometimes, as in the case of artists and scientists, it acquires a secondary autonomy, which leads to constructive activities, often of the highest order. At other times it remains tied to the parents, serving the purely defensive function of isolating the individual from their critical blows or views (the harsh superego). This is the daydreaming kind of child who escapes into a world of his own to avoid or block out parental disapproval. In still other cases, there are mixtures in varying degrees of the two kinds of narcissism.

Selfishness and self-love (Fromm, 1939), other terms for narcissism, are at opposite ends of a continuum, in that selfishness as a rule is a manifestation of self-hatred rather than self-love.

The Social Order

In order to be happy a human being has to find his place within some social order. Recognition of this requirement in one sense provides the most important conceptual change in psychoanalysis since Freud. However, it is well to remember that in theory Freud drew no distinction between individual and social psychology (1921).

The Nature of Culture

Anthropologists Kroeber and Kluckhohn (1952) offer this definition of culture:

> Culture consists of patterns, explicit and implicit, of and for behavior acquired and transmitted by symbols, constituting the distinctive achievements of human groups, including their embodiments in artifacts; the essential core of culture consists of traditional (i.e., historically derived and selected) ideas and especially their attached values; culture systems may, on the one hand, be considered as products of action, on the other as conditioning elements of further action.[1]

Within these areas of differences and similarities the individual must find his way in the world into which he is born. It is to be noted how strongly the anthropological emphasis is on the psychic situation.

The psychological aspects of culture have been investigated by psychoanalysts in four areas: (1) cultural universals—the unity of mankind; (2) cultural effects on personality—the diversity of mankind; (3) critical remarks on American (and Western in general) culture; and (4) group behavior as an essential aspect of all cultures.

Cultural Universals: The Unity of Mankind

For biological reasons (Ashley Montagu and Dobzhansky), certain features are universal in all known societies. Kardiner (1939) lists these as follows: (1) family formation; (2) in-group formation; (3) presence of larger groups, like class or tribe, based on family organization or on common interests; (4) techniques for deriving sustenance from the outside world; (5) basic disciplines; (6) control of aggression; (7) cohesiveness determined by recognizable psychological forces; (8) definite and distinctive life goals that vary widely and even change within the same culture.

Culture and Personality: The Diversity of Mankind

The physical differences among men, as compared, say, with dogs, are small; the range of heights, birth weights, foods consumed, and hair colors is relatively narrow. It is in the psychological realm that major variations must be sought. These variations have been formulated in terms of the effects of culture on personality.

To clarify these issues, the concept of social character or basic personality structure was developed. Fromm (1941) defined social character as a selection of traits; it is the essential nucleus of the character structure of most members of a group that has developed as a result of experiences and modes of life common to a group. Linton (in Kardiner, 1945) defined the basic personality type as that personality configuration which is shared by the bulk of the society's members as a result of the early experiences that they have in common.

The notion of a basic personality structure or social character has come under severe attack from a number of sources (Levine, 1973, and Harris, 1968). The counterarguments are that human behavior is shaped by the coercive pressures of social survival, involving the maintenance and enhancement of career, reputation, status, and the esteem of others. Hence the environment is more important than the intrapsychic processes. Then there is growing evidence that the basic personality applies to only a small percentage of the population. There are even some who allege that the way populations differ psychologically is of little social significance.

These antipsychological arguments miss the point that there are noticeable psychological differences among men and that the psychological environment in which man lives shapes him and is shaped by him to varying degrees.

Critiques of American Culture

Almost from the very beginning it was observed that there is a wide gap between the statistical average and the analytic ideal. In *The Interpretation of Dreams* (1900) Freud noted that those who could not interpret dreams should not be treating patients, thereby implicitly condemning the entire profession of that day as grossly inadequate (a criticism with which we would agree today). Once he had discovered the pernicious effects of sexual repression, he stressed its harmful consequences for society at large, though for personal reasons he did not choose to engage in any reform movement.

Because of the shattering experiences of this century, especially after the two world wars, analysts and analytically oriented writers have frequently had occasion to comment critically on the prevailing psychological attitudes in American and Western culture in general. Severe sexual repression is one aspect that has had a strong impact and in the past decade at least appears to be changing rather rapidly.

Riesman (1950), following Fromm, stressed the loneliness and other-directedness of American culture. Protests against the exploitation of human beings by one another have a long history in American culture and have been brought into sharper focus by psychoanalysts. The oppression of women can be tied up with the need of men to seek power and glory, what William James called the "bitchgoddess" success. Child abuse has been brought out into the open, with the recognition that severe physical punishment in childhood can have deleterious effects for the rest of the individual's life. Marital harmony has been called into question with the realization that marriage as a rule represents a neurotic equilibrium and that when a disturbed person marries, it is virtually certain that another disturbed generation is in the making. Work should not be dull and monotonous, so efforts to make it meaningful and rewarding have been numerous. In short, every component of the analytic ideal at one time or another has been used as a criterion by which to judge the social reality, and usually the social reality has been found wanting. In this way psychoanalytic theory has become a significant basis for meaningful social reform.

Group Behavior

Group behavior is essential to human existence. In fact, it is surprising how all the higher animals integrate group activity into their lives. Ethologists have been puzzled by the mechanisms by which this group interaction is successfully maintained, such as the dominance–submission patterns.

Just as the individual moves from one relationship to another, with its attendant libidinal conflicts, throughout his life, so he moves from one group to another, likewise with its attendant conflicts, throughout his life. The first group is the family, which is universal. Thereafter each society provides different group affiliations, although the progression is similar, apparently dictated by basic human needs and capacities. On the whole, however, group development has been studied much less intensively than individual.

As soon as the child leaves the family, he is thrust into a peer group (in our society, at school). The groups he belongs to become part of his identification; without groups there is something inherently missing in the individual's sense of identity. Eventually groups can enlarge into a community, which has a special aura about it (Kanter, 1977).

All human behavior lends itself to ritualization, but group behavior particularly so, because the group is more interested in conformity with its rules than in the inner experiences of its members. Mary Douglas (1970) has made an exceptionally good point in stressing the reciprocal relationship between ritual and inner experience (discussed later).

This reciprocal relationship becomes especially clear in the history of religion. What begins as a divinely inspired form of revelation and inner light soon turns into a series of rituals, the performance of which becomes of the highest importance to the established clergy. Revolts against the dominant theology almost invariably begin by attacking the rituals, which have beome empty forms (Spiro, 1970).

COMMUNICATION

As people must live in social groups, so they must communicate with one another. Roheim (1950) once hypothesized that the origin of culture can be traced to the need of one human being to tell his dream to another. However that may be, the staggering effects of a dream on the primitive mind (it is staggering enough today) can well be imagined, as can the relief obtained from sharing this with another person.

The normal rational method of communication is language, and the study of language has created a new discipline, linguistics. But rational linguistics is interfered with in many ways by the emotional needs of the individual. McLuhan popularized this idea years ago with his formulation: "The medium is the message"—that is, content is less important than the way in which it is put across, the typical trick of the advertising man. Psychoanalysis has studied the many ways in which emotional conflicts interfere with the normal methods of communication.

To begin with, the process of psychoanalysis focuses in the most intimate detail on the ways in which two people communicate both verbally and nonverbally. Actually, it could be said that interpretation in adult (and often in child) psychoanalysis represents the attempt to put into words what the patient is trying to communicate in other ways, either by actions or by linguistic utterances from an earlier stage of development.

From the very beginning it was realized that all aspects of psychoanalytic theory relate to communication in one way or another. The *dream* was the first mental product subjected to extensive analysis. Through that analysis it became apparent that a great deal is communicated at an unconscious level, so much, in fact, that in ordinary life many essential facets of communication are simply left out. Thus the dream deepens and enlarges our understanding of the communicative process.

Similarly, it appeared that neurotic symptoms, such as hysterical conversions of all kinds, become intelligible as symbolic ways of communicating with other people. Freud had early observed that the hysterical woman executing the famous *arc de cercle*, in which she arches her body back, seemingly without rhyme or reason, is really putting herself in a position where she can offer coitus. It could be said that Freud's early work, in the 1890s, involved an unraveling of the many disguised ways in which communications were presented to him. The very first patient in psychoanalytic history, Anna O. (Breuer and Freud, 1895), who invented the term "talking cure" (in English), had a linguistic distortion in that for a while she could speak only English instead of her native German. Making the unconscious conscious is a way of putting into intelligible, communicable form that which is in unintelligible, disguised form.

Schizophrenia, the most extreme form of mental illness, is obviously a disorder of communication. Even to the layman the salient characteristic of the schizophrenic is that he is "unintelligible," and traditional psychiatry gave up on him because of this unintelligibility. Actually, as a rule he comes to the attention of his social circle or to professionals only when his utterances and/or actions reach the point of unintelligibility, even though careful examination would have revealed other serious sources of difficulty much sooner. In principle, psychoanalysis offers a method by which the seemingly bizarre utterances of the schizophrenic can be decoded and understood.

There has been a strong and growing realization that the entire process of alienation, neurosis, and psychosis represents a failure in communication (Ruesch, 1957, 1961; Ruesch and Bateson, 1951; Freedman and Grand, 1977). As with all mental phenomena, there is a continuum of gradations from the normal to the psychotic, indicating that difficulties in communication are widespread.

The extraordinary power displayed by propaganda in the totalitarian countries has emphasized that communication should not be taken literally. George Orwell, in his satirical novel *1984*, satirized this as "newthink," which could prove beyond the shadow of a doubt that black is white. Since World War II and the obvious misuses of propaganda (Hitler's "big lie is best"), interest in communication has escalated enormously.

A primary distinction must be made between *manipulative* and *expressive* communication, as in emotion. Expressive communication, a manifestation of the autonomous ego, suits the communication to the rational purpose for which it is intended. Manipulative communication, however, as the name implies, is designed either consciously or unconsciously, to manipulate another person to do something. A certain amount of manipulative communication is quite consciously dishonest, even cynical, as in propaganda (Lifton, 1969). But a good deal of it is unconsciously determined. The manipulation is then directed just as much at the introject as at the other person. In schizophrenia, communication is generally manipulative and generally fails, because the outside person is so different from the person's introject. A person "talking to himself" is talking to his introject.

CREATIVITY

To be mentally healthy involves a certain amount of creativity. This is one of the surprising findings of modern psychology. "Creativity" is used here, however, in the sense of an attitude toward the world, a willingness to take a fresh look, to see things never seen before, to appreciate what has previously been ignored or denigrated.

Artistic and Aesthetic Attitudes

A distinction must be drawn between the artistic and the aesthetic attitudes to life. In the artistic, there is a wish to create new forms, enjoy new experiences, and seek out new ways of doing things, not just for the sake of the novelty, but because doing so adds zest and meaning to life. It is a pleasure gain. The aesthete, on the other hand, wishes to appreciate what is there, to be a happy spectator; he is more content to look at the masterpieces that others have created than to try his hand at some small undertaking that will leave others unmoved.

Both attitudes can be creative in life. The danger is that the artistic will deteriorate into a search for anything that is different, as in the drug addict or in the sadistic murderer, like Nero, while the aesthetic may bog down in a constant deprecation of the living by ceaselessly comparing them with the dead.

The Creative Artist

The most notable contribution of psychoanalysis in this area has been the intensive study of the creative artist, which began with Freud's book on Leonardo da Vinci in 1910. Today, thousands of such monographs (psychobiographies) are in existence.

To begin with, the artist is closer to his id than the average person. He is in contact with wishes, desires, and instinctual impulses that are ordinarily repressed. Berkman (1972) used the telling phrase "to seize the passing dream." The artist is indeed capable of seizing the passing dream, and the analogy is an apt one, for the dreamer too must make use of primary process material, which has to be apprehended in a moment. Schneider (1950) calls this the creative thrust, which is then molded by the ego in an act of creative mastery. For true art both are necessary, id and ego, thrust and mastery, to seize the passing dream and expand it.

The artist, always attuned to a new inspiration and thus closer to his id, becomes narcissistic. This narcissism may be healthy or it may be pathological (that is, defensive). In either case, the narcissism is transferred to his work rather than remaining focused on himself. Thus he shares his narcissistic experiences with an audience.

A number of possibilities now arise:

1. Frequently the process fails because the artist is dealing with psychologically dangerous material. The narcissism is turned back on the artist, and suicide or psychosis may ensue (for example, Van Gogh).

2. When the process succeeds it may often do so through a regression in the service of the ego (Kris, 1952).

3. In another kind of artist there is an acceptance of impulse all the way around. This is the Renaissance man—a hearty individual capable of enjoying life to the full. Otto Rank (1932) saw such a man as normal, in contrast to the conforming average and the will-crippled neurotic.

4. Quite often the artist remains stuck in his narcissism. He has intimate contact with only a small portion of reality.

5. Because of the opportunity for narcissistic gratification, many people are attracted to art as an avenue of release for their narcissism. They may have little or no talent for art, or little or no interest in it. They play artist in order to be bohemian rather than embrace bohemianism because it is indispensable for their art.

6. The narcissistic release may be temporarily frightening, and as a result the artistic productivity comes to a halt. This is the creative block, the most common problem that brings artists to analysis.

7. The narcissistic absorption may become so fatiguing that the artist gives up his art to return to ordinary living. This is not so much creative block as creative fatigue. Sometimes the retreat is permanent; more often it is temporary.

None of this is intended to cast aspersions on the artist's native ability, which, as Freud pointed out, does not lend itself to analytic explanation, any more than any other native ability.

Inner and Outer Creativity

Two forms of creativity can be distinguished: inner and outer. In inner creativity, seen most clearly in the growth of the child, what counts is the growth process. The child sees something new, though it is old hat to everybody around him. In this form of creativity expression is the principal need.

In outer creativity the artistic product says something new to the outside world. This is the creativity of the professional artist or the expert in any field (the "creative" idea).

Inner creativity is essentially unrelated to the achievements of others. This point of view is similar to that of John Dewey, who stresses art as experience. Ideally the analytic process is one of inner creativity. It is a continued growth toward the ultimate goals of maturity, love, and work.

Outer creativity, inasmuch as it is a form of social communication, requires a strong ego. It is here that the ability of the artist to use a symbol that will mean many things to many people comes into play.

Frequently there is a conflict between inner and outer creativity. The latter is affected by many social circumstances over which the artist has little or no control. It is here that the common conflict crops up between pure art and commercialism. (This topic will be developed further in Chapter 11.)

WORK

Although work and love are the two cornerstones of analytic philosophy, relatively little has been written by psychoanalysts about work. Most of the material comes from psychoanalytically oriented psychologists who have devoted themselves to the problem.

The idea that work can make man happy is a fairly novel one in human experience. Aristotle did not think so, nor did the Christians for many centuries look upon work as anything but interference with service to God. In keeping with this ideology, the classical economists assumed that man works only to make money (Heilbroner, 1973).

The most significant departure from classical theory was Max Weber's concept of a Protestant ethic, which has such a compelling quality that it has virtually become part of the language of every cultured man today (Weber, 1905). His central thesis is that modern capitalistic man is dominated by a special ethos, called the Protestant ethic because it is far stronger in Protestant (especially Calvinist) than in Catholic countries. This ethic emphasizes the virtues of industry, thrift, sobriety, work, and the accumulation of wealth, all of which have religious sanction. The *summum bonum* of this ethic is the earning of more and more money, combined with avoidance of the spontaneous enjoyment of life.

McClelland (1961), following out Weber's ideas, has shown that what is basic to capitalism, as well as to any other form of society that grows rapidly, is a certain frame of mind that stresses achievement, responsibility, enterprise, and growth. He sees the desire for achievement as more basic than the desire for money.

Contemporary Views

Many contemporary economists have become critical of the classical theory of work as motivated only by money, especially since the Keynesian revolution has compelled all economists to re-evaluate their basic assumptions. John Kenneth Galbraith in *The New Industrial State* (1973), as well as in many other works, has offered a total revision of the psychological-economic bases upon which modern man lives. He makes free use of the findings of modern psychology and psychiatry.

Galbraith enumerates four motives that lead modern man to work: pecuniary compensation, compulsion, identification, and adaptation. The last two are the features that characterize work in the modern corporate system, which he calls the technostructure. The "organization man" has powerful incentives to stick to his organization and make the most of his opportunities there. (For a fuller discussion see Chapter 9.)

Frederick Herzberg is perhaps the best-known and the most important of the empirical investigators of work satisfaction. He distinguishes between motivators and dissatisfiers (Herzberg, 1966, 1974). He found five strong motivators of job satisfaction: achievement, recognition, the work itself, responsibility, and advancement. The main factors that stand out as dissatisfiers are company policy and administration, supervision, salary, interpersonal relations, and working conditions.

One principal result of Herzberg's theory is to bring work into line with the psychoanalytic image of mental health. For him the "hygiene factors" or maintenance of them must lead to job dissatisfaction because of a need to avoid unpleasantness; the motivators lead to job satisfaction because of a need for growth or self-actualization.

Modern Critique of Work Satisfaction

The demand that work should be gratifying, partially stimulated by psychoanalytic thought, has brought about a searching reevaluation of the meaning of work to man, especially as the hold of religion and the Protestant ethic lessen. The most comprehensive examination of the American work experience is found in the report of a special task force to the Secretary of Health, Education, and Welfare, published in book form under the title, *Work in America* (1973).

A large percentage of the workers queried expressed much dissatisfaction with their work lives. The sources can be summarized as follows: (1) blue-collar blues—work problems spill over from the factory into other life activities; (2) worker mobility—opportunity to advance has decreased or become non-existent; (3) white-collar woes—managers are also discontented; (4) the young worker versus the work ethic—fewer than half of young people queried believed that hard work pays off; (5) minority workers—these are serious casualties of the work system; (6) women and work—in 1971 Department of Labor Studies showed that nine out of ten women will work outside of the home at some time in their lives;[2] (7) older workers and retirement—retired workers often find life much less rewarding; (8) work and health—a surprisingly positive correlation exists between work satisfaction and physical and mental health. In one fifteen-year study of aging (Palmare, 1969), the strongest single predictor of longevity was work satisfaction.

Thus psychoanalytic theory has been in part responsible for stirring up a lively debate on how to make man's work life more gratifying. If no all-inclusive answers are available at present, at least important questions have been raised for the first time. (A further discussion of this topic will be found in Chapter 4.)

PSYCHIATRIC SYMPTOMATOLOGY

Every mental health professional knows that the current situation in psychiatry, as in all the mental health fields, is chaotic. Even as this is being written, *The New York Times* carries an article that excessive tranquilization of mental patients in New York State has led to an excessive number of deaths among them. The chaos can be grasped only with the help of a thorough understanding of both history and theory.

Kraepelin, in *One Hundred Years of Psychiatry* (1917), described the treatment of the mentally ill a century earlier:

> The broad outlines of psychiatry as it existed a century ago have been revealed by our cursory survey: negligent and brutal treatment of the insane; improper living conditions and inadequate medical care; beclouded and false notions concerning the nature and cause of insanity; senseless, haphazard, and at times harmful therapeutic measures which aggravated the plight of those afflicted by mental illness.

But if the treatment of the mentally ill was barbarous and cruel before Kraepelin, under his system the schizophrenic was shocked, injected almost to death, castrated, and lobotomized; had all his teeth extracted and his intestines removed; and was bound hand and foot, beaten by careless attendants, and largely neglected in filthy, poorly kept mental hospitals, which are now being systematically dismantled.

Somatic Factors

Inasmuch as the psychiatrist has a medical degree, the search for organic factors has gone on apace. Beginning with the 1930s, various organic treatments were instituted, particularly insulin coma, electric shock, and lobotomy. Almost all of these have disappeared, to be replaced by the drug revolution of the 1950s. The drugs led to a new era of optimism in psychiatry. Since then psychiatrists have been trained in a mixture of somatic and psychological therapies, generally adopting an eclectic position somewhere between the psychological assumptions of psychoanalysis and the organic ones of Kraepelinian psychiatry. But in spite of all the hullaballoo, somatic treatment today still remains a highly speculative affair.

The Expansion of Psychiatry through Psychoanalysis

Even though psychoanalysis, like general psychiatry, could rarely treat mental patients successfully, it could at least explain their symptoms and suggest possible treatment approaches that made more sense than what had been done in the past. Through psychoanalysis, a psychological understanding was brought into psychiatry, which became an essential part of the training of every psychiatrist from about the 1950s on.

"Illness" as Distance from the Analytic Ideal

The psychiatric diagnostic system commonly employed, which follows Kraepelin, has come under much criticism. Since its adoption in 1917, it has been changed almost every ten years. The last revision was in 1980; another revision has been announced.

Instead of labels and diagnoses, analysts have preferred to develop a profile of ego functions, since the total personality has to be considered. The best known of these are Anna Freud's developmental lines (1965) and Bellak's ego functions profile (1973).

Anna Freud stressed that there are developmental lines valid for every area of the personality. In every instance they trace the child's gradual outgrowing of dependent, irrational attitudes to an increasing mastery of his internal and external world. A full catalogue of each individual's stage of development and failures in development must be provided to understand any person. In almost all persons development is uneven and has proceeded much farther in certain directions than in others. Freud (1937) had even pointed out that the normal individual varies in his functioning from normal to psychotic.

Bellak singled out twelve ego functions for his profile: (1) reality testing, (2) judgment, (3) sense of reality of the world and of the self, (4) regulation and control of drives, affects, and impulses, (5) object relations, (6) thought processes, (7) adaptive regression in the service of the ego, (8) defensive functioning, (9) stimulus barrier, (10) autonomous functioning, (11) synthetic-integrative functioning, and (12) mastery-competence. In his pioneering research project he and his collaborators were able to show that the systematic measurement of these ego functions could provide valid and useful personality profiles.

The analytic ideal and its twelve components, fully discussed throughout this book, have also been used successfully for clinical evaluations and have again proved far more fruitful than the conventional diagnostic categories.

Insanity and the Social Structure

It has become increasingly clear that psychosis and neurosis are both intimately related to the social structure. Rosen (1968) has gathered much evidence to show that this has always been so. Thus every culture produces its own brand of psychosis and other emotional disturbances. This observation likewise shifts the weight more strongly to psychological than to somatic factors.

Current Practice

Current practice is dominated by widespread eclecticism in theory, together with considerable dissatisfaction about actual treatment. Marmor (1975) has documented the hit-or-miss character of much contemporary psychiatry. (A further discussion will be found in Chapter 5.)

Concluding Comment

Such, in brief outline, are the essentials of mainstream psychoanalysis. It will now be shown how this system provides the most meaningful approach to the problems of psychology and supplies a core framework for all the social sciences, thus unifying them into one science of man.

It is worth noting how the present formulation of psychoanalysis differs from others now extant, for example, Rapaport (1960) or Arlow and Brenner (1964). The main differences are the following:

1. Theory is sharply distinguished from therapy. Psychoanalysis is a comprehensive system of psychology, and its applications to therapy depend on the nature of the patient and the cultural milieu.

2. All unnecessary references to physiology have been eliminated. The neurological substrata that make the psychological functioning possible pose important questions in their own right. But these are neuropsychological and neurophysiological problems faced by all approaches to psychology. The fact that Freud spent so much time ruminating about physiological origins can be ascribed to his early education and the realization that when he began his work psychology in the modern sense really did not exist at all.

3. Because of the elimination of physiological speculation, the entire jargon of metapsychology, with the complexes of cathexes, libido theory, psychic energy, and the like, can be totally discarded as not essential to the psychological system of psychoanalysis. They often pose important questions that require research and resolution in their own right, but again these questions relate to all of psychology and not to psychoanalysis as such.

4. The formulations are offered in terms of human goals and purposes rather than in terms of an abstract concept like information

processing. Certainly the human mind processes information, like any other computer-like machine, but this should be looked upon as a way of clarifying some of the processes involved, not as a substitute for psychoanalytic theory. Above all, in systems like information processing the essential psychoanalytic vision gets lost.

5. Mainstream psychoanalysis combines the best thought of all the "schools" without entering into any doctrinaire school of its own. On the current scene, the Freudians and the culturalists represent the two largest groupings. The theory presented here includes features from both approaches.

6. The central vision of psychoanalysis, of what man is and what he might become through therapy or analytically oriented education, is kept in mind throughout. This accomplishes two principal goals. First of all, everything psychological that is observed in the human subject is included; there are no "taboo" topics. Second, the element of change is viewed continuously as an indispensable aspect of human behavior, even if the facilities for such change are not immediately available, or even if the change methods are inadequate, as in traditional philosophy and religion.

7. In accordance with this central vision, there is a full incorporation of all relevant data from all other disciplines. There is, as will be developed further throughout the book, only one science of man, and the division into many "disciplines" is another of those historical accidents that have caused endless wastage of human research resources. In the development of the self-image, for example, history, sociology, anthropology, group behavior, family background, and many other considerations must be properly evaluated to arrive at a full account.

Part II

The Social Sciences

Chapter 4

The Vision of Experimental Psychology

THERE ARE TWO basically contradictory attitudes toward psychology today: the behavioristic-experimental and the dynamic-psychoanalytic. In general, the behavioristic has dominated the universities for a hundred years; more recently the psychoanalytic has come to dominate the thought and practice of clinicians.

The Historical Setting

In his standard work *Historical Introduction to Modern Psychology* (1972), Gardner Murphy has this to say by way of introduction:

> Wherein lies that unity of subject matter which leads us to speak, compactly enough, of "contemporary psychology"? From behaviorism or Gestalt psychology to psychoanalysis or the objective measurement of character, the eye wanders over an interminable range of experiments, measurements, hypotheses, dogmas, disconnected facts, and systematic theories. . . . Whatever difficulties there may be in finding unity in the various psychological disciplines, there is at least one unity to which we can cling for orientation and perspective, for appreciation and synthesis; and this is the tranquil unity of history.[1]

The sharp rejection of psychoanalysis by academic, behavioristically oriented psychology is a historical fact that cannot be ignored. Though this rejection is somewhat weaker, it is still true that anyone with a strong analytic orientation must find his way outside the recognized departments of psychology. Yet it is our thesis in this book that psychoanalysis represents the heart of psychology. Thus arises a paradox that cries for resolution.

The Clash of Two Visions

The experimentalist rejection of psychoanalysis was total and was carried out in an authoritarian manner. Psychoanalysis, Sears stated bluntly in his 1942 survey, was simply "bad science." In this way he was simply repeating what psychologists had been saying since the time of Wundt, the acknowledged father of experimental psychology.

Wundt, who held both Ph.D. and M.D. degrees, was a professor of philosophy at the University of Leipzig from 1874 until his death in 1920. He was the leading world figure in psychology when Freud made his epochal contributions in the 1900–1914 period. Wundt ignored them entirely; to him they were not psychology and they were not science. Science for him, as the title of his major work, *Principles of Physiological Psychology* (1873–74), indicates, meant experimental investigation by purely physiological methods.

In this view Wundt was adhering to the famous Helmholtz program, which had also had a strong influence on Freud in his early days. The Helmholtz program was formulated in this way by du Bois-Raymond in 1842:

> Brücke and I pledged a solemn oath to put into power this truth, no other forces than the common physico-chemical ones are active within the organism; that, in those cases which cannot at the time be explained by these forces one has either to find the specific way or form of their action by means of the physico-mathematical method, or to assume new forces equal in dignity to the chemical-physical forces inherent in matter, reducible to the force of attraction and repulsion.[2]

Most of the early American psychologists did postgraduate work in Germany, where they were heavily influenced by Wundt. According to Murphy, the most important single factor in saving America from becoming a branch office of Wundt's laboratory was the influence of William James.

Thus the vision of Wundt and of Freud's other psychological contemporaries was methodological. Experiment enough psychologically and all the problems of human functioning will be resolved. There is no image of happiness, no concern with human problems, not the remotest awareness of man's love life.

After a hundred years, it is possible to form some opinion of the effectiveness of various methodologies. In 1938, when Woodworth published the first edition of his *Experimental Psychology* (rev. 1954), he remarked on the youth and immaturity of experimental psychology and noted that experimental psychology was itself an experiment. Hull, in the 1930s and 1940s, was determined to find mathematically correct laws of learning that would solve psychology's problems, even if it took 300 years to do so (1943).

Many philosophers and scientists have been highly critical of this model's attempt to reduce psychology to physiology by experimental methods. Bertrand Russell (1948) once commented that the behavioristic denial of introspection was so absurd that he would not even take it seriously were it not for the fact that an influential school of psychology had placed such stress on it. Ernest Nagel, in *The Structure of Science* (1961), correctly observes that behaviorism at that date (almost a hundred years after Wundt began) was clearly a program of theoretical and experimental research, and then commented: "The objectives of the program have certainly not been attained, and perhaps never will be."[3]

The biologist Wheeler, who wrote several standard works on the social insects, commented in 1923:

> After perusing during the past twenty years a small library of rose-water psychologies of the academic type and noticing how their authors ignore or merely hint at the existence of such stupendous and fundamental biological phenomena as those of hunger, sex and fear, I should not disagree with, let us say, an imaginary critic recently arrived from Mars, who should express the opinion that many of these works read as if they had been composed by beings that had been born and bred in a belfry, castrated in early infancy and fed continually for fifty years through a tube with a stream of liquid nutriment of constant chemical composition. To put it drastically, most of our traditional psychologies are about as useful for purposes of understanding the human mind as an equal number of dissertations on Greek statuary would be to a student eager for a knowledge of anatomy.[4]

The Basic Error in Experimental Psychology

The basic error in experimental psychology is that it rests on the nineteenth-century assumption that man is rational, conscious, and subject to control by powerful external forces, and hence that it is the business of psychology to uncover what these powerful forces are. Totally unrecognized is the psychoanalytic discovery that while these powerful external forces may at times exist, in many cases man is irrational, unconscious, and governed by powerful internal forces, which can be brought to consciousness by psychotherapy and thereby put under control. Much ink has been spilled on the distinction between "nomothetic" and "idiographic" sciences, or Dilthey's distinction between *erklaerende* and *verstehende Wissenschaft* (causal and descriptive science), which he saw as basic to the distinction between the natural and the social sciences. But the most significant error of all, the assumption that internal forces are by and large of no real importance, has been overlooked entirely. The experimentalists simply perpetuated this error in their writings, endlessly repeating the Helmholtzian assumptions of nineteenth-century science, without being aware of the tremendous changes that have occurred since.

Nagel has been particularly caustic about the lack of philosophical sophistication in the average experimental psychologist. He writes:

> [Proponents] of these conflicting psychological schools are often divided by commitments (sometimes, though not always, explicit) to different philosophical conceptions of what constitutes scientific knowledge and how such knowledge is to be established. These conceptions frequently involve gross oversimplifications and misunderstandings of the logic of inquiry in other natural sciences; in particular, they sometimes contain crude empiricistic notions of scientific research that fail to do justice to the complex substantive and methodological assumptions which enter into the collection and interpretation of empirical data. But in any event, such conceptions are commonly acquired by psychologists from the parochial intellectual traditions which they imbibe in an unquestioning manner during their professional training.
>
> Accordingly, it does not seem unreasonable to suppose that the progress of psychology as a natural science would be helped, and the level of the theoretical discussions raised, if psychologists were philosophically more knowledgeable than they usually are and had in particular competence in the logic of theory construction.

One of the main goals of the present work is to offer some constructive suggestions for the reformation of psychology along adequate philosophical lines.

The Growth of Psychology

Although the American Psychological Association was formed in 1893, it is really a post–World War II phenomenon. In 1940 its membership was less than a thousand. As of 1978 its membership was 46,891.

This extraordinary growth can be attributed almost entirely to the rise of clinical psychology, which did not exist as an independent Ph.D. discipline before the war.

Clinical psychology is essentially a mixture, in varying degrees, of three streams of thought: psychoanalysis, experimental psychology (including learning theory), and psychological testing. In terms of its practical applications, by far the most important of the three is psychoanalysis. The division of experimental psychology in the APA in 1978 numbered only 1,392 persons, while the clinical membership numbered 4,137. Thus, psychology has become a largely clinical science.

The advent of clinical psychology left the old theoreticians flabbergasted. Nevertheless, power is attractive, and the old theoreticians maintained their hold in the universities. As in other fields, a deep split emerged in the body psychological: In practice psychologists became clinicians, dealing with human beings, understanding them, trying to help them; in theory they were experimentalists, questioning every device adopted in any clinical situation as "unscientific" or "unproved." One prominent professor of psychology even seriously suggested around 1950 that all psychotherapy be discontinued for ten years, during which time large-scale experiments should be set up to determine the most appropriate methods; then psychotherapy could be resumed on a "scientific" basis. The university where he taught dropped clinical psychology from its degree program and limited itself to "pure" and "theoretical" psychology. Back to Helmholtz and Wundt!

Most clinicians themselves remained confused about what they were doing. Brainwashed by the academic insistence on experimentation as the only real basis of science, they tended to see themselves as "applied" psychologists, a kind of second-rate citizen. Wittgenstein, looking at the situation from the outside and gifted with a logical mind, correctly observed that there was something wrong with "experimental psychology;" as he put it, problem and method pass each other by. But most clinicians, not sufficiently trained in the history of science (cf. Nagel, above), timidly agreed that their approaches and their findings could not be dignified with the name of "science." Those who insisted that psychoanalysis and clinical methodology were quite scientific as a rule left the larger association of psychologists.

In spite of this enforced split, a sizable number of psychologists remained faithful to the clinical tradition, pursued it, and pushed the science ahead. Henry (1971) has shown that a higher percentage of psychologists take postgraduate psychoanalytic training than of either psychiatrists or social workers. When the writer and a group of colleges sent out a call in 1978 to form a division of psychoanalysis within the APA, polling only the members of the divisions of clinical psychology and of psychotherapy, about 1,000 replies were received. Allowing for duplications, this means that some 15 to 20 percent of the members of these two divisions wished to be classified as psychoanalysts.

Science, Methodology, and Psychology

The traditional argument has been that psychoanalysis is "bad" science while experimental psychology is "good" science. Even eminent psychoanalyts have been taken in by this objection.[6] Yet an increasing number are doubting it. It is essential to look at the arguments and at the evidence.

Following Wundt, psychology was supposed to experiment, using primarily the methods that had pushed physics and chemistry to such peaks of excellence. On the contemporary scene B. F. Skinner remains the most eloquent spokesman for this position, and it will be easiest to consider his arguments, which are highly valued by many psychologists.

To begin with, Skinner continues the diatribe against "mentalism," using the same arguments that Wundt used a century ago and Watson a half-century ago. In *Beyond Freedom and Dignity* (1971) Skinner reaffirms the positions of his lifetime: Mentalism is to be rejected because "the world of the mind steals the show. Behavior is not recognized as a subject in its own right."[7] Skinner ignores the fact that while this objection may apply to astrology and fortune-telling, it has no relevance whatsoever to psychology. For the psychoanalyst, behavior is not only recognized as a subject in its own right, *it is accorded even more weight than in experimental work*. The analyst examines every bit of his subject's behavior, no matter how slight: his walking, his manner of talking, his dress, his intonation, and so on. The difference lies not in that psychoanalysis ignores behavior but in its conviction that no bit of behavior can be properly understood without reference to the context. This statement seems self-evident, yet the behaviorists ignore it almost entirely.

Consider a very simple example. John meets Fred and says, "You." Is he angry, is he friendly, is he indifferent, is he objective? No one can tell without knowing the relationship between John and Fred and what John's intentions are. To describe this situation as one where two men meet and greet each other not only does not do justice to the situation but is a completely incorrect analysis of behavior. And yet this, on a larger scale, is what the behaviorists are doing all the time.

Skinner also takes strong exception to the concept of "autonomous man" and to the concepts of freedom and dignity. Actions have antecedents; without understanding these antecedents, he argues, one cannot understand what is going on. There is no argument whatsoever here. Skinner is setting up a straw man, which he then knocks down. His statements to the effect that there is a longstanding conviction that for much of human behavior there *are* no relevant antecedents does not apply in the slightest degree to psychoanalysis, which has always insisted that *all* of human behavior can be understood, regardless of how irrational it may appear on the surface. In fact, the paradox is that psychoanalytic research has come to the conclusion that no bit of human behavior is really irrational; at the unconscious level there is always some rational explanation for what the person is doing.

The fact that physics and chemistry do not have to consider intentions, aims, and purposes is another bit of irrelevancy that Skinner makes much of. Intentions and purposes are of no importance in charting the course of the stars or the physics of a nuclear explosion. But human beings *do* have intentions and purposes, and without talking about them it is impossible to understand the human being.

Skinner's dilemma can be resolved by introducing the concept of the unconscious (even though it is anathema to him). Consider the conditioning paradigm. Is the conditioned animal (and by extension the human) conscious of what he is doing or unconscious? He is not conscious of the threat or reward; if he were he would make a simple choice, and we would not call it conditioning. Bandura in fact has stressed this point, insisting that "conditioning is a myth, since the subject must see some connection between the stimulus and the response; there is no mechanical coupling of the two."[8]

Human learning is not based on conditioning, except in a trivial sense. The major rewards are the approval and/or disapproval of important people, to begin with the parents. When the child is very young, he cannot yet verbalize these feelings; the analyst speaks of the unconscious, and the learning theorist prefers to use the word conditioning. Essentially they are describing the same phenomenon. Only the radical behavior theorist like Skinner then goes on to deny the reality of the internal world, while the psychoanalyst explores the nature of the internal world further.

The Logic of Experimentation

Skinner would have us believe that all that is necessary to build up a true science, what he calls a "technology of behavior," is to acquire sufficient information about antecedents and consequents. Here he is merely perpetuating an ancient error. The formula for learning should read S-O-R (stimulus = organism = response), not just S-R (stimulus = response). Actually, the behaviorists fail to realize that the formula in physics or chemistry is also S-O-R, the organism in that case (since Einstein) being understood to stand for the contextual environment in which stimulus and response occur, including temperature, pressure, fields of force, gravity, catalytic agents, and so forth.

Other objections have been raised to the glorification of experimentation. Rosenthal (1976) has amassed an enormous amount of data to show that all too often the expectations of the experimenter seriously color the results obtained; in other words, the experimenter finds what he is looking for, even in animal experimentation. The difficulties in generalizing from animal work to human situations have often been noted. Even more surprisingly, Silverman (1977) has shown that it is extremely difficult to generalize from a laboratory situation with humans to a real-life situation. He argues that subjects in psychological experiments act in ways that bear little relation to their behaviors in the life situations to which psychologists seek to generalize their findings.

Still, the main objection to experimentation remains the pragmatic one, that it has not proved possible to experiment on material that is of serious significance to the human being. Experimentation has thus remained close to the physiological realm, where Wundt wanted to keep it. Thus, in the latest revised edition of Woodworth's basic *Experimental Psychology*, in 1971, the topics covered by the seventeen distinguished contributors are: psychophysics, neural function, the cutaneous senses, the chemical senses, audition, vision, perception, learning (selected topics), positive reinforcement, aversive behavior, motivation, verbal learning, theoretical and experimental approaches to human learning, transfer, interference, and forgetting. There is nothing here about love, sexuality, death, work, self-esteem, or any of the other subjects so central to human happiness.

The Psychoanalytic Vision and the Experimental Vision

If experimentation has proved so sterile with regard to the central human issues, why then does a powerful body of psychologists cling to it as a fundamental solution to human ills? Skinner, for example, still calls for a technology of behavior, to be established by experimental methods, with suitable schedules of reinforcement, for all antecedents and all consequents. In itself this would be less important were it not for the fact that so many psychologists (and others in the social sciences) have made Skinner a kind of hero. *Contemporary Psychology*, the journal of reviews of the APA, devoted extensive space to Skinner's book in 1972, shortly after the book appeared, lavishing effusive praise on his ideas and conclusions, even though the book said nothing that Skinner had not said before and was essentially a worthless political tract.

As usual, hidden behind this battle about methodology is a more crucial one. The real issue is psychotherapy: Should psychologists, following Freud, start doing psychotherapy and trying to make individuals happier, or should they putter about in their laboratories, hoping for an eventual discovery like DNA?

Going farther behind the façade, we find that experimental psychology is allied in practice to organic psychiatry and to milieu social work, and in theory to various approaches in the other social sciences. All of these have in common an opposition to psychotherapy (which they generally fail to understand). Searles once eloquently warned his fellow psychiatrists that the phenothiazine-genetics approach to schizophrenia, which most psychiatrists today favor, would usher in "the long dark night of the human soul." At best psychologists would allow for behavioral modification or behavior therapy (of which more anon), which is stuck in the thinking of the 1890s, when Freud began.

A second commonality in these three approaches is that they are all acceptable to the totalitarian countries. This fact has been even less appreciated than the opposition to psychotherapy. They all (experimentation, organic, psychiatric, milieu social work) stay away from the deeper psychological problems afflicting mankind. Skinner does not even recognize that his theories lend themselves to a Nazi type of experimentation on human beings, as when he says:

> The technology of behavior which emerges is ethically neutral, but when applied to the design of a culture, the survival of the culture functions as a value. . . . . It is not the benevolence of a controller but the contingencies under which he controls benevolently which must be examined.[9]

There is nothing in Skinner's philosophy that would condemn the Nazi experimentation on human beings by medical doctors, which horrified the world, the thought control of the Chinese (Lifton, 1969), the psychiatric terror of the contemporary Russians (not to mention the gruesome mass murders of Comrade Stalin). All of these have "survival value;" they keep the culture going.

In recent years these questions have become particularly pertinent in the American culture because of the proliferation of behavior modification. Following Skinner, behavior modifiers merely wish to change behavior without regard to values. Thus they have applied electric shocks to the testicles of child molesters, incarcerated rebellious subjects in boxes where they could scarcely move, withdrawn (or threatened to withdraw) welfare money from recipients who refused to work, and so forth. On an even broader level the whole structure of behavior therapy as now practiced denies or ignores the fundamental values of our democratic society by focusing on trivial symptoms and leaving out the central issues. In justifiable reaction to such techniques, behavior modification has been restricted in the federal prison system and is often looked upon with suspicion elsewhere.

In the early 1970s some behavior modification approaches with prisoners brought the ethical questions into the courts and regulatory agencies (Friedman, 1976). In one program, known as START, prisoners were selected without their prior consent or knowledge. When this practice was challenged, the courts held that a prisoner brought into such a behavior modification program is entitled at a minimum to a hearing. In 1973 the Task Force on Corrections of the National Advisory Commisssion on Criminal Justice Standards and Goals recommended strong precautions for the use of behavior modification techniques with prisoners (Milan and McKee, 1977). And in 1974 HEW proposed additional regulations providing more safeguards for vulnerable groups, such as prisoners and the mentally disabled. The furor around behavior therapy in prisons also led in 1974 to the establishment by Congress of a Commission for the Protection of Human Patients (Friedman, 1976). Trotter and Warren reviewed the whole situation in an article in the *APA Monitor* entitled "Behavior Therapy Under Fire" (Trotter and Warren, 1974).

Science and Vision

The issue, then, is not one of science; psychoanalysis in its own way is just as good a science as experimental psychology. The real issue is the philosophy of living. Psychoanalysis is banned in the totalitarian countries because of its fundamental emphasis on love, friendship, happiness, self-esteem, and the like, while experimental psychology and its corollary behavior therapy are welcome because they do not in any way challenge the basic values of the society.

Likewise the academic resistance to psychoanalysis in the democratic countries on the pretext that it is "bad science" is exactly that: nothing more than a pretext. College professors would rather stay in their laboratories, exploring the intricacies of intermittent reinforcement (which can never be resolved in the form in which they explore it), than go out into the everyday world and tackle the basic problems that face mankind.

It is against this perversion of the significant democratic vision that clinicians have risen in protest. Only, since "psychoanalysis" has been a taboo word, they have failed to see that they are pursuing a psychoanalytic vision of science and human happiness. It is high time to get away from the useless (and grossly incorrect) argument about science, experiment, and methodology and face the real question: Should science pursue the cause of human welfare, no matter where that pursuit leads, or should it hide behind a variety of trivialities and irrelevancies?

In his well-known book *The Scientific Revolution* (1962), Kuhn distinguishes between preparadigmatic and paradigmatic phases of science. A more useful distinction for our purposes is that between the stages of science where large-scale errors occur and the stages where these large-scale errors have for all practical purposes disappeared. In the physical sciences large-scale errors have for all practical purposes disappeared. They may reappear for political reasons, as in Lysenko's resurrection of the Lamarckian theory of the inheritance of acquired characteristics in Soviet Russia. But barring such events, scientists pursue common goals with a common method and form an international community.

Nothing of this kind exists in the social sciences and psychology. There large-scale errors still occur. In one study of Chinese psychology after the revolution, all reports ceased from 1966 on; psychology in effect had disappeared. It was not until 1979 that a Chinese journal of psychology resumed publication. Some American psychiatrists still wish to serve as apologists for Soviet psychiatric terror[10] rather than recognize that it is a way of brutalizing and dehumanizing the human being.

On a broader scale, the usual ways in which psychology is taught represent a large-scale error in that the image of science presented is grossly incorrect; likewise the history of physics and chemistry, on which it is allegedly based, is also incorrectly presented. Second, the more basic human concerns are omitted from consideration or are treated in a deplorably superficial manner. And third, in the conflict between precision and relevance the student is encouraged to pursue precision, no matter how irrelevant it might be.

We are speaking here of the broad trends still prevailing today. It is also to be noted that there is a large-scale commotion in the psychological organizations, in conscious or unconscious protest against such a state of affairs. How far such a protest goes is hard to say. So far the academic psychologists' objections to the serious study of psychology have carried the day and forced clinicians to go elsewhere for their more basic training, such as to psychoanalysis and projective methods. At the same time the institution of new doctoral programs, the expansion of clinical facilities, and the incorporation of much of psychoanalytic thinking augurs well for the future.

To make these constructive trends maximally effective it is imperative that the psychoanalytic vision be fully grasped by all psychologists. From a scientific point of view, this involves the recognition that psychology is essentially a clinical science—that is, dependent on careful observation rather than laboratory experimentation, useful though that might be at times. There must also be a recognition that allied to this clinical science is a philosophy of living that makes more sense than any previously known to man.

It is a heartening sign that a Division of Psychoanalysis was established by the APA in 1979. Such a development would have been unthinkable even ten years ago.

On the Nature of Psychological Science

Many definitions of science are available. The most appropriate one is that science is an honest inquiry into any state of affairs, which is prepared to present its evidence and draw conclusions appropriate to that evidence. Ernest Nagel in *The Structure of Science* (1961) offers a similar definition when he says that "the distinctive aim of the scientific enterprise is to provide systematic and responsibly supported explanations."[11]

Now the state of affairs that interests psychological science is man. What kind of a creature is he? How does he function? What does he want? Is he happy or unhappy? These and similar questions are the proper concern of psychology.

If we return to Skinner for a moment and evaluate him by the above canons, a surprising conclusion presents itself: Skinner (and the behaviorists in general) rule out from their domain of inquiry a large part of what is ordinarily called human. Intentions, aims, goals, purposes, freedom, dignity—all of these, Skinner tells us, are illusions, not worthy of serious consideration. Stones have no goals; why should humans? There are only antecedents and consequents, only S-R formulas.

In part Skinner is making a correct observation. The stated goals and purposes of men are not their goals and purposes; quite often, in fact, they do not know what their real goals and purposes are. The logical conclusion is that these goals are unconscious. But Skinner recoils from such an obvious conclusion. Instead he takes the entirely illogical step of ruling goals and purposes out of human existence. This is not science at all.

In this way behaviorists exclude large segments of human behavior. Not infrequently college sophomores interested in psychology avoid behavioristic departments because they teach only "rat psychology" and instead go to the English department or the philosophy department to study "real" psychology. In this choice their native intuition serves them well, for in fact behaviorism is not psychology in the correct sense at all. From a philosophical point of view it does not investigate goals and purposes, which are the essence of the human spirit. From a technical point of view it omits dreams, fantasies, and other mental products, which differentiate the human from the animal. The college student's intuition that philosophy and literature are psychology is correct.

Behaviorism as a Large-Scale Error

It has already been pointed out that all the social sciences have made an incorrect assumption of the nature of man, that he is rational, conscious, and manipulated by powerful external forces beyond his control. In each discipline this assumption has led to different mistakes. In psychology the large-scale error deriving from this view has been behaviorism.

Like experimental psychology, with which it has always been closely allied, behaviorism started out as a methodological revolution: Explore behavior, avoid mentalistic assumptions, seek out the antecedents and consequents of behavior, and you will have a psychological science. That was its vision, and that remains its vision.

Behaviorism has attempted to buttress this vision by ascribing to itself the aura of science while branding approaches, such as psychoanalysis, "unscientific." In this connection the term "science" acquires an honorific character: To be scientific is to be good and worthy, to be unscientific is to be anecdotal, unworthy.

It is about a hundred years since Wundt established his first experimental laboratory. Unfortunately, as Nagel and many others have pointed out, behaviorism has not fulfilled its promise. In his 1971 book Skinner deeply laments the fact that we have no "technology of behavior," in effect, that the program he espouses has led nowhere. Instead the science of psychology has moved in a markedly clinical direction.

For this failure of the behavioristic program three principal reasons can be ascribed, all of considerable consequence for the growth of the science.

1. *The facts unearthed by psychology are often unpalatable.* A realistic appraisal of the human scene discloses many grim realities that people are reluctant to face. Mass murder has been more the rule in history than the exception. Man has been more insane than sane, more infantile than adult, more primitive than civilized. Tragically, genocide seems to continue today in various countries.

Careful studies undertaken after World War II disclosed an enormous amount of suffering and conflict in the average population. Rennie, in his study of New Yorkers (1962), estimated that some 80 percent of them were disturbed. Leighton (1963), in his exploration of the Maritime Provinces of Canada, reached similar conclusions. In psychotherapy the shift in clientele from the bizarre to the normal population has been one consequence of this growing awareness.

It is no accident that psychoanalysis was catapulted into world-wide popularity by two disastrous world wars that cost the lives of hundreds of millions of people. While mental illness was not so obvious in World War I, by World War II it had become clear that there were a number of psychotic dictators around. Psychoanalysis had the conceptual tools with which to grasp such phenomena; behaviorism did not.

Further, when faced with such a wholesale reversal of ordinary standards of human decency two reactions are possible: revolution or retreat. Psychoanalysis has offered a revolutionary approach; behaviorism beat a hasty retreat and is still beating a retreat from the realities of evil (see Becker, 1968).

2. *The data of psychology are often not reproducible or not easily reproducible.* This factor has made the scientific pursuit of psychological problems difficult. Freud did pursue these hard-to-get-at data, such as dreams, slips of the tongue, neurotic symptoms, artistic productions and the like. His system was built in part on inferences from these data.

By contrast, behaviorism has eschewed anything that is not readily reproducible in the laboratory, proclaiming such reproducibility to be one hallmark of science. It has been pointed out that a variety of disciplines, such as history, astronomy, paleontology, much of biology, and the like, also deal with material that is highly evanescent or that cannot ever again be reproduced. Thus the behaviorist's insistence on reproducibility drastically and needlessly limits his observation of the human scene.

Here too the problem is one of pursuing the data offered by the human subject or creating artificial situations from which information about the human subject can be extrapolated or inferred. The device of the artificial situation is the one pursued by the behaviorist; that of observing the human being as he is, by the psychoanalyst. It would appear that on most of the issues that really count psychoanalytic research has gone farther than behavioristic.

3. *The observer is often biased.* Still another problem that has bedeviled those who have tried to make psychology scientific is the bias (or biases) of the observer. Mostly these are unconscious; sometimes they are near the surface.

These biases stem from the anxieties aroused in the observer by the material he is observing. Such biases first became noticeable in the therapeutic situation, where the principle was laid down at an early stage that no analyst can go farther with a patient than he has gone with himself. Accordingly, as we have noted, since about 1930 personal analysis has been an indispensable requirement of all psychoanalytic training.

The question raised here is whether personal analysis may not also be a reasonable requirement for research into any aspect of human behavior. The kinds of questions asked, the areas of research pursued, the sophistication with which the replies are sifted; these and numerous other issues relating to psychological research depend very heavily on the objectivity of the observer. In the areas of deepest concern, such as sexuality, love, or affect, such objectivity is always interfered with by some personal bias. For example, research into the prevalence of neurosis depends very strongly on what the observer takes "neurosis" to mean. If he confines himself to the extreme aberrant symptoms, such as hand-washing compulsions or hysterical crying fits, he comes up with a small percentage. If, however, he broadens his view to include character problems, such as dissatisfaction with life, low self-esteem, lack of love, excessive hatred, and the like, he comes up with a much higher percentage. Sociologists who have taken the narrower view estimate that 3–5 percent of the population is neurotic; those who take the broader view find 60–80 percent of the population neurotic (Dohrenwend and Dohrenwend, 1969).

It will be seen that these three factors—unpalatable material, uniqueness of the data, and observer bias—will enter into every discussion of psychology and all the social sciences. How they are handled depends ultimately on the vision of the scientist more than on anything else.

Psychology as a Clinical Science

The shift from the experimental paradigm to the clinical, which characterized the field after World War II, was inspired primarily by the psychoanalytic vision, even though many clinicians were unaware of it. It was only then that enough psychologists and psychiatrists had gone through a personal analysis, of greater or lesser depth, and it was only through this personal analysis that they began to see what was happening in their own lives and in the lives of other people.

Nevertheless, relatively few realized that the clinical approach was just as scientific as the experimental. Paradoxically, one of the few who did was Edwin Boring, the eminent author of *The History of Experimental Psychology*, widely respected as one of the deans of American psychology. In the APA symposium on "Psychoanalysis as Seen by Psychoanalyzed Psychologists" (1940), Boring wrote:

> It seems strange that a psychologist after his psychoanalysis should not have a message for his colleagues, when there has been so much questioning of psychoanalysis by the orthodox psychologists; and yet it is true that four years after my analysis I still cannot assess with assurance the significance of the experience in my life. Since, nevertheless, my hesitation is a datum in itself, I welcome this opportunity to make it in specific detail a matter of record. Apparently psychology is not yet in a position to validate or invalidate psychoanalysis experimentally—with selected groups and carefully chosen controls. Hence we are reduced to the collection of case histories; and critical autobiographical histories by sophisticated, scientifically minded persons ought to be worth more than the enthusiasm of naive persons about an event which has helped them.[12]

In this passage Boring admits that experimentation in the traditional sense had not yet been able to evaluate psychoanalysis. Yet even today, after the publication of Fisher and Greenberg's *The Scientific Credibility of Freud's Theories*, which summarized, in a positive fashion, all the available experimental evidence, it is still true that there is no strictly experimental proof of any of the doctrines of psychoanalysis. But this is generally true of psychology, except for such global matters as the fact that human beings, like other organisms, learn.

The three factors mentioned above and several others correlated with them make it virtually impossible to determine anything in this field with absolute precision. Thus arises the problem of relevance versus precision. Science, to be science, must be relevant; if it cannot attain absolute precision, it can but increase its efforts to make its findings more precise, rather than abandon the enterprise.

Under these circumstances reasonable inference from imprecise data becomes one of the main methodological tools. The term "imprecise" is used here in comparison with purely physiological data or data from some other fields. For example, that a person actually did have the dream he relates to an observer is likely but not absolutely certain.

Theory and Therapy

It is inevitable that confusion should arise in the clinical field between theory and therapy, especially since the two, historically, have generally gone hand in hand. By now certain hoary confusions have been, or should have been, completely dispelled. The analytic patient is not "sick" in the conventional sense but represents a cross-section of the population. The material he presents is not different from that presented by other people. It is not suggested by the therapist. In fact, it can be, and has been, obtained by many other methods as well: interviews, autobiographies, personal documents, projective techniques, and so on.

Today the relationship of therapy to theory is still widely misconstrued. That people can change, and change in directions indicated by psychoanalytic theory, is a datum of overwhelming significance. It is also a datum ignored by all the nonclinical approaches. The degree of change, the nature of the process, the desirability of the changes produced—these and many other questions can now be discussed intelligently on the basis of clinical experience. They provide an entirely new dimension for psychology.

A clinical science is one that relies on observations more than on experimentation. Although these observations are inaccurate and merely form the basis for an inferential process rather than serve as absolute data in their own right, they still are far more valuable than anything else available, as Boring rightly saw a generation ago. This state of affairs decrees that psychology (and all the sciences of man, which extend from psychology) must be first of all a clinical rather than an experimental science.

When experiments are possible, by all means let them be performed. But human affairs rarely lend themselves to the pure kind of experimentation seen in physics or chemistry. (For that matter biology does not lend itself readily to experimentation either, and much of our knowledge depends on careful observation there too.)

The cry for experimentation and the erroneous belief that only experimentation makes true science possible have placed psychology in the famous double-bind position. It cannot get anywhere with experimentation, but the demand that it should do so cripples constructive research and needlessly puts the clinician in a second-rate position. It is high time to recognize the obvious fact that most of our knowledge of human beings derives from clinical rather than experimental data.

The Conceptual Framework of Psychology

In his book *Patterns of Discovery* (1965) the philosopher Norwood Hanson shows how fundamental the conceptual framework is to all science. Any perception, he stresses, is theory-laden. Progress in science has come about through conceptual analysis, criticism of criteria, and revision of methods and ideas. He quotes Einstein's famous remark from *The Method of Theoretical Physics* that "there is no inductive method which could lead to the fundamental concepts of physics . . . in error are those theorists who believe that theory comes inductively from experience."[13]

If what Hanson says is true of physics, it is all the more true of psychology. What Freud gave us was a conceptual framework with which the data of psychology can be organized; without it, the organization collapses. Thus the concepts of transference and resistance illuminate the therapeutic enterprise as nothing else does, while the concepts of development, fixation, and regression offer extraordinary illumination in the areas of psychopathology.

Much vitriol has been poured on the basic psychoanalytic concepts. Concepts such as the unconscious, transference, introjects, and the Oedipus complex have all been severely mauled as unwarranted "reifications" or at times simply figments of the analyst's imagination. Skinner, for example, erroneously accuses psychotherapists of restoring the image of the daimonic and says that psychoanalysts have distinguished three personalities—the id, the ego, and the superego.[14]

All of this misses the point of science, in fact represents a gross misunderstanding of science (apart from the fact that Skinner's accusations are entirely without foundation and that he fails to understand what psychoanalysts are saying). Without adequate concepts no science is possible. Nor can concepts be said to be true or false; they are either useful or not useful.

For clinicians the concept of the unconscious is enormously useful. Without it the repeated denials of patients, their lapses, their forgetting, their distortions, their resistances, their transferences, and their rationalizations all remain utterly incomprehensible. Further-more, anyone who has had any psychotherapy almost immediately recognizes in himself that he has at times been actuated by motives of which he was not conscious.

To the experimentalist, however, the concept of a dynamic un-conscious that can motivate people without their being aware of what motivates them is much less useful. His concern is to make his controls precise, to define his terms, to specify his problem, and to get a result. Whether this result is applicable to everyday human af-fairs is really no concern of his. What he fails to see is that the net consequence of this kind of experimentation is an impoverishment of the human spirit. Without the concept of the unconscious, the field of psychology is constricted to a narrow range where man behaves more like an animal than a human.

No doubt the term "happiness" defies exact definition. What does not defy definition is that all men seek and have sought happi-ness, however they define it. And there is equally little doubt that this search for their definition of happiness is one of the central con-cerns of their lives. Thus how men choose to define happiness is, or should be, one of the central concerns of psychological science. That their conscious definition may conceal some entirely different un-conscious quest does not alter this statement in the slightest.

As indicated in the previous chapter, the science of psychology can now be built up along these lines. Man seeks happiness, a work-ing definition of which from the analytic point of view would be the twelve components of the analytic ideal listed in Chapter 3. Within these broader goals he has many subsidiary goals, purposes, aims, and intentions, which must be explored. The study of these twelve components, from both a philosophical (value) and a psychological point of view, would then provide the framework for the science of psychology. It is in this sense that we can say that psychoanalysis *is* psychology, in that it provides the most meaningful framework for pursuit of the field.

On Values and Biases

Two objections have been raised to the approach suggested above. First of all, science should be above values; it should be ethi-cally neutral. And second, this approach has inbred biases that will necessarily color the data.

With regard to the first, that human beings are dominated by value systems is beyond dispute. So any science that studies human beings must also study these value systems. Any kind of psychology that does not have anything to say about values is not really science in the serious sense, though it may deal scientifically with a small part of the human enterprise.

As for ethical neutrality, experience shows that to be impossible. At the same time it is not essential for the scientist. The physicists who made the first atomic bomb certainly deplored the enormous loss of life it caused, yet they could still go ahead and make a good bomb. A psychiatrist who examines a convicted killer can be revolted by his inhuman acts and yet be objective about his state of mind. What is required is not ethical neutrality but objectivity.

The second objection, that any value system will color the data, is likewise contradicted by experience. It is the general analytic conviction that severe emotional deprivation in infancy will have deleterious effects on later personality functioning and that such effects are to be deplored. Yet we can still consider objectively any evidence that is presented to contradict the assumption that early deprivation does cripple the personality. The same holds for any other data. Honestly, integrity, and full disclosure of all data are sufficient to correct any biases that might creep in.

The Significance of Change in Personality Theory

Personality theory of the nonanalytic variety usually concentrates on enduring constellations of behavior that operate over all or most of an individual's lifetime. In so doing, it makes the correct observation that human beings after their early years do not change much in certain essential respects. But it overlooks the equally cogent observation that psychotherapy is a procedure that does get people to change, sometimes in dramatic ways, though usually in less dramatic ones. But even when the changes are less dramatic they are nonetheless changes.

In this respect psychoanalysis has a great advantage over other personality theories, because it is always concerned with the possibility of change. The analogy should be drawn between radioactive matter and personality constellation, rather than between insert matter and personality, which was the traditional assumption. Stones, after all, do not change unless some external force comes along, so why should people? The inner forces that lead people to alter their personality structures are more similar to the inner forces that lead certain radioactive compounds to decay and alter over periods of time.

If this dimension is not added, a one-sided view of the human enterprise results. Actually, even without therapy change enters into human existence in many ways. The analytic focus on development stresses the changes that a person must cope with in the course of life. This developmental process is now generally recognized as valid, and life-development studies of all ages have become an integral part of psychology. Thus it becomes essential to distinguish those aspects of an individual that are alterable under certain conditions and those that are not, and to specify the conditions under which these alterations can be said to take place.

Some Comments on Behavior Therapy

Of recent years, behavior modification and behavior therapy have become the vogue, especially among psychologists, who pride themselves that at last here is a form of therapy that derives from well-established principles of science. More careful investigation of this claim does not substantiate its allegations that it is the only scientific therapy, that it is scientific in its base, or that it is remarkably effective.

London (1972) has specifically tried to refute the notion that behavior therapy is an application of scientific principles. Mackenzie has concluded that behaviorism as a scientific movement has failed: "There is no methodological substitute for good ideas, at every stage of research."[15] Strupp in a review of Wolpe's 1968 book found that he used a large number of ad hoc devices that had nothing to do with science as such. Even many behavior theorists have viewed behavior therapy as a "fuzzy entity," and admittedly it defies exact definition.

In a review of Wolpe's latest book, *Theme and Variations*, the present writer found that Wolpe had used at least eleven different techniques in his treatment cases, none of them significantly related to any experimentally established principles of learning. Wolpe himself is critical of some of his fellow behavior therapists, such as Albert Ellis and Arnold Lazarus. Furthermore, Wolpe's stress on reciprocal inhibition would not meet with agreement among learning theorists, who attribute learning to a variety of other factors.

Thus in practice behavior therapy has become a kind of fad. In this writer's experience, it generally gives the therapist carte blanche to do what he wants to, in some hit-or-miss or commonsense way, without going through the difficult and exacting training required of the psychoanalytically oriented clinician. The advent of behavior therapy does not alter the theoretical arguments in favor of structuring psychology around a psychoanalytic core.

Furthermore, a careful comparison of behavior modification reveals the following. Whatever the theory, in practice behavior modification seeks to rid the sufferer of some troubling symptom. In general the origin of this symptom is traced to some noxious stimulus in the person's life that he has been unable to master (thus again the assumption that man is subject to powerful external forces, not internal ones). The methods designed to free the sufferer of his symptoms may rely on tracing them to past events, desensitization, or some other more general approach, such as relaxation. Even in the behavior-modification literature considerable dispute exists about the effectiveness of the various methods employed and their relevance to different kinds of patients.

By contrast, Freud in the development of psychoanalysis went through four stages: (1) making the unconscious conscious (1890s), (2) working out the transference and resistances (1900–1914), (3) replacing the id with the ego (1920s), and (4) establishing the optimal conditions for the functioning of the ego (1937 paper: "Analysis Terminable and Interminable"). The subsequent analytic literature has elaborated these four stages in various ways.

In deconditioning, if the question is asked whether the subject is or was conscious of the noxious stimulus the answer would have to be no, except perhaps for a momentary awareness. Thus both conditioning and deconditioning are another way of saying that the noxious stimulus was unconscious or became unconscious.

Consequently behavior modification, despite the elaborate ingenuity of some of its methods, is most similar to the Freud of the 1890s. It attacks a symptom and makes the unconscious conscious. It does not concern itself with transferences and resistances, does not as a rule consider the replacement of the id with the ego, and has no philosophical position about how man can become happy.

Nor should it be surprising that behavior modification became popular after World War II, with the usual claims of "scientific exactitude," "laboratory evidence," and the like, which do not stand up to careful scrutiny. For by that time there were scores of mental health professionals available for the pursuit of psychotherapy, and they needed a technique that could be learned easily and had wide applicability. At first psychologists overresponded to Rogerian therapy, which in the 1940s claimed that it could cure almost anybody in eight sessions and trained practitioners in six weeks. Gradually these claims have faded into oblivion, and today Rogerian therapy has become a variant of psychoanalysis.

Today psychologists are overresponding to behavior therapy for similar reasons; that is, that it can be learned easily and has wide popular appeal. The innumerable disputes among behavior therapists arise from the overemphasis on symptoms, apart from the inherent difficulties in the field. It can be anticipated that as behavior therapists become more sophisticated and more experienced with the practical problems of handling patients, they will recognize the significance of transference, will deal with resistances, will consider the ego–id dichotomy, and will pay much more careful attention to the philosophy of living. In other words, behavior therapy has taken the first step along the route of psychoanalysis, and it may reasonably be anticipated that many honest practitioners will go farther and become full-fledged analysts.

Psychoanalysis and Cognitive Psychology

Traditional psychology has now been rebaptized cognitive or rational psychology, and its relationship to psychoanalysis must be more closely examined. George Klein put his finger on some of the essentials in a paper on "The Role of Consciousness in Psychological Theory" (1959).[16] Cognitive psychology deals with human behavior under certain limiting conditions. It is behavior in a laboratory setting, where there are no distractions, where motivation is provided from the outside, and where emotional needs do not interfere.

Experimentalists often argue that one of the great triumphs of this kind of approach is the establishment of the learning curve by Ebbinghaus, with his introduction of the nonsense syllable. No one of course sits around voluntarily memorizing nonsense syllables. So this technical innovation was viewed as providing a "pure" learning curve, in contrast to the impure ones resulting from everyday learning activities. Obviously the analogy with chemistry or physics is clear: Hydrogen and oxygen in certain proportions combine to form water, but this cannot be ascertained from ordinary observations.

Ebbinghaus (1850–1908) was more or less contemporary with Freud, and his introduction of the nonsense syllable is regarded by experimentalists as a stroke of genius. (Titchener referred to it as the most important methodological advance since Aristotle. However, Titchener had nothing to say about Freud's explanation of everyday slips, parapraxes, which have since been called "Freudian slips.")[17] Ebbinghaus's work has long since been superseded by more refined methods. In the area of memory the human being today can be looked upon as a computer, with storage and retrieval processes; this computer analogy explains both the cognitive and the affective aspects of memory.

From the standpoint of a total science, Freud's work looms just as large as, if not larger than, Ebbinghaus's. For Freud at least observed the human being as he functions in everyday life, while Ebbinghaus created an artificial situation, extrapolation from which proved to be very difficult. Ebbinghaus's paradigm of an artificial situation led to an immense body of literature and to experimentation in many areas. Yet its value is still questionable, and when applied to problems where the emotions play a role it almost invariably leads to equivocal or uncertain results.

As a consequence psychologists have confined themselves to looking for generalizations without inquiring whether or not such generalizations can validly be made or how they apply to real-life situations. Consider, for example, the famous "Zeigarnik effect." In its original form, Zeigarnik maintained that uncompleted actions are recalled more often than completed ones. Her explanation, in line with Kurt Lewin's theorizing, was that the interruption leads to an "unresolved tension," which tends to maintain the memory trace of the task in question.

Subsequent extensive research on the Zeigarnik effect led to conflicting results. After a very detailed review of the literature, van Bergen concluded that "the problem of the selective recall of uncompleted and completed tasks must be regarded as one of those questions which seem to lead nowhere."[18]

It could have been predicted that the experimentation would lead to conflicting conclusions since it paid no attention to the state of the subject, his involvement in the task, and other variables. From a methodological point of view it is in fact so stated that it does not allow of a reasonable solution, because the prime factor, the individual, is left out of the formula. Yet this is precisely what Ebbinghaus's work led to. The image of man as rational, conscious, and subject to external forces beyond his control dictated the search and the experiments. This is but one more indication that this image leads and has led to large scale scientific errors.

Toward the Construction of Psychological Science

The first requirement of a science is that it deal with its subject matter by means of a sensible conceptual framework. Because the subject matter of psychology is man, science must deal with man as he is, not as he might be or as he is under peculiar conditions (though these could be pursued, provided that they were used as data from which to infer conclusions, not as absolute facts).

In this way four questions emerge as basic to psychological science:

1. How do people function?
2. Within what limits, and by what means, can this functioning be altered?
3. What are the effects of such alteration?
4. How should we (if at all) try to change people (the issue of social change versus social understanding)?

How Do People Function?

As soon as we ask the question of how people do function in reality, formidable obstacles appear. It will already be necessary to alter our whole mode of thinking about people and to question every assumption, no matter how dear. Such a reorientation is an inevitable outcome of the psychoanalytic vision.

Certain objective facts about human beings can be ascertained easily enough. The visible spectrum extends over a range of 320 to 1,000 millimicrons.[19] Appropriate wavelengths can be assigned to each of the colors in the visible spectrum. Above and below these limits the human being cannot see. The height of the average person varies between 5'3" and 6'6", with only rare adult individuals falling below or above these limits. Further, so far as can be ascertained, these limits have existed for at least several hundred thousand years. And so on.

But as soon as we get to more affect-laden questions, disagreements of the sharpest kind appear. For example, consider the basic problem: How happy is the human being? There have been two approaches to this question: One is the surface-statistical interview, the other the depth-therapeutic.

Andrews and Withey (1976) used a surface-statistical interview method to determine how Americans view their well-being. They interrogated 5,422 subjects.[20] In general they came up with the finding that most people are reasonably content with their lives and that problems appear only in certain contexts, which they call life concerns. In a parallel earlier study by Hadley Cantril (1965) the results were similar.

However, they were surprised to find that well-being did not correlate with any of the unusual sociological variables, such as education, income, or socio-economic status. They were baffled by this finding but reported it as they found it.

On the other hand, Bradburn (1969) reported widely differing findings from a study conducted just a few years earlier. His samples were close to 6,000 subjects from a variety of communities. He found: "To those who have the attributes that go with positions higher in the social structure, such as higher education and income, also go the psychic rewards of greater happiness."[21]

Bradburn also found a marked lack of correlation between positive and negative feelings: Happiness was one thing, unhappiness another. He maintained that the difference between the numbers of positive and negative feelings is a good predictor of a person's overall rating of his own happiness. In his study relatively few people (mostly between 5 and 20 percent) rated themselves as "not too happy,"[22] and the highest percentage of those who felt "not too happy" (36 percent) were those with an income of less than $2,000 per year.

In still another surface-statistical study, this time of sexuality, Kinsey, working in the 1940s and 1950s, would venture no opinion about whether his subjects were content or discontent with their sex lives; he merely reported "outlets." The significance of his work lay primarily in the objective finding that the actual sex lives of people vary widely from the socially accepted (and legally sanctioned) norms.

On the other hand, Kinsey let his "objectivity" slip in several places. Finding that the average American male ejaculation occurs very quickly (often within ten or twenty seconds after coital entrance) he concluded:

Far from being abnormal, the human male who is quick in his sexual response is quite normal among the mammals, and usual in his own species. . . . It would be difficult to find another situation in which an individual who was quick and intense in his responses was labeled anything but superior, and that in most instances is exactly what the rapidly ejaculating male probably is.[23]

In his book on female response, Kinsey called the vaginal orgasm a "biologic impossibility."[24] In fact, this remained the predominant opinion among nonanalytic authors until Masters and Johnson (1966) were able to photograph orgastic response and specify other details long known to analysts (cf. Reich, 1927). Since then, everyone recognizes vaginal orgasm, and the argument has shifted to its value rather than its existence.

Contrariwise, investigators who have a more clinical orientation have reported findings markedly contradictory to the above, both in general happiness and in sexuality. Hendin (1975) interviewed four hundred college students, paying them for participating in five depth interviews. He found suicidal preoccupation high, depression common, the drug problem proliferating, impotence and frigidity frequent, homosexuality popular, and much enmity between young men and women. Many young people find themselves increasingly driven toward defensive maneuvers that can allay depression, stave off impotence, or check rage. College students are very frightened of emotional intimacy, and their feeling of vulnerability enters into many of their other interactions, including study and work. Work is often used as a barricade and a protection, as are drugs and certain forms of extreme political activism. The modal college student is afraid to feel, especially to love.

At an earlier date Rennie and his co-workers (1962) investigated by careful interview a substantial sample of the inhabitants of a portion of Manhattan in New York City. In a by now widely quoted study, they found that of 1,660 respondents only 18.5 percent could be considered well, while 36.3% had mild symptom formation, 21.8% moderate symptom formation, 13.2% severe symptom formation and 2.7% were incapacitated.

Criticism was leveled at Rennie's study in that he picked the denizens of New York, a notoriously "neurotic" environment. Accordingly Leighton (1963) investigated the inhabitants of the Maritime Provinces of Canada, which would ordinarily be considered a haven of mental health. His results, also obtained by careful interviewing, were equally staggering: He found that 24 percent of the people of Stirling County had suffered significant impairment from psychiatric disorder during their lives, while another 33 percent had experienced psychiatric disorder without significant impairment.[25]

Still earlier, Eli Chinoy (1955) tried to see the relationship of the American dream to the lives of auto workers. On the basis of seventy-eight long and searching interviews with sixty-two workers he found the factory to be the locale of largely meaningless work and poignantly futile gestures of independence, with life outside the plant almost forced to become the locale of genuine self-expression.[26] However, the total life-style of the factory worker was found to be unsatisfying in profound respects.

Worth mentioning here too is the work of Frederick Herzberg, the only non-Russian social scientist who has ever been permitted a look behind the public facade of Soviet society.[27] In 1964 Herzberg was invited to Leningrad to discuss his publications on job attitudes and to consult on the problems of job dissatisfaction in the Soviet Union. The method was a questionnaire administered face to face to a sample of 2,665 workers. While Herzberg found his motivation-hygiene theory to be applicable to the Soviet situation, all workers rated themselves as highly content.[28] It is interesting to cite his quotation from the Soviet sociologists:

> In the case of the unskilled manual laborer, the widening of his mental horizons and the increase of his education does not improve but, rather, worsens his attitude to work and it impels him to quit his job. In this case the appeal to the social value of labor hardly helps, since other work is more useful to society due to its greater productivity. It is not by accident that the manual laborer was found in our research to be the least stable.[29]

More studies could be cited. Enough has been presented to show that the question of how people function (reports of happiness) is answered in an entirely different manner by different investigators, *depending primarily on their theoretical orientation.* Thus it becomes a matter of ultimate vision rather than of statistical manipulation. There is certainly enough empirical evidence available to justify the assertion that the psychoanalytic vision is fundamental to the science.

The same or similar results could be shown to occur in every aspect of the analytic ideal: love, sexuality, work, family structure, social role, self-esteem, creativity, and the rest. The three questions of unpalatable findings, material that cannot be reproduced, and observer bias remain fundamental to scientific investigation. They cannot be sidestepped by any recourse to authority. Their inevitability shows once more that psychoanalytic theory is the core of all of psychology, not just a peculiar system grafted on to rational psychology to explain a few abnormal individuals.

The Psychoanalytic Retreat: Freud and His Reformulators

The vision of a psychoanalytic reform, of the social sciences, and of society in general was with Freud from an early date. It has been mentioned that in the introduction to *The Interpretation of Dreams* in 1900 he wrote that anyone who has failed to understand dreams can scarcely be qualified to treat neurosis, thereby disqualifying the entire profession of his day. In a paper on "Civilized Sexual Morality" in 1908 he called for reform but argued that it is not the business of a physician to engage in reform (and why not?). After the war, when things looked brighter for a while, he contended that whole civilizations can become neurotic and that psychoanalysis can provide a needed corrective to the pressures of civilization.

Yet for all that, Freud remained ambivalent. His concern, he said, was with science. "We do not know enough yet" was his constant cry. And in his final formulation, in *The Outline of Psychoanalysis*, he was content with a pure exposition of psychoanalytic theory, omitting the vision.

Many of Freud's followers have demonstrated a similar ambivalence. In an article in *The Psychoanalytic Movement* in 1933, Hartmann criticized Freud's narrow view of a *Weltanschauung* (philosophy of life) and urged a broader position. Thirty years later, when he returned to the topic in a lecture at the New York Psychoanalytic Institute on "Psychoanalysis and Moral Values," he had retreated to a position where he saw psychoanalysis as a technology and denied that there were values inherent in it. The flirtation with Marxism in the 1920s was soon abandoned by the analysts, especially when the Marxists unleashed their most savage fury at psychoanalysis, at times dubbing it "the last resort of capitalism."

The current reorganization of psychoanalysis dates essentially from 1945, the end of World War II, although the form is not different from that set up by Freud in 1910, when the International Psychoanalytic Association was founded. Like all organizations, the American Psychoanalytic Association (as well as the International) has been primarily concerned with the maintenance of its power. All the serious battles that have erupted, and that still erupt, revolve around the training of analysts, specifically, who shall have the right to train prospective analysts. In this struggle for power the central vision of psychoanalysis, for the betterment of mankind, has often been lost. Political compromises of the most unsavory kind have by no means been infrequent. Many analysts trained since World War

II are not even aware of the revolutionary history and implications of psychoanalysis (Pollock, 1974).

Apparently influenced by those critics who have maintained that psychoanalysis is not "scientific," many theoreticians have attempted to reformulate the main doctrines of psychoanalysis. Rapaport attempted it in 1960, although he stated that he did not feel psychoanalysis was yet ready for systematization. His theoretical structure stressed particularly the various metapsychological points of view. As the greatest need he saw methods to obtain data that can lead beyond the clinical relationships to theoretical relationships of the type discussed in his essay. His work has virtually been forgotten.

Peterfreund (1971) attempted to reformulate psychoanalysis in terms of information systems theory. Gedo and Goldberg (1973) set up hierarchical models of the mind. Gedo (1979) sought to "reintroduce" aims and goals, as though these had never existed. Pribram and Gill (1976) tried to show that Freud's 1895 Project, in which he offered a neurological basis for psychology, was still viable. Schafer (1976) has urged a new language for psychoanalysis, which sounds more like behaviorism than anything else. Lacan (1977) has set up various formulations—among others, that the unconscious is structured like a language, a proposition that obviously is far from the basic tenets of psychoanalysis.

All of these have one element in common: They attempt to set up a different kind of psychology, sometimes physiological, sometimes otherwise, which will make the findings of psychoanalysis more coherent. This new psychology is then to be grafted on to the more traditional cognitive psychology to make a total science.

One person who has moved against this trend is the late George Klein. In *Psychoanalytic Theory: An Exploration of Essentials* (1976) he argued for scrapping metapsychology and sticking to clinical observations, which are the essentials of psychoanalysis. This writer, in agreement with Klein's thesis, has attempted to elaborate on it in *Psychoanalytic Psychology* (Fine, 1975).

In the meantime bitter battles have raged within psychoanalysis for and against Freud. These battles have covered up the struggle for power within the organizations (see Rubins, 1978, or Fine, *A History of Psychoanalysis*, 1979). Since ideology has been secondary to politics, the presentations of Freud, both in his favor and against him, have all too often been incorrect, sometimes grossly so. The result has been, within the organizations, an emphasis on technique and technical questions to the exclusion of philosophy.

Outside the organizations there have been many visionaries, like Erich Fromm, Herbert Marcuse, the Frankfurt school of sociology, or even eccentrics like Wilhelm Reich. The trouble with these visionaries is that while they grasp some of the dreams of psychoanalysis, they lose touch with the psychological realities. The consequence is that their visions suffer the same fate as other philosophical visions in the past: scorn, ridicule, and ultimately neglect.

Thus the field has become divided into visionaries who lack technique and technicians who lack vision. It would be an enormous step forward if the two, vision and technique, could once again be combined. Such a synthesis is one aim of the present work.

Should All Psychologists Be Trained in Therapy?

From the time of Wundt, the ego ideal of every psychologist has been to be a researcher, with the dream of contributing some fundamental theorem or discovery to the field. "Applications," of which therapy has been considered one, have been regarded as secondary. And yet three paradoxes immediately stare one in the face. First of all, the greatest impetus to psychology has come from Freud, a man who spent by far the greatest part of his life as a therapist. Second, Freud's observations have in the main proved to be right (though with many exceptions), as Fisher and Greenberg have recently shown in their review of the literature (1977). And third, when research is guided by solid analytic principles, as in Hendin, Rennie, or Leighton, the findings are in marked contrast to those resulting from an eclectic or experimental philosophy, as in Bradburn, Kinsey, or Withey and Andrews.

We are considering broad philosophical problems here, which include the reorganization of both psychological science and psychological practice. What would happen, then, if *all* psychologists were to become trained therapists, some to engage in purely clinical work, others to become involved in research that may not be clinical yet is guided by clinical understanding? In particular, what would happen if the three problems stressed over and over again—unpalatable material, unreproducible data, and observer bias—were tackled by means of analyzing all psychologists? The results could indeed be remarkable.

In point of fact, some movement in this direction is already noticeable. Clinicians have come to dominate more and more of the psychological world. And almost all clinicians do some therapy.

At a minimum the clinician-researcher could be expected to have some personal analysis; have done some therapy; and be aware of the contrast between depth-therapeutic findings and surface-interview findings.

It is not to be supposed that analysis of the prospective social scientist will produce any dramatic change immediately. But in the long run it will help the field to move to more meaningful research and more useful kinds of social change.

There is currently a broad move toward the therapizing of the entire population. But because of the shortage of therapists, and especially of competent analytically trained ones, this therapy often takes brief and superficial forms, such as weekend encounter groups or brief behavior therapy to counteract some isolated symptoms. To be effective, therapy should be inspired by the analytic vision of a complete science of man, comprising both a method of understanding him and a method of changing him.

Ideally, if sufficient facilities could be made available, it would be desirable to have therapy as an essential part of every college program, as essential as physical hygiene. Out of the group of therapized individuals, those who respond best would be encouraged to continue in the social sciences, while those with a bent in the other direction could specialize more in the natural sciences. Eventually some unified core curriculum could be set up, including all the information pertinent to the human situation. Such a core curriculum could serve as a base for all future social scientists. Out of the group trained in this way, with a knowledge of the science of man and maturity gained through personal therapy, could be chosen those who would go on to become full-fledged therapists and those who would go on to become researchers.

No doubt this scheme will be called a "mad Utopia." Yet it offers a program for meaningful alteration of the entire educational system along lines that make sense. Some statistics indicate that persons in the social sciences actually do enter therapy more often than those in the natural sciences. In a way, then, the scheme would systematize something that is already going on.

Alteration of Functioning

No understanding of human functioning is complete without specifying the conditions under which it does or can change. This is most evident with children. For example, the six-year-old child can be understood only in terms of the fact that he was five years old a year ago and will be seven a year from now. But it is equally true with persons of all ages. Growth, decay, progress, and change are all essential components of human existence.

It is at this point that another important connection can be drawn between traditional cognitive psychology and psychoanalytic affective psychology. In the study of cognition (including perception, memory, and learning), the change process is ordinarily left out of the picture. One consequence is that the theoretical results obtained can be applied to real life situations only with great difficulty. Thus these laboratory and experimental results apply only to certain limiting conditions. As applied to these limits they are of value. But the limits within which they do apply must be specified. Here too it becomes apparent that cognitive psychology is a branch of the broader science of which psychoanalysis remains the core.

Psychosocial Change Versus Psychosocial Understanding

Every one of the social sciences is troubled by the question of how its findings can be translated into the realm of action. If change were included as a special dimension of every investigation, the dilemma could be resolved more easily.

In psychology proper three contingencies can be enumerated. First there is the traditional realm of cognitive factors in which the aim is to establish certain limiting laws applying to specific conditions—for example, the mixture of blue and green producing yellow, or other color mixtures. Unless there is some special purpose, there is no reason to suggest one color to people rather than another.

The second contingency is that where cognitive factors are predominant and have their principal applications in the learning situation. Thus the study of memory would lead to better methods for memorizing, the study of language to better methods for learning reading, and so on. In other words, with the affective factors at a minimum the primary area of concern here is education.

The third contingency is that where affective factors are predominant. These have their chief applications in therapy—for example, the numerous studies of schizophrenia must find some applicability in the general problem of the treatment of the schizophrenic.

This tripartite division actually is representative of some of what is going on at present. There are purely theoretical investigations, with little or no relevance to real life; there are educational-learning problems; and there are affective-therapeutic problems. What is added here is the theoretical recognition that the element of change or changeability must be included in all psychological discussions.

Of course, people, governments, and institutions will have differing reactions to any attempt to change them. The failure of Project Camelot is but one of numerous indicators that there are serious limits imposed on any application of social science to the political realm. The ban on behavior therapy in federal prisons is proof that therapeutic measures cannot be dispensed in a vacuum. Nevertheless, the extraordinary growth of psychology and psychiatry in the past thirty years is proof, if proof were needed, that there is a great hunger for accurate knowledge of how change can be realistically effected in all areas of people's lives.

Some Special Problems

Certain special problems have proved to be persistent headaches throughout the history of psychology. Because they cut through to the heart of the science, it is worth discussing how psychoanalysis has dealt with them. Four problems are particularly important: the relationship between body and mind, the nature of consciousness (and the unconscious), the relationship between cognition and affect, and the question of free will.

THE BODY-MIND PROBLEM

The question of how mental events can arise on a corporeal base has occupied the most profound philosophers for centuries. Three answers have been offered: dualism, monism, and psychophysical parallelism. Psychoanalysis has actually sidestepped all of these solutions and instead offered some weighty empirical data.

Inasmuch as Freud emphasized his biology heritage so often (he said of *Three Essays on Sexuality* in 1905, for example, that it was to be regarded as a contribution to biology), this statement may come as a surprise. We are referring to the broad sweep of Freud's thought, not to specific details. This broad sweep, as he himself recognized at an early date (cf. letters to Fliess in the 1890s), is a system of psychology with little or no relation to its physiological (or biological) underpinnings.

Specifically Freud, but also later analysts, showed that it is possible to investigate an extensive range of mental phenomena without reference to their physiological base. The specific psychoanalytic contributions here are two: the distinction between primary process and secondary process, and the exploration of the affective life.

Primary-process phenomena are either physiological or psychological; their main characteristic is that they impinge on the person from the inside, distracting his attention, disturbing his equilibrium, and calling for peremptory action. The secondary process is the rational self that takes this primary-process material and molds it into a form that is acceptable to the ego and superego. In many cases, however, the primary-process material does not lend itself readily to such molding, and considerable inner conflict may ensue.

The second area in which progress has been made with the body–mind problem is in affect. For the analyst an emotion is a total psychophysiological phenomenon, involving conscious, unconscious, somatic, and (frequently) motor responses. Furthermore, the human being is seen as one who is constantly experiencing some emotion, in contrast to the more traditional view, which saw emotion as an emergency response.

Psychoanalysis does not per se, and need not, subscribe to any particular psychophysical theory. It explores mental phenomena as they come up without regard to physiology. In this way it can adjust itself to any new neurophysiological data, such as the recently discovered split-brain phenomenon or the view of the nervous system as a kind of computer. The commonly expressed view that psychoanalysis is a "reductionistic" system, in which the mental is reduced to the physical, is erroneous.

CONSCIOUSNESS AND THE UNCONSCIOUS: THE INNER WORLD
OF MAN

The problem of consciousness has been approached in two ways: through the study of free associations and through the exploration of the unconscious. Freud assumed from a very early date that

consciousness is primarily a surface expression of deeper unconscious trends.

The study of the unconscious is a specific contribution of psychoanalysis to psychology and has proved enormously fruitful.
While it is true that some philosophers and psychologists had theories of the unconscious before Freud, he was the first to devise a
workable system for getting at the unconscious and showing how it
operated in a variety of life situations. If we realize that when Freud
was writing about the unconscious, the other psychologists of that
day were lost in the famous "imageless thought" controversy of the
Würzburg school, we can see the quantum jump psychoanalysis represented over the psychologies that were contemporary with it. Thus
when Freud was writing his *Three Essays* (1905), the academic psychologists were arguing the trivial problems of whether thought is
possible without images (Murphy, 1972).

The theory of the unconscious has led to the recognition that
there is in every person an extensive inner world, or representational
world, through which he sees the outside. One task that psychology
must set itself is to find out what this inner world is for each person,
as it can be expected to differ. In general, the internalization process
begins early and leads the infant to approach the world in terms of
his or her caretakers, primarily the mother. Later the father and
other persons are internalized, leading to a series of introjects, which
eventually culminate in the superego at the close of the Oedipal period. However, the inner world embraces more than the superego, for
it includes symbols, attitudes, values, perceptions, and a total way
of living.

This inner world is never directly available; it must always be
inferred from its external manifestations. The self-image is never
made clear directly; we always have to read between the lines to see
what a person thinks of himself.

Here too psychology must rely heavily on a process of reasonable inference. Like behaviorism, it examines every bit of behavior,
but unlike behaviorism it assumes that there is some inner psychological structure that determines the behavior. In this way it can be
said to include behaviorism, whereas it is impossible for behaviorism to include psychoanalysis because of the faulty logic of behaviorism. Here too we must conclude that psychoanalysis represents
the core of psychological thinking.

Observer bias is particularly important with regard to this internal world. Anyone who has been through analysis and done any

clinical work immediately becomes aware of it. By contrast those who stick to purely experimental methods, especially when their subjects are animals, frequently find it difficult to fathom.

Further distinctions can be made in terms of age and pathology. For the very young child, up to eighteen months of age, in what Piaget calls the sensorimotor period, consciousness is still a highly bewildering experience. True, recent research has shown that there is some organized ego activity from birth on, but the organization at this time is still extremely rudimentary. The weak ego is one factor that explains the strong attachment to mother, who represents the security that the child is unable to find on its own. Thus consciousness grows in strength and importance as the child gets older. Piaget himself has made significant contributions to the ways in which consciousness comes to apprehend causality, the external world, moral judgment, logical operations, and so on.

The second distinction, in terms of pathology, is equally important, if not more so. In psychosis the individual is guided by purely unconscious motives; what he is conscious of is merely a rationalization. The degree to which the "normal" individual is actuated by unconscious motives must be inferred for each case and each situation. But even if he is not conscious of motives, he can become conscious of them more easily than the psychotic, whose defense of his deeper unconscious secrets is impenetrable under ordinary conditions, even under ordinary therapeutic conditions. The unconscious is repressed because it makes the person anxious, hence theoretically the repression of the psychotic is so severe because the material that would come to consciousness would create a panic-like state; to avoid this panic he exerts every effort to keep it hidden from himself as well as from others.

COGNITION AND EMOTION

The Aristotelian dictum that man is a rational animal has been questioned by psychoanalysts, who see him rather as an emotion-ridden animal. For many people, as Stanley Hall once put it, "the intellect is a speck afloat on a sea of feeling." Nevertheless, it is beyond dispute that many persons do act rationally in many areas of their lives, so that the relationship between cognition and emotion defies easy formulation.

In this area age and pathology again play a significant role. The infant is presumably unable to distinguish clearly between thought and feeling, nor can it distinguish between either of these two and somatic processes. Life thus begins in a relatively undifferentiated state in which cognition, affect, and soma are all intertwined. It is only in the course of life, as the ego grows, that the three are separated.

The infant obviously has less control over his affect than the adult has. Even in the behavioristic studies of Goodenough, it was easy enough to show that temper tantrums decrease with age, until for many children after a certain age they virtually disappear. However, while the overt manifestation may disappear, the unconscious resentment may very well remain.

In terms of pathology three observations emerge. First, all of pathology involves an excess of affect and a relative inability to control it. The classic Kraepelinian distinction between affect disorder (manic-depressive psychosis) and thought disorder (schizophrenia) is wholly erroneous. Jones (1929; in Jones, 1948) was the first to make explicit the analytic assumption that early frustrations produce a weak ego, which lies at the basis of all of the severe mental disturbances. On the basis of this weak ego there can then ensue manic or depressive, schizophrenic, or other pathological states.

Second, the affect that is most strongly brought to the fore in pathology is hostility. Thus all emotional disturbance involves a fixation at, or a regression to, the early infantile states of rage. This rage may be directed at other people or inward, at oneself. The somatic consequences may be widespread or may be minimal. Because of these somatic consequences, the psychosomatic disorders, as well as the addictions, are generally classified together with the more severe forms of emotional disorder, even though no obvious mental symptoms may be present.

Third, the seemingly irrational manifestations of the psychotic all turn out to be capable of explanation at the unconscious level, where they turn out to be perfectly rational. It is the premises that are mistaken, not the reasoning. Thus paradoxically psychoanalysis comes up with the conclusion that the human being is always rational but that in the more disturbed individual the rationality operates at an unconscious level.

Further relationships between cognition and emotion are necessarily complex and again do not lend themselves to any easy formula. Perhaps the most important conclusion that emerges from infant studies is that a good relationship with a warm, empathic mother is more likely to lead to superior cognitive functioning (Brody and Axelrad, 1978; Ashley Montagu, 1976).

FREE WILL

If human actions, like everything else in the universe, are caused, how man can feel himself free to choose what he is going to do poses a puzzle. Once more age and pathology provide clues that offer at least a partial solution, though much remains unresolved.

The development of voluntary independent action in the child can be traced easily enough. It requires the growth of self-awareness and of the differentiation of self from object (other person). Some intimation of such differentiation is present as soon as the infant is able to operate independently of mother, at about one year of age. Some time in the third year of life the child begins to talk of himself (me, I) in terms that indicate his awareness of some psychic emancipation from mother.

Thereafter there is a steady growth toward independent activity. However, this growth is gradual and is punctuated by various critical phases (*rites de passage*) that pose problems for the developing organism. At these critical passages, when more autonomy is achieved, breakdowns are more likely to occur than at other times, indicating that there is always a conflict between freedom and subservience or attachment.

The study of pathology sheds further light on the matter. Compulsive actions and obsessive thoughts, over which the individual has no control or feels he has no control, are characteristic of more severe psychopathology. All severe mental disturbance involves a harsh superego, which acts as arbiter of the individual's destinies. After a certain point the superego takes over from the parents, replacing external control by internal. In the disturbed individual these harsh internal controls are obeyed even though the reality consequences may be harmful or even disastrous (for example, suicide). Freedom of the will is thus seen to be characteristic of the mature conscious person who is not seriously disturbed.

In all of these problems, psychoanalysis has made its distinctive contribution by considering age, pathology, and the inner world, with its psychic structures determined by operations of the unconscious. While the problems in no case are fully resolved, at least some resolution is offered on the basis of empirical evidence. It is noteworthy that other psychological approaches have merely avoided the problems.

Psychology as an Integrative Discipline

A narrow definition of psychology, or restriction of its activities to certain delimited realms, is always self-defeating. As Gardner Murphy has observed:

> Hardly had the challenge and the response been clearly defined when it became evident (early in the present century) that science was a larger enterprise than had been grasped. If the living individual is to be scientifically studied, so likewise is the group to which he belongs; if the interrelations of his tissues and of his sensory and motor acts are proper subject matter for science, so are the interactions of men in their linguistic, their economic, their political behavior.[30]

From a very early date Freud began to extend the area of his interests outward. Psychiatry has become aware of this extension, so that today such a book as *The American Handbook of Psychiatry* covers every conceivable science that deals with man, from sociology to neurology to linguistics. The question then becomes one of clarifying the interrelationships among the various disciplines.

Two approaches have been taken toward this need to enlarge the scientific enterprise. One is to set up a "pure" discipline and then apply it; this has been done in both psychoanalysis and academic psychology. It has not been especially successful, because as a "pure" discipline what it offers is some generalization, such as the psychoanalytic principle that man is motivated by drives or the learning theorist's insistence that for learning to take place there must be some reinforcement.

The second approach is to divide the field into different disciplines. The trouble here is that the domain of each becomes narrow, so that when the specialist wishes to investigate any significant question he is compelled to expand his horizons beyond his discipline. Added to that is the human wish to be important, so that each discipline acquires the honorific title of "science." Anyone who has ever done any work in any of the social sciences soon becomes aware that very early he has to touch base on all of them, so that the notion of separate disciplines is contradicted.

A third approach, the one suggested here, is to unite all the disciplines around psychology as the science of man. Such a psychology would naturally be dynamic, deriving from the principles of psychoanalysis as enunciated above. Each discipline has more information about certain types of functioning than others: Economics knows more about economic man, linguistics more about linguistic man, and so forth. Psychoanalysis has derived most of its information from the study of neurotic man, but this is only one aspect of its activity.

Hence this approach would stress above all else integration of information from all sources. In fact, this is the way I have worked. Our understanding of sexuality is enriched by anthropology with its experiments of nature; history with its recital of past efforts to handle the sexual problem; linguistics with its knowledge of sexual words; sociology with its research into current sexual customs; and so on.

To build up a complete science every aspect of the analytic ideal must be thoroughly investigated. There is a great deal of information available; what is needed mainly is integration. While psychology remains the core of such integration, it should by no means be considered the "pure" science with the others as "applications." Rather, it is simply a convenient center, like the hub of a wheel, to which all the spokes can be attached. But each spoke plays a vital role in the total balance. If, for example, the anthropologist tries to understand the peculiarly complicated kinship systems of primitive tribes, material can be brought in from history, from folklore, from psychology, from psychiatry, from linguistics, even from economics, and each of these areas will shed some light on the problem. The main trouble has been that each discipline has tried to elevate its own subject matter to a special plane. These attempts will be examined in detail when the specific sciences are examined more closely.

Recapitulation

Psychoanalysis is dynamic psychology. The more traditional psychology, like many of the social sciences, has lost its way with the large-scale error of behaviorism. With the introduction of the clinical point of view and the advent of clinical psychology after World War II, a needed corrective has been added.

The image of science pursued by many experimental psychologists has been incorrect. It has led them to the erroneous conviction that somehow psychoanalysis is unscientific. This has created a kind of double bind: Traditional psychology has strayed away from science by avoiding too much of the subject matter of psychology, while it has forbidden psychoanalysis to investigate areas considered taboo.

Three problems have persistently appeared: the unpalatability of the material, the unreproducibility of the data, and the bias of the observer. In each case psychoanalytic psychology has made a significant contribution by showing how to handle these problems in a dynamic manner.

Psychology must necessarily be an integrative discipline, drawing its knowledge from many different sources. All the sciences that deal with man have their own special fund of information but are also parts of psychology. The psychoanalytic vision sees all the sciences of man, unified around psychoanalytic psychology as the core and pursuing by both understanding and social change the psychoanalytic vision of happiness.

Chapter 5

The Vision of Organic Psychiatry

ANY REFLECTIVE DISCUSSION OF PSYCHIATRY immediately calls to the reader's attention that the field is in an "identity crisis." Recently Engel (1977) has even commented that all of medicine is in an identity crisis. Where psychiatry came from, where it is, and where it is going are all much-disputed questions. The situation is so troublesome that the authoritative *American Handbook of Psychiatry* devotes a whole chapter to the topic. To clarify this crisis, we must seek first the underlying vision of psychiatry and second its historical development.

Griesinger: "Mind disease is brain disease."

The underlying vision of psychiatry is that all mental and emotional illness is basically organic and that adequate research will sooner or later show what the organic causes are. Historically this goes back to the Greeks but in more recent times to the assumptions of nineteenth-century German psychiatry, epitomized in the famous statement by Wilhelm Griesinger, cited above. Griesinger was the foremost German psychiatrist of the nineteenth century, Kraepelin's most illustrious predecessor.

Today it is generally accepted that the psychiatrist practices psychological as well as organic medicine; in fact, in the public mind he is frequently confused with the psychoanalyst. But this is a misconception; only about 10 percent of the 28,000 psychiatrists in this country are fully analytically trained (Marmor, 1975). There is no question, of course, about the psychological component of organic disease. What is at issue is the relevance and extent of the organic factor. This chapter will focus mainly on this question of organicity.

Historical Background

In the light of the contemporary position, which stresses psychosocial factors, the first question that arises is, How did medicine get into the picture at all? As late as the end of the eighteenth century philosophers like Kant were credited with more insight into insanity than medical men.

The answer lies three centuries earlier, before the French Revolution. Essentially, modern psychiatry was a product of the French Revolution and its enlightened hopes for the betterment of mankind. Previously Europe was dominated by a clergy-run persecution of "witches," which had led to the torture and death of hundreds of thousands of innocent victims. Christian psychiatry of the fifteenth and sixteenth centuries, if it may be called that (and it was the dominant official position of that day), was a system of delusion, destructiveness, and paranoia. Somehow, as will be apparent, the eighteenth century and above all the French Revolution brought about a revulsion against the brutality of previous centuries and a wish on the part of many for an entirely different kind of world.

To take the psychotic out of the hands of the clergy required a theoretical rationale. This lay at hand in medicine's hope that some form of brain damage would be found in the severely mentally ill that would explain their symptoms; Griesinger gave voice to this faith. Further, it was medicine's hope that the psychotics would be treated kindly (Pinel's famous freeing them from their chains), placed in good homes (hospitals or asylums—both are humane concepts) and provided with proper medication.

There were thus four ingredients to the psychiatric vision when psychiatry was born in 1800: humane treatment, custodial care, the search for the causative bacillus, and the use of appropriate drugs. Sciences have a way of holding on to the prejudices of their founders, especially when these are unverbalized. Not surprisingly, then, "traditional" psychiatrists today subscribe to essentially the same philosophy. Allied with it is an attitude of therapeutic nihilism, most clearly formulated later by Kraepelin (see below).

But psychiatry also inherited the more pernicious aspects of Christianity, also unverbalized and undiscussed. The demons of the Christians turned into the diagnoses of the psychiatrist. There were bad demons, like schizophrenia, which could not be exorcised, and good demons, like manic-depressive psychosis, which would leave the afflicted person for no apparent reason. The job of the psychiatrist, as far as Kraepelin could see, was to separate out those who had bad demons (dementia praecox) from those who had good ones.

Furthermore, the patients were irrational people to whom one could not talk, just as the Christians could not "talk" to witches, who were allied with the devil. Essentially these people were regarded as "bad" or "demented" (literally: without a mind). Because there was no benefit in talking to them, they had to be locked up and subjected to physical treatment. The Christians applied torture to elicit confessions about the pact with the devil; the psychiatrists used physiological methods to elicit sane behavior. While at times these physiological methods were relatively benign, at other times they were brutal in the extreme. Many of them did (and do) cause death or permanent damage in the subjects. These "side effects" are accepted by organic psychiatrists as unavoidable. Later on, psychoanalysts were to offer as a rationale for "shock" and "drug" treatments that their purpose was to punish the patient; the patients who benefited did so because they were reacting to what they regarded as just punishment for their guilty feelings, in much the same way as a Catholic benefits from the penance imposed on him by his confessor. And since the patients had asked for punishment, the doctors who administered it were placed in a position where they could gratify their own sadistic wishes (Fenichel, 1945; Sullivan, 1940). If they were unanalyzed, these sadistic wishes could be quite strong, especially in a culture where hatred and contempt for the deviant "lunatic" were normal attitudes. The term "furious lunatic," which was common currency in the nineteenth century, expresses the feelings of the culture more graphically than the common term today, "violent psychotic."

The only way out of this Christian hangover was through personal analysis. In time many psychiatrists did go through a personal analysis and discovered to their dismay what they had been doing. But many did not and remained fixated at the organic level; we call these "traditional" psychiatrists. As Mora and many others have pointed out, there is a generation gap between the traditional psychiatrists, who still form the majority of the profession, and the analytic psychiatrists, who have acquired a deeper understanding of the field. The battle between the traditional, organically oriented psychiatrist and the modern, analytical psychiatrist (now supplemented by at least three new professions) is still raging.

The psychiatric vision that dominated the thinking of the latter part of the nineteenth century had two essential components that

Freud was forced to combat. One was the hypothesis that there is a sharp dividing line between health and disease; the "mentally ill" are diseased, entirely different from other people, and should be confined to hospitals, like any other sick person. The second hypothesis was that psychological forces are secondary to physiological forces. Sooner or later some organic factors would show up to explain any illness that could occur in man, whether physical or psychological. In a very real sense, it has been the work of the twentieth century to destroy both of these hypotheses.

By 1880, when Breuer treated Anna O., often called the first psychoanalytic case, the organic hypothesis had no facts to verify it. The consequence was that the psychiatrist of that day was near the low end of the totem pole in the medical hierarchy. To begin with, he divided the world into psychotics, neurotics, and normals. The psychotics were all "hopeless," "hereditarily tainted," and in need of hospitalization. The neurotics were incomprehensible, but at least they could stay out of hospitals. They were amenable to suggestion and to drugs such as phenobarbital, chloral hydrate, or, above all, one of the innumerable opium compounds then on the market. The frequency of addiction to opium and its derivatives was higher in the United States in the nineteenth century than in any other country, mainly because the art of medicine as yet had relatively little to offer except rest and hope.[1] The normals were "normal" and were not the province of the physician in any way.

There were as a result very few psychiatrists, in our modern sense, around, and very few people ever consulted one. Most mental illness, except for extreme cases that violated the society's mores too openly, went unnoticed and untreated.

In pursuit of the medical model in the nineteenth century, various diagnoses were offered by many clinicians. These were combined toward the end of the century into what from 1896 has been called the Kraepelinian system, devised by the German psychiatrist Emil Kraepelin. Kraepelin divided illnesses into psychotic, neurotic, and normal on the basis of the psychiatric vision of his day. Under psychotic he included schizophrenia (then called dementia praecox) and manic-depressive psychosis. Schizophrenia he classified as a "thought disorder," manic-depressive psychosis as an "affect disorder." That this makes no sense psychologically made no difference to him. His assumption was that schizophrenia was genetic and unresponsive to treatment, while manic-depressive psychosis was an off-again-on-again disease, getting better and then worse from time to time for unknown reasons. Nor did he realize that he was merely re-casting Christian demonology in pseudoscientific terms (Reider, 1955).

Looked at sociologically, such a psychiatry (which still prevails in many parts of the world) served as an apology for the status quo. It is not surprising that in such an atmosphere Freud's early discoveries aroused the intense antipathy and opposition of his medical colleagues. The situation even led to police action in several notable instances: In 1906 Ernest Jones was jailed overnight for asking two schoolgirls about their sexual feelings. Although the case was dismissed, Jones, then already a Harley Street neurologist of distinction, found his reputation so tarnished that he had to leave England for Canada.[2] In 1913 the Boston police threatened to prosecute the psychiatrist Morton Prince, editor of *The Journal of Abnormal Psychology*, for the "obscenities" he was publishing in the *Journal*, which consisted of psychoanalytic papers. Prince, who had at one time been mayor of Boston, managed to get out of it through his political connections.[3]

When police action was not invoked, as in the case of German psychiatrist Wilhelm Weygandt at Hamburg in 1910, psychoanalysts were summarily dismissed from their posts or could obtain no advancement. In 1910 the government of Ontario ordered the *Asylum Bulletin*, of which Ernest Jones was editor, to discontinue publication. M. Wulff was dismissed from a German institution in 1909 and emigrated to Russia, then freer than Germany in such matters, where he was one of the founders of a psychoanalytic movement later destroyed by the Revolution.[4]

The story could be continued indefinitely. What is important is that in many countries in the world today it is no different. Psychoanalytic psychiatry, as it is practiced in the United States today, is limited to a few democratic countries; in the rest of the world it remains unknown and, if introduced, would result in police action or threats.

The first important change in the psychiatric picture did not occur until the 1930s, when four major events took place. First of all, the psychiatric residency was introduced, so that at least some training was made available for psychiatrists, and specialization boards were set up. Second, Hitler chased most of the leading analysts of Europe into the safe havens of America and, secondarily, England. Once out of Germany, these analysts took the lead and helped to train a large number of psychiatrists in the basic principles of psychoanalysis. In 1933 psychoanalysis, in a bitter fight led by Harry

Stack Sullivan, Abraham Arden Brill, and Clarence Oberndorf over the opposition of the more traditional psychiatrists, became an official branch of the American Psychiatric Association.

A third change was the discovery of new and effective treatments for syphilis, in both the early and the late stages, and for epilepsy, two of the greatest scourges of mankind. The malaria treatment for the last stage of syphilis—paresis, or general paralysis of the insane—was discovered by Julius Wagner-Jauregg; later it was replaced by more refined fever treatments and still later by penicillin. After the invention of the electroencephalogram in 1929 it was soon discovered that the brain waves of epileptics were different from those of normals, and several drugs were developed that could control the seizures.

These discoveries, together with the spectacular growth of medicine in all fields, continued to spark the psychiatric vision that some organic factors would be uncovered to account for mental illness. In the 1930s many physiological treatments were introduced: metrazol (or convulsive therapy), electric shock, insulin coma, and brain surgery. Electric shock and brain surgery are still in use, though on a much less extensive scale. The other techniques, introduced as a rule with great fanfare and extravagant promises, eventually disappeared.

Fourth was the impact of World War II, when the groundwork was laid for the extraordinary growth of the mental health professions that was to take place after the war. The events of the war and the postwar period dramatized the widespread incidence of mental illness. Particularly striking was the realization that men who wielded enormous power over other human beings, like Hitler and Stalin, could be suffering from serious mental illness. If world leaders could be so disturbed, what about lesser mortals? The myth of the "happy normal" was punctured once and for all. In the American army up to 21 percent of the draftees had been rejected for mental defects, and for those who were drafted neuropsychiatric disabilities were the most common cause for discharge.[5] Later these disabilities called for a large network of mental health facilities to take care of them.

The Revolution of the 1950s

Because most of the drugs now in common use were discovered in the 1950s, it is usual to talk of the drug revolution of that period.

But drugs were not the only novel factor in the psychiatric picture. In fact, in all essential respects modern psychiatry could be said to have been born during World War II. A number of historical forces contributed to the profession, which, though it retained the language and trappings of the old one, became an essentially new kind of enterprise. It is essential to find out what happened to the vision in the midst of all these changes.

The New Drugs

The change that has impressed the traditional psychiatrist most is the introduction of a whole host of new drugs: thorazine for schizophrenia; lithium for manic-depressive psychosis; ritalin for hyperactivity in children; meprobamate, valium, and librium for ordinary anxiety; various new barbiturates and any number of new hypnotics for insomnia; and so on. Sometimes these drugs have a theoretical rationale, sometimes they do not. Sometimes, as in the case of thorazine, the rationale is circular: The drug influences dopamine metabolism, therefore dopamine metabolism must somehow be involved in the physiology of schizophrenia. This leaves unanswered the question of what effect the drugs do have in schizophrenia. Primarily, then, the drugs remain an empirical *materia medica*. But side effects of the drugs are by no means uncommon. Their dangers cannot be discounted, and the full story is not in yet.

Improved Training: A New Profession

Less noticed in all the hullabaloo about the drugs is that psychiatrists after World War II for the first time began to receive some training. The residency program, initiated in the 1930s, became a universal requirement for specialization after the war. In these residency programs, instruction in theoretical or dynamic psychiatry increasingly came under the direction of psychoanalytically oriented psychiatrists, or psychoanalysts. Thus the aspiring doctor for the first time received an intensive course in psychoanalytic theory.

Personal analysis is harder to evaluate than theoretical courses. As noted, according to Henry (1971), in his survey of four thousand psychotherapists, including the three major mental health professions, 74 percent of the entire sample and more than 60 percent of each professional group had undergone psychotherapy.[6] Naturally, about the quality of the psychotherapy nothing can be said, except that, it having been undertaken on a voluntary basis, presumably these persons, all with graduate degrees, chose the best they could find.

In addition, psychiatrists went in for other postresidency training. According to Henry the mean number of years of training for the psychiatric group after the residency was 3.3.[7] Thus psychiatrists average at least six years of training beyond medical school and internship, a far cry from the old days, when the psychiatrist was little more than a formal custodian of incurable psychotics.

THE INCORPORATION OF PSYCHOANALYSIS INTO PSYCHIATRY

Residency and postresidency training for the psychiatrist have been heavily influenced by psychoanalysis. This influence has taken two forms: first the personal analysis, and second the inclusion of psychoanalytic theory in the psychiatric curriculum. It has already gone so far that in the public mind at least—and the official bodies make no effort to educate the public more clearly—the terms "psychiatrist" and "psychoanalyst" have become virtually synonymous.

At the same time the reality is that the analytic training of the average psychiatrist is far inferior to that of the full-fledged psychoanalyst. Most psychiatrists currently tend to identify themselves as "eclectic," which means that their true opinions are uncertain and the extent of their analytic training is unknown. With the rise of the other mental health professions this ambiguity has become particularly nettlesome for both practitioner and client. For example, Judd Marmor's (1975) study of practicing psychiatrists indicates that the average psychiatrist sees patients on a once-a-week basis for an uncertain duration with unclear goals. Thus, whatever theory may dictate, practice remains confused.

THE GROWTH OF OTHER MENTAL HEALTH PROFESSIONS

Another striking feature of the postwar period is the growth of other mental health professions, especially psychology and social work. Psychotherapy is the same no matter who practices it; hence these two professions have taken on an increasing share of the psychotherapy done in the community. The training program for psychologists, if they go into analytic training, is as long as that for physicians, but they begin their psychotherapeutic work at an earlier stage. The training program for social workers is much shorter than that for either of the other two professions. As a result, the sheer pressure of numbers is increasingly relegating psychiatrists into administrative and supervisory positions, thus increasing what one keen observer has called the "flight from the patient" (Strean, 1974).

Increasing competition from other professionals has forced psychiatrists to take a closer look at their organic biases. From the hyperactive child to the schizophrenic, alternatives to organic treatment are now readily available. Psychiatrists have recommended that the "first line of defense" should be the family physician. But because this physician has no training in psychology or psychiatry and may be as disturbed emotionally as his patients (medicine was and is the leading profession in frequency of addiction, and the profession was commonly believed to be a cause of most other addictions),[8] shifting the responsibility to him is no solution. The recent incident with presidential adviser Dr. Peter Bourne has further damaged the image of the drug-prescribing physician.*

The Development of Psychosomatic Medicine

In the meantime, again since the 1930s, a great deal of research has taken place in psychosomatic medicine. Since Franz Alexander's pioneering work in Chicago in the 1930s, many others have followed. By now the term "psychosomatic" is well established in the English language.

Without trying to summarize the results of this research, one surprising outcome can be noted. The effect of the mind on the body has consistently been shown to be greater and more lasting than the reverse. Various forms of stress have been implicated in a whole host of illnesses, from coronary-prone patients to allergies to colitis, even possibly to certain forms of cancer. As a result many forms of relaxation have become popular, from biofeedback to meditation and, of course, psychotherapy, which is slower but most effective in the long run.

*Dr. Bourne was dismissed from his post for prescribing a drug for a patient without using her real name, in violation of the medical code.

CHANGE IN THE CULTURAL CLIMATE

A noticeable change in the cultural climate has come about as well. In several states, including New York in 1977, it has been mandated that all insurance policies covering illness must include provisions for psychotherapy. There is hardly any stigma attached to going to a psychiatrist, and the offices of the practitioners are overflowing. It is often stated that America is the most therapized community in the history of the world, not because it is sicker but because it is more aware of the problems.

Psychology has become the most popular subject in the college curriculum. Even children's joke books contain references to "shrinks." The notion that police action should be taken against psychoanalysts, so common in the early 1900s, seems ludicrous indeed today. When Richard Nixon's Watergate crew was apprehended and sentenced, many popular periodicals speculated openly on what kinds of psychiatric disturbances could have motivated these people to do what they did.

THE DISMANTLING OF THE MENTAL HOSPITALS

Once it had become clear that psychosis involved a sense of terrible loneliness and despair, the old-fashioned mental hospital, into which thousands of patients were crowded with nothing to do and hardly anyone to take care of them, no longer made sense. Besides, with the spread of knowledge about mental illness, it was realized that only a small percentage of those incarcerated in such hospitals are actually dangerous; the rest are depressed and apathetic.

The weight of research led to some significant legal decisions in the 1960s. In the case of Donaldson *v.* Florida the courts held that a mental patient had the right to treatment, by which they meant psychotherapy. Similar decisions in other states forced the authorities to take a closer look at the structure of the hospital. Ahmed and Plog (1976) have documented the position that the care of the mentally ill in America is a national disgrace.

In a widely publicized research study, Rosenhan introduced eight journalists into different mental hospitals to see what treatment they would get.[9] When they entered they said that they heard voices, but once they were in they behaved exactly as they would on the outside. Some of their fellow patients recognized that they were normal, perhaps newspapermen, but *none* of the hospital authorities did.

One reporter found that the average patient had seven minutes' contact per day with *any* member of the hospital staff—nurse, attendant, physician. Thus neglect and incompetence were shown to be the order of the day in the average mental hospital.

Since the 1960s there has been a determined effort to get rid of large mental hospitals. Theoretically, the patients are to be discharged into the community, where they are to be given careful attention. Unfortunately, the community care offered leaves much to be desired. Nevertheless, the hospitals *are* disappearing. Today the mental hospital population of the United States is less than 200,000; twenty years ago it was well over 500,000.

Still, as Talbot (1978) points out, the process of deinstitutionalization has created a backlash as well. For eighteen months beginning in 1972 the *Bulletin* of the New York State District branches of the American Psychiatric Association published a series of critical articles entitled: "Who Will Care for the Patients?"[10] The New York City Commission on State Policy Relations issued a report on the problem entitled *State Policy and the Long-term Mentally Ill: A Shuffle to Despair*, and the director of psychiatry of the Department of Social Services of New York City wrote an editorial in the official journal of the American Psychiatric Association again branding care of the mentally ill a national disgrace.[11] This characterization has been repeated a number of times by others. Talbot concludes his survey by saying:

> No longer can anyone maintain that state hospitals must be emptied simply because they are "so awful"—because the settings we have allowed to replace them are just as bad as their predecessors. No, the answer lies in looking at the problem again. And the problem is the *treatment and care* of the chronic mental patient. Unless we are able to address this population and this problem it does not matter what we call the buildings—state hospitals, community mental health centers, or nursing homes. What we must do is establish and fund adequate programs for the treatment of the chronically mentally ill. It is this approach that is most lacking in our current discussion about the merits and demerits of de-institutionalization.[12]

What Happened to the Psychiatric Vision?

Once all these widespread changes have been recorded, the question reasserts itself: What about the psychiatric vision that some day an organic cause would be discovered for all mental and emotional disturbance, with appropriate physical treatment for each condition? Since the discovery of abnormal brain waves in epileptics fifty years ago, the results have been meager indeed: many theories, few facts. Treatment by drugs remains on an empirical basis, with the outcome uncertain or questionable; many drugs have also turned out to be more dangerous than had originally been thought.

The trend is rather toward increasing recognition that human warmth, caring, and sympathy are far more effective than any drugs known. Certainly there seem to be some cases of organic impairment, but they seem to be in a small minority. The problems the mentally ill suffer from are fear, depression, jealousy, anger, and the like, all exaggerations of emotions that everyone goes through. Psychotics simply have these emotions more intensely than others. Their reactions are understandable and treatable. Thus the psychoanalytic vision that man is irrational, governed by the unconscious, and subject to internal forces over which he can acquire control by making the unconscious conscious has proved more enduring than the psychiatric vision.

It is almost fifty years since Aldous Huxley caricatured the psychiatric vision in his novel *Brave New World*, in which he depicted a society where everyone could be fed soma pills that would cure any imaginable distress, leading to a mechanical world in which love was taboo. The soma pills are here, but a world in which they would replace warmth and love seems horrible indeed. Once more basic values take precedence over mechanical arrangements.

The Concept of Diagnosis

Scarcely anything in the whole field of psychiatry is in greater disarray than the diagnostic system. First published in 1917, the *Diagnostic and Statistical Manual (DSM)* of the American Psychiatric Association has been in almost continual revision ever since. The latest revision, the product of a Task Force appointed in 1973, was issued in 1979 (Rakoff, Stancer, and Kedward, 1977). Spitzer, chairman of the Task Force, proceeded on the basis of the medical model. He writes:

> We regard the medical model as a working hypothesis that there are organismic dysfunctions which are relatively distinct with regard to clinical features, etiology and course. No assumption is made regarding the primacy of biological over social or environmental factors.[13]

In discussing Spitzer's work, Feinstein condemned virtually the whole approach. He described the medical model as illogical, "an eclectically assembled chronologic polyglot of different terms and ideas that reflect every layer of nosologic thinking and technologic data from antiquity to the present."[14] Thus even in anticipation very little is expected of the 1979 revision of the *DSM*. And yet it is the required system of classification for any kind of legal work, such as insurance reimbursement.

Because we are reconsidering fundamentals in this book, it is necessary to go back to the history of psychiatric diagnosis to find out what is wrong with it.

Post-Kraepelinian research, particularly in America, has deprived Kraepelin's system of whatever support it may have had. Analysts (Jones, 1929; in Jones, 1948) have viewed personality as developing from an early ego structure that derives from the warmth or destructiveness of contact with the mother. If the ego is weak, it may branch out later in many different directions, whether schizophrenic, manic, psychopathic, or other. This perspective fits in with clinical observations, tying up the therapeutic material with our understanding of early childhood experience, whereas Kraepelin's system makes no sense psychologically.

The neuroses were first adequately classified by Freud in the early 1900s, when he coined the terms "hysteria" and "obsessional neurosis" and showed where they came from and how they could be treated. Surprisingly, after his early thorough work, these neuroses as illnesses seemed to disappear. If they are seen today, it is only as syndromes within a wider picture, not as illnesses in their own right.

In 1914 Freud made an even more fundamental distinction, dividing illness into transference and narcissistic neuroses. This was a classification based on a therapeutic reaction, an entirely novel idea. Some people react to the therapist with transferences; Freud called their disorders the transference neuroses. Some people do not react to the therapist at all; he called their neuroses narcissistic. His own work he saw as confined to the transference neuroses. As far as the narcissistic neuroses were concerned, he expressed the hope that improvements in technique would someday be found that would make these patients accessible. These improvements have actually been found; today by far the largest percentage of psychiatric patients are amenable to psychotherapy properly administered by a well-trained therapist.

The exploration of the neuroses (and psychoses) led to further unexpected results when the field blossomed out after World War II.

With the new requirement that anyone wishing to practice analysis must undergo a personal analysis himself, the analyses of culturally "normal" individuals became an everyday occurrence. These analyses, surprisingly, did not proceed any differently from those of the patients seen earlier. Thus, through an experiment of training, it was shown that the culturally normal individual in our society suffers from a variety of emotional disturbances that are disabling in many ways and difficult to eradicate. The idea was born and nourished that there is an image of mental health that goes well beyond the way the average person lives. For this image the present writer has suggested the term "analytic ideal"; various other terms have been proposed.

As understanding of the analytic ideal progressed and grew, another unexpected development occurred. The persons who came to analysts for help seemed to be less and less disturbed. Friends and relatives wondered why they had to go to analysts at all. Yet within the analytic situation they described a whole array of symptoms that they felt to be extremely debilitating. The shift of the patient population from the abnormal to the normal had begun. This shift has continued, until today more and more people are aware that analysts can be of great assistance with all kinds of human problems and are not exclusively involved with the chronically insane.

Thus Freud's premonition was fulfilled: Analysts woke up to find that they did indeed have the whole world as their patients. This was an extension of the analytic vision, but what could conventional psychiatry do with it?

Caught up in the medical model, psychiatrists had to continue to make "diagnoses," irrelevant though these had become. At one point the psychopath became the focus; at another the "pseudoneurotic." In more recent years the term "borderline" has become very popular, a wastebasket diagnosis into which everybody can be fitted. But it sounds medical, so the patient is brought back under the aegis of medical psychiatry.

Once the Task Force of the American Psychiatric Association had admitted the existence of social and environmental factors as causative, in addition to biological ones, in effect it destroyed the value of the medical model. Then the question becomes a psychological one: What are people like, how do they function, how do they react to the slings and arrows of fortune?

In a similar predicament, psychologists long since abandoned the global image of intelligence (smart, dumb, and so forth) and replaced it with a variety of component parts. In the same way, analysts have attempted to replace diagnosis with total assessment profiles, sometimes called ego-assessment profiles (Anna Freud, Bellak), in which all aspects of the individual's functioning are taken into account. The emphasis shifts from pathology to the total personality.

As far as pathology is concerned, analytic progress has revealed another problem that conventional psychiatry did not have the conceptual tools to handle. Every culture places demands on its subjects to conform to certain requirements. Most people in every culture do conform to whatever is asked of them, even to the point of self-destruction. For example, in World War II Japanese pilots by the thousands were ready to die in suicide attacks, and many actually did so. Suicidal attacks of this kind involve psychological factors that are quite mysterious in our culture, yet apparently the Japanese had no shortage of kamikaze pilots; what they lacked was planes.

At a less extreme level conformity produces adjustment to the culture. But this adjustment is bought at a price. The normal population now going to analysts is trying to maintain itself within the culture without paying too heavy a price. Some, however, are so frustrated by the culture that they are scarcely able to function. Thus the population can be divided into those with adjustment neuroses and those with maladjustment neuroses. Here, too, the traditional psychiatric classifications are false or misleading.

Carefully reviewed, diagnosis is thus seen to derive from an unwitting holdover of demonology and a lack of adequate vision on the part of the psychiatrist. In some mechanical way he applies the medical model to a patient population, then discovers that his classification is misleading or useless. Another group then takes over to revise the model. But as long as the underlying assumption of some organic disturbance remains, nothing changes.

Once more the analytic vision turns out to be fundamental. If it is ignored, as in psychiatric diagnosis, confusion and chaos result.

The Problem of Schizophrenia

Under the impact of psychoanalytic critiques, organic psychiatry has gradually come to focus on schizophrenia as the basic form of psychosis. Although by now most psychiatrists have at least some familiarity with analytic theory, they remain convinced that schizophrenia is an essentially organic illness. This medical approach has prevailed for about two hundred years.

Yet a paradox immediately appears. Society has entrusted the care, treatment, and prevention of schizophrenia to the psychiatrist of organic persuasion. But history leaves no doubt that organic psychiatry has consistently been wrong in its approach to this psychosis. There is little reason to doubt that it is still wrong.

Two polar extremes stand out in the approach to psychosis: Kraepelin's and Freud's. They were even contemporaries, born within a few months of each other. Thus once more two visions developed side by side: the organic and the psychological.

Kraepelin is generally given credit for the diagnostic system in almost universal use since the beginning of this century. What is most striking is the extraordinary degree of therapeutic pessimism that dominated Kraepelin's thought in contrast to Freud's therapeutic optimism. In a summing up near the end of his life, in 1917, Kraepelin wrote:

> We must openly admit that the vast majority of the patients placed in our institutions are according to what we know forever lost, that even the best of care may never restore them to perfect health. Our treatment probably makes life endurable for a vast number of mental cripples whose plight would otherwise be intolerable, but only rarely does it effect a cure.[15]

The dominant note in contemporary psychiatry is still that struck by Kraepelin: The cause of schizophrenia is heredity, the prospects for psychotherapeutic success almost nil. Thus ever since Kraepelin a diagnosis of schizophrenia stigmatized the sufferer as a freak afflicted with an incurable illness. Subsequent generations of organic psychiatrists have echoed Kraepelin's spirit, using, it is true, new methods and sometimes offering variations of theory, but always with the same underlying foreboding: This is a hereditary illness, which can be alleviated but not cured.

With such a theory it was at least a step forward to liberate the psychotics from the cruel and barbarous forms of punishment and custody to which they had been subjected for several centuries. The "snake pit" is an old form of treatment that sought to terrify the patient. Chains, beatings, starvation, and exposure to humiliating conditions were the order of the day in the eighteenth and nineteenth centuries. Confinement to a mental hospital was a virtual death sentence.

It is again striking that in spite of the belief in heredity and incurability, forward-looking psychiatrists (earlier known as alienists—even the name indicates that they regarded their charges as strange and alienated creatures, only half-human) repeatedly made progress by providing humane treatment for the psychotic. The work of Dorothea Dix in this country is well-known (Deutsch, 1949). But there were many earlier attempts. Kraepelin himself gives credit to English alienists for the elimination of many cruel practices. In 1839 John Conolly, superintendent of the asylum at Hanwell, removed all restraining instruments from the patients in his institution. Kraepelin reports:

> The experiment was remarkably successful . . . but only because, as Conolly never tired of repeating, a complete revolution in the handling and care of patients was simultaneously executed. Instead of using physical restraint to repress external manifestations of disorders, he had to find some means of exerting a favorable influence on the mental life of patients, preventing accidents, and eliminating evil tendencies or diverting them into harmless channels. Conolly achieved all this by giving patients comfortable accommodations, conscientiously caring for their needs, treating them sympathetically, consoling them, familiarizing himself with their individual problems, and providing them with appropriate activities and diversions. He observed that patients were far less dangerous than they had earlier appeared; indeed, that many unpleasant, obstructive, and dangerous traits had actually been the product of the treatment intended forcibly to suppress the symptoms of their disease. As in the fable of the contest between the sun and the wind for the traveler's coat, *the warm sun of human love quickly achieved what was beyond the reach of brutal force.*[16]

Kraepelin could observe the effects of the "warm sun of human love," but because there was no biochemical formula for such effects he continued to maintain his belief in hereditary origin and therapeutic hopelessness. Although he prided himself on being an empirical scientist, his correct observations were drowned out by his eighteenth-century hangover.

Freud himself was not personally optimistic about the therapeutic prognosis for psychotics, chiefly because he never functioned as a therapist in a mental hospital. The spirit of organic psychiatry was a spirit of pessimism; the only hope lay in the discovery of biochemical approach or in some eugenics program. The psychiatrists realized that they did not have enough evidence to justify any system of screening parents, so they focused on the biochemical route. Vast quantities of money and labor were poured into biochemistry, seemingly undeterred by the absence of results and by the everyday observation that kindness and understanding had always been shown to be more effective than drugs.

THE PARADOX OF PSYCHIATRIC HISTORY

Even a cursory knowledge of psychiatric history reveals the curious paradox noted earlier: In the roughly two hundred years in which the psychiatrist has been charged with the care of the mentally ill, *the science has always been wrong in its handling of schizophrenics*. It has not even been able to name the "illness" correctly. Kraepelin's term "dementia praecox" means premature senility, which it is not. It was replaced by "schizophrenia," or split mind, Bleuler's term, beginning around 1911; this is also wrong. Actually, Bleuler's term was the "group of schizophrenias," which recognized that he was dealing with a variety of disturbances, not one concrete medical entity, but careless followers ignored his cautious warnings. The American Psychiatric Association has changed its mind every ten years or so about how to classify the illness.

The basic assumption of organic psychiatry has always been that there is something wrong with the brain of the schizophrenic. In the process of testing out this theory virtually every part of the patient's body was implicated at one time or another: Schizophrenics have had their colons removed and their teeth pulled, have been castrated, lobotomized, injected with thyroid extracts, given enormous doses of vitamins, knocked over the head, electrically shocked, driven into convulsions, pushed close to death with large quantities of insulin, and so on. Whatever fad was popular at the moment was followed by the psychiatrist, regardless of the lack of progress.

TODAY'S DRUG REVOLUTION

But, the reader may well argue, these misguided efforts of the past have largely disappeared; today the treatment of choice is the major tranquilizers or neuroleptics, and these seem to be "miracle drugs" similar to penicillin and other antibiotics in many organic conditions. They fit in, it is claimed, with what is known of the biochemistry of the schizophrenic's brain, and they seem to produce lasting therapeutic results. True, precautions must be observed in their administration, and some side effects, at times serious, may be anticipated, but these are a small price to pay for such a major advance. It is appropriate to subject these claims to a critical examination.

The drug revolution that began in the middle of the 1950s with the introduction of thorazine (chlorpromazine) seems less impressive today, thus repeating the experience of psychiatry with all the seemingly miraculous physiological treatments of the past (Magaro et al., 1978). Critical observers have noted the following:

1. While the drugs provide relief to some patients, the kinds of patients who are benefited are the same as those benefited by other forms of treatment, namely, those with the best premorbid history.

2. Long-term studies (e.g. by Manfred Bleuler and Achte and Niskanen) show a high relapse rate and no significant change in the percentage of patients who are permanently helped. In other words, the drugs, when they do work, are merely a temporary palliative.

3. The use of the drugs has coincided with a change in hospital policy leading to the discharge of large numbers of mental patients into the community. While they are able to maintain themselves in the community, although frequently rehospitalized for brief periods, they are unable to function as full-fledged members of society. As Tissot (1977) puts it in what is probably the most objective review of the situation: "their future as human beings still remains very gloomy."[17]

4. The percentage of admissions and readmissions to hospitals depends primarily on the attitude of the community toward hospitalization, not on how "disturbed" or "socially adapted" the patients are. For example, Zwerling points out that in 1979 California and New York had approximately the same population. Yet California, which had developed an extensive network of outpatient facilities, had only 11,000 patients in hospitals while New York had 47,000.[18] Nevertheless, the majority view, as voiced by Davis and Cole (1975), is that the accelerated discharge of mental patients from hospitals "is, perhaps, the most convincing proof of the efficacy of these agents" (drugs).[19]

5. The side effects of the drugs are by no means as minor as many psychiatrists have claimed. Tissot states that two patients out of three develop extrapyramidal syndromes, or difficulties with the brain structures that control bodily movements. In his small-scale series he observed two cases of malignancy, of which one was fatal.[20] A large percentage of patients who take the neuroleptics over a long period of time develop tardive dyskinesia, or loss of control of

various muscle groups. No treatment is known for this effect. Further, a recent paper (Mehta et al., 1978) reported that there is a higher mortality rate for patients with tardive dyskinesia. The authors conclude: "Our results, if confirmed by prospective studies, indicate that tardive dyskinesia is a more serious problem than has been generally acknowledged."[21]

6. Family care of the mentally ill has been practiced since the twelfth century. The Belgian city of Geel became famous for its capacity to handle the mentally incompetent, at first ascribing its powers to divine Providence, later simply accepting the fact that it could care for these unfortunates in the homes of the inhabitants. In other countries family care has been tried with varying degrees of success; even Kraepelin spoke of it favorably[22] (see also Roosens, 1979).

7. Thus the introduction of the mental hospital in the eighteenth century and its current dismantling represent the beginning and the end of a long-term experiment, in which the pessimistic theories of Kraepelin and organic psychiatry have actually been proved wrong. Nevertheless, the belief in biochemical causation is so powerful that it tends to overshadow all the objective evidence.

8. At present it is widely recognized that in the long run the rehabilitation of the schizophrenic must be carried on in the community (Chiland, 1977; H. Lamb, 1976), although the drugs offer more relief in some cases. Nevertheless, in practice the situation remains deplorable. Ahmed and Plog, summing up the dissolution of state mental hospitals in 1976, wrote that

> . . . the question that we have answered till now is not where to care for chronic patients, but where not to care for them. In order to take care of the chronically disabled, we need a total care system which would see to their housing, use of drugs, training for a job, opportunity to work, and ways to ease the burdens of the community. We are nowhere close to achieving such a total service system.[23]

9. Finally, it should be stated that the alleged untreatability of the schizophrenic is to a considerable extent a myth. A good deal depends on when the patient enters treatment, but if he does enter early enough the percentage of improvement is fully as satisfactory as with drugs (Sullivan, 1931; in Sullivan, 1962) and from a human point of view far more rewarding. This fact has been known for fifty years but its proper application would require a thoroughgoing reformation, which the psychiatric profession is not prepared to undertake. In practice, however, it is being carried out by the introduction of other mental health professionals into the field.

Once more a curious historical paradox appears: In the eighteenth century the care of the mentally ill was entrusted to the medical profession because the clergy was so cruel. By the twentieth century the medical profession had become so cruel that the care of the mentally ill was increasingly being turned back to nonmedical practitioners. Freud's wish to turn his teachings over to a new profession, lay curers of souls, seems to be coming closer to realization than many realize (Hughes and Brewin, 1979).

THE PSYCHOANALYTIC HYPOTHESIS: SCHIZOPHRENIA AS A STATE OF DESPAIR

Once psychoanalysts after World War I began to study schizophrenia dynamically, a new, entirely different formulation came to the fore. First of all schizophrenia was seen as a psychological disorder, though physiological factors could enter in, as in any psychological disorder. Second, it was seen as a state of despair, a feeling of hopelessness that any meaningful human relationships could ever be established. Clearly this state of despair must be related to the early mothering process, since its roots extend far back into the infantile period. Third, once the despair was recognized, more effective new methods of psychotherapy could be devised.

While the vast mass of psychiatrists in the 1920s were still lost in the morass of Kraepelinian hopelessness, an increasing number of analysts began to pay attention to the illness and to make meaningful progress with its elucidation and therapy. Ernest Jones, in his address at the opening of Columbia University's Psychiatric Institute in 1929, put the matter most clearly:

> All mental morbidity is . . . a state of schizophrenia, although Professor Bleuler has proposed to reserve this term for the most striking of its forms. What we meet with clinically as mental disorder represents the endless variety of ways in which the threatened ego struggles for its self-preservation. In the nature of things, therefore, our conception of it can be cast only in terms of dynamic strivings.[24]

About the same time Harry Stack Sullivan was even more explicit in his condemnation of the Kraepelinian approach. In 1930 he wrote:

> As I am but one of many who no longer entertain [Kraepelin's] views, I shall be content with stating that his formulation—the dementia praecox concept—has been a great handicap to psychiatric progress, a

death sentence to many schizophrenic individuals, and an important factor in justification of the continued anachrony of the Institutional Care.[25]

The subsequent fifty years have witnessed an ongoing battle between the analytically oriented psychiatrists (later also psychologists and social workers) and the organically oriented. The dramatic changes especially in the past twenty years have resulted primarily from the increasing absorption into psychiatry of the analytic point of view.

EVIDENCE FOR THE ANALYTIC POSITION

The evidence that has accumulated in favor of the analytic position that schizophrenia is a state of despair brought about by grossly inadequate mothering in the early part of life is by now considerable. The theory that there is a continuum from normality to psychosis appears much more plausible than the disease theory, which holds that psychosis is primarily an inherited biochemical disorder, afflicting only a few individuals and separating them from the rest of the population (the Kraepelinian hypothesis). Historically, the analytic image of man as irrational, unconscious, and subject to the control of powerful internal forces has received ample substantiation. The evidence for the analytic position derives from at least five sources: (1) the family background (2) the cultural factor (including the historical), (3) the effects of psychotherapy, (4) more careful long-term studies, and (5) the diagnostic confusion.

The Family Background

For Kraepelin the environment, including the family environment, had nothing to do with the illness. This assumption has been completely exploded by subsequent research. Analysts from Sullivan on have repeatedly shown that schizophrenia arises from a malevolent family structure, particularly from bad mothering. Sullivan's most eminent student, Frieda Fromm-Reichmann, coined the term "the schizophrenogenic mother." By a gradual process of successive degrees of frustration, the schizophrenic symptomatology eventually evolves out of this deprived childhood environment. Fromm-Reichmann put it as follows in 1948:

The schizophrenic is painfully distrustful and resentful of other people, because of the severe early warp and rejection that he has encountered in important people of his infancy and childhood, as a rule mainly in a schizophrenogenic mother. During his early fight for emotional survival he begins to develop the great interpersonal sensitivity which remains his for the rest of his life. His initial pathogenic experiences are actually, or by virtue of his interpretation, the pattern for a never ending succession of subsequent similar ones. Finally, he transgresses the threshold of endurance. Because of his sensitivity and his never satisfied lonely need for benevolent contacts, this threshold is all too easily reached. The schizophrenic's partial emotional regression and his withdrawal from the outside world into an autistic private world, with its specific thought processes and modes of feeling and expression, are motivated by his fear of repetitional rejection, his distrust of others, and equally so by his own retaliative hostility, which he abhors, as well as the deep anxiety promoted by this hatred.[26]

The bad experience with the mother is repeated with the father, later with other figures. In a very real sense this discovery of the long prehistory of schizophrenia is similar to another great discovery of psychoanalysis, the long prehistory of sexuality.

Why does the mother engender such serious hostility and distrust in her child? Because she herself is seriously disturbed. Indeed, as Silvano Arieti (1974) points out, although he does not fully agree with the theory of the schizophrenogenic mother, there is one unanimous finding in all careful studies of the families of schizophrenics: In every case serious family disturbance was found. M. Bleuler likewise has stressed what he calls the "horrible childhood" of his patients.

It is again not too surprising that this observation of family disturbance is not new. More than a hundred years ago Griesinger, in spite of his organic predilections, noted the frequency of eccentric parental behavior and commented that, aside from genetic influence, the influences of such parents upon their children must be taken into account.[27] But the preoccupation with biochemistry swamped any concern with familial and social features. Once more it becomes clear than organic psychiatry has followed a pure theory, regardless of much available evidence contradictory of the theory.

Lidz and his co-workers at Yale published the first careful statistical examination of the families of schizophrenic patients, seventeen in all (1965). The investigation went on for almost a quarter of a century and in many phases is still continuing. They produced ample evidence of family disturbance.

Lidz's group was the first to show how pathological the fathers were in these families, as well as the mothers. They divided fathers into five groups: (1) fathers of girls who were in constant battle with their wives and tried to use the daughter in these battles; (2) fathers of boys who hated their sons as rivals; (3) fathers characterized by a sense of paranoid grandiosity; (4) fathers who have failed in life; and (5) fathers who are virtual nonentities, functioning as children to their wives.

Other investigators have stressed other aspects of the family pathology. Bateson (1956) introduced the concept of the double-bind, in which the child is exposed to contradictory commands, so that he can never learn to please his mother. Ackerman (1958) stressed the disturbed child as the family scapegoat. Wynne and his collaborators have shown how the "transmission of irrationality" occurs. Laing and Esterson published studies of the various kinds of disturbances in the families of their schizophrenic patients. By now the literature is so extensive that in one of the latest compilations (Wynne et al., 1978) an entire section is devoted to family relationships and communication.

It has been argued by those who favor the organic approach that these data could just as well be explained on the hypothesis of genetic transmission. Cromwell (in Wynne et al., 1978) states that schizophrenic genetics has had a history of redoing and superseding older studies and data with better methodologies, yet finding evidence to some degree again that genetic factors exist. Yet even he admits that we are in the dark about how such genetic transmission occurs, if it does.

Contrariwise, in the same symposium, Kringlen (in Wynne et al., 1978), who studied a more adequately classified group in Norway, concluded that the risk seems not as high as previously maintained. His results, he says, give no support to any simple dominant or recessive genetic transmission. Perhaps of the greatest importance from both a theoretical and a practical standpoint is that three-fourths of the offspring of schizophrenic couples do not in fact develop schizophrenia.[28]

Thus the theory of genetic transmission, which has been around for several centuries, explains little of what actually goes on in the lives of people. The theory of early deprivation explains much more.

The Cultural Factor

If it could be shown that cultural factors play a role in the formation, treatment, and outcome of schizophrenia, that would weigh heavily against the organic hypothesis. By now a considerable body of evidence along these lines is available, though often subject, as usual, to differing interpretations.

In 1939 Faris and Dunham published their now classic study of the relationship between mental disorder and urban area. They were able to show that the incidence of mental disorder is by far highest in the center of the city and decreases progressively as one moves outward toward the suburbs.

Stimulated by this and many other studies, Hollingshead and Redlich (1958) then undertook a more thorough examination of social class and mental disorder in the New Haven area. They found, for example, that age- and sex-adjusted rates for schizophrenic patients in psychiatric treatment were more than *nine times greater* in the lowest social class than in the highest.[29]

The Hollingshead-Redlich study was the first of many that demonstrated the inverse ratio between poverty and mental disorder. Almost invariably, even in a country as different from ours as Japan, this inverse ratio has been shown to hold.[30]

Looked at from the opposite point of view, that of cultures where schizophrenia is rare, it has been found that in integrated communities where alienation was uncommon, schizophrenia was likewise uncommon. Eaton and Weil (1955), in their examination of the Hutterite communities in North America, found schizophrenia to be almost nonexistent. Spiro, in his study of the Ifaluk, found only one peculiar individual, and he had been taken off to another island by the Japanese during World War II. Carothers (1970) found that the incidence of schizophrenia among blacks in Africa was much higher among men living away from home than among those who remained with their tribes.

Thus a consistent picture emerges: An alienated culture produces individuals who are severely frustrated in their childhood, which in turn predisposes them to mental breakdown. If later events worsen the earlier instability, there will be a high incidence of schizophrenia. If the culture is integrated and subjects the individual to relatively few traumatic breaks, the incidence of schizophrenia will be comparatively low. All this fits in very well with the conceptualization that schizophrenia is essentially a state of despair about ever having meaningful relationships with other people.

The culture of poverty. Why is there such a high incidence of psychiatric casualties among the poor, and why, as so many studies indicate, are they so untreatable by psychological methods? As an explanation the sociologist Oscar Lewis in 1959 suggested the concept of a "culture of poverty" which characterizes many cultural groups. The main characteristic of such a culture are (Lewis, 1966):

1. the lack of effective participation and integration of the poor in the major institutions of the larger society
2. on the local community level, poor housing conditions, crowding, gregariousness, but above all a minimum of organization beyond the level of the nuclear and extended family
3. on the family level, the absence of childhood as a specially prolonged and protected stage in the life cycle, early initiation into sex, free unions or consensual marriages, a relatively high incidence of the abandonment of wives and children, a trend toward female- or mother-centered families and consequently a much greater knowledge of maternal relatives, a strong predisposition to authoritarianism, lack of privacy, verbal emphasis on family solidarity, which is only rarely achieved because of sibling rivalry and competition for limited goods and maternal affection
4. on the level of the individual, a strong feeling of marginality, of helplessness, of dependence, and of inferiority

The most important omission in Lewis's description is the preponderance of sentiments of rage, hostility, resentment, and anger, and the frequency of acts of violence. As Green had shown in a well-known paper, physical punishment and violence as measures of getting the child to obey are far more common in the lower class than in the middle class, which tends to rely much more on the threat of loss of love (Green, 1946; Davis and Havighurst, 1946). In his study of Polish-Americans, Green writes:

> In exasperation and fear of losing all control over their Americanized youngsters, parents apply the fist and whip rather indiscriminately. The sounds of blows, screams, howls, vexatious wails of torment and hatred are so commonplace among the rows of dilapidated mill-houses that the passer-by pays them scant attention.[31]

Thus in the culture of poverty the child is brought up with hatred rather than love, is beaten unmercifully (at times to actual death), is deprived of real affection, is denied much schooling, thereby stifling his chances for advancement, and is disadvantaged in many other ways. Small wonder, then, that he soon reaches a state of despair that is virtually irreversible by our present techniques. And small wonder that both as a child and as an adult he becomes filled with hatred and violence, which spill over easily. Psychotherapy, which attempts to get people to give up their hatred and violence, is understandably helpless with such people.

The re-evaluation of history. The naive assumption has been that man is in general sane and that psychotic or insane individuals have some peculiar psychology or biochemical make-up that accounts for their bizarre behavior. A more careful study of history reveals that this assumption is of recent origin and that there is every reason to believe it is false. What we call "psychosis" has been the average mental state of men in many civilizations from ancient times to ours. This can be appreciated only if we remember that by "psychosis" we mean a state of despair induced by intolerable suffering. (The evidence on this point will be presented more fully in Chapter 17.)

Investigators have examined the psychiatric beliefs and methods adopted in other cultures, both primitive and modern. It is always the case that psychiatry is profoundly dependent on the culture's value system. Kiev (1964), in his compilation of psychiatric practices from a large number of contemporary relatively primitive groups, demonstrated that culture, or a group's shared system of beliefs, practices, and behavioral patterns, contributes not only to personality formation and psychic conflict but to the development, perpetuation, and management of whatever is called mental illness in that culture. As a rule it can be shown that what is called mental illness in any culture represents an exaggeration of personality traits that are relatively normal to that culture. Thus schizophrenia in our own society can be seen as an exaggeration of the trends toward separateness, despair, blocking of feeling, and irrational thinking, which can be found in every person in Western civilization. As the anthropologist Bernard Diamond has suggested, ours can be called a schizoid or a schizophrenic culture.

Alexander Leighton, influential in the development of social psychiatry, has summarized this point of view as follows:

> It is widely recognized that when circumstances force isolation on an individual he is apt to show psychophysiological disturbances and symptoms of psychiatric disorder. . . . Those circumstances that force isolation on individuals are usually imbedded in society and culture.[32]

The Results of Psychotherapy

While Kraepelin was reiterating his conviction that schizophrenics were hopeless mental cripples, others were adopting a diametrically opposite position and proving it by actual results. The first of the large-scale studies was Harry Stack Sullivan's landmark paper in 1931, "The Relation of Onset to Outcome in Schizophrenia."[33]

Sullivan's work. Sullivan reported on seven years of research. About 250 young male schizophrenics were subjected to "more or less elaborate investigation."[34] Of these he chose 100 of the first 155 serial admissions, eliminating 55 for various administrative reasons. Of these 100, the onset of mental illness was insidious in 22, acute in 78. Of those with acute onset, 48, or somewhat over 61 percent, showed marked improvement; "in a considerable number the change has amounted to a recovery from the mental disorder."[35]

At a time when the vast majority of psychiatrists in the world were, with Kraepelin, beating the drum of therapeutic hopelessness, Sullivan's report that he had improved or cured 61 percent of those with acute onset branded him either a genius or a madman. His contemporaries rationalized their own embarrassment by calling him a madman; later generations have agreed that he was a genius.

Nevertheless, even a genius cannot do the impossible. Sullivan was practicing analysis and analytic theory in the 1920s. His orientation toward his young schizophrenics was so different from that of Kraepelin that they may be said to have lived in two different worlds. In any discussion of therapeutic outcome, the enormous gap between the hopeful, therapizing, analytic psychiatrist and the pessimistic, custodial, organic psychiatrist must be borne in mind.

Sullivan's was only the most brilliant of many analytic researches that showed over and over that the schizophrenic is treatable (Fine, 1979a). But he is treatable only by a therapist who has genuine warmth, empathy, and understanding of his "irrational" productions. The personality matters, not the degree. The psychiatrists who objected so strenuously to Sullivan's formulations and therapeutic results were holding onto the vision of psychiatry that they had started with in 1800 and were also protecting their own personal and professional backgrounds.

The Whitehorn-Betz studies. In 1954 Whitehorn and Betz published their first study of the relationship between patient and psychiatrist, followed by a number of others. They found that one group (Group A) had much more success with schizophrenic patients than another (Group B). Group A psychiatrists had an improvement rate of 75 percent in their patients, while Group B psychiatrists had an improvement rate of only 27 percent with a comparable group of patients. Betz concluded that with schizophrenics at least the determinants of therapeutic success lie in the physician, or perhaps in the "fit" between the therapist's characteristics and the patient's.* Jerome Frank, reviewing this material in 1974, concluded that "features of the therapists' personality and style that counteract demoralization are more important determinants of their success than are their specific procedures."[36] Truax and Mitchell (1971) found warmth, genuineness, and empathy characteristic of the successful therapist.

Even though nothing has been conclusively demonstrated, the overwhelming evidence is that a therapist who is warm, genuine, understanding, and actively a participant can be much more successful with the schizophrenic patient than one who is objective, diagnostic, puzzled, and passive, the characteristics of the average psychiatrist trained in the Kraepelinian tradition.

The Yale studies: A-P and D-O psychiatrists. Myers and Bean (1968), following up the Hollingshead-Redlich studies, also investigated the orientations of the psychiatrists treating schizophrenic patients. They found, as had been the case earlier, that social class of the patients played a decisive role in their ultimate disposition: Those at the lowest end of the SES ladder were hospitalized more often, were more often regarded as hopeless, and made less progress than those higher up.

They also found that the psychiatrists fell into two groups: A-P, those with an analytical and psychological orientation, and D-O, those with a directive and organic orientation. In training, the A-P psychiatrists went through full or partial psychoanalytic or psychodynamic training and orientation. D-O training was more closely oriented to the organic medical approach, and considerable training was undertaken in neurology and basic biological sciences. This dichotomy persisted for the more than ten years of the study. Thus once more it is the personality and training of the psychiatrist that are decisive in the outcome.

The May study. In 1968 Philip May and his associates published the results of a comparative study of five treatment methods: (1) individual psychotherapy alone, (2) ataraxic drugs alone, (3) individual psychotherapy plus ataraxic drugs, (4) electroshock, and (5) milieu, a control group which received none of these specific treat-

---

*The types also showed different patterns on the Strong Vocational Interest Blank. As so often happens, despite fifteen years of research, the value of this discrimination has remained controversial (Meltzoff and Kornreich, 1970).

ments. The patients were hospitalized schizophrenics. Release rates were: (1) 65 percent, (2) 95–96 percent, (3) 95–96 percent, (4) 79 percent, and (5) 58 percent. The main conclusion was that analyses indicate that *drug* had an extremely significant effect in increasing the release rate, while there was relatively little effect from *psychotherapy*.[37]

May's study has been widely cited as conclusive evidence that drugs are the treatment of choice for schizophrenics, while psychotherapy adds little or nothing. However, his study has numerous flaws.

The patients were "randomly selected"—228 schizophrenics admitted for the first time to Camarillo State Hospital. Nothing further is said about them, in spite of the overwhelming evidence that different kinds of patients respond in different ways. The historical perspective by Dr. Tuma in the first chapter of May's book discloses no real familiarity with the literature; thus he pays a good deal of attention to Eysenck, but Freud and Sullivan are not mentioned at all. When the qualifications of the therapists are examined, we are told only that "the patients were treated by physicians with six years or less of psychiatric experience who were either in residency training or had completed it."[38] The amount of psychotherapy is not broken down clearly, though the instructions were that each patient should have an average of not less than two hours per week, with a minimum of one hour per week.[39] Those assigned to psychotherapy alone and psychotherapy plus drugs who were successfully released received from seven to eighty-seven hours of psychotherapy (12–106 interviews).[40]

Further, the milieu was so generally therapeutic that it contributed substantially to whatever results may have been achieved. In fact, the psychologist Dr. Luther Distler in his evaluation said:

> [T]he addition of *psychotherapy* to such an intensive *milieu* treatment program appears to add little or nothing of value in the treatment of the general run of hospitalized schizophrenics. This may be due not so much to *psychotherapy* not working as to the amount of "psychotherapeutic" contact already available from the nursing staff. *Milieu* in the present study may not constitute an adequate control group for assessing whether *psychotherapy* works for hospitalized schizophrenics.[41]

Thus the May study really sheds no additional light on the overall question of the treatability of schizophrenics. It failed to consider the patient, the therapist, the intensity of therapy, the hospital milieu, and other factors.

How Treatable Are Schizophrenics?

Like all questions relating to treatability, that of schizophrenics is extremely complex. In the May study, even though the emphasis was on drugs, the overall discharge rate *without* drugs was incredibly high by Kraepelinian standards. In other words, May showed, unwittingly, that the Kraepelinian doctrine of therapeutic hopelessness is no longer justified in the present environment. As Bleuler was also to emphasize (see below), the doctrine of chronic, irreversible hopelessness of the schizophrenic has to be given up.

As to the effect of psychotherapy on the individual schizophrenic, clearly it depends on so many factors that overall figures mean little. Because a disproportionate number come from the lower classes, whose state of despair in the culture of poverty is so great, their reaction to therapy must be colored more by the bleak and grim nature of their lives than by the "illness," which is merely a reflection of this environment.

In any case, whatever figures are produced, it seems beyond dispute that a considerable number of schizophrenics do respond to psychotherapy when properly administered. This also shatters the vision with which psychiatry started several hundred years ago and tends to confirm the overall analytic position.

LONG-TERM STUDIES

It has been observed that schizophrenics tend to respond to any dramatic change in their environment. More than one hundred years ago Jarvis (1855; reprinted 1971), in reviewing the cases of patients hospitalized in Massachusetts, noted that a preponderant number were discharged in *less than a year*. Jarvis wrote:

> [T]here are manifold disorders of the brain . . . classed under the general term of insanity. These are usually grave diseases; and yet they are among the most curable of maladies of their severity, provided they are taken in season and the proper remedies applied. In recent cases, the recoveries amount to the proportion of 75 to 90% of all that are submitted to the restorative process . . . they become more and more difficult to be removed with the lapse of time.[42]

Hence care must be taken with the evaluation of any new therapeutic modality. As some wit has said, schizophrenia is the easiest disease in the world to cure, for a new cure is announced every week. Only long-term studies can definitively establish what happens to these patients.

In the era of insulin coma and electric shock, some thirty to forty years ago, numerous cures were also reported in the beginning, only to disappear as time went on and patients were submitted to follow-up examination (Bellak and Loeb, 1968). Follow-up studies of the drugs are now coming out, and the results point in similar directions. Achte and Niskanen (1972), studying Finnish patients, could establish no essential difference between those treated with drugs and those treated without drugs. But by far the most exhaustive and definitive study that has appeared is the one by Manfred Bleuler, son of the great Eugen Bleuler. One paper was published in 1970, followed by a book, recently translated into English under the title *The Schizophrenic Disorders* (1978). This is undoubtedly the most important single work on schizophrenia that has appeared in the past quarter-century.

The Bleuler study. Bleuler's work is based on a quarter-century follow-up of 208 patients admitted to the Bürghölzli Clinic after he became its head in 1942. He had personally treated all of them and followed each one until death, or for at least twenty-two years, together with the destinies of their parents, siblings, marital partners, and children. He was also in touch with other investigators who had studied carefully the course of 950 more schizophrenics. Many of his conclusions were in marked contradiction to those of Kraepelin and the contemporary drug therapists.

1. On an average, after five years' duration, the psychosis does not progress any further but tends, rather, to improve. This tendency to improvement becomes evident only if the conditions of these patients are considered in detail.

2. At least 25 percent of all schizophrenics recover entirely and remain recovered permanently.

3. On the other hand, about 10 percent of schizophrenics remain permanently hospitalized as severe psychotics.

4. Of the 25 percent who had reached a long-term favorable condition, *not one was under long-term neuroleptic or other pharmocologic treatment*, nor were most of the recovered patients cared for by the welfare agencies.

5. So-called catastrophic schizophrenia, which is characterized by an early acute onset with no improvement, resulting in lifelong deterioration (the typical patient as described by Kraepelin), has virtually disappeared.

6. The most common type of patient is the phasic-benign.

7. A careful analysis shows that the factor that contributed most to patient improvement was the advances made in social and environmental therapy. Bleuler emphasized what his father had always stressed, that no patient should ever be given up.

Thus Bleuler's careful work restores intensive long-term psychotherapy to its rightful place. It also shows, as does the work of many others (Chiland, 1977; Achte and Niskanen, 1972), that the drugs have primarily the effect of providing temporary relief. In the long run, it makes no difference whether drugs are used or not; it may well be that with many patients they do more harm than good.

An interesting and unexpected development is the greater awareness among patients of what is being done to them. A *New York Times* article on December 11, 1978, reported that a group of mental patients was challenging the use of thorazine because it leads to incurable tardive dyskinesia. They were also questioning the entire jargon of psychiatry. Howie Harp, a founder of Project Release, a self-help group of mental patients in New York City, put it this way:

> I do not think there is mental illness, which is only normal reactions to abnormal situations. And I certainly don't think that psychiatrists should be free to oppress us with forced drugging. Their orientation is one of control, of imposing their values on you, a concept of normality and of abnormality we cannot accept.
>
> If you are poor you are nuts and if you are rich you are eccentric. No, there is nothing in psychiatry that is of help to people.

Howie Harp, though labeled a schizophrenic, shows much more insight here into the real nature of mental disorder than most psychiatrists on the current scene.

The Diagnostic Confusion

The confusion of organic psychiatry is nowhere more clearly demonstrated than in the area of diagnosis. Diagnosis is a concept taken over from organic medicine; its application to "mental" illness is of relatively recent origin. As I have noted, the first classification of mental disorder in the United States was published in 1917. Since then it has been changed almost every ten years. The current classification appeared in 1979, and already people are discussing how it should be changed the next time.

Patchwork and arbitrary groupings characterize the system. In 1952 schizophrenia was changed to schizophrenic reaction; in 1968 it was changed back to schizophrenia; in 1979 it became schizophrenic disorders. The dishonest reclassification of homosexuality is well known (Socarides, 1974). Suddenly in 1973 homosexuality was classified as a "sexual orientation disturbance." In 1978 this became "ego-dystomic homosexuality,"[44] and in 1979 "homodysphilia" (a term no one can understand).[45] In explanation, Dr. Spitzer stated that this term refers to homosexuals who are distressed by their homosexual arousal. Asked whether he and his committee had considered the unconscious anxiety of the homosexual or his capacity to repress, he replied that while they had considered the unconscious they did not know what to do with it. We also find Dr. Stoller asking whether heterosexuality could not be considered a disorder; this classification was actually considered by the committee, but a majority retained enough rationality to vote against it.

The current analytic literature, which is designed to keep analysis within the framework of medicine, shows just as much confusion as the psychiatric. The favorite diagnoses are "borderline" and "narcissistic personality disorder." In practice "borderline" generally points to some countertransference problem on the part of the psychiatrist: If you do not like a patient, call him borderline. "Narcissistic personality disorder" refers to people who are too "narcissistic." Everybody is to some degree narcissistic (self-involved or self-loving), so where the line is to be drawn becomes a moot point. The term has been popularized by the followers of Heinz Kohut. In a casebook issued by his students, the six cases presented are all typical analytic problems, but mysteriously at some point each therapist discovers that he is dealing with a "narcissistic personality."

The current diagnostic manual dispenses with the term "neurosis." In reality the various definitions of neurosis since Freud's day and the various classifications have been remarkably similar: people who are unable to work, have difficulty in loving, are excessively angry, and so forth. Doctors are paid to make diagnoses, so the charade continues indefinitely, even if the diagnoses are utterly senseless.

In sum, reviewing the family studies, cultural background, therapeutic results, long-term studies and the diagnostic confusion, the following conclusions seem justified:

1. Schizophrenia is primarily a psychogenic disorder deriving from long-standing inner conflicts going back to earliest childhood,

particularly the struggle with a rejecting or schizophrenogenic mother.

2. It is not a medical illness in any significant sense but a state of despair about ever having meaningful loving relationships with other human beings.

3. It is much more apt to surface in alienated or poverty-stricken societies, because these factors make for a state of despair in their own right.

4. The diagnostic category of "schizophrenia" as such tells us little; it should be replaced by a full-scale description of the personality.

5. Many patients diagnosed as schizophrenic do respond to analytically oriented psychotherapy. Some achieve a full recovery.

6. The tranquilizing drugs in some cases provide temporary relief from the symptoms, but in the long run they do nothing. In fact, they may do more harm than good in some some cases. The side effects are often serious and lasting, sometimes permanent, and on rare occasions fatal.

7. The average hospital-trained psychiatrist with little more than the standard three-year residency does not have the competency to do psychotherapy with schizophrenics. This is the real conclusion to be drawn from May's study, paradoxical though it may seem, for it was his main aim to simulate ordinary hospital conditions as much as possible.

8. Therapists with the capacity for warmth, empathy, and understanding have a much better chance to help the schizophrenic than those without. The professional degree is of secondary importance.

9. On the current scene, and for the past thousand years, the care and treatment of the psychotic have been a disgrace.

The Adjustment Neurosis and the Maladjustment Neurosis

Sociopsychological knowledge plus the understanding of the analytic ideal lead to the conclusion that there are two types of difficulties people suffer from: adjustment neurosis and maladjustment neurosis (see pp. 141–144). Traditional organic psychiatry has confined itself to the maladjustment neurosis; it has had no concepts or techniques available for the adjustment neurosis. Hence the effort is made to declare the prospective patient "sick" or "mentally ill," totally ignoring the cultural environment in which both psychiatrist and patient find themselves. The addition of the adjustment neurosis enlarges psychiatry with psychoanalysis but also creates an entirely new discipline.

An adjustment neurosis arises inevitably in every culture because the demands of human beings are not met adequately by the culture. This has actually been known since the days of Rousseau, but he and his contemporaries thought that man had but to go back to a primitive state of being to find happiness, and we know now that they were wrong. There are primitive cultures even more psychotic than ours—paranoid cultures where the natural cause of death is denied, for example, so that every death becomes a homicide calling for punishment. There are other primitive cultures that in many respects seem to be models of mental health, eschewing violence and rage and living peaceably for hundreds of years. It seems impossible to set up any rule.

But by now the developmental processes in all cultures are reasonably well understood. The early experiences of the child with the parents are incorporated by the child into a psychic entity known as the superego. This superego then increasingly dominates the individual's sense of well-being. Almost always he is caught between the demands of the superego and the demands of reality. The ensuing conflict may be intense or it may be mild, but there is always some conflict (Brenner, 1976). Through the agency of the superego the culture produces some modal personality, typical of a considerable percentage of the members of that culture. Judged by the standards of the analytic ideal, this modal personality is always to some extent inadequate. Hence we can speak of the adjustment neurosis of any culture.

This distinction between the adjustment and the maladjustment neuroses, which follows directly from psychoanalytic thinking, is far more profound and more meaningful than the usual psychiatric diagnoses. It allows for a dynamic understanding of each individual in relation to his past and in relation to the position in which he finds himself in the culture. It allows for no easy formula, but then again all the easy formulas have to be discarded anyhow. Further, it ties in the individual with the kind of therapy and/or education for which he is best suited.

The Biochemical Factors: Organic Psychiatry

As I have pointed out, extensive claims have been made in the past twenty years for the existence of organic factors in psychiatric illness and the effectiveness of various drugs in treating these illnesses. Among the claims are (1) the dopamine theory of schizophrenia, (2) the biogenic amine theory of depression, (3) the minimal brain damage theory for hyperactive children, and (4) the autonomic nervous system disturbance for anxiety.

If the claims were substantiated, the psychological theories would certainly be invalidated or at best would become secondary to the more significant physiological theories. But a careful reading of the literature reveals over and over again that these claims are put forth tentatively, without widespread testing, without a fully satisfactory rationale, and without paying attention to negative results and factors tending to invalidate the theories involved.

It is certainly true that a variety of drugs have been developed that change the moods of people. Once the hallucinogens had become widely popular, from the 1950s on, historical and cultural research revealed that such drugs had been used by a variety of cultures from time immemorial. Coca, for example, has been chewed by the inhabitants of Peru for hundreds of years. Marijuana was known to the ancient Chinese. Every culture, in fact, has turned to the use of some drugs to ease the suffering that seems to be universal.

But it is a far cry from the relief of pain or the change of mood to the understanding of personality structure. Alcohol is still the most common and the most venerable substance used to alter the mood of people; every culture seems to have devised some means of producing alcoholic beverages. But no one would seriously argue that the careful study of alcohol would resolve the problems of psychology. Yet such is precisely the kind of argument put forth by the proponents of biological psychiatry.

It would take us too far afield to examine the literature of this subject in detail. It will have to suffice to quote some typical summary statements made by researchers who have worked extensively in the field and have no special axe to grind.

In a recent review, Snyder (1978) examines the evidence for and against the dopamine theory of schizophrenia. He states: "The only way to state definitively that dopamine plays a role in the pathophysiology of the disease is to demonstrate a specific abnormality of dopamine-related biochemistry in brains or body fluids of schizo-phrenics. This has never been done."[46]

The dopamine theory states that the schizophrenic symptoms result from the release of excessive dopamine in the brain. One piece of evidence that is heavily cited is that the phenothiazines have been shown to block the release of dopamine, which explains why they "work" so well. Yet it will be remembered that in Bleuler's careful study, of the 25 percent of his schizophrenic patients who recovered after a schizophrenic episode *not a single one had neuroleptic or other pharmocologic treatment.*[47]

With regard to the experimental study of psychological proc-esses in schizophrenia, one function that has been extensively inves-tigated is attention. It is obvious that schizophrenics cannot pay at-tention as well as normals. Yet attempts to quantify this observation by experimental methods have not succeeded. To cite Sutton et al. (1978):

> Where does all of this leave us with respect to the nature of attentional organization in schizophrenic patients? Unfortunately, at this stage, not very far. The virtue, or, perhaps from another point of view, the fault of tight experimental paradigms is that it is not easy to talk one's way around results that do not fit some formulation. Hopefully, *these inconsistencies eventually will yield to ingenious experimentation.*[48]

These two quotes are good illustrations of the biases and faulty thinking of the organic psychiatrist–experimental psychologist. Clear evidence for the drugs is not available, so push farther; experi-mentation has gotten nowhere, so experiment some more. There is no recognition of the other side of the picture, that we are dealing here with clinical entities arising from sociopsychological distur-bances, which have to be approached, understood, and treated in clinical terms.

Hartmann: The Sleeping Pill

An example of more enlightened research is provided by Ernest Hartmann, one of the leading sleep researchers, in his recent book *The Sleeping Pill* (1978). Hartmann views insomnia as a psychologi-cal problem that has to be dealt with by psychological methods; pills at best bring only temporary relief. But his careful research has convinced him that in the main sleeping pills, even when used for relief, do more harm than good. He states:

> Sleeping pills are presently overprescribed and overused. I have examined some of the practical and psychological reasons for this . . . my conclusion is that the overall risks outweigh the overall benefits. If a drug is used only for very specific indications, if the drug to be used is carefully chosen, and if new drugs are developed that relate specifically to the biology and chemistry of sleep, this low benefit-to-risk ratio will no longer obtain.[49]

The Personality and Training of the Psychiatrist

We have emphasized that Freud's self-analysis was the real revolution in the history of the field. It seems self-evident that the personality of the psychiatrist would be of crucial importance in the outcome of any therapeutic undertaking, especially with psychotics. Yet it took a long time to appreciate this elementary fact, and strong resistance to it is still present.

The most elaborate study of psychiatrists in private practice is one published by the American Psychiatric Association in 1975, edited by Judd Marmor, a former president of the association. This reveals that the modal form of treatment is once-a-week analytically oriented psychotherapy. It also discloses a marked disproportion of psychiatrists in various parts of the country, with the Northeast overrepresented and Southeast underrepresented.

What training the psychiatrists had for doing analytically oriented psychotherapy is not considered by Marmor's report, a significant omission in itself. The researchers did find out that 29 percent of the respondents claimed to be analysts, in contrast to the factual finding that 10 percent of the total profession are so trained. Lebensohn says that informal investigation showed that only 14 percent of the psychiatrists who claimed to be analysts were not really trained in analysis; he mentions this statistic without comment.[50] It seems to make no difference to him that 14 percent of psychiatrists were deliberately lying about their background in a questionnaire that was to be kept confidential. Most people on the current scene would judge the figure to be higher—a considerable percentage of psychiatrists who are not analytically trained nevertheless continue to make this claim to their patients. According to Henry in his 1971 survey, more than one-third of the psychiatrists had never even had any therapy, much less formal analytic training.[51]

Little is known about what kinds of persons enter psychiatry. What little is known (Henry et al., 1971, 1973; Schuster et al., 1972) indicates that psychiatrists are more or less normal characters in our culture who enter psychiatry as a comfortable way of making a living (Knight, 1953). The idealism that marked the early beginnings of psychoanalysis has gone. At the same time the psychiatrist increasingly is pushed to take on for treatment other people more or less like himself; that is, the patient population has shifted from those with maladjustment neurosis to those with adjustment neurosis.

Training has become a medley of every conceivable school of thought. Here a sharp distinction must be made between psychiatrists whose training is more or less limited to their hospital residency, who make up by far the bulk of the profession (Henry et al., 1971), and those who go on to become psychoanalysts. For now we are talking only of the 90 percent of psychiatrists who do not take formal analytic training. In *The American Handbook of Psychiatry*, George Mora has the following comments to make about training:

> Serious efforts have been made toward offering a comprehensive type of training, including experience in state institutions, outpatient clinics, special facilities (for example, for children or for delinquents), and presenting a manifold philosophical orientation (genetic, organicistic, psychodynamic, and epidemiological) and various therapeutic approaches (chemotherapy, individual as well as group and family therapy, and others). In view of the vastness of each new field of psychiatry, such an ambitious program can be realistically carried on in very few places.[52]

It is obvious that everything is thrown at the psychiatric resident in the three years of his residency. Relatively few take systematic training beyond that point, so that what they really know they must learn in residency. Small wonder that Tischler (1968), when he looked at the progress reports of Yale University psychiatrists, found that the characteristic prelude to each resident's report was the frank statement: "I for one felt very insecure in psychiatry not knowing what I was doing."[53]

The Rosenhan (1973) study has already been mentioned (pp. 127–128. While Rosenhan attempted to show from his study that the definition of insanity remains completely unclear, what he really did was to paint a gruesome picture of contemporary psychiatric incompetence. Studies such as his have contributed to the accelerated dismantling of the mental hospitals.

Without any reflection on the caliber of the persons who enter the field, three things become clear from this examination of the psychiatrist. First of all, the resident is faced with an impossible task. To master so much material in such a short time is simply impossible. Second, the most essential ingredient of all training, the personal analysis, is left to chance. At least a third of residents do not enter into it at all. Many of the others choose grossly inadequate therapeutic encounters. Third, on the present scene the psychiatrist has become at best a half-trained analyst, at worst one-third or one-sixth trained.

Here the value of the extensive training offered to the psychoanalyst becomes apparent. Kris once spoke of the "formative decade." It seems impossible to acquire the necessary skills for the adequate practice of psychoanalysis and psychotherapy in less than ten years. Once acquired they raise the psychoanalyst to a considerably higher level than the psychiatrist.

It is therefore all the more surprising that the American Psychoanalytic Association in 1972 reached the agreement with the American Psychiatric Association referred to elsewhere (pp. 104–105), which in effect nullified all differences between psychoanalysis and psychiatry. As the review here indicates, the education of the average nonanalytic psychiatrist is far inferior to that of the analyst; in fact, for the purpose of long-term psychotherapy it is inferior to that of both the clinical psychologist and the social worker as well. Once more it becomes clear that the analytic vision has time and again been sacrificed to political and financial considerations, by analysts as well as others.

Organic Psychiatry: A Re-evaluation

Almost any reflective book on psychiatry today raises the question of the adequacy of contemporary theory and practice. As noted, the editors of the standard *American Handbook of Psychiatry* (Arieti 1974–75) included "A General Assessment of Psychiatry." The author, Dr. Alfred Rifkin, begins with the comment that we do not ordinarily begin a discussion of any medical specialty, such as cardiology or pediatrics, by assessing its worth, yet that seems necessary in psychiatry. He explained:

> The question reflects a certain uneasiness, a need to clarify the scope of psychiatry, to fix the proper limits of its concern, to determine the na-

ture of the problems to which it should address itself, and to study the conceptual and technical tools fashioned for the solution of problems.[54]

Rifkin goes on to discuss the contributions of psychology, sociology, history, and other social sciences to the work of the psychiatrist. He discusses the pros and cons of the much-disputed medical model. He neglects to state, however, that medicine itself is in a state of crisis because of the awareness of its vast social and cultural implications (Engel, 1977).

It is certainly not possible to sum up the merits and demerits of organic psychiatry in one facile sentence. Much has been uncovered, much remains mysterious. But one fact is clear: Psychiatry in the twentieth century made its greatest strides by incorporating the psychological doctrines of psychoanalysis. Officially this can be dated from 1933, when a section on psychoanalysis was established in the American Psychiatric Association against the bitterest of opposition. Unofficially, it has gone on as long as psychoanalysis has existed.

Unfortunately, however, the incorporation of psychoanalysis into psychiatry is anything but complete. Henry's figures indicate that one-fourth of psychiatrists do not even have any personal therapy, much less formal psychoanalytic education. A large percentage of psychiatrists limit themselves to the formal three-year psychiatric residency in spite of its obvious inadequacy.

We have noted that while psychiatry has been entrusted by society with the care of the mentally ill for some two hundred years, it has always been wrong in its theoretical position, in its diagnostic systems, and in its treatment approaches. Rosen comments that throughout a large part of the nineteenth century psychiatric theory had been a "tangle of confusion,"[55] and the twentieth century has not really been much better. New drugs are reported in almost endless profusion, only to be followed by a period of disillusionment and discouragement. Officially and unofficially, psychiatry has turned to mental hygiene and relies principally on adequate humane care for all patients. But again, for his role as an expert in mental hygiene, which involves a profound knowledge of many social sciences, the psychiatrist is as a rule very poorly prepared. The alternative nonmedical professions, clinical psychology and social work, have in fact grown more rapidly than psychiatry and have taken over much of the domain previously reserved to the medical practitioner, often against fierce opposition by organized medicine.

From the "Sick Patient" to the Unhappy Person

In order to bolster its claim to priority, psychiatry has labeled the subject a "sick patient," thus obviously one in need of medical care. Psychosis and neurosis (both misnomers deriving from medical ignorance) are aspects of "mental illness." As time has gone on, it has become increasingly clear that all of these designations are tragic misrepresentations. The shift in the patient population since World War II has been to the normal person, the average citizen, in our country and in Western Europe. Because of reactionary governments, including both fascism and communism, this unhappiness is denied in other parts of the world.

Far-seeing observers were aware of the potentialities for the future at an early date. In 1929, Ernest Jones made the following prophetic statement:

> The most outstanding [change in American psychiatry], and one on which [the United States] has every right to congratulate itself, is what might be called the social consolidation of psychiatry. So much impressed is the outside observer by this that it does not seem unmerited to say that America has actually created a new profession. *In a very important respect one can almost say that the profession of psychiatry does not exist in any other country in the world.*[56]

Jones attributed the growth of the new profession to America's social conscience, which he valued highly. In the ensuing fifty years many of his prophecies have been fulfilled, though much remains to be done.

Naturally Jones did not foresee World War II and the enormous disasters and transformations connected with it. But he was right in his prediction that psychoanalysis would emerge as one of the dominant intellectual movements of the twentieth century. By contrast, organic psychiatry, in spite of all the hullabaloo, has become less and less impressive, even though most of the new miracle drugs now in use were virtually unknown in 1929.

The situation today in fact is not dissimilar to that in 1839, when John Conolly dispensed with all restraints in his asylum (see p. 134). It is ironic that Kraepelin was impressed by Conolly's humanitarian form of treatment but remained stuck in his own biochemical formulas and hopes (or fantasies, one might say). With a revolutionary step suggesting itself before his very eyes, he could not take it because of his medical bias. This is one more proof that sciences often fail to overcome the biases of their founders.

Kraepelin's pessimistic stance in 1917 can be contrasted with Sullivan's remarkable therapeutic successes only ten years later. Sullivan was quite justifiably strong in his insistence that traditional Kraepelinian psychiatry led to many needless deaths and to the stultification of the lives of thousands of others.

The situation today is not essentially different from what it was in 1939. New drugs are available, offering at times better relief than before. But the lives of those whose schizophrenia or depression has been ameliorated temporarily remain for the most part hopelessly gloomy, as Tissot points out (see p. 136). The soma drugs that Aldous Huxley fantasized about in *Brave New World*, which would automatically make people happy, are still a fantasy. And one tragic consequence of these fantasies is that millions of young people have turned to drugs, both medical and nonmedical, to alleviate their pain in living. In spirit at least, this wholesale resort to drugs has been encouraged by the medical attitude regarding the use of drugs in severe "mental illness."

It has been shown repeatedly that whatever temporary relief is brought about by drugs, in the long run kind and warm treatment of the unhappy person produces the best results. It is for this reason that psychiatry has attempted to include in its curriculum all of the social sciences. In spite of this inclusion, in the mind of the medically trained individual the pharmacological approach must necessarily have primacy. This grievous error has caused untold harm.

Conclusion: Psychoanalysis Is Primary, Psychiatry Secondary

The important conclusion that emerges from these considerations is that psychoanalytic psychology, or psychoanalysis, is the primary science. Psychiatry represents an application of this primary science to certain types of patients, historically those too disturbed to function in society. That psychiatry may also make use of drugs or other physical treatments does not alter this position. To take a homely analogy: Glasses are often needed in reading, but one need not be familiar with the science of optics to teach reading skills.

Inasmuch as psychoanalysis is primary, it is no surprise that one writer after another finds psychiatric education hopelessly inadequate. The most basic requirement, the personal analysis, is either omitted entirely or left to the whim of the student. Without a personal analysis, the psychiatrist places excessive reliance on drugs or somatic manipulation, as he has always done; the drugs may be new, but the ideas are old. The vast amount of material from the behavioral and social sciences that is offered to the psychiatric resident cannot be absorbed in the time allotted. The result, as Marmor's study shows, is a poorly prepared and poorly functioning profession. Nevertheless, since society would rather rely on physical manipulation than rational amelioration of psychosocial difficulties, in practice medicine is still given top priority.

Ideally again, the psychoanalytic vision should prevail. As with psychology, a personal analysis should *precede* entry into any training program in psychiatry. Only those who benefit from this analysis, showing a capacity for psychological insight, should be admitted to further training. In essence, full psychoanalytic training should be required of all psychiatrists. Only in this way will psychiatry be able to fulfill its great promise for humanity's future.

Finally, one can only be impressed by the persistence and power of a vision that arose two hundred years ago. The idea then was that the psychotic suffered from a brain disease (the unknown bacillus) and was therefore essentially incurable by psychological means. However, his condition could be ameliorated by humane and kind care given to him in specially constructed hospitals or asylums. Drugs could also be of help. Yet no matter what was done, the essential element was the search for the bacillus: Unless that was found, no permanent alleviation of the condition could be expected. Kraepelin formulated this vision in the pseudo-scientific terms of his day, replacing the older concepts of good and bad demons by the newer ones of curable and incurable diseases. This is the vision still adhered to, partly unverbalized, partly verbalized in a different way, by the majority of psychiatrists today. Currently it is referred to as organic or traditional psychiatry. Above all, it is based on the nineteenth-century image of man as rational, conscious, and under the sway of powerful external forces. In the case of psychosis, this external force is an organic impairment that science will someday uncover.

By contrast, the psychoanalytic vision is that the psychotic suffers from a horrible childhood in which he experienced severe frustration and rejection in his efforts to obtain warmth from responsible parents. This rejection left him with a weak ego, which further exposed him to a variety of deviations at later stages. All of the mental "illnesses" are variations of reactions to this earlier ego weakness (Jones, 1929; in Jones, 1948). They are not illnesses in any significant sense, though they may lead to organic illnesses, but difficulties in living. They should be handled by psychotherapy administered by specially trained practitioners who have an abundance of warmth, empathy, and understanding. When so treated under proper conditions, the outlook becomes much brighter. The care and treatment of the psychotic on the current scene remain a national disgrace. This disgrace can be remedied only by improving the culture of poverty and providing a large number of therapists and allied professionals who are able to influence other people in a constructive manner.

Chapter 6

Toward Clarification in the Social Sciences

To any objective observer there is an astounding amount of controversy in the social sciences. Even the nomenclature is unsettled: Many wish to call them the behavioral sciences. Some people include in them what is also called the "humanities"; others do not. Which disciplines should be included and which should not occupies some theoreticians. The proper subject matter for each discipline is unclear; as long ago as 1908 Franz Boas, the father of modern anthropology, noted that the subject matter of many disciplines is a matter of historical accident.[1]

Most accounts of social science today state that the two greatest formative influences in the conceptualization of these sciences have been Marx and Freud.[2] Nevertheless, they show little understanding of Freud and as a rule indoctrinate their students against anything psychoanalytic. The contradiction, now virtually absolute, between Marx and Freud is also overlooked. Not surprisingly, the result is endless argument and endless confusion.

The Cultural Context

It has already been pointed out that the social sciences in their modern form are a development of the twentieth century and that their growth has proceeded *pari passu* with that of psychoanalysis. To this a further fundamental historical observation is necessary. The world today could be said to be divided into three major ideological camps: Marxist, Freudian, and religious, to which a fourth, eclectic, could be added. The form the social sciences take in countries where Marxist or religious ideology predominates is entirely different from their form in countries where Freudian or eclectic influences predominate. The conceptualizations, the professions, the applications, and the contents of the textbooks are all radically different. Yet if we are really dealing with "sciences," how could such differences exist? Obviously the ideological preconceptions of the culture play a heavy role in everything about the social sciences, actually determining many of their methods and even dictating a certain number of their conclusions. For example, a Christian country could not admit that sexual abstinence is injurious and would thus reject any research pointing in that direction. A Marxist country could not tolerate awareness by the masses of the class structure dictated by power considerations that has replaced the class structure dictated by economic considerations. Many other examples could be given.

Ideology also plays a large role in determining the activities of the professions. Simirenko (1969) has detailed how systematic destruction and persecutions of the ablest social scientists in the Soviet Union began in the 1920s and did not let up until 1938, when most of them had been destroyed. This persecution extended to persons not ordinarily thought of as involved in any ideological work: Almost all of the museum directors, ethnographers, and archaeologists were either arrested or dismissed from their positions, and dismissal meant in plain language extermination.[3] Once all the older social scientists were wiped out, the newer ones merely parroted the official ideology; in effect, then, the professions were reorganized to subserve Communist doctrine. The mental health professions—psychiatry, psychology, and social work—numbering perhaps 200,000 in the United States, scarcely exist in the Soviet Union.

In this country ideology likewise plays an enormous role, though it is less readily acknowledged. Nisbet sums it up as follows:

> It is this essential conflict regarding the purposes of the social sciences, the relation of the social sciences to government and society, and the role of the individual social scientist in the society of the twentieth century that bids fair at this moment to be the major conflict of the years ahead.[4]

Naturally, in the democratic countries we are all committed to an impartial search for the truth, wherever that may lead. We cannot be concerned further with ideological distortion of all the social facts. In what comes now we shall limit ourselves to the conflicts and controversies that have arisen and that arise in the democratic countries.

The Methodological Morass

At the turn of the century the great methematician Henri Poincaré remarked that while physicists dealt with their subject matter, sociologists (by which he meant social scientists) were engaged almost entirely in considering their methods. Every social discipline, today as well, devotes an inordinate amount of time to the question of the proper "scientific method" in that discipline. Consensus social science, pursued in an academic atmosphere, has built up a certain image of what the proper methods are. Presumably the scientists should experiment, establish facts, then go on to derive theories and laws from these well-established facts. It goes unnoticed that despite unremitting research and efforts in this vein these laws and theories are still conspicuous by their absence. Equally unnoticed is the fact that this consensus procedure, which is supposed to be derived from the more mature physical sciences, is almost never discussed by the physical scientists, who rather take scientific method for granted. Thus the consensus image of scientific method should more properly be called a group fantasy than a sober statement of how scientists should proceed. Morris Cohen, a distinguished American philosopher of science, comments that Poincaré's remark is

> . . . a just rebuke . . . to those romantic souls who cherish the persistent illusion that by some new trick of method the social sciences can readily be put on a par with the physical sciences with regard to definiteness and universal demonstrability. The maximum logical accuracy can be attained only by recognizing the exact degree of probability that our subject matter will allow.[5]

One of the most influential works of our time in this area is Thomas Kuhn's *The Structure of Scientific Revolutions* (1962). Kuhn, who began as a physicist, turned to a study of the ways in which physical science actually did develop. His search of the historical record revealed an entirely different image of the concept of science. In particular he was struck by the importance of what he calls "paradigms" or models for scientists to follow. Of the social sciences he comments: "Particularly, I was struck by the number and extent of the overt disagreements between social scientists about the nature of legitimate scientific problems and methods." Or, to use his language, social science has not yet reached a consensus on what paradigm to follow in its research and theoretical programs.

It is within this context that the widespread social science criticism of psychoanalytic methodology must be evaluated. The vast majority of academic social scientists still echo Sears's dictum (1942) that psychoanalysis is simply "bad science." What they are really saying is that social scientists have not yet reached any agreement on what constitutes the proper scientific method (see Mitroff and Kilman, 1978; Shye, 1978) and that the psychoanalysts do not adhere to the paradigm that Sears set up. Ignored is the fact that Sears's paradigm is only one of many, that on the whole it has failed to produce any notable results in any of the social sciences, and that his authoritative pronouncement on science is wrong (see Chapter 4).

The attempt to apply the methods of the natural sciences to the social sciences without further consideration stumbles on the obstinate fact that social events are of far greater complexity than physical and are connected with different ideological preconceptions. Cohen notes that with the greater complexity of social facts are connected (1) their less repeatable character, (2) their less direct observability, (3) their greater variability and lesser uniformity, and (4) the greater difficulty of isolating one factor at at time.[7]

I have already noted that the social sciences developed more or less within the same period as psychoanalysis (roughly since 1900). Attached to this time framework is an image of man, universally accepted in 1900, as rational, conscious, and subject to influences beyond his control. This image of man provided the basis for the consensus approach to methodology, although numerous controversies persist, primarily because of the paucity of results. In this way one paradigm was set up, with a number of variations. All of them have in common the superficial study of large numbers of cases in an effort to discern underlying similarities and/or attributes, regardless of their meaning to the individual.

By contrast, the psychoanalytic paradigm was based on an image of man as irrational, unconscious, and subject to internal forces over which he can gain control by self-study (analysis). This led to a paradigm of intensive study of relatively few cases. Increasingly this paradigm has come to exert a greater influence on the thinking and methodology of the social scientist.

Stung by the outright rejection of psychoanalysis by their academic colleagues, psychoanalysts reacted in two contrary ways. One was to reformulate analysis in a manner more acceptable to the consensus scientist, for example, as information theory (Petefreund, 1971); action theory (Schafer, 1976), a form of behaviorism, or physiological theory, as Freud himself had done.* The other reaction was to overemphasize certain discoveries about the individual, an error accurately termed "vulgar Freudianism." Instances of this are Gorer's explanation of the Russian character as due to excessive swaddling in infancy (Gorer and Richman, 1949), or Loewenstein's (1951) interpretation of anti-Semitism as due to the excessive castration anxiety aroused in the Christian by the Jewish practice of circumcision.

Both reactions are neither necessary nor desirable. Instead it must be recognized that psychoanalysis has made a fundamental contribution to methodology as such by showing how the individual case can be investigated more thoroughly and more effectively. This in no way destroys the methodology based on superficial examination of large numbers of cases but merely places it in proper perspective. Certain facts can be ascertained only by large-scale statistical research. However, the meaning of these facts to the individual can be determined only by careful study of the individual.

Skill Versus Bias

Various significant, and generally overlooked, differences between the natural and social sciences can be singled out. One of the most important is the relative weights of skill and bias. The natural sciences started out, in the seventeenth century, by freeing themselves from the clerical bias, which had weighed them down for centuries. Galileo's is only the best known of the many ordeals scientists went through in those centuries in order to free themselves from the church and to study nature dispassionately.

But by the eighteenth century this battle was won, for all practical purposes, in the more civilized countries. Thereafter subjective bias no longer played any significant role in the natural sciences, and no progress could be made by putting bias to one side.

Instead, progress came about through the refinement of skill. Mathematicians refined their proofs and explorations to give physics more powerful new weapons. The microscope introduced biologists to a hitherto unknown world; the telescope did the same for astrono-

---

*I have attempted to show elsewhere (Fine, 1979a) that Freud's physiological speculations derived from his uncertainties about his momentous psychological discoveries and that the value of psychoanalysis in no way depends on these physiological theories.

mers. Once the initial step was taken, one invention followed another to produce ever more accurate results. The early crude microscope led eventually to the current electron microscope; the early telescope to current radio astronomy. This process is continuing and every day seems to bring new instances of advances in technical skill.

By contrast the problem in the social sciences, including psychology, from the very beginning has been the subjective bias that enters into the measurement of psychosocial events. As a result social scientists move in rarefied circles of their own choosing, in a kind of mutual-admiration society that excludes the outside world. When outsiders do come to look upon their works, they are either critical or unimpressed.

Psychology itself presents some of the clearest examples of this kind of bias. While academic scientists have prided themselves on being experimental scientists, dated their "science" from Wundt in 1879, and tried to exclude everything from the science that is not experimental, an outsider like Wittgenstein could rightly observe that in experimental psychology all too often problem and method passed each other by. Objections to the experimental method were ruled out, and objecters were simply kicked out of the university.

And yet in 1979, when the *Annual Review of Psychology* came to celebrate the hundredth anniversary of the founding of the science, its historian, Conrad Mueller, could not find any real progress that had been made by experimental methods since Wundt's day. He wrote:

> The plan to solve psychology's systematic differences by being quantitative, precise and explicit, the plan to formulate issues in such a way that they would be testable against alternative formulations did not succeed in any general way. Formulations that could be solved to many decimal places included terms that could not be contained. The broad programmatic formulations were still found to be remarkably immune to disproof . . . the changes . . . in the last 75 years cannot be viewed as a permanent progressive development, a systematic mainstream.[8]

Mueller even points out that the deification of the experimental method by Wundt's followers did violence to Wundt's own thinking. Wundt himself had insisted that many problems, expecially those of the higher mental processes, could *not* be solved by experimentation. Thus the extreme reliance on experimentation that has been so characteristic of academic psychology can only be viewed as a group fantasy, with no real evidence to sustain it.

On the other side, psychoanalysts have pursued their own group fantasy about the nature of their science by linking it with medicine. The *Bulletin* of the American Psychoanalytic Association states that psychoanalysis is a branch of medicine, in defiance of the members' own knowledge and experience.[9] Psychoanalysts build up a group fantasy along the opposite dimension to justify their own organizational hunger for power and prestige.

The political struggle has obscured, if not wholly obliterated, the real ways in which progress has been made and can be made in the future. One of Freud's chief contributions to method lay in his ability to overcome his subjective biases and look at the human being objectively. His conclusions were not palatable to his contemporaries: Religion is a universal neurosis; most men are seriously disturbed; sexual repression, the official morality of the day, leads to illness; psychologists and psychiatrists (of that day) live in an ivory tower and refuse to see what human beings are really like; and so on.

The rejection of Freud as "unscientific," as in the famous Sears book of 1942 (which was commissioned and published by the Social Science Research Council), is thus seen as an expression of a group fantasy, not the sober assertion of objective science. It is most unfortunate that psychoanalysts themselves for the most part reacted with a group fantasy of their own instead of probing into what Sears was calling science (see Hartmann, 1944).

Yet psychoanalysis made its way until by 1977 Fisher and Greenberg could find, in a review of some two thousand carefully done studies, that psychoanalysis is the best-researched and most securely validated personality theory extant. However, they too ignore the real contributions of psychoanalysis to psychological methodology: overcoming subjective bias and providing a vision of how man can change and become happier, even if ultimate happiness should prove elusive.

As will be seen in more detail later, what is true of psychology is also true of all the other social sciences. The glorification of the experimental method has led nowhere, yet it remains glorified, the essence of a group fantasy similar to what the psychologists build up.

The Social Consequences of Social Science

Another vital difference between the natural and the social sciences is that the latter are *inherently* involved in social criticism in the inception of their theories, in their application, and in their practical implementation. Note the word: inherently. The physical sciences likewise have been involved, especially recently, in the question of social consequences. Some of these are of fundamental importance. One example is the argument that chemical substances are literally stripping the atmosphere of sufficient ozone, which screens the ultraviolet rays of the sun, and will in time lead to an excessive heating of the planet, with possibly disastrous consequences. The nuclear accident at Three Mile Island created the fear that civilian use of nuclear energy could destroy large segments of the population. The dangerous consequences of many chemicals and pesticides are becoming increasingly obvious. All of these, however, are secondary to the science as such.

Not so with the social sciences. Any examination of the social scene, whether in the psychology of individuals or in the structure of large organizations, is motivated by a wish to change the human condition and carries with it various implications of such changes. Scientists in general have not been aware of this aspect of their science because of their lack of philosophical sophistication, together with the faulty conceptualization of scientific method, which has been commented on over and over.

A recent compilation of six studies by social scientists from various fields on this topic (Weber and McCall, 1978) generally recognizes that the social scientist must become an advocate. Thus Laue states that

> . . . doing sociology in all its forms is social intervention, . . . there are no neutrals in terms of their impact on given power configurations, and any sociologist claiming to be "neutral" in anything other than the strictest technical sense is naive, misinformed, and/or devious.[10]

The other contributors to the work all indicated that they favored an advocacy position for the various branches of social science represented (social work, law, community psychology, urban planning, action anthropology, and sociology). In each case they indicated that ideally the practitioners and the theoreticians seek some goal beyond immediate neutral knowledge, though that is included in the goal. Thus in social work the goal becomes the redistribution of wealth; in law, public interest; in community psychology, human welfare (though this concept lacks a unitary definition); in anthropology, the vision of a just society; in urban planning, redistribution, and in sociology, social justice.

Vision Versus Technique

In every case in the Weber–McCall symposium (and in all the social sciences, as will be seen later) a tension is created between vision and technique. The fields are all full of visions of redistribution, of justice, of an ideal society, and the like, while the practice involves compromises, often of the most humiliating kind. Clarence Darrow, one of the most esteemed lawyers of his day, wrote that "litigants and their lawyers are supposed to want justice, but in reality there is no such thing as justice in or out of court. In fact, the word cannot be defined."[11] While every adult recognizes that a lawyer's job is to win the case for his client, regardless of the facts or where justice lies, few recognize that a similar predicament occurs in all the social sciences. Thus when Sol Tax and his students started out to do traditional anthropological research on the Fox reservation in Iowa, they concluded that "the malaise of the community and sympathy with individual Indians . . . conspired to turn us into actionists."[12] In spite of their good intentions, the anthropologists could do little to help their chosen clients. They had the vision but lacked the technique—or the means, to use more ordinary language.

In all the social sciences this gap leads to a sharp dichotomy between visionaries who lack technique and technicians who lack vision. This conflict so pervades all the social sciences that it may be said to be one of the core conflicts that differentiate the social from the natural sciences. To take but one example: In historiography Toynbee offered a grandiose vision, which was sharply criticized by his fellow historians for lack of accuracy. By contrast, Ranke offered a perfection of technique that was totally lacking in vision (Gay, 1978). The study of revolutions and political processes has uncovered similar dilemmas, usually put in terms of means versus ends: Does this end really justify these means?

Looked at from this perspective, psychoanalysis is in an ideal position. It has both the vision (a happier mankind) and the technique (psychoanalysis and psychoanalytic therapy). But as so often, lack of awareness of the dilemma has polarized psychoanalysts into the two familiar camps of the visionaries without technique (such as Erich Fromm or Carl Jung) and the technicians without vision (the average practitioner). Because of his own background, Freud tended to stress technique much more than vision. But though he failed to make the distinction sufficiently explicit, a careful reading of his works shows that he had both vision and technique.

Customarily, in the early stages of development of a social science the vision has been prominent (as witness Comte, Durkheim, Marx, and Weber in sociology). Later, as more knowledge accumulates, the vision becomes watered down. The original formulations are seen as oversimplifications (the large body of critical examination of Weber's theory of the Protestant ethic). Mathematics is set up as an ideal, without any real understanding of its limits and underlying assumptions. Statistics, mathematical "proofs," and computer counts take over more and more, all in search of what Morris Cohen stigmatized as "some new trick of method," which forgets that "the maximum logical accuracy can be attained only by recognizing the exact degree of probability that our subject matter will allow" (see above, p. 166).

Today most of the social sciences have lost track of the vision that marked the thought of the great founders. They place their faith in ever more minute dissection of ever more minute pieces of the pie. Thus Boas published more than 10,000 pages on the Northwest Coast alone,[13] most of them without the barest information that would be needed to render them intelligible to the reader. To call Boas's approach historical particularism is to overlook the fact that when the anthropologist displays a mass of facts without trying to make sense of them he is exercising sterile technique without vision. The same observations and objection hold for much of the recent work in history, involving use of computers and large-scale demographic studies; without a vision these become meaningless or end up in obviously nonsensical theses, such as Fogel and Engerman's claim that slavery was not "such a bad institution after all."[14]

Here once more psychoanalysis offers a much-needed additive to the social sciences by presenting a vision of how man can achieve happiness. The anthropologist, the economist, the historian, and all other social scientists are called upon to decide whether the systems they study are beneficial or harmful to human welfare; if they avoid this central question they become technicians without vision. Because psychoanalysis offers us the clearest definition of what human welfare is, it must be incorporated into the empirical data to gain a fuller picture of the human estate, or that portion of it under investigation.

This notion of a vision has been obscured by the various misconceptions of psychoanalysis current and past and by the bitter internal rivalries of the psychoanalysts themselves, who have stressed power rather than vision. Eissler, for example, has recently written of the American Psychoanalytic Association that "at present it can be safely said that the beliefs, convictions, principles, and professional aims of members can no longer be brought to a common denominator."[15] The result is that psychoanalysis has mistakenly been identified with a specific technique (which the psychoanalysts themselves have not been able to agree upon, except in certain broad essentials) rather than a systematic approach to psychology and a philosophy of living.

What has happened is that suddenly new words have been invented, such as psychohistory, clinical psychology, or psychological anthropology. All of these represent primarily the introduction of psychoanalytic concepts to give meaning to the empirical data gathered by other investigators. However, the construction of a meaningful theory, with both data and a vision, has a powerful effect on the empirical data uncovered. Thus, under the impact of psychohistory numerous aspects of the analytic ideal, such as love, work, sexuality, family relationships, and the like, have been investigated in past societies. The material was always there; it was merely ignored.

Bias, Theory, and Empiricism

The uncertainties in the social sciences have in turn obscured the close relationship that exists among bias, theory and empirical research. No anthropologist today would repeat Boas's feat of producing 10,000 pages on the Northwest Coast or anywhere else without some attempt to order the data into a meaningful body of human experience. This in turn would lead him to unearth new data that Boas had ignored, such as dreams, projective mechanisms, and fantasy productions in general.

Every field is full of evidence that any given theory produces a consistent bias that colors the empirical research unduly. Thus investigation of the "mental health" of Americans leads to varying conclusions, for instance, that between 28 percent (Florida) and 82 percent (New York) of Americans are "mentally disturbed" or "emotionally disturbed." The lower figures leave out of account the more refined data, such as free associations, deeper dissatisfactions, and the like, that point to the kinds of deeper conflicts recognized by psychoanalysts. Hence what is being measured is largely the biased theory of the investigator, while the empirical data are highly censored and highly colored. The rejection of fantasy material by nonanalytic authors is particularly pronounced (e.g. Gesell's view of dreams).

The Measurement Problem

Physicists have long known that when a measuring instrument comes up against the object or thing to be measured, the interaction between the two affects the result, sometimes microscopically, sometimes on a large scale. Ultimately the principle of indeterminacy was reached, which helped to establish the primacy of the theory of relativity (Nagel, 1961).

It is surprising that the first person to point to a measurement problem in psychology was a physicist, Niels Bohr. In *Atomic Physics and Human Knowledge* (1958), Bohr wrote:

> Indeed, the necessity of considering the interaction between the measuring instruments and the object under investigation in atomic mechanics exhibits a close analogy to the peculiar difficulties in psychological analysis arising from the fact that the mental content is invariably altered when the attention is concentrated on any special features of it.[16]

As the psychological community has become more sophisticated, it has become increasingly aware that the older, naive behavioristic views of measurement (S-R phenomena) are grossly oversimplified. Rosenthal (1976) has accumulated large quantities of experimental data to show the significance of both experimenter and observer effects in the standard psychological experiment. These, he argues, are so strong that complete bias can scarcely be eliminated. Berg (1967) has summarized the data on response set, showing that in general the responses of subjects to psychologically significant questions fall into one of three categories, determined respectively by social desirability, acquiescence, and deviance. Thus a large body of evidence has already accumulated showing that when a subject in a psychological situation is asked a seemingly simple question, the replies are complex indeed. Clearly this invalidates a substantial body of the questionnaire studies that are so popular among social scientists, largely because of their ease of administration and ease of manipulation. Yet, social scientists continue to make extensive use of this kind of material. Nor can any romantic notion of mathematical ingenuity undo the underlying unreliability of the original data. As the computer people nowadays say: Garbage in, garbage out.

While the measurement problem entered into physics and chemistry only at an advanced stage of the sciences, in psychology it has been present from the very beginning. Throughout the years a great deal of sophistication was put into the question of how to measure psychological variables more accurately. Thus physiological measures whenever available have been preferred to psychological, because they are more easily repeatable and less subject to falsification by the subject. Unfortunately they are all too often also irrelevant to the main purposes of the study. In the analysis of emotion, for example, the physiological responses play only a small part in the total picture. An emotion is a total psychophysiological reaction, which defies equation with any specific physiological variable. Or again: The recent discoveries of REM and NREM sleep have added much physiological knowledge to our understanding of dreams but have not altered the underlying Freudian theory (Arkin et al., 1978). An example of the difficulties encountered in this area is that the mere question—What is a dream?—has posed thorny problems of measurement that have led to widely contradictory empirical findings.

Although not couched in the form common in academic psychology and social science, psychoanalysis has always been keenly aware of the theoretical and methodological problems involved in psychoanalysis as a scientific approach. The foundation of science is observation alone, Freud wrote in 1914,[17] and the next year he said:

> We have often heard it said that sciences should be built up on clear and sharply defined basic concepts. In actual fact no science, not even the most exact, begins with such definitions. The true beginning of scientific activity consists rather in describing phenomena and then in proceeding to group, classify and correlate them. Even at the stage of description it is not possible to avoid applying certain abstract ideas to the material in hand, ideas derived from somewhere or other but certainly not from the new observations alone. Such ideas—which will later become the basic concepts of the science—are still more indispensable as the material is further worked over.[18]

What was lacking in his work was an extended discussion of these problems. This discussion has been filled in by many later workers.

In essence, psychoanalysis maintains its claim to being the most scientific approach to psychology because it has paid due attention to the measurement problem (though again not in so many words) from the very beginning, while the other approaches have not. Actually, behaviorism could be seen historically as an attempt to sidestep the measurement problem by limiting itself to direct observables. After more than fifty years this detour can fairly be said to have failed completely, both in its intent and in its results. The internal human environment cannot be sidestepped; it must be handled with reasonable inferences, as psychoanalytic psychology has always done.

What is observed cannot be properly understood without reference to these internal variables.

An equally important way of phrasing this is to cast the problem in terms of transference. When one human being asks another a question, a transference has been set up, and how the second human being responds depends on this transference (what Berg more conventionally calls the response set). These transference reactions may be conscious or unconscious, but they will always be there. And the more significant the material is to the individual, the greater role will the transferences play. These considerations help to explain the wide discrepancies in empirical findings that are displayed in every piece of social science research. Many examples of this will be offered as we go along.

The Psychological Factor

It seems intuitively evident that any science dealing with man must give consideration, in greater or lesser degree, to the psychological factor. The reason this on the whole has not been done is simply that when the social sciences began to develop, at the turn of the century, psychology in its modern sense did not yet exist. Hence the pioneers in every field—history, economics, sociology, anthropology, and the rest—had either to wait until psychology matured or ignore the psychological element in favor of other, more abstract concepts. In general they chose the latter course and persisted in it until the advances of psychoanalytic psychology called their error to their attention.

These observations can be confirmed by the study of the works of any of the great pioneers in any of the social sciences. Thus Boas, in *The Mind of Primitive Man* (roughly contemporaneous with Freud's *Totem and Taboo*, 1911), writes:

> A close introspective analysis shows these reasons [for opposition to change] to be only attempts to interpret our feelings of displeasure; that our opposition is not by any means dictated by conscious reasoning, but primarily by the emotional effect of a new idea which creates a dissonance with the habitual.[19]

Boas continually emphasizes in this book that primitive man is dominated by emotion, not by reason; his reasons for his actions are rationalizations (though he did not know the term and did not use it).

From this it is but a short step to the psychoanalytic or psychodynamic mode of thinking, using Freud's equation of the primitive, the dreamer, the child, and the psychotic. But Boas, knowing only the primitive, could not draw the obvious parallels that have been drawn since.

It also becomes quite clear that anthropology, as Boas developed it, is primarily psychology; the reasons for distinguishing the two and creating two separate disciplines are purely the result of historical accident, as Boas himself, incidentally, frankly admitted at one point.

Had psychology been adequately developed in 1900, the elaboration of a host of disciplines, with its attendant quarrels and confusions, need never have taken place. Instead there would have been the study of man in the past (history), of man in other cultures (anthropology), of how man works and regulates his productive efforts (economics), of man in the contemporary culture (sociology), and so on. With the increasing importance of interdisciplinary efforts, it is tacitly admitted that the traditional division into separate disciplines was an error.

This argument should not be misinterpreted to mean that everything is psychology. In every area of human existence there are external factors and internal (psychological) factors. Only the interaction of these two helps to explain the total picture. This position had already been stated by Freud in 1913 when he wrote:

> There are no grounds for fearing that psychoanalysis, which first discovered that psychical acts and structures are invariably over-determined, will be tempted to trace the origin of anything so complicated as religion to a single source. . . . Only when we can synthesize the findings in the different fields of research will it become possible to arrive at the relative importance of the part played in the genesis of religion by the mechanism discussed in these pages. Such a task lies beyond the means as well as beyond the purposes of a psychoanalyst.[20]

The Conceptual Framework

One of the chief contributions of psychoanalysis to psychology has been the provision of a unique conceptual framework, without which much of the data of psychology remains unintelligible. As Hanson (1958) has emphasized, concepts are fundamental to any scientific enterprise, and as a rule they cannot be deduced from the observations but enter into the observations themselves.

Much ink has been poured into attacks on the conceptual framework of psychoanalysis. It has been excoriated as "muddled," "unscientific," "incapable of verification," "poorly defined," and the like. All these charges have been refuted over and over again as based on a faulty understanding of the analytic position (Canning, 1966). At the same time, within the ranks of psychoanalytic theorists a continual active discussion goes on about the viability of various constructs in the light of the clinical and experimental data available. As a result of this constant self-criticism, at present the construct of psychic energy has been virtually discarded; earlier the concepts of the libido theory (in its 1914 sense), actual neurosis, the death instinct, biogenesis and phylogenesis, sublimation, and numerous others have either been discarded or superseded by more refined views.

Nevertheless, much of the thinking of Freud and the mainstream psychoanalytic tradition remains intact: the unconscious, psychosexual development, the life cycle, the id-ego-superego formulation, the anxiety-defense combination as part of the core structure of all personality, and so on. What the present writer deems essential to psychoanalysis has been presented in Chapter 3. It is this conceptual framework that remains one of the main contributions of psychoanalysis to the science of man. Even more emphatically, it is within this conceptual framework that the science of psychology must be established and must make further progress.

Freud was brought up in the Leibnizian tradition, which encouraged original minds to forge their own conceptual frameworks. Whatever the weaknesses of this tradition may be, it has offered the world extraordinarily fruitful systems, such as Freud's psychology, Einstein's physics, and Marx's economics. By contrast, Americans and British have been more steeped in the Lockean *tabula rasa* tradition, which stresses ideas and concepts emerging from the empirical data. Naturally, both traditions are important. But in psychology at least the attempt to derive fundamental concepts from a mass of empirical data has been anything but successful. As will be seen, in all the social sciences there has been an overemphasis on empiricism, leading to an enormous accumulation of facts without a meaningful ideological framework within which to place them.

From Freud on, psychoanalysts have offered psychologically meaningful frameworks within which to place the empirical material gathered by other investigators. In general psychoanalysts have not been in a position to engage in empirical research, with some notable exceptions (Roheim in Central Australia, the Rennie mental health study in New York). Logically this should lead to more meaningful empirical research inspired by a psychologically coherent structure. Illogically instead it has led to useless acrimony, more meaningless accumulation of unassimilated facts, and more confusion.

Actually, as mentioned before, in all the social sciences there have been explicit or implicit psychological assumptions about the organization of the empirical material uncovered. The choice is not between psychology and (say) sociology, but between one psychological approach to sociological facts and another psychological approach. The painful contradictions and absurdities into which the social sciences have frequently forced themselves because of the avoidance of this obvious fact will be examined in detail in later chapters.

The Publication System

Too little attention has been paid to the nature of the publication system, especially in the social sciences. Every association has its own limited point of view. Those who agree with it can publish in the association's journal; those who do not agree will be rejected. This leads to a system where the articles in any one journal become markedly repetitious, merely emphasizing or re-emphasizing points made by the intellectual originators of that point of view.

Within the broad framework of Western versus totalitarian countries, the censorship is quite obvious. Recently the prestigious journal *Science* editorialized:

> [T]he laws of nature are invariant across jurisdictional and geographic boundaries. . . . The social sciences start from a very different perspective. The laws of economics, social structure, political process, and human psychology are not invariant across national boundaries. In the social sciences and humanities we accept the profound importance of cultural, historical, and national differences. Social science findings in one society are tested against the experience of other societies. Variation through time and across cultures is turned to scientific advantage.[21]

This observation is of course quite correct; the image that this is used to "scientific advantage" is, however, completely unrealistic. Instead it is used to reaffirm in a most dogmatic manner the veracity of whatever point of view happens to prevail in that culture. The experience of Galileo with the Catholic Church in the seventeenth century is not at all foreign to many social scientists in the twentieth.

As the social sciences are now constituted, even within the Western countries, a seriously repressive form of censorship operates within every field. In the main this has been directed at the psychological, particularly the psychoanalytic, point of view. For example, when Harold Lasswell, who was already a noted political scientist in 1930, became convinced of the value of psychoanalysis for political science, he could not publish another paper in a standard political science journal for twenty years thereafter.[22] It has not been uncommon to speak of "consensus sociology," "consensus psychology," or "consensus economics" to designate this state of affairs. New ideas are rejected, not because the evidence is not there but because they do not fit in with the prevailing consensus.

Among the other consequences of this publication problem, two in particular are serious for the progress of science. One is that mistakes of the most fundamental kind abound in the literature. In general, social scientists have grossly misunderstood the nature and purport of psychoanalytic psychology. But even within the field of psychoanalysis proper practitioners of one persuasion (e.g. Freudians) have grossly misunderstood theoreticians of another persuasion (e.g. culturalists). The second serious consequence is that few people are really adequately educated in all the necessary ramifications of what they are approaching or what they are doing. For a great many, as they go on in the field there is just as much unlearning as learning to be done.

The Lesser Certainty of Social Facts

Another important source of methodological complexity is that social facts are inherently less certain and less observable than physical. Whatever the technical tools devised, a wide area of uncertainty always remains. To take but one simple example: The mere census enumeration of the number of persons living in the United States (or the world, for that matter) at any one time is subject to considerable error.

Morris Cohen's comments on the greater complexity of social facts have been noted above (p. 166).[23] In addition, to the extent that social facts have an essential historical character they are essentially unrepeatable. Yet consensus scientific methodology stresses this element of repeatability above all others. Hence the contradiction results: No laws of social science comparable to those of physical science can really be established.

If social facts are inherently less reliable, obviously their interpretation must be even more so. It is not surprising, then, that wide areas of disagreement, not infrequently gross contradictions, are found in all the social sciences. These disagreements are then concealed behind the notion of "schools," and every social science has its collection of schools from which the student is asked to choose. Or more correctly, every department has its own dogmatic approach to which the student must conform if he wishes to get a degree in that school. This results in further confusion. In every social science authors are found who wish to jettison the entire body of previous knowledge. Andreski has written a book entitled *The Social Sciences as Sorcery* (1972), Dell Hymes has edited *Reinventing Anthropology* (1972), and Braginsky and Braginsky have written *Mainstream Psychology: A Critique* (1974). This list could be extended indefinitely.

In a recent book Shulamit Reinharz (1979) describes in a series of introspective essays her struggle and disillusionment with the research approaches she was taught. Then she says:

> Although I have been trained as a sociologist, I frequently speak of social science in general terms. My reasons for doing so are because the boundaries between the content areas and the perspectives of the various social science disciplines are, in my opinion, almost meaningless. The only real distinction can be found in the professional identification of the various constituencies.[24]

Even without resorting to psychoanalysis, Dr. Reinharz reports her private discovery that solutions to many problems could emerge only from honest and careful examination of her experience as a researcher. "A crucial component of an alternative direction for sociology, therefore, was precisely the concept of self, particularly the researcher's self, *which is suppressed in mainstream methods.*"[25]

While the social sciences for a hundred years have prided themselves on their empirical attitudes and empirical research, it is only too clear that much of this pride derives from self-deception. The social facts described in textbooks are neither so certain nor so clear and easily interpreted as investigators would have us believe. Everything must be re-examined from a critical point of view.

Summary

A number of significant criticisms of all the social sciences as currently constituted have been presented. These may be summarized as follows:

1. In all areas considerable controversy exists.

2. The social sciences exist only within a certain cultural context, which highlights the role of ideology.

3. The social sciences are bogged down in a methodological morass. What could be called "consensus social science," as usually taught in academic departments, offers a seriously misinformed account of the nature of science.

4. Important advances in the physical sciences have come from the perfection of skills or tools, such as the telescope or the microscope. Important advances in the social sciences, however, have come from the elimination of pre-existing biases. Technical advances in the accumulation of information as yet have not made any fundamental contribution.

5. The social sciences all have social consequences. Often these are not made explicit.

6. There is in all a dichotomy of vision versus technique, as a result of which the fields are divided into visionaries without technique and technicians without vision.

7. Pure empiricism has been impossible because of bias and lack of clarity of theoretical framework.

8. The measurement problem in human affairs is of major significance and has largely been ignored.

9. In all the social sciences some psychological factor is at play. The degree to which this psychological factor is important varies.

10. A satisfactory conceptual framework is offered by psychoanalytic psychology, which offers the basis for a science of man.

11. The publication system in social science shows marked deficiencies and errors. As a result, large-scale errors appear in the works of even leading thinkers, while students are poorly and dogmatically prepared.

12. Even under the most ideal circumstances social facts are less certain than physical.

Toward a Positive Program: One Science of Man

It is only against this background discussion that the essential contribution of psychoanalytic psychology can be evaluated. Because man is involved in all social activities, the psychological factor must always be given some weight. If it has not in the past (as in Ricardo's Iron Law of Wages), such omission can only be stigmatized as an error. Psychoanalysis is in a better position to supply and evaluate this psychological factor than any other approach.

This should not be misconstrued to mean that everything should be interpreted psychologically; that would merely repeat the blunder of "vulgar Freudianism." Psychoanalytic psychology provides us with a new image of man. While psychoanalytic therapy has existed for only about a hundred years, psychotherapy in one form or another has always been there. Its role in the social structure must not be ignored.

As will be demonstrated in detail, an approach of this kind leads to a thorough reconstruction of all the social sciences. Goals, methods, facts, conclusions, and interpretations must all be re-evaluated to see how they fit in with what we know about the essence of man.

One important consequence of this approach is that in one form or another all of the social sciences have been presenting us with psychological conclusions. The choice is between a commonsense, unsophisticated psychology and the deeper penetration of the human psyche that we get from psychoanalysis.

No doubt this approach will be criticized as excessively bold, speculative, or the product of a heated imagination. Nevertheless it represents one important direction in which many thinkers have been moving since Freud gave us the fundamental insights. It must be tried if the vast body of information that has accumulated about the human being is to be put to more constructive use.

Chapter 7

The Dilemmas of History

BOTH OUR AGE AND OUR CULTURE are extremely historically oriented. Time capsules have been planted at the United Nations to record for posterity what things are like today. Historical societies abound everywhere, and history remains a popular academic subject.

History stands at the center of all the social sciences. No mathematician would think of introducing the subject of calculus with more than a paragraph about its historical development, but no sociologist would think of discussing any sociological topic without extended references to its historical roots.

By contrast, history is of little or no importance in the totalitarian countries. There are few historians, and those who do write are regarded as inferior by Western standards.* This sharp difference between the Western and the totalitarian countries immediately calls for some explanation.

History acquired its leading role in Western thought largely since the end of the eighteenth century.[1] For most of Western history prior to that time, men were imbued with the notion that Christianity represented the acme of earthly happiness and development. God, it was felt, inspired the course of man with a "higher wisdom." The last book in which this delusion was proclaimed seems to have been Bossuet's *Discours sur l'Histoire Universelle* in 1681.[2] Thus history became important only when men realized that they had not reached perfection. Obviously this explains the difference between

*Patai (1973), for example, makes the interesting observation that before contact with the West the Arabs had no available histories written in Arabic after the end of the Middle Ages. They were thus blissfully unaware of their cultural decline, which had begun in the fifteenth century. Instead they focused on the great Arab golden age, while the subsequent centuries of stagnation remained largely unknown or at least unconsidered (p. 256).

185

the Western and totalitarian worlds today: The totalitarian systems proclaim themselves as perfect, which means everything that happened before their advent is of little or no consequence.

Every other dilemma noted in the preceding chapter applies with no less force to history. In all areas considerably controversy exists; facts may be agreed upon, but interpretations will vary, so it can be said that every age rewrites its history in its own way. The cultural context within which history is written is obviously of prime importance. The methodological morass of the historian derives from the absence, in greater or lesser measure, of the primary sources, making history an art rather than a science. Significant technical advances such as the current stress on "cliometrics" merely shift the problem; they do not resolve the underlying issues of bias or point of view. The social consequences of history are enormous, so interpretations become the subject of bitter battles. For example, the theory of evolution, while accepted by all biologists after Darwin, encountered virulent opposition from certain theologians and, at times, politicians. In the United States the fundamentalist religions demanded the literal acceptance of the Bible as part of their credo. The famous Scopes "monkey" trial of 1925 was one outcome of this insistence. Tennessee's anti-evolutionary law was not repealed until 1967.

In the Southern part of the country the Civil War is still referred to as "the war between the states" (Fitzgerald, 1979). Visionaries such as Hegel, Spengler, and Toynbee have been roundly criticized by professional historians for disregarding facts, and consequently most historians have turned into technicians who prefer to report in minute detail on isolated periods without drawing any meaningful conclusions.

Perhaps most central to our thesis here is that the psychological factor has always been present in historical writing and has not been given its due weight. Currently we are in the midst of an argument between the technicians who stress "cliometrics," that is, advanced statistical techniques (which many do not understand too well) and visionaries who stress the newer psychological insights (the "psycho-historians"). Overlooked is the fact that neither of these is in any significant respect new, and that the basic question remains one of psychology and of ideology. History, after all, is the record of what men were like in the past, and there is absolutely no evidence that they were ever in any essential respect different from men today.

Traditional History: The Ideology of Victory

Given that history, like any social science, must always be driven by some ideology, what is the theory behind traditional or consensus history? We refer here to the usual compendiums on "world history," "American history," "Chinese history," and the like.

The oldest extant history, in a modern sense, is the work by the Greek Herodotus from the fifth century B.C., in which the "father of history," as he has been called described the wars between the free Greek peoples and the enslaved Persians, in which the Greeks won out. The next significant work of history described in textbooks is that of Thucydides in the latter part of the fifth century B.C., telling of the long battle between Athens and Sparta in which his native Athens was defeated. It will be argued that both of these works set the ideological tone for all of subsequent history until the most recent shift to psychohistory, which is really the first real revolution in historical writing. That ideology is the ideology of victory: History is a series of battles. The first question is, Who won? The next question is, How did they win?

In spite of all the trappings added by the more careful sifting of evidence, the rise of scientific history, and so forth, the ideology has remained the same until today. The Romans described their victories. The Christians saw history as moving toward the conquest of the world by Christianity. Even Marx was in the same tradition, merely adding a new twist to the age-old story of conflict in that he saw history as a class struggle.

Even highly sophisticated historians fall into this ideological trap. As an example we may take the work of William H. McNeill, *A World History* (1967). These comments are not to be taken as a reflection on Professor McNeill, one of our most accomplished historians, but on his underlying assumptions. In accordance with the trends of modern thought, McNeill stresses large regional groupings rather than individual nations. Thus his work is divided into three parts: (1) the emergence and definition of the major Eurasian civilizations to 500 B.C.; (2) equilibrium among the civilizations, 500 B.C.–A.D. 1500; (3) the dominance of the West after A.D. 1500. The underlying ideology involves five tacit assumptions, all of momentous importance for the way in which history is presented (or misrepresented): (1) the role of violence, including wholesale massacres (rebaptized genocide in the twentieth century), (2) the role of slavery,

(3) the incidence of psychosis among the ordinary population, (4) the relationship between the victors and the vanquished, and (5) reliance on a commonsense kind of psychology that ignores the basic human emotions and makes all kinds of assumptions about motives that cannot be accepted by modern science.

THE ROLE OF VIOLENCE AND MASSACRES

While McNeill correctly chronicles the course of victory throughout the ages, no serious consideration is given to the human cost of these victories. It has long been known, however, that this human cost has run into thousands and millions of lives. In view of the experience of our century with the sadistic madness of Hitler and Stalin, it is certainly important to know how different they were from previous rulers and mass murderers.

The only mention of numbers to be found in McNeill relates to the French Revolution:

> The Convention declared France a republic, executed King Louis, and instituted a reign of terror against "enemies of the people," in the course of which several thousand persons were summarily judged guilty and beheaded with a new efficiency and humanity, thanks to Dr. Guillotin's machine for cutting off human heads.[3]

Even in terms of French history, McNeill makes no mention of the lives lost through the inhuman practices of the *ancien regime* that preceded the Revolution. Nor does he even mention the well-known historical fact that in 1572 some three thousand Huguenots, assembled in Paris, were murdered in cold blood *in one night*.[4] Nor does McNeill note the process by which France was consolidated in the thirteenth century, when the so-called Albigensian crusade exterminated untold thousands of Christians in southern France.

The great Swiss historian Jakob Burckhardt once wrote that history is the record of what one age finds of interest in another. Our own age is particularly concerned with violence and massacre; today for the first time in history the very existence of the earth as a planet is threatened. What then happened with regard to violence and massacres in previous generations? On this the traditional texts like McNeill are strangely silent, even though the material is readily available. At one point McNeill writes that "barbarian violence was at last partially Christianized through such enterprises as the Crusades and by the development of a knightly ideal that asked men-at-arms to aid the weak, serve womankind, and protect Mother Church."[7] Surely the historian is then required to document the degree to which this "partial Christianization" did stem the tide of "barbarian violence." On both of these questions ample evidence is actually available. In 1258, when the Mongols, who could presumably be classified as barbarians, overran Baghdad, they massacred the Caliph and the entire population of 800,000 inhabitants.[8] Of the Mongols in general, the *Encyclopaedia Britannica* says that "although it was undoubtedly policy to sap resistance by fostering terror, massacre was employed for its own sake."[9]

Certainly such wholesale slaughter for its own sake qualifies as barbarism. But what is the Christian record?

To the dispassionate observer the Crusades represent a peculiar dichotomy: The popes, presumably dedicated to peace, sent their followers to exterminate infidels (Muslims). According to McNeill's own account, if such matters can be measured, Muslim civilization was at a higher level at that time than Christian. When the Christians conquered Jerusalem in 1099, all Muslim men, women, and children, as well as Jews, were slaughtered by the victors.[10] Somewhat more than a hundred years later, in 1204, when the Crusaders took Constantinople, with the permission of the leaders the city was subjected by the rank and file to pillage and massacre for three days.[11]

Nor were the Christians much kinder to their fellow Christians. In the religious wars of the seventeenth century, murder and massacre were virtually everyday occurrences. At one time it was held that Germany lost almost half of its population during the Thirty Years' War (1616–48). Gay and Webb note that "not all, perhaps not even most, of these losses were the results of massacres. The indirect effects of war [famine and disease] were probably worse than the spectacular killing and looting by undisciplined soldiers."[12]

What is important for our present thesis is not the precise number of persons murdered in cold blood in the name of God—that can never be ascertained with precision—but the fact that this human cost is ignored by McNeill (and most other historians) in his recital of the course of victory. Even for our present day, when the facts are much better known, the extent of the violence is glossed over. Thus McNeill says: "Hitler also invented an enemy—the Jews—upon whom to focus hate and blame for all of Germany's difficulties and failures."[13] No mention is made of the holocaust, in which six million

Jews were murdered. Stalin he describes as having a "tyrannously heavy hand."[14] Again there is no reference to the systematic terror that Stalin practiced for a quarter of a century.

That the omission of these massacres from traditional history leads to catastrophic distortions scarcely requires any emphasis. It will be sufficient to cite one example. In 1915 the Turks decided to "liquidate" the Armenians by deporting the whole Armenian population of 1,750,000 to Syria and Mesopotamia. It was intended as a "final solution," and it is estimated that about 600,000 persons died or were massacred en route.[15] In the next generation Hitler was to emulate this "final solution," using the slogan: Who remembers the Armenians? He was right—few did. The victory ideology leaves the student thoroughly confused about what really happend.

Weber's Protestant Ethic

Even the great social scientist Max Weber remained rather oblivious to the role of violence and massacre in history. With the Protestant ethic he coined a new term and a new concept—that Western capitalism had triumphed because it attached a religious sanction to a certain way of life, which he called the Protestant ethic, with its emphasis on industry, sobriety, and hard work. Weber frankly admitted that he was dealing with a psychological notion but maintained—and rightly so—that psychology (including psychiatry) had not yet advanced to the point where it could contribute to his thinking.[16]

In his analysis Weber stressed asceticism and hard work. Because he did not have either the ideology or the technical psychological tools at his disposal, he left out of his account the role of hostility and violence in those who espoused the Protestant ethic. Marx in *Capital* had already directed attention to the miserable conditions under which the English laboring classes lived in the nineteenth century. But he made the mistake of ascribing the hostility to capitalism rather than to the psychology of the capitalist. Others have since documented in considerable detail the appalling cruelties practiced by those who espoused the Protestant ethic. If today this cruelty is less apparent, it is only because of the efforts of centuries of reform.

The colonial revolutions of the twentieth century have produced much evidence that nineteenth-century imperialism was frequently based on nothing but wanton violence. When Leopold of

Belgium took over the Congo in 1878, murder and violence were the order of the day. Gay and Webb diplomatically comment that "Leopold II's barbaric exploitation of the Belgian Congo proved that a really determined entrepreneur could drag a good deal out of his miserable subjects."[17] In another part of the world Hemming (1978) estimates that the number of Indians in Brazil has been reduced since 1500 from 2,431,000 to 100,000. Of the 230 tribes extant in 1900, more than 35 percent were extinct by 1960.[18]

On the other hand, the totalitarian countries have been even more destructive in their exploitation of their subjects. Even today, how many Russians are dying in labor camps is completely unknown and unknowable. The purges of China, the Pol Pot regime in Cambodia, and the mass murders of Idi Amin in Uganda are all atrocities of recent years. Violence and wholesale massacres have been present throughout history and are still there.[19]

Thus the traditional historian's emphasis on victory produces a completely one-sided image of the past.

THE ROLE OF SLAVERY IN HISTORY

If victory has been attained by atrocity and violence, it has been maintained, historically, by slavery. The significance of slavery for mankind in general has been obscured by the particular role it has played in American history, unique and special to our country. But the one problem should not be confused with the other.

It is in fact rather remarkable that slavery was the dominant form of human relationship until roughly the French Revolution. It has been estimated that during the first two centuries of the Roman Empire three out of four residents of the Italian peninsula—21 million people—lived in bondage. Eventually slavery was converted into the milder institution of serfdom, which was the characteristic condition of labor in Europe during the Middle Ages.[20] Thus the analytic ideal of love and work, described by Freud as the core of normality, could exist only in the last two centuries.

Up to the eighteenth century even the most enlightened did not protest against the inhumanity of slavery. It was mentioned in the Bible with evident approval. In 1375 Pope Gregory XI ordered the enslavement of excommunicated Florentines whenever they were captured. Even John Locke did not see slavery as unjust, arguing that "if the hardships of bondage should at any time outweigh the value of life, he could commit suicide by resisting his master and receiving the death which he had all along deserved."[21]

It is amazing that beginning in the late eighteenth century slavery was abolished, at least in principle, all over the world within one century. It vanished from its last American bastion, Brazil, in 1888.[22] This dramatic revolution in men's fortunes has attracted too little attention from the traditional historians, whose ideology failed to sense its significance.

Historians have made odd psychological comments about slavery. It is argued that in many societies slaves and freemen were not so sharply separated.[23] Nevertheless, a slave was not considered a human being. Hebrew law provided that if a master beat a slave to death he went unpunished because "the slave is his money."[24] Another source alleges that "slavery was regarded as a misfortune but not as a wrong, and slaves felt no resentment against their masters unless they were ill-treated."[25] In Aztec society, where young men and women knew a year ahead of time that they were destined to be sacrificed to the gods, they allegedly felt no anger about their fate.[26] Documentation for these extraordinary observations is of course lacking.

The disappearance of slavery certainly cannot be attributed to purely economic motives. There is some evidence that beginning about 1800, that is, after the French Revolution, a real change in men's feelings began to emerge, shifting from violence and hatred to peace and love. Shorter (1975) has tried to show that the family has moved toward love and companionship as its base continuously since about 1750.

Naturally, these are broad generalizations with all-too-glaring exceptions. The twentieth century will not take a back seat to any previous century when it comes to murderous brutality. Nevertheless, as a trend in history these facts are important. Historians are too accustomed to tracing continuities; when discontinuities arise they are baffled. It has already been argued that psychoanalysis represents a discontinuity in intellectual history. In the same vein it can be argued that the shift toward more loving human relationships after the French Revolution was accompanied by an enormous increase in the world's population and a significant lengthening of the life cycle, which represents another discontinuity that separates the world after 1800 from that before it.

REASON AND MADNESS IN HISTORY

The catastrophic events of our age have forced a total re-evaluation of all familiar views. One subject with which this has occurred
is madness. The thesis is simply that throughout recorded history
man has been more insane than sane.

This position, which derives from an application of psychoanalytic knowledge, has been underplayed because of the enormous
weight given to conventional psychiatry. The problem has been approached primarily in terms of overt psychosis in the Kraepelinian
sense—outright craziness, in the ordinary sense of the term.

Even in terms of technical psychosis there is little accurate
knowledge before 1800. The well-known study by Goldhammer and
Marshall (1953) and the careful work by Jarvis (1855; reprinted
1971) both show that admissions and discharges from mental hospitals in Massachusetts in the nineteenth century did not differ markedly from admissions and discharges in the twentieth. But what happened before 1800 is unknown, because mental hospitals scarcely
existed. Actually, as noted in the preceding chapter, psychiatry as a
medical specialty was for all practical purposes nonexistent before
the French Revolution, the occasional liberal physician like Vives or
Pinel notwithstanding.

It would be an interesting technical venture (that so far no one
has undertaken) to determine how much overt psychosis in the conventional sense did exist in former centuries. Freud showed that a
neurosis of demonic possession in the seventeenth century corresponded in certain essentials to what we would call today a psychosis. Freud says: "We need not be surprised to find that whereas the
neuroses of our unpsychological modern days take on a hypochon-
driacal aspect and appear disguised as organic illnesses, the neuroses
of those early times emerge in demonological trappings."[27] Likewise
Ernest Jones, in his famous study of the nightmare, has shown that
the accusations against witches in former centuries corresponded to
projections of sexual delusions on the part of the clergy, who were
projecting their own psychoses onto innocent women, whom they
then burned at the stake. Thus the witchcraft persecutions, which
took the lives of hundreds of thousands of innocent victims (Gay
and Webb, 1973)[28] over several centuries, represented in modern
terms an acting out of the psychosis of the clergy, who were then the
dominant psychiatric power in the world. The counter-argument

that this was merely the "spirit of the times" and not an actual psychosis will be considered later.

The similarity between religious beliefs and psychotic delusions has long been known, though not properly appreciated. Even in our own day the peculiar phenomenon of glossolalia is widespread. In this experience a member of a church group suddenly falls into some sort of trance and begins to talk gibberish. Everybody then becomes convinced that the voice of God is speaking through him, and he is looked upon as divinely inspired. How many such instances have appeared throughout history no one knows, but the phenomenon itself is quite familiar to any student of the history of religion.[29] Now, looked at analytically, glossolalia represents an infantile regression to the period when the child could not understand the language of its parents. In outright psychosis such talk is referred to as "verbigeration"; it becomes the mark of craziness for the ordinary individual. It seems to be a psychotic manifestation, but one admired by large numbers of people.

That political or religious figures may be clinically psychotic is a valuable piece of information in its own right. As this book is being written, Ghotbzadeh, the Foreign Minister of Iran, has reportedly said that the Ayatollah Khomeini is "out of touch with reality." George Rosen, in *Madness and Society* (1968), has put together much material showing that throughout history madmen have often been recognized as divinely inspired and accordingly granted extraordinary privileges. Even Plato remarked that no one achieves inspiration and prophetic truth when in his right mind.[30] In the *Phaedrus* Socrates is made to say: "the greatest blessings come by way of madness, indeed of madness that is heaven sent." Socrates further divided madness into four types: prophetic, telestic (mystical), poetic, and erotic. All four are regarded as praiseworthy.[31] Indeed, the word "enthusiasm" derives from the Greek *enthousiasmos*, which means divine madness. Some nineteenth-century psychiatrists regarded enthusiasm as an illness, which they confused with mania and "erotomania."

Nietzsche, who eventually became mad himself, had an inkling of the desperate struggle the Greeks were going through when he wrote: "The fanaticism with which all Greek reflection throws itself upon rationality betrays a desperate situation; there was danger, there was but one choice: either to perish or—to be absurdly *rational*."[32] In a sense Nietzsche here foreshadows the modern concept of rationalization. In a similar vein the modern emphasis on science or rationality may frequently be a defense against an underlying psychosis. It is not uncommon to regard scientists as "mad," and in fact many of them have had episodes of overt psychosis (Fine and Fine, 1977). Even Ellenberger, in considering this phenomenon among psychiatrists, regards their work as part of a "creative illness" (1970).

Modern anthropological studies of shamans, the priest-doctors of many primitive tribes, have revealed the most bizarre forms of mental illness in them. Julian Silverman wrote in 1967:

> In primitive cultures in which such a unique life crisis resolution is tolerated, the abnormal experience [shamanism] is typically beneficial to the individual, cognitively and affectively; he is regarded as one with expanded consciousness. In a culture that does not provide referential guides for comprehending this kind of crisis experience, the individual [schizophrenic] typically undergoes an intensification of his suffering over and above his original anxieties.[33]

The statement that overt psychosis has been by no means unusual throughout history meets with disbelief for two reasons. First, psychiatry in modern times has largely operated with a grossly incorrect conceptualization of schizophrenia, in accordance with Kraepelin's erroneous theories, which sees the schizophrenic as an individual who becomes increasingly bizarre until his illness is manifest to everybody around him (see Chapter 5). Among other things, Bleuler shows that the most common type of psychosis is the phasic-benign, in which the individual has episodes of psychosis from which he recovers with or without treatment (almost always without before modern times, and frequenty with almost none in modern times), and then remains clinically or culturally normal for many years. Several such episodes may occur in the lives of many persons. In ordinary parlance this is referred to as a "nervous breakdown."

This phasic-benign view would explain much of the psychosis in history better than the genetic Kraepelinian position. The conclusion is inescapable that overt psychosis has been much more common than is ordinarily thought.* Further, it is particularly in the area of religion that the most bizarre psychotic material has been encountered.

In 1978 the world was horrified by the mass suicide of some nine hundred believers in the Reverend James Jones, leader of a small sect

---

*Quantitative data obviously cannot be offered here; nevertheless, in anticipation of the objections of the cliometricians, "many" is a respectable mathematical term.

encamped in Guyana. At that time the *New York Times* published an article by the historian Theodore K. Rabb describing a somewhat similar incident in the sixteenth century. In 1534 two preachers arrived at the German city of Münster and began proclaiming a powerful new vision of salvation. The faithful had to promote God's plan by taking up the sword against unbelievers. Under two psychotic leaders, Matthys and John, the entire city was transformed into a madhouse. Attacks from the outside eventually led to the death of all the inhabitants. When the city finally fell, only three hundred men were left, all of whom were massacred (we are not told why). Rabb, a prominent modern historian who is not at all psychologically oriented, after recounting this horror story, writes:

> When the dust of all the interpretations, from the psychological to the economic, finally settles, these extraordinary moments become the landmarks of history because they offer us a chance to test comfortable assumptions. However much the normal, the prosaic, and the recurrent may tell us, the unique, the bizarre, and the disturbing remain the best proving grounds for our conclusions about human nature, society, and the temper of a particular time or place.[34]

While the gruesome massacre of all the inhabitants of Münster was an exception, the mass psychosis displayed by the official Christian church has been underestimated by historians, who have merely ascribed it to the Zeitgeist. The available material (neglected by almost all traditional historians) is too overwhelming; bizarreness and psychosis virtually drip from every incident.

Consider as an unusual concern what Deschner (1974) calls the "foreskin problem." As late as 1728 a pope made a pilgrimage to the foreskin of Abraham.[35] A long series of church fathers bewailed the uncertain fate of the foreskin of Jesus. Did it putrefy, or did it become smaller or larger? Did the Almighty God give him a new one? In 1907 a Dominican monk, A. V. Muller, wrote a monograph on *The Most Holy Foreskin of Jesus* in which he enumerated thirteen places that claimed to have the "real" foreskin. One of them, Rome, reputedly received the relic from Charlemagne, who had received it from an angel. The Jesuit Salmeron celebrated the foreskin of Jesus as a suitable engagement ring for his brides (the nuns). A regular foreskin cult developed. In 1427 a brotherhood of the holy foreskin was founded.[36]

Enough of this, one can say. All of it is obviously outright psychosis. Yet it not only was sanctioned by the highest officials of the church, but played a significant role in the lives of many people.

This brings us to the second reason why the psychosis of religion (and the incidence of psychosis in general) has been underplayed by traditional history. The average historian, unschooled in technical psychiatry, assumes that a psychotic must be completely unable to function. This was also the assumption of Kraepelin and his followers. Subsequent work has shattered this assumption completely. Few persons are so completely psychotic that they cannot function at all. Most are incapacitated in certain areas but can function in others. Modern analysis approaches this in terms of ego functions. Freud had already commented that normality is a fiction, that most normal persons have egos that range from the normal to the psychotic (*Analysis Terminable and Interminable*, 1937). Subsequent work has fully borne out this evaluation (Fine, 1979). Saul and Wenar (1965) have remarked that "if all children were properly reared we would have a world of emotionally mature men and women. What we see instead is not human nature, but a variety of characterological disorders which are so nearly universal that we mistake them for human nature."[37]

The careful, detailed individual study of millions of individuals on which statements like the one above are based cannot be duplicated for past eras. The best we can do is make educated guesses. The most plausible guess is that throughout history characterological disorders of all kinds have been the rule, not the exception. Among these disorders outright psychosis in the literal sense has been not at all unusual and has played a variable, often major, role in shaping the forces of destiny.

The argument is customarily offered that in a society where everyone holds to some bizarre belief, such a belief cannot be considered a sign of psychosis or neurosis. No doubt this argument has some merit, but it is not as simple as it appears.

In the first place, bizarre beliefs must be divided into those on which the individual has no information and those he can test out himself. An example of the former would be the idea that the earth is flat; of the latter, that supernatural beings come and torture one during the night. No one would classify misinformation of the first kind as mental illness in any sense. But the second is in an entirely different category.

When the belief is so strange that it cannot be confirmed by the individual, sooner or later someone comes along and points that out, as in the tale of the emperor's new clothes. Strict adherence to such beliefs is an indication that there is something wrong with the mental atmosphere of that society.

These ideas have been confirmed by the study of various cultures in the contemporary world. In a paranoid society where no natural cause of death is admitted, for example, it is assumed that every death is the result of sorcery or murder on the part of an enemy, who is then made the object of a hunt of revenge. The society then alternates between murdering and being murdered.[38] The average individual in such a culture is paranoid in every sense of the term.

To the analyst it has become an everyday observation that most of the people with whom comes in contact are seriously disturbed. The famous Rennie mid-Manhattan Study of the 1950s gave some quantitative base to this observation. To the nonanalyst the situation is puzzling because he confuses the statistical average with the analytic ideal (Offer and Sabshin, 1974). A further source of confusion derives from acceptance of the psychiatric error that "mental illness" is a disease in some sense of the word. More careful research indicates that what we call mental illness is a reaction to life stresses and that under extreme circumstances many or most of the persons in any culture may respond with a psychosis or near-psychosis. This seems to have been the case throughout much of history. Thus the conclusion is justified that madness has been of more importance in human affairs than reason.

Witchcraft: A Typical Example of Madness

It needs no detailed presentation of the events to show that the whole system of belief in witches and of methods for their persecution seems stark staring mad by modern standards. Traditional historians have been baffled by this phenomenon. At first the naive explanation—that witchcraft was simply an expression of a primitive mind unable to think rationally—prevailed.

As time went on, this explanation has come to be seen as oversimplified. Some other psychological factor must be at play. A typical attempt at clarification is the following in the *Encyclopaedia Britannica* (1978):

> Beliefs in witchcraft in the generic sense are conspicuous in most small-scale communities (e.g. in preliterate cultures), where interaction is based on personal relationships that tend to be lifelong and difficult to break. In such societies belief in witches makes it possible for misfortunes to be explained in terms of disturbed social relationships.[39]

However, this attribution of witchcraft to the small group does not serve to clarify the extraordinary delusions and outright murders connected with the institution. A more sophisticated account is given by Rosen (1966):

> The overwhelming impression one carries away from the witch pamphlets is one of consternation at the human predicament. Through these pages we come to know the desperation of lives played out in restricted surroundings, and to feel the helplessness of people before a succession of natural catastrophes which they did not in the least understand. . . . The profound mental effects . . . the obsessions and mental peculiarities, are very much part of the story of witchcraft.[40]

Next come those writers who see madness as part of the structure of witchcraft, but not all or even most of it. Thus Russell writes:

> The concept of madness is of only limited use in explaining the medieval witch phenomenon, for not all witches were psychologically disturbed or psychotic individuals. An alleged witch or Inquisitor, holding views of the supernatural that appear mad to the commonly accepted philosophical materialism of our own day, cannot in any meaningful way be assumed to have been mad, because these views were commonly accepted in his society.[41]

Social tension in the Middle Ages, expressed in terms of transcendental Christian myth, Russell writes, produced crazes of fear that were directed against outcasts from Christian society.[42] Mental order, he says, deteriorates in times of social crisis.[43] Fears were reinforced by social alienation in periods of stress.[44] The obvious meaning of the accusation that the witches had kissed the devil's backside is denied by Russell, who says that the meaning "goes beyond the obvious."[45] Finally he admits that the phenomenon of witchcraft, whether we are talking about the persecutors or the witches, was the result of fear expressed in supernatural terms.[46]

Russell agrees that "the possible permutations of mental illness in witches are almost infinite,"[47] but stops short of saying the same of the witch-persecutors, who were after all the culpable psychotics. In his careful work Russell has actually outlined the normal development of a psychotic state in both the witches and their persecutors. He refrains from reaching this final conclusion only because he is misled by the conventional psychiatric image of psychosis. Analytically, fear leading to delusions and murder (loss of control of violent urges) is a typical course of psychosis. Thus, whatever the social structure, it would seem that belief in witches represents a serious form of mental derangement. And all authorities agree that such beliefs are extremely widespread. This is but one small instance that presents confirmation of our thesis that madness has played a more central role in human history than reason.

The Emergence of Psychiatry in the Nineteenth Century: A New Hypothesis

If man has been more mad than rational throughout history, the emergence of psychiatry in the nineteenth century requires some clarification. Why did man suddenly take an interest in certain types of schizophrenics, confine them to hospitals, and build up a "science" of psychiatry, allegedly a medical specialty, with the hypothesis that all of these peculiar manifestations derived from a disorder of the brain? For broadly speaking psychotics (and neurotics) can be subdivided into two types: those who vent their hostility against themselves and those who vent their hostility against others. Hostility, or hatred, research reveals, lies at the root of all mental disturbance.

The emergence of psychiatry focused on those psychotics who took it out on themselves, resulting in peculiar speech, withdrawal from people, and an apathetic attitude toward life. By contrast those psychotics or neurotics who took their hatred out on others (like Hitler or Stalin) instead moved into positions of power, as had happened all through the ages.

The common illusion that psychotics are dangerous lunatics who are going to destroy others must be seen as a projection by the victors of their own destructive impulses.

The first century of psychiatry concentrated on the incarceration of the self-punitive psychotic. As has been seen, until Freud came along psychiatrists really had no inkling of what they were doing. There were, however, many kindly men among them who gave their wards some humane treatment, in contrast to what had been done before. As noted in Chapter 5, the care of the mentally ill passed from the clergy, who had been murdering them en masse for several centuries, to the medical profession.

The second century of psychiatry has seen a broadening of horizons all along the line. But confusion persists because of the difficulty in accepting the appalling realization that most men are seriously disturbed mentally. Today this confusion is buttressed by the current fad among psychiatrists of labeling their patients "borderline." This keeps them within the ranks of psychiatric patienthood but avoids recognition that the real revolution lies in the shift of the population from the aberrant to the normal, from the maladjustment neurosis to the adjustment neurosis.

McNeill himself, in an excellent book, *Plagues and Peoples* (1976), has offered the arresting thesis that the centuries from 1300 to 1700 should be viewed as those in which the preliminary steps toward the eradication of infectious diseases were taken; the process began in 1700 (roughly) and flowered in the twentieth century.* It may be that future generations will see 1800 as the turning point in the eradication of mental disease. First the focus was on the deviants who internalized their hostility. Finally it has turned to the mass of mankind and the caricatures of mental health that they present. With this realization the course of history may be changed as much as by the gradual eradication of the majority of physical illnesses and the extraordinary increase in the life span that has taken place since 1800.

THE SHIFT IN INTEREST FROM THE VICTORS TO THE VANQUISHED

In the ideology of victory the greatest interest naturally attaches to those who are victorious. A peculiar assumption, unstated of course, begins to make itself felt: Those who are victorious must somehow "have something." They may be despots, tyrants, or mass murderers, but they have some kind of genius, they know how to organize, they have extraordinary insights into others, and so forth. Thus Ian Grey in a recent biography of Stalin sees him as the man who forged a new nation out of Russia; his paranoia, his wholesale massacres, and his narcissistic grandiosity are all forgotten. Similarly with Hitler. Scarcely a generation has passed, millions of the survivors are still alive, and some have already suggested that the story of the annihilation of the Jews is a concoction. The Poles insist that only Poles were massacred; the Russians say only Russians; the Nazis (or neo-Nazis) deny that any massacre occurred. Instead, some (Maser, 1971) see Hitler as a genius who created a new spirit and a new nation in Germany, who could organize, plan, and ad-

---

*Yet this hypothesis, which obviously gives a central role to disease in human history, is omitted by the same author in *The Rise of the West*, where the ideology of victory takes over.

minister as no one had before him. Actually Hitler ruled for twelve years, in the course of which at least 10 million Germans died, while countless others were maimed for life. The story of these Germans is omitted. History deals with the victorious, not the vanquished.

Our vision of the past has similarly been blurred by the traditional historians. Witchcraft persecutions, which flourished in Europe for two whole centuries, sent several hundred thousand innocent women (perhaps several million; who can count?) to their deaths. Historians argue over whether or not these witches were "psychotic" and ignore the obvious psychosis of the Catholic Church in those centuries. But Catholicism has survived; it was "victorious" against the "heretics" and infidels, so it must "have something"—a genius for organization, an insight into human nature or whatever. Freud once remarked that religious penance for past murders permits new murders to be committed, as in Christianity (Freud, 1938), but few historians have taken his remark seriously. They should. The strength of Christianity, as of many other victors, derives from the willingness to kill. The Romans and Mongols made no bones about it; the Christians covered it up so effectively that many were misled into thinking that their murderous proclivities were simply part of the *Zeitgeist*.

Since World War II, many historians have turned their attention to women, children, blacks, Indians, Hispanics, immigrants, and other groups previously slighted. This switch is a good illustration of Burckhardt's comment, quoted earlier, that history is the record of what one age finds of interest in another. As a result of the spread of psychological knowledge, it becomes clear that history is the record of what men did in the past, and *all* men must be included, the unimportant as well as the important, the ruled as well as the ruler, the vanquished as well as the victor, the underdog as well as the top dog. The change, still in its infancy, represents a real revolution in historical writing.

Yet even today it is hard to convince people of the psychological origin of their difficulties or the psychological aspect of their lives. In a revealing sidelight on the psychiatric disturbance known as the Watergate conspiracy, John Dean's *Blind Ambition* (1976) describes a conversation he had in jail with a fellow con, a Mafia man. The Mafia man said: "Let me ask you something, if you don't mind. You look a little wet behind the ears to be the President's lawyer. How'd you get there so young? Your old man put you in the fix?" "No, I just

kissed a lot of ass, Vinny. A lot of it."[48] Yet Dean shows no awareness that his criminal behavior resulted from inner conflicts. Apparently his only regret was that he did not win. Nixon in his memoirs
displayed the same psychology—or pathology.

THE RELIANCE ON A COMMONSENSE PSYCHOLOGY

The arguments about psychohistory (to be discussed below)
arise from the mistaken notion that psychology has never played a
role in historical writing. Quite the contrary. Traditional historical
writing is highly psychological on every page, but it is the commonsense psychology of the schools, not the depth psychology that has
emerged in the twentieth century. Man is rational; his motives are
what he says they are; at worst he is dominated by hidden economic
motives but nothing worse; feelings are unimportant except when
they flow over; psychosis is a rare malady encountered in only a few
aberrant individuals; the wish for victory dominates human history
and requires no explanation ("blind ambition").

Consult any history text, and psychological comments appear
everywhere. Barbara Tuchman describing an incident in the Hundred Years' War: "at Modena the mercenaries aroused the fury of the
citizens, which the Pope almost tearfully begged Coucy to appease.
[After heavy rains and assaults] amid general lack of enthusiasm the
offensive disintegrated."[49]

Peter Gay and R. K. Webb say of Alexander I of Russia:

On occasion the tsar still showed signs of his early dedication to liberal
ideas, but he was preoccupied with foreign affairs and sought political
counsel. . . . His increasing withdrawal into religiosity finds its most
celebrated evidence in his brief infatuation with the famous mystic, the
Baroness Julie de Krudener. In short, Alexander's fragile temperament
could not bear the strains he himself had placed upon it.[50]

William McNeill (1967), writing of the Iranian Empire, states:

The difficulty lay in creating a system of society that could support a
sufficient number of suitably armored and trained cavalrymen near
enough to the frontier to provide effective and continual protection
against steppe raiding. The Parthian monarchs had allowed (perhaps
they even encouraged) the growth of a military class of landowners
who equipped themselves as heavy cavalrymen and were perpetually
on the alert to protect their own lands from destruction.[51]

These comments, taken at random, could be augmented indefinitely. History has always involved both an objective description of events and a characterization of the psychological motives of the actors involved. Thus history has always been psychohistory; the difference lies in the kind of psychology used, not in the use of psychology itself. Further, the oversimplification of psychological motives casts considerable doubt on the "science" in scientific history. A skeptic could reasonably ask: How do we know that the soldiers lost their enthusiasm? What is the evidence that Tsar Alexander was so temperamental, and what caused his temperament? Who is to say that the dominant motive of the Iranian nobles was to protect their lands? These trivial examples show once more that history has always dealt in gross psychological inferences, the evidence for which has always been either tenuous or absent.

The Philosophy of History

The conventional view of historiography is that history aims at reconstructing an accurate record of human activities and at achieving a more profound understanding of them. About the need for an accurate record and the procedures for arriving at one there is no argument whatsoever. Here new techniques often open up new vistas. For example, the discovery of Carbon 14 dating, stemming from the nuclear physics of World War II, has allowed a much more accurate determination of many significant dates in early history, where objective man-made records are lacking. In an earlier age, the advance of astronomy could allow the dating of an eclipse centuries past with unbelievable precision. The opening up of hitherto unavailable archives and records has cast much new light on old problems, and continues to do so.

It is in the attempt to achieve a more accurate understanding of historical events that controversies have arisen. These controversies have centered on what has become known as the critical or analytical philosophy of history, which has only risen to prominence during the twentieth century (Gay, 1978).[52]

In previous centuries many scholars held some form of the belief that there must be some general scheme or design in human history, some all-encompassing purpose or pattern. Among these theories may be mentioned the Christian view that history moved toward the triumph of Christianity, the Hegelian view of the evolution of the spirit, the Marxist view of the dialectical process that would eventually lead to the victory of the proletariat, the Enlightenment credo that history moved toward the establishment of freedom, Toynbee's theory of the cyclical growth and decline of cultures, Spengler's assumption that the West was doomed to decline, and many others. For none of these theories is there any real evidence. Clearly history is made by man, and the historical record must focus squarely on what men have done with one another. There is no order or design other than that which man has created.

Another question that has concerned philosophers is whether social science (in history) and natural science are the same or different in their fundamental purposes and methods. Here too it seems clear that the two are radically different, although social science will and must use the findings of natural science wherever it can. As Collingwood once put it, the time has come for history to be released from "its state of pupilage to natural science."[53]

We come back then to the fundamental question of how a deeper understanding of history is to be achieved. One view, deriving from the Italian Benedetto Croce and the British scholar Robert Collingwood, is that history must be a re-enactment of past experience; that is, the historian must try to see each age in its own terms. Opposed to this is the position that history must serve a purpose: As Croce put it, past history is always contemporary history. Some similarity, no matter how vague, always exists between the present and the past; accordingly, what the past shows is of some use for the present. However, these two positions need not necessarily be put into opposition; the re-enactment of the past can be carried out in its own terms, and then whatever lessons it may carry for the present may be drawn. Another way of saying this is that history is pursued not only for its own sake but because of the light it throws on today's problems.

Still, this does not answer the question of how the deeper understanding of the past can be achieved, or how the past can be re-enacted. Collingwood offered an answer to this in terms of psychology: The historian must imaginatively reconstruct or re-enact in his own mind, rather than by showing the events to be instances of general uniformities or regularities that are established by induction.[54] Collingwood also maintained that most historical writing has been either theocratic or mythological, a thesis that we have attempted to document here. However, Collingwood did not have command of the insights of modern psychology, so he did not carry his theories far enough.

While the factual data on which history is based cannot be disputed by objective historians, they are clearly insufficient for a deeper understanding. For even the most superficial examination of treatises on any area of history uncovers considerable disagreement among the various authorities. Why did Rome fall? Why did slavery cease? These and numerous similar questions invariably lead to considerable dispute. On this point Gay writes:

> It is notorious that disputes between historians as to the "true" causes of occurrences such as wars or revolutions often appear to resist resolution at a purely empirical level, and it has been persuasively maintained by some philosophers that the basic grounds for such disputes may often be traced back to the historian's adherence to a moral or political standpoint not shared by his opponent.[55]

In other words, the historian is driven, whether aware of it or not, by some theoretical point of view, which he uses to choose his facts and to interpret them. On this point there can be no doubt that Gay is completely correct. Hence his view that history is critical reflection on the past. Understanding, in other words, is reached by such critical reflection.

But how is this critical reflection to be carried out? To answer this it is first of all necessary to dissect history a little further. Collingwood (1946) lists four characteristics of history: (1) it is scientific; (2) it is humanistic (or asks questions about things done by men); (3) it is rational (bases its answers on appeal to evidence, not authority); and (4) it is self-revelatory (exists in order to tell man what man is by telling him what man has done).[56] In a similar vein Morris Cohen wrote:

> The tragic view of human history widens our sympathies and prevents us from becoming dull to the finer possibilities which wiser conduct or a different turn of events might have realized. Above all, it enables us to do our best in an actually imperfect world, and if it warns us in the language of Kant man is a crooked stick and that we cannot build a perfect kingdom of heaven on our own limited earth, it also provides us with the vision of an ideal which, even though not completely attainable at any one time, illumines the direction in which our efforts should be exerted if the history of the future is to be brighter than the history of the past.[57]

Brilliant minds like Burckhardt, Croce, Collingwood, Cohen, Hegel, and Gay have always sensed that there was something wrong with history as it has been written. They have stressed the need for understanding, the role of values, and above all the need for critical reflection. What they lacked was a deeper knowledge of psychology, which can now be supplied via psychoanalysis.

It is clear that history involves three elements: (1) factual data, (2) psychological understanding, and (3) inferences about causes. Traditional historians, unschooled in deeper psychological analysis, have tended to see the causes of events in past events. Even revisionists have not changed this attitude but have merely altered its contents. Thus the traditional image of the American Revolution is that it was a rebellion against British oppression. The revisionist view (Charles Beard, *The Economic Interpretation of the Constitution*) maintained that it was an expression of economic self-interest by the wealthier colonists, who used the notions of justice and freedom to cloak their economic objectives. Marxists have claimed that it was, like the French Revolution, a bourgeois affair in which no real shift of power among the classes occurred. Progressive historians have claimed that it was in reality two revolutions—an external one in which the British yoke was cast off, and an internal one to determine whether the upper or lower classes would rule once the British had departed. Still others have claimed that the distinctive character of the American Revolution, as contrasted with the French or Russian, was that it was dominated by men like Jefferson, Franklin, and Adams, who were mature enough to eschew the fanaticism and violence that has marked other revolutions. The empirical data are the same; the interpretations vary widely.

Historians spend their lives delving into the past; hence, like other social scientists they tend to value the material that they discover very highly. Accordingly, the usual tendency is to interpret any historical event in terms of the events that preceded it, as a rule without reference to psychology. If psychological factors are brought in, they too are interpreted in terms of the preceding events. Yet, as Cohen says: "Wisdom here as elsewhere consists in analyzing our questions before we attempt to answer them."[58] Any such analysis would reveal that the nature of historical (as of all social) causation is exceedingly complex, more complex in fact than that of physical causation (see Chapter 6).

We have here the crux of the real argument about psychology and psychoanalysis, an argument that will be seen to recur in every discussion of a social situation. The social scientist uncovers a mass of facts. These become his source of self-esteem and wisdom. The natural reaction is to interpret causation, including psychological causation, in terms of these social facts. The psychologist demurs. He points out that the same social situation, in this case the same or a similar historical situation, could have led to entirely different consequences. If many similar situations are created, they will in fact lead to entirely different outcomes. Hence the social situation as such cannot be the cause of the subsequent event. British tyranny as such cannot explain the Revolution; the same or worse tyranny in other places did not lead to revolution. Economic motives have had similarly variable consequences. Therefore psychological factors must have played a role. Here too caution is necessary. Just as similar social situations lead to different results, so similar psychological situations lead to varying forms of behavior. A certain unpredictability about human beings must be allowed for here. Just as our clinical experience warns us against making exact predictions about what will happen to our patients, study of the larger scene leads to a similar warning.

It therefore becomes necessary to combine social and psychological factors in seeking the causes of any social events. In the case of history, both extremes have been seen. At times theories about a design or purpose in human affairs independent of the individual have been paramount (Christianity, Marxism, and so forth). At other times, in simpler terms history has been seen as the actions of leading figures (the great man theory). Neither of these is adequate.

To redress the balance it is essential to bring in the insights of depth psychology. These insights still will not bring certainty about the course of history. But at least they will make our explanations and inferences more plausible.

The Illusions of "Cliometrics"

Technically, a significant development of the past decade has been the rise of "cliometrics," or more precise measurement of historical forces. It is alleged by its proponents that this more precise measurement would answer many of the unresolved questions.

One of the outstanding products of this cliometric approach is a book by Fogel and Engerman, *Time on the Cross* (1974). These authors claim that although masses of data have been available for some time,

. . . the techniques required to analyze and interpret them systematically were not perfected intil after the close of World War II. Then a series of rapid advances in economics, statistics, and applied mathematics, together with the availability of high-speed computers, put information long locked in obscure archives at the disposal of a new generation of scholars.[59]

They then try to apply these "new" techniques to the question of slavery. Technically, they limit themselves to the economics of slavery. But the gist of their argument is psychological, repeated over and over throughout the book: The severity of slavery has been exaggerated.[60]

An examination of the book (as well as of similar treatises in other fields) reveals that the authors who now call themselves cliometricians are merely repeating the ideology and errors of behavioristic psychology. In the first place, statistics did not develop after World War II; it has existed for several hundred years. Second, the book contains all the typical errors involved in the use of statistics in any social field: sampling errors, incomplete data, and oversimplification (for example, the term "average" is used throughout without reference to its three principal meanings in statistics—mean, median, and mode—or to the standard deviation).

Above all, the authors fail to appreciate that cliometrics is merely a new name for an ancient device. Since the end of the eighteenth century historians have been persistently involved in refining the tools with which they uncover the factual data; this refinement could have been called cliometrics from the beginning. Hence they fall into the same trap that historians who deny their philosophical underpinnings have always fallen into (see quotation above from Gay, p. 206): The empirical data assembled could lead to many different conclusions, and the conclusions they have chosen to stress reveal their own biases or moral preconceptions and are not dictated by the data.

For, while they go to great pains to deny it, their work serves as a moral tract to justify slavery. "Slavery was not as bad as it has been made out to be" is the thesis repeated over and over. As bad for whom? And made out to be by whom? For the two-thirds of the blacks who perished in the voyage from Africa to America (these are not mentioned). For the innumerable slaves who rebelled against their owners throughout the slave era (also not mentioned; only a passing reference is made to the Nat Turner rebellion)? For the slaves who were so brutalized that they could not even run away when given a chance to do so (not mentioned, or ignored)? (See Aptheker, 1943.) For the blacks who returned to Africa during the revolution and afterward to live in their own country (Wilson, 1976)?

Above all the central question of how happy the slaves were under slavery is not discussed:

> It is, for example, much easier to obtain data bearing on the frequency with which slave families were broken up . . . than on the inner quality of the family life of slaves. . . . *And while the cliometricians have been able to construct reasonably reliable indexes of the material level at which blacks lived under slavery, it has been impossible, thus far, to devise a meaningful index of the effect of slavery on the personality or psychology of blacks.*[61]

But this is after all the central question, together with the other question of why, after three thousand years, slavery suddenly disappeared within one century; peacefully in all countries except the United States, where admittedly the slavocracy went to war to defend its right to mistreat fellow human beings. On all of these, the real questions that would lead to historical understanding, the authors admit in advance that their data are irrelevant. Certainly there is no critical reflection here, no serious attempt to reach understanding. As will be seen, such efforts to heap up quantitative data without reflecting on their meaning are typical of many social science approaches. (See also Rose, 1970; Davis, 1966.)

Some Comments on Psychohistory

In the 1960s interest in the study of history seemed to be languishing. In New York State the Education Department ordered two doctoral programs in history closed down because of the absence of jobs for the graduates.

Then along came psychohistory, and the situation changed. Kren (1977), reviewing the offerings, found that while in 1967 there were only two courses in psychohistory offered in American universities, by 1977 there were more than two hundred. The one element that appears to be paramount in these offerings is the need to introduce psychoanalytic ideas to students. The problem, says Kren, is conceptual. Students find Freud difficult and the vocabulary of psychoanalysis strange and are not really convinced of the value of the approach. As a rule no help is forthcoming from the psychology departments, which are solidly behavioristically oriented. Thus paradoxically psychohistory serves to introduce students to a kind of psychology that they cannot learn either in the psychology departments or elsewhere.

Psychohistory has been attacked as the fantasies of wild revolutionaries who lack the patience or the skill to engage in serious historical research. This is of course sheer nonsense. History, as we have seen, has always been psychohistory; only historians have failed to recognize it. The difference lies in the introduction of psychology as such. Naturally, there have been extremes in this kind of history as in all others. Psychoanalysts themselves have rejected these extremes and have gone to great lengths to write scholarly treatises. If they have not always been successful, that is due as much to the difficulty of the material as to the injection of psychological ideas.

The use of the prefix "psycho-" seems to represent a stage in the growth of understanding. "Psychoneurosis" has been replaced by "neurosis"; psychosomatic is now being replaced by psychogenic, or an awareness of the role that the psychological factor may play in any disease. Likewise with psychohistory. The term is transitional. Eventually it will become clear to professional historians that they have always been making psychological inferences, merely using an antiquated and inadequate kind of psychology. The main problem will always be to determine to what extent psychological factors do or do not play a role in the events recorded.

The psychohistorians have already directed attention to many aspects of history that previously went unnoticed. No one today would seriously think of writing a biography without a careful search into the subject's childhood. No one would any longer question that the role of women in history has been almost totally neglected. De Mause, in his *History of Childhood* (1974), has produced a masterpiece of research that will be essential to any future historian. As interest shifts from the victors to the vanquished, more and more individuals will come under the historian's scrutiny.

History and the Analytic Ideal

A persistent question has been that of human happiness. How happy have men been in the past, under different systems, at different epochs? We have noted Hegel's comment that happiness is found in the empty pages of history. Others have either ignored the problem or have gone from the extreme of assuming that all men have been reasonably happy to the extreme of assuming that all men have been miserable. There seems little reason to believe that men in the past have been very different from men in the present, whose lives show varying amounts of happiness and unhappiness in different spheres of existence.

Psychologically, we can approach people in terms of the analytic ideal (see Chapter 3). Because this explains how men function today, history should examine how the various components of the analytic ideal have fared in the past. What has the love life of men been like? What have family relationships been? How have individuals fitted into the social structure or departed from it? How mad have rulers and ruled been? These and analogous questions are being asked by a number of researchers today. They are questions that were scarcely posed before.

For many of these questions the available historical data may be insufficient. That has always been the case. However, the experience of the past twenty years has been that the material is available; it has simply been passed over because its significance has not been appreciated. As the ideology of victory gives way to the ideology of a science of man, more of these questions will be carefully researched, and more meaningful answers will be given.

History and Psychology

Enough has been said to support our fundamental thesis that psychology is essential to all historical work. Eventually, as Langer (1972) once recommended, psychology will be regarded as a basic tool for all historians, who will be trained in psychoanalytic institutes or their equivalents (suitable doctoral programs in psychology offered along dynamic lines). Inferences about historical causation will no longer be made without considering whether and to what extent psychological factors were involved. Thus history will involve: (1) the description of the record (not different from what is done now except in the details of material to be unearthed), (2) psychology of the individuals or peoples involved, and (3) inferences about historical causation combining social and psychological forces in different measure.

It has been said that history is rewritten by every age to suit its own specific needs. Our age is the first in which an adequate psychology is available to any student. It can only be anticipated that history in the next generation will be rewritten to give due weight to the psychological forces.

Chapter 8

Society Versus the Individual: Sociology and Anthropology

THE PROBLEM OF THE RELATIONSHIP between the individual and society lies at the root of the sciences of society, which have, as a result of various historical accidents, been rather arbitrarily divided into two: sociology, dealing with our own society, and anthropology, dealing with other cultures, especially those considered "primitive" or "pre-literate." Because of their differing concerns and differing development these two sciences will be considered separately, even though theoretically they are identical.

Sociology

Sociology is defined by the dictionary as the scientific study of society, social institutions, and social relations,[1] specifically the systematic study of the structure, development, and function of human groups. This definition is so broad that in theory it may extend to almost any human activity; the same is true for the other social sciences.

In practice, however, sociologists have tended to focus on social relationships or forces that in their opinion are beyond the control of the individual. In this respect they have been under the influence, knowingly or not, of one of the great pioneers, Emile Durkheim, who emphasized the central significance of *social facts*, which he defined in 1895 as follows:

> A social fact is to be recognized by the coercive power which it exercises or is capable of exercising over individuals; and the presence of this power is, in turn, to be recognized by the existence of some determinate sanction or by the resistance which this fact opposes to every endeavor which tends to do violence to it.[2]

In more or less similar terms the other giants of sociology have likewise placed the greatest stress on social facts or social forces. Since these are the forces most intensively studied by sociologists, they become the factors best known by them. There ensues a process similar to that described above in the study of history: Sociologists uncover (1) social facts—the social record—and (2) psychological factors, and then make inferences about the causation of these psychological factors. It becomes almost a dogma that the social fact or social force is more likely to be seen as the cause of events, while the psychological is relegated to a secondary role.

In Chapter 6 I pointed to the lesser certainty of social facts, among other factors to be considered in the methodology of the social sciences. This lesser certainty is accepted by everyone. Argument centers more on the way in which this uncertainty is to be approached, and I have suggested that the prime need in the social sciences is for a reduction of bias, whereas increased technical skill is the *via regia* in the natural sciences. Numerous instances of this have been cited before and will be cited throughout these chapters.

Whatever the social facts may turn out to be, the chain from them to psychological events is generally approached by the sociologist as one in which the social is primary. It is here that the greatest arguments have arisen, and it is here that the main thrust of our discussion will lie.

In addition, the social facts turned up by the sociologist are those now in existence in our contemporary society. Like all other intelligent human beings sociologists are disturbed by these facts. Hence they are moved, more than other social scientists, to social criticism, either in word or in deed. Since, again most likely for historical reasons, Marx has been esteemed more highly by sociologists than by other social scientists, there has been a strong tendency for sociologists to be left-wing critics. While there can be no argument about the undesirable and disruptive character of many social forces on the current scene, here too a clash with the psychological approach arises.

The wide range of sociological investigation and its closeness to social criticism have led to a domain of inquiry less well defined than other fields. Faris, himself a leading sociologist, says:

It is evident that sociology has not achieved triumphs comparable to those of the several older and more heavily supported sciences. A variety of interpretations have been offered to explain the difference— most frequently, that the growth of knowledge in the science of sociology is more random than cumulative. . . . Critics have attributed the slow pace to a variety of factors—the appetite of sociologists for neologisms and jargon, a disposition for psuedo-quantification, and excessive concern with imitation of methods of the natural sciences, overdependence on data from interviews, questionnaires and informal observations. All these shortcomings can be found in contemporary sociology, but none is characteristic of all areas. . . . The dispute about the main purpose of sociology, whether it works to understand behavior, or to cause social change, is a dispute found in every pursuit of scientific knowledge, and such polarization is far from absolute.[3]

As in the other social sciences, it will be our thesis here that the conflicts in sociology arise primarily from the incorrect image of man on which so much research has been based and that these conflicts can most readily be overcome by a better appreciation of psychology and closer cooperation with adequate psychological methods.

Sociology and Psychology

The most casual perusal of any sociological work reveals that it is concerned with psychological issues approached via the social circumstances leading to those issues. As we saw in the preceding chapter, this is not any different from history, and in fact many theoreticians deal with history and sociology together. But if psychological issues are to be properly comprehended there must be some familiarity with modern psychology. Unfortunately this is all too often lacking.

The Durkheimian position, which has been dominant in this respect, made a great point of differentiating sociology from psychology. In 1900 Durkheim wrote that

. . . social phenomena do not have their immediate and determining cause in the nature of individuals. If they did . . . sociology would dissolve into psychology. It is certainly true that all functional phenomena of the social order are psychological in the sense that all constitute a way of thinking or acting. But if sociology is to have its own field, collective ideas and actions must be different in nature from those that have their origin in the individual consciousness and must be subject to laws of their own. Social physiology may be said to be psychology, but only if the proviso is added that it must in no way be confused with the science so designated, which aims exclusively at studying the mental constitution of the individual.[4]

Durkheim was writing at a time when psychology was still in its infancy. Like Max Weber (see pp. 190–191) he could have admitted frankly that psychology had not yet developed to the point where it could shed light on the problems he was studying. Instead he chose to rule it out entirely. His editor, G. Catlin (*Rules of Sociological Method*), rightly criticizes him for this, pointing out that his distinction is of an entirely artificial nature, deriving from his arbitrary limitation of psychology.[5]

Again the situation is similar to that in history (and in the other social sciences as well, as will be seen). Whether admittedly or not, scholars have been writing on psychology. The only question is whether or not they will use the insights of modern psychology. Durkheim did not have them at his disposal, so he approached the problems sociologically. Weber sensed that something was being developed, so he really deferred his final views until more knowledge was available. Modern sociologists have vacillated. As late as 1978 Faris could write that the psychologists on whom sociologists have relied most heavily have been Dewey, Mead, and Cooley[6]; Freud is noticeably absent, as well as everyone else who wrote after 1920. Parochial views of this kind have naturally met with strong objections from many sociologists. Barry (1940) writes:

> What does seem defunct, at any rate in writing about politics, is the notion, introduced by Durkheim and elaborated by Parsons, that the way to explain some feature of a society is to show how it relates to other aspects of the society to form a functional whole—not to explore the way it came about or the reasons people have for maintaining it.[7]

The Image of Man

Thus the image of man becomes one of the central issues in the dispute, if not the central issue. Reference has already been made to the work of Peter Roche de Coppens on the ideal man in classical sociology. This will be given more extended discussion here, together with the views of Marx and Freud.

De Coppens maintains that social theory rests implicitly or explicitly on four basic sets of interrelated assumptions, or perspectives: (1) a theory of human nature, (2) a theory of human society, (3) a theory of the nature of history, and (4) a theory of the nature, scope, and purpose of sociology. He proceeds to examine these assumptions for each of four thinkers, widely regarded as founding fathers of modern sociology: Comte, Weber, Pareto, and Durkheim.

According to Comte, in its youth humanity was forced by natural necessity to labor to survive; thus it discovered and developed science and technology, which freed it from this fatality. In the course of unfolding knowledge and activity, humanity will reach a point, in Comte's vision, where science and labor are transcended, where the essence of human nature will be free to express itself fully in beauty, truth, and goodness. Toward the end Comte believed that he had become this ideal man, destined to become the priest of a new humanity.

For Durkheim, the ideal man is the goal of education and moralization. This person is content with what he is and what he has; he is adjusted to his sociocultural milieu and is in full harmony with the best of his *Zeitgeist*, being particularly sensitive to its noblest and highest aspirations. The highest psychic reality is the "hyperspirituality" of society. The ideal man is a child of his society in the same way that the traditional man is a child of God. Man needs ideals. Further, the great ideals contain not only the secret of the social order but also the blueprint for the unfolding and realization of man's personality; they contain the highest forms of psychic activity, or human consciousness (hyperspirituality), which he saw as the true essence and substance of humanity.

For Pareto man is basically a biological entity and an instinctive animal with no higher nature or potentialities. Hence he is eternally destined to remain an egocentric and selfish being, and society and human affairs are ruled by force and cunning, which should be used to personal advantage. Not surprisingly, in his own life Pareto retreated more and more into a detached pessimism.

Weber's ideal man was a *"Kulturmensch,"* a well-rounded universalist. His last great ideal was the genuinely charismatic or spiritual man. This person, through love and faith, has established a continuous inflow of spiritual inspiration in his own psyche and acts as a channel through which spiritual light and energies are released into his community and into the world.

For all four thinkers, whatever the ideal man might be, the way to transform humanity was by imitating his example. Man, they assumed, was rational, conscious, and subject to powerful external forces. It was the task of a social reformer to take hold of these social forces and to mold them in the direction of the development of the ideal. None of these thinkers, it must be emphasized, grasped the Freudian concept of inner forces. Their main emphasis, therefore, had to be on external rather than internal change.

Marx and the Alienated Man

In view of the importance of Marx for sociology, some notion of his image of the ideal man must be extracted from his writings. Marx concerned himself primarily with alienation and alienated man. It is only rarely that he offered some comments about what ideal man would be like.

In the *Economic and Philosophic Manuscripts* of 1844 he wrote:

> Man is directly a *natural* being. As a natural being and as a living natural being he is on the one hand furnished with *natural powers of life*; he is an *active* natural being. These forces exist in him as tendencies and abilities—as *impulses.* On the other hand, as a natural, corporeal, sensuous, objective being he is a *suffering*, conditioned and limited creature, like animals and plants. That is to say, the *objects* of his impulses exist outside him, as *objects* independent of him; yet these objects are *objects of his need*—essential *objects*, indispensable to the manifestation and confirmation of his essential powers. To say that man is a *corporeal*, living, real, sensuous, objective being full of natural vigor is to say that he has *real, sensuous, objects* as the objects of his being or of his life, or that he can only *express* his life in real, sensuous objects.[8]

Obviously these are not very profound remarks. Marx was preoccupied with alienated man, and he paid little attention to what man would be like ideally, once this alienation had disappeared. The alienation, furthermore, was a state imposed by external forces; in his famous phrase, it is not consciousness that determines society but society that determines consciousness. It also scarcely needs emphasis that his main concern was with the class struggle, both historically and currently for his age, including political activity to assure the victory of the proletariat. Once that victory was assured, the rest would follow automatically. It may well be that Marx's refusal to consider the nature of the ideal man contributed to the later chaos and extraordinarily destructive violence of the Communist countries.

The Freudian Revolution

Freud's image of man cannot be placed on a par with that of the sociologists we have mentioned. It was based on an intensive study of many individuals over a lifetime. It approached man not from his social situation (as the others did) but from his psychological situation. Confusion has arisen because Freud worked as a psychiatrist, dealing allegedly with "neurotic" men or with "Victorian" women. The subsequent development of psychoanalysis has revealed that he was dealing with all mankind.

A further unique feature of the Freudian image has already been alluded to: its connection with psychotherapy. Freud's discovery of psychotherapy was a real revolution in human affairs. It meant that he had uncovered deep-seated internal forces (the unconscious) governing men's lives, which could be brought under control by a specialized technique. At first it was applied only to a few aberrant individuals. Later it became clear that it can be applied to all humans.

Thus Freud's unprecedented attachment of personality theory to psychotherapy represents an extraordinary advance, not a weakness, as has commonly been supposed. Quite simply, it points to a new way of creating the ideal man. All the others recognized only external forces; hence the way to reach the ideal man was to change these external forces. As Mitzman observes, the central historical experience of our time has been the transformation of the dream of social and technological perfection into the nightmare of bureaucratic petrification and ecological apocalypse.[9] As the cynical French saying goes, *Plus ça change, plus c'est la même chose* (the more it changes the more it remains the same). Freud offered a way out of this impasse through his technique for uncovering the internal forces and directing them to a real change. Thus among other things psychoanalysis becomes a technique for social reform, as well as for individual reform (Fine, 1972; 1979a).

Interpretations of Freud in terms of the scientific jargon he used have entirely missed this central point. We have seen how analysts themselves have all too often bogged down in senseless fratricide or the polishing of minute technical details and have lost sight of the central vision. It is this central vision that must be used to illumine the problems of sociology, as well as of all the social sciences.

Alienation and Community

The central observation about the social malaise of the twentieth century that has come from sociology has been the widespread sense of alienation. Many different terms have been used: Durkheim's anomie, Marx's alienation, Riesman's loneliness, Tönnies's *Gesellschaft* (estranged community), Bleuler's schizoid personality, and many others. The observation has been confirmed and reconfirmed in myriad studies: Modern man is suffering from a sense of isolation from his community. What is in question is the causes of this alienation and the measures that should be taken to combat it. Inasmuch as sociologists have been preoccupied with social forces, their general answer has been: Restore a healthy community. After the bloody wars and revolutions of the twentieth century this answer does not seem so simple. Nazi Germany was a solidified community; Japan was so unified that many thousands of pilots were willing to go voluntarily to their deaths in suicidal attacks on American ships.

The Romance of Community

Apart from a few individual examples it is essential to examine the idea of community in much more detail. By and large sociologists tend to offer community as a central guiding beacon in the understanding of human behavior and the restoration or establishment of community as the essential form of therapy. Both of these assumptions are open to serious question.

Nisbet (1966) provides an excellent discussion of the role of community in the sociological tradition. He calls it "the most fundamental and far-reaching of sociology's unit-ideas." He then defines it (or more correctly misdefines it) as follows:

> By community I mean something that goes far beyond mere local community. The word, as we find it in much nineteenth and twentieth century thought, encompasses all forms of relationship which are characterized by a high degree of personal intimacy, emotional depth, moral commitment, social cohesion, and continuity in time.[10]

The main objection to this definition is that it refers to one ideal of a good community, not to community in general. It is one of the many cases in the social sciences where a moral judgment is concealed behind a definition. Its main emphasis is on cohesiveness, without regard to the purposes of this cohesiveness, the cost at which it is achieved, or the effect on the outsider. Even though the terms "in-group" and "out-group" have been household words since Sumner's famous *Folkways* (1906), they are ignored in the definition.

According to Nisbet, it was Tönnies in the latter part of the nineteenth century who gave community its lasting terminology: *Gemeinschaft* and *Gesellschaft*, two words as a rule used in their original German, thereby further confusing the issues. It would be simpler to speak of cohesive and noncohesive groups.

Tönnies himself defined the difference as follows:

> The theory of the Gesellschaft deals with the artificial construction of an aggregate of human beings which superficially resembles the Gemeinschaft insofar as the individuals live and dwell together peacefully. However in Gemeinschaft they remain essentially united in spite of all separating factors, whereas in Gesellschaft they are essentially separated in spite of all uniting factors.[11]

It becomes clear that the essential distinction between *Gemeinschaft* and *Gesellschaft* has to do with unity as contrasted with separateness. Other factors are completely disregarded.

As Nisbet shows, the emphasis throughout the history of sociology has been on the "good" community, or *Gemeinschaft*. Durkheim took some of the deepest states of individuality, such as religious faith, the categories of the mind, volition, and the suicidal impulse, and explained them in terms of what lies outside the individual: community and moral tradition.

Marx was obviously well aware of the deep-seated hatreds that separate the classes. But he recognized that "it is essential to educate the educator himself."[12] Yet he too went along, without thinking it through with particular care, with the general sociological idealization of community. In *The German Ideology* (1845–46) he wrote:

> Only in community [with others has each] individual the means of cultivating his gifts in all directions; only in the community, therefore, is personal freedom possible. In the previous substitutes for the community, in the State, etc. personal freedom has existed only for the in-

dividuals who developed within the relationships of the ruling class, and only insofar as they were individuals of this class. The illusory community, in which individuals have until now combined, always took an independent existence in relation to them, and was at the same time, since it was a combination of one class over against another, not only a completely illusory community, but a new fetter as well. *In the real community the individuals obtain their freedom in and through their association.* [13]

In more recent years (since World War II) this image of the good community has been applied therapeutically in the field of group therapy. Here too the assumption has been that somehow "the group heals."[*]

In a recent article Rosbeth Moss Kanter (1976) has made some telling points about the romance of community, which she says captured the American imagination in the late 1960s and early 1970s. After a historical survey showing that the image of communes and community is as old as man, she enumerates six commitment-building processes in strong communes: sacrifice, investment, renunciation, communion, mortification, and transcendence. Although it does not enter the center of her discussion, Kanter is one of the few sociologists who point to the dangers involved in community:

> [T]he danger of the highly organized community is that it loses its human feeling and leaders use their power toward destructive rather than constructive ends. . . . Communes also face the specter of the tyranny of group pressure for conformity.[14]

The Psychoanalytic Contribution: The Psychology of Community

Without denying in any way the real value and merit of many of the sociological observations on community, psychoanalysis enters in by pointing to the absence or paucity of psychological understanding of what makes people adhere to communities and how they really behave in them. Le Play's classic study of *The European*

---

[*]E.g., in *The Healing Community* (1974) Richard Almond describes a number of therapeutic groups, within and without our society. He finds that two guiding principles underlie the effectiveness and survival of these unusual organizations. One is *communitas*, a special sense of cohesive group life that makes all members fundamentally important, regardless of external status or role in the group. The other is *healing charisma*, an intense and therapeutic quality that pervades interactions among members of the group, especially in relation to the healing process. Here too other factors, such as sublimated homosexuality and the release of hostility against insider or outsider, are ignored.

Working Classes (1855; expanded and revised 1877–79), although based on a close examination of forty-five working-class families, likewise lacks any deep psychological understanding of what made them tick; such understanding was out of the question before modern psychology was established.

However, even before Freud many thinkers were cognizant of the dangers inherent in groups. Thus Sumner in his classic *Folkways* wrote:

> The relationship of comradeship and peace in the we-group and that of hostility and war towards other-groups are correlative to each other. The exigencies of war with outsiders are what makes peace inside, lest internal discord should weaken the we-group for war . . . sentiments are produced to correspond . . . brotherliness within, warlikeness without—all grow together, common products of the same situation. . . . Virtue consists in killing, plundering and enslaving outsiders.[15]

Sumner also emphasized the group's resistance to reform in its emphasis on irrational beliefs and customs, which he described in detail in his work. The significance of these insights for the theory of community was not appreciated by other sociologists; they were too psychological and failed to idealize the community as an inherently positive experience.

Freud made his initial contribution in *Totem and Taboo*, the cornerstone of cultural anthropology (1913), which has been widely misquoted and misunderstood by anthropologists and sociologists. The essential thesis is that the same kinds of psychological motives are to be found in all human societies. The central themes of incest and parricide are found everywhere, though they may be and are interpreted in different ways.

In *Group Psychology and the Analysis of the Ego* (1921) Freud used his new structural theory to make some comments about the psychology of groups. Groups are bound together by a common superego. This superego has the task of regulating the instinctual drives, particularly sexuality and aggression. Hence the relationship of every group to these two basic drives must be examined in detail.

Subsequently the psychology of groups (and community in general) has been examined in considerable detail by a host of theoreticians. Transferences, resistances, acting out, impulse release, impulse control, love, hate, and everything else are found in groups as well as individuals. The distinction between individual and group psychology, as Freud pointed out in 1921, is artificial. What happens in a group (and in any community) depends on the psychology of the members more than on anything else. There is no "group mind" or superordinate "society" or "culture" that exists independent of the individuals involved. One can, however—and this is all-important—speak of *group fantasies*, which take hold of and dominate the thinking of various groups. These may range from the relatively harmless group fantasies of working constructively for a socially acceptable purpose to delusional beliefs that justify the extermination or enslavement of millions of people.

The reflections of most of the sociologists and anthropologists who have discussed the idea of community rely heavily on historical reconstruction. Here the observations of the preceding chapter are pertinent. Traditional historians (which includes most of these thinkers) have seen history in terms of the march to victory of rational men who operated on the basis of conscious motives. Marx is no different in this respect: His main difference lies in his emphasis on the alienation of the vanquished or oppressed. This alienation is an old psychiatric concept; but Marx attributed it to the class struggle and cherished the illusory belief that the abolition of private property would end it once and for all.

Love Cultures and Hate Cultures: An Essential Distinction

The consistent application of psychoanalytic thinking to the nature of the community leads to an essential distinction between love cultures and hate cultures (see Chapter 3, p. 36). A love culture is one where the predominant mode of interrelationship among human beings comprises love, tenderness, affection, cooperation, and other positive feelings (what Rado called the "welfare emotions"). In the hate culture the predominant mode of interrelationship is one of hatred, competition, jealousy, envy, overachievement, and the like (negative or neurotic emotions). Although no culture is exclusively one or the other, the distinction is fundamental for the clarification of the psychology of any culture.

All cultures, as Freud showed, have had to struggle with feelings of love and hatred; in some one predominates, in others the other. Although hate cultures have been far more common, the significance of love as a liberating force in mankind should not be underestimated. There are cultures in which the concept of warfare is so foreign to the people's thinking that they cannot even understand it when it is described to them. Ruth Benedict (1934) quotes Rasmussen, who told of the blankness with which the Eskimos met his explanation of what warfare is. Benedict herself says that she tried to talk of warfare to the Mission Indians of California, but it was impossible.

Margaret Mead struck a powerful blow in the sexual revolution of the twentieth century when she described the sexual freedom of the Samoans and their relative freedom from guilt and hatred. In the old Samoa there were, however, many expressions of hatred. It is interesting that the Samoans have been able, according to Mead, to absorb the positive values of Western civilization and resist the negative ones.

Of primitive peoples in whom aggression is virtually absent the Ifaluk in the Western Pacific are probably best known. Spiro (Spiro and Burrows, 1953), who investigated them, found that the only expression of aggression was their belief in malevolent ghosts. Otherwise the outstanding sentiment in their ethos is the feeling of kindliness. Obedience, to his surprise, was exacted by love rather than by reward or punishment.

Within our own society the Hutterites have been seen as an instance of a love culture (Eaton and Weill, 1955). In the early 1950s a team of a sociologist, a psychiatrist, and two clinical psychologists examined every member of the Hutterite group. At that time there were 8,542 persons living in ninety-eight hamlets or colonies. Only nine persons were discovered who had ever had any of the classical symptoms of schizophrenia, which has been associated with isolation from the community. On the other hand, depression was not infrequent, with a rate of 9.3 per 1,000 in those aged fifteen or older, though the severity of the depression was not clear. In a century there have been no homicides, suicides, severe psychoses, or divorces in this community. Of course, this cohesiveness has been achieved by eliminating any questioning of religion and by avoidance of any advanced occupations; thus all professionals (lawyers, doctors, and others) come from outside the community.

With regard to feelings that are found within various cultures, William Goode (1959) has done considerable research in the subject of love. He summarizes his main conclusions as follows:

1. Falling in love is a universal psychodynamic potential in the human being. Most human beings in all societies are capable of it. It

is not, as some anthropologists have asserted, a psychological abnormality about as common as epilepsy.

2. We must look for the ways in which this potential is handled to prevent a disruption of the family structure.

3. Far from being uncommon, love relationships are a basis of the final choice of mate among a large minority of the societies of the earth.

By stressing the universal significance of love and the tension between its personal and social aspects, Goode has made an important contribution. In the light of his work the meticulous, detailed dissection of the love lives of millions of people by psychoanalysis carries even more weight. Goode's work points to one way in which a truly fruitful collaboration between the social and the individual-psychological should be carried out.

In contrast to Goode, the analysis of feelings by sociologists like Simmel leaves out an essential feature of the whole experience. In his 1923 essay on faithfulness and gratitude, for example, Simmel overstresses the social aspect. Thus he says that "faithfulness is significant as a sociological form of the second order, as it were, as the instrument of relations which already exist and endure." In this as in his comment that "such a term as 'faithful love' is somewhat misleading"[16] Simmel confuses the individual and the social. It is certainly true that human relationships require some affective bond if they are to endure, but this bond may vary widely, from outright hatred to deep love. In ordinary language "faithful" does indeed have the double meaning of an inner feeling and an outer form of behavior; it is essential that these two meanings not be confused.

This error is typical of much sociological writing. If something is socially acceptable, it is argued, certain feelings must go along with it; thus marriage implies love, and lasting relationships imply faithfulness. This ignores the psychological observation that any form of behavior may be determined on the basis of a variety of inner feelings. The confusion of the social and the individual is a continuation or an expression of the erroneous behavioristic view of human nature (see Chapter 4). It also underlies the arguments about sociological interpretation. As we have seen, the typical sequence is: establish the social record, observe the psychology, and make the inference that the social is the cause of the psychological. We have every reason to believe that this sequence, as a general proposition, is erroneous; it leaves too many variables out of account. The whole situation calls for a much more meticulous examination of the concept of social causation, which is the subject of Chapter 12.

The Mental Health of the Contemporary World: Community and Reality

The psychoanalytic position on community or group behavior has never been clearly formulated, largely because of the political struggle in this country between the "Freudians" and the "culturalists." Since the significance of the group was stressed by the culturalists while the significance of the individual experience was emphasized by the Freudians, it seemed preordained that never the twain would meet. But as the author has shown in detail elsewhere (Fine, 1979a), the split has been maintained for political purposes and leads to nothing but scientific confusion if maintained to the extreme. The outlines of a clear theory exist in the various psychoanalytic treatises. They could be formulated as follows:

1. Group formation is part and parcel of the formation of the self-image and identity of any individual. The earliest group (genetically) is the family. From there the child proceeds to peer groups, clearly demarcated by age level, thus the nursery school, the elementary school, cub scouts (or the equivalent) at about age eight, pre-adolescent unisex groupings (now changing to mixed sexes), adolescent gangs and parties, and so on, depending on the structure of the culture.

2. The meaning of the group to the individual, and of the individual to the group, cannot be easily summed up in any glib formula. A group is an aggregate of individuals, and the nature of the group depends on the individuals that compose it. No inferences can be drawn from group formation as such without reference to its individual components.

3. Groups may vary from constructive to destructive to meaningless or peripheral. The inner dynamics of a group are complex, again depending on the inner dynamics of the individual members. Cohesive groups have a common superego, but cohesiveness must not be equated with desirability.

4. Accordingly the value system of a group must be carefully examined. Many groups, both historically and currently, have been highly destructive of their members, their enemies, or both. The value system is more important than the cohesiveness.

5. Groups may be used for therapeutic purposes. When they are so used, evaluation of the outcome is a complex problem. As with group formation, it may be constructive, destructive, or meaningless (see Chapter 15).

6. The primary contribution of sociological research to the understanding of groups lies in an elucidation of social forces; the primary contribution of psychoanalysis, in the elucidation of inner dynamic forces. *Neither can be properly understood without the other.* Inasmuch as the social element has been stressed much more heavily by the social sciences, psychoanalysis serves as a counterbalance. This should not be interpreted to mean that the psychodynamic factor is always basic. The question of social causation remains difficult (see Chapter 12).

7. On the current scene one of the great advances that has resulted from psychoanalytic thought has been the spread of psychotherapy. As stressed elsewhere, the patient population has shifted from the maladjustment neurosis to the adjustment neurosis, that is, to the entire population.

8. Inasmuch as the evaluation of groups depends on the inner dynamics of its members, theoretically the degree of disturbance of these members must be taken into account in any conclusions reached about these groups. In general, this has not been done by sociologists; there is very little material on the psychology of the different social classes. For example, Warner in his classic *Yankee City* (1963) does not even list psychology in the index.

9. Changes in the social system can be brought about either by changing the individual psychodynamics through psychotherapy or by changing the social structure through revolution or evolution, or both. In this way psychoanalysis, in addition to being a theoretical system of psychology, becomes a method of social reform as well.

Studies of Mental Health and Psychotherapy

Although Freud had realized from an early date that he really had all mankind as his patient, it took a long time for this realization to become part of the make-up of the average intellectual. The process is still incomplete, still meets with strong resistance, and is still going on. Just as the recognition of the ubiquity of madness marks the need for a decisive change in historical writing, so appreciation of the wide incidence of mental disturbance requires extensive rethinking of all research done in sociology and social forces. Durkheim's "social facts" cannot be adequately understood without reference to the mental health or sickness of the population being described.

The events of World War II, coupled with the growth of psychoanalytic knowledge, brought home the significance of mental illness as never before. Two mad dictators ruled much of the world and brought disaster to the lives of hundreds of millions. In the American army a large percentage of the draftees were rejected for mental reasons, and a considerable percentage of those discharged from the service as unable to meet the needs of war were neuropsychiatric cases.

In line with these observations, the field of social psychiatry was born. One of its earliest accomplishments was to offer some quantitative estimate of the degree of disturbance in America. This was the contribution of the Midtown Sudy, originally published in 1962, then in revised and enlarged form in 1978.

Two important findings emerged from the Midtown Study: The overall percentage of Manhattan residents who could be considered "well" was only 18.5 percent, leaving 81.5 percent of the population regarded as emotionally disturbed, 23.4 percent of them fairly seriously incapacitated.[17] Second, emotional disturbance varied inversely with socioeconomic status, thus providing evidence for the theory of the "culture of poverty" (see pp. 142–143).

The authors reported that the findings were viewed by many as "staggering in magnitude, and of dubious credibility."[18] Subsequent replications yielded widely varying figures. On careful examination, however, it appeared that the percentages of emotionally impaired individuals found depended very strongly on the methods of investigation used and on the assumptions guiding the research (see Chapter 6). These variable figures show once more how social scientists often become tehnicians without vision, producing material that is biased, not relevant to the main theses, and poorly researched. Thus the Baltimore study, done shortly after the Rennie study, found a mental disorder frequency of 10.9 percent. But upon closer examination it was found that the investigation was conducted largely by internists, and on patients who came to the hospital. By contrast, the Midtown Study was carried out by trained mental health professionals and through intensive personal individualized visits to the home.

The methodological innovations of the Midown Study were of great importance. The authors list five:

1. a shift in focus from an inpatient aggregate to a large sample of a community's general population
2. in primary mode of data gathering, a change from census-type counts of institutional case records to multihour, face-to-face interviews with sampled subjects
3. a shift from incidence to prevalence as the more defensible measure of frequencies of mental morbidity
4. a turn toward classifying mental health on an innovative, inclusive gradient of degrees of symptom formation instead of reliance on psychiatry's embattled diagnostic categories (see Chapter 5).
5. in breadth of statistical analysis, a shift from the traditional cross-tabulation of one or more potential predictors of mental health toward controlled analysis of up to five such explanatory variables simultaneously.[19]

The Shift to Psychotherapy as a Means of Social Reform

The Midtown Study is but one of many instances of a major shift in social thought that occurred in the aftermath of World War II. There has been a change to a feeling that somehow the problems of society cannot be solved by any kind of large-scale social change as long as the inner dynamics of the individuals involved remain unchanged (Fine, 1972). This feeling has been fed by two sources: first the disillusionment with the Communist countries, which have practiced large-scale violence, mass murder, and genocide on an unprecedented scale, and second the growth of a new mental profession that is capable of handling large numbers of troubled individuals by therapy.

In the years just before the Midtown Study was launched, Srole estimates that an annual total of one million Americans had one or more contacts (as a patient) with a mental health professional in a hospital, clinic, or office.[20] A decade later the number had doubled, by 1970 it was doubled again, and by 1975 it probably reached a total of five million. This represents a jump in twenty-five years from 0.7 percent to 2.4 percent of the national population.

Again this phenomenal growth in psychotherapeutic services must be evaluated not in terms of sickness (the medical model) but in terms of the growth of awareness (the philosophical model). Crime, alcoholism, suicide, divorce, violence, discontent, and many other social facts previously attributed to the community as such are now seen as due to a combination of social and psychological causation, both of which must be tackled if any real change is to effected.

The growth in psychotherapy will be discussed in more detail Chapter 13. Suffice it to say here that neurosis is not largely an American phenomenon. There is no reason to believe that the mental health of the rest of the Western world, the developing countries, almost all of which are ruled by violence, or the Communist countries, which maintain slavery in disguised form (*Gulag Archipelago*), or exert overpowering pressures for conformity (Lifton, 1969), is any better. Quite the opposite: There is every reason to believe that these countries are much worse off and that their reliance on social amelioration rather than individual change produces new and even worse problems in the long run.

Class Structure (SES)

In the years following World War II most American sociologists assumed or at least hypothesized in their studies the strategic function of class position, or socioeconomic status (SES), in the structuring or functioning of a wide variety of behavior patterns, attitudes, and values. These correlates include power, elitism, social disturbance, social mobility, organizational membership and participation, religious affiliation and belief, dating customs and marital choice, marital discord and divorce, sexual tastes and practices, consumption patterns and use of leisure, educational performance and opportunity, delinquency and crime, physical and mental illness, prejudice and discrimination, modal personality and character, political attitudes and behavior, and many other aspects of human behavior. Thus the tendency has been to see class or SES as the principal causative factor in human psychology and conduct.

Without denying in any way the significance of these sociological contributions, it is still pertinent to note that almost all the variables listed above, and many others, are psychological in nature. Furthermore, the relationship between SES and any behavior pattern is rarely complete; there are always many exceptions and many deviant resolutions. Thus some members of the lower classes are deeply religious, while some are completely agnostic; some have virtually no barriers to sexual experience, others have the most severe sanctions against such experience. As with the anthropological findings on different cultures, the differences, even among classes with a shared background, are as wide as the similarities.

Two other factors emerge as objections to the ascription of causative effect to class status. First of all, the United States, or the capitalistic system in general, has shown more fluidity in movement from one class to another than had been anticipated by scholars in previous generations, particularly Marx and the Marxists. Second, social sanctions have to be evaluated in the light of the amount of force that the legally constituted, or illegally constituted, authorities are prepared to use. In the case of delinquency and crime, for instance, the kinds and degrees of punishment meted out by the society play a significant role in the subsequent behavior. Third, as Parsons in particular never tired of pointing out, social sanctions are internalized in the superego, which then becomes as much of a real force as the external pressures. And the superego is a highly variable entity, even within the same person.

In addition, when men become aware of the social forces impinging on them, as they inevitably do, what are they going to do about it? Here, as noted in Chapter 6, the social scientist becomes a social critic and an advocate of social reform. Then the reform movement becomes as much a social-psychological force as the social behavior, thereby complicating the picture immeasurably. Studies that have demonstrated inequality of opportunity among the different classes have led to reform movements to increase opportunity, such as education, housing, welfare, and other reforms. Attempts to remedy inequalities have in turn led to a variety of reactions, some anticipated, many unanticipated. Again the complex nature of social causation looms here, without any simple solution.

Finally, the most significant question arises in terms of consciousness: Does class status operate impersonally or in terms of the individual's awareness of it? Related to this is the observation that the belief systems of men have a powerful determining influence on their behavior, regardless of how true or false these beliefs are. For example, Americans will generally resent the imputation that they belong to the "lower class," but they will accept designation as the "working class."

The Psychology of the Class Struggle

The central significance of the class struggle throughout history and on the current scene has been one of the fundamental tenets of Marxist thought. Marx contended that the hostility of one class to another was an inevitable accompaniment of this struggle. The only way out was to overthrow the existing governments by force and establish the dictatorship of the proletariat. "The proletarians have nothing to lose but their chains. They have a world to win."[21]

Intellectually, Marx's thesis can be faulted on two counts. First he oversimplifies history, with the main stress on victory, just like the traditional bourgeois historians. Second, and more important, the notion is put forth that hostility or hatred is a result of the ownership of private property; abolish private property and you will abolish hatred. In the light of what has happened in the communistic revolutions of the twentieth century this seems like a gruesome joke. In both cases the psychological roots of hostility and hatred are almost entirely disregarded.

It is paradoxical that Marx's own thesis that society determines consciousness and not consciousness society should lead to the conclusion that the communistic societies formed since World War II have produced an enormous amount of hatred in their citizens. Because of this obvious conclusion the societies involved have had to go to great lengths to deny the wholesale violence committed. Thus history is falsified, and sociology as a discipline virtually disappears.

A more careful reading of history would suggest that in some cultures the class struggle has been intense, in others mild. These variations are similar to those seen in the Oedipus complex, which may also vary from the most intense violence to the deepest love. In both cases social and psychological forces must be considered to arrive at a true picture of the stituation.

Another quandary faced by Marxist theory has been the fact that the first large-scale revolution broke out in Russia, where it was least expected; in fact it contradicted Marx's predictions. Likewise the peaceful resolution of industry–labor conflicts, which has been the hallmark of Western capitalism, was unforeseen by Marx. Germany, long the most violent of countries, unforeseeably became the country with the greatest degree of cooperation between labor and management in the post-war world. Sweden, which sent one-fifth of its people to America in the nineteenth century, gradually turned to a social-democratic form of government, which has ruled for many decades. These and many other examples show that human beings may become aware of the social forces involved, change their psychology, and give a different turn to the social movements in which they are taking part. The inevitability of *any* historical or sociological event is questionable because of the possible change of mind of the participants.

Durkheim's Work on Suicide

Many sociologists regard the work of Emile Durkheim on suicide (1897) as a model of sociological research. Thus Lowry and Rankin in their textbook on sociology state:

> Durkheim's study sets the stage for the work presented throughout this book. It is a model of the scientific method for investigation. . . . It points out clearly that acts which might seem to reflect individuality are to be understood, in large part, as determined or influenced by a social pattern.[22]

What Durkheim did was to examine the suicide rates for different countries at different times. His research showed that these rates vary greatly from one time to the next and from one society to the next. They are higher in Protestant countries than in Catholic. Until recently the rates were lower for Jews then for other ethnic groups. They are higher in periods of social distress than in periods of social cohesiveness. He enumerates three types of suicide, all related to the person's attitude toward his culture: egoistic, altruistic, and anomic. His numerical results certainly reflect differences in the social structure, although there have been some changes since.

But these changes do not affect the chief flaw in Durkheim's argument (and that of the sociologists who emulate him). Suicide rates are invariably low, even in times of the greatest social distress. The highest rate Durkheim recorded was 334 per million inhabitants in Saxony in the period 1874–78.[23] If social conditions really determine suicide in any sense, why is the absolute number always so small? This question, which any psychologist would think of immediately, is completely ignored by Durheim. In other words, most of the empirical data are left out, since his thesis lies elsewhere. Durkheim explains his rationale as follows:

> We do not accordingly intend to make as nearly complete an inventory as possible of all the conditions affecting the origin of individual suicides, but merely examine those on which the definite fact that we

have called the social suicide-rate depends. The two questions are obviously quite distinct, whatever relation may nevertheless exist between them. Certainly many of the individual conditions are not general enough to affect the relation between the total number of voluntary deaths and the population. They may perhaps cause this or that separate individual to kill himself, but not give society as a whole a greater or lesser tendency to suicide. As they do not depend on a certain state of social organization, they have no social repercussions. *Thus they concern the psychologist, not the sociologist.*[24]

In this way Durkheim reasserts his sharp distinction between sociology and psychology. It is clear here that he is still relying on the nineteenth-century image of man as rational, conscious, and subject to external forces. In *Suicide* he seeks to establish the external forces and locate them in the constitution of society. By his own admission this leads to oversimplification of the problem. Further, it ignores the modern image of man that has grown since Freud. Suicide seems a particularly poor choice of subject for sociologists, for the rates are so low that it plays a negligible role in the constitution of society. If it is taken as an example of a social force independent of psychology, it is one that has almost no impact on the whole culture.

The editor of the English translation of Durkeim's book on suicide, George Simpson, comments that the chief advances in our knowledge of the subject since Durkheim have come from actuarial statistics and psychoanalytic psychiatry. Neither has been able to formulate any thoroughgoing, systematic, and consistent hypothesis concerning the causes of suicide, which is what Durkheim is after. Simpson faults the modern scholars for failing to formulate such general hypotheses; he does not recognize that they have punched such deep holes in Durkheim's theory that it falls apart. Whatever the social conditions involved, the motives for suicide can never be properly understood without considering the individual. Put another way, sociology can never be divorced from psychology.

Summary Comments on Sociology

Our main thesis throughout has been that the psychoanalytic vision sheds an irreplaceable light on all the social sciences. In sociology, three questions are involved: (1) the social facts, (2) the psychology involved, and (3) the causal inferences that can be drawn. Because of their adherence to a nineteenth-century image of man, in which inner dynamic forces were essentially ignored because they had not yet been discovered, sociologists have tended to place their greatest emphasis on external social forces. Two of these were considered in some detail: community and class structure. In both there has been a strong tendency to see the social force as causative, without regard to individual psychology. In this way an essential methodological flaw has crept into much contemporary sociological thinking. This is not to say that much other thinking has avoided this methodological error; when it does, it becomes a psychoanalytic sociology, in which both social and psychological forces are considered. The social facts remain the same in all approaches, but the causative inferences will vary widely.

From a positive, constructive point of view, it is always essential to research both the social and the psychological factors. However, when that is done properly sociology loses its distinctive characteristic and becomes another branch of psychology. What is at issue is the psychology of the human being in the social sphere. Some social forces will submerge the individual, some will be on a par with him, some will be submerged by him. Generalizations are impossible. Instead, a research strategy is indicated.

Anthropology and the Mirages of "Culture"

In the science of anthropology, the dispassionate observer is immediately confronted with a peculiar dilemma. How did anthropology get to its present state, where it embraces in the usual academic department cultural anthropology, physical anthropology, linguistics, and archaeology? Offhand, cultural anthropology would seem to be the study of other peoples, which is psychology; physical anthropology is a branch of physiology, including medicine; linguistics is the study of human language, thus a branch of psychology too, and archaeology is a branch of history. It would seem that, like Topsy, anthropology just "growed." As has been noted, Boas once said frankly that the subject matter of anthropology was a matter of historical accident.

Etymologically, anthropology is the science of man. Today this definition would apply more to psychology. Of its four customary branches, psychoanalysis does not concern itself with two: physical anthropology and archaeology. A third, linguistics, is increasingly being given independent status and will be considered later (Chapter 11). It is with cultural anthropology that this section will be primarily concerned.

ON THE NATURE OF CULTURE

For a number of centuries thinkers have exerted themselves to offer a definition of culture. Primarily the idea has been that culture must be something superorganic, something over and above the individuals involved. The question then is: What is it that makes culture superorganic?

Innumerable attempts have been made to answer this question. In their summary book Kroeber and Kluckhohn (1952) enumerate no fewer than 164 different definitions. Clearly no agreement has been reached in this field.

The attempt to define culture is a continuation of the age-old wish to find the "one" unifying underlying factor in human affairs, on the basis of which everything else is to be explained. Hegel stressed "spirit"; Marx stressed the class struggle; Durkheim emphasized collective representations.

Different terms have been coined to highlight various aspects of the definitions: cultural diffusion, culture traits, culture patterns, culture areas, culture circles, and so forth. The latest in this long line is cultural materialism (Harris, 1979), which states that human social life is a response to the practical problems of earthly existence, and sociobiology (Wilson, 1975), which maintains that human social life can be explained by means of Darwinian and neo-Darwinian evolutionary biology. Like much of what has been written about culture, these two points of view take one aspect of human existence and blow it up to include the whole—again the wish to find "the one" unifying factor.

Thus the concept of culture does not differ particularly from that of a larger community or the more commonsense image of society. Of this there can of course be no doubt, and the contributions of many anthropologists have helped to clarify what is common to all cultures and what is divergent. Nor can there be any doubt that cultural forces, in some hitherto unexplained way, exert a powerful influence on the individual. What the nature of this influence is and how these forces operate create the area under dispute.

Culture and the Individual

Pre-Freudian anthropologists could always see that the societies they studied produced different kinds of individuals. They went through the usual attempts at explanation: evolution, primitivism, tradition (the "force of custom"), magic, economic determinism, and the like. Not until Freud wrote *Totem and Taboo* in 1913 did anthropologists really acquire a psychology that could cope with the myriad customs that had been described and a methodology that could get at the relevant facts in any culture.

Paradoxically, *Totem and Taboo* has had a checkered history among anthropologists. It sometimes seems as if contemporary anthropologists have to take a solemn vow first not to read this book carefully and second to misquote it by emphasizing the discarded primal horde–murder theory. Harris's otherwise excellently researched work *The Rise of Anthropological Theory* (1968) is a good example. His reasoning is worth some extended discussion, for it hits at the roots of the problem.

First Harris notes that psychologizing is a deeply rooted habit among cultural anthropologists.[25] Then, after reviewing a number of the standard studies (Mead, Benedict, Malinowski, and others) in which field workers had provided ample confirmation of the basic psychoanalytic hypotheses, he attacks Freud's book as "representative . . . of the worst form of evolutionary speculation."[26] He fails to observe what others have since stressed (see Fortes, discussion pp. 25–26), that Freud was the first to bring any real order into the vast mass of undigested anthropological data, that he dealt with the best field material available to him, and further, that the thrust of the book lies in its psychological framework: the concepts that totem and taboo in primitive cultures can best be explained by their relationship to the two aspects of the Oedipus complex, that incest is a powerful drive in all cultures,* and that in general psychological forces operative in our culture can be found in all cultures, thereby establishing the essential unity of man.

One of the most basic and most fruitful Freudian methodological approaches, looking for the parallels among primitives, psychotics, dreamers, and children, is dismissed out of hand. Dreams and psychosis are not even listed in the index. It is clear that this is sim-

---

*Incidentally, it may be noted that Freud's treatment of the incest taboo is still among the best in any literature and that Harris's discussion of the topic is woefully incomplete and superficial in the extreme.

ply an aspect of psychology with which Harris, like many other anthropologists, is not familiar. The acceptance of many psychoanalytic positions by anthropologists is tossed off as due to the "irresistible lure of Freudianism,"[27] but no reason is given as to why Freudianism should be so irresistible. Harris does quote Malinowski as confirmatory of Freud (1923): "By my analysis, I have established that Freud's theories not only roughly correspond to human psychology, but that they follow closely the modification in human nature brought about by various constitutions of Society."[28] By way of summary Harris writes:

> The meeting of anthropology and psychoanalysis has produced a rich harvest of ingenious functional hypotheses in which psychological mechanisms can be seen as intermediating the connection between disparate parts of culture. Psychoanalysis, however, had little to offer cultural anthropology by way of scientific methodology. In this respect the meeting of the two disciplines tended to reinforce the inherent tendencies toward uncontrolled, speculative and histrionic generalizations which each in its own sphere had cultivated as part of its professional license.[29]

In the next chapter learning theories of the type espoused by Clark Hull and, to a lesser extent, Skinner receive high praise as "the outcome of a deliberate attempt by operationally minded psychologists to raise the standards of intersubjectivity and verifiability."[30] There is no recognition that behaviorism is largely a catastrophic blunder or that the claim of learning theorists to be the leading representatives of scientific psychology must be dismissed as entirely without foundation.

Thus the objection to psychoanalysis is not based on lack of empirical data or even inadequate theorizing. It is based on the assumption that behaviorism (or learning theory) is a more scientific form of psychology than psychoanalysis. Harris does not assume any superorganic theory of culture, implying that anthropology is after all another version of psychology, that of primitive peoples.

Regardless of the strictures of many contemporary anthropologists, it may be taken as well established that different cultures turn out different kinds of personalities and that these differences can be scientifically investigated and understood by the techniques deriving from Freud's original work. *Totem and Taboo* remains one of the cornerstones of anthropological theory because for the first time it provided a sound psychological basis for comprehending the wide variety of customs and traditions found throughout the world.

Anthropology and Psychology

A more central question arises with regard to anthropology: If culture is not a superorganic entity (and virtually no anthropologist today holds that it is) and if culture and personality represent an intricate psychosocial network, how are we to delineate the difference between the two disciplines? Theoretically what the cultural anthropologist does is investigate the psychology of other (primitive or preliterate) peoples. If again, as seems well established, there is no essential difference between this psychology and the psychology of the civilized peoples, then anthropology is simply psychology in another form.

The main reason this has been overlooked is that the anthropologist still holds to the nineteenth-century image of man (as in Lévi-Strauss, for example) as conscious, rational, and driven by powerful external forces. From that perspective, the main job of the anthropologist is to clarify the nature of these powerful external forces in other societies. But if we move on to the more sophisticated image of man provided by psychoanalytic psychology, the role of the external forces becomes much more complex.

Finally, it may be noted that much of the anthropological animosity to psychoanalysis has been based on a serious misunderstanding of what psychoanalysis has had to say about social and biological forces. As long ago as 1945 Fenichel wrote:

> The instinctual needs are the raw material formed by the social influences; and it is the task of a psychoanalytic sociology to study the details of this shaping. . . . Different "biological constitutions" contain manifold possibilities; yet they are not realities but potentialities. It is experience, that is, the cultural conditions, that transforms potentialities into realities, that shapes the real mental structure of man by forcing his instinctual demands in certain directions, by favoring some of them and blocking others, and even by turning parts of them against the rest.[31]

Chapter 9

The Myth of "Economic Man"

ECONOMICS IS WIDELY REGARDED as the most highly developed of the social sciences. As Sidney Weintraub comments in his compendium *Modern Economic Thought* (1977), there has been a century of advance since 1950, and economics is generally considered to be a concerted discipline. Economists have become identified as specialists with expertise in studies affecting the daily life of mankind. At times Marshall's dream that through economics poverty might be alleviated seems closer to realization that ever before. In such a scientific enterprise psychology seems to have no place.

And yet many voices of dissent are heard. In a recent work Benjamin Ward (1979) presents the three ideal worlds of classical economics liberal, radical, and conservative. He argues that the evidence available could be adequately interpreted in terms of any one of these three ideal world views, so that none is really conclusive. He then adds:

> Surely the major implication is that economics as presently taught in American universities fails a fundamental test of scholarly objectivity. . . . If ideologies are powerful, our scholarly approach has been transformed into a system of indoctrination in liberal values and how to use such values in dealing with economic policy and the interpretation of society.[1]

The mathematical and statistical treatment of economic problems in most textbooks (including Weintraub's compendium) is imposing indeed. To a nonmathematician it looks like absolute proof that economics is a finished science. Yet to one who looks behind the equations at the underlying assumptions the mathematical facade becomes no more than that—a façade. Ward is not alone in his charge that economic science is nothing but a form of indoctrination—Keynes, Galbraith, Heilbroner, Weisskopf, Lowe, and many others have insisted that it is a grave mistake to ignore ideology in economic discussion. And if ideology is important, psychology must also be important.

The Idea of "Economic Man"

Behind the formulas of the economists lies the assumption of an "economic man."

> The "economic man" is not a "social animal," and economic individualism excludes society in the proper human sense. Economic relations are *impersonal*. The social organization dealt with in economic theory is best pictured as a number of Crusoes interacting through the markets exclusively. . . . The relation is theoretically like the "silent trade" of some barbarian peoples.[2]

This "impersonal economic man," who is not a social animal but a kind of Robinson Crusoe, has been the dominant image in the minds of many economists. The reader will immediately recognize, in virtually prototypical form, the nineteenth-century image of man that has been much discussed before. In economics it seems more "intuitively" obvious than in other fields, for man must take measures to meet his economic needs or perish. Hence he is likely, it is argued, to be rational and conscious, to seek out the powerful external forces impinging on him, and to act in an adult, sensible manner. And in some instances he does behave in this way. But in others he does the exact opposite. Psychology cannot be avoided. The "economic man" is a myth (Lowe, 1965). Or, more precisely, economists have based their science on an inadequate image of man. How this came about is highly pertinent to our main theses.

On the Ideology of Economics

Weintraub's *Handbook* contains a discussion of ideology in which Warren J. Samuels emphasizes that there is considerable disagreement over the possibility, the actuality, and the content of a nonideological economic science. "Economists are generally uncomfortable with the question of ideology . . . for the problem challenges professional identity and belief in the discipline's collection of tools, concepts, research procedures and analyses."[3]

A number of factors point to the need to consider psychological questions more carefully than has traditionally been done by economists, who, as Samuels notes, find their professional identity challenged. The situation sounds familiar to us from the discussion of the other social sciences: Psychology, particularly of the psychoanalytic variety, disturbs customary grooves; questions the assumptions on which mathematical, statistical, or empirical data are collected; and forces a complete rethinking of the fundamentals of every science. This has been the case with economics as well.

A number of factors operate against the acceptance of economics as a mathematically exact science. First of all, traditional theory, of whatever variety, has failed over and over again to predict economic events. From Adam Smith's fantasy of the "invisible hand" guiding economic destinies to Keynesian and post-Keynesian governmental regulation, economic problems have remained unsolved. The energy crisis beginning in 1978 is one of many instances where economists have simply been unable to control all the forces involved in such a complex problem, nor does anyone have the confidence that they could on their own resolve the problem.

Second, the same observation made about the other social sciences holds for economics. An entirely different kind of economics exists in the Soviet Union and other Communist countries. How could two such entirely different economic systems operate side by side? Clearly the Communist countries have rejected all of the cardinal tenets of Western economics and still have some kind of economy going.

Third, there is the constant change in theory over the years. Heilbroner has documented the fact that these changes embody different philosophical assumptions and views of the world, and that further they all contain a variety of psychological hypotheses that will not stand up under close scrutiny.

And finally there are many direct psychological questions involved in economics that have been largely ignored by the traditional scholars. Among contemporary economists Galbraith has particularly called attention to the fact that economists have largely neglected the problem of motivation, both in work and in consumption. Many others have pointed out that consumption, particularly when leisure is available, is not nearly as simple as the classical economists made it out to be. Still others (such as Weisskopf) have shown how classical economics avoids the problem of deep-seated alienation in modern society.

Psychological Factors in the History of Economic Thought

As ordinarily presented, the history of economic thought offers up a wide variety of theories about the operations of the economy and the market place. Almost always psychology is avoided. Again, as in the other social sciences, this situation is familiar (see particularly Chapter 7 on history) and derives from the incorrect image of man.

Heilbroner (1973) and earlier Lowe (1965) have been particularly cogent in clarifying the psychological assumptions inherent in all economic theory. In fact, as Heilbroner unrolls the panorama, what emerges is a history of psychological theories applied to the economic scene.

The history of economics as a separate discipline does not really begin until the end of the eighteenth century, with the publication of Adam Smith's *The Wealth of Nations* in 1776. What happened before then? We discover that the profit motive, which Smith and subsequent theoreticians assumed to be part of "human nature," is only as old as modern man. In the Middle Ages the Church taught that "no Christian ought to be a merchant."[4] Not until the eighteenth century was the world that had prohibited merchants from carrying unsightly bundles, had worried over "just" prices, and had insisted on carrying on in its fathers' footsteps on the wane.

It was then that "economic man" was born—a pale wraith of a creature who follows his adding-machine brain wherever it leads him. This was the economic man glorified by Adam Smith.

Guided by self-interest, economic man makes only rational choices. Accordingly he is led by the law of supply and demand. The market is central; leave it alone, and it will be self-regulated by the principle of competition. Capital will accumulate, profits will rise, wages will increase, and a veritable Utopia will result. The workings of society are guided by an "invisible hand," which cannot fail the welfare of mankind. Faulty though it is, Smith's reasoning is still repeated almost verbatim by many orators who praise the virtues of traditional capitalism.

After Smith a number of major and minor works made a profound impact on men's minds. Thomas Malthus's 1798 *Essay on Population* for the first time signaled the danger of. overpopulation, a danger even more acutely felt today. David Ricardo, in *Principles of Political Economy* of 1817, saw the economic world as a tragic system in which the landlords would eventually destroy the capitalists. The Utopian socialists rebelled against the idea that industrial life, with its squalor and depravity, was the only and inevitable social arrangement. Their happiest hunting ground was in the United States, where at one time in the nineteenth century there were at least 178 actual Utopian groups, with memberships ranging from fifteen to nine hundred.[5] All of them foundered on human passions and disappeared. John Stuart Mill, in *Principles of Political Economy*, 1848, after diligent study of the subject over a period of thirty years, discovered that economists had entirely neglected the problem of distribution, which lifted the whole economic debate from the stifling realm of impersonal and inevitable law and brought it back into the arena of ethics and morality.

But after Smith the man who made the most powerful impression on the world was Karl Marx. For Marx, as for Smith, economic man remained—impersonal and subject to inexorable laws of history. These laws dictated that inevitably capitalism must destroy itself and unknowingly breed its own successor. Violent revolution was the only effective way to produce real historical change; the other socialists he decried as Utopian, men who failed to realize that change can be brought about only by revolutionary means, since no ruling class in history has ever given up its privileges without a fight.

Economists have been quick to point out that Marx's economics was all wrong. Surplus value as the basis of capitalism could not be confirmed, because his mathematics were incorrect. Historical change is not inevitable. And so on.

Yet, whatever sober scientists may say, the lure of his vision persists for many men. For it presents a simple picture of the world that anyone can grasp: The bad capitalists will do anything to preserve their power; the good workers are increasingly ground down into a life of degradation and misery (the *"Lumpenproletariat"*); capitalism should collapse of its own weight; there should be a revolution; the workers have nothing to lose but their chains.

Heilbroner comments that Marx was not so much wrong in his economic vision as he was mistaken in assuming that the psychological and sociological preconditions underlying that economic vision were fixed and unalterable. What has remained for the social scientist is first the conviction that economic motives are of fundamental importance, second that it is the business of the social scientist to bring about change, not mere understanding, and third that this change can be achieved only by a total transformation of societal structure.

At the opposite extreme from Marx was the Englishman Alfred Marshall, who dominated academic Victorian economics to the end of World War I. Marshall envisioned a quiet world in which equilibrium was the guiding idea. Directly and indirectly, he fathered the quantitative development of specific ideas that became a hallmark of the science, especially after World War II. But he too ignored the psychology of the individual; it was still economic man in operation.

Among Marshall's contemporaries the iconoclast who has had the most impact on subsequent intellectuals was Thorstein Veblen. His most celebrated book, *The Theory of the Leisure Class* (1899), is still read with pleasure today. On the surface this book is a treatise, as Heilbroner puts it, on economic psychopathology. But it has a much deeper and more serious message. For man, Veblen argued, is not to be comprehended in terms of sophisticated "economic laws" in which his innate ferocity and creativity are both smothered under a cloak of rationalization. He is better dealt with in the less flattering but more fundamental vocabulary of the anthropologist or psychologist (the two were still identical at the time): a creature of strong and irrational drives, credulous, untutored, ritualistic. Leave aside the preconditions of another age, he told the economists, and find out why man actually behaves as he does.

Thus Veblen may be given credit for being the first to introduce into economics the powerful role of actual psychological forces—man as he behaves, not the mythical economic man or the Robinson Crusoe of his contemporaries. While Veblen wrote in the right spirit, what he, like his great contemporary Max Weber, lacked was an adequate psychology.

After World War I the man who gave economics its most powerful impetus was John Maynard Keynes. In *The General Theory of Employment, Interest and Money* (1936), written in the midst of a worldwide depression, Keynes pointed out that the catastrophe facing America and, indeed, the whole Western world was only the consequence of a lack of sufficient investment on the part of business. And so the remedy was perfectly logical: If business was not able to expand, the government must take up the slack.

Keynes's book was written in language so technical that scarcely anyone reads it today. Yet his ideas made such a profound impact that economists rightly speak of the Keynesian revolution and the age of Keynes. Even more important than the economic aspects of this revolution are its psychological aspects: Man is not subject to immutable economic laws; he can be the master of his economic destiny as much as he can be the master of his destiny in other fields. Although not directly influenced by psychoanalysis, so far as anyone can see, his notions were in the spirit of the psychoanalytic vision. For he emphasized that his position was a moral one above all. In reply to Hayek's *The Road to Serfdom*, written during World War II, Keynes said:

> I should say that what we want is not no planning, or even less planning, indeed I should say we almost certainly want more. But the planning should take place in a community in which as many people as possible, both leaders and followers, wholly share your own moral position . . . the curse is that there is also an important section who could be said to want planning not in order to enjoy its fruits, but because morally they hold ideas exactly the opposite of yours, and wish to serve not God but the devil.[6]

As Shackle (1977) points out, after Keynes not merely the detailed design of the economist's account of things needed to be changed but its fundamental assumptions, its purposes and ambitions, and what it claimed to do had to be essentially reconsidered. Such a reorientation was hard to accept and is still mainly unaccepted. In our terms what he is saying is that economics can no longer be considered an isolated impersonal science; it must give proper weight to psychological and philosophical considerations. But since this threatens the professional identity and daily activities of the economist, it is still a position that is hard to accept.

Galbraith's Reanalysis of Our Economic System

In a series of witty, highly readable, yet scholarly works, Galbraith has depicted the changed nature of the economic system, its advantages and faults, and has proposed a system of reform.

The New Industrial State (first published in 1967) paints a picture of modern economic life and discusses the question of motivation in much more detail than is found in any other economic treatise. The modern industrial society is large and technical, and requires extensive planning. Nearly all communications, nearly all production and distribution of electric power, much transportation, most manufacturing and mining, a substantial share of retail trade, and a considerable amount of entertainment are conducted or provided by large firms. The numbers are not great; five hundred or six hundred huge firms dominate the economy. This is what he calls the technostructure.

Six consequences of technology and the domination of the technostructure are enumerated by Galbraith: (1) an increasing span of time separating the beginning from the completion of any task, (2) an increase in the capital committed to production, (3) with increasing technology, the ever more inflexible commitment of time and money, (4) specialized manpower, (5) organization, and (6) planning. Clearly all of this calls for conscious rational decisions on the part of government and large organizations, a far cry from the "invisible hand" of Adam Smith. Laissez faire would lead to chaos. Modern economic man must adjust himself to the technostructure.

Three chapters in Galbraith's book are devoted to motivation. As he rightly observes, these matters have not been much studied by economists.[7] The motives he examines are those that tie a person to an organization. "What an organization will seek from society will be a reflection of what members seek from the organization."[8] Traditionally the two motives that have been stressed in leading men to work have been money (pecuniary compensation) and force. To these he now adds identification and adaptation (that is, fitting into the structure of the organization). The better the individual fits into the organization—the more he identifies his own goals with what of the larger group—the more efficient he will be. As evidence for this he quotes a careful postwar study of the Nazi doctrine of slave workers dragged in from all over Europe. It was found that these slave workers were not as efficient as the women and domestic workers whom Britain brought into its labor force.[9]

In a subsequent book, *Economics and the Public Purpose* (1978), Galbraith stresses the theme of unequal development and the associated inequality in income, both of which are socially damaging. This makes it most urgent to revise the traditional views of economics.

Samuelson, whom Galbraith regards as the most influential teacher of our times, defines economics as "how . . . we choose to use scarce productive resources with alternative uses, to meet prescribed ends."[10] This, Galbraith argues, is based on the notion that the individual is still all-powerful, disregarding the technostructure, in which organizations are central. In the tradition of Adam Smith, Samuelson's definition still makes economics serve a private purpose, the self-interest of the individual. Instead, Galbraith maintains, economics must serve a public purpose, the needs of society at large. In his concluding statement he stresses that economists will, in contradiction to Keynes's prediction, remain vitally important provided that they pay sufficient attention to the public purpose and the psychosocial factors involved:

> Or economists can enlarge their system. They can have it embrace, in all its diverse manifestations, the power they now disguise. In this case, as we have seen, the problems of the world will be part of their system. Their domestic life will be less passive. There may be a contentious reaction from those whose power is now revealed and examined. And similarly from those who have found more comfort than they knew in the fact that economists teach and discuss the wrong problems or none at all. But for a very long while to come economists will thereby escape the fate [triviality] that Keynes foresaw.

In the last section of his book Galbraith outlines a general theory of reform. Surprisingly, he regards the first and most vital step in reform as the emancipation of belief—specifically, from the traditional economic wisdom that the purposes of the planning system are those of the individual. The power of the planning system depends on instilling the belief that any public or private action that serves its purposes serves also the purposes of the public at large. This depends, in turn, on popular acceptance of the proposition that the production and consumption of goods, notably those provided by the planning system, are coordinate with happiness and virtuous behavior.[12]

Galbraith's further proposals for reform stem from this primary emphasis on the reform of belief. To discuss them in detail would take us too far afield. Suffice it to say that Galbraith's arguments, which can scarcely be refuted, demonstrate that psychology and philosophy are just as central to economic thought as mathematics and statistics.

For centuries it had been taught that if one could divine the nature of the economic forces in the world, one could foretell the future. This view derived from the nineteenth-century image of man, in which the only forces that counted were external to the individual.

In 1942 Joseph Schumpeter published his famous *Capitalism, Socialism and Democracy*. Heilbroner regards this book as a turning point because it is the first time a great economist carried his economic analysis of capitalism to its final optimistic conclusion and then, disregarding the outcome of his economic thinking, pronounced doom on the economic system for a noneconomic reason. Thus the era that saw economic determinism as the major force in the world was beginning to crumble. Economics can no longer be written without reference to psychology. If it is, it becomes a hollow exercise in semantics or a mathematical model with no reference to the real world.

Alienation and Economics

With the abandonment of the fantasy of a pure, value-free science whose problems would be solved by mathematical techniques, psychology moves back into the center of the picture. A writer who has stressed this above all else is Walter Weisskopf. In *The Psychology of Economics* (1955) he tried to explain certain aspects of economic thought as the result of psychocultural trends: the substitution of a business ethic for the Christian ethic; the substitution of rationalism for a religious interpretation of history and society; the gradual substitution of ethical relativism for a belief in objective values.

In a subsequent work, *Alienation and Economics* (1971), he expanded this thesis to show that conventional economic theory neglects essential nonmaterial—intellectual, psychological, and spiritual—human needs. Critical of the principle of growth, he asks the insistent question: growth for what and for whom? We must know how to produce goods, but we must not neglect the meaning of this production, the values involved in it, the affective dimension (the feelings involved), and even the realm of close relations to the other, the realm of love. In conclusion he says:

> A general simplification of life should be attempted. . . . There is a fantastic waste of precious life-time for things that do not touch the substance of existence. Wherever there is a choice between making more money and simplifying life, the latter road should be taken. . . . Trends in these directions are already visible in some of today's subcultures. Whether they will prevent the destruction or dissolution which technical and economic one-dimensionality threatens to bring about and take us closer to a balanced way of life lies in the hands of fate.[13]

In a presentation of the ideas of current economists, Leonard Silk (1976) essentially agrees with the thesis that ideas are more basic to economics than techniques. Samuelson he regards as a philosopher of the mixed economy, Milton Friedman as a prophet of the old-time religion, Galbraith as an advocate of socialism without tears, Leontief as the apostle of planning, and Boulding as the exponent of peace and love. In short, for economics, as for all the social sciences, the quality of life is more basic than mathematical manipulation.

The Psychology of Work

With changing economic conditions, the problem of what motivates people to work looms ever larger. In his view of normality Freud stressed love and work, but the problems inherent in work have received too little attention from analysts. Perhaps it is because their own profession offers such great spiritual and financial rewards that they have tended to ignore the work experience of the vast mass of mankind, who consider work more a curse than a blessing.

Again we find that a significant historical jump occurred around the time of the French Revolution. To the Greeks work was a curse and nothing else. Their name for it, *ponos*, has the same root as the Latin *poena*, sorrow. For the Hebrews work was painful drudgery, a hard necessity. Primitive Christianity followed the Jewish tradition in regarding work as a punishment laid on man by God because of man's original sin.[14]

These views are understandable in the light of the prevalence of slavery until the nineteenth century. If the slave will do it, why should a gentleman? Historical forces cannot be dated with precision, however. Protestantism seems to have been the first moving force that established work in the modern mind as the base and key of life, and the first voice of Protestantism in this matter was Luther. It was with Luther that the German word for profession, *Beruf*, took on a religious color. Eventually every man had to have his *Beruf*, or calling (*rufen*-call), which in today's world translates into the fact that a man's occupation is an essential part of his self-image.

In this connection it is vital to note the changed image of the self that gradually took in the eighteenth century. Lyons (1978) has traced this evolution in literature before the middle of the eighteenth century. It was only when man was provided with the ideal of an integrated self rather than an immortal soul that he could go on to experience the revolutions, romanticism, and alienation of subsequent ages. Similarly Gagliardo (1969), in his study of the German peasant, has shown how the self-image changed between 1770 and 1840 from that of a pariah to that of a patriot, making it ideologically possible to usher in the psychological and social upheavals of the next two centuries, including the nightmare of total warfare.

Once slavery was abandoned and man had to clarify his self-image in all areas, including that of work, some rationale had to be found to get men to work. For a long time, as Marx so amply documented, impoverishment and force ruled the day. But they could not continue indefinitely; man needs rationalizations. One of these was the Protestant ethic (discussed above, pp. 190–191), which made work a source of religious salvation. David C. McClelland's study of the achievement motive has provided a brilliant confirmation of Weber's underlying idea that work must have some spiritual sanction and that even when the religious sanction vanished, some substitute could be found.

The recent decline in force of religion has been accompanied by a decline in the power of the achievement motive. Unrestricted achievement, unchecked growth, it is now recognized, can be as bad as its opposites. Some new ideology is needed, some more modern philosophy of living that would place work and achievement in better perspective. This is what economics has been struggling with, to greater or less effect. Economists like Galbraith and Weisskopf recognize it; others tend to deny it.

Empirical Analyses of the Work Experience

Instead of the global directives that dominated the past, such as the Protestant ethic and the achievement motive, modern scholars have moved in a different direction, toward the empirical improvement of the work situation, without much benefit from underlying theories. Or, rather, the underlying theory may be said to have become that of the analytic ideal, which insists that because love and work form the basis of normality, careful attention must be paid to the work experience to make it more meaningful and rewarding.

It is in this spirit that the numerous improvements of the work place should be viewed. Some of these have been mentioned: Herzberg, the HEW report on *Work in America*. But few outside the profession are aware of how extensive the experimentation has become. Flexitime, profit-sharing, labor-management cooperation, educational incentives and provisions for education in industry, adjustment of the worker to his level of competence, whether that be up or down, pressure to treat people well, and even large-scale support of psychotherapy for discontented workers are now accepted policies in many large companies.

It is difficult to sum this movement up in any easy way, other than to say that a strong effort is now going on to make man's work life more meaningful, and by man here we also mean woman, who as a rule is no longer satisfied with the traditional role of housewife.

In 1951 Ackerman published a seminal article on social role and total personality, stressing that every aspect of the individual's functioning interacted with his total personality; naturally this is also true of his work life. It is not an accident that even today many of those who come to analysis are in one of the mental health professions or allied to it (Knapp et al., 1960); psychotherapy is so disruptive of normal rationalizations that it becomes a threat to many occupations, such as that of the politician. As a result they tend to avoid psychotherapy or seek some glib formula such as est. It is a matter of common observation that the work patterns in many fields (e.g. salesmen) are so antagonistic to humanistic values that the persons in those occupations are all too often torn apart by psychological conflicts.

Yet to give up work altogether, as some urge, is no solution. Obviously work is essential to the fabric of society. What is necessary is to provide a new rationale for the work experience that will give it an adequate place in the psychic economy. It is here that the analytic ideal can make and does make a significant contribution.

The Psychoeconomic Disorders

Failures in the work role lead to a variety of disturbances, which are usually handled by economic analysis. This is too one-sided. By analogy with the psychosomatic disorders, the psychoeconomic disorders can be singled out. In these disorders inner-psychological disturbances lead to economic symptoms. It is just as ineffectual to handle them economically as it is to handle the psychosomatic symptoms medically. Six kinds of psychoeconomic disorders can be distinguished: (1) total inability to work, (2) work incapacity, (3) work instability (4) work dissatisfaction, (5) underachievement, and (6) paradoxical overachievement. Characteristically these problems are receiving increasing recognition from industry. One of the surprising developments in the past decade has been the vast increase in insurance for psychotherapy allocated by the large corporations, which thus move toward the recognition that the need to maintain worker satisfaction is as important a part of their enterprise as the need to show a profit.

Psychotherapy and the Economic Situation

The motives for entering psychotherapy will be considered in detail in Chapter 17. Here I wish to direct attention to an interesting economic aspect of psychotherapy. It has long been known that psychotherapy with the lower classes either is impossible or must take an entirely different form from that with the middle and upper classes. Various reasons for this have been offered.

One that has received little attention is the effect of therapy on the economic functioning of the patient. Many patients come to therapy with a history of job instability, underachievement, or such dissatisfaction as to reduce their earning capacity. Quite often within a fairly short period they find themselves working better and their incomes increasing. One study found that after a year of fairly superficial therapy (once a week) the majority of patients experience a sizable increase in income.[15]

Such a result is possible only in the upwardly mobile middle classes and under satisfactory economic circumstances. It is not possible for the members of the lower classes, who generally (but not always) see themselves as tied to menial jobs from which they can never escape. Nor is it true of the very wealthy, who would derive no benefit at all from earning more money. Accordingly the very poor and the very wealthy make the worst subjects for psychotherapy. This would indicate that economic underachievement may be even more of a prod to psychotherapy than other forms of personal suffering.

Economics and the Psychoanalytic Vision

It has been made clear that in every one of its main concerns economics must tie itself to psychology, which means that the psychoanalytic vision is highly relevant to all economic enterprise. Why men work, why men consume, why the market functions, and what kind of new men make the technostructure function more effectively are all matters intimately related to our vision of what man should be and what man needs to be happy.

Our analysis again brings out some change in the psychological attitude of the world, beginning some time in the eighteenth century. Up to now this change in emotional climate has received scant attention from historians; perhaps it is too complex to unravel. Yet as we go from one social science to another a pattern begins to emerge. In the world of economics men searched for great external forces, as they did in all other fields. Man was despised, and the lot of the average man was miserable indeed. Only victory counted, regardless of the cost.

Intellectually, men had to disprove one after another of the theories regarding external forces, in all the social sciences. Once men had unleashed their internal forces, it became clear that they were not bound by any immutable laws of economics. Like any other human enterprise, the economy could be manipulated for the public purpose, to assure the greater happiness of mankind.

Chapter 10

Believers and Skeptics: Religion and Philosophy

FOR ALL THEIR wide diversity of views there is one point on which virtually all psychoanalysts are united: the rejection of religion as a desirable force in human existence. Freud himself was clear on this subject. In 1907 he wrote a paper showing that religion has many similarities to the obsessional neuroses he had studied in such detail. In *Totem and Taboo* he tied up religion with magic and the Oedipus complex. In *The Future of an Illusion* 1927 he wrote: ". . . in the long run nothing can withstand reason and experience, and the contradiction which religion offers to both is all too palpable."[1]

The next year, in a letter to Pfister he went further:

> I do not know if you have detected the secret link between the *Lay Analysis* and the *Illusion.* In the former I wish to protect analysis from the doctors and in the latter from the priests. I should like to hand it over to a profession which does not yet exist, a profession of *lay* curers of souls who *need* not be doctors and *should not* be priests.[2]

In spite of the spread of pastoral counseling, psychoanalysis thus opposes, on both theoretical and practical grounds, the practice of turning to a clergyman for help with any emotional problem.

Advocates of religion have naturally strongly resented the psychoanalytic view. To the bombardment by the French *philosophes* of the eighteenth century, who called religious ideas and practices absurd and irrational, had now been added the psychoanalytic charge that religion is a universal neurosis. Not ancient or modern religion, not Western or Eastern, but religion as such.

Just as the intellectual attack on Christianity after Darwin forced the growth of the "higher criticism" to reconcile the teachings of the Bible with modern science, so the psychoanalytic diagnosis of religion has had two momentous consequences on the current scene. First the established religions (Christianity, Judaism) have found it difficult or impossible to justify certain practices to their faithful. How can the Catholic church expect a young woman today to distinguish between "normal" virginity, seen as the highest state attainable, and "neurotic" virginity, in which the state of chastity is chosen as a defense against irrational fears? Few young woman can make such a distinction, and the number seeking out convents and nunneries has diminished markedly. Why should priests maintain lifelong celibacy? Many do not wish to do so, and the manpower situation for the priesthood is steadily becoming more of a problem. And so on. Religion is shot through with psychological assumptions that are in sharp contradiction to modern psychological knowledge, just as the previous scientific assumptions were in contradiction to the post-Darwinian science of the nineteenth century.

A second consequence of this psychodiagnosis of religion has been the enormous growth in popularity of the Eastern religions— Buddhism and its offshoots, many of the Indian sects, even the adoption of Islam by blacks. This shift has been motivated primarily by the feeling that Christianity (and to a lesser extent Judaism) has failed modern man. In part it derives from the immersion in a totally new way of life offered by these unfamiliar religions.

Furthermore, psychoanalysis has subjected the various types of religious experience (for example, those described in the classic by William James, *The Varieties of Religious Experience*) to careful scrutiny and found them to be neurotic reactions of various kinds: conversion as a search for the father, saintliness as a reaction formation against hatred, mysticism as a retreat from reason, sometimes catatonic in nature, and so on.

Some students find that religion has played a significant role in all known human societies and conclude that it has some positive values for mankind. In spite of a diversity so great that religion defies exact definition,[3] they tend to see religion as a socially unifying force. A typical view is that of Goode (1951), who sees religion as a level of integration, offering common societal values which help to direct the society as a whole. Religion *expresses* the unity of society but it also helps to *create* that unity. Yet Goode has reservations about the utility of such unity and its effects on other aspects of social functioning. The main trouble with Goode's position is that no religious believer would accept it: for him religion is always revealed truth.

Religion as a Stage in the Development of Psychotherapy

One point of central importance has escaped attention, in both the psychoanalytic and non-analytic accounts. Historically and currently one of the major functions of religion has been psychotherapy.

There is no way of knowing how anxious primitive man was. Roheim (1955), the first trained analyst to do field work, merely commented that the amount of one's anxiety was related to the security experienced with the mother. Thus he found that while the Central Australian tribes reside in a desert area where death by starvation is well within the realm of possibility, they have no anxiety about starvation. On the other hand, the Normanby Islanders, who have plentiful supplies of food, continually and anxiously practice magic both to increase the food supply and to spoil their appetites.[4]

Magic is ubiquitous, and magic is a regressive defense against anxiety (Odier, 1956). That magic necessarily reduces anxiety cannot be definitely maintained; it may merely involve the individual and the society in an endless round of rituals, as is often seen today. Still, the intent of the magic is to lessen the anxiety. At times magic is the forerunner of religion, and at times it goes hand in hand with religion. Virtually all primitive religions are full of magical practices.

In his posthumous book *Magic and Schizophrenia* Roheim drew attention to the numerous parallels between the two. Magic he saw as counterphobic (an attempt to deny fear), and schizophrenic magic as "imagination" magic. However, it is often difficult to separate the two. Because schizophrenia is a reaction to a panic state (Sullivan, 1940), it follows that the widespread use of magic covers up panicky feelings of all kinds. Nor need we fully agree with Roheim that maternal security is sufficient to defend against anxiety, since our own culture and practices provide numerous examples to the contrary.

Thus it seems plausible that religion in general defends the individual against otherwise overpowering anxieties and that this defensive ability explains the powerful hold it has had on mankind.

In the religion that concerns us most in Western civilization, Christianity, there can scarcely be any question of the overwhelming position that fear plays. Oskar Pfister, a minister who became an analyst and a friend of Freud, gave the title *Christianity and Fear* (1944) to his last important work. Reviewing salient historical turning points, he found that fear is predominant over and over. For example, he found that the public and private practice of Catholicism is saturated with fear and with ideas and symbolical actions born of fear and designed to alleviate it; such phenomena are so pervasive that the first idea to suggest itself is that the problem of fear is the only one existing for a Catholic. But he also regards Luther as the typical sufferer from fear. Later Erikson, in his well-known *Young Man Luther*, was to show that the founder of Lutheranism had a psychotic episode as a prelude to his religious conversion, and psychosis means panic.

Because of this preoccupation with fear, Pfister argues, Christianity often became a compulsion neurosis, erected preposterous dogmas, and turned into a hell on earth: The "history of Christianity rather has the appearance of a gigantic misunderstanding or of a pathology of Christianity."[5] Pfister felt (and this is relevant to our main theses) that the only way to make men good Christians was to analyze them.

For centuries the only kind of psychotherapy ever seen was religious. Faith healers abounded in the Middle Ages (they are still found today) and were credited with all kinds of miraculous powers. Certainly an age that saw whole populations wiped out by epidemics and violent death at the hands of soldiers needed a belief in miracles to keep it going.

It is interesting to speculate on how much good faith healers actually did. One study of Lourdes (Saunders, 1940) saw the shrine as a place where poor people were exploited by the church hierarchy. However, Smiley Blanton (1940) examined one alleged cure at Lourdes and found it to be authentic. At that time it was reported that there were about eight to fifteen authentic cures per year. Blanton concluded that the patient's healing was quickened by the emotion aroused by the transference to an all-powerful, all-loving Virgin Mother and that phenomena of this kind have not yet been recognized or accepted by the medical profession. However, the original founder of Lourdes, Bernadette, had been examined by Charcot in 1858 and found to be hysteric. In any case, even by the official statistics the number of real cures is negligible, so what faith healers have done through the ages is questionable. What is most important for our thesis is that faith healing for centuries was a form of psychotherapy.

The other side of religious "healing"—witch persecution—is equally important. This has been touched upon above (pp. 198–199). Here the psychosis of the clergy was acted out, with catastrophic results.

Either way, constructive or destructive, Christianity has for many centuries been a form of psychotherapy. Theoretically this hardly needs proof. The whole theology of Christianity revolves around fear, guilt, and other negative emotions, and their conquest by faith. While scientists no longer hold to the evolutionary schemes of the nineteenth century (which Freud also went along with), which viewed history as a progression from magic to religion to science, it is true that psychotherapy has in the past and currently been approached via magic, religion, and medicine before the scientific psychotherapy that derives from Freud took over.

Religious Ethics

Proponents of religion have stressed three factors in favor of the continuation of religious systems: They are true, they unite society, and they promote ethical behavior so strongly that without religious sanctions man would be completely amoral. As to the "truth" of any religious system, no adherent of any religion takes the truth of any other system seriously, and even many believers have all kinds of questions about their own theology. That religion may serve to unite society is certainly correct, but it leaves out of account the manner in which this unification is achieved. As with community or culture, religion is a group phenomenon, which may have either destructive or constructive consequences. In general the shockingly destructive aspects of religion have been grossly underemphasized.

There remains then the argument that religious sanctions are essential to maintain man's ethical behavior. Here historical and contemporary evidence may be brought in to test the statement. History speaks overwhelmingly against it. In the religion best known to us, Christianity, wholesale massacres and genocide, even apart from ordinary everyday persecution, have been common in every century. Even in the days of the Romans, when the Christians were a severely persecuted minority, one of the Roman emperors sarcastically commented: "How these Christians *love* one another." In World War II one of the hit songs in the United States was "Praise the Lord and Pass the Ammunition."

Enough evidence is available to show that man can be deeply moral and ethical without being restrained by fear of supernatural sanctions. Among Western countries today, the one that has taken the strongest measures against violence is Sweden, and Sweden, although nominally Lutheran, in reality is almost totally irreligious (Tomasson, 1970). Confucianism, another religion devoid of the supernatural, for centuries produced a code of conduct superior to any extant in Christian Europe. It is therefore an open question whether official religion adds to or detracts from desirable norms of ethical conduct.

Religion and the Psychoanalytic Vision

Our inquiry leaves no doubt that religion should play no role in the psychoanalytic vision of happiness. Whatever merits it may have had in the past (social unification, moral codes, differential roles) may be accomplished much better by other means.

Philosophy

Because psychoanalysis is a philosophical science, its relationship to other philosophies must be carefully examined. Immediately a paradox presents itself, for, as with the other social sciences, there is already disagreement on how philosphy should be defined. Levi states: "It is a paradox faced by all of those who attempt to write the history of philosophy that the 'philosophy' whose history they write probably would not have been defined by any two of the major figures whom they judge it fitting to include in their account in the same way."[6]

Even the most cursory examination of philosophical works displays the wide variety of views adopted by leading thinkers. Will Durant sees philosophy as "the synthetic interpretation of all experience."[7] Bertrand Russell regarded philosophy as essentially one with science, differing from the special sciences merely in the generality of its problems and in its concern with hypotheses where empirical evidence is lacking.[8] Randall saw philosophy as primarily a means of criticism, a leverage for either attacking or defending tradition.[9]

Morris Cohen (1961) commented that at the turn of the century, when the American Philosophical Association was founded, no field of philosophy was so discredited as the philosophy of history, yet he had come to feel that the difference between the philosopher and the historian could be only one of degree and emphasis.[10] R. G. Collingwood, who is ranked as both a philosopher and a historian, took essentially the same position: The philosopher must come to grips with history.

The more conventional view of philosophy is represented by Höffding (1900), who states that the nature of philosophy can be understood only in the light of its history, and that the purpose of studying the history of philosophy is to shed light on what philosophy really is.

If we turn from the general consideration of philosophy to its relationship to psychoanalysis, we are again confronted with paradoxes and contradictions. Russell states that since the Middle Ages the prestige of philosophy has been going steadily downhill. Yet philosophers feel that they are dealing with questions of vital importance, so to them being ignored represents a deep humiliation. And there can be no question that since the rapid rise of empirical social science at the turn of the century the role of philosophy has been of less and less importance. Just as the mathematician has replaced the speculative philosopher in the study of logic, so there has been a strong tendency for psychoanalysts to replace philosophers in their domain.

Naturally this has aroused a strong protest on the part of philosophers. Most of them (Wolheim, 1974) prefer to continue their philosophical speculations without admitting that psychoanalysis exists, or that it is of any importance. Others echo the behaviorist psychologist (Ryle, 1949) and assail psychoanalysis as a congeries of philosophically untenable assumptions. Unfortunately, the vast majority (Hook, 1959; Ricoeur, 1977) fail to show any real understanding of psychoanalysis or appreciation of its relevance to the traditional problems. Ricoeur asserts that "psychoanalysis has never quite succeeded in stating how its assertions are justified, how its interpretations are authenticated, how its theory is verified,"[11] thereby annihilating at a single blow the entire corpus of psychoanalytic literature. In reality his statement that psychoanalytic theory is merely the codification of what takes place in the analytic relationship is a restatement of one of Freud's fundamental insights. Wittgenstein, one of the gods of modern philosophy, once described himself as a "disciple of Freud." "I sat up in surprise; here was someone who had something to say," he reportedly commented when he read Freud. Later he rejected psychoanalysis as "offering or imposing upon one a mythology."[12]

It has been widely supposed, even by some psychoanalysts (Gedo, 1979), that the modern philosophy of science has decisively refuted some of the basic constructs of psychoanalysis. This too seems to be based on some misunderstanding, as Canning (1966) has shown and as is clearly demonstrated in the recent synthesis by Fisher and Greenberg (1977).

Traditionally, philosophy is divided into four branches (Höffding): (1) the problem of knowledge, (2) the problem of existence, (3) the problem of the estimation of worth, and (4) the problem of consciousness. More commonly, these are called, respectively, epistemology, metaphysics, ethics, and logic and esthetics. Epistemology represents the interface between physics and psychology and thus ceases to be a speculative philosophical problem. Metaphysics is relevant insofar as it concerns itself with a way of living more happily, not with the origins of the universe, which is a problem in astronomy or history. Neither ethics nor esthetics can be pursued without reference to psychology. Thus in all its branches philosophy is necessarily intertwined with psychology.

Psychoanalytic Observations on Two Age-Old Philosophical Problems

All the problems with which philosophers have wrestled through the ages are at some point related to psychology, since they deal with human beings; thus the pursuit of philosophy without reference to psychology is no longer fruitful. In the case of two specific problems, the problem of free will and the relationship between body and mind, it has been shown that psychology can advance them much further, though as yet without offering any ultimate resolution (cf. Chapter 4).

Ethics and Psychology

Another area in which psychological (psychoanalytic) considerations supersede philosophical speculation is ethics. It would be superfluous to consider in detail the innumerable systems of ethics that have been proposed through the ages. But it is appropriate to comment that none of these has taken into consideration the role of the superego or the psychological capacity of the individual to respond to ethical demands. Because of this neglect, ethics most often deteriorates into a superego game, in which certain commands are either obeyed or disobeyed, with consequent reward or punishment. On the whole, philosophers have simply disregarded the psychological aspects of their ethical precepts; e.g., Ricoeur (1967) discusses basic ethical questions, such as sin and guilt, with no reference whatsoever to the psychological realities involved.

Indeed, the same point arises here that was made earlier with regard to religious ethics. If a man is going to behave ethically, much more is at stake than the verbal decision to do so. Our language is full of aphorisms indicating that the average man has always been aware of this discrepancy: "He does not practice what he preaches" or "The road to hell is paved with good intentions" and so forth. Or again, ethical standards may be set at such a high level that it is impossible for anyone short of a saint to live up to them. This is just as true for Kant's categorical imperative as it is for the Ten Commandments. Obviously ethical standards that are impossible to fulfill merely lead to hypocrisy, guilt, and disappointment.

On the other hand, the philosophical ideals by which our lives should be led cannot be deduced from psychology alone. There are many different ways of living that are entirely consonant with psychological possibilities. Man is free to choose among them.

Philosophy as a Way of Living: The Search for Happiness

Most interest still attaches to the ways of living advocated by various philosophers. In *The Idea of Happiness* (1967) V. J. McGill takes the position that this question has now been relegated to the psychotherapists:

> In this final chapter we shall confine ourselves to the most important current development of the theory of the good life, i.e. the good-enough, the better, and the best or ideal life. The disciplines that are obliged, more than any others, to say what they mean by an improvement of the individual's general condition, and hence what they mean by a satisfactory or ideal life, are personality theory and psychother-

apy. Both are concerned with undesirable symptoms and their removal, but their interest often goes beyond this negative result to a
positive conception of "mental health" which is close to what we have
been discussing under the name of "happiness." The fact that this conception is logically connected with medical therapy or with objective
tests and controlled studies gives it a significance lacking in earlier theories.[13]

Apart from the recognition that the search for the *summum
bonum* has now passed from the philosopher to the psychologist,
McGill's statement is significant in that it marks one of the few explicit acknowledgments by a philosopher that philosophers have in
fact been engaging in one form or another of psychotherapy from
time immemorial. For our central thesis this is an essential building
block. On the road to the real psychotherapy of today, as will be
seen in more detail in Chapter 14, many other attempts have been
made. Among these have been magic, religion, philosophy, and
medicine; all are still found, in one form or another, on the contemporary scene.

That philosophy has been a form of psychotherapy is thoroughly obscured by the intellectual manner in which the history of
philosophy has ordinarily been presented. As Scharfstein and Ostow
point out (1970), the idea that knowing the truth will protect the philosopher and grant him a tranquil or ecstatic eternity is one of the
oldest and most persistent in all of philosophy. Consequently the
philosopher, serene in his intellectual convictions, has generally ig
nored the question of how these convictions are to be conveyed to
other people and what they will do with them once conveyed. The
history of philosophy too has in general attached much more importance to ideas than to the way in which the ideas have been dissemi-
nated and applied.

Philosophy itself is as old as mankind. As long ago as 1927 the
anthropologist Paul Radin wrote the fascinating book, *Primitive
Man as Philosopher.* He showed that wherever we turn, man, no
matter how primitive, has shown keen interest in the same questions
that have concerned philosophers in more modern times. Nor does
he think that the answers primitive man came up with are in any
sense inferior to what more famous thinkers have propounded. In
conclusion he says:

> [T]he higher natures among primitive people can have a true moral
> sense and an intuitive insight into right and wrong. That they can also
> possess true wisdom, that they can envisage life in a critical and half-

pessimistic manner, that they can face fortune and misfortune objectively and with equanimity, that they can in fact accept life in all its realities and still enjoy it, for that the reader is not prepared any more than the ethnologist who discovers it. And yet there is no escaping recognition of the fact, for it is borne in upon him in numerous songs, speeches, myths and proverbs and is to be encountered in every tribe in the world.[14]

Moving on into the Western tradition, the close connection between philosophy and psychotherapy among the Greeks has been largely overlooked. Entralgo (1970), Drabkin (1954) and Simon (1978) have all documented the fact that the Greeks, with the Sophists, developed a rather sophisticated form of psychotherapy, which was not surpassed before Freud. The word "sophist" has indeed persisted in our language, with the dual meanings of "sophistry," or fraudulently persuasive arguments, and "sophisticated," or more cultivated than the masses—the same kind of ambivalence that our patients display toward us today.

The usual emphasis on the Sophists as teachers conceals their activity as therapists, which was at least as important. Their theory centered on the force of persuasion. Gorgias, the first prominent Sophist, elaborated the theory of persuasion extensively. The word, he thought, "is a powerful sovereign, for with a very tiny and completely invisible body it performs the most divine works. It has in fact the power to take away fear, banish pain, inspire happiness and increase compassion."[15]

What is of concern here is not so much the ideology of the Sophists, although their ideology was a direct inspiration to Freud, but the fact that they were practicing psychotherapists, translating their philosophical ideas into action. A number of Sophists, for example, applied the theory of persuasion to the treatment of mental and emotional disturbance. How widespread this kind of psychotherapy was is hard to tell, but of its existence there can be no doubt. From one point of view, the chief objection Socrates had to them was that their thinking was unclear. Socrates too, by holding public discourses without fee, was also a psychotherapist of sorts, and the accusation that he was corrupting the youth, which led the Athenian reactionaries to put him to death, is not unlike that leveled against contemporary psychotherapists, who are looked at askance but are not usually put to death.

Throughout the history of mankind, innumerable other forms of psychotherapy can be uncovered. In Western civilization most of these have been tied up with religion in one form or another, which is perhaps one reason why their importance has escaped the traditional historian. A more important reason, however, is that the traditional historian, as pointed out in Chapter 7, has been so focused on victory that everything else becomes secondary. And psychotherapy does not contribute to military victories; if anything it works against them.

Within the secular tradition three forms of psychotherapy that were prominent in the Hellenistic world were Stoicism, Epicureanism, and skepticism. The importance of these schools lies in the fact that they attracted large numbers of disciples, who adopted their precepts as guides to living. Thus Stoicism, although founded around the turn of the third century B.C., took several centuries to become fully developed. In the periods of the rising monarchy and of its established rule (first century B.C.) Stoicism became the religion of the republican opposition. The Stoic takes a position above the rest of mankind, looking down on their struggles as on a spectacle. With this doctrine, Stoicism could give consolation, composure, and fortitude to many in times of trouble and despair.

The philosophy of Zeno's contemporary Epicurus likewise offered a philosophy of defense in a troubled world and likewise attracted a large following (not unlike that of existentialism today). Skeptics, neo-Pythagoreans, and neo-Platonists also had strong followings in the ancient world, until Justinian I in A.D. 529 ordered all the philosophical schools closed because of their "pagan" character. Thereafter Christianity dominated the theory of salvation, and *ipso facto* the field of psychotherapy, until modern times.

There were, however, a number of exceptions. Montaigne (1533–92) in his famous *Essais* described a kind of self-analysis (Gedo and Pollack, 1976) and even tried to do a little psychotherapy, applying to some others what had worked so well on himself, but his work never attracted a wide following. By contrast Spinoza (1632–77) eventually became the founder of a psychotherapeutic sect, which continues to this day. His views have also been compared to Freud's.

In the eighteenth century Mesmerism, which began as a psychotherapy, for a while turned into a popular movement, offering a full philosophy for living. By the nineteenth century, when religion was fast losing its hold on men's minds, innumerable new sects began to flourish: phrenology, faith healing, mind cure, occultism, and Christian Science are but a few of the better known (Bromberg, 1954).

In Freud's day the most popular philosophical-therapeutic movement in America was the Emmanuel Movement, founded by the Reverend Elwood Worcester. Worcester described the numerous evils plaguing the society of his day, such as drugs, sexual libertinism, and divorce. To combat these evils he inauguarated a cheerful crusade combining liberal Christianity, the "powers of the Subliminal Self," and the latest in medical psychotherapy (not Freud) (N. Hale, 1971). On November 11, 1906, in the vestry of Emmanuel Church, the first class was held for the "moral and psychological treatment of nervous disorders.[16] For the next four years the Emmanuel Movement, as the newspapers christened it, spread across the country among a number of Protestant denominations. After World War I the movement disappeared as suddenly as it had arisen.[17]

After the Enlightenment, philosophy became an official subject in almost all universities all over the world. For the most part, however, its doctrines have been couched in such abstract language that they have had little effect on anyone, either the intellectual or the man in the street. The neglect of psychotherepy, which is philosophy in action, has led to endlessly verbose disquisitions without clear referent. Levi, in discussing the history of philosophy, puts it as follows:

> [T]here seems little prospect for philosphical unification. The scientific and the metaphysical tempers still pursue their opposite courses, and the subjectivity of Existentialism and the objectivity of Logical Positivism still express their opposition in mutual contempt. Thus, in the contemporary philosphical universe, multiplicity and division still reign.[18]

Existentialism

In our own day, and especially since World War II, the philosophy that has attracted the widest attention has been existentialism; in many ways it has proved for many people the most attractive alternative to psychoanalysis. Rollo May, its leading American exponent, defined existentialism as "the endeavor to understand man by cutting below the cleavage between subject and object that has bedeviled Western thought and science since shortly after the Renaissance."[19] This approach is contrasted with Freud and psychoanalysis, which, he alleged, could not understand man in personal relation with fellow men and man in relation to himself. May goes on to make the extraordinary statement that "it does not detract, of course, from the genius of Freud to point out that probably almost all of the specific ideas which later appeared in psychoanalysis could be found in Nietzsche in greater breadth and in Kierkegaard in greater depth."[20]

Basing his ideas on this peculiar notion of history, May then goes on to list six contributions of existential psychotherapy: concern with being; anxiety and guilt as being ontological; being-in-the-world; the three modes of the world (biological, fellow men, self); consideration of time and history; and transcendence of the immediate situation.

It is noteworthy that May, like other existentialists, scraps the entire understanding of mankind that had been so carefully pieced together by Freud and the psychoanalysts, attempting to replace it by a philosophy. This philosophy owes much of its popularity to the devastation of World War II. It has properly been called a philosophy of despair.[21] Being a rationalization of the reaction to the horrors of the war and the bitter defeatism that followed, it does not lend itself readily to rational discussion. Despite the fact that it is historically false (as in May), philosophical gibberish (as in Heidegger), psychologically misperceived (as in Sartre); and philosophically without hope (as in Frankl), it has been able to appeal to many modern intellectuals.[22]

One aspect of this appeal can be highlighted here. The philosophy of psychoanalysis derives from a rational optimism about the human condition and the possibilities of improving it. Opposed to it is the emphasis on irrational demonic forces in human nature and the world, beyond the capacity of any one individual or even one country to combat. Many such situations have arisen historically. Within the Roman Empire Christianity itself represents one, and it too was prey to the irrationality, hopelessness, and discouragement of that period.

When the world looks so bleak and dismal, reason holds out little hope for amelioration. Accordingly, many embrace the seeming power of dark irrational forces they do not understand but which at least offer some relief from the oppressive gloom by providing easy magical solutions.

Within the field of psychotherapy, the existential therapist in effect says to his patient: The ultimate solutions do not exist, live from day to day, enjoy yourself and make the best of it. Childhood origins, transferences, resistances, and the like are entirely beside the point; anyhow, there is no time for them. Like Omar Khayyam in a similar epoch they say: Take the cash and let the credit go. In addition, the fierce existential attack on psychoanalysis serves as an outlet for the otherwise insatiable feelings of hatred and destructiveness that are never brought into the analysis.

Psychoanalysis as a Philosophical System

The principal thesis of this book is that psychoanalysis is a philosophical system based on a sound psychology and that as such, it replaces all previous psychological systems.

"Philosophy" can be viewed (following Randall, Cohen, and others) as critical reflection on a body of experience. If the analyst engages in critical reflection on what he has been doing and how he helps his patients work out a meaningful philosophy of living (which may or may not agree with his), he is a philosopher in the truest sense of the word.

Such critical reflection leads to two conclusions, one in terms of scientific understanding, the other in terms of happy living.

In terms of scientific understanding, psychoanalysis provides the core of a science of man in which all disciplines are included. It has been seen over and over that philosophy, like the social sciences, defies exact definition. This lack of clarity can now be comprehended: It derives, to put it most simply, from the fact that the "independent" disciplines simply do not exist as such: all refer to man and his functioning. Sociology looks at man in our society, history at man in the past, anthropology at man in other cultures, economics at man in his economic functioning, and so forth. The notion that philosophy must embrace a "synthetic unity of all experience" is too grandiose a goal, impossible of fulfillment in that it searches for one unifying principle that will explain everything.

Instead, the science of man as it comes out of our psychoanalytic critical reflection must deal successively with man in his various roles: social, historical, economic, artistic, and so on. In each case factual data must be gathered. In this data-gathering the chief role of psychoanalytic theory is to indicate the directions in which the most fruitful research should be done; it does not contribute to the actual accumulation of data as such. That is the province of other approaches, which, in this limited sense, and only in this limited sense, may be called disciplines.

Nowhere does the accumulation of factual data solve any of the underlying theoretical or practical problems. Again these problems call for critical reflection after as much of the data as can be gathered are in. In this sense psychoanalysis provides a unique guide for research, one that is sorely needed in areas that have seen such stupendous waste of time and energy.

But even with the available evidence, which is woefully incomplete in so many domains, some useful conclusions about the human condition can be drawn. Man is not merely subject to powerful external forces; he is also driven by powerful internal forces. Only by knowing both can we reach rational conclusions about the management of human difficulties. Our current knowledge permits a guarded optimism about the future.

One of the most important of all conclusions comes from the other side of the philosophical stance of psychoanalysis: Man can find happiness here on earth. Neither God nor the devil, neither the stars nor mythical forces like inexorable laws of history or an invisible hand, need be called upon. Man creates his own misery, and having created it he can undo it as well.

The psychoanalytic image of happiness centers on the concept of the analytic ideal. This analytic ideal differs markedly from the statistically average individual in any culture yet studied. Yet it is an ideal capable of realization, by education where available, by psychotherapy if education has miscarried.

The analytic ideal has been described in Chapter 3. This assumes that man can find the greatest degree of happiness if he can love, enjoy sex, have pleasure, feel yet be guided by reason, have a role in the social structure, be part of some kind of family, have a strong sense of identity, communicate with his fellow men, be creative, work, and be free from psychiatric symptomatology. Other analysts have offered somewhat divergent images of the ideal: fearlessness, freedom from guilt, integrative living, and the like. There is actually more agreement on the ideal goals of analysis than on the techniques needed to reach those goals.

In the literature directed at the public, and in most of the technical literature, too little attention has been paid to the philosophy of living espoused by psychoanalysis. One reason is that the term "philosophy" carries such repellant connotations of wordy and windy abstractions, never touching the ground, that most people tend to fight shy of it. But philosophy also teaches us that there is no such thing as a technique without some underlying theory; man craves directions and goals for his life as much as he craves food and sex.

Philosophy and the Psychoanalytic Vision

Thus philosophy does become an essential part of the psychoanalytic vision, in two equally important senses. First, as critical reflections on man's experience: Because they had no adequate psychology with which to buttress their insights, past philosophies no longer have anything of significance to offer. Second, from a positive point of view psychoanalysis offers a constructive way of living. Those analysts who hold to the view of psychoanalysis as pure technique (Hartmann, 1960) err by underplaying the larger meaning of psychoanalysis for the world.It is still true that the technical roads for reaching the goals are lined with many obstacles and that many patients fall by the wayside. It is also true that in the actual practice of therapy to talk of goals too early prejudices or even ruins the therapeutic process. Despite these caveats, it is essential to bear in mind that psychoanalysis does offer people a guide to happy living. And for many this image of happiness (as represented in the numerous self-help books on the market, for example) draws them, and rightly so, to the analyst.

Chapter 11

Creativity and Communication: Art and Language

SOME WILL ARGUE that the topics of this chapter belong under the humanities; others will disagree. The distinction is artificial. Everything that is psychological and human is included in our scheme, is illuminated by the psychoanalytic vision, and must be given due consideration in our total enterprise.

Art

As usual, the attempt to render a precise definition of art meets innumerable obstacles. The *Encyclopaedia Brittannica* (1978) offers the simplest and widest definition: Art is anything that is man-made.[1] This sidesteps the question that has concerned philosophers of aesthetics: What is "good" art, and how is it to be distinguished from "bad" art? Beyond the question of good and bad art, how are we to understand the creative urge in man? What is creativity? What is genius? How does the creative individual differ (if he does) from the uncreative? It is to these and related questions that our inquiry is directed.

GENIUS AND MADNESS

Once more we are confronted with age-old clichés. The genius, we are told, is inherently mad. Art is essentially a divine "inspira-

tion," literally a gift of the gods. Even psychoanalysts have fallen into this trap: Niederland (1976) states, "As a clinician I have never
seen a creative individual who did not have serious, all-pervasive
and disturbing conflicts."[2] Freud spoke in 1930 of the "riddle of the
miraculous gift that makes an artist."[3]

More sober consideration will show that observations of this
kind are wide of the mark. Like any other human experience, creativity can be analyzed, its childhood origins grasped, its social functioning appraised, and its role in human existence put in proper perspective.

PSYCHOANALYTIC OBSERVATIONS ON CREATIVITY

Creative artists were among the first to appreciate the value of
psychoanalysis, at a time when the professionals still expressed violent opposition to Freud. In psychoanalysis they saw a psychological
approach that helped them to make some sense out of what they
were doing. Still, their acceptance was limited, for in our culture the
creative artist is primarily interested in the successful reception of his
work by the public, not in its psychological ramifications. The common fear of artists that analysis will rob them of their inspiration is
contradicted by everyday experience.

Psychoanalytic thought on creativity is somewhat skewed because it began at a time (the early 1900s) when Freud was looking
for some confirmation of his psychosexual theories (cf. Chapter 3,
pp. 64–66). The first observation was that the creative artist gives
expression to the same forbidden impulses that the neurotic deals
with, but for him they are permitted, whereas for the neurotic they
create illness. The problem of creativity then shifted to a different issue: How is it possible that one person releases his impulses with
pleasure and gratification while for another the release leads to pain
and suffering? This basic question about creativity remains to be answered.

The question can be answered in two ways. First of all, the creative artist frequently suffers far more than he is willing to admit. A
whole literature of studies of artists has brought to light the deep
anxieties and conflicts, leading to neurosis and even at times psychosis, with which their lives are permeated. Thus the artist who releases his impulses is playing with fire, and it is not surprising that
many artists are burned in the process. Second, the pain and suffer-

ing do not come from the impulse release as such, as had originally been thought, but from the superego prohibitions, which go back to the parental attitudes. In this way the scene once more shifts to the family and the social structure in which the artist (or nonartist) lives and flourishes.

Studies of the psychosocial backgrounds of artists have led to a variety of unexpected findings. Art is just as much a social as an individual product, and the degree of creativity displayed depends on both external and internal factors. Further, there are many avenues to art and creativity. As with so many other human functions, the early oversimplifications had to be abandoned in favor of a more sophisticated theory. At a panel on creativity in 1972 Bernard Meyer said:

> [I]t would seem unlikely that so universal an activity . . . that is begun so early in the course of each individual life could possess a single mental significance. It would appear more plausible to view the creative impulse as comparable to a biological function, like breathing or parturition, which under certain circumstances may become the vehicle for a host of other psychological meanings and consequently to wide fluctuations of functioning.[4]

Theoretical work thus led to the conclusion that creative work could stem from many different sources and could flow in many different directions. Terman in his studies of gifted children found that at an early age they were gifted in many ways. Those who later became eminent scientists could just as well have become eminent artists, had they developed those talents. Creativity is thus just as much a matter of consistent application as it is of sudden inspiration.

By this time thousands of artists and nonartists have undergone psychoanalytic treatment. Two observations emerge. Artists do not lose their talent as a result of analysis: on the contrary, they may overcome what stands in the way of releasing their talent, so that they can function more effectively than before. Second, new talent is not born in the course of psychoanalysis, with rare exceptions. Freud once used the metaphor of sculpture and painting. In sculpture the finished figure is there in the stone (or other medium) before the sculptor starts; he has only to pick away at it and bring out the desired form. In painting the artist starts from scratch and adds something entirely new to the canvas. Analysis, Freud argued, is more akin to sculpture than to painting: It can only bring out what is there; it cannot create something entirely new.

THE IIMPULSE TO CREATIVITY

What is it that leads a person to be creative? What role do the creative impulse and creativity play in human existence? These and similar questions call for a comprehensive psychology of creativity.

The ordinary psychological approach has little to say on this subject. Guilford (1950) in his book on creativity viewed it as "divergent production" but did not try to explain why the creative individual should want to be divergent, or of what use it was to him to be so. Arieti (1976) although writing within a psychoanalytic framework, still clings to the old image of the artist as a genius: Creativity is a "magic synthesis." Barron (1972), studying art students at the San Francisco Art Institute, found his subjects to be notably independent and unconventional, vivid in gesture and expression, and rather complex psychodynamically, but with an emphasis on openness, spontaneity, and whimsicality rather than neurotic complicatedness. "They choose to do what they value most, and this itself sets them apart from many apparently better adjusted people who are doing what they would rather not."[5] This seems to be part of the glorification of the artist as a genius; in psychoanalytic theory Otto Rank had stressed this feature above all features. However, as a general proposition it is contradicted by the observation that so many artists are seriously miserable and disturbed, to such an extent that psychosis and depression are often regarded as everyday occurrences among them.

Getzels and Csikszentmihalyi (1976) studied several hundred artists who were still in school and followed up a number after graduation. Their main conclusion was that despite personal and social obstacles young artists whose cognitive approach emphasizes problem-finding over problem-solving are more successful in their creative careers.[6] This generalization seems both too glib and too shallow; it still tells us little about the psychology of creativity.

Artists themselves have had almost no insight into the psychological forces that drive them to creativity. The English poet Francis Thompson once wrote:

> We speak a language taught we know not how
> And what it is that from us flows
> The listener better than the utterer knows.

When artists do call upon psychologists, as a rule it is for help with their circumstances or with a creative block, not in order to understand themselves better. Thus Virginia Woolf (who ended up a suicide in the course of a schizophrenic episode) wrote in 1929:

> Accentuating all these difficulties is the world's notorious indifference. It does not ask people to write poems . . . it does not need them. . . . Here the psychologists might come to our help. For surely it is time that the effect of discouragement upon the mind of the artist should be measured.[7]

Art critics (including literary critics) have been concerned primarily with "greatness," either in their own estimation or in that of others. This reminds one of the traditional historian's tacit assumption that his job is to trace victories; the vanquished are left to others. Similarly, the art critic portrays the history of art as a series of victories, paying little attention in the process to the inner psychological struggles the artists had to go through or to the artists who were less popular or less successful.

Thus Edmund Wilson could write: "The letters and records of writers of genius are one of the ways we have of finding out how life was really lived in any given time and place."[8] Wilson was an only child, described as the son of a brilliant, moody, melancholy father, often hospitalized for what was then called "neurasthenia," and a deaf and strong-willed mother. He himself suffered from repeated depressions throughout his life, for one of which he too was hospitalized. The connection between these depressions and his life and work is entirely omitted; the only possibly pertinent comment found is a statement about Dickens; that "lasting depressions and terrors may be caused by such cuttings-short of the natural development of childhood."[9]

Henry McBride shared the view that the job of the art critic is to clarify the work of genius and that it is almost in the nature of genius to be misunderstood by contemporaries. At one point he wrote: "Directly in proportion to the vitality of an artist's work is the reluctance of the public to accept it."[10] Then again he said:

> Gertrude Stein's friend, Alice Toklas, says that she has met three geniuses in her lifetime and that each time a bell within her rang, and she was not mistaken. I am that way myself. Alice's three geniuses were Gertrude, Pablo Picasso and Alfred Whitehead. My latest is Walt Disney. The moment I walked into the Kennedy Gallery where the Mickey Mouse originals are shown, the bell rang sharp and clear.[11]

Speaking of literature, the book reviewer Nona Balakian (1978) writes

Taking part in a recent symposium on literary criticism, a noted critic confessed that criticism for him was "all a matter of individual opinion." Apologizing for the low level of criticism today, he bluntly concluded: "The decline of creation has led to the decline of criticism." And still more sourly, he added: "Nothing very much is happening in the novel."[12]

Psychologists who have tried to find what is excellent in art have stressed above all the inherent sense of order and harmony (Arnheim, 1974). This has led to the field of experimental aesthetics and the need to find universals that explain aesthetic appeal. Anthropologists who have examined primitive art have discovered that the peoples of tribal societies had many aesthetic ideas and that their artistic productivity was often of a high order (Jopling, 1971; Biebuyk, 1973). It is well known, however, that in primitive cultures the identity of the artist as a rule remains unknown. In spite of this lack of individual identification they often produced works of great beauty. As long ago as 1520 Albrecht Dürer, on observing objects brought in from Mexico, wrote: "All the days of my life I have seen nothing that rejoiced my heart so much as these things, for I saw amongst them wonderful works of art and I marvelled at the subtle ingenuity of men in foreign lands. Indeed I cannot express all that I thought there."[13]

From this discussion it becomes clear that artists, psychologists and critics have all approached the topic with the same image of man that has so often appeared before: rational, conscious, and moved by external forces. With such an image art and creativity can only appear to be a divine inspiration, a shaft of illumination, as it has often been put. Those who have it are geniuses, or at least very gifted, and they are the important ones in the world of art. Manifestly a deeper psychological approach must come from psychoanalysis. Once more it must be noted that the difference between the analytic approach and the commonsense or academic-psychological approach lies in the more profound questions that psychoanalysis has had the courage to ask, even if the replies tend to be somewhat more speculative. In other words, psychology, again, has always been used; what is at issue is what kind of psychology it should be.

Toward a Theory of Creativity

A satisfactory theory of creativity must take into account all the evidence, psychological, psychopathological, sociological, historical, and anthropological. Because much of this is already available, the construction of a theory is largely an integrative effort. However, there is no intimation here that all the problems have been solved. The psychoanalytic approach becomes on the one hand a work of coordination, and on the other a program for further research.

The Nature of Fantasy

In all cultures, at all times some fantasy life has existed. Because of his preoccupation at the time with neurosis, Freud in his early work made the mistake of assuming that fantasies are inherently pathological: "A happy person never fantasizes, only an unsatisfied one."[14] This error has misled many subsequent analysts to act and write as if they were dealing with pathology rather than with an inherent capacity of the human mind.

Fantasies may develop spontaneously or as a result of stimulation from surrounding people. Either way, in the beginning and for a long time to come, they deal with the basic human needs—life, birth, death, sexuality, aggression, fear, and the like. Whatever branch of art is approached, the same facts emerge. The oldest known artifact of sculpture, a figure from Willendorf in Germany, depicts a pregnant woman with large, pendulous breasts. Thompson, who devoted his life to the study of the folktale, detected persistent similarities among the products of many cultures, even though he had no use for any special kind of psychology:

> No one will doubt that we are dealing everywhere with essentially the same human activity, and that the interest in a story is practically universal. Moreover the actual subject matter of folktales shows many striking resemblances from age to age and from land to land. And although the patterns differ somewhat, there is a tendency for the tales to range themselves into certain well-recognized formal groups, depending on style, purpose, or occasion for which they are used.[15]

The Id

Since fantasies deal with basic human needs, they are an expression of the id. Fear, love (including sexuality), and aggression (including hatred) are reflected in all artistic endeavor.

One of the earliest psychoanalytic discoveries in this field was that the sexual and aggressive drives, which play such a vital role in the psychology of any neurotic, find an outlet in art as well. But while the neurotic is driven into illness by his conflicts about the drives, the artist is able to use them constructively. The neurotic will be "shocked" by the sight of a nude body, for example, and the artist will simply paint it.

On closer inspection, however, it turns out that the artist's concern with the basic impulses was not as innocuous as had been supposed. The question then arose: How does the artist manage to handle these impulses, which others find so dangerous?

Narcissism: Healthy and Unhealthy

Because of the nature of his work, the artist becomes more narcissistic than the average person. However, the narcissism is transferred to his work, and he shares it with an audience rather than focusing it on himself. This has been treated in Chapter 3 (pp. 53–58).

The Ego

The outcome of the narcissistic struggle over the impulses depends on the strength of the ego. With a strong ego as a rule the narcissism is healthy; with a weak ago it is pathological.

It is always the ego's task to control the impulses. The contrast between control and release of impulse leads to the dichotomy between classical (control) and romantic (release) forms of art. Otto Rank's description of this distinction was especially noteworthy (Rank, 1932).

Inner and Outer Creativity: Every Man an Artist

One of the most important outcomes of psychoanalytic treatment of all kinds of individuals is the discovery that everybody can find some creative outlet. The stifling of creativity is characteristic of neurosis; its release is one sign of mental health. This point has also been touched upon before (Chapter 3, pp. 65–66).

This should not be mistaken to mean that every man is a potential Shakespeare or a Michelangelo. Quite the contrary. The creativity released by psychotherapy is the capacity to do things and is not related to talent as such. To come back to Freud's sculptural metaphor cited above, analysis brings out the person's stifled capacities but does not create new ones.

The experience of spontaneity that is let loose by the psycho-analytic process could be called inner creativity. This stands in contrast to outer creativity, which is the capacity to produce something new to the world. Ordinarily discussions of creativity center exclusively or too heavily on outer creativity, while the vastly more important question of inner creativity is neglected. This goes along with the emphasis on victory and success in all the social sciences.

The recognition that inner creativity can be released by proper education or by psychotherapy carries the implication that every man is potentially an artist. The quality of the work will vary, but the artistic outlet is available to all. We have already mentioned the awe with which many modern masters have reacted to the productions of unknown "primitive" artists.

Reference may also be made here to technical experiences with the projective techniques (Rorschach, Draw-a-Person, Thematic Apperception Test, and so on). These are devices in which the individual is asked to perform some artistic task, such as drawing a picture, telling a story, or constructing a play. From the way in which the subject performs these tasks many inferences are drawn about his personality. There is a vast literature on the relationship between the artist's personality and his work; in their book *The Creativity Question* Rothenberg and Hausman (1976) note that some nine thousand references are available.

Originality, Competence, and Popularity: The Question of "Great" Art

If there is one question that has concerned theoreticians and artists more than any other, it is: What makes art great? The philosphy of aesthetics has been kicked around for centuries without any really conclusive result. Little has been added to the cliché, Beauty is in the eye of the beholder.

In this area cultural factors play a vital role. For several centuries now the artist has liked to see himself as a critic of the culture, one who has "deeper" insights into what his fellowmen are doing than anyone else. As a result he has generally been on the side of the rebels and has often led a rebellious life himself (Egbert, 1970). However, many artists have led conventional, conservative lives, hence the element of rebelliousness is not essential to art. And in previous centuries, as well as in other cultures, a different role was often reserved for the artist. In a study of a traditional African artist, Abatan of Nigeria, Robert Thompson showed that the two aspects of art, tradition and innovation, normally held to be antithetical, form in this woman's works a dynamic unity—that is, her art is embedded in culture and yet is autonomous.[16]

Then again it may be observed that many works of art, some even held to be masterpieces, have achieved enormous popularity only to be forgotten by later generations, sometimes even the very next one. This is particularly the case in literature, where a list of the best-sellers of an earlier generation would elicit little more than blank stares today. In *Culture and the Crowd* (1969) Deric Regin traces the shift from elitist to proletarian culture over the past two centuries. It was about two hundred years ago that men in most artistic and intellectual fields began to rebel against the forms and formulas of the classical world. There lies the watershed between the stable classical and the restless modern way of life. It divides cultural history into two periods, one of hierarchical values and elitist judgment and one of mass consensus. McLuhan's well-known book *The Medium is the Message* carries this kind of thinking further.

Thus popularity need not at all be an index of the inherent worth of any artistic product; it may and often does reflect instead the inherent tensions between the artist and the audience. The man who can express these tensions carries the crowd with him and may achieve immense popularity for a while, only to be forgotten when the tensions change and he cannot change with them. This explains the frequent observation that many writers have only one book in them, and after the first have less and less to say, if indeed they write at all.

Thus no definition of great art is possible without reference to the social and cultural conditions in which the work was produced, distributed, and appreciated (or despised). Critics never tire of pointing to one artist or another who was ignored by his generation only to be revered as a great master fifty or a hundred years later; van Gogh and Shakespeare are two famous examples.

In *The Social History of Art* Arnold Hauser (1951) tried to draw parallels between the art of any epoch and the cultural productions of the time. But as he was the first to admit, these parallels, while valid in general, admit of innumerable exceptions.

Consequently, the social pressures that impinge on the artist in any generation must be given full weight in any definition of great art or simply of art. As Hauser shows, in ancient Greece and Rome the artist occupied a low rung in the social ladder. Seneca said: "We offer prayers and sacrifices before the statues of the gods, but we despise the sculptors who make them."[17]

Actually periods when the artist was held in high esteem—the Italian Renaissance, Western culture in modern times—have been rare. For most of history the artist was dependent on the bounty of patrons whose generosity varied with their vanity.

Today the artist is dependent on those who hold the purse strings, what Faye Levine calls "the culture barons." The commercial element in all art in the current scene is decried by most artists, yet there is little they can do about it. Consequently the conflict between artistic purity and commercial success has become particularly acute. Levine (1976) documents the manner in which money has come to dominate every art form but neglects to point out that it is only the form that has changed, not the control.

Work and Creativity

Picasso turned out 35,000 works of art in his life. Michelangelo, in painting the Sistine Chapel ceiling, lay on his back every day for four years. August Strindberg's *Collected Works* run to more than fifty volumes. Obviously the creative individual is a person who can work.

This close connection between creativity and productivity must be accorded great theoretical weight. Ordinarily in a theory of creativity the emphasis is placed on the "inspiration," the "creative idea," the "spark of genius," and the like. However, no matter how many sparks are there, they still have to be kindled, and this is where the element of work comes in.

Chaim Gross, in his introduction to a book by Edrita Freid, *Mental Health in the Creative Individual*, expresses some surprise at the usual psychoanalytic theory of creativity as a neurotic expression, stating that what he loved most in life was his artistic work and that the same was true for most of the artists he knew. And they spent most of their time at it.

Ideally the capacity for work derives from healthy narcissism. As a child the future artist produces some product that is praised by the parents. On the basis of this praise, he reacts with healthy narcissism and produces more. The combination of work and praise eventually leaves him with a feeling of great self-confidence and high self-esteem. Artur Rubinstein, who conforms to this pattern, tells us in his autobiography that despite an extraordinary capacity to memorize musical scores, he would often improvise when he played the piano in public, and the audiences, not sufficiently sophisticated musically to know the difference, would still applaud enthusiastically.

An intuitive appreciation of the different roles that work plays is seen in the reaction to a work block on the part of creative and uncreative individuals. If the creative individual stops creating, we say that he is suffering from a creative block and try to get him past it. If the uncreative individual does not want to work, we say it is only natural, and he deserves a vacation.

The antithesis of work in the creative artist is depression. The depressive may be seen as a person who is unable to work but instead longs for the comforts of infancy. In a hospital situation one technique for getting him past his depression is to force work on him (occupational therapy) or provide some creative outlet (recreational therapy). There is an important hint here for a proper distinction between satisfying work and unsatisfying: Satisfying work is an aspect of inner creativity, unsatisfying a routine performance without meaning.

Neurosis and Creativity

Our analysis provides no basis for the commonly held belief that the artist is inherently neurotic; this would appear to be a relic of the old idea that the artist is either a madman or a genius. It is of course true that many artists are neurotic or, not infrequently, psychotic, but the connection between their art and their illness is complex.

The early analysts were so impressed by the frequency of neurosis among artists that many tended to assume that art per se was an infantile fixation. This is clearly erroneous. The artist is a human being, and like other human beings he has to struggle with mother, father, sexuality, Oedipal conflicts, and the like. If he falls ill in this struggle (becomes "neurotic"), the reasons may not be different from those that lead to neurosis in other humans. The art per se has nothing to do with it.

CREATIVITY AND THE PSYCHOANALYTIC VISION

The psychoanalytic vision sees creativity as the birthright of everybody. The creativity envisioned however is inner creativity, the release of spontaneity and the capacity for growth. This release may take place either through education or through psychotherapy. Like any other aspect of the analytic ideal, it may be repressed, distorted, or exaggerated out of all proportion, but this should not obscure the fact that creativity is one of the most desirable features of a happy life.

Within our own culture, the emphasis on creativity as a rule is concealed behind the wish for notoriety or success. As soon as anyone begins to write, paint, or engage in any sport, the first thought commonly is how well he is doing. Many persons stay away from any creative endeavor at all because they are "no good at it." By shifting the emphasis from success to the inner experience creativity can be fitted into its proper place.

Language and Communication

In accordance with the nineteenth-century image of man, it was held that communication follows an orderly, rational procedure, embedded in language. Neurosis was seen as an expression of "irrationality," largely incomprehensible. At best it was viewed as an outcome of brain damage, and any communicative value of the symptoms was totally disregarded.

Naturally psychoanalysis changed all that; hence in a sense the problem of communication was virtually discovered by Freud and psychoanalysis, although it has of course branched out considerably since then. To put this in another way, one of Freud's great discoveries was that the classical symptoms of neurosis are unconscious forms of communication. In hysteria the patient speaks in symptom language, which is made possible by the fact that the listener does not understand the meaning of the symptom. Thus the typical scene of the Victorian lady who fainted in the drawing room and was promptly given smelling salts has disappeared today, because everybody would know that she was just trying to get attention and would call in the nearest psychiatrist. The hysterical woman's *arc-de-cercle* position, which neurologists of Freud's day regarded as part of her "degenerate" weakness, vanished when Freud pointed out that such a woman was presenting herself in the sexual position.

Kubie and Israel (1955) present a fascinating case of a five-year-old girl admitted to the hospital with a diagnosis of "mutism." Kubie examined her and heard the faint words, "Say you're sorry." He thereupon called a conference of all the professionals, with the child present, and instructed each one in turn to say loudly "I'm sorry." Thereupon the child began to talk. Her "mutism" had been a single-track demand that certain words be spoken, not mutism at all.

The Development of Linguistics

The twentieth century has seen an extraordinary growth in the science of linguistics, to such an extent that it is sometimes listed as a separate department in universities (e.g. New York University). By now many of the formal aspects of language use have been unraveled. Most striking and best known is Noam Chomsky's conception of transformational grammar (Chomsky, 1967), which claims that every person has an unverbalized conceptualization of deep linguistic structures in accordance with which he patterns his own linguistic utterances. Other linguists have criticized Chomsky for ignoring semantics, or the communicative content of language. The generative semanticists have attempted to replace his grammatical transformations with transformations of meaningful units (Winograd, 1972).[18] Thus, in spite of the extensive knowledge uncovered, linguistics still tells us almost nothing about the essential human problem connected with language, that of communication.

In Sapir's (1921) definition, language is a purely human method of communicating ideas, emotions, and desires by means of a system of voluntarily produced symbols. While language subserves rational thinking, its chief function in human affairs, he emphasizes, is communication. Thus while linguistics has investigated the forms of communication, it has remained for psychoanalysis to examine its disturbances and failures, as well as the realities of what human communication is all about. (This is in no way changed by the recent remarkable demonstration that chimpanzees can learn a considerable amount of American Indian or other sign language.)

It has long been known that language gratifies significant emotional needs. The twelfth-century chronicle of Salimbene reports a linguistic experiment of Frederick II. King Frederick wanted to find out what kind of speech children would have when they grew up if they spoke to no one before. So he bade foster mothers and nurses to suckle the children, to bathe and wash them, but in no way to prattle or speak with them. He was interested to know whether they would speak the Hebrew language, which is the oldest, or Greek, Latin, Arabic, or perhaps the language of their parents. But he never found out, because all the children died. They could not live without the loving words of their foster mothers. Perhaps apocryphal, the story is still relevant to the twentieth-century concern with autistic children.

The Realities of Linguistic Communication

While the facts surrounding language universals and linguistic development are both useful and interesting, they tell us no more about the realities of linguistic communication than the physiology of the brain tells us about the thoughts a person is thinking. As the problems have been unraveled in the course of psychoanalytic research, the following conclusions have emerged:

1. Schizophrenia, the last ditch of mental illness, is a disorder of communication. Even to the layman the outstanding characteristic of the schizophrenic is that he is "unintelligible." Actually he comes to the attention of his social circle or professionals only when his utterances and/or actions reach the point of unintelligibility, even though more careful examination would have revealed serious sources of difficulty much sooner. Nothing in human behavior is totally irrational; what seems irrational is the expression of some unconscious conflict, and once the unconscious roots are known everything falls into place (see also Chapter 3, pp. 61–63).

Lyman Wynne and his collaborators at the National Institute of Mental Health have been in the forefront of researchers investigating the background of the communication disorder in schizophrenia. Their subject population has included approximately six hundred families (Wynne et al., 1978). Their principal finding has been that disordered styles of communication are a distinguishing feature of families with young adult schizophrenics. In these families, communication processes appear to be disturbed when the basic phase of focusing attention and sharing foci of attention begins. In the families of borderline, neurotic, and normal individuals communication problems also occur but are more evident later on in communicational sequences, after an attentional focus has been initially shared by two or more persons. The researchers set up a hierarchy of "communication deviance" categories and found that schizophrenics have difficulty from an early age not only with thinking but also with sharing their experience. They suggest that instead of thought disorder the term "communication disorder" should be used.

2. Dreams are a form of communication. It is for this reason that Freud's epochal work *The Interpretation of Dreams* marks a turning point in the history of psychology. The same kind of analysis that makes dreams intelligible makes many other seemingly meaningless communications intelligible. Psychosis has in fact been designated a "waking dream."

3. Many neurotic symptoms, such as hysterical conversions and obsessional rituals, were "decoded" by Freud and his co-workers as symbolic ways of communicating with other people. The very first patient in psychoanalytic history, Anna O. (Freud and Breuer, 1895), who invented the term "the talking cure," had a linguistic problem in that for a while she could speak only English instead of her native German. We are reminded of the nineteenth-century observation that most people have a "burdensome secret" that they are ashamed to reveal and of which the final disclosure brings great relief (Ellenberger, 1970).

4. The process of psychoanalysis focuses in the most intimate detail on the ways in which two people communicate with each other, both verbally and nonverbally. Actually, it could be said that interpretation in psychoanalysis represents an attempt to put into adult words what the patient is trying to communicate in other ways, either by actions or by linguistic utterances from an earlier stage of development.

Freedman and Grand (1976) have presented a large number of research studies bearing on this topic. Spitz (1965) had already shown that the basis for dialogue is laid down in the growth of the infant's capacity to say no or to differentiate between yes and no, which occurs about the age of fifteen months. Others, building on Spitz's ideas, focus upon the more or less derailed maternal dialogue and try to demonstrate, in analysis of the behavior of preschool children, how completed or uncompleted cycles affect the child's later ability to initiate social contacts, engage in shared play, and manifest empathy.

In the area of nonverbal communication few reliable generalizations are possible. Freedman and Steingart (1976) have shown in several ingenious experiments how there is often a close connection between body movements and inner conflicts.

5. While truth and honesty are highly valued in all cultures, lying and dishonesty are more common. Even though lying is of fundamental importance, it has received almost no attention from psychologists, even analysts. Most people would look upon the utter-

ances of politicians as conscious lies, but clearly much unconscious distortion goes on as well. Ludwig (1965) has one of the few extended discussions of this topic in the literature.

6. The extraordinary importance attached to propaganda in the totalitarian countries has emphasized more than any other single factor the distortions of communication that prevail in the everyday world. Hitler's notorious emphasis on "the big lie" has unfortunately been all too often imitated. In many social and political areas truth is hard to come by.

Harold Lasswell pioneered in the attempt to grasp the connections between political power and language (Lasswell, Leites, et al., 1949). Central to his analysis was the concept of the *political myth.* This comprises the whole body of beliefs existing in any given age, generally traceable to certain fundamental assumptions which at the time, whether actually true or false, are believed to be true by the mass of the world with such confidence that they hardly appear to bear the character of assumptions. Perhaps a better way of phrasing this is to speak of *group fantasies,* which operate in many realms of life.

7. In everyday life, a primary distinction must be drawn between *manipulative* and *expressive* communication. Expressive communication is rational behavior, the main kind recognized by traditional psychology. More common however is manipulative communication, in which the intention, conscious or unconscious, is to manipulate another person to do something or feel a certain way. In schizophrenia the communication is almost always manipulative; it is less so in less disturbed conditions.

Rose Spiegel (1959) has suggested a fivefold classification of manipulative communication: (1) grossly destructive, (2) authoritarian, (3) disjunctive, (4) pseudo-communication, and (5) noncommunication (nonverbal).

COMMUNICATION AND THE PSYCHOANALYTIC VISION

For many people (especially women) the complaint "no sex, no communication" has become the rallying cry that brings them to analysis; they sense that analysts favor a sane sex life and interpersonal communication. The "silent American husband" has become a cliché of our times; unfortunately it is not merely a cliché, it is often a reality. One of the principal discoveries of psychoanalysis is that ours is a world in which people do not communicate with one another. Many people even turn to animals because the human beings around them are so detached.

Very often communication is carried on through a fantasy world. Psychoanalysis has a systematic approach that makes fantasies intelligible. In our own age films have become a powerful communication medium. Raymond Durgnat has written: "*We* are the Immortal Gods, watching the screen characters live their anguished lifetime in 90-minute lives. . . . Art doesn't really make the artist immortal, but it makes the audience *feel* immortal."[19]

As fantasies change, their expression must necessarily change. Whether it knows it or not, the audience responds more to deeply felt unconscious strivings than to surface wishes. It is this alteration in the inner fantasy life that serves to clarify the differential popularity of various fantasy productions.

But the psychoanalytic vision calls us away from fantasy, back to reality. It is better to change the reality than to drift off into fantasy. The proper study of communication and the ways in which it can be improved thus chart a course back to a more realistic, constructive attitude to other people and to life.

Chapter 12

The Complexities of Causation

IT SEEMS AS though every year some scholars issue a new pronouncement that the social sciences have proved nothing and lead nowhere. One of the latest such assertions comes in a book by Lindblom and Cohen, *Social Science and Social Problem Solving* (1979). These authors, one a professor at Yale, the other at Harvard, say the record of social science is deplorably meager. "With relatively few exceptions social science does not in fact produce and confirm generalizations."[1] The number of such exceptions is so paltry that the authors do not even give any examples. Instead, they argue that since analysis of the situations is useless, we should promote "professional social inquiry."

This kind of nihilistic view, though quite popular in certain circles, must be rejected as unscientific. The issue relates primarily to the question of social causation: What causes what in the social field? To this question some reasonable answers can be given, even if they are not as pat as those in other fields of inquiry.

The Problem of Causation

It is well known that the course of modern physics has brought into dispute the age-old principle of causality, once thought to be an a priori characteristic of the world and of the human mind. With quantum mechanics and the Heisenberg principle of indeterminacy, it seems as though causal laws of the precise kind envisioned by

Newton and his age have vanished. This is an oversimplified version of the situation.

Nagel (1961) has an excellent discussion of this topic, and we follow his reasoning here. The traditional principle of causality was most clearly formulated by John Stuart Mill as the principle of the uniformity of nature: "There are such things in nature as parallel cases; that what happens once will, under a sufficient degree of similarity of circumstances, happen again."

It is this formulation that has come under attack because of the requirement of parallel cases. But, as Nagel points out, it is this formulation and not the principle itself that is made dubious by modern physics. He proposes the following formulation instead:

> The function of the principle [of causality] is to make explicit a generalized goal of inquiry and to formulate in general terms a *condition* that premises proposed as explanations are required to satisfy. Moreover, it is also clear why on this interpretation the principle cannot be disproved by any experiment or series of experiments, although *special forms* of the principle may be abandoned as ill-advised in the light of experience. For the principle is a *directive*, instructing us to search for explanations possessing certain broadly delimited features; and even repeated failures to find such explanations for any given domain of events is no logical bar to further search.[2]

Thus causality remains a general principle of inquiry, both in the natural sciences and in the social sciences. The differences between these two fields lie in the nature of the material to be investigated, not in any alteration of the principles of science as such.

In his early years, and even almost to the end, Freud insisted over and over again on the principle of determinism in psychic life. In later formulations of psychoanalysis this has been dropped, for it is now clear that all natural events, and that includes psychological as well, come into being by certain decipherable courses of events and not by chance.

In psychology proper, the partisans of "pure" science have stressed the stimulus–response principle (S-R), and in the main this principle has been cited as the chief objection to psychoanalytic theorizing. But as a directive for inquiry, the S-R principle is completely faulty, because it ignores the role of the organism, either animal or human (Fine, 1969). The correct formula is S-O-R. As many have noted this basic correction cuts through to the heart of many of the misunderstandings (see Chapter 4).

In what we have been calling the nineteenth century image of man, the assumption is that the organism, or the person, plays at best the role of a mediating telephone circuit; in Thorndike's classical terms, connections are stamped in or stamped out, and the only role the person plays is to allow these stampings to take place. Skinner makes essentially the same error with his exclusive stress on schedules of reinforcement (Fine, 1975). Even though his own followers have made trenchant critiques of his position (Breland, 1961; Glaser, 1971), Skinner has remained adamant and allows no intervening variables.

These psychological theories have naturally had a profound impact on the social sciences, which must depend on others for their underlying psychological assumptions. The elimination of the person as a vital force in any stimulus–response system corresponds to the nineteenth-century image of man; the introduction of the person as affecting every S-R system moves on to the twentieth-century image. In the social sciences the assumption of man as an inert connecting mass emerge most clearly in the definition of economic man (see pp. 242–243) as one who is impersonal and unsocial. Our detailed analysis has shown how similar assumptions underlie all the social sciences and have vitiated their inquiries and their results.

The principle of inquiry leading to an understanding or explanation of social phenomena must therefore include the role of the person if any meaningful conclusions are to be drawn from the data. The directive (in Nagel's terms) is to seek out all the factors involved, including whatever the individual does or does not contribute.

Michael Scriven (1965) has attempted to show that there is an essential unpredictability in human behavior. His argument is that predictions embody a contrapredictive effect, which is unavoidable, so in many cases no predictions can validly be made at all. This is similar to what the sociologist Robert K. Merton has termed the "self-fulfilling prophecy."

In principle, however, this argument does not hold. If predictions arouse a contrapredictive reaction that spoils the prediction, this is simply one more fact, unwelcome though it may be, to make predictions about human events so much more difficult than predictions about natural events. Once more it underlines the extreme complexity of social phenomena and social causation (see Chapter 6).

Nagel also discusses why statistical laws have become the rule in the social sciences, whereas mathematically precise laws are the goal and often the rule in the natural sciences. He points out that the

universal form in which physical laws are cast is the fruit of a successful logical strategy.[3] In many cases it is possible to state laws as
universally valid under certain ideal conditions and for pure cases of
the phenomena under investigation, and then to account systematically for any discrepancies between what the laws assert and what
observation reveals.

This strategy is not customary in the social sciences because it is
far too difficult. (Nagel somewhat dubiously offers the reason that
adequate theoretical notions have not been developed in the social
sciences.) Attempts in this direction are seen over and over again, for
example, the body of mathematical psychology or mathematical
laws in economics. Even Marx's inexorable laws of history are steps
in this direction. But the discrepancies from observation become too
great, and the mathematical system has to be dropped.

It follows that social causation is so complex that it cannot be
approached adequately with the mathematics currently available.
This need not, however, be a deterrent to closely reasoned and accurate inquiry. If the data do not permit greater exactness, to attempt
such greater exactness is clearly foolhardy. Generalizations have to
conform to the data at hand.

Nevertheless, as has been seen, inquiry is possible; causative
connections can be ascertained with some degree of probability; and
social science can proceed as a rational domain of inquiry, provided
that the data are not distorted to force them into a mold that calls for
more quantification than is theoretically possible. This is the error
many social scientists have made, attempting a degree of precision
and exactness greater than the data warrant.

Psychoanalysis and Social Inquiry

The role of psychoanalysis and psychoanalytic psychology in
social inquiry must be evaluated in the light of the above considerations. It is only then that their true contribution to social science can
be appreciated.

From Freud on, no responsible psychoanalyst has offered a total
explanation of any social phenomenon. In *Totem and Taboo* Freud
inserted the following disclaimer:

> There are no grounds for fearing that psychoanalysis, which first dis-
> covered that psychical acts and structures are invariably overdeter-

mined, will be tempted to trace the origin of anything so complicated as religion to a single source. . . . Only when we can synthesize the findings in the different fields of research will it become possible to arrive at the relative importance of the part played in the genesis of religion by the mechanism discussed in these pages. Such a task lies beyond the means as well as beyond the purposes of a psychoanalyst.

Thus psychoanalytic psychology fully recognizes, and has always recognized, the complexities of social causation. What it contributes is an understanding of the psychological factor, the importance of which may vary from great to small. And, as has been stressed throughout, this contribution is particularly important because in the other approaches to social science the psychological factor has been either omitted entirely or approached in terms of an outmoded nineteenth-century image of man.

Two Examples of Social Research: Social Influence Processes and Homosexuality

The issue involved can be clarified more easily in terms of specific problems. Two such problems, much discussed, have been chosen almost at random: social influence processes and homosexuality.

SOCIAL INFLUENCE PROCESSES

In order to focus the discussion, the comments here will center on one book, *The Social Influence Processes*, edited by James Tedeschi (1972). Its preface states that the current status of theory and research in the area of social power and influence is clearly inadequate from almost every point of view. The editors then set themselves the goal of providing some new beginnings and stimulating new directions for social psychological research. "The emphasis is upon the development of scientific theory."[4]

The introductory chapter reviews some of the theoretical discussions of social power. Most of the definitional problems concerning the concept of power are identified as philosophical or prescientific. The authors then say that the "modes of influence are those that exist between two persons—the source of influence and his target." However, there is no further attempt to classify in terms of important people, merely "sources" and "targets." Immediately one flaw in the research procedure becomes obvious: premature generalization without regard to the empirical data.

The succeeding chapters consider in turn (1) how people define the psychological situation; (2) personality as a power construct; (3) the notions of cognitive complexity recently developed; (4) the relationship between the source of influence and the target individual; (5) social power within the context of exchange theory; (6) various questions concerned with the source of influence; and finally (7) a general theory of the social influence processes as they affect the target individual. "All interpersonal interactions are interpreted in terms of tacit or explicit communications of threats, promises, warnings, or mendations."[5] By a "mendation" Tedeschi indicates he means an influencer's positive prediction of a contingency between a target's behavior and a favorable outcome, where the outcome is not controlled or affected by the source of influence.[6]

The chapter that comes closest to discussing what happens to real people is the one by Walster and Abrahams. However, it is discussed in terms of learning theory rather than in terms of real-life experiences. About romantic love we are told:

> When we discussed romantic love, we suggested that a mixture of emotions might be a common prelude and accompaniment to romantic love. Schachter's . . . research suggested all that was necessary to produce "love" was strong physiological arousal accompanied by the cognitive label "love." The physiological arousal so necessary to a romantic experience could presumably come from a wide variety of sources.[8]

The theory offered in the last chapter is called the subjective expected value theory of social influence or belief probability. We are told that decision theory is derived from classical economics, but changed to fit men, who are not omniscient. Many of the generalizations reached are so obvious that one wonders why they are stated: People like to be liked, the effect of a source of influence depends on the status of the source in the target's mind, and so forth. Finally the editors sum up their theory as follows:

> A rather uncomplicated theory was built upon the expected value definitions. Source characteristics of attraction, status, prestige and esteem were defined as orthogonal factors which serve to bias the target's estimations of the probability component of the expected value of the message and hence affect the influenceability of the target. The reader should also be reminded that the present theory concerned a

rather passive target in a dyadic influence process in which predictions were of a binary nature. The theory does present, however, a firm framework for a more dynamic conception of human interaction. The evidence, where it exists, is generally encouraging for a subjective expected value theory of influenceability. However, individual differences factors, when considered, may well produce a number of interactions and destroy the simplicity of the present formulation, *which has deliberately omitted personality theory.*[8]

This conclusion is typical of the methodological morass and confusion that come out of work of this kind. In effect it offers a personality theory, then denies it. And how can human interactions be discussed in any reasonable way without reference to some theory of personality? Emotions are as usual disregarded or oversimplified. Love is certainly more than a physiological arousal to which a cognitive label is attached. (I have devoted two whole chapters of the present book to the topic of what love really means to people and has meant to them.) Four major criticisms of this work can be made:

1. It is based on an image of man as "rational"[9] and involved in some form of communication, explicit or tacit. The latter is obviously true but completely unexplored in terms of real-life communication.

2. Together with the image of rationality goes the image of decision therapy similar to that in classical economics. We have already seen (p. 242) that this image is the nineteenth-century version of man, completely contradicted by everything we know.

3. The evidence for statements rests very largely on experimental situations. In these the main social influence mechanisms, such as force, violence, sex, and actual rewards (not tokens), cannot be duplicated. The value of the experiments as such is therefore open to question. Psychoanalytically oriented research would instead examine the real-life experiences of people and their various reactions to influence.

4. The final sentence acknowledging that the authors ignore personality theory, is the clue to what is going on. In reality, they are merely reformulating personality theory in terms they consider "scientific." But in the process they omit all consideration of such vital elements as transference, the unconscious, the developmental process, the changes in personality, age, SES, pathology, cultural background, and so forth. As a result the conclusions reached are almost entirely worthless, from both a theoretical and a practical point of view.

HOMOSEXUALITY

In the past ten years there has been a marked upsurge of interest in homosexuals and homosexuality. As it is usually put, gay sex has come out of the closet. In its revision of its diagnostic system in 1979 the American Psychiatric Association even reclassified homosexuality as not pathological unless accompanied by distress. A number of large-scale studies of homosexuals, mainly men, have appeared in print. How is all this to be evaluated? And what is its cause, or what are the causes, of overt homosexuality?

Two theories are prominent in this area. One is analytic, and at the same time the common sense, position that a man becomes homosexual because he is sexually frustrated and has had poor inter-personal relationships in childhood. The other is that homosexuality is simply a deviant form of sexual expression. It is noteworthy that no one who offers the theory of deviance offers any explanation of why one man becomes homosexual while another does not; it seems to be regarded simply as a naturally occurring variation.

The deviance theory has been stressed particularly by the homosexual groups and buttressed by the Kinsey Institute for Sex Research. In the first large-scale study from the Kinsey Institute (1974) Weinberg and Williams state:

> Our final suggestion is that homosexuality be conceptualized in terms of social statuses and roles rather than as a condition. "Homosexual" is a social status, and the role expectations surrounding it account for the types of homosexuality that any society produces. . . . In other words, the notion of the "homosexual," for some purposes, can useful-ly be seen as a cultural product, a status. This status is not inherent in the individuals associated with it, but it influences them by organizing other persons' reactions to them and giving those persons who occupy the status a stereotyped set of traits to orient their own behaviors and attitudes toward themselves.[10]

In a more recent study from the Kinsey Institute (Weinberg and Bell, 1978) this position is maintained. What the authors seek to demonstrate now is the relationship between homosexuals' life-styles and their social and psychological adjustment.[11] They then proceed to construct a typology of sexual experience among male and female homosexuals. No attempt is made to consider the more significant question of what causes homosexuality. Some material on this topic is promised for a third volume.[12]

If the evidence is examined critically, some extraordinarily ex-treme positions become evident in the pro-homosexual group. As

Socarides (1974) has commented, homosexual groups have resorted to violence to prevent sober scientists from presenting their findings objectively. In the APA revision of the Diagnostic and Statistical Manual III, the bizarre term "homodysphilia" was coined to refer to homosexuals who are distressed by their homosexual arousal.[13] In a referendum held among the members of the American Psychiatric Association, 58 percent of the respondents upheld the Board's reclassification of homosexuality.[14]

However, the notion that only distress is pathological, as assumed by the APA vote, is the exact opposite of our analytic views of mental health. Distress about an abnormal condition would be normal and would lead to proper remedial measures; lack of distress is repression or denial. Thus the APA vote merely indicates that most psychiatrists are not familiar with the simple notion of repression. The only conclusion to be drawn is that the APA is in a state of serious moral and intellectual decline, a conclusion reached from other directions in Chapter 5.

The "evidence" often cited for this "vegetarian" view of homosexuality (some like meat, some like vegetables), as it has been called, is grossly inadequate and in a number of cases outright nonsense. In her "questionnaire" study of women Shere Hite (1977) found that only 30 percent of her subjects experienced orgasm in intercourse, from which she inferred that sexual intercourse was a plot foisted on unsuspecting women by men who wished to deprive them of the pleasures of masturbation. The studies by Hooker (1957, 1958) have been completely refuted in a number of ways (Fine, 1973). First of all, evidence contradicting her main thesis was simply rejected out of hand. Second, even her own analysis revealed a consistent difference between homosexuals and heterosexuals, which she disregarded. Third, what she was examining was whether judges working blind from written protocols could distinguish between homosexuals and heterosexuals; they could not, but this in itself proves nothing. And fourth, no mention is made of the fact that subsequent studies of the Rorschach protocols of overt homosexuals have consistently shown a dynamic pattern different from that of the heterosexuals (Stone and Schneider, 1975). Even though Hooker's studies were not up to professional standards and prove nothing, they continue to be quoted by persons favoring the sociological position described above.

While investigators like those of the Kinsey Institute and Hooker find no substantial differences in adjustment between heterosexuals and homosexuals, others find enormous differences. Ollendorf (1966), after studying 292 cases, concluded that juvenile homosexual experience has a markedly pathological effect on later personality formation. The classic study by Bieber and his associates (1962) found that a considerable percentage of homosexual men could become heterosexual as a result of psychoanalysis; the percentage was higher in those who were originally bisexual than in those who were originally exclusively homosexual.

The objection has been raised to studies like those by Bieber and by Socarides (1978) that analysts treat only the "sick" homosexuals and do not see the "well" ones. First of all, as any analyst knows, in the course of the analytic treatment of any patient, reports are received from the patient on hundreds, often thousands of others. Thus the analyst actually has a very wide sample, even though it is unsystematized. And second, this view derives from a serious misunderstanding of the nature of psychotherapy and a denial of the adjustment neurosis, which has led virtually the entire population to seek out therapy as a means of salvation. And finally, as a method of research, the course of analytic treatment reveals far more about the personality characteristics of patients, homosexual and otherwise, than do superficial questionnaire studies.

Curious results were reported by the Masters–Johnson group in their study of homosexuality (1979). That sexual responses of homosexuals are no different from those of heterosexuals scarcely needs any proof, since for both sexes sexual responsiveness in masturbation and intercourse is the same. More interesting is the outcome of what they call their "10-year program for treatment of homosexual patients."[15] Sexual dysfunction in homosexuals was found to be highly treatable. Then they state that they also "achieve surprisingly positive returns from treating homosexual men and women with a more difficult problem—the desire to convert or revert to heterosexuality."[16] Among men they had nine "conversion" clients, of whom seven were successful and two were failures, and forty-five reversion clients, of whom thirty-six were successful and nine were failures. The professional world was startled by these figures, especially when it is recalled that the Masters–Johnson team uses a two-week educational reorientation program, which is not really therapy. The high percentage of persons who wished to become heterosexual and did so in two weeks is further proof that the psychological set of the patient is more important than anything else.

Anthropological and historical knowledge can be applied here as well. No sexually permissive society ever known has led to a wide incidence of overt exclusive homosexuality (which is what is under discussion here.) Wherever it has been investigated, an exclusive homosexual orientation has been found to result from deep-seated heterosexual frustration. This commonsense notion has been amply confirmed by analytic theory and analytic experience.

What is there to say, then, about the currently widespread belief that homosexuality is just a "normal" deviation, of no more significance than wearing a hat or not wearing one, which also varies with the times? Two comments: It is first, totally devoid of objective foundation. Second, it has become part of a profound political battle. Within psychiatry it is the battle against a humanistic psychoanalysis led by the reactionary organic psychiatrists. Within a number of the professions it is a battle led by militant homosexuals who are out to assert their power: The Association of Lesbian Social Workers and the Association of Gay Psychologists are examples. Within the culture it is a battle against a healthy resolution of life in terms of the analytic ideal.

Looked at more closely, the "vegetarian" theory of homosexuality makes two gross blunders. First of all it uses entirely inappropriate research methods that prove nothing and that could not prove anything because the investigation lacks any depth. And second it is totally devoid of any theory of homosexuality. For even if one were to assume that homosexuality is simply a deviation within the "normal range," as Hooker and others allege, this would not explain why it occurs. After all, the basic sexual physiology of all human beings is the same; the variations are so minor as to be negligible. How then can such a basic physiological apparatus lead to widespread psychological variation without a great deal of input from childhood and the family constellation? Not even an S-R theory is offered by the advocates of homosexuality; no theory at all is put forth. This makes no sense.

Clearly the topic of homosexuality has become a political football. The intellectual arguments in its favor need not be taken seriously.

The Psychoanalytic Vision and the Problem of Social Causation

Our main conclusion is that the problem of social causation is extraordinarily complex and simply has been avoided by almost all theoreticians. What psychoanalysis contributes is an understanding of the psychological factor and a methodology for getting at this factor in specific instances. Without this methodology, much of the empirical research is simply worthless; much of it needs considerable refinement before it can be used.

Two points have consistently been stressed throughout. First, psychoanalysis provides a more refined image of man, giving full weight to both internal and external factors. Second, since social scientists become better acquainted with social than with psychological forces, they tend to see the social as causative. This costly error has vitiated much of their work. The problem of causation, as Nagel observes, is a problem of a method of inquiry, a directive for research. Full discussion of the causation of any social phenomenon is bound to be extremely complex and must include the psychological factor. The problem, however, is not so difficult as to lie beyond the means currently at our disposal. What is most essential is to get rid of the bias against psychology, especially of the depth variety.

Part III

Psychotherapy

Chapter 13

The Emergence of a New Profession

IN ONE FORM or another, psychotherapy has always existed. Man, frightened by pain, has sought ways to eliminate it, deny it, face it, or relieve it. For thousands of years the difference between physical and mental pain was virtually indistinguishable. The crystallization of the existence of anxiety, a psychic pain entirely different from, though related to, physical pain, is one of man's great cultural achievements. Even today this distinction is a mystery to the lower classes and to many professionals in the field of mental health.

Historically and currently, five stages of psychotherapy can be enumerated. In the first, magic played the dominant role. For most of human history, including today in many parts of the world, systems of magical belief have been dominant. In the second stage, magic gave way to religion, where the emphasis is on supernatural powers that must be placated to avoid otherwise inevitable suffering. Many men have valued the ethical precepts of religion while disavowing the supernatural. This led to the third stage in psychotherapy, philosophy. The numerous philosphical schools that have thrived and thrive today have been discussed in a previous chapter.

About the time of the French Revolution, philosophy gave way to medicine, the fourth stage. Finally psychology came in with Freud.

Before that can be discussed, some comments must be made about the role Christianity, as the precursor of our current system, played in the management of mental illness.

Christianity as Delusion, Destructiveness, and Paranoia

Whatever its professed tenets might be, in the centuries preceding the French Revolution Christianity *functioned* as a ruling system based on delusion, destructiveness, and paranoia. Its replacement by medicine in the nineteenth century can only be understood as a reaction to this age-old madness.

The climax of the Christian delusional system came in the fifteenth and sixteenth centuries with the persecution of "witches," although the roots of this persecution extend back a long way. Even today historians (Gay and Webb, 1973) underestimate the depths to which humanity sank in those ages, possibly because those were also the centuries of the Renaissance and of the growth of modern science.

Bromberg (1954) comments: "The science of witchcraft of the medieval period was a discipline that strove to explain wrongdoing, madness, senility, impotence, hysterical and psychopathic symptoms in terms of demon possession."[1] What makes this "science" of such fundamental significance is first that it was fully sanctioned by the official church, from the pope down, and second that it led to the outright murder of hundreds of thousands, perhaps millions, of innocent people, mainly women (see Chapter 7).

The notion that witchcraft merely reflected the Zeitgeist has already been discussed (see pp. 198–200) and rejected. It is the same kind of rationalization that leads to the justification of homosexuality as a "sociological status" (see pp. 298–301). Its realities must be given more weight.

The early Christians built up a paranoid system. Humanity, the Christian fathers asserted, had to be preserved from the "thousand demons to the right and ten thousand to the left."[2] In the third century Tertullian insisted that a malevolent angel was in constant attendance on every person and that only the most energetic Christian action could combat its evil influence. Origen explained that demons produce disease, famine, infertility, corruption in the air, and pestilence. They hover concealed in clouds in the lower atmosphere, attracted by blood and incense, which the heathen offers to them as gods.

After the publication of *Malleus Maleficarum* in 1484, the inquisitors had a bible, which was a textbook of pornographic sadism.

The theme was that "woman is a temple built over a sewer." All witchcraft comes from carnal lust, which in women is insatiable.

Faced by such a delusional paranoid system, it was only to be expected that the church would move on to murder the enemy, which it did. Torture of the most horrible kind, no less monstrous then the tortures of Hitler, Stalin, and Idi Amin in modern times, were inflicted on the innocent victims until they died.

From the Priest to the Doctor: Revulsion Against Torture and Murder

Somehow, the fury spent itself. By the time the French Revolution rolled around, the world had had enough of being tortured and murdered by a psychotic clergy. Yet, even though the practices were given up, the theory espoused by the church has never changed. The Witchcraft Act of 1735 in England, based on the delusion of "trafficking with the devil," is still in force.[3] And the Catholic Church still believes in demons as the cause of many ailments, and recommends exorcism of demons as the cure. The film of the best-selling novel *The Exorcist* attracted enormous crowds some years ago, proving that the delusions are still in force in a considerable segment of the population.

To get the patients away from the clergy, recourse was had to the theory that there must be something wrong with the brains of these abnormal people. Hence the physician, trained in medicine, should handle them. Someday science would discover the cause of the illness through the advances of biochemistry (see Chapter 5).

Thus was psychiatry born. But its derivation as a replacement of Christianity left it with important residues. First of all, the "patient" had to be a deviant, obviously "crazy" even to the layman. Hence psychiatry dealt only with the maladjustment neurosis. It had nothing to say about the disturbance in the general population, which we know today to be infinitely more important. Second, the language of demonology was translated into the language of psychiatry: Instead of demons psychiatrists now spoke of "diagnoses" (Reider, 1955). Third, the practice of torture was continued in greatly modified form. While the excesses of the eighteenth century were removed, others gradually took their place. Patients were housed in large, ill-kept hospitals (now being dismantled); they were kept there involuntarily without real treatment, put in straitjackets, brought close to death in insulin coma; and they were subjected in the course of time to a wide variety of assaults against the body, such as electric shocks, dangerous drugs, and extraction of many parts of the body, from the teeth to the intestines, or even castration. Before the modern era, they were kept in hospitals until they died. If they got better, many times they were ignored, or in some cases the psychiatrists, guided by Kraepelin, changed the "diagnosis"—they had selected the wrong demon. Just as the realities of Christianity have been ignored in favor of its words and ideals, the realities of organic psychiatry have been ignored in favor of learned discussions about heredity, neurotransmitters, diagnoses, and the like.

Anton Boisen, the founder of pastoral counseling, had a breakdown in the early 1920s and was hospitalized at Elgin State Hospital. In *The Exploration of the Inner World* (1936) he writes:

> The doctors did not believe in talking with their patients about their symptoms, which they assumed to be rooted in some as yet undiscovered organic difficulty. The longest time I ever got was fifteen minutes during which the very charming young doctor pointed out that one must not hold the reins too tight in dealing with the sex instinct.[4]

Some fifty years later, the simulated schizophrenics whom Rosenhan introduced into mental hospitals (see previously) fared little better: They averaged eight minutes a day with the staff. Psychotherapy with the mentally ill is still as rare as hens' teeth. In line with its Christian origin, the notion that the demons could not be exorcised was translated into the scientific jargon that the patients were incurable.

From the Doctor to the Analyst: The Freudian Revolution

The Christian-psychiatric tradition continues to this day and remains dominant in most parts of the world. Change has come about only through the discovery of an entirely novel element: psychology. In one sense this is the most fundamental contribution of the Freudian revolution: the revelation of the inner life of man. We have stressed throughout how this leads to an entirely new image of man.

Many of the consequences of this changed image of man have already been spelled out; there is no need to repeat them here. What

is of consequence now is to show how this entirely new image of
man has led to an entirely new image of psychotherapy, and hence
to a therapeutic revolution.

In traditional psychiatry, as in Christian demonology, the patient is a "sick" person, a deviant. He must be secluded from the majority, for the good of the community, as well as for his own good. If
he should turn out to be afflicted with a certain illness (demon)
known as schizophrenia, the outlook is hopeless. Therapy is useless;
even if modern drugs bring some relief from the symptoms, the prospects for a happy life remain gloomy. No comment can be made
about the "normal" person who does not suffer from a "psychiatric
disorder."

With the Freudian revolution all of this had to be changed in its
entirety. The "patient" is not sick; he is unhappy. He may or may
not be deviant from the majority. To seclude him does more harm
than good. The outlook for schizophrenia, as for other forms of unhappiness, is not at all hopeless (Bleuler, 1970, 1978). The prospects
for a happy life are not at all so bad if a happy life is sought. The
average individual in the culture may be seriously unhappy. There
is, however, a technique that can lead to more happiness, and that is
psychotherapy, based on the principles of psychoanalysis. The adjustment neurosis is as painful as the maladjustment neurosis. All the
world needs therapy.

Psychotherapy: The New Profession Created by Psychoanalysis

Once Freud had made sure of his fundamental discoveries, as
early as 1900, he visualized the creation of a new profession that
would follow in his footsteps. For even then he realized that the neurologists and others of his day had no competence whatsoever in the
real practice of psychotherapy. A new training system was needed.
And just as his own work had come primarily out of his self-analysis, eventually he was to see that this new profession had to rest securely on one foundation: personal analysis.

In this respect once more Freud took a revolutionary step forward. If the emphasis was to be on the analysis, then the degree was
irrelevant. And in fact among the members of the Vienna Psychoanalytic Society there were persons from every walk of life: lawyers,

musicians, editors, psychologists, and philosophers, in addition of course to doctors of medicine.

From this radical approach two problems emerged that have plagued the profession ever since. First of all, if psychoanalysis is a broad philosphical systematic approach to life, then its practitioners can come from anywhere, not merely medicine; this is the problem of lay or nonmedical analysis. And second, if analysis is so essential, at what point in training should it be undertaken? In particular, if a person has an advanced degree, how can he be influenced to be psychoanalyzed? Conversely, if he has been psychoanalyzed, why should he take an advanced degree? But before these problems can be discussed more fully, the training system itself must be described in some detail.

The Psychoanalytic Training System

Although Freud was still alive and active in Vienna, the first psychoanalytic institute with a systematic training program was set up in 1920 elsewhere, in Berlin. Its founders include some of the most distinguished names in the history of psychoanalysis: Karl Abraham, Karen Horney, Sandor Rado, Hanns Sachs, Otto Fenichel, Franz Alexander, and many others. Although it has been subjected to severe criticism from many quarters, the training system is still maintained today in all psychoanalytic institutes, Freudian or neo-Freudian, with virtually no substantive changes. Since it has been faulted as the cause of so many of the bitter disputes in psychoanalysis, that system is worth examining in more detail.

The program had four constitutents: (1) the training analysis, (2) the theoretical courses, (3) control analyses, and (4) control of training by the analytic society. These still remain in all institutes.

The Training Analysis

To begin with, the candidate for analytic training must undergo a "training analysis." This immediately raises the question: Why? After all, the candidates are all doctors of medicine or have advanced degrees in some other field. How can they be so "sick" that they require "treatment"? And why is it called a training analysis, rather than simply analysis, or personal analysis?

The answer to these questions contains a discovery about modern man (really by generalization all men) first brought to light by Freud's self-analysis. All men seem to suffer from disturbances in love, work, sexuality, communication, and other aspects of the analytic ideal. Furthermore, it soon became an established principle that no analyst could take a patient farther than he had gone himself, that the blind spots of the analyst inevitably interfered with the analytic process.

What was initially called a "training" analysis (literally learning analysis, *Lehranalyse*) was later referred to as a "didactic" analysis. The term "didactic analysis" disappeared long ago, when it became evident that the analysis of the prospective analyst did not differ one whit from the analysis of any patient. Thus ideally the training analysis serves to demonstrate to the candidate that he too has always suffered from neurotic problems in some measure and that these problems can be overcome by analysis.

The need for a personal analysis has been affirmed and reaffirmed by every analytic institute. No person can analyze others who has not been through a successful personal analysis himself.

When the Berlin Institute was founded in 1920, it admitted both medical and nonmedical persons, although the medical contingent was by far predominant. (The question of lay analysis will be discussed more fully below.) All the candidates were eager to go through the new method of analysis. The world, as sick then as it is now, was licking its wounds after World War I and the revolutionary changes in government that had come in its wake. A kind of missionary spirit prevailed. Candidates were only too happy to be analyzed and to partake in this new way of transforming the world. As part of their practical experience, they donated their time to the Berlin Clinic, which was financed by Max Eitingon, one of Freud's most devoted admirers. All the patients then were given full, intensive analyses, at no fee or at fees that they could afford.

In 1920 psychoanalysis was still a neglected stepchild. At the annual meeting of the American Psychoanalytic Association that year, one of the members suggested that the organization be disbanded because of the lack of interest in the field.[5] Fees were correspondingly low; even Freud charged American and British physicians, then the wealthy ones, only ten dollars a session.[6]

Not until after World War II did psychoanalysis became a source of wealth and power for its practitioners. In a recent text on technique, the author actually lists as one of the reasons for becom-

ing an analyst that it "provides a good income,"[7] while another analyst recently stated that one good reason for maintaining the ban on
lay analysis in the official medical institutes is that man is after all
homo economicus and accordingly physicians have a right to make
more money.[8]

In this changed situation, and with the changed requirements
for admission to institutes, the personal analysis acquires a different
coloring. It is resented as an encroachment on the individual's sense
of personal adequacy and is bitterly fought. Consequently, the analytic institutes have complained about the decreasing number of candidates who are willing to submit themselves to this rigorous regi-
men, as well as about the caliber of those who do.

The July 1979 Newsletter of the New York Psychoanalytic Institute, the oldest, largest, and most prestigious society in the world,
contained a variety of complaints and lists of disappointments.
Twenty-four applications had been received, as compared with
thirty applications the previous year. Of those applicants, *two* were
accepted and *eight* rejected; fourteen had not yet been processed.
Since the last annual report there had been only one graduation, but
it was stated that there would probably be several more during the
next few months. The number of Treatment Center applicants was
declining. The total membership had declined from 323 to 319 in the
past year, but the total number of regular members had declined
from 284 to 258, a drop of almost 10 percent in one year. Two suits
were pending from disappointed students. Legal fees were reported
to be $58,450. In his concluding remarks the outgoing president of
the Society, Dr. Leo Stone, said "As to the future, I would make one
suggestion: that we give up our insular view and position in the psychoanalytic and medical world, heed the pleas and warnings of various official colleagues, and intensify our connections with and in related organizations."[10]

As early as 1952 Robert Knight, in his presidential address to
the American Psychoanalytic Association, had complained that the
majority of candidates were "normal characters," not introspective,
inclined to read only the literature assigned to them, and eager to get
through with the training requirements as quickly as possible.[11] Obviously, such persons, who were merely sitting through a series of
required courses, one of which was a personal analysis, could not be
expected to have any real vision of what analysis might do for the
world. The ideal had already been sacrificed for the sake of success,
monetary as well as organizational.

The preliminary requirement of an advanced degree for admission also created an entirely new problem. Many people are impelled to enter analytic training by their personal problems. In a study of Boston psychoanalysts, Zinberg (1967) found that no fewer than one-third had had some therapy while they were in high school or college.[12] Many persons in the course of their analyses experience such an extraordinary amelioration of their life situations that they naturally wish to communicate this amelioration to other people, especially when they realize how unhappy so many human beings are. Analysts who view the profession as a business see this desire as a "symptom" rather than a step forward.[13]

Again, the dilemma has arisen: If a person has a degree, usually an M.D., why should he be analyzed? And if a person has been analyzed, why should he get a degree? No adequate solution to this dilemma has ever been found, and it continues to haunt the profession. It also interferes with the psychoanalytic vision.

In the beginning, the institutes grossly underestimated the time needed for the training analysis. Karen Horney stated in 1930 that it should take at least one year.[14] In 1956 the American Psychoanalytic Association regulations stated that "experience indicates that at least 300 hours of analysis, and usually more, are required."[15] In 1960 Lewin and Ross found that the length of training analyses varied from less than 200 to 1,950 hours and that there were enormous discrepancies from one city to another.[16] For many years now the New York Psychoanalytic Institute in its Bulletin has stated:

> The preparatory analysis is the foundation for the training in psychoanalysis. Its objectives are not different from those of a therapeutic analysis and include freedom from personality factors that would interfere with the ability to conduct psychoanalytic treatment. Therefore, no fast rule can be applied to the duration of the preparatory analysis which is determined by the analyzing instructor. *It will be seen that any statement of a definite number of hours of analytic treatment is incompatible with this concept.*[17]

Thus the length of the training analysis still varies widely. It is not surprising that the system has created innumerable "training transferences" (Glover's phrase), which form the background for the seemingly interminable dissensions and splits within the ranks of every institute.

Ideally the personal analysis should occur before the candidate seeks training. it can then be conducted like any other analysis, with maximum benefit to the patient. (Karen Horney did in fact suggest such an arrangement in the earliest discussions of the Berlin Institute.[18]) From the ranks of those who have had a successful analysis, by the usual criteria of the analytic ideal, the most promising candidates for analytic or therapeutic work can be chosen. Such an ideal is hard to realize, but like all ideals at least it points to a direction out of the present impasse. The assessment of the crucial quality of personal aptitude can then be made on the realistic basis of how much change has occurred as a result of the individual's analysis. In comparison with this, all current methods of assessment of talent are crude and have led to confusion.

Thus the conclusion emerges: Without a personal analysis no one can do therapy properly. But the complications involved in setting up the requirements for the personal analysis are enormous. The present system has led to innumerable and interminable controversies. Once a person has a degree in one of the professions (M.D., Ph.D., M.S.W.), the conflicts surrounding the personal analysis are insuperable. In fact most people with degrees—perhaps 90 percent—do not get an adequate personal analysis; many of them get no analysis at all.

The New Profession

In his psychoanalytic vision Freud called for a new profession whose members "need not be doctors and should not be priests."[19] The new profession has been created, especially in America, but still leaves much to be desired.

Looking first at the most clearly defined group, the American Psychoanalytic Association, the report of the Committee on Professional Education and Research (COPER) after much preliminary study held a special conference in 1974, the results of which were published in 1977 (Goodman, 1977). These bear meaningful comparison with the earlier survey done by Lewin and Ross, published in 1960.

The mean length of the training analysis was about 20 percent longer in 1974 than in the survey done twenty years earlier.[20] Further, wide variations occurred from one group to another. In 1960 the range was from an average of 463 hours in Philadelphia to 963 in Cleveland, and in 1974 the range was from 506 hours at Duke University at Durham, North Carolina, to 1,386 at Cleveland.[21]

How is it possible that there should be so much difference from one location to another? Are the candidates in Cleveland so much "sicker" than those at Duke, or the reverse? And why should the average training analysis last 20 percent longer in 1974 than in 1957? No answers are forthcoming from the figures.

According to Goodman, the absolute number of new students entering analytic institutes has remained unchanged for twenty years, in spite of the large increase in population and available professional pool. The numerical increase in the American Psychoanalytic Association can be ascribed to the opening of new institutes.[22]

Particularly intensive criticism was leveled at the quality of research done by graduate analysts. The commission stated:

> The commission [on research] concludes that all is not as well as it might be with the scientific life within the Association. A flow of fresh data and new and solidly based additions to theory, particularly clinical theory, are needed; and these must come from an organized research effort. The commission feels that there is a dampening of research effort within the psychoanalytic profession at two levels. It occurs at the level of scholarly inquiry, where research is often inappropriately equated with restrictive experimental and laboratory models, rather than broadly defined and adapted to the particular discipline of psychoanalysis. It is also manifested at the socio-organizational level, where the major emphasis has been upon those training activities which are the source of important career awards. As a result there are too few personal incentives or organizational structures to reinforce research activity.[23]

In general, the conference concluded that the training system, essentially unchanged since 1920, had produced many excellent clinicians but few adequate researchers. Furthermore, at all levels, and in relation to all pertinent questions, considerable disagreement remained. It was frankly admitted that they were dealing with "inherently difficult and complex problems."[24] It is now also openly admitted that there are economic factors that "restrict and even coerce career choices."[25]

It has always been known that political considerations, which play a role in all organizations, have shaped many of the decisions within the American Psychoanalytic Association and have influenced many of the bitter battles.

Although the training analysis is the absolutely indispensable base for all further analytic work, in the United States the American Psychoanalytic Association chose to ally itself with medicine and psychiatry, thus shifting the emphasis from the analysis to the degree. This has led to some highly complex and unsavory political maneuvering.

Many analysts have felt queasy about the fact that the term "psychoanalyst" has no legal standing. Repeated applications to the accreditation section of HEW to restrict the title to persons approved of by the American Psychoanalytic Association have been rejected. This is part of the long quest for official recognition, which was denied to Freud by his own university and has remained the rule ever since.

In the search for such recognition, some members in 1958 proposed that psychoanalysis be made a subspecialty of the American Medical Association's Board of Psychiatry and Neurology. This proposal, contradictory to all the basic principles of psychoanalysis, was defeated by the Board of Professional Standards the next year, after vigorous debate in the component societies. It has never been officially revived.[26]

An extraordinary piece of political legerdemain took place in 1972. In the preliminary discussions about coverage for national health insurance, the American Psychiatric Association issued a paper in which it recommended exclusion of psychoanalysis and long-term psychotherapy from national health insurance coverage. After considerable soul-searching the American Psychoanalytic Association came up with the following compromise:

> As a result of that meeting [with the psychiatrists] the Committee on Health Insurance concluded that a Position Statement of the American Psychoanalytic Association should *not* emphasize the special and unique features of psychoanalytic treatment, but rather the similarities and commonality of psychoanalytic treatment with the mainstream of psychiatric and medical care. *It was felt that such an approach would be much more effective in offering a strong case for its coverage under national health insurance.*[29]

Surely no clearer example could be given of the fact that many psychoanalysts have completely lost sight of the psychoanalytic vision, replacing it with the conventional search for power and wealth. Thus the long, intensive training analyses have not made them any less power-hungry or money-grubbing than the next fellow.

Looking at the larger picture of all the mental health professions, the issue of the training analysis becomes completely confused. In the first place it is not a requirement for work in any of the fields, so that it becomes a purely private arrangement for practitioners. Some of them do it, some do not. It is hard enough to evaluate the quality of any training analysis done under the auspices of an official institute. It is utterly impossible to evaluate the training analyses of the profession at large. Even the grossest forms of psychopathology, such as psychosis, criminality, and sexual perversions, which at least are eliminated by the official system, are found at times among unanalyzed or poorly analyzed practitioners.

A further peculiar restriction has occurred with the principle of "society control of training." This principle states that the individual practitioner must refrain from training unless he has the permission of the society to undertake it. Presumably the training analysts represent the cream of the crop. Barring persons who are not official students from training (which includes analysis as its main basis) further restricts the availability of competent analysts for the rest of the profession. Once more, sight is lost of the psychoanalytic vision, and emphasis is placed on the assertion of power.

Summing up, the training analysis is indispensable for all therapeutic work. Yet even within the official institutes it has varied widely and led to interminable disputes. For the profession as a whole its effects are impossible to estimate with any precision. It can only be concluded that without a personal analysis no one should be permitted to carry on any form of psychotherapy, but the quality of such an analysis is so hard to gauge that by itself it is insufficient to guarantee the competence of any therapist. In many cases the drive for power and wealth has replaced any idealism. A drastic overhauling is needed to restore the psychoanalytic vision.

THE CURRICULUM: THEORETICAL COURSES

The curriculum of the first psychoanalytic institute has likewise survived, in expanded but essentially unaltered form, in all later institutes. There were two years of theoretical courses covering (a) normal psychology, (b) psychopathology, (c) Freud's writings, (d) technique, and (e) applications of psychoanalysis to art and literature. The third year was devoted to practical experience with supervision ("control analyses") and a technical seminar.[28] On paper, at least, little has changed except that the theoretical length of the course has usually been expanded to four years, the actual length to something like ten. Naturally, as new discoveries have come in, new writings have been added to Freud's.

Inasmuch as the vast majority of students entering the analytic institutes today have already covered this material in their previous training, the question arises: What is the justification for maintaining this curriculum today? In fact, complaints that the course material is extremely redundant or much too elementary are heard all the time.

The analytic candidate is exposed to much repetition on all counts. About 75 percent of those applying to institutes of the American Psychoanalytic Association had had previous treatment;[29] 42 percent had even been analyzed. Still, they had to have more analysis by an analyst assigned to them rather than chosen by them (as is true of the average patient), and the analysis was to be of indefinite duration, with results often open to question. Likewise, the theoretical material offered repeats much of what had previously been covered in psychiatric residencies or graduate programs in psychology and social work.

The bias in the personal analysis has gone hand in hand with considerable theoretical confusion. Roger Shapiro rightly comments that differences in theory frequently become part of a political struggle rather than a scientific investigation within psychoanalysis.[30] Schafer points out that Freudian psychoanalysts have been steadily assimilating what is best in Object Relations Theory, Sullivan and the Culturalists, and the existentialists, in spite of official condemnation of these positions.[31] Yet for them to admit this publicly would be tantamount to courting political ostracism. The result is that many of the current articles, deriving from so many different approaches, are so obscure that they are really unintelligible. The analytic student, who is required to parrot this literature or leave the institute, remains confused.

It need come as no surprise that the Committee on the Ideal Institute of the American Psychoanalytic Association found that the current institute structure has apparently been least effective as a means of achieving a continuing dialogue and mutually influential exchange with the wider world of science and scholarship housed in the university.[32]

The analytic institute grew up in response to determined opposition from the universities. Though considerably diminished, this opposition continues today. Nevertheless, there are enough positive forces within universities for a meaningful course of psychology, which is what psychoanalysis really is, to be taught.

Proposals to this effect have been forthcoming for many years. Dr. Lawrence Kubie first described such a plan thirty years ago.

Freud himself had already suggested it in his 1926 book *Lay Analysis* but he could not foresee that it could actually be adopted at some future time by universities. The Kubie plan was elaborated by the Chicago Psychoanalytic Institute, under the leadership of Dr. George Pollock, and approval was obtained from the Illinois Department of Education for granting a Ph.D. in psychoanalysis. The Chicago Institute, being a constitutent member of the American Psychoanalytic Association, had to obtain approval of its plan, now known as the Chicago Proposal, from the parent association. Surprisingly, such approval was denied, and the plan had to be shelved.[33]

A somewhat similar plan, developed by Dr. Robert Wallerstein at the University of California, has been in operation for some years. The California group has sought to obtain approval of its graduates for admission to the institutes. Thus the theoretical work would be done under university auspices, which makes sense, and the clinical work done privately, which also makes sense. Approval of this plan has been postponed by the American Psychoanalytic Association. Lurking behind this hesitation lies the fear of training too many non-medical analysts. For such programs would obviously stress psychology and broad social science training rather than medicine.

The Commission on the Ideal Institute in 1974 stressed that collaboration between psychoanalysis and the university structure was a highly desirable goal. All of the above proposals likewise conform with their recommendations and, further, with the psychoanalytic vision. Nevertheless, they have been consistently rejected by the official body. Since this official body has not hesitated to play ball with untrained psychiatrists for the sake of getting insurance coverage, it is obvious that power and money have been more important than vision (Fine, 1979a).

CONTROL ANALYSIS

A "control analysis" is one in which the student-practitioner presents the contents of his sessions with patients to a more experienced analyst, who guides him in the management of the case. It is called supervision in all similar situations and could just as well be termed supervision here; in fact, it would simplify matters to use the term "supervision," because control seems to imply a degree of authority that supervision does not.

The concept of a control analysis as an integral part of the analytic training grew out of the medical setting (Maetze, 1970). In ordinary medical practice the fledgling physician can carry out his activities in the presence of and under the watchful eye of a more experienced physician. Obviously this is impossible in analysis. So the next best device was to record the sessions and present them separately.

In light of the difficulties encountered in psychoanalytic treatment, this procedure amounts to an intensive tutorial experience. It is used in all the healing professions in one form or another; social work has elaborated it most extensively. Of the various aspects of analytic training it has given rise to least question.

Society Control of Training

Within the standard institutes individual psychoanalysts are strictly forbidden to conduct any training. All training is limited to the formal track prepared and supervised by the directors.

This startling rule is unique to the psychoanalytic profession. It has never been seriously challenged as an educational principle, although it has been challenged as a legal prerogative of the societies. Even more curious, it has been taken for granted so completely that it is never even discussed. So far as the present writer has been able to discover, there is not a single article in the psychoanalytic literature that has ever considered its pros and cons.

To begin with, it comes up in the selection of students. Naturally, for official admissions some official rules with the usual criteria for evaluation must exist. But for psychoanalytic training the criteria are notably vague or even nonexistent.

The Goodman (1977) report states that the number of applications has remained relatively constant since 1959. However, the number of acceptances, after fluctuating only minimally around the 50 percent point, increased to 60 percent in 1971–72. As usual, there was a wide disparity in the acceptance rate from city to city.[34]

As to the basis on which 40 percent to 50 percent of those applying are accepted or rejected, all agree that the decision derives from personal judgment. As Karen Horney noted in the initial report of the Berlin Institute, personal aptitude for the field is essential, yet on how this is to be evaluated there is neither "clarity nor unity."[35] Lewin and Ross comment:

> The requirement that a student be "analyzed satisfactorily" defies academic definition, is bound to rest on individual or "jury" opinion, and

can be subjected to measurement as little as "true scholarship" (as distinct from official pedantry) or, for that matter, as little as love, which notoriously, "N'a jamais connu la loi."[36]

The commission charged with considering the whole tripartite system (Goodman, 1977), evidently realizing that the selection process has rested so heavily on personal subjective judgments, simply ignored the problem in its discussion.[37]

Thus the selection process is arbitrary, evaluation of the training analysis uncertain, many aspects of the training procedure highly variable, and graduation postponed for many years. Yet through it all society control must be maintained at all costs.

In his initial paper on the training analysis, Hanns Sachs (Maetze, 1930) made some remarkable statements. The future analyst must learn to recognize things that others easily overlook, particularly if these observations conflict with his own feelings and wishes. So far, all is in accord with the psychoanalytic vision. But then Sachs goes on to say: "Analysis requires something which corresponds to the novitiate of the church."[38]

It would seem that the facet of the analytic training system corresponding most closely to this demand for a novitiate is the emphasis on society control. Especially today, when there are so many conflicting points of view, the student must learn to agree with his masters. As in the churches, which demand absolute obedience to superiors, the analytic candidate must either obey or leave the institute.

Society control has been strictly enforced, despite its dubious legal base. When the American Psychoanalytic Association tried to expel William Silverberg and Clara Thompson in 1950 because they were conducting "unauthorized" training, they retained a legal firm to challenge the right of the association to regulate training. Thereupon the suit was dropped. Further efforts to acquire the legal authority to punish members who were involved in unauthorized training were forestalled.[39] Instead, an undeclared system of intimidation was instituted. Members who violated the rules were denied patients, appointments, and other privileges.

Looking at the matter from a larger perspective, society control has had a number of undesirable effects, all particularly harmful to the psychoanalytic vision. First of all, the number of applications to the institutes has remained quite small in relation to the enormous growth in the mental health professions. Undoubtedly many people are deterred by the rigid requirement of a "novitiate." Second, in practice it has proved unenforceable. And third, it has hampered the activities of the best talents in the societies but has had little or no effect on the others.

The fact remains that the nature of psychoanalytic training is such that it defies strict regulation. Personal analysis is open to anyone who finds a competent analyst. Theoretical courses are available in various mixes; even the highly regulated institutes offer "extension" courses in which the same material is taught as in the standard curriculum. And controls or supervision can be bought.

Thus in every institute, sometimes almost unofficially attached to it, there has been a kind of black market where anyone who wished to do so could get training, perhaps inferior in quality to the official offerings, but certainly not very different. The qualities of talent and personal aptitude have always carried more weight in the long run than the required training.

The hunger for power has gone so far that currently a battle is going on in the American Psychoanalytic Association that might result in the expulsion or inactivation of about five hundred, or one-fourth, of its active members. This battle ostensibly again centers on "certification." All graduates of component societies, even though members of the association, would be required to be "certified" as competent psychoanalysts by a national board. While most members have complied, apparently there are about five hundred or so who do not wish to do so.[40] Considerable debate now rages about whether to allow these five hundred persons to remain as regular members of the association. The action of the board in requiring certification, like the earlier attempts to expel members in the 1950s (Fine, 1979a), may well be in violation of the charter, but no member has as yet had the courage to challenge the authorities.

In other disciplines the equivalent of society control works because the institute has a legal right to offer a degree (M.D. or Ph.D. or M.S.W.), without which a person cannot practice. The only way in which analytic society control coerces the individual is by admitting or rejecting him; it does not have the right to grant a degree. Hence allied to society control is the attempt on the part of the institute to convince the public that it has a monopoly on all the competent practitioners. This attempt has not been notably successful. It often seems that the less adequate practitioners have more of a following than the more adequate ones, primarily because they offer the patient more gratification of his dependency needs. The elimination of society control could vastly enlarge the availability of psychoanalytic teachers and thus prove a boon to the furtherance of the psychoanalytic vision.

Disciples and Deviants: The Splits in Psychoanalysis

As everybody knows, the analytic world is divided into many factions. The two largest groups in the United States are the American Psychoanalytic Association, which sees itself as "Freudian," and the Academy of Psychoanalysis, formed in 1956, which categorizes itself as "neo-Freudian." There are many other groups of varying sizes and dimensions and varying theoretical persuasions, medical and nonmedical, individual and group, all calling themselves "psychoanalysts." These splits have been extensive and serious, and serious attention must be paid to their causes and consequences.

Lest it be thought that these splits are all past history or that they involve only fringe groups, it can be mentioned that within the rigidly controlled American Psychoanalytic Association public notification was given of a split that occurred in the Los Angeles Institute in 1976. An ad hoc investigating committee, headed by Dr. Joan Fleming, stated that while the ostensible cause was the theoretical differences between Freudians and Kleinians, "of much more concern was the unrelenting hostility and distrust among various groups and individuals, whatever their theoretical orientation."[41] The Spring 1978 issue of the *Journal of the American Psychoanalytic Association* reported that on June 28, 1978, twelve training and supervising analysts in Washington, fed up with what they described as their futile efforts to correct "bad psychoanalytic teaching and example," had announced their intention to withdraw from the older Washington Psychoanalytic Society and to form a new group "to develop a program clearly within the mainstream of American psychoanalysis."[42] The details of the theoretical dispute there are not given, but presumably the same kinds of unrelenting hostility and distrust are at play, for it is stated that this group for years had been trying to correct the situation from within and had been unable to do so.

While criticisms of various analytic practices had been common enough from the outside, a wholly new factor was introduced in 1978 with the publication of a survey of psychoanalytic practice in the *Journal of the American Psychoanalytic Association.*[43] This paper was the report of a committee appointed several years earlier because of the concern of the association with the decline in psychoanalytic practice.

The conclusions were devastating. The percentage of analysts with three or fewer patients in analysis had increased to 40 percent. Ten to fifteen years earlier almost half of the members were treating four to seven analytic patients; by 1976 this proportion was down to one-third. The mean number of analytic patients had dropped from 6.2 in 1966 to 4.7 in 1978. Seventy-two percent of the membership feared that the practice of analysis would shrink drastically without insurance coverage. Criticisms of the profession and of some aspects of the professional organizations were widespread.

Nor is the situation any different in the rival organization, the American Academy of Psychoanalysis, which is smaller in numbers but quite influential in that almost every city in the country has an "orthodox" Freudian group and a "liberal" culturalist group. Marianne Eckhardt, the daughter of Karen Horney and now an analyst herself, reports on the splits in the cultural groups after 1941 in the 1979 anthology *American Psychoanalysis:*

> I took no active part and remained an observer. Being young and idealistic, I felt disillusioned. I experienced the events as an outcome of personal rivalries and clashes, and I agreed with those who later emphasized that the so-called issues were red herrings. . . . Schisms in psychoanalytic organizations are a particularly active and apparent manifestation of a spirit of conflict or dissension pervasively present in these organizations.[44]

Nor have these splits been confined to the United States. Between 1964 and 1968 the French Society split four times (Barande and Barande, 1975). In 1977 a dissident group in the Buenos Aires Society applied to the International for recognition as a provisional separate group.[45]

While ostensibly the splits are based on theoretical differences, as Fleming indicated in her report, underneath these differences lie bitter personal rivalries and hostilities. These rivalries seem to stem from many different sources. The Argentine analyst Leon Grinberg has suggested that analysts displace their hostility toward their patients, which they are forced to repress, onto their fellow analysts. The extreme rigidity of many of the leaders in the field is another important cause. Eitingon, for example, who founded the Berlin Clinic and Institute, was so slavish an admirer of Freud that he never wrote a paper, stating that Freud had already said everything. This rigidity has been worsened by the political system of psychoanalysis, which rewards obedience and punishes defiance. The result is a surface acquiescence, followed later by a violent rebellion.

Obviously all too often analysts lose sight of the psychoanalytic vision and start bickering like children. Doctrinaire positions are adhered to with stubborn tenacity, often in the face of a weight of evidence to the contrary. As in all other organizations, excessive power granted to the leaders tends to be corrupting.

Politics Versus Vision: The Attempt to Define Psychoanalysis

After World War II, the American Psychoanalytic Association made a serious attempt to achieve conceptual unity in the organization, for the lack of which it had been severely criticized. In 1947 a Committee on the Evaluation of Psychoanalytic Therapy was established.[46] In six years this committee was never able to arrive at definitions of psychoanalysis, psychoanalytic therapy, and transitional forms acceptable to a majority of its members. Incredibly, it was even forced to conclude "that a strong resistance to any investigation of this problem existed among the members of the American Psychoanalytic Association."[47]

The original committee was accordingly discharged and replaced in 1952 by a Central Fact-Gathering Committee, chaired by Dr. Harry Weinstock and charged with the responsibility of setting up a method for pooling the data of psychoanalytic practice (Hamburg et al., 1967).

Initial enthusiasm ran high. Questionnaires were sent out to all members of the association and to all advanced students. The design was simple enough: to compare the state of the patient at the beginning of treatment with his state at the end. Nevertheless numerous unforeseen difficulties arose. Returns began to fall off. This committee was therefore discharged in 1957. Incredibly, the association at its business meeting in 1958 voted that none of the accumulated material should be published. In May 1960 it was recommended that this action be reversed.[48]

Subsequently, a second committee, chaired by Ives Hendrick, reviewed the project and reported principally on the methodological difficulties encountered. Interest lapsed until a third committee was appointed in 1961 to prepare a report that would clarify the methodological problems and derive any substantive findings that might be stimulating to psychoanalysts generally and to future investigators particularly. The report, published in 1967, was prepared by the third committee, by then chaired by David Hamburg.

While the report per se was noncommittal in its remarks, it was devastating to the illusion that conceptual unity existed among the members of the American Psychoanalytic Association. The two largest areas of unresolved difficulty were in the areas of diagnosis and in judgments of treatment outcome. The approach of the committee had been along conventional psychiatric lines, using accepted diagnostic categories rather than more extensive ego profiles, such as those pioneered by Anna Freud (1965), Bellak et al. (1973), and others. Although most of the patients who finished their analyses were regarded as "improved" (as in the earlier studies going back to Fenichel, 1930) a dynamic clarification of this improvement was not offered. The whole episode must be regarded as a great fiasco.

Regrettably the sorry story has been repressed by the society. Only rarely has any mention of it been seen in subsequent issues of the *Journal*. Such repression is highly damaging to the image of integrity and full disclosure of all suitable material relating to analytic practice. It can only be concluded that the monolithic organization of the American Psychoanalytic Association conceals enormous differences under the surface, which erupt from time to time into open battle, as curently in Los Angeles, Washington, and Detroit. Lest this be taken as singling out one society unduly, I would like to express my feeling that it is true of all psychoanalytic societies.

This protective repression can only be interpreted as meaning that psychoanalytic organizations, like all organizations, are primarily concerned with the power and economic well-being of its members; idealistic wishes take a secondary role. Obviously this is equally true of physicians, lawyers, psychologists, accountants, and all other professional groups. They are there to protect their members, not to serve the public or pursue broad humanitarian goals. It is certainly regrettable that psychoanalytic organizations should be no different.

Hartmann (1956) once emphasized that psychoanalysis requires a "freedom from myth."[49] This can be achieved by focusing squarely on the essentials of the psychoanalytic vision, wherever that might lead.

Mainstream Psychoanalysis: Toward Conceptual Unity

Careful sifting of the arguments discloses that there is a common base for all analysts, which we have called *mainstream psychoanalysis.* It stems from Freud and embodies his major insights. But in many areas analysis has gone well beyond Freud. For example, about the early relationship between infant and mother he wrote almost nothing; today a voluminous body of literature exists on the subject. Subsequent theoretical disputes in psychoanalysis, to make sense, must be fitted into this mainstream development.

While theoretical disputes can go on for a long time without resolution, when it comes to therapy both the therapist and the patient have to behave in certain ways. Hence the splits here are sharper than in theory.

In spite of the inability to define psychoanalysis with any precision, certain aspects of the therapeutic procedure are common to all those who today call themselves analysts. These aspects derive from Freud's discovery of the central importance of transference and resistance. In fact, Freud at one point defined psychoanalysis as any approach that starts with the observations of transference and resistances, "even if it arrives at results different from my own."[50]

Freud's immediate collaborators, Adler and Jung, did not understand the principles of transference and resistance; Freud's papers on these topics were written after they had left the analytic organizations. (It may well be that he wrote them in order to clarify his technique for future students, so that they would not make the same mistakes Adler and Jung had made.) Their technical approaches therefore cannot be called psychoanalysis in any real sense of the word.

The approaches today that call themselves deviant, such as the culturalist school, the Object Relations school, or the recent Kohut technique for treating narcissistic personality disorders, all continue to regard transference and resistance as fundamental. However, within this technical framework considerable differences of opinion continue. Should the transference be tackled at once, as Melanie Klein used to do, or should one wait? Can the transference be completely dissolved, or will it always remain to some extent? Should termination aim at completion, or should one be satisfied with partial improvement? These and many other questions keep on plaguing contemporary analysts, who fill the journals with discussions of their relevant experiences.

Within the psychoanalytic procedure, however, more seems to depend on the warmth and empathy of the analyst than on any specific technical procedure he decides to adopt. Further, what works with one patient may not work with another. Hence, while psychoanalysis may be viewed as a technique deriving from Freud, the contemporary divisions into "schools" of psychoanalysis becomes misleading. This is one reason why the Fact-Gathering Committee could reach no consensus. In a review of the work of British analysts in 1938, when there were only twenty-nine in the entire country, all of whom had been trained either directly or indirectly by Ernest Jones, Edward Glover likewise found wide divergencies.[51] It may be assumed that all analytic work is characterized by careful attention to transference and resistance, although different techniques may be adopted at various stages to deal with them.

A sharp distinction, however, can be drawn between analytic forms of psychotherapy and nonanalytic forms, such as behavior therapy or "Gestalt" therapy. These systems should not be considered analytic in any sense, though they frequently make use of the insights of analysis. In general, they are all decidedly inferior to analytic therapy (see Chapter 14).

The Shift in the Patient Population

One of the most far-reaching changes that has occurred since Freud has been the dramatic shift in the patient population. In Freud's day the patients were still the deviant, bizarre outcasts of society. For example, the Wolf Man, one of Freud's best-known patients, who came to him in 1910, was a young Russian nobleman who was totally disabled by neurotic illness. Because of his great wealth he could afford to travel around Europe with his own retinue of servants, including his personal physician. For years he made the rounds of most of the leading psychiatrists in Europe for help, coming to Freud only out of desperation and as a last resort. Freud in fact was able to use his psychoanalytic technique of seeing patients six days a week because they were unable to carry on the functions of normal living.

Today, however, the situation is entirely different. Most of the patients who come to analysts are functioning human beings suffering from inner conflicts that cause them various degrees of distress. For example, in the recently published collection of case histories from the Chicago group (Goldberg, 1978), the first of the six cases presented is a twenty-five-year-old engineer who is too promiscuous sexually. The others are a thirty-year-old writer whose wife had left him for another man; a thirty-one-year-old housewife suffering from tension, depression, and diarrhea; an artist in his twenties caught up in an unhappy marriage; a thirty-three-year-old housewife, depressed, fearful, and dissatisfied with herself; and a twenty-six-year-old graduate student in sociology in the process of getting a divorce. These people are not markedly disturbed in any traditional psychiatric sense, and a psychiatrist who is not analytically trained would not know what to do with them.

Thus the notion of the analytic ideal has penetrated to the consciousness of many people on the current scene. Aware that there is much lacking in their lives, they seek out analysts for help. Again, unlike Freud's patients, they come with a considerable knowledge of psychoanalytic theory (though they may not be able to formulate it in technical terms) and a considerable realization of what psychoanalytic treatment is about.

Kadushin, in his study of why patients go to psychiatrists, divided them into three groups. The mentally ill, those who have been hospitalized and have recovered, go to hospital clinics or psychiatrists, who treat them with drugs, shock, and other physical methods. Those with family problems go to church-oriented or church-directed marital-counseling clinics. The analytic group consists of those who feel some inner needs or dissatisfactions. It is this third group that is ever expanding and ever seeking more help from psychoanalysts.[52]

The existence of this growing group partly explains the rivalry among therapists for patients and the alleged division into schools. The so-called YAVIS patients—young, adult, verbal, intelligent, and sexual   make the most responsive analytic subjects, in contrast to recovered schizophrenics or those narrowly focused on family problems. The competition seeks to attract these YAVIS patients to analysis; hence the emphasis in each school that it alone provides the right kind of analysis.

Whatever kind of therapist they go to, this group represents the core of the normal population. The self-awareness of the normal core explains the shift of psychoanalysis away from the small percentage who are psychiatrically disturbed in the traditional sense.

Our culture, however, has been too sick to catch up with the idea of a different way of living for the normal person, though it is moving in that direction. Hence many euphemisms come into vogue to describe these "new" kinds of patients, although analysts should know them well, for that is what they themselves were like when they started. Some rationalization must be advanced to allow these people to come to treatment. Because the dominant emphasis is still on medicine and psychiatry, new diagnostic terms are invented.

Kohut and his group in Chicago have classified many such patients as "narcissistic personality disorders," thus bringing them within the purview of psychiatric treatment. Narcissism is their illness; psychoanalysis their treatment.

The term, however, is merely a confused classification in a confused field. Strictly speaking, everybody is narcissistic to some degree, so the diagnostic category of narcissistic personality disorder, without specification of degree of narcissism, is pure myth, merely a cloak to justify psychiatric treatment. But the same purpose could be served, and served more honestly, by saying that these are average people in our world who have recognized how far they are from the analytic ideal and wish to make more sense of their lives.

In a very real sense, the public has moved ahead of the profession. Increasing recognition of the analytic ideal and of the availability of therapists who understand it and can treat in accordance with it has led to an extraordinary growth and expansion in the number of people who seek help. Through the analysis of these people the psychoanalytic vision can be broadened and deepened in the entire culture.

The Charismatic Figure in Psychoanalytic Societies: A New Dilemma

Freud's discovery that children have sexual feelings and that dreams embody wishes has been denied by many, including a large percentage of the healing profession. Such massive denial of the obvious can be explained only on the basis of the sickness of the culture in which psychoanalysis has developed. Those who are now analysts have been brought up in this culture; hence they too have been indoctrinated with massive denials from early childhood. This has had two consequences. First, they have found it very difficult to understand the basic doctrines of psychoanalysis, although these seem to be simplicity itself, once they are past a certain point. And second, they seek out and gather around charismatic figures who oversimplify the material or go off on wild goose chases. The history of psychoanalysis is filled with these charismatic figures.

The first, and still the foremost, is Freud himself. The minutes of the Vienna Psychoanalytic Society show clearly that Freud's immediate followers failed to grasp much of what he was saying. They attached themselves to him as to a great man who was leading mankind out of the wilderness, but they often could not see what he was driving at.

Add to this that Freud constantly was changing his mind about important issues. The direct sexual theory of the 1890s was abandoned for the more sophisticated theory of infantile sexuality. Id psychology was given up for ego psychology. Sexuality as the only instinct was replaced by a dual instinct theory. Many other changes occurred.

C. Oberndorf, one of the early leaders of psychoanalysis in America, has testified to the difficulties the members of the New York Psychoanalytic Society had in understanding Freud's works as they appeared after 1911. He states that the rapid changes in theory created one critical situation after another in the society.[53] Abraham Brill, Freud's first English translator, made the astounding statement that psychoanalysis was "practically a finished product when he became acquainted with it in 1907,"[54] thus throwing all of ego psychology out of the window, apart from the numerous changes in the other theories. Eitingon, a great administrator who worshiped Freud, seemed to have little understanding of him. On the other hand, Ernest Jones, who eventually became Freud's biographer, was critical of many of Freud's theories, such as the first theory of anxiety, the paper on narcissism, the death instinct, the image of female sexuality, and so on. To him, unlike the others, Freud was a genius but not a god.

There are still many today who, like Eitingon, would not change a word Freud ever wrote. In France, Jacques Lacan insists that he has gone back to the original Freud, even though Lacan's writings show no real understanding of what Freud was trying to do. Many Freudians are unaware that the self-analysis is the real turning point in the history of psychoanalysis, or that in his writings of the 1890s Freud was not really very original. The consequence is that many Freudians today, just like the neo-Freudians and the anti-Freudians, are misinterpreting Freud in various ways.

A further complication arises from Freud's increasing stature as time goes on. Many have tried to replace him and have been forgotten. In spite of all his errors, his basic insights are so profound that no one as yet has made a comparable contribution. As some have put it, psychology has had its Newton but has not yet found its Einstein.

When analysts become aware of the profundity of Freud's work, they often become envious that one man could have seen so much and gone so far. At first this envy may be masked by uncritical adulation. Later, not unnaturally, the envy may break through and lead to the formation of a new "system." If the person is in a position of power, as has often been the case, he may then break off and start a new trend or a new school, thereby becoming a charismatic figure to his followers. That seems to have been the case with Jung.

The organization of psychoanalytic training unfortunately lends itself all too readily to the formation of charismatic figures. The training analysis is experienced partly as an introduction to profound wisdom, partly as a novitiate. All institutes have a narrowly prescribed reading list, which discourages questioning and promotes ignorance. Thus Freudians tend to ignore observations of the culturalists, even though the significance of culture in personality formation is probably the most important advance in theory since Freud, and by the same token culturalists tend to ignore the Freudian emphasis on inner psychological reality. The result is that it is rare to find an analyst who has a fully rounded picture of the whole field.

Many charismatic figures have dotted the psychoanalytic landscape since Freud; apart from Jung and Adler, there were Horney, Sullivan, Lacan, Schultz-Hencke, Melanie Klein, Hartmann, Bion, Kohut, and Kernberg, to name only a few. When their views are examined critically, in the light of the entire history of mainstream psychoanalysis, some novel ideas come to light for each one, but not a total system.[55] Still, their followers inject a total system into them, sometimes in spite of their wishes. Thus Hartmann felt he had never deviated from Freud, yet others have seen him as the head of a new "ego-psychological" school. Melanie Klein was one of the first to explore the infant's earliest feelings about mother, but in most other respects she simply followed Freud. Kohut, in his theoretical writings, sounds like Jung, but the casebook published by his followers demonstrates good analysis without need of a new theory.

In a recent critical review of the contributions of Otto Kernberg, who has placed so much stress on the "borderline" concept, Calef and Weinshel write:

> We very much wish that we could offer convincing and comprehensive explanations for what we have referred to as the "social phenomena": the recurrent waves of efforts to introduce significant alterations in basic psychoanalytic theory and practice, the tremendous "bandwagon" popularity of Kernberg's contributions, the cult-like atmosphere that has surrounded so much of his work, the reluctance (or at least, the open reluctance) to question its derivation and its validity. We do not believe, however, that we are capable of doing so. It may

be necessary, perhaps, for more time and distance to intervene before a psychoanalyst can undertake such a critique; and, perhaps only someone who is outside of the profession of psychoanalysis can bring both the objectivity and the necessary complex perspectives in humanistic studies to accomplish this task.[56]

The uncritical adulation afforded many charismatic figures interferes with the furtherance of the psychoanalytic vision. To repeat: The bases of the psychoanalytic system come from Freud, but much has had to be changed since. Many ideas have been put forth, some of which are valid, some not. What is of value can be integrated into mainstream psychoanalysis; what is not of value can be rejected. There is no need for new systems and new heroes.

Psychoanalysis and the Social Sciences: Toward a Science of Man

While the initial steps were taken by Freud, the expansion of psychoanalysis to the social sciences has made considerable headway since his time. Nevertheless, for the most part its role has been considered peripheral; it is usually listed as one of many approaches to the data. Our contention is that psychoanalysis, the core of normal psychology, is central to all the social sciences. It is only by adopting this view that a fundamental viable science of man can be constructed.

It will be recalled that the point was made earlier that Freud's self analysis initiated a different approach to the study of man, the intensive study of individuals. With few exceptions, the social sciences have all developed concurrently with psychoanalysis; thus the American Psychological Association was founded in 1893, the American Sociological Association in 1900, the American Anthropological Assocation in 1908, the American Psychoanalytic Association in 1911. From the very beginning they moved in different directions, with different methods and different goals.

One hundred years ago all the social sciences were regarded as branches of philosophy. They did not have any separate status in the university. Even psychology was seen as part of philosophy; in one large Eastern university it did not become a separate department until 1940.

To emancipate themselves from philosophy and become independent disciplines, all of the social sciences had to stress their commitment to empirical research. Furthermore, they all subscribed, wittingly or unwittingly, to the prevailing image of man as rational, conscious, and at the mercy of powerful external forces; inner needs and desires played a secondary role in this image. Clearly behavioristic psychology (though the term had not yet been invented) was much more to their liking than psychoanalytic. On top of that, by being objective and scientific, they could not be regarded as enemies of the social system, although sharp criticism of existing conditions in all the social spheres was widespread in the latter part of the nineteenth century, as well as earlier.

Today, all these positions must be carefully re-evaluated. For a long time now there has been an insistent demand for interdisciplinary research, thus implicitly recognizing that the division of the social sciences into a large number of different disciplines is arbitrary and unwarranted. The unity of the social sciences can be restored by linking them with psychodynamic psychology. A detailed effort to effect such a unification has been made in Chapters 4–12.

As for empirical research it is clear that such research must be made theoretically meaningful. The mere accumulation of facts without a theory leads nowhere; facts have a way of multiplying without end. It is here that psychoanalysis can serve as a meaningful guide. For example Rennie's study of Manhattan residents (1962; revised and enlarged, 1978), the exploration of the authoritarian character by Adorno and the California group (1950), the investigation of a Mexican village by Fromm and his associates (Fromm and Maccoby, 1970), and the study of American Indians by Boyer (1979) are all examples of large-scale research with a meaningful point of view.

Further, the existence of the two equally valid approaches to the study of man mentioned earlier—one involving a superficial examination of large numbers of people, the other the intensive study of small numbers—must be reorganized. The psychoanalytic study of individuals and the psychodynamically oriented study of individuals are valid empirical methods, yielding meaningful results.

In the main, the social sciences have operated on the basis of an incorrect image of man. Man is not per se a rational animal in the traditional Aristotelian sense; rather, he is dominated by needs, passions, and desires that seriously interfere with his ability to think clearly. At the conscious level rational motives do not suffice to explain why man behaves the way he does. Paradoxically, it may be noted here that psychodynamic psychology has reached the conclusion that all behavior is rational at the unconscious level; that is, given the situation as seen from the unconscious, the consequences are perfectly rational. Many men simply reason correctly from false premises of which they have no real awareness.

Nor is man in general conscious of his motives. As Thomas Mann could sense fifty years ago, it is the task of psychoanalysis to lead the way to a freer, more conscious humanity. Consciousness is characteristic of the analytic ideal, but it is not a hallmark of the culturally normal person, who is often closer to the dreamer, the child, the psychotic, or the primitive. How much is based on conscious and how much on unconscious motives cannot be ascertained beforehand; this is a matter for empirical research. It is a total caricature and distortion of psychoanalysis to see every car as a penis and every body of water as a birth symbol. It is, however, perfectly true that some people see a car as a penis without realizing it and that some people view bodies of water as birth symbols without being aware of it.

There are, of course, powerful external forces that impinge on every individual. But there are also powerful internal forces. What psychoanalysis contributes to the social sciences is an understanding of these internal forces and a methodology for clarifying them. No science of man can be complete if it fails to grasp these internal forces. As was noted in Chapter 6, this is the battle that has been fought, and is being fought, in every social science, from economics to linguistics to anthropology. It is by a careful analysis of these internal forces that the unity of man and all the sciences of man can be restored.

Toward a Reform of the Training System

The experience of the past sixty years calls for a thorough overhaul of the training system, not the patchwork devices that have been applied. Conditions today are vastly different from what they were in 1920. The emphasis has shifted from the deviant psychotic to the normal population, the more intelligent portion of which is clamoring for psychological help. The climate of public opinion is strongly positive toward the general tenor of psychoanalytic ideas. Spock's book on childrearing, which is a translation of these ideas into ordinary language, has sold in the millions. Such other books as Gail Sheehy's *Passages*, which present psychoanalytic concepts in everyday language (as they should be presented), have also become bestsellers. In fact, the self-help market is growing all the time. The chief dangers to the field stem more from poorly trained professionals than from antagonistic laymen. The agreement of the American Psychoanalytic Association with the American Psychiatric Association placing untrained or partially trained psychiatrists on a par with fully trained psychoanalysts in order to get insurance coverage is a disgrace. Above all, the reform of the training system should be inspired by a full awareness of the psychoanalytic vision.

The training analysis certainly remains indispensable as a basis for any kind of therapeutic work. But the term should be dropped, just as the older euphemism of the "didactic" analysis has been dropped. Instead we should speak of the personal analysis. In theory, personal analysis is highly desirable for a large percentage of the population, perhaps 60 or 70 percent. Hence there should be an enormous expansion of the opportunities for analysis. This may require insurance, a lowering of analytic fees, or both.

Furthermore, the personal analysis of students must be kept independent of the later training program. The common practice of analyzing people *after* they have received an advanced degree and before they start their training has created an impassable dilemma. Some institutes require extensive analysis before admission to courses, but this merely creates another problem, because the analyst is then given the right to determine when his patient is ready to start studying, a blatant violation of analytic principles, as Anna Freud has pointed out; the analyst should never have the right to intervene in the patient's life.

It was the hope of many of the pioneers (see Maetze, 1930) that the personal analysis could be completed long before the training program was started. That never-realized hope should be put into effect. If large numbers of college students could be analyzed, those who showed the most aptitude for the profession could be chosen from the body of analyzed persons by applying the basic analytic criteria of mental health. That is, candidates for training should be selected on the basis of the degree of progress in their personal analysis rather than for their academic grades, as is now the case.

The *curriculum of theoretical work* should be taught in a university-based program granting a degree in psychology. Many plans have been suggested: Freud's 1927 scheme, the Kubie plan, the Chicago proposal, the Berkeley doctorate, the doctoral program proposed by the present writer. All are basically similar in that they take psychoanalysis as the core of psychology and teach a unified science of man.

The students for such a program should be selected from the body of those who have had some successful personal analysis. Everyone is agreed that the prime requirement for a good analyst is success in his own analysis, yet the principle is not applied in practice.

Furthermore, a university-based program would allow for more diversity of opinion than the current analytic institutes. The novitiate would be eliminated. Instead there would be a reasoned marshaling of all the evidence, including, with strong emphasis, the evidence gleaned by the student in his own personal analysis. In this way a good background would be created for both competent practitioners and competent researchers. As things stand now, a certain body of analytic folklore has been built up in each institute, and this folklore is passed on unquestioningly from one generation to the next. Few realize that the folklore varies from institute to institute, each of which tends to come under the sway of strong charismatic figures. There is wide room for a public airing of all the issues that trouble analysts and divide them, and it is only through such a public airing that these issues can be resolved.

The system of *control analysis* requires no essential change. It represents a tutorial rather than a classroom approach. Since the tutorial is far more intensive, it is far more effective. The term "control" has so many undesirable connotations in English that it would be just as well to use the more common term "supervision." Close personal supervision is certainly desirable for all those who seek to help others.

Finally, *society control of training*, with its implications of a religious novitiate, should be radically altered. If there is a degree in psychoanalytic psychology, the analytic institutes, which arose because the universities would offer no such degree, would lose their *raison d'etre*. Since they would not offer training analyses and would not teach the theoretical courses, they would be limited to advanced practitioners and research. They could continue as bodies of fellows, persons of eminence within the profession, akin to the fellowship status offered in other disciplines or in the various branches of medicine. Membership in such a society of fellows would then be a real distinction rather than a sign that the person had passed through the novitiate without questioning his superiors.

Can such a scheme to further the psychoanalytic vision be realized? If enough people in the professions get behind it, there is a good chance that it can be.

Chapter 14

Vision Versus Technique: Psychotherapy and Social Reform

N O SOONER HAD the new profession been established than its nature came to be questioned. In name it resembled medicine, and the lay public, as well as the medical profession, tended to see it as part of medicine. But in practice and in training it was entirely different.

There was with time a gradual shift in emphasis from the particular to the general and from the individual to the family to society at large. Technically this has been discussed as the shift from symptom analysis to character analysis. But it has much broader implications.

It soon appeared that any "neurotic" symptom was part of a larger complex. First it was discovered that it is not the symptom that is important but the whole character structure. Then it was seen that in many instances the "patient" was not only not as "sick" as the other members of his family but often healthier in a real sense. Analysts began to talk of the "family neurosis" and of sick and healthy families. Then this was enlarged to societal neurosis and sick and healthy societies.

But if all of society is disturbed, as in the witchcraft period, for example, what becomes of the concept of illness and of the technique of psychotherapy? Clearly entirely new conceptualizations were required. It is here that the problem of vision versus technique entered. If all of mankind is sick, then psychoanalysis represents a vision of a healthier society, a utopia. If it is just a question of a few neurotics, then it becomes a matter of improved technique. Freud himself took a long time to become aware of the problem, and his hesitation resulted in a great deal of subsequent confusion.

Freud as an Ambivalent Revolutionary

The ambivalence in many of Freud's theoretical views has already been traced in Chapter 2. Here we wish to document the ambivalence of his views about psychotherapy, especially with regard to its connection with the social structure.

Originally, Freud started out like any other medical practitioner, taking patients who were supposedly "neurotic" and treating them by the means standard to that day—electrotherapy, hypnotism, suggestion. Only gradually did he come to perfect his own instrument, psychoanalysis. It changed constantly and did not receive a definitive formulation until 1914, almost thirty years after he had begun to practice.

As has been seen, Freud realized at an early date that he had all mankind as his patient. He always insisted on the continuum from normality to psychosis, stressing that only quantitative factors separated one from the other. This alone presented a sharp contrast to other psychiatrists of his day, who maintained the image of the neurotic and psychotic as incomprehensible outcasts.

The logical next step from this discovery was to extend analysis to all of mankind. But here Freud's ambivalence entered in: It was too much of a jump for him to take. Some of his followers wished him to do so; he held back for a long time. Instead he remained focused on scientific progress and on technique. Hence he was already caught up in the inner conflict that bedevils every analyst.

Technique Versus Vision

Freud's first serious encounter wih the issue of analysis as personal and social reform came in his exchange with the American neurologist James Putnam. Putnam, a distinguished professor at Harvard, became a follower of Freud when he was already in his sixties. The two men conducted a lively correspondence from 1909 to 1916, which has been published.

Putnam argued that psychoanalysis must bring about moral improvement. In 1911 he wrote: "I consider that no patient is really cured unless he becomes better and broader morally, and, conversely, I believe that a moral regeneration helps toward a removal of the symptoms."[1]

Freud was not in agreement. He continued to stress the development of the basic principles of the science, fearing that concern with morality and moral improvement would interfere with scientific work. But then a subtle change, perhaps under the influence of Putnam's bombardment, began to emerge. Yes, moral and philosophical improvement are desirable, but only after the repressions are lifted. In a letter of May 14, 1911, he wrote:

> If we are not too satisfied with saying "Be moral and philosophical" it is because that is too cheap and has been said too often without being of any help. Our art consists in making it possible for people to be moral and to deal with their wishes philosophically. Sublimation, that is, striving toward higher goals, is of course one of the best means of overcoming the urgency of our drives. *But one can consider doing this only after psychoanalytic work has lifted the repressions.*[2]

Thus was born the first statement of what has since become a standard viewpoint: Analyze first, reform later. However, this carries with it two implications. First, reform without previous analysis is merely a shuffling of pieces, yielding nothing. Second, analysis itself becomes a method of reform, for it is the main instrument by which any rational reform can be brought about.

Nevertheless, at this stage technique remained uppermost in Freud's mind. All very well for reform, but let the analyst analyze, let others reform. In a letter of March 30, 1914, he wrote to Putnam:

> I quite agree with you that psychoanalytic treatment should find a place among the methods whose aim is to bring about the highest ethical and intellectual development of the individual. Our difference is of a purely practical nature. It is confined to the fact that I do not wish to entrust this further development to the psychoanalyst.[3]

About the same time he also stated, in his critique of Adler (*History of the Psychoanalytic Movement*, 1914), that "psychoanalysis has never claimed to provide a complete theory of human mentality in general." This too was to be changed after the war.

After World War I Freud turned directly to more philosophical questions. Theoretically, he saw psychoanalysis as a system of psychology (*Autobiography*, 1925). With regard to therapy, it could become a virtually universal panacea. In *The Question of Lay Analysis* (1926) he wrote:

> Our civilization imposes an almost intolerable pressure on us and it calls for a corrective. Is it too fantastic to expect that psychoanalysis in spite of its difficulties may be destined to the task of preparing mankind for such a corrective? Perhaps once more an American may hit on the idea of spending a little money to get the "social workers" of his country trained analytically and to turn them into a band of helpers for combating the neuroses of civilization.[4]

Yet only a few years later he wrote in *Civilization and Its Discontents*: "The program of becoming happy, which the pleasure principle imposes on us, cannot be fulfilled; yet we must not—indeed we cannot—give up our efforts to bring it nearer to fulfillment by some means or other."[5]

Many other examples of Freud's ambivalence could be given, but enough has been cited to demonstrate the main tenor of what was happening. It could be said that in his later years Freud did pursue philosophy, did hold that psychoanalysis provides the basis for a general psychology, and placed his faith for the amelioration of man's lot in a universal analysis to be offered by lay curers of souls, a new profession. However, these positions are contradicted by others and obscured by linguistic considerations. All his life Freud was preoccupied with the conflict between vision and technique. Most of the time he stressed technique, but occasionally he would let the vision show through. This conflict has disturbed and still disturbs many other analysts.

Vision Versus Technique

Just as it took Freud almost thirty years to reach the first clearcut exposition of his technique, it takes many years of training today to reach a state of maturity as a therapist. The nature of this training is such that the heaviest stress is placed throughout on the perfection of technique. Whatever ideals he may have brought with him into the field, the practitioner soon learns that he has to understand transferences, master resistances, and bow to numerous practical exigencies. Kris once spoke of the "formative decade," and indeed, it is rarely possible to acquire any great skill as an analyst in less than ten years. Most of the time it takes longer, so that for many the perfec-

tion of technique becomes a lifelong process. At analytic confer-
ences, one notices over and over again that the stress is on technique—what should I do in this or that situation, how should such
and such a problem be handled, and so on. Numerous and divergent
points of view are expressed, so the analyst frequently remains in a
quandary about the best procedure. Furthermore the variety of practical problems encountered by the analyst is so great (suicide, psychosis, divorce, drugs) that technical considerations must predominate. Faced by a suffering human being in his office, the analyst is
primarily concerned with how to help most effectively.

On top of that, the analytic training system is highly authoritarian. Disputes are not allowed, especially on technical matters; the
student must either adopt the technique espoused by his institute or
leave. As a student, then, the analyst is mainly preoccupied with getting through the training program. He must learn a certain theoretical position and master certain technical devices in the management
of people. He must avoid what Anna Freud called the "odium" of un-
orthodoxy—and the orthodoxy of one institute is the heterodoxy of
another. So little technical variation is permitted that it becomes understandable for the student to stick to the prescribed technique reli-
giously. After all, his main wish is to graduate.
The emphasis on medicine and medical training makes this obsession
with technique even stronger. For the medical man is required by
both law and custom not to deviate too much from accepted practice. If he does, the punishment is not only exclusion from the sociey
(that he might tolerate) but legal liability. In this age of high insurance premiums and extensive malpractice suits, the legal consequences of being a maverick may be quite costly.

When the pressures to master technique in a prescribed direction are so great, there is a strong tendency to lose sight of the
analytic vision. To use Freud's language, first the repressions must
be lifted, a task that requires so much effort that the vision is forgotten. The youthful ideals are put to one side in favor of a comfortable
middle age, in which the main concern is to avoid trouble.

A further complication arises in that many analysts conceal
their ideals behind technical precepts. For example, it has been
pointed out that Hartmann, in his work on neutralization, was really
espousing the progressive neutralization of libidinal drives as a philosophical ideal. Freud's ideal of love and work lay behind his analytic thinking, yet his technical prescriptions for working through the
transferences and resistances, or later for replacing the id with the

ego, make up the bulk of his writing, while the significance of love for human welfare receives relatively scant attention—so little, in fact, that many people overlook that love was the essential basis of his philosophy. On the current scent Kohut, with his new "diagnosis" (demon) of "narcissistic personality disorder," is plumping for a solution to life's problems in terms of narcissistic gratifications instead of the more traditional image of object love. Yet his works offer no discussion of the relative merits of object love versus narcissism as ideals of living, but merely technical considerations.

Actually the battle of techniques in the field is just as much a battle of visions. Conventional psychiatry espouses a return to establishment functioning in contrast to analytic psychiatry, which advocates inner growth toward the analytic ideal.

It therefore becomes all the more important for the analyst to hold on to his youthful ideals, even if the cost is high; to maintain his vision of what the good life could be, for himself as well as for others; and to subordinate his technical concerns to this vision all the way through. Even if it is not applicable to certain patients, it certainly becomes applicable to the majority, especially in this day and age, when the patient population has shifted to the normal person.

The Redefinition of Psychotherapy in Light of the Analytic Vision

One of the consequences of the analytic vision is a total redefinition of psychotherapy. Historically, one reason for this redefinition is that all of scientific psychotherapy stems from Freud, even though it may and does deviate from the strictly classical analytic technique. For Freud marks a watershed in the history of psychotherapy. Everything that preceded him was uninformed, hit-and-miss procedures based on no rational theory, of dubious effectiveness, handled by poorly trained or totally untrained practitioners.

The analytic redefinition of psychotherapy compels a re-evaluation of everything connected with it.

THE PATIENT

The older image of the patient as a deviant struggling with problems that the "normal" person has resolved has to be completely abandoned. In light of the continuum theory, there has been a shift, as mentioned, to the entire population. Where before the only persons who came were those suffering from a maladjustment neurosis, today the adjustment neurosis is fully understood and recognized. In fact, the analytic patient population is made up of adjustment neuroses more than of maladjustment.

No longer is the patient population confined to those who suffer consciously from distress. Everybody seems to suffer from distress in one form or another; the differences are of degree. Analysis has brought out the mechanisms of denial and repression, which many people use to cover up their deep unhappiness. The educational dissemination of analytic ideas has helped many people to become aware of problems that they never recognized before, to get over rationalizations they had been using all their lives, or equally to get over professional misinformation. For example, a homosexual man came to our clinic as a patient after he had read a book by Edmund Bergler that explained the genesis of homosexuality; prior to that he was convinced that he had been born that way (which many nonanalytic professionals might tell him even today).

Another important change in the self-image of the patient is that in a culture where so many people are disturbed, the analytic patients form a superior rather than an inferior group. This process began with the training analysis, which required anyone who wished to practice analysis to undergo analysis himself. It was found that in these training analyses the problems were identical with those found in other patients. The original term "didactic analysis," which was used to indicate that the patient was a student rather than a typical person with problems, was eventually dropped when it was realized that the analyses of students proceeded in entirely the same manner as those of the more traditional patients. Today it is widely recognized that all persons suffer from inner difficulties and conflicts that can be helped by analytic treatment. The alternative is one of the many paranoid defenses or compromises available in the culture. Hence to enter an analysis would be considered by many as a sign of mental health per se rather than of illness.

THE "ILLNESS": THE REDEFINITION OF NEUROSIS

To remove the stigma attached to "neurosis" and "psychosis," the euphemism of "mental illness" was developed. And in fact the public has been sold on the idea of mental illness. Unfortunately this term has also sown considerable confusion.

In the first place, the notion of mental illness fails to separate out those conditions in which an actual physical illness results from those in which it does not. A large number of such psychosomatic conditions are known—for example, peptic ulcers, bronchial asthma, hypertension. Harold Wolff, one of the foremost researchers in this field, produced evidence to show that emotional factors could facilitate the appearance of any physical illness, even those that are demonstrably biochemical in origin and course. Lynch, in *The Broken Heart*, maintained that the primary cause of heart attacks and heart conditions, should be sought in the loss of important people; the term "a broken heart" should be taken literally. He seriously questioned the methodological adequacy of studies such as the famous Framingham report, which did not consider the effect of emotional loss.

However, once the illness has reached the stage of physiological damage, and before it reaches that stage, various physiological measures could be more effective than psychotherapy, or more essential. Medicine continues to provide numerous drugs that offer relief and even reversal of many dangerous physical conditions. It would of course be a serious mistake to ignore or sidestep these medical measures. Paradoxically, one of the resistances to analysis is attaching an omnipotent fantasy to the analyst with the thought that he can cure any physical as well as psychological disturbance.

A second source of confusion, of equal importance, is the fact that the notion of "mental illness" carries with it the implication that emotional disturbances of all kinds, but especially the more severe ones like psychosis, have some unknown physiological cause, which science will unravel in time. This is one of the basic fallacies of organic psychiatry and could be said to be a carryover of the Christian theory of paranoia. Like academic psychology and the social sciences, it relies on the old nineteenth-century image of man and cannot envisage the significance of powerful internal forces originating in a disordered childhood.

"Illness" as Distance from the Analytic Ideal

The redefinition of illness that emerges from this discussion is that it represents the distance from the analytic ideal. For many reasons the culturally defined image of normality has become unacceptable (see below) and has been replaced by the analytic ideal. But here large numbers of people fall short. When they realize that their sex lives are unsatisfactory, that they are unable to communicate with their spouses, or that their social role is frustrating, and that they themselves contribute to this dissatisfaction, they consult a therapist in order to get over the felt difficulty.

The expansion of psychotherapy on the current scene is thus due to the growth in awareness of large numbers of persons. Naturally this growth in awareness is more prominent in those who are sophisticated, young, and open to new ideas.

The "Presenting Symptom": Redefinition of the Referral Situation

Traditionally a patient came to a psychiatrist because of some felt distress, much as the Christian clergy took to prosecuting a witch when complaints were lodged against her by some member of the community. The first break in this attitude came with the analytic training system.

It has been stressed that Freud's major insights, and the revolutionary changes, stemmed from his self-analysis. In the same way, the personal analysis gradually became the indispensable requirement for all further training as a therapist.

This personal analysis was required of all prospective candidates, regardless of whether they had felt distress or not. Here a curious discovery emerged: Those who felt that they had inner problems they wanted to work on were found to be much more promising candidates for analytic training than those who insisted that everything was fine in their lives. This helped to crystallize the recognition that the popular image of neurosis as overt anxiety, an image that the nonanalytic profession shared and shares, is the opposite of what takes place dynamically. Those who "feel no problems" are relying on the defense mechanism of denial or repression. Another way of putting it is that since people without problems do not exist, the difference lies between those who are aware of them and those who are not.

In a similar vein, Merkle and Little (1967) described what they called the "beginning psychiatry training syndrome." They found that many psychiatrists at the beginning of their residency training experienced considerable anxiety, but those who went through this anxiety came out much better psychiatrists than those who did not.

Numerous other examples could be given. The main thesis is that under many circumstances anxiey is a sign of health rather than of sickness while the absence of anxiety would be one of the most pathological signs ever found. In more human terms, the anxious person can be helped; the detached person is beyond human contact. His unhappiness is so great that it cannot be assuaged by any mortal means.

These considerations place the referral situation in an entirely different light. In the main people still come because they have some distressing symptom. Often they are referred by well-meaning but uninformed professionals, including doctors, lawyers, and psychologists, who operate in accordance with the traditional ideology.

What analysis emphasizes is the need for referral on the basis of character problems or ways of living that are detrimental to the general well-being of the individual. All too often these character problems arouse no conscious anxiety in the person; it is only education to the analytic ideal that helps him to see that there is something wrong with the way in which he is living. Homosexuality is a good example. As noted previously, many homosexuals feel no anxiety about their situation; this is a serious sign, far more serious than the opposite, excessive anxiety about homosexual activities. If they can be motivated to recognize their plight, they can be helped.

Thus the referral system that generally exists today is based on a total incomprehension of psychology and inner dynamics. Professionals who attempt to decide whether or not Patient A "should have therapy" generally do not know what they are doing. Since the illness is distance from the analytic ideal, therapy is called for in all those who experience such a distance in any of its components. Our general finding today is that this includes most of the population.

THE REDEFINITION OF "TREATMENT"

The Freudian redefinition of treatment is in reality a definition of treatment; before Freud nothing existed that was of any value, and even the alternatives today are largely derivatives of his ideas or, if not, as useless or confused as the pre-Freudian techniques.

Freud's conception of analysis went through four distinct phases in terms of goals: (1) making the unconscious conscious (1890s), (2) working through the the transference and resistances (culmination 1914), (3) "where the id was the ego shall be" (1923), and (4) creating the most suitable conditions for the functioning of the ego (1937).

Prior to Freud therapeutic techniques were entirely of a hit-or-miss nature, using suggestion, hypnosis, advice, and anything else that would "work" (or not work). Because the positive transference guarantees that some patients will respond to almost anything the therapist does, all these pre-Freudian techniques could report some successes. After Freud the alternative techniques, as will be seen in more detail below, took out one part of the analytic framework and emphasized it to the exclusion of the rest.

In its ideal form, the analytic procedure goes through four phases: establishing a relationship, understanding the dynamics, working through the transferences and resistances, and termination by reaching some suitable goal. It is based on the image of neurosis as the distance from the analytic ideal. The patient talks; the analyst listens. In the course of listening the focus shifts more and more to transference manifestations, and through the understanding of these transferences everything else is effected. As Freud once put it, whatever the analyst does the patient responds to with transferences; hence transference is the core tool around which all psychotherapy revolves.

There are a large number of studies in the literature dealing with all aspects of the analytic treatment, including evaluations of results. Although it is not conclusive, there is certainly objective evidence that psychoanalysis as a treatment procedure is far superior to anything else that preceded it or that attempts to subplant it today. The first such study was done by Fenichel at the Berlin Psychoanalytic Institute, covering the period 1920–30. Other such studies, including ones by Franz Alexander (Chicago) and Ernest Jones (London), have found a similar result: that most patients treated by analysis make substantial progress in growth toward the analytic ideal. By now even the most severe critics of analysis admit that its techniques help people (Garfield and Bergin, 1978).

A rather widely cited exception is Hans Eysenck, who has maintained that psychotherapy not only does not help but actually does harm in many cases. The study by Eysenck is typical of the shoddy work offered by so many critics of psychoanalysis (Fisher and Greenberg, 1977). In a review of Eysenck's evidence and claims, Meltzoff and Kornreich (1970) note that in his 1960 paper Eysenck relied on four studies, one of which had nothing to do with psychotherapy. In his 1965 paper he added seven, for a total of eleven (by his count). Meltzoff and Kornreich relate that by 1964 there had been at least seventy controlled studies on the effects of psychotherapy. The evidence was available largely in a positive direction. Thus Eysenck's claims simply ignore the available data.

Further, the critics of psychoanalysis fail to give any credit for the meticulous self-criticism and self-observation that has been typical of the best analytic work. As an instance of an evaluation of effectiveness, Fenichel's original report can be examined (Maetze, 1970). In the period from 1920 to 1930, 604 patients were analyzed, with all possible diagnostic categories, including schizophrenia. Of these, according to Fenichel, 111 were cured, 89 appreciably improved, 116 improved, 47 unsuccessful, and 241 broken off prematurely. In all, ninety-four therapists were represented, of whom sixty either were or became members of the International Psychoanalytical Association. Fenichel states:

> The concept of "cured" has been interpreted as strictly as possible. Only those cases are included in which there was not only a disappearance of symptoms, but an alteration of character structure that was analytically comprehensible, and where possible, supported by life histories. This strictness is such that most of the "much improved" category should be considered "cured" for all practical purposes.[7]

Most nonanalyst critics consider the Fenichel type of study (which has been duplicated many times) grossly inadequate because there are no controls. On this score it is worth recalling what Freud once said: The only real control is to let the patient live his life over again without analysis. Controls may be totally misleading because of the assumption that all possible variables are spread evenly throughout the sample. On the other hand, credit must go to Fenichel and his co-workers for the meticulous care and stringent criteria, including determined self-criticism, with which they prepared their data. It should also be remembered that Fenichel's is one of the few studies where the patients experienced real analysis at the hands of reasonably competent analysts.

But even the general question about psychotherapy tends to be answered in the affirmative nowadays. Bergin and Lambert, as a rule critical observers of the scene, had this to say in 1978:

> In contrast to the chapter on this topic in the previous edition of the *Handbook*, wherein it was concluded that psychotherapy had an average effect that was modestly positive, recent outcome data look more favorable. A growing number of controlled outcome studies are analyzing a wide variety of therapies. These findings generally yield clearly positive results when compared with no-treatment, wait-list and

placebo or pseudotherapies . . . we believe that a major contributor to these newer findings is that more experienced and competent therapists have been used in recent studies. Our review of the empirical assessment of the broad range of verbal psychotherapies leads us to conclude that these methods are worthwhile when practiced by wise and stable therapists.[8]

The notion that there are many alternative therapies radically different from Freudian analysis will be discussed below. For the moment it will suffice to say that after half a century of determined negation and doubt, the professional community has at last grudgingly admitted that analysis produces positive therapeutic results in a considerable number of cases. Thus the basic ideas of listening to the patient, establishing a relationship, and working out the transferences and resistances may be said to be reasonably well established.

The Redefinition of the "Doctor"

If the patient is not a patient, the illness is not an illness, the reason for referral not the real reason, and the treatment is just talking, what kind of a person is the "doctor" who performs such a procedure? Certainly not a doctor in the medical model. Then what is he?

Reference must first be made to the nature of analytic training. The most essential prerequisite for such training is the personal analysis; without it no one is permitted to practice analysis, regardless of what degrees he may possess. Yet this personal analysis itself creates many obstacles and problems and is rewarded with no official certificate or diploma.

We have noted that the curricula of psychoanalytic institutes are all essentially the same and have not changed in any basic manner since the first one was founded in Berlin in 1922 (Fine, 1979a). Further these curricula consist of various courses in aspects of psychology, "normal" as well as "abnormal," which can be summarized as psychoanalytic psychology. Finally, there is the requirement of doing psychoanalysis under supervision, usually referred to as controls.

Thus the person who performs the analytic treatment is one who has gone through a successful personal analysis, studied psychoanalytic psychology, and handled several control cases under the supervision of more experienced analysts. Nothing is stated here about the practice of medicine, familiarity with branches of psychology that are nonclinical, or the acquisition of any recognized degree. No degree is granted for analytic training, but merely a certificate of membership in a society of psychoanalysts.

This situation has proved very confusing both for the public and for the professions. The three professions from which analysts are recruited, medicine, psychology, and social work, all terminate in established degrees—M.D., Ph.D., and M.S.W., respectively— which are recognized and regulated by the state. Legally they are licensed to carry out psychotherapy. But if they do not have psychoanalytic training in their background, what is there in their training that prepares them adequately for the performance of psychotherapy? One never knows.

Various statistical studies show that not more than 10 percent of the three major professions enter analytic training (Henry, 1971; Marmor, 1975). Thus for 90 percent of the mental health professionals there is no way of knowing how they have prepared for their life work of psychotherapy, or if they have prepared at all. This will be considered more carefully in Chapter 15, in the evaluation of the cultural reaction to the redefinition of psychotherapy.

The Redefinition of "Cure"

Here we can be brief, in the light of the extended discussion beforehand. If there is no illness, if the treatment is talking, and if the doctor is not a doctor, the notion of "cure" has to be dropped in favor of improvement. Psychotherapy is a way of reaching more happiness by coming closer to the analytic ideal. There is never any point at which it can be said: He has reached it. Allowances for growth must always be made. Hence the stress has shifed from termination in the medical sense of an illness treated and cured to growth in the psychological sense, and it is recognized that this growth process can go on all through life.

Chapter 15

The Half-trained Professions: Diplomas Instead of Analysis

The Cultural Reaction to the Redefinition of Psychotherapy

AS WAS SEEN before, the psychoanalytic vision was virtually complete by the time of Freud's death in 1939. The new image of man, the redefinition of psychotherapy, and the need for a new profession were all there in Freud. Six years passed before the madness of World War II came to an end. There then emerged, as Jones had predicted as far back as 1929 (see p. 160), a new profession, that of psychotherapist. The trouble was, however, that the nature of this new profession was completely misunderstood. Its practitioners displayed as much interest in acquiring more power as in educating the public. The net result has been tremendous confusion, incomprehension, and mismanagement, together with great development, reform, and new directions. As in analysis itself, growth was attended by fratricide.

The Half-trained Professions Struggle for Power

In 1945 three established professions existed that dealt with mental health: psychiatry, psychology, and social work. In none of these had psychoanalysis made any significant headway as yet. But the need for psychotherapists was enormous. Neuropsychiatric discharges had been a common cause of manpower difficulty in the army; now these men demanded treatment at Veterans Administration hospitals and clinics. Personnel had to be supplied to treat them. In the civilian population as well, the incidence of "neurosis" was seen to be stupendous. Who was to treat these unfortunates? Who was to be in charge? Not surprisingly, a scramble for power ensued.

THE MEDICAL MODEL

Closest to tradition and most readily comprehensible to the layman or even the professional was the medical model. These people were sick; they needed doctors to treat them. But established doctors had no training and no background in psychotherapy. It was not at all unusual for a man with his boards in psychiatry, requiring at least five years of experience and training, to be an absolute beginner in psychoanalysis and psychotherapy.

When the present writer was a graduate student in psychology in 1945, the head of the department of neurology at the university was also head of the department of psychiatry; the two were merged. He was a well-known neurologist but had absolutely no background in psychiatry. For training the new residents he offered extensive work in biochemistry, genetics and neurology, and Kraepelinian psychiatry (traditional diagnostic categories). The residents rebelled and sent an appeal to Washington, which was supporting the training for most of them, for education in psychoanalysis. The head of the department had to retreat and appoint psychoanalysts to teach. Such scenes were repeated all over. Even though psychoanalysis had been admitted as a respectable branch to the American Psychiatric Association in 1933, the great majority of psychiatrists had not yet accepted it.

Increasingly the residency training programs in psychiatry were taken over by psychoanalysts. In 1960 Lewin and Ross reported that of the eighty-three professors in the 1958 American Medical College Dictionary, eighteen were members of the national psychoanalytic organization or of a local society.[1] They also found that residency training programs differed widely in the extent of their "psychoanalyzation." But whereas by 1960 many programs made training in individual psychoanalytic psychotherapy the core of their residency experience, Goodman (1977) reported that the trend a decade later was to decrease that emphasis.

Almost all students in medical institutes still come from psychiatry, but the percentage of psychiatrists who enter analytic training remains small. Goodman found that the interest of psychiatric residents in psychoanalytic training remained stable at 10–30 percent but does not comment further on these extraordinarily low figures.

The interpenetration of psychiatry and psychoanalysis remains uncertain. As pointed out in an earlier chapter almost one-third of the psychiatrists surveyed by Henry (1971) had had no experience in psychotherapy at all, thus missing what analysts have always considered the most fundamental and indispensable part of their training. Marmor (1975) states that only 10 percent of psychiatrists complete full psychoanalytic training.

What, then, are the background and training adequacy of the psychiatrists who do not go into analysis? These are the men who have been most insistent on the medical degree as essential for the practice of psychotherapy. They have been active for thirty years in legislative efforts to bar nonmedical persons from practicing psychotherapy, even though these efforts have been uniformly unsuccessful. Even the attempt to restrict insurance reimbursement (third-party payments) to licensed physicians has largely failed.

There is no way of knowing what qualifies the nonanalytic psychiatrist to do psychotherapy. From an analytic point of view, he is either untrained or at best half-trained. The survey by Marmor (1975) discussed earlier revealed the deplorably low standards that prevail in the office practice of psychiatry today.

Apart from the medical analysts, since World War II two new analytic professions have sprouted on the American scene: Clinical psychology and social work. Neither of these requires medical training yet members of both do therapy with patients who were formerly the exclusive province of the physician. Hence the battle between the medically trained and the nonmedically trained revolves primarily around psychotherapy: Is it useful, who should do it, how should one prepare to do it?

Here the education and sophistication of the public play a highly important role. According to Lewin and Ross in their survey twenty years ago, the widest discrepancies were already evident. In one city the patients insisted on being treated only by analysts, so the local analytic institute was flourishing. In another city, the public knew little and cared less about analysts; there general medical men and Miltown ruled the roost.[2] So the kind of education offered to the public assumes central importance.

There is a natural tendency in everybody to keep strangers away from their turf; the psychiatrists formed no exception. Because the nonanalytic psychiatrists formed the vast majority and often had questionable qualifications to do psychotherapy, the understandable reaction was to stress the physical aspect of "neurosis." It must be a medical illness, and only physicians are competent to treat it. The psychiatrist always has medical training, so he can always fall back upon that, and does.

It is in this light that the "drug revolution" has to be carefully evaluated. If drugs are truly effective for psychosis, neurosis, or both, then only the medically trained person should be permitted to do psychotherapy, for drugs should then be used in conjunction with therapy. If drugs are ineffective, then the psychologically trained person can be equally competent, and it is a waste of time and money for society to insist that all psychotherapists have a medical degree. Obviously both sides have a lot at stake.

As has been seen, for political reasons medical analysts either have sidestepped this struggle or have taken the side of the psychiatrists in violation of their own convictions. The nonmedical world has thus had to fight without the help of what they consider the most competent and strongest group of physicians.

It is surprising and heartening that the nonmedical professions have grown so rapidly in spite of intense and at times rabid opposition from the medical fraternity. Cleary the public has not been convinced by the physicians that psychotherapy should be their exclusive province. While the battle continues on many fronts, on the whole the medical profession is on the defensive.

The sophistication of the public is seen in an article on the "war between the shrinks" by Hillel Levin, which appeared in *New York* magazine on May 21, 1979. The article concerns itself with the activities of Dr. Donald Langsley, installed in May as President-elect of the American Psychiatric Association. The author correctly observes:

> Essentially, psychiatrists and psychologists can offer the same treatment. No medical background is necessary to conduct either psychoanalysis or psychotherapy, although both techniques require extensive training and experience. . . . The major difference between the professions is that only psychiatrists can prescribe drugs.[3]

Levin then goes on to detail some of Langsley's activities. Apparently Langsley has set himself the task of eliminating any kind of psychotherapy done by psychologists (or other nonmedical health personnel). Levin shows that many of Langsley's statements are either unfounded or misleading. He quotes some wild accusations made by Langsley, including unfounded charges of medical malpractice by nonmedical therapists, and goes on to observe that in a study published in August 1978 in the *American Journal of Psychiatry*, of ninety-eight psychiatrists surveyed, none routinely performed physical examinations; 53 percent admitted that they no longer felt competent to do so, and some hospitals, in order to ward off malpractice suits, will not even allow psychiatrists to do physicals. Levin directly makes the point that Langsley's compaign is based on no scientific evidence. On the contrary: All the scientific evidence available is in the opposite direction. Langsley is conducting an economic campaign to bolster the financial well-being of his medical colleagues, without regard to the scientific realities or the patient's welfare.

The one point that Levin does not discuss is the training that nonanalytic psychiatrists receive in order to do psychotherapy; as indicated before, this may vary from nothing to full or almost full analytic training. However, there is nothing in the officially sanctioned residency training program that particularly equips the potential psychiatrist to do psychotherapy; if he learns it; he does so by his own extracurricular efforts. Many do learn it, but many others do not.

In the meantime the nonmedical psychotherapeutic professions have been growing by leaps and bounds. Psychologists and social workers fit into a long-established degree system. Of late even a fourth group is being added, the mental health counselors, persons with a master's degree in some other field. There is thus every reason to believe that the medical model, which is devoid of established scientific foundations, is constantly losing ground to an increasingly better-educated public.

Psychology as a Profession

The situation in other professions shows the same kinds of confusion, self-seeking, and distortion of scientific facts in the interests of economic advancement as in psychiatry. Until the end of World

War II psychology was very largely an academic discipline, almost unconcerned with the real problems of real human beings. Then came the crisis of the war and the postwar period, and everybody who had the remotest knowledge of what to do with troubled human beings was drafted into the field.

In psychology the same battle ensued as in psychiatry: the degree versus training. And a similar process took place: degree first, training second. The clinical psychology programs that began to appear after the war (there were none before) offered the student little opportunity for training in psychotherapy. No personal analysis or therapy was required. No special training was needed. The psychologist knew the "normal," so he could simply apply his knowledge to the "abnormal."

In his image of psychotherapy the psychologist reacted much like the average individual. Pathology was simply a bad "habit," to be undone by various devices. Thus Knight Dunlap advised stutterers to utter as many dirty words as they could, having reasoned that stuttering resulted from the fear of using filthy language. (Evidence? None.) Because learning theory was the special province of the psychologist, it soon became fashionable to argue that neurosis was simply learned behavior (which nobody had ever denied, least of all Freud), so all you had to do was teach the patient to unlearn it. Therapy could be a simple, rational process, as Albert Ellis claimed. It need not take years; it could be done in months or even weeks.

All of these arguments were offered for much the same economic reasons as those of the psychiatrists. Psychologists for the first time had been offered a lucrative opportunity to do psychotherapy, so they were not going to seek out the painful and expensive analytic approach. Carl Rogers became the hero of the day in 1945. He proclaimed that all you had to do was accept the patient and allow him to ventilate his feelings; anybody could be cured in eight sessions. As training he offered a six-week course. It is true that Rogers eventually changed his position and moved to a deeper appreciation of people's problems, but that took a long time. For at least twenty years after the war Rogerian therapy seemed to be the dominant note at all psychological meetings; analysis was "unscientific."

Thus each half-trained profession fell back on its own rationalizations and its own brand of expertise. The psychologists were adamant in their insistence that psychoanalysis is unscientific. That they did not properly understand the nature of scientific method, as has been shown previously, escaped notice. As usual, those who agreed with the official line could get ahead; those who did not had to go elsewhere.

In spite of all this ballyhoo, many psychologists, perhaps as a result of doing psychotherapy, began to see into the problems more deeply. Large numbers went to analytic institutes either officially or unofficially. There were enough analytically trained psychologists to teach them and guide them. And in spite of the official ban on lay analysis, the official medical institutes would give bootleg training to anyone who wanted it and was willing to pay for it. Nor was bootleg training inferior to the official kind; after all, as we have seen, personal analysis, theoretical courses, and supervised analysis can all be had outside the framework of an official institute.

As with the other professions, gradually the feeling toward psychotherapy became more hospitable. The Fisher–Greenberg synthesis on psychoanalysis, which appeared in 1977, could scarcely have been published earlier; the antagonism was too great. Even today most psychologists prefer to ignore its disturbing findings, which contradict their absurd diatribes against psychoanalysis.

But given the kind of society we have, it seems inevitable that here too the emphasis would be first on the degree and then on the training. Thus the Ph.D. in psychology became an important degree; it brought with it licensure, stature, patients, and money. What training went into it, as with the M.D., no one cared.

As in other professions, since most psychologists still shied away from analytic training, they remained dubious about psychotherapy. Extensive surveys were conducted. Eysenck was widely quoted in spite of the flimsiness of his evidence, which would have been unacceptable in a term paper if the issue had not been so vital. Again the decision remained up to the public, which had to be educated to know what psychoanalysis is, what psychotherapy is, and what psychology is.

Social Work

The situation with the third of the three mental health professions is quite similar to that in the other two. The M.S.W. has existed for some sixty years, but the degree was not standardized until after World War II. Again, even though the social worker was often called upon to do psychotherapy (euphemistically named "casework"), no real training was offered. It is true that social work developed a much more extensive supervisory process than any other profession, but this supervision could not be said to take the place of more thorough training. Social work remained a practical degree. The nature of the training, in spite of the superficial standardization, varied all over the lot, as with the other professions. Some social work schools were frankly psychoanalytic; most were equally frankly antipsychoanalytic. Since social workers for the most part dealt with the poorest, most downtrodden segment of the population, they placed their hopes more in social amelioration and social change than in individual change. One large agency in New York, the Community Service Society, discontinued all individual psychotherapy in the 1970s because it was no longer "germane" to the needs of the times. Others, while continuing to offer therapy, placed little faith in it. Systems theory became all the vogue; the suffering individual was only part of a bad system. The system had to be changed, and the individual could do nothing. We see here the same kind of thinking that has dominated so much of sociology, with its idealization of the community."

Again, as in the other professions, social workers increasingly began to get postgraduate training in psychoanalysis and psychotherapy. Many became competent and sincere therapists. Many others simply hung out a shingle upon graduation and started to practice. There was no way to know how much training any therapist had.

Summary Comments on the Half-trained Professions

The cultural reaction to the discovery of psychotherapy by Freud and his followers was dual. On the one hand it fell back on the "diploma disease," as Dore (1976) has named it. Let people get degrees; then they can do what they want. Traditional schooling in the professions became more and more a ritualized process of qualification-earning. But since the public values degrees, and insurance companies do not know what to do with professionals who have no degrees, the degree became mandatory.

Too little attention was paid to the persons who granted the degrees and to how the degrees were obtained. Here certain similarities are seen. In all the professions, the official degree-givers were not trained in psychotherapy and were opposed to it. All of them developed rationalizations to justify their own professional existence and to exclude the others. Thus the physicians stressed the medical model and drugs, the psychologists the learning model and quick therapy, the social workers the evils of society and the futility of individual attempts to change. The arguments in favor of these positions were all ritualized, so that no counter-argument was possible. The scene is reminiscent of the tale of the emperor's new clothes.

Because the official institutions were opposed to psychoanalysis and rationalized their opposition in various ways, they were in a dilemma when it came to preparing students to do psychotherapy. Their first reaction was natural: Favor the briefer therapies as more effective and more pertinent than long-term analysis, which could be afforded only by the "rich and idle." Thus a host of therapies grew up, sponsored by one or another of the schools. Largely these were technique without vision; what the schools produced then was technicians without vision. The intellectual and therapeutic status of these therapies will be considered below.

The second reaction was less expected: Many persons in the field, out of personal conviction, drifted into the psychoanalytic orbit and undertook long and expensive training of their own volition. They became analysts, some fully trained, some partially. Because of the struggles within the field, they could not usually identify themselves in that way. But the public did. And anyone who did therapy became a "shrink"; the differences were not readily apparent to a layman.

Psychoanalytic Dissension: Charismatic Figures and the Battle Against Lay Analysis

In all of these struggles the official psychoanalytic community played an ambivalent role. On the one hand it was in favor of psychotherapy, and the whole world needed it. Then again, many patients were not amenable to therapy or analysis; they should be either left alone or treated in other ways. Only physicians should be permitted to do analysis or therapy, but then again their medical training was worse than useless. For example, a psychiatrist with his boards (five years' experience) would have to begin from scratch in any analytic institute. At the same time, unofficially they cheerfully trained nonmembers of the institute, medical and nonmedical, in hospitals, clinics, and private practice, as long as they were willing to learn. Dominated by one or another charismatic figure, analysts moved in whatever direction he or she indicated.

THE QUESTION OF LAY ANALYSIS

"Lay" analysis refers to the practice of analysis by persons who are not medical doctors. In the United States the official institutes since 1938 have banned nonmedical candidates. In all other countries in the world nonmedical persons are admitted, as a rule on a par with medical.

The significance of the problem may be inferred from the fact that Freud once commented that "the resistance to lay analysis is the last mask of the resistance against analysis and the most dangerous of all."[4] As Jones tells us in his biography, it was the source of greatest concern to Freud in the post–World War I years. His own daughter Anna became a lay analyst and one of the leaders of the field in England but was discouraged from taking a stand on the American scene.

The question goes back to the 1920s. In his original Viennese circle Freud admitted a number of persons who were not physicians. After World War I, when institutes were established, the question of admission and preanalytic qualifications came to the fore. A symposium on the subject was held in 1927 and published in the *International*; opinions were naturally divided. The strongest stand against lay analysis was taken by the American group, while the strongest stand for it was taken by the Hungarian. This was paradoxical in that in 1927 the Americans had no training facilities, very small institutes, and few analysts of any prominence, while the Hungarian institute was one of the most prestigious in the world.

In 1938 the American Association rebelled against the International Association, declared itself independent, and passed a "Resolution Against the Training of Laymen," which has remained the legal position until today. The rival Academy of Psychoanalysis, founded in 1956, has taken the same stand. While the rules have been modified somewhat in recent years, the ban still remains. However, an official ban is one thing, reality another. As pointed out before, it is virtually impossible to regulate psychoanalytic training strictly. Thus unofficially many nonmedical persons have been trained. Actually the prohibition has had little more effect than that other great American experiment in prohibition, that of alcohol. After the war analysts who had been unofficially trained by the official institutes formed institutes of their own. In 1979 an unofficial count by the present writer revealed that there were at least eleven training groups in the New York area, with about six hundred members and two thousand students.[5] By 1974 Burness Moore, in his presidential address to the American Psychoanalytic Association, said:

> A piece of reality has been overlooked. We have no exclusive prerogative to Freud's heritage. Lay analysis is here to stay. It is only a question of whether our Association will play a significant role in guiding and promoting its development along lines that we believe advantageous to psychoanalysis.[6]

WHY THE OPPOSITION TO LAY ANALYSIS?

Since the question of lay analysis is a purely American phenomenon, the reasons for the adamant, at times rigid, opposition have to be sought in the cultural factors on the American scene.

First of all there is the ubiquitous diploma disease. What gets you somewhere is a diploma; inner qualitative factors do not count. Even the history of psychoanalysis has been misrepresented in this respect, for it is only gradually that analysts have come to realize that the decisive turn in their history came with Freud's self-analysis, not with his functioning as a neuropathologist. In the United States the M.D. places a man near the top of the list in the status hierarchy of occupations; it is hard to give that up.

Second there is the ever present uncertainty about psychoanalysis. For it is no secret that psychoanalysis from the very beginning has been torn by splits and dissensions. Theoretical disputes are still going on. Thus a committee of the American Psychoanalytic Association tried for years to reach consensus on a definition of psychoanalysis and failed. Even today, in a 1979 special issue of the Journal of the *American Psychoanalytic Association,* devoted to problems of therapy, no agreement is reached on a definition of classical analysis.

This uncertainty has had two important consequences. One is that the analytic societies have chosen to remain small as a way of controlling obstreperous deviants. A small society allows for more control than a large one. Thus between 1978 and 1979 the New York

Psychoanalytic Society, the largest in the country, actually lost members.

A second consequence is that the charismatic figure continues to play a leading role, and from time to time new cults are formed around such figures. In the July 1979 issue of the *Psychoanalytic Quarterly* Calef and Weinshel devote an extensive article to a careful critique of the work of Otto Kernberg.[7] They point to the bandwagon popularity of Kernberg's contributions, the cult-like atmosphere that has surrounded much of his work, and the reluctance to question its derivation and its validity. They argue that Kernberg and his theories on the borderline personality represent a major change in psychoanalytic theory, a fact that has not been properly appreciated:

> [T]here is a significant tendency to depart from . . . very basic technical precepts. . . . In their place, we see more and more instances in which the patient is being viewed through a prism of prefabricated ideas, and his treatment is predicated on *what* is believed contained within a given diagnostic label and preformed ideas about *how* that diagnostic label should be approached.[8]

A relevant point that they do not make is that the current popularity of the diagnosis of "borderline personality," which they thoroughly demolish on theoretical grounds, serves a political purpose. For if the patient is borderline (and, as they show, this has been expanded to include virtually all patients), he remains within the purview of psychiatric control and treatment, since by definition he must be very close to psychotic. If the patient is seen as an average citizen of a culturally miserable population, then the lay analyst could do just as well as the psychiatrist in treating him.

The same issue of the *Psychoanalytic Quarterly* carries an article by Lacan, the French analyst, and an article about him. Lacan is another charismatic figure on the current scene. He proclaims a "return to Freud," but his critics (Anzieu and others) point out that he seems never to have read Freud. His language remains so obscure that it requires a commentary; people tend to excuse his obscurity because he is writing in French, forgetting that French is the language of precision.

It is an old truism, demonstrated by Freud, that leaders are close to their followers. If a sizable group of American analysts has to rally around Kernberg and his overinsistence on the borderline diagnosis, then they are as confused and uncertain about psychoanalytic theory as Calef and Weinshel demonstrate Kernberg to be. If Lacan has a large following on the basis of a return to Freud, whom he has never read carefully, his followers likewise are making Freud a totem figure without having read him.

The analyst's uncertainty about his work leads him, like any other mortal, to increase his insistence on his worth and look for an enemy on the outside. As Santayana has observed, the fanatic is someone who redoubles his efforts after he has lost sight of his goal. I have elsewhere suggested that the American opposition to lay analysis smacks of an identification with Freud's peculiar misjudgment of Adler and Jung: Adler was the hated enemy, Jung the beloved friend. In America the psychiatrist became the beloved friend, the lay analyst the hated enemy. Although psychiatry officially has embraced much of psychoanalysis, it still remains an open question whether the embrace is oral-erotic or oral-sadistic—whether the object is to include it or to destroy it. Certainly, if one examines the writings of people like Marmor and Langsley, they seem more determined to destroy analysis than to further it.

Our prime concern here is with the cultural forces that have led American psychoanalysis in the directions in which it has gone. Among other factors the struggle for power remains primary. As Knight observed at an early stage, all the battles within psychoanalysis have revolved around who shall be the training analyst, the person who has the real power in the institute (see pp. 335–337). A full discussion of the numerous problems surrounding the training analysis is found in Chapter 14. Here it must be re-emphasized that the system which prescribed the degree first and then the training has failed in many ways. This need to maintain power cannot be stigmatized as all bad; it is true of all psychoanalytic instistutes and has positive implications as well. Nevertheless, it is an old observation that power corrupts. There is every reason to believe that excessive power has corrupted the psychoanalytic movement in many ways.

Psychotherapy and the Need for a Scapegoat

A third factor in the struggle is the therapist's need for a scapegoat. In some ways this too is a reflection of the historical derivation of psychiatry from Christian theology, only the scapegoat is now re-clothed in fancy diagnostic terms—he is the "incurable" schizophrenic. If some people are analyzable while others are not, as standard psychoanalytic theory has maintained, then there is a perpetual supply of scapegoats available for custodial care, which provides the bulk of the psychiatrist's income. If everybody is analyzable to some degree, then the scapegoating maneuver can be avoided.

It may come as a surprise to learn that psychoanalysts have joined in this scapegoating, naturally under the guise of scientific jargon. Psychoanalytic meetings are filled these days with extensive discussions of the differences between psychoanalysis and psychotherapy. No clear consensus is ever reached, but it is generally held that "true" psychoanalysis must be confined to a very small portion of the population, while the mass must be treated by special techniques of therapy that are not essentially analytic. We do not wish to take the space to discuss this problem scientifically (see Fine 1980). The point to be stressed here is that the distinction is a way of maintaining power. For if psychoanalysis is defined in such a way as to confine it to a small elite, then the practitioners likewise will form a small elite, and the power struggles will be brought under better control. If everybody can be psychoanalyzed, as I have consistently tried to show, then the analytic profession must undergo a large-scale reorganization (see also Pollock, 1974).

THE ANALYST'S RESISTANCE TO ANALYSIS

Finally a peculiar phenomenon must be commented upon. As time has gone on, the most intense opposition to the spread of psychoanalysis has come from certain psychoanalysts. These are the ones who, in spite of all evidence to the contrary, regard analysis as a procedure that can be performed only on certain individuals and only by the medically trained.

In his final paper on technique, "Analysis Terminable and Interminable" of 1937, Freud alluded to the analyst's resistance to analysis and recommended that in order to overcome this resistance the analyst should not be ashamed to go back to analysis every five years or so. There are no statistics on how often this has been done, but it does seem to be rare. As a result analysts, like other mortals, merely cover up their resistances with polemical statements that are either questionable or devoid of empirical foundation. Much of the argumentation within the psychoanalytic field must be evaluated in this light, as a rationalization of the analyst's own unresolved problems or as a scientific disguise for political power struggles (see

Shapiro 1978). Theory as well has often been distorted for these reasons (Fine, 1979a, 1980). It would appear that with his remark that the resistance to lay analysis is the last and the strongest of all the resistances to psychoanalysis, Freud was again demonstrating prophetic insight.

A consequence of this is, as noted, that analysts all too often bog down in technique and lose sight of the vision. If the vision is restored to the technique, then the battles can be resolved and psychoanalysis will again be seen as the great liberating force in man's history it was intended to be.

Psychoanalysis and Its Alternatives

What has been said should not be taken as an attempt to destroy the careful structure that the psychoanalytic organizations have built up over the years. Rather, it embodies a wish that they would extend their efforts in socially desirable directions rather than lose themselves in adherence to charismatic figures or socially useless power struggles. For with all its faults, psychoanalysis is so far superior to its alternatives that no meaningful comparison can really be made. Nevertheless, in a culture widely inimical to psychotherapy because it does not wish to look at itself, it is only to be expected that inferior psychotherapies will flourish. One could even set up a kind of Gresham's law, that bad therapy tends to drive out good, because it is more seductive and offers more immediate and tangible gratifications. It is necessary to look at these alternative forms of therapy more closely now.

THE MYTH OF "SCHOOLS"

The untutored person who approaches the field today is immediately barraged by a host of different "schools," all claiming great therapeutic successes based on a variety of theories. Without considerable sophistication it is easy to get lost in the maze. As a rule these other techniques begin with a vigorous attack on Freud and psychoanalysis, which they seriously misunderstood and misrepresent. Then various aspects of the Freudian schema are singled out and made into a complete therapy. It is pertinent to re-examine these various claims in the light of competent psychoanalytic knowledge.

Before that is done, a word may be said about the origin of these various therapies and the cultural milieu in which they arose. Almost all stem from the post–World War II period, when the demand for therapeutic services greatly exceeded the supply. Accordingly anyone with any kind of degree in even remotely connected fields was drawn into the picture. These therapists were almost never analyzed and almost never trained. Unaware of the profound effect of transference, they evolved various technical devices based on questionable theory and with dubious results. However, because of the transference they were bound to help some patients. Because their professional position depended on reporting successes, serious self-criticism as a rule was lacking. The public, beguiled by their seductive claims and often in resistance to serious analysis, provided some support. In order to avoid going too far afield, some of the systems described in the popular survey edited by Corsini, *Current Psychotherapies* (1978), will be considered.

BEHAVIOR THERAPY

Currently the technique with the greatest vogue among psychologists is behavior therapy, or behavioral psychotherapy, as Chambless and Goldstein name it (Corsini, 1978, Ch. 6). The American Psychiatric Association has officially endorsed it as a valuable procedure. (Given the association's antagonism to psychoanalysis, this may well look like a kiss of death rather than a sign of approval.) It has become so widespread that an annual reviewing all its applications and ramifications has been published since 1973.

Behavioral psychotherapy in Corsini's compendium is defined as consisting of two related systems of treatment: behavior *therapy*, based on the work of Joseph Wolpe, and behavior *modification*, based on the work of B. F. Skinner. The first system follows a classical conditioning model and the second is derived from operant conditioning. (Here the authors fail to state that the difference between the two forms of conditioning is by no means clear, and many researchers today deny that it is of any significance.)

In both systems, it is argued, problematic behaviors (affective, cognitive, or motoric) are seen as responses to stimuli, internal and external, and psychological distress is viewed as the result of ineffective or maladaptive learning. Behavioral treatment is based on implementing experimentally derived laws of learning so that desirable behaviors replace less functional ones. Although many presentations of behavior modification engage in violent diatribes against psychoanalysis, the one by Chambless and Goldstein considered here does not.

A basic assumption of the behavioral approach to therapy, they say, is that people have become what they are through learning processes, or more accurately through the interactions of the environment with their genetic endowment. Problems, therefore, are generally learned and can be unleared.

Statements of this kind, which are quite common in the writings of behavior therapists, seem to derive from the naive notion that they are saying something new. In reality, the notion that neurotic reactions are learned phenomena has been basic to Freudian thinking from the very beginning, although because of the different audiences to which it was directed these exact words were not used.

Chambless and Goldstein continue to make a number of commonsense statements with which no one would disagree. "Most human problems are comprised of numerous components. . . . No one of these components is the 'real' problem or causes the real problem."[9]

Other statements, however, represent dogmatic assertions without evidence. Thus they state:

> Once it is clear what change the client wants to make, behavioral techniques seem effective in bringing about changes. . . . Much time and money can be saved when the therapist has specific ways of helping the client learn new behaviors or unlearn maladaptive ones, rather than just waiting for the client to stumble on a good approach. Thus the desired changes are likely to occur more quickly through behavioral treatment than with other therapies.[10]

This claim, basic to most behavior therapists, runs counter to both common sense and observation. Many symptoms are completely refractory to any kind of behavioral technique—psychosis, stuttering, alcoholism, drug addiction, and so on. Every therapist deals mainly with people who in spite of tremendous efforts are unable to change their behavior no matter what the therapist tells them or does to them. In fact, on p. 237 these authors admit frankly that on the whole little attention has been devoted to the development of a behavioral model of personality theory. As an exception they cite Eysenck's work on defining personality through factor analysis, work that most psychologists regard as worthless because the factor analysis, which is merely a convenient way of reducing a series of correlations, is based on meaningless tests. The absence of personality theory (a statement incidentally made by many of the nonanalytic therapists) allows the therapists to use the analytic model.

In their description of the process of psychotherapy, the authors place primary emphasis on establishing a working relationship. They fail to see that what they are describing is establishing a positive transference. Because they do not use the word "transference" they create the impression that they are doing something new. They also fail to note that the mere establishment of a transference not infrequently has an ameliorative effect on many symptoms; in analytic terminology this is known as a transference cure or transference effect.

As we read further, we find that "behaviorists maintain a rather constant skepticism about the mechanisms responsible for change in behavior. 'Explanations' are viewed as hypotheses."[11] Thus they operate without a personality theory and without any real hypotheses about the effects of what they are doing. Their main concern is "to see if it works"; if it does, why is of secondary importance. In this way they become technicians without vision.

The virtual absence of values in behavior modification has exposed it to the justifiable criticism that it does not evaluate properly what it does. The authors agree with this criticism insofar as behavior modification has been used in a repressive manner to further the ends of "the system."[12] But they allege that while this has been the case all too often, it represents the actions of particular individuals, not of behaviorism as such.

To an experienced therapist the case history presented smacks of magic. The patient was a thirty-year-old woman with three children. She felt inadequate and indecisive as a mother and unloved as a wife. She described her husband as critical and "emotionally unsupportive." At one point he too was referred for very brief therapy. In the fifteenth session the client complained that all her symptoms were back after initial progress. The therapist interpreted this as a reaction to termination and reassured her that she could come back. In the eighteenth session she was terminated. "At one year follow-up she stated she was enjoying life, felt fully functional, and had experienced no recurrence of depression."[13]

Looked at analytically, one would say that this woman made a positive transference to the therapist and grew somewhat through this transference. What other changes were made is hard to say, because the material one would like to see is simply omitted. What were her relationships with her children? Did she really get over her father's death so quickly? What did she mean by "becoming orgasmic again"? And so on. There is actually little more here than a recital that the woman came in depressed and after eighteen weekly sessions left feeling better. The authors also say, referring to the first interview: "Talking provided her with some support and temporary relief and also served to form an emotional bond on which to base the working relationship."[14] Thus they almost confirm the impression that this is essentially a transference improvement, which could have come about with any warm relationship.

Behavior Therapy and Ethics

Alone among the alternative therapies, the ethical question has come up quite often with behavior therapy. The 1978 edition of the *Annual Review of Behavior Therapy* again has a section on ethics,[15] apparently prompted by the reactions of the profession and the public to certain measures adopted by some behavior therapists.

Originally, and to a large extent currently, behavior therapy could be classified as a technique without vision. But Franks and Wilson, in their discussion, now recognize that since behavior therapists have to make some value judgment about what aspect of behavior they wish to change, they are beginning to espouse moral principles. However, in this area they are hobbled by the views of some of the founders. Thus Skinner's book *Beyond Freedom and Dignity* sounded a highly discordant note in an age when these concepts were attacked wholesale by ruthless dictators. Skinner goes farther in his book when he states:

> The technology of behavior which emerges is ethically neutral, but when applied to the design of a culture, the survival of the culture functions as a value. . . . It is not the benevolence of a controller but the contingencies under which he controls benevolently which must be examined.[16]

At another point he says: "The archetypal pattern of control for the good of the controlee is the benevolent dictator."[17]

One wonders whether Skinner was aware of what he was saying. The Nazis justified their murders and enslavement in the name of survival, as did the Communists. If the archetype of control is the benevolent dictator, who is to rule on his benevolence? All dictators, from Nero to Idi Amin, have proclaimed themselves benevolent and have murdered anyone who dared to say otherwise. In effect, then, Skinner is condoning any tyrannical system so long as that system survives. Surely there is reason enough here to make others quake if such beliefs gained the upper hand. In their review Franks and Wilson admit it frankly: "On more than one occasion we have drawn attention to the fact that behavior therapy lacks a philosophy of man and his personal responsibility."[18]

But if behavior therapists have no philosophy, and yet must make value judgments on the basis of a philosophy, there is an obvious contradiction. Wolpe confuses the matter further when he states that he accepts the basic goals of therapy as formulated by psychoanalysts, but that psychoanalysts never follow them: An absurdity of this kind does nothing to help the situation.[19] When we read further in Franks and Wilson that the characteristics of behavior therapists are now less clear than they were twenty years ago[20] and that they are unable even to arrive at a clear definition of the field, the confusion and dangers multiply.

Almost all definitions of behavior therapy stress the idea that it involves the application of scientifically determined principles of behavior. This is clearly not the case, as has been shown innumerable times. Consequently behavior therapists begin by offering a definition contrary to fact, which many would consider unethical from the start.

The dilemmas of behavior therapy are so great that the *Annual* now has more commentary than reprinted papers (1978).

In 1971 Lazarus published a paper on where behavior therapists go for therapy; he had found that half went to psychoanalysts. Although this *gaffe* has since been corrected by juggling other statistics, the implications are clear. Behavior therapy is an ad hoc procedure, ready to use any and every device available, with little regard for the outcome. In the 1976 *Annual Review of Behavior Therapy* Bandura wrote: "Although abuses of institutional power arise from time to time, it is not totalitarian rule that constitutes the impending peril."[21] How is this fantastic statement supported by experimentally derived principles of learning? It is not surprising that behavior therapy with its use of aversive conditioning (read: punishment) has been restricted in some institutional settings. Wolpe quotes a study by MacLean in which welfare clients were threatened with the loss of their welfare checks if they did not go back to work. Wolpe is critical of this study because "breaking the motor habit does not diminish anxiety."[22] He has nothing to say about the ethics involved in starving a welfare client to death.

One last point: The names chosen by the alternative therapies frequently reflect their propagandistic intent rather than their scientific origin. The name "behavior therapy" is taken to imply that psychoanalysts do not deal with overt behavior, a nonsensical charge.

ROGERS'S PERSON-CENTERED THERAPY

Person-centered therapy is the current name for what Rogers until 1974 called "client-centered" therapy. Its central hypothesis is that the growth and potential of any individual will tend to be released in a relationship in which the helping person is experiencing and communicating realness, caring, and a deeply sensitive, nonjudgmental understanding. So far this is simply a reformulation of the analytic emphasis on psychotherapy as the key to growth, differing from Freud only in the word used.

Meador and Rogers explain further:

> The basic theory of person-centered therapy can be stated simply in the form of an "if–then" hypothesis. If certain conditions are present in the attitudes of the person designated "therapist" in a relationship, namely, congruence, positive regard, and empathic understanding, then growthful change will take place in the person designated "client." The hypothesis holds true, theoretically, in any relationship in which one person assumes the attitudes of congruence, empathy and positive regard, and the other person perceives these attitudes.[23]

If this basic theory is looked at critically, it immediately becomes apparent that it relates to the *therapist*, and not to the patient or client at all. At best there is a qualification at the end, if "the other person perceives these attitudes." And what if he does not? No allowance is made. And what if he does and reacts with teasing, negativism, or violence (as in Richard Wright's famous novel *Black Boy*)? No comment. Thus in reality this theory is not person-centered at all but completely therapist-centered. It prescribes what the therapist should be or do but leaves out of account the reactions of his client.

A joke that was current when I was in graduate school in the late 1940s, a time when Rogers was all the vogue among psychologists, tells of a suicidal patient who goes to a Rogerian therapist and says: I feel terrible. THERAPIST: You feel terrible. PATIENT: I'm going to kill myself. THERAPIST: You're going to kill yourself. PATIENT (*walks over to the window*): I'm going to jump. THERAPIST: You're going to jump. PATIENT (*opening the window*): This is the end. THERAPIST: You feel that this is the end. (*Patient jumps*.) THERAPIST: Plop.

Many a true word is spoken in jest. The joke brings out the real weakness in Rogerian therapy: Its high-flown ideals cover up the simple fact that it pays almost no attention to the real feelings of the person. In this respect, a significant parallel can be drawn with Christianity. Nor does the 1978 article reveal the tremendous changes that have been forced on Rogerian therapy by the need to consider the client. The original eight-week miracle cure, with six-week miracle training of the therapist, has disappeared so completely that most psychologists today are unaware that this was the prevalent theory for many years. Instead, Rogerian therapy has become a kind of psychoanalytic therapy, fully as long and as difficult as any other form of psychoanalytic therapy.

As with behavior therapy, Rogers espouses no special theory of personality.[24] His focus is "on the manner in which change comes about in the human personality."[25] How the manner of change can be studied without some theory of personality is unexplained. It is in the same tradition as other nonanalytic therapies: technique without vision.

At another point, however, Rogers does offer some assumptions about human nature. He defines hostility and irrationality but stresses rationality and self-actualization:

> I have little sympathy with the rather prevalent concept that man is basically irrational, and that his impulses, if not controlled, will lead to destruction of others and self. Man's behavior is exquisitely rational, moving with subtle and ordered complexity toward the goals his organism is endeavoring to achieve.[26]

In theory this is not essentially different from psychoanalysis. But it is so broad that it omits any attempt to explain the obviously irrational destructive aspects of man's behavior. Rogers does not care to face the fact that the world today is full of destructiveness and irrationality, as it has been for thousands of years, with more of the same promised for tomorrow. In this respect he repeats the Christian myth that kindness and love will cause the enemy to lay down his arms. All of human history brands this as an unrealistic fantasy.

As is customary, Rogers reveals a profound ignorance of what psychoanalysis is about, and by comparing his system with psychoanalysis he distorts the "enemy" beyond recognition:

> In psychoanalysis, the analyst aims to interpret for his patient the connections between his past and his present. In person-centered therapy the therapist facilitates the client's discoveries of the meanings of his own current inner experiencing. The analyst . . . takes the role of teacher. . . . The therapist in person-centered therapy presents himself . . . as simply the person he is. . . . Person-centered therapy has not found the transference relationship, central to psychoanalysis, a necessary part of a client's growthful change.[27]

But then again he says:

> The process of therapy is, by these hypotheses, seen as being synonymous with the experiential relationship between client and therapist. Therapy consists in experiencing the self in a wide range of ways in an emotionally meaningful relationship with the therapist.[28]

This latter statement is simply a reformulation of what analysts mean when they refer to the transference. Rogers' background has been shown to derive from Otto Rank, who emphasized the here-and-now of the therapeutic relationship exclusively. The same criticism applies to Rogers as was applied to Rank at an earlier day: Granted the vital significance of the here-and-now of the transference (therapeutic relationship), why should the therapist put aside the extraordinarily useful tool of correlating it with the patient's past experiences, particularly with his parents?

The concept of "self-actualization" has been strongly stressed by Rogerians and other advocates of the human potential movement and somehow has been contrasted with psychoanalytic theory. Actually it is merely a reformulation of psychoanalytic theory, which has been concerned with the self and the growth process from the very beginning, even if other words are used. What Rogers and the human potentialists leave out of account entirely is the psychology of the person under consideration. Whatever the origin of such feelings may be, it is a truism that people are dominated by feelings of hatred, anger, insecurity, resentment, and rage, and frequently resort to violence and destructiveness in their relationships with others. If a theory of personality and therapy does not offer some technique for dealing with these powerful irrational forces it is either utopian or totally oblivious to clinical realities. That is, it alternates between being a vision without technique and a technique without a vision.

RATIONAL-EMOTIVE THERAPY

Rational-emotive therapy, the creation of Albert Ellis, dates from the 1950s. It emphasizes rational cognitive discourse and has acquired a considerable following. Neither extensive training nor extensive theory is required of the practitioner. It is again a technique without a vision.

Ellis states that rational-emotive therapy holds that when a highly charged emotional consequence (C) follows a significant activating event (A), A may seem to cause C but actually does not. Instead, emotional consequences are largely created by the individual's belief system (B). When an undesirable emotional consequence occurs, such as severe anxiety, this can usually be traced to the person's irrational beliefs. If these beliefs are effectively disputed (D) by challenging them rationally, the disturbed consequences disappear and eventually cease to recur.[29]

The theoretical statement by Ellis can be compared with various statements by Freud. For example in *Totem and Taboo* Freud wrote:

> What lie behind the sense of guilt of neurotics are always *psychical* realities and never *factual* ones. What characterizes neurotics is that they prefer psychical to factual reality and react just as seriously to thoughts as normal people do to realities.[30]

Clearly Ellis is repeating Freud in different language. Had he used the same language he could not have pretended that he had a new system.

The second part of Ellis's statement is his therapeutic hypothesis: Challenge the false psychical beliefs rationally and they will disappear. This is again the same as Freud in the 1890s: Make the unconscious conscious. And again the experience of the transference and resistances, which, as Freud discovered, interfere with the simple rational process, must make their way into Ellis's therapy as well, but he prefers to disregard them. Thus he can operate only in a state of positive transference, and then only with regard to superficial aspects of the personality.

Later Ellis states: "After practicing classical psychoanalysis and psychoanalytically oriented psychotherapy for several years, . . .

Ellis discovered . . . that [clients] rarely lost their presenting symptoms."[31] This statement is usually made about analyses conducted
by other people; it is surprising that Ellis makes the claim that he
practiced psychoanalysis for several years. There is nothing in his
writings to indicate that he has the remotest knowledge of the theory
of psychoanalysis. Although he is an omnivorous reader, he never
even cites popular psychoanalytic literature, let alone the technical
writings of Freud or others. He makes no allowance for transference,
resistances, working through, acting-out, ego structure, superego
strictures, or any of the other concepts of psychoanalysis. We can
only conclude that his allegation that he "practiced classical psychoanalysis" is totally devoid of foundation.

Unlike other alternative theorists Ellis does present a theory of
personality. It is completely eclectic, drawing on every theory in the
book. But then he says:

> RET holds that humans' environment, particularly childhood parental
> environment, *reaffirms* but does not *create* strong tendencies to think
> irrationally and to over- or underemote. Parents and culture teach
> children *which* superstitions, taboos and prejudices to abide by; but
> they do not originate their basic tendency to superstitiousness, ritual-
> ism and bigotry.[32]

Thus he takes a completely genetic view: Neurosis is inherent in
man's condition. At the same time he denies the existence of instincts, instead alleging that people have "instinctoid" tendencies
(whatever that might mean). He thus denies the validity of the vast
body of literature showing that happy children come from happy
families and that unhappy children come from unhappy families.
Such dogmatic assertions are typical.

In therapy his main emphasis is on reducing the severity of the
superego (naturally he declines to use that most useful term). He
states: "The many roads taken in RET are aimed at one major goal:
minimizing the client's central self-defeating outlook and acquiring a
more realistic, tolerant philosophy of life."[33]

But again, as in Rogerian therapy, the reactions of the client are
largely disregarded. Ellis states that RET practitioners quickly "pin
the client down to a few irrational ideas."[34] They "logically analyze
these ideas and make mincemeat of them," then teach the client to
"think scientifically, so he can observe, logically parse, and thoroughly annihilate any subsequent irrational ideas."[35] The enormous
aggression in these statements is right out in full view: The therapist
is to *pin* the client down, *make mincemeat* of his ideas, teach him to

annihilate any subsequent irrational ideas. Are we to believe seriously that this tremendous aggression has no effect on the patient?

Thus the "system" of Ellis goes back in theory and practice to
the Freud of the 1890s: Find the person's psychic state, make it conscious, and it will disappear. The difference is that in RET the process of making it conscious requires a direct, active attack on the
patient's belief systems by the therapist. No mention is made of the
patient's reactions. Again, technique without vision. As in other systems, it is highly doubtful whether the technique, which uses far
more therapist aggression than other systems, has desirable practical
consequences.

GESTALT PSYCHOTHERAPY

Gestalt therapy is a system introduced by Fritz Perls in the
1950s. As Simkin describes it now, it is a noninterpretive, ahistoric,
existentially based system of psychotherapy in which awareness is
the primary focus in the here-and-now.[36] Cognitive explanations or
interpretations of "causes" or "purposes" are rejected. By concentrating on what is going on (the *process*) rather than what could or
should be going on (the *content*), the patient is encouraged to take
responsibility for what he is doing. "Choice and growth are thus en-
hanced through organismic self-regulation."[37]

The name of this system is rather odd, inasmuch as the only
other way in which "Gestalt" is used in psychology is in the now almost forgotten system of Gestalt psychology, with which the Perls
technique has nothing in common. Perls was also one of the few analysts who practiced analysis for a time and then moved on to an entirely different approach. What kind of analytic training he had is
not wholly clear. We are told that he was analyzed by Wilhelm
Reich in the 1930s and that from him he learned "the function of the
motoric system as an armor."[38] In the published lists of members of
the International Psychoanalytical Association Perls is included as a
member of the Society for Dutch Psychoanalysts in 1934 and 1935,
but not afterward.

The literature of Gestalt therapy impresses by its vagueness.
Perls saw man as a "biological event"[39]; who could quarrel with
that? Kempler, one of his main disciples, wrote in 1973:

> There is nothing in Gestalt Therapy that can be considered original.
> All its theoretical considerations can be found throughout man's his-

tory. Furthermore, there is nothing in its activity that has not been done by someone, somewhere, sometime. The most that can be said is that it represents an updated language, and recommendations for behavior that hopefully apply more effectively knowledge which man has known for a long time.[40]

Later, referring to the first summer-long workshop in Gestalt therapy on the West Coast led by Perls, Simkin, and Kempler in 1963, Kempler wrote:

"I and Thou" and the "Here and Now" were popular phrases that characterized the theoretical essence of the day. Their difference was over the issue of "I and Thou." In theory everyone was in full accord. In practice it was another matter. . . . In no way could Perls' behavior be called "I." He was the puppeteer, the manipulator, the director and that was how it had to be. Any remark inviting Perls to look at his own behavior met with the invitation for the subject to look at *his* own motives in making the suggestion.[41]

As Simkin describes it, Gestalt therapy has become a variety of existentialism. Still, after Perls's death in 1973 Kempler described it as "a bit like an anthill that has been uncovered. People are scurrying about uncertain how to proceed. There is no clear leadership."[42]

Perls himself toward the end rejected all individual therapy. In 1967 he wrote: "I have come to consider that all individual therapy is obsolete and should be replaced by workshops in Gestalt Therapy."[43] Nevertheless, most Gestalt therapists continue to do individual work.

The reader will already have sensed the outsider's difficulty in coming to grips with the Gestalt approach. It would appear to be a method devoid of theory, widely eclectic in technique, and extremely vague in its philosophy, like Perls himself. The central concept of "awareness" is taken over from the analytic notions of free association and transference. Although there are a number of Gestalt groups around, there seems to be no systematic doctrine and no organized training.

In such a situation, the therapist has permission to do whatever he wants. Perls himself, as Kempler describes, was a narcissistic individual who always demanded the center of the stage. The Gestalt school evidently allows the therapist to identify with Perls and "do his thing," wherever that will take him. It has neither a clear-cut vision nor a clear-cut technique, but a bit of each.

REALITY THERAPY

Reality therapy is a system developed by William Glasser in the 1950s. It is a series of theoretical principles, Glasser tells us, applicable to individuals with behavioral and emotional problems as well as to individuals or groups seeking either to gain a success identity for themselves and/or to help others toward this same goal. Focusing on the present and on behavior, the therapist guides the individual toward an ability to see himself accurately and to fulfill his own needs without harming himself or others. "The crux of the theory is personal responsibility for one's own behavior, which is equated with mental health."[44]

Glasser claims to have developed reality therapy around 1956, while he was still a resident in psychiatry at UCLA. Thus he rejected the long and difficult training of which residency is usually only the beginning and struck out on his own. In New York Daniel Casriel, whose approach is similar to Glasser's in many ways, did something similar.

Apparently the main emphasis in reality therapy is on success. Reality therapy, Glasser says, views identity as the single basic requirement of all mankind, transcending all cultures and existing from birth to death. Although identity can be seen from several viewpoints, "it is most useful to regard identity from a therapeutic vantage point, as *success identity* versus *failure identity*."[45] To achieve this success eight principles are laid down: (1) personal (the therapist cares), (2) focus on behavior rather than feelings, (3) focus on the present, (4) value judgment, (5) planning, (6) commitment, (7) no excuses, and (8) eliminate punishment.

Glasser attempts to differentiate his therapy from "conventional" therapy in a number of ways. First of all, he describes most forms of mental disturbance as irresponsibility. The past is irrelevant. The therapist is not to be treated as a transference figure. The unconscious is irrelevant. "The reality therapist does not permit patients to use unconscious motivations as an excuse for misbehavior."[46] People must be guided in great detail.

Three comments are in order here. First of all, one element in personality theory, identity, is singled out as superseding all others in importance. Glasser does not give any credit to Erikson (or any other analyst) for writing about identity and does not link identity to other aspects of the personality, as would ordinarily be done. What he is really talking about is success, a basic premise of the American ethic. His therapy is a kind of punishment device, even though verbally he eschews punishment. "You have failed, and I will show you how to succeed. Just listen to me and you will succeed." This is the essential message that he conveys, even though he is unaware of it.

Second, there is the usual misconception about psychoanalysis. Glasser says the therapist "does not allow himself to be used as a transference figure," as though the therapist, not the patient, created the transference. Transference is a universal aspect of all interpersonal relationships (Fine, 1979); as Freud once put it, whatever the analyst does the patient responds to with transferences. Thus Glasser can only work in a positive transference; he has no technique for handling a negative transference.

Third, the emphasis is on the activity of the therapist. The patient is guided, chided, and derided. He has to obey. If he does not, he is irresponsible and will suffer for his faults. He has to learn responsibility. The therapist thus is expected to function as a stern parent, while the patient is expected to be the obedient child. That this model fails quite often even in the good family is of no concern to Glasser.

Thus reality therapy's only vision is success, the standard American ethic. There is no conception of love, affection, creativity, self-actualization, or any of the other aspects of the analytic ideal. The technique is forceful direction. While this might be effective with some psychotic patients (with whom Glasser was working when the idea of reality therapy occurred to him) at certain times, as a general principle of psychotherapy it is patently absurd. And of course as usual there is no training required of the prospective reality therapist. Any degree will do. It seems to be no accident that the therapy was devised while Dr. Glasser had just begun his training.

Summary Comments on the Alternative Therapies

We have discussed some of the more important therapeutic systems avilable today. Many more are in existence, but space considerations preclude a more detailed or comprehensive examination. The general conclusions would not be different from those that come out of the ones scrutinized. The following considerations are offered as a wind-up of this section:

1. All of these techniques were developed after World War II when there were a number of persons with degrees but no training in

psychotherapy who did not know what to do with the hordes of patients society had thrust upon them.

2. All of the founders and their followers avoided the long and difficult but spiritually rewarding path of psychoanalytic training. A common feature of all of these methods is that no training is required to learn them or to practice them; the degree suffices. No personal therapy is needed, no self-scrutiny, no control by more experienced therapists. "This is what you should do; go out and do it" is the message.

3. As a rule no theory of personality is offered. In practice bits and pieces of the analytic theory are incorporated here and there, commonly with insufficient understanding of analysis.

4. All of them begin with an attack on psychanalysis as "ineffective." Misrepresentations, often of the grossest kind, are usual. In fact, one feature that all these systems have in common is an almost total failure to grasp what analysts have been talking about. This can best be understood by realizing that all (except for Perls) were started by persons who refused to go into analytic training. They are thus expressing a negative transference, not a reasoned reevaluation of all the clinical data.

5. For the most part the emphasis is on whatever works. This is most explicit in Glasser's reality therapy, which explicitly adopts the American success ethic without reflecting on its consequences. Insofar as this is so, they represent technique without vision.

6. Some, like Rogers and the Gestaltists, do have a vision, usually expressed in self-actualization. Rogers stressed the therapist's need to care for the patient, ignorant of the fact that this has always been one of the cardinal tenets of psychoanalysis. Rogers's system is reminiscent of Christian faith healing. The Gestalt vision of awareness or self-actualization is a partial reformulation of the analytic ideal.

7. Most have adopted names that carry propagandistic messages directed against analysis. Thus Rogers is client-centered (now person-centered), implying that analysis is analyst-centered; behaviorists deal with behavior (allegedly analysts do not); reality therapists deal with reality; RET therapists are rational (presumably analysts are irrational); and so on. These names serve to obscure one all-important similarity: *None of these therapies pay any real attention to the patient.* They are all directives for how the therapist should behave and largely ignore the clinical and theoretical realities of the patient's responses. These clinical realities immediately lead to

the observations of transference and resistance, which all have a need to deny. Whatever they call themselves, they are thus all essentially intellectual approaches without feeling.

8. For the most part these techniques go back to the Freud of the 1890s, when the main formula was: Make the unconscious conscious. Because of a lack of flexibility about their language, they do not realize that they have really merely reformulated the early Freud. Ellis speaks of "belief systems" rather than Freud's "psychic reality," although the two are the same. Behavior therapists speak of conditioning and deconditioning, neglecting to ask whether the subject is conscious of the S-R situation or not. If they but asked, they would immediately realize that conditioning works only if the subject is unconscious of the goal of what is being done to him, and that deconditioning involves making the unconscious conscious.

9. Most of them make vague claims about results, often supported by a variety of "confirmatory" studies. The usual statement today is that all therapies do some good, and no one can be shown to be better than any of the others. This ignores the qualitative aspect of behavior change. In terms of research procedures, in the evaluation of results the fantasy life of the subject is almost always ignored in nonanalytic studies. There is still no reason to alter our principal claim that psychoanalysis is the most effective form of psychotherapy known.

10. Thus all of them represent the cultural reaction to the discovery of psychotherapy and the need for therapy after World War II. Their appearance, programs, and claims can only be understood in light of the cultural conditions of the past thirty-five years.

The Public's Reaction

In the meantime, the public, after World War II, was exposed to a barrage of literature that described the analytic ideal and the benefits of psychotherapy but was not given a chance to try personal therapy because so few therapists were available or because the cost was prohibitive. In addition, many who had a chance to try therapy were dissuaded by well-meaning but half-trained professionals, as well as by the natural resistances found in all people when it comes to revealing their inmost lives. It was in this environment that the human potential movement developed.

It was only to be expected that Americans, when informed of the benefits of therapy, would immediately demand quick routes to success. Analysts have also searched unremittingly for ways to shorten the process; Freud's final paper on technique, "Analysis Terminable and Interminable" of 1937, was devoted to this issue, and many others have considered it in great detail. But the analytic response in general has been negative. Freud himself, in the paper cited, concluded that character analysis or a change in life style and life goals, which is what most people want, cannot be brought about quickly. Under these circumstances it was comprehensible that the public would turn to others.

Vision Without Technique

Popular literature on psychoanalysis and its concepts has burgeoned spectacularly. Many of these popularizations are of extremely high quality; for example, Gail Sheehy's *Passages*, which has sold hundreds of thousands of copies, is in essence an excellent presentation of psychoanalytic theory. Spock's *Book of Baby Care*, which has sold in the millions, is also a translation into ordinary language of many psychoanalytic views on childrearing. The self-help literature has reached mass-market proportions, and every bookstore seems to have a special section devoted to it. But to clarify and rephrase all of this excellent advice into a method of curing suffering and neurotic problems is an entirely different matter. The books thus offer a vision without a technique.

Encounter Groups: The Attempted Technique

Beginning in the 1960s, group therapy, which had originally developed in response to pressing therapeutic needs, expanded into a variety of led and leaderless therapeutic groups. Because the average person, it was recognized, had numerous problems to contend with, what was more natural than for him to meet with his peers and "talk it out"? Leaders might help or they might hinder. Anyhow, there were not enough trained professionals, so anyone who had experienced some personal growth could become a leader. Thus was born the idea of the encounter group.

By the 1970s encounter groups were to be found everywhere. Lieberman and his colleagues (1973) wrote:

> Today's American is fairly likely to come face to face with the question of membership in an encounter group. If he is not personally considering enrollment in a "growth center" or joining a "living room group," he may be evaluating encounter groups connected with his work or with his church, or he may be puzzling over a request from his offspring to sign a permission slip for participation in a school group.[47]

Sometimes these encounter groups were similar to groups with psychoanalytic psychotherapy. Sometimes they were extreme shortcuts, like the popular est. Sometimes they were inspirational groups sponsored by the churches. Or again they could be T-groups, most suitable to educational milieus. Most of these groups are short-lived. Some are very intensive, like marathon groups, some as light as a church social. It has been estimated that currently some five million Americans attend encounter groups of one kind or another every week. Some prefer to see this as an "American disease." Others, more informed, recognize the deeper import of the movement.

The encounter groups represent group-therapy situations. But they do not use any disease or medical model; they prefer the growth model. In this way they are rephrasing analytic theory without knowing it. As always, however, the problem is one of vision versus technique. The vision is there, but the technique is inadequate.

Group therapy also began with a tremendous explosion after World War II, with the idea that groups could do the same thing as individual therapy. Essentially these groups also operate on the principle of making the unconscious conscious. It is fairly easy to teach any reasonably intelligent person about sexuality, aggression, anxiety, interpersonal relations and so forth and to train him in interpreting the actions, words, and motives of others. Indeed, this is done all the time; the only difference is that with increased analytic knowledge, it is done on a sounder basis.

Sooner or later, resistances and transferences enter the picture. Certain material cannot be "revealed." Quarrels erupt between group members, which are not easy to resolve. Members feel slighted and drop out. Bion, in his theory of group therapy, distinguishes three reactions: fight, flight, and pairing off. All these are found in the encounter groups. As a result, sooner or later these groups break up. It is impossible to estimate their therapeutic effectiveness. Theory would predict that change achieved in such group situations cannot be very great or lasting.

Back to the Eternal Problem: Vision Versus Technique

Thus we come full circle to the eternal problem of vision versus technique. The public has greeted the analytic vision with enthusiasm, but what to do with it? Analytic therapy is long and expensive, and there are too few analysts around. The alternative therapies by and large offer technique without vision. The public encounter groups by and large represent vision without technique.

At least it is plain that the discovery of psychotherapy has had a profound impact on society. Man has discovered through Freud and his followers a technique for making people happier. Suffering and misery can never again by countenanced as the "will of God" or as inherent in the human condition. Here once more we find that a quantum jump has occurred in human history.

Chapter 16

The Meaning of Love in Human Experience

ALTHOUGH THEY COME from different directions, a surprising confluence has become observable between the theoretical and the clinical approaches to man's well-being. Theoretically it has become clear that man must give up violence if he is to survive on this planet, a prospect that no longer seems as certain as it once did. Clinically, it has been established that hatred is the characteristic emotion of all the more severe forms of psychopathology, while love is characteristic of all the more mature forms of behavior. This confluence can be utilized to draw up a complete theory of love. For love is socially vital as the binding force that keeps men living together in harmony, and it is individually vital as the central facet of every person's experience.

This discussion will also provide an opportunity to show how the various critical comments on methodology made in the foregoing pages can be used as a guide to a more satisfactory theory and practice. This chapter may be viewed as an attempted model for how interdisciplinary barriers can be broken down and a single science of man can be constructed. Because data are available from many different sources, we must begin by relying on the different disciplinary approaches that have existed in the field; however, we shall end by formulating a single integrative theory.

Historical Data

In previous chapters I have noted the destructive aspects of man's behavior, which have been largely ignored by traditional historians. It was necessary to stress destructiveness in order to make an essential point. But obviously there must have been many constructive forces in human history as well; otherwise the race would never have survived. It is to these that we now turn.

Inasmuch as our primary concern is Western society, historical comments will be confined to that. Much information is already available, and new material is coming out all the time, in accordance with the changed orientation introduced and elaborated by the psychohistorians. Still the best available summary is Morton Hunt's *The Natural History of Love* (1959).

Hunt describes eight periods in Western history, from the Greeks to the present day.* Each period has struggled with the problem of the conflict between tenderness and sexuality and come up with a different solution. But all can be understood in terms of Freud's formulations of the development of sexuality toward mature love, or the union of tender and sexual feelings toward a person of the opposite sex.

The Greeks

The Greeks had two names for love: eros, or carnal love, and agape, or spiritual love. Characteristic of both was the lowly state ascribed to women and marriage. "Marriage brings a man only two happy days," said one Greek writer, "the day he marries and the day his wife dies." According to Aristotle, the wife, being inferior to her husband, ought to love him more than he loves her.

Most striking in the Greek culture was the high value placed upon homosexuality among men, particularly the love of a mature man for a pubescent boy. Aristotle wrote: "Love and friendship are found most and in their best form between men." Homosexuality is related on the one hand to contempt for women and on the other to the narcissistic overevaluation of instinctual gratification for its own sake. The release mattered, not the person. Freud was to comment on this several thousand years later in his *Three Essays*:

> The most striking distinction between the erotic life of antiquity and our own no doubt lies in the fact that the ancients laid the stress upon the instinct itself, whereas we emphasize its object. The ancients glorified the instinct and were prepared on its account to honor even an in-

---

*More conventional historians argue that he has oversimplified the case. That is to some extent true, but without some oversimplification no historical trends can ever be properly drawn. Accordingly his outline can be extremely useful.

ferior object; while we despise the instinctual activity in itself, and find excuses for it only in the merits of the object.[1]

The Romans

The Romans took over the contempt for women characteristic of the Greeks, but not the homosexuality—at least not until much later. Sex was for man's pleasure; woman should submit. But to this view they added the Roman specialty of cruelty.

There were several other differences from the culture of the ancient Greeks. From the old patriarchal system, in which woman was the mother, silent and untouchable in her home, there gradually emerged the sexual emancipation of women, who sought to gratify their desires as much as men, and with the same kind of sadism.

Thus Roman love flourished in the context of the disintegration of family life, and even accelerated it. In fact it produced a problem of utmost seriousness—the voluntary infertility of the native Roman stock. Historians searching for the reasons for Rome's fall have uncovered the gradual diminution of the noble Romans and the need to replace them more and more with conquered peoples. The Romans' love life was dominated by conquest rather than by tender feelings; in the end the noble families died out.*

Early Christian Asceticism

In reaction against the sadism and sexual profligacy of the Romans, the Christians at first tried to abolish all sex. They devised the institution of the continent marriage, then spiritual marriage. In both cases there was little or no sex. They even instituted a "trial of chastity" in which two people were required to sleep together and yet remain chaste.

According to a legend recorded by a medieval scholiast, an Irish holy man of the sixth century named Scuthin always shared his bed with two beautiful virgins. When Saint Brendan the Navigator chided him for taking such risks, Scuthin challenged him to prove himself equally capable of virtue. Brendan tried it and managed to resist temptation; however, he found himself quite unable to sleep, and so cut the experiment short.

---

*A similar pattern was observed among the Marquesans, and to some extent among the French in modern times. Hence the need to consider the children in the evaluation of the whole love pattern.

In this period woman was again an ambivalent figure. Saint Augustine said: "Through a woman we were sent to destruction; through a woman salvation was sent to us."

For all their exaggerations, the Christians did make one step forward in their consistent emphasis on love as opposed to hatred. It is true that this ideal has been violated over and over again, yet it is there, and as long as Christianity exists somebody comes back to it. Further, there is the notion that love should be directed to one Being in heaven rather than to anyone here on earth, with the implication that even though the greatest love is reserved for God, much love can be distributed here on earth.

Historically, the theoretical emphasis on love created through the course of Christianity two diverging groups: those who sought love directly, and those who sought power. As an institution, the Church has sought power more often than love, finding it necessary to stamp out all "heretics" who take Christ's message too seriously. Nevertheless, it would be an error to forget that both sides exist and have always existed.

The Romantic Ideal

Somehow, toward the end of the eleventh century, the Romantic ideal, which still exerts a powerful hold over men's minds, came into being. In southern France the game of courtly love was established, soon to spread to all parts of Europe. A treatise by Andreas Capellanus became one of its principal texts. He wrote: "Love is a certain inborn suffering derived from the sight of and excessive meditation upon the beauty of the opposite sex, which causes each one to wish above all things the embraces of the other and by common desire to carry out all of love's precepts in the other's embrace."[2]

In this image love, depression, and suffering go together, as is still frequently the case today. Shakespeare, who represents the culmination of five centuries of the development of this notion of suffering love, expressed the connection between love and suffering beautifully in one of his sonnets:

> When in disgrace with fortune and men's eyes,
> I all alone beweep my outcast state,
> And trouble deaf heaven with my bootless cries,
> And look upon myself, and curse my fate,
> Wishing me like to one more rich in hope,
> Featured like him, like him with friends possessed,

Desiring this man's art and that man's scope,
With what I most enjoy contented least;
Yet in these thoughts myself almost despising,
Haply I think on thee, and then my state,
Like to the lark at break of day arising,
From sullen earth, sings hymns at heaven's gate;
For thy sweet love remember'd such wealth brings
That then I scorn to change my state with kings.

Since the eleventh century, men and women throughout the Western world have lived by and taken for granted a number of the principal concepts of the romantic ideal, such as the close connection between love and depression. Just as a lover today feels lost if separated from the beloved, even if for a brief while, so Shakespeare's beautiful poem describes the torments of the deserted lover who is pulled out of his depression by the thought of the beloved.

One of the cardinal tenets of courtly love was that it could not exist between man and wife. Love and sex were thus sharply differentiated. It is here that the image of the unattainable woman, the beautiful virgin, arises. Perhaps it is some corporealization of the Virgin Mary.

The Romantics even continued the old practice of temptation, playing a game they called *amor purus*, in which the lover and his lady played around in bed in the nude without consummating the act. This was considered the highest achievement.

The Lady and the Witch

Perhaps in inevitable reaction to the idealization of the woman characteristic of the age of the troubadors came a period in which there was another sharp cleavage, but this time with intense persecution of the "bad" woman, the "witch." The pathology of witchcraft has already been mentioned several times (see pp. 198–200). Most striking is the hatred of the clergy for women. In *Malleus Maleficarum* the two demented monks Heinrich Kramer and James Springer wrote:

A woman is beautiful to look upon, contaminating to the touch, and deadly to keep . . . a foe to friendship . . . a necessary evil, a natural temptation . . . a domestic danger . . . an evil of nature, painted with fair colors . . . a liar by nature. [She] seethes with anger and impatience in her whole soul. . . . There is no wrath above the wrath of a woman.[3]

Puritanism

Although Puritanism is usually regarded as an antisexual reaction, this impression is historically inaccurate. It was more a kind of attempt to create a married love that would make both partners happy, and a married love that was quite compatible with sexual pleasure. One Puritan theologian, Daniel Roger, wrote: "Husbands and wives should be as two sweet friends, bred under one constellation, tempered by an influence from heaven, whereof neither can give any great reason save that mercy and providence first made them so, and then made their match."[4]

The image of Puritanism that we have comes from the nineteenth and twentieth centuries. Seventeenth-century Puritanism was tight-lipped, severe, and pious, but it was simultaneously frank, strongly sexed, and somewhat romantic. It was as much an offshoot of the Renaissance as a reaction against it. Its primary historical importance to our argument is that it represents an attempt to raise women to a higher level and to combine love and sex in marriage, apparently the first such attempt in human history.

The Eighteenth Century

"Love," wrote Jonathan Swift in 1723, "is a ridiculous passion which hath no being but in play-books and romances." (Incidentally, Dean Swift's father died before he was born, his mother separated from him while he was still an infant, he never knew the love of a mature woman, and he became psychotic in his old age.)

To Casanova, a typical product of the same century, love was pure sexuality, but without the overtones of sadism so typical of the Romans. Casanova's memoirs deal as much with violence as with love; one goes with the other in this context, but the violence is the fight among men. Interestingly, the only woman Casanova ever wanted to marry turned out to be his daughter.

The Nineteenth Century

The Angel in the House is the title of a book by Coventry Patmore, a spokesman for Victorian English morality. Victorianism represented an attempt to restore married life in that it sought to combine love and sexuality in marriage. To do so the sexual excesses of the past had to be strictly banned. To the Victorian mind the free enjoyment of sexuality was the surest path to destruction of the home.

But again, as love was emphasized, sexuality withdrew more and more into the background. The greatest outcome of this period was actually Freud, who in his own love life was a typical product of his time. Freud's lack of the historical knowledge discussed here (much of it acquired in recent years) has contributed to many fruitless arguments about Freudianism. His image of the union of tender and sexual feelings toward a person of the opposite sex as the end stage of development was the resultant of centuries of social thought and experimentation, much of it never consciously verbalized.

Contemporary Times

Hunt calls our age "by love obsessed." No more so than other ages, apparently. What is happening today, and it has been going on since Freud wrote, is an attempt to put the Freudian ideal into practice in the face of all the other difficulties that have beset modern man. The problem remains, as it always has existed, of how sex and love can best be combined in marriage or some other satisfactory institution.

The History of Childhood

The previous section deals with love between man and woman. What about love between parent and child? On this topic an extremely worthwhile contribution has been made by Lloyd de Mause in *The History of Childhood* (1974). Since this publication numerous others have appeared (De Mause himself publishes the *Journal of Psychohistory*), and a full account would have to consider all the various complexities. Still, it is useful to examine de Mause's summary, which essentially confirms his claim that the "history of childhood is a nightmare from which we have only recently begun to awaken."[5]

One might think that giving affection to children is the most natural thing in the world and has existed from time immemorial. Nothing could be farther from the truth. Children have been literally murdered (infanticide), beaten, starved, chained, forced into early labor, enslaved, sold, abused sexually and otherwise, misused, and manhandled in every conceivable way. Often the rationalization offered was the same as with psychotics: Children have no feelings. Children were simply considered the property of their parents, who could do anything they liked with them, just as they could do whatever they liked to any other kind of property. The long chronicle of mistreatment and outright crime documented by de Mause is appalling. In both England and America societies for the prevention of cruelty to animals were established before similar societies for children.[6] Illegitimate children continued to be killed regularly well into the nineteenth century.[7]

In a broad sense, de Mause delineates attitudes characteristic of various historical epochs: (1) the Infanticidal Mode (antiquity to the fourth century A.D.), (2) the Abandonment Mode (fourth to thirteenth century A.D.), (3) the Ambivalent Mode (fourteenth to seventeenth century), (4) the Intrusive Mode (eighteenth century), (5) the Socialization Mode (nineteenth to mid-twentieth century), and (6) the Helping Mode (mid-twentieth century to present).

De Mause explains these terms as follows. (1) the *infanticidal* mode involved direct murder of the child when unwanted. (2) In the *abandonment* mode the child was directly abandoned by the parents, whether to the wet nurse, to monasteries, or to foster families, or by severe emotional abandonment at home. (3) In the *ambivalent* mode the parents construed their task as one of molding the child into shape, an attitude that implied considerable ambivalence. (4) In the *intrusive* mode the parents intruded extensively into the infant's life, both physically and emotionally. The object was to conquer its will. (5) In the *socialization* mode the raising of a child became less a matter of conquering its will than of training it and guiding it into proper paths. (6) Finally the *helping* mode is based on the proposition that the child knows best what it needs at each stage of life, and it is the duty of the parents to conform to these needs.

Critics have understandably found fault with de Mause's broad outline and have attempted to correct many particulars. Still, there does seem to be some trend toward paying more attention to children and treating them with more care and affection. Rousseau is often credited with giving an impetus to this modern development. Louise Despert, in her book *The Emotionally Troubled Child*, comments that the concept of an emotionally troubled child did not exist before the present century.

We have previously had occasion to comment on a subtle but noticeable change in men's feelings from the French Revolution on. While barbarism and violence certainly did not disappear (and are far from gone today) there does seem to have been some revulsion against the barbarism of the past and some increased wish to become more loving and affectionate. If the twentieth century can be considered the century in which childhood was discovered, then it is reaping the fruits of this evolution after Rousseau.

The Making of the Modern Family

That there has been some change in the nature of conjugal relationships over the past few centuries seems obvious. What are the changes, and how can they best be described? On this subject Edward Shorter has contributed an interesting study, *The Making of the Modern Family* (1975).

At the end of the eighteenth century, he tells us, young people began to pay much more attention to inner feelings than to outward considerations, such as property and parental wishes, in choosing marriage partners. They began to court those they liked rather than those whom their parents thought most suitable. In the 1950s and 1960s people of all ages, but particularly adolescents, began to strip away the sentimental layers from the romantic experience to get at its hard sexual core, apparently having decided that eroticism was the most precious aspect of what human relationships have to offer and impatient with the delays feelings once imposed. These historic changes of mind have been sufficiently widespread and consequential for the rest of the social order to be considered revolutionary. Shorter suggests that the phenomenon he designated "the two sexual revolutions."

Our primary concern at the moment is with developments since about 1750. Shorter's thesis is that since that time there has been a shift from a cold, property-dominated, businesslike attitude to marriage toward a stress above all on inclination, affection, and romance. In other words, a greater growth toward love in marital relationships.

In a chapter entitled "The Rise of the Nuclear Family," he argues that the nuclear family is a state of mind rather than a particular kind of structure or set of household arrangements. What really distinguishes it is a special sense of solidarity that separates the domestic unit from the surrounding community. Its members feel that they have much more in common with one another than with anyone else on the outside—they enjoy a privileged emotional climate that they must protect from outside intrusion, through privacy and isolation. He then presents a variety of historical data to buttress his thesis that since about 1750 there has been a continual growth *toward* a nuclear family.

SUMMARY COMMENTS:
THE GROWTH IN IMPORTANCE OF LOVE

We are well aware that the historical trends drawn by Hunt, de Mause, Shorter, and others have been criticized over and over. Nevertheless, there does seem to be some trend noticeable in the course of human affairs, similar to what has been commented on before.

Anthropological Data

The literature contains no consistent discussion of the anthropological investigations into love. Where they have occurred, they have centered more on sex than on any other element of the love experience. What is being sought here must be integrated from many different sources.

Previously (Chapter 3) a fundamental distinction among cultures was proposed: love cultures and hate cultures. In the love cultures greater emphasis would be put on feelings of tenderness, affection, gratification, cooperation, and all the outgrowths of these feelings. In the hate cultures the greater emphases are on feelings of hatred, warfare, competition, achievement, success, and the like. Naturally these descriptions are not absolute; probably no culture ever known has been completely love- or completely hate-oriented. But the balance of forces can be estimated as weighing more heavily on one side or the other. In that case our own culture would be viewed as a hate culture, but with many forces on the side of love.

One basic thesis is that the whole love experience would be evaluated differently in a love culture and in a hate culture. In a love culture love is more diffuse, less intense, more gratifying, less ringed with violence (in cases of desertion or unfaithfulness, for example), less confined to the family. In the hate culture the opposite of all of these would hold.

Love Cultures: Ashley Montagu's Summary

In a paper on *Aggression and the Evolution of Man* (1974) the anthropologist Ashley Montagu has put together data on a number of the most peaceful cultures ever found. His thesis is that man developed as a highly cooperative creature, and that aggression, when it is found, is culturally conditioned. Some of his examples are instructive.

The Eskimos

Most persons who have lived among and written about Eskimos have expressed unfailing admiration and enthusiasm for the way they regulate human relationships. Kaj Birket-Smith (1959) describes them as individualists who consider aggressiveness and violence repulsive and who see far-reaching helpfulness as a primary duty. Lubart (1976) states that Eskimos rate generosity very highly. It is a common practice for Eskimos to give away their possessions.

Although murder is not unknown among the Eskimos, it is rare; the traditional way of settling disputes is for the contestants to assult each other with reproachful songs. Even the murder of a relative may be settled in this way.

By and large the Eskimos are a gentle, cooperative people who place a high value on loving and being loved; as such they pursue a wholly unaggressive way of life.

Central African Pygmies

The Pygmies of the Ituri Forest of Central Africa live in a world that for them is good, in peace and amity with all about them. They are unaggressive, both emotionally and physically, as is evidenced by their lack of any form of warfare, feuding, witchcraft, or sorcery.

The Australian Aborigines

Several hundred aboriginal tribes were discovered in the late eighteenth century. They too were by and large a highly cooperative and unaggressive group of peoples. In one group there was ceremonial fighting, after which the air was cleared and there were no grudges. Once their quarrel was settled, the ex-combatants assisted each other with first aid.

Tribes as a whole seldom made war; this was a concern for local groups or clans. There were no wars for territorial aggrandizement. On rare occasions they did carry out a sanctioned killing in much the same manner in which a state-appointed executioner executes a condemned felon.

The Bushmen of South Africa

The Bushmen have been somewhat romanticized. They are not so gentle as many of us have been led to believe, but neither are they violent. One Bushman witnessing a loss of temper remarked: "If you want to help people don't get angry with them. Keep calm." One anthropologist who made a special study of them found that Kung parents do not physically punish children; because aggressive postures are avoided by adults and devalued by society at large, children have little opportunity to observe or imitate overtly aggressive behavior. Quarrels occur, but they soon blow over. There is no aggressiveness toward other groups, no raiding, no war. When quarrels do break out between members of different bands they are almost invariably occasioned by adultery. On rare occasions someone is killed with a poisoned arrow, but when this occurs hostilities cease and everyone joins in a trance dance, a kind of ritual healing of wounds.

Gatherers-Hunters

Ashley Montagu maintains that many groups of gatherer-hunters are extraordinarily cooperative and unaggressive. The Ifaluk have been mentioned previously. Many, even under conditions of famine and considerable social change, preferred to express their anger in words rather than in physical violence. Among American Indians, such as the Hopi and the Zuñi—and the Pueblo peoples generally—any form of aggressive behavior is thoroughly condemned.

The Tarahumara Indians of Mexico

The Tarahumara can run a hundred miles or more at an average speed of 6 to 7 miles per hour without resting. They are equally remarkable for their dignity, respect for others, good humor among themselves, and helpfulness toward strangers. Intergroup or intragroup violence is unknown. In the past quarter century there have been no suicides and only one homicide among the 50,000 tribes-men. All this prevails under the most bleak and trying conditions, where hunger and disease are the daily experience of all.

CONCLUSIONS ON COOPERATION AND AGGRESSION

More examples could be cited. Ashley Montagu concludes:

It should be said that the evidence considered in this essay strongly tends to confirm the high probability that man developed as a highly cooperative creature. It further seems highly probable that aggressive behavior has not been genetically built into him as an "urge to kill his neighbors" but that, on the contrary, what has probably been genet-ically built into him is an urge to cooperate with his neighbors. Potentialities for aggressive behavior exist within the brain of *Homo sapiens,* but in order to be expressed in overt behavior they must be appropriately stimulated by the cultural environment. And the same holds true, of course, for cooperative behavior.[8]

The evidence cited by Ashley Montagu, which has been over-looked by most anthropologists, serves to buttress the thesis that man is inherently a loving creature just as much as a hating one; the outcome depends on cultural conditions. The fact that our own Western culture has been so filled with hatred through the centuries must be ascribed to social events, not to the genes. And what society has done society can also undo. Anthropology, a study of nature's experiments, tends to confirm the view that love is a reasonably at-tainable goal for mankind.

LOVE AND SEXUALITY AND THE INCEST TABOO

All cultures ever investigated have had some form of incest ta-boo, which is closely connected with the regulation of sexuality and love. These feelings, however, have posed some knotty problems for theoreticians.

The Incest Taboo

While explanations of the origin of the incest taboo are still con-troversial (Meiselman, 1978), there is no question of its universality within the nuclear family or of the powerful emotions connected with it. Murdock (1949) had already shown that in the 250 societies thoroughly studied by anthropologists all had banned nuclear-family incest. Further, incest taboos and exogamous restrictions, he claimed, are characterized by a peculiar intensity and emotional quality. He described the "grisly horror" that incest inspired in most peoples, as evidenced by the frequency with which the death penalty was prescribed for offenders. In other societies there is no legally institutionalized sanction for violation, because there the taboo is so strongly internalized that the consummation of an incestuous act is simply unthinkable.

What Freud contributed in *Totem and Taboo*, in which the first of the four parts is devoted to incest, is the demonstration that the internalization of the incest taboo has profound repercussions on the entire personality. In particular, in Western culture it leads to the conflicts of the Oedipal situation and later to the sharp split between love and sexuality, which has been discussed before. The "good" woman is the mother, who is sexually forbidden to the boy (or the father to the girl in the parallel case), while the "bad" woman is the one who is so different from mother that she is sexually approachable.

While it is easy enough to recognize the universality of this process (although the range of the tabooed women or men varies widely), it is harder to see how much suffering the child must undergo before these taboos are thoroughly internalized so that he can become a member of society. As Fortes pointed out in a passage quoted earlier (p. 28), anthropologists knew about the sanctions against incest long before Freud, but it remained for him to show that the coercive power of these sanctions derives from the parents and is internalized at great cost to the individual. In general, even a casual perusal of the literature will show that anthropologists, with rare exceptions, have chosen to ignore the price that any culture pays in terms of suffering for its incest taboos.

LOVE AND SEXUALITY

The experience of love is universal, as are the sexual drive and the incest taboo. What has to be evaluated is how these three are emotionally intertwined.

For our own culture, Freud showed that love is aim-inhibited sexuality. When the man is confronted with a "good" woman, with whom he is not permitted to have intercourse, he "falls in love" (and similarly for the girl). Contrariwise, he will not love a woman who makes herself sexually available. While the various sexual revolutions of the twentieth century have shaken this psychological attitude to its depths, clinical experience shows us over and over that it still plays a powerful role in the psyche of modern man.*

Explorations of other societies have in general tended to confirm the Freudian hypothesis in one direction but not in another. That is, when there is free, unhampered adolescent sexuality, the love torments so common in our own culture are absent. But where sexuality is severely inhibited, as in our culture, there may or may not be strong love feelings displayed.

A typical example of a sexually free culture is Mangaia (literally: peace), one of the Polynesian islands. According to Marshall (1971), Mangaian informants were quite interested in the European concept of "love." The components of affection and companionship, which may characterize the European use of the term, puzzled the Mangaians. Informants stated that "when the Maori gets old, that's the time to 'get close' to his wife; but this is when they are over fifty years of age." And some Maori have no good feeling between husband and wife at all, for they feel only sexual jealousy. For a Mangaian to show any affection toward his wife in public would bring public ridicule. Still, despite an initial lack of relationship between affection and sexual involvement, there develop an emotional attachment and a spirit of affection and willingness to sacrifice between long-married couples.

On the other hand, if the proposition is examined in terms of the effect of sexual repression on love, the pattern of Western culture seems to be rather rare. Anthropologists in general have not been sufficiently interested in the problem of love, so any conclusions from their writings must be read between the lines. However, Messenger (1971), writing about Inis Beag, one of the most sexually naive of the world's societies, notes that sex is never discussed in the home when children are present. Sexual misconceptions are myriad. Men feel that sexual intercourse is debilitating. Messenger could not determine the frequency of marital coitus. There is not even a "dirty joke" tradition (see below). The style of dancing allows little bodily contact among participants.

*One of my patients coined the acronym "PUM" for the "presently unattainable man," after discovering that she always feels attracted to the unavailable man and rejects the available one

But all of this sexual repression is not replaced or sublimated by love, as it has been among at least some people in our society. Rather, the only outlet for the inhabitants seems to be emigration, and the population has been dwindling for a long time. Blanshard writes:

> When all the reasons for a flight from Ireland have been mentioned, there still remains a suspicion that Irish young people are leaving their nation largely because it is a poor place in which to be happy and free. Have the priests created a civilization in which the chief values of youth and love are subordinate to Catholic discipline?[9]

Likewise, Harris (1971), in his study of a small Brazilian town where there was a sharp double standard and women were severely repressed sexually, found that the culture was highly individualized, had a low order of economic and political cooperation, a weak sense of community spirit, a dominance of capital as the organizing factor in group labor, and a high incidence of impersonal transactions lubricated by cash rather than by family or friendship. No special sign of love in this community.

Still another culture sheds some light on the subject. Turnbull (1972) describes the Ik in Africa, a people whose only goal is individual survival and who have learned that the price of survival is to give up compassion, love, affection, kindness, and concern, even for their own children. These people are sexually free, even promiscuous. But the sexuality has a hostile, self-aggrandizing flavor to it— sex is a way to get something from another person.

Contemporary anthropologists have become so obsessed with the structure of society that they have tended to ignore human feelings. In the compendium by Harris (1968), for example, there is no index entry for love. While it is certainly true that the sexual patterns of any culture are molded by the superego of that culture, this tells us nothing about the price the inhabitants pay for obedience to different kinds of superegos. In other words, as has so often been mentioned, the vital question of happiness is simply sidestepped.

The repression of sexuality, as it has been attempted in Christian culture, is rare. The only societies with a probable general sex taboo, according to Murdock, are the New England Yankees and the Ashanti and the Timne of West Africa.[10] Among the New Englanders the attempt at least has been made to elevate love to a superordinate position; what happened in the other two societies is not recorded.

When sexual repression is less complete, one intermediate step is a mild joking relationship.[11] Here Freud's examples in *Jokes* (1905) are of surprising relevance, except that Freud emphasized the sexual element and did not pay much attention to the relationship between the joking partners (although he did not neglect it entirely). Jesting revolves largely about the subject of sex, often between grandparents and grandchildren. Each party delights in calling the other his husband or wife, accusing him of sexual advances, and playfully initiating sexual overtures of his own. This doubtless provides both with some substitutive gratification, and the age disparity makes it apparent to everyone that the behavior is merely "good clean fun" with no ulterior overtones. But joking relations with kinsmen of the opposite sex who are closer in age reveals quite a different emotional quality.

It is noteworthy that some cultures, such as the Irish, are so thoroughly repressed that even joking relationships are absent. Love is likewise absent. These people seem thoroughly miserable and can find an outlet only in leaving the community entirely.

Most cultures allow greater or lesser degrees of sexual freedom. To evaluate what happens there the quality of this freedom must be examined more carefully. In some cases, as among the Ik, the freedom is completely exploitative and totally unrelated to any kind of pleasure derived. In others, such as the Mangaia, a free and easy sexuality forms the basis for a rather happy life. In still others (e.g., the Turu of Tanzania), sexual freedom is accompanied by extraordinarily high rates of assault, murder, and divorce.

The ideal combination of sexual freedom and love seems to have been approached in some cultures (perhaps the Chinese of the fifth century B.C.) but also seems to be rare. Still, if any generalization can be made, it is that sexual freedom is possible with or without love, and that sexual freedom of the pleasurable kind frequently leads to love relationships later in life, or could be the essence of love relationships in adolescence. On the other hand, love with complete repression of sexuality is virtually impossible. This was one of Freud's most fundamental discoveries, and it has been confirmed by anthropological research.

KINSHIP AND LOVE

Kinship is one of the fundamental aspects of social structure in all known societies. In our culture the domestic family is primary. In tribal societies kinship has even more far-reaching effects. Yet the relationship between kinship and love has been little explored.

The term "kith and kin," derived from the old English, highlights the affectional qualities of kinship, since it means familiar friends, neighbors, acquaintances, or countrymen; clearly the emphasis is on feelings of friendship. This tends to be obscured in the usage of the word "kin," especially as the kinship systems of more primitive peoples turn out to be so extraordinarily complex. It is hard enough to uncover the rules that govern kinship and kinship behavior, so the psychological meaning of those rules is often left out. For our purposes, however, it is essential.

The elucidation of kinship rules has been one of the chief preoccupations of anthropologists for a hundred years, and definitive solutions are not yet in sight. Why do so many peoples have such incredibly complex systems, and what purposes do these systems serve?

To this question of the purpose of kinship systems two answers may be given. One, favored by Lévi-Strauss, is that these systems are a set of rules by which all persons within the culture are forced to abide. His emphasis is always on the formal aspects of kinship, and he has made a notable contribution in his mathematical analysis of the various systems. Nevertheless, he omits the feelings of the participants, laying almost exclusive emphasis on sociological causes. Thus he writes:

> The sense in which infrastructures are primary is this: first, man is like a player who, as he takes his place at the table, picks up cards which he has not invented, for the cardgame is a datum of history and civilization. Second, each deal is the result of a contingent distribution of the cards, unknown to the players at the time. . . . One must accept the cards which one is given. . . . To explain the noticeable frequency of certain sociological solutions, not attributable to particular objective conditions, appeal must be made to form and not content.[12]

At another point he writes: "The question of how far and in what proportion the members of a given society respect the norm is very interesting, but a different question to that of where this society should properly be placed in a typology."[13] Thus he is limiting himself to formal considerations, and it is not surprising that words such as "love" are not to be found in the indexes of his books. Even when he frankly admits that the degree of deviation is an "interesting" question, he refuses to pay any attention to it.

This kind of approach has been discussed before. Social forces are easier to grasp, and more intensively studied, so they are made into the causes of events, while the individual and his feelings are disregarded.

A more meaningful psychological approach is taken by Meyer Fortes (1969). Whatever the system adopted, kinship implies love and friendship. The kin become an outlet for the essential feelings of warmth and affection; this is primary, while the particular structure in which the kin is housed is secondary. Fortes puts it thus: "Though the structural connotation which the notion of kinship carries varies widely, the central value premise associated with it is uniform. Kinship predicates the axiom of amity, the prescriptive altruism exhibited in the ethic of generosity."[14]

Thus anthropologists like Levi-Strauss have failed to tackle the central problem of human society, how love and hate appear, and how they are regulated by the social structure. Fortes comes much closer and gives us the most important clue to the universal prevalance of kinship systems: They provide an institutionally acceptable framework within which feelings of love and affection can find an outlet. It is here that the greatest feelings of love should be found; if they are absent here, the society can be said to be a hate culture and is in bad shape. As Goode has shown (1959), all human societies have to come to terms with the feelings of love, and all recognize it and attempt to regulate it in some way.

THE PRINCIPLE OF RECIPROCITY

Human beings in all cultures recognize their obligations to one another and express them through gifts. The classic work in which the anthropological material was first clearly presented was Mauss, *The Gift* (1925). Men give gifts, and they expect gifts in return; these feelings exist in all known societies. Or one could say more psychologically: Man wishes to feel related to his fellow men, and the gift is one way in which this relationship can be expressed. Since Mauss this has been rebaptized the principle of reciprocity, and widely applied.

However, reciprocity again touches on basic human feelings. It is not just a legal or moral obligation or a "rule of the game." It is an expression of the deepest human emotions. In a passage from the Eddas which Mauss quoted it was said: "Generous and bold men have the best time in life and never foster troubles. But the coward is apprehensive of everything and a miser is always groaning over his gifts."[15]

LOVE AND MONOGAMY

Anthropology teaches us that the rule prescribed by our culture—that love and marriage must go together and be confined to one person—is a rare occurrence in human history. It is a relatively recent development, not even implied in Christian doctrine. Polygamy was legally practiced and accepted by the church in the Middle Ages, and it occurred sporadically until the seventeenth century.[16] But monogamy as pattern and prototype of human marriage is universal, for it rests upon the biological fact that the production of a child requires essentially two people.

In the current widespread discussions of alternative forms of marriage these observations are often forgotten. The rule has been that marriage must be entered into, but the feelings involved in marriage have varied widely from one society to another. Up to the present century prescribed marriage was more common than the exception. In fact, Lévi-Strauss goes so far as to say that there is no difference between prescribed and preferential marriage, a typical error.

What psychoanalysis adds to the discussion is that marriage should be based on love and affection and should not be merely a ritual performed for the sake of the elders. While this is not novel as an experience, since many cultures seek to base marriage on preference, it is novel as an ideal. To combine love and sexuality in marriage exclusively with one person has rarely been tried. It may well be that the current rapidly rising divorce rate is a reaction to this wish to have a meaningful marriage, so that it can be regarded as an index of social optimism rather than of social distress.

SUMMARY COMMENTS ON ANTHROPOLOGICAL OBSERVATIONS ON LOVE

Love is a universal experience, sought in all societies and esteemed as an inner feeling that leads to happiness. There are cultures in which love predominates and cultures in which hatred predominates, with many in between.

Love is expressed most easily within the family structure (kith and kin). To move from the family to strangers the individual must overcome the incest barrier, another universal aspect of cultures. The incestuous desire always operates to tie the individual to the family.

Love and sexuality are intimately related. All possible combinations have been found, from cultures in which both love and sexuality are highly prized to those in which both are condemned. In general, sexual freedom seems to make love possible provided that it is pursued in a positive manner, while love with a complete restriction of sexuality proves to be chimerical. The current image of marriage, in which love and sexuality are combined in exclusive marriage with one other person, has never been tried before. Here too Freud set up a new ideal for mankind.

It would appear, then, that Western culture has made two innovative attempts to regulate human affairs. One is to have love without sexuality—the ideology of Christianity. This seems humanly impossible; its psychological impossibility would account for the enormous hatred, psychosis, and destructiveness that have characterized Western civilization for the past two thousand years.

The second is the union of love and sexuality as an exclusive relationship with one other person—the ideal of the monogamous marriage. As part of the analytic ideal, analysts naturally subscribe to it on paper, but its ultimate fate is still open to question.

Ethological Data

Animal investigations have by now conclusively established the fact that affectional needs exist in a wide variety of mammals. Even animals as ostensibly ferocious as gorillas thrive on love and affection. Schaller states that gorilla groups remain stable, on the whole, even though there may be no receptive females for months at a time: "Gorillas always gave me the impression that they stay together because they like and know one another. The magnanimity with which Big Daddy shared his females with other males, even though some were only temporary visitors, helped to promote peace in the group."[17]

Affection in animals has been studied through the examination of the mother–infant situation, separation experiences, and aggression. Each of these may be considered in turn.

THE MOTHER–INFANT SITUATION: HARLOW'S MONKEYS

It is pertinent to begin with the striking series of experiments by Harlow, summed up in *Learning to Love* (1974). Harlow begins with the relevant comment that the subject of love has been almost completely neglected:

> In the area of love the lowly layman should not stand in awe of the professions, since there is objective evidence to suggest that psychologists, psychiatrists, psychoanalysts and social workers are either unaware of or are afraid of love, in fact or in fancy.
>
> In an effort to assimilate the best that had been said and thought about love by the professionals, I scanned the *Psychological Abstracts* from 1950 to 1970 for abstracts on love. Even though love is at least as concrete as it is abstract, the results were startling. There were almost no abstracts on the theory and facts of love.[18]

Harlow defines love as affectional feelings for others. On the basis of this definition, he finds it possible to distinguish at least five basic kinds of interactive, interpersonal love in monkeys: (1) maternal love, (2) infant love, (3) peer or age-mate love, (4) heterosexual love, and (5) paternal love. Each system evolves from the one that precedes it, and the faulty development of any system, or the faulty transition from one system to another, may arise from any number of variables.

Maternal Love

Maternal love is genetic, based on the happy triumvirate of hope, health, and hormones. There may also be inherent differences in the central nervous system between females and males. Harlow breaks the mother–infant stage down further into three substages: a stage of care and comfort, a stage of maternal ambivalence, and a stage of relative separation. It is impossible to define exact temporal periods for any maternal affectional stage in either monkey or man, for there are large individual differences, and variables of experience play an increasing role in the later stages. In general, however, the stage of care and comfort in monkeys evolves into the stage of maternal ambivalence when the monkey infant is about five months old, and the stage of maternal ambivalence evolves into the stage of maternal separation four months to a year later. This stage depends on the monkey mother's ability to enjoy contact comfort, including pleasure in clinging and nursing. Experiments showed that when the infant did not respond to the mother's offer of contact, the mother would turn away and lose interest. But if another infant was provided and proved responsive, her interest was immediately rekindled.

When the infant is old enough to go off on his own, the process is facilitated by the mother, who rejects and punishes actively. Maternal rejection during this period is truly one of the many forms of mother love; a mother who loves her infant will emancipate him.

Infant Love

Infant love, the love of the infant for the mother, is entirely indiscriminate at birth; the neonate eagerly and equally attaches to any maternal object, animate or inanimate, that is endowed with adequate physical properties. Contact seems to be the primary factor. Thus in Harlow's classic study infants who had been provided with a lactating wire mother-surrogate showed decreasing responsiveness to "her" and increasing responsiveness to a nonlactating cloth mother-figure, which meant they preferred body contact to food.

The infant love system proceeds through at least five stages: (1) organic affection and reflexive love, (2) comfort and attachment, (3) security and solace, (4) disattachment and environmental exploration, and (5) relative independence. Anatomically the monkey neonate is roughly equivalent to the human one-year-old, and its physiology and behavior are correspondingly advanced. While it is always risky to draw parallels between monkeys and humans, the similarities are so marked, allowing for the age differential, that they cannot be avoided.

A most revealing sidelight in view of the theme of this chapter is that monkey maternal punishment is usually gentle and restrained, but even when it is harsh and vigorous no mother has ever been seen to injure her own baby or even to attempt to do so. Again man turns out to be the most ferocious of all animals.

Age-Mate or Peer Love

Once the monkey infant has loosened the bonds to mother, it seeks out its peers. The primary positive variable pervading peer love is that of play. Previous investigators had failed to see play as the primary factor in integrating the earlier forms of love, in fulfilling the inexhaustible social needs of the peer affectional or love system, and in organizing the experiences of the individual in preparation for the requirements of heterosexual or adult attachment. Harlow differentiates presocial from social play. Under presocial play he includes free play, creative play, and formal play.

Harlow maintains that all primates are born with aggressive potential, but aggression itself is a relatively late-maturing variable. Further, one of the primary socializing functions of age-mate or peer affection is the opportunity for the formation of personal love bonds.

Heterosexual Love

The heterosexual system appears with the development of mechanical sex and secretory sex. One of Harlow's most surprising findings, confirmatory of analytic theory, was that the failure to develop affectional bonds early in life has a profound impact on the naked realities of sexual performance.

Beyond mechanical and secretory sex, there is a third one, referred to in humans as romantic and in monkeys as transient heterosexual attachments or preferences. The affective component goes beyond the emotions of mechanical-secretory sex and identifies the basic nature of the entire system. Monkeys who as infants had been reared by inanimate surrogate mothers could not function normally in the heterosexual situation, even though they were physiologically ready for it; males were more deprived than females.

Indiscriminate promiscuity is not the normal pattern among primates. Their relationships are characterized rather by affectional compatibility of individual pairs. This new principle of affectionate sex sets primates apart from more primitive animals and is a common element in all primate heterosexual behavior. Harlow suggests that the variations in human, ape, and monkey heterosexual relationships may be viewed as differences in the degree of affectional influence on the time and behavioral content devoted to the courtship phase, the conquest phase, and the consequent phase of the heterosexual bond.

Paternal Love

The paternal affectional system is the affectional relationship of an adult male for an infant. Biological kinship between the adult male and the infant is not a defining characteristic of paternal love, since substitute fathers are not infrequent.

The paternal affectional system and the variables that affect it have been far less adequately studied in both monkeys and humans than the other affectional systems. While the data are limited, they nonetheless suggest that innate biological variables are minimal in paternal affection, and experimental variables are maximal, along with a great degree of cultural determination of human paternal love. In monkeys the paternal affectional system lacks the duration and strength it has in some cultures, such as our own.

THE INCEST TABOO IN MONKEYS

While no clear-cut evidence is available, there is some that is suggestive of an incest taboo in the higher primates. Among Japanese macaque monkeys there is later mother–son avoidance,[19] while Jane van Lawick-Goodall could find no instances of mother–son incest among the chimpanzees she studied. Temerlin, a psychologist who "adopted" a female chimpanzee, discovered to his surprise that when it reached estrus it presented itself "shamelessly" to every human male that came along but avoided him, seemingly a manifestation of an incest taboo. With increased research along these lines more evidence may soon be available.

SEPARATION AND DEPRESSION

In the wake of the analytic emphasis on separation anxiety and the depression that ensues upon separation, much research has accumulated (Scott and Senay, 1973; Bowlby, 1973; Ashley Montagu and Matson, 1979). The most important conclusions are as follows:

1. In both human beings and the higher animals, evidence exists of a general social-motivational system associated with attachment, separation, and cooperative behavior. Either interference with the development of this system or disruption of its function through prolonged separation at later stages is likely to produce various forms of maladaptive behavior.

2. Differences in the effects of brief, repetitive, and prolonged separations are important, as are the immediate and later effects of any separation. The various parameters of separation—the situation from which one is removed, the environment and associations during the separation, and the age of the subject—play an important part.

3. Species and individual variations in the severity of depressive symptoms indicate that strong genetic, even evolutionary factors are involved. All the higher organisms have a strong need for contact (Ashley Montagu and Matson, 1979).

4. Successive adaptive responses are based on the available biological response systems and mediated by neural mechanisms. If the initial agitated distress reaction is not relieved, the depressive conservation–withdrawal reaction sets in.

5. Conservation–withdrawal is a biological threshold mechanism for adapting to a deprivation that is intolerable but cannot be actively avoided. It may even mean survival.

6. An important contribution supports the findings that life-change events, by evoking faulty adaptive efforts by the human organism, lower bodily resistance and enhance the probability of disease occurrence. Early childhood experiences, particularly permanent loss of a parent, and the kind of substitute care available can contribute significantly to the risk of depression in human adults. Further, life events experienced at the time of onset of depression confirm the importance of separation from persons in the immediate social field.

MONOGAMY AMONG LOWER ANIMAL SPECIES

Even animals lower down the evolutionary scale than the primate often develop patterns that gratify feelings of affection and solidarity. Wickler (1972) has shown that permanent monogamy is widespread among such animals as cichlids, butterfly fish, small birds, ravens, pigeons, geese, parrots, moles, jackals, dwarf antelopes, marmosets, and gibbons. In each case there are also closely related species that live in polygamy or without pair-bonding. Hence his main thesis: The development of the family is not an artificial human device but exists throughout nature.

STUDIES OF AGGRESSION

Studies of aggression in both man and animals have generally focused on the overall question of whether aggression is innate or acquired. Among those who hold to an innate theory the most prominent is probably Konrad Lorenz, but, as has been pointed out, while Lorenz knows animals he has no more than the average man's familiarity with humans. Typically symposia on the topic (e.g. Whalen, 1974), reach no clear-cut conclusions.

It has gradually become apparent, however, that by and large man is more aggressive than almost any other animal. As one anthropologist commented some years ago, genocide occurs only among humans, and anthropologists refuse to recognize it. A few species have so much innate aggression that if the conspecifics are left alone in an enclosure, after several hours some of them will be dead. But this is an exception. In by far the greatest number of species, through the dominance-submission patterns an order is established that does away with almost all violence. Best known are the pecking order among chickens and the sham battles among wolves, but there are many other examples. Social order is a way of curbing aggression, and virtually every animal species has developed mechanisms to maintain order of this kind. Thus there are built-in aggressive urges in animals and built-in mechanisms for curbing those aggressive urges.

In human beings the record is so colored by cultural patterns that firm conclusions are difficult to establish. Freud's theory of the death instinct has been universally rejected. Some have replaced it with a dual-instinct theory, in which equal weight is given to libido and aggression (e.g. Hartmann, 1964). Others disagree (e.g. Fenichel, 1945) and insist that all human behavior can be explained within the pleasure principle, so that there is no need to go beyond it. Insofar as the ethological data are relevant, there is no real evidence of an innate aggressive drive in human beings that will break through any cultural barrier.

Whatever the genetic factors may be, the actual behavior depends on how the environment teaches man to handle his genetic endowment (Dobzhansky, 1973). To separate genetics from the environment is a serious error. Ashley Montagu (1976), after reviewing all the evidence, emphasizes man's malleability: "The only way one learns to love is by being loved. This is neither a fantasy nor a theory. It is a fact—a verifiable fact. . . . Our true inheritance lies in our ability to make and shape ourselves, not the creatures but the creators of our destiny."[20]

This quotation may serve as a summary comment about what we can learn from animal psychology about the nature of love. In his desire to love, or in his wish to create a more loving environment, man need not be constrained by any genetic factors. Aggression is made by man and can be unmade by man. Likewise love is part of man's inherited capability.

Sociological Forces

The sociological question is: Which institutions in our society encourage the experience of love and which discourage it? Further, to what extent does the love experience break through regardless of institutional restraints, and to what extent does it merely conform to what is required? Inasmuch as sociologists have generally paid little attention to these questions, any conclusions reached as a rule will have to be based on broadly drawn inferences. However, as will be seen, in every case some empirical information is available.

THE FAMILY

Theoretically the family is the place where the greatest exchange of love and affection should take place. No attempt can or will be made here to assess the general theory of the family; that is far too vast an undertaking. But it is possible to focus on the question of the degree to which love and affection do occur within the family setting.

The sociological literature contains a large number of studies of success and failure in marriage. Typically these operate from the outside, casting little light on the inner dynamics. For example, C. Kirkpatrick (1955) found five general influential factors on marital adjustment. Roughly in order of decreasing substantiation by the evidence, they are (1) early and adequate orgasm capacity, (2) confidence in the marriage bond and satisfaction with affection shown, (3) an equalitarian rather than a partriarchal marital relationship, with special reference to the husband role, (4) mental and physical health, and (5) harmonious companionship based on common interests and accompanied by a favorable attitude toward the marriage and spouse. On this last point, other studies have tended to show that in "adjusted" marriages (by which is meant marriages that last) the partners are quite similar in outlook and interests (Grey, 1970).

Commenting on studies of this kind, George Simpson (1966) writes:

> [T]here is something definitely wrong with this literature. It is naive, though well-intentioned, and it is scientifically misguided. It shows little or else barbarized appreciation of unconscious factors. . . . If neurotic tendencies make for failure in marriage, then all marriages in the U.S. must be failures, which is nonsense.[21]

Hence it will be more useful to examine the literature that looks at marriage from a deeper point of view. One valuable study is *The Significant Americans* (1965), by John Cuber and Peggy Harroff. They begin with a quotation from John O'Hara: "A married couple always presents an absurdly untruthful picture to the world, but it is a picture that the world finds convenient and a comfort."

Instead of a superficial questionnaire approach, the Cubers (Harroff is Mrs. Cuber) personally interviewed 437 distinguished Americans. The interviews were unstructured, lengthy, and open-ended and gave the respondents a chance to express all their feelings, pro and con, about their marital lives. The subjects chosen were a roughly representative group of the leadership echelon, the decision-making, policy-forming people, the most clearly successful, as success is currently conceived.

Of the sample of 437, at the time of the interviews, 406 were married, 15 divorced, 4 widowed, and 12 never married. All were between the ages of thirty-five and fifty-five.

The Cubers had anticipated that many of the people approached would be unwilling to discuss the subject with candor. "We could not have been more wrong."[22] They evidently discovered, as many others do, that many people are only too eager to share themselves with others, if the interviews promise to be of any help to them. Evidently the interviews had a quasi-therapeutic effect. One corporation executive said:

> You seem to be up to something more honest and complete than the stuff I've read on this subject. There's a lot of humbuggery that passes around for truth. . . . I even tried to do that with you at first. But I got carried away with the idea that some good could come of this. And even if it doesn't, it's quite an experience to sit down and talk for all these hours. . . . I don't know why I've trusted you with all of this— my God, you could blackmail me—but I know you won't, any more than my doctor or my priest would. . . . If you want to repay me, just write a damned honest book.[23]

In summarizing their findings, the interviewers eschewed glib generalizations. They did, however, find a gross sorting of marital life into "Utilitarian" and "Intrinsic Marriages." Utilitarian were further broken down into conflict-habituated, passive-congenial, and devitalized. Intrinsic were divided into vital and total. By far the largest number fell in the Utilitian category.

The most important conclusion reached is that regardless of technical statistical differences between social levels, there are appreciable numbers of people whose conduct is not consistent with the expectations of the monolithic code, and these people tried to find expression through various social customs that fitted the circumstances of their own climate. In other words, in terms of the immediate inquiry, love is either absent or of minor importance in most American marriages. It exists only in the Intrinsic Marriages, of which they say:

> Even if the Intrinsic Marriages decorate the brighter spot in the montage, the brightness is dimmed somewhat by the twin facts that they are a minority and that not all people capable and needful of vital relationship have found it possible to form and to hold on to one within the structure of monogamous marriage.

They even go so far as to state that "the Intrinsic Marriage is a minority arrangement by the middle years for the clear and sufficient reason that it is not really suited to many and it doesn't fit smoothly with deeper commitments to the responsible goals of adult life."[24]

VIOLENCE IN THE FAMILY

In the past ten years increasing attention has been paid to the obvious fact that the family, idealized as the source of love, sympathy, and understanding, is often in reality the source of assault, violence, and even homicide. Clearly in the violent home love is conspicuous by its absence. Nevertheless, the incidence of violence has been almost entirely ignored until recently. One investigator, consulting the index of the *Journal of Marriage and the Family* from its inception in 1939 until 1969, found not a single entry under the title "violence."[25]

Obviously statistics on this subject are hard to obtain; still, there are some facts known. Gelles (1972) interviewed eighty families in Manchester, New Hampshire, and found that violence had occurred in 55 percent of the families. Moreover, in 26 percent of the entire sample, conjugal violence was a regular occurrence, ranging from a dozen times a year to daily. Although the sampling of families was not chosen to be representative of any population, it became clear that there is generally a high level of conjugal violence even among families that present a public façade of harmony. The only meaningful generalization the author allowed himself was that while violence occurs at all levels of the social structure, it seems to be somewhat more common among the lower classes. In any case the violent home is not a place where love and affection are learned, so once more it is found that while love and marriage may go together like a horse and carriage, the horse and carriage are now museum pieces (Davidson, 1978).

NEUROTIC INTERACTION IN MARRIAGE

While it is again impossible to substantiate this in any meaningful statistical way, one of the outcomes of the psychoanalytic and analytically oriented investigation and treatment of families is the consensus that marriages are often, if not usually, the result of a neurotic interaction. A passive man marries an aggressive woman, or the reverse, and both are superficially satisfied. One might even set up a principle of "regression in the service of the spouse," which means that each spouse unconsciously becomes more infantile in order to gratify the unconscious demands of the other (Strean, 1979). Such marriages may be extraordinarily stable, but it is a stability without meaning. This is one of the facts that vitiate the usual statistics about stable marriages; stability (duration) may have nothing to do with happiness. In unhappy marriages often one partner enters therapy, as a result of which the neurotic equilibrium is broken and divorce threatens. The other partner may also enter therapy, or the two may be divorced. In social terms the high incidence of divorce is deplored, but actually such divorces are a measure of the individual's desire to have a happy marriage, not a social distress syndrome.

HAPPY AND SUCCESSFUL FAMILIES

It is by now well established that the most important determinants of personality structure are the early family influences. Consequently, personality runs in families. In analysis we no longer look for the single decisive event that made the individual neurotic; it is rather the total emotional climate of the early family that is thoroughly explored.

Beavers (1977) divided families into severely dysfunctional, midrange, and healthy (see also pp. 51–53). The characteristics of the optimal family were described as follows: The structure was definite and clear, and it was not experienced by the members as a burden. Family members concerned themselves with functioning. Change in methods, goals and choices did not threaten the family; even the youngest children contributed to family plans. Everyone enjoyed negotiations and welcomed new input. This input was examined and evaluated, but the family members viewed it positively. They respected human biological drives. There was little embarrassment when a family member showed fear or anxiety, and anger was considered a sign that something needed to be corrected; it had less of the impotent or intimidating overtones seen in less effective families. Sexual interest was considered a positive quality both in parents and in children. The parent did not demonstrate concern with the masturbatory activities of the children. "When a system, whether person or family, is not at war with itself and is able to accept and affirm its basic qualities, an adaptive and differentiating state can develop."[26]

Without realizing that he was doing so, Beavers was describing the core of the analytic ideal as the essence of these optimal families.*

INEQUALITY AND SUCCESSFUL FAMILIES

Inasmuch as the ideology of America stresses it as a land of equal opportunity, the question of how much inequality exists becomes a burning issue. In 1972 the sociologist Christopher Jencks and his colleagues at Harvard University published their detailed investigation into the subject in the book *Inequality*, which met with a stormy reaction. Seven years later it was followed by another significant book, *Who Gets Ahead?* (1979).

In the second work, after attempting to correct certain errors in the earlier one, Jencks and his group concluded that family background as a whole explained about 48 percent of the variance in occupational status and 15 to 35 percent of the variance in earnings among men aged twenty-five to sixty-four in the early 1970s. These estimates imply that those who do well economically typically owe almost half of their occupational advantage and 55 to 85 percent of their earnings advantage to family background. Thus the family is

---

*Unfortunately in his book Beavers engages in a pointless diatribe against Freud and psychoanalysis, which he does not understand, mistakenly assuming that what he is advocating is radically different.

seen to be the most decisive single factor in economic and educational success. Jencks and his collaborators conclude:

> It does not follow . . . that *Inequality*'s major policy conclusion was unjustified. *Inequality* argued that trying to equalize men's personal characteristics was an unpromising way of equalizing their incomes. This argument had two parts. *Inequality* first argued that even if personal characteristics were equalized, this would have very marginal effects on the distribution of income. This conclusion, while still plausible, may have been premature. But *Inequality* also argued that past efforts at equalizing the personal characteristics known to affect income had been relatively ineffective. This assertion, sad to say, remains as true as ever. Thus, if we want to redistribute income, the most effective strategy is probably still to redistribute income.[27]

Again, then, the family is seen as a prime determinant of the individual's fate in life. Similar reports have recently come out of the Soviet Union, which would indicate that even after a violent revolution family influence counts more than any other single factor (Ward, 1979).

The Abolition of the Family: The Soviet Union and Psychoanalysis

It had long been recognized that the family could be a conservative, even reactionary institution that impeded man's progress more than it advanced it. Before World War I both communism and psychoanalysis were in agreement that the family often did more harm than good. Engels, in *The Origin of the Family* (1884), argued that the bourgeois capitalist family was essentially an economic arrangement in which love was less important than property, the wife was enslaved and exploited by the husband, and the husband's authority was enforced by Church and state. In the socialist society, Engels argued, the female would be liberated and the family as an economic unit of society abolished. Women would work equally with men, property inheritance would cease to play a decisive role, and there would be no other motive left for marriage except mutual inclination. Once the communist revolution came, the family, like the state, would "wither away."

In the early period of psychoanalysis (before World War I) the family was not the center of interest; the focus was on the instincts. Freud recognized that these instincts had to be repressed or molded by the family; to that extent the family became a hindrance to full growth. He agreed with the evolutionists that in the primitive family the will of the father remained unrestricted.[28] Hostility to the parents is easily aroused; the demands of the Oedipal situation are powerful. However, Freud was not in favor of abolition of the family, as some of his contemporaries urged, but his reasons were rather peculiar. At one point he argued that family life is the basis for the striving for propagation;[29] at a later stage he merely objected that if the family were abolished and complete sexual freedom established, hostility would still remain.

In the first extended discussion of the family by a psychoanalyst, Flugel's *The Psychoanalytic Study of the Family* (1921), the stress throughout is on the danger attached to the sexual emotions aroused within the family. "The relations of the members of a family to one another are in many respects of such a nature as to call forth hostile emotions almost if not quite as readily as they call forth love."[30] Little can be found in Freud or in Flugel pointing to the protective or security-providing functions of the family; that was to come later.

In line with these theories, the Soviets in the early days of the Revolution, from 1918 to 1926, enacted a variety of laws and practices to do away with the old patriarchal family. "Free love" was proclaimed and practiced by many, as it was all over the world in the wake of the horrors of World War I. Abortion became legal; divorce a private matter and easy. Marriage had to be voluntary on both sides; women were given the same rights as men; household duties were collectivized, and a concentrated effort was made to attack the authority of husbands over wives and of parents over children (Zelditch, 1964).

Analysts in the 1920s still saw the family as often doing more harm than good. Thus Fenichel, who was a member of the Marxist opposition in psychoanalysis in the 1920s (Fine, 1979a), in his encyclopedic work in 1945 defined the family as "a situation in which a couple who have sexual relations live together with only a few children, one of this couple being the more or less absolute ruler."[31] More extreme but still true to the analytic theory of the time were A. S. Neill, whose school at Summerhill (England) abolished all instinctual inhibitions in the expectation that this would eliminate neurosis, and Wilhelm Reich, whose Sexpol movement in Germany attempted to combine free sexuality with communal ownership of property, again with the expectation that such a combination would prevent neurosis. In their analytic work analysts likewise attached little importance to the protective functions of the family. For example; the Wolf Man, the classic patient of Freudian psychoanalysis, was viewed only in the light of his psychosexual development (Wolf Man, 1971; Fine, 1973).

Eventually it was recognized in both communism and psychoanalysis that the family serves more vital functions than merely warding off instinctual needs. From 1936 to 1944 the Soviet Union completely reversed itself on its rules about family life in an effort to "stabilize" the society.[32] Likewise, in psychoanalysis the gradual shift to interpersonal theory, the discovery that mother love was as important as air for the neonate, and the change to a structural theory rather than a purely instinctual one all combined to lead to an entirely different evaluation of the family. Ackerman (1958), in *Psychodynamics of Family Life,* was perhaps the first to give a clear description of the vital functions of protection and security which the family served for the child. Today no one seriously questions the essential importance of a family life for both child and adult (see pp. 51–53).

Thus a similar development occurred in both communism and psychoanalysis, which otherwise are at opposite ends of the ideological spectrum. In the 1920s, the family was seen as a patriarchal relic, a holdover that did more harm than good. Abolish the family, abolish all sexual restrictions, and happiness will result. The consequent release of violence, in both the individual and the social spheres, was totally unexpected. Theory then reversed itself. The family was seen as the bulwark of order and security. Instinctual release was tabooed by many communists, while in psychoanalysis it frequently was rebaptized "acting-out." The main lesson to be learned is that the family gratifies certain essential needs in human nature and cannot be abolished by fiat.

Women's Liberation and Changing Family Patterns

The events of the world move with such dazzling speed that it is difficult to isolate clear-cut patterns or, if they are isolated, to know what they mean. There can be no doubt that, particularly since World War II, vast changes in the structure of the family have come about all over the world. Goode (1970) set up an ideal type in the conjugal family but could not say to what degree empirical observation would fit his theory. Even with modern high-speed computers, statistics in this field are more bewildering than enlightening.

In any case, when changes in the family are recorded, they are of a factual nature. But the meaning cannot be inferred from the bare facts. Whether marriages stay together or dissolve, whether children leave home or stay at home, whether communal families can replace or are replacing the nuclear family—these can all be measured. But the inner dynamics of these changes remains elusive.

Our concern has been with the relationship between love and marriage. With all the different kinds of marriages studied, little love shines through. The only sociological conclusion is that by and large marriage serves varied functions, changing in a changing world, but that love relationships remain rare.

WORLDS OF PAIN: WORKING-CLASS FAMILIES

If love is so rare even in the families of the more affluent, what happens in those at the lower and lowest rungs of the economic ladder? The most recent answer comes from Lillian Rubin, who after studying fifty working-class families in the San Francisco area, with twenty-five professional middle-class families as a kind of control, titled her book *Worlds of Pain* (1976).

The scientific study of the poor family has received considerable impetus since World War II. In 1962 Mirra Komarovsky opened her study of blue-collar marriages with the Durkheimian idea that anomie was the most common condition among them and produced great misery. Her results were contrary, and surprising. Most unusual in her methodology was that she attempted to estimate the degree of happiness found among these families. Her general conclusions were:

> Glenton's families are generally stable, respectable and law-abiding, sharing deeply internalized and common values. Stable though they are, one-third of these marriages fail to rate our assessment of "moderately happy." In 14% of the cases the marriages are "very unhappy." There is no doubt about this latter diagnosis; in these very unhappy cases all but one of the wives (and she was also wretched) voiced strong regrets about their marriages. Slightly over one-third of the marriages are rated as moderately happy. At the other extreme, slightly less than one-third are happily or very happily married. . . . Some violations of social norms were no doubt concealed from us . . . deviant behavior plays only a minor role in the marriage problems of our respondents.[33]

The Komarovsky study was based on interviews with 116 persons (58 couples). The modal occupation of the husbands was semi-skilled; 38 of the wives were under thirty and the remaining 20 were thirty or older; 23 couples had been married less than seven years and the rest seven years or longer. The approach was a personal interview, and we are told that a minimum of six hours of interviewing was devoted to each family.

Even though Komarovsky rated a higher percentage of the married couples as happy than the Cuber and Harroff study did, the meaning of this is not entirely clear. For example, one of Komarovsky's most striking findings was that among those married twelve years or longer, 59 percent of the wives felt that lack of conversation with the husband was a genuine problem. Five husbands whose wives had been interviewed refused to be interviewed. Generally husbands resented intrusion into their private lives. In terms of our main concern in this section, some love must have been present in some of these marriages, but it was apparently absent in a very high percentage; even where the respondents rated themselves as "happily married," This response seems to correspond more to Cuber's categories of passive-congenial or devitalized than to vital or total.

The Studies by Oscar Lewis

A number of notable studies of lower-class families were published by the anthropologist Oscar Lewis, who coined the term "culture of poverty." He particularly examined the Mexican and Puerto Rican-New York cultures. While there was a great emphasis on family solidarity, it was "an ideal only rarely achieved."[34]

Although Lewis did not consider the matter explicitly, it is clear that there was little love and security in these families. The realities of poverty were much too harsh, leaving little room for the amenities of life. Though often gay and bubbling on the surface, underneath they were deeply sad and mournful; the surface gaiety corresponds more to what Melanie Klein called the "manic defense."

The Moynihan Report: The Black Family

The worldwide push for liberation spurred American blacks to seek greater economic and social equality. Beginning with the

famous decision in Brown *v.* Board of Education in 1954, school de-
segregation became a national issue. In March of 1965 Daniel P.
Moynihan, then Assistant Secretary of Labor, wrote a report on the
condition of the American Negro (the term had not yet changed to
black), which has since become known as the Moynihan Report.

The report stressed the disintegrated condition of the Negro
family as the main root of the evils plaguing blacks. In 1965 nearly a
quarter of urban Negro marriages ended in divorce or desertion;
nearly one-quarter of Negro births were illegitimate; almost one-
fourth of Negro families were headed by a female, and the breakdown of the Negro family had led to a startling increase in welfare
dependency. Moynihan concluded with a call for national action:

> Three centuries of injustice have brought about deep-seated structural
> distortions in the life of the Negro American . . . a national effort to-
> wards the problems of Negro Americans must be directed towards the
> question of family structure. . . . The fundamental importance and ur-
> gency of restoring the Negro American family structure has been evi-
> dent for some time . . . the programs of the Federal government bear-
> ing on this objective shall be designed to have the effect, directly or
> indirectly, of enhancing the stability and resources of the Negro Amer-
> ican family.[35]

Although the vast majority of social scientists fully agreed with
Moynihan's analysis of the situation, there were some dissenting
voices. Frank Riessman (1967) argued that the Negro has responded
to oppressive conditions by many powerful coping endeavors. "One
of the most significant forms of his adaptation has been the extended, female-based family."[36]

A similar argument has been propounded by a number of historians (see Chapter 7) who maintain that the black was not so much
deprived as a person who developed a unique culture of his own.
Fogel and Engerman (1974) tried to show that slavery was "not as
bad as it was supposed to be." In a similar vein Herbert Gutman
(1976), reinterpreting the historical evidence, contradicted the Moynihan Report by stating that enslavement and poverty did not shat-
ter black family ties, that blacks adapted to the harshness of enslavement with a remarkable degree of strength and solidarity and faced
freedom with a courage and an integrity that "until now have not
been credited to them."[37] Numerous scholars have torn Gutman's argument to pieces (Modell et al., 1979).

Once more we are confronted with the nineteenth-century image of man and the claim that social forces must somehow be work-

ing for the good if they persist. The black matrifocal family must "somehow" be the nucleus of a different kind of culture, since it has persisted for so long. Gutman does not actually deny Moynihan's statistics, nor does he really deny that numbers of white slaveowners treated their slaves cruelly, but since he cannot find the exact number he passes it over. Thus he says, "A vast scholarly literature . . . discloses that variations existed in the behavior of owners toward their slaves. *Nothing in this study contradicts that finding.*"[38]

It is well established by now (Labov, 1968; Williams, 1970; Dillard, 1972) that "black English" is not a dialect but a full-fledged language, with its own grammar, its own rules, and its own rationale. The question is: Why do black children learn this language rather than standard English? Or, to put more directly: Are we dealing with language that is deficient or with language that is different?

The argument about black culture is similar. Are we dealing with a culture that is deficient or with one that is different? The Moynihan position (the consensus, actually) is that the black culture is deficient in certain essential human respects, which militate against happiness and mental health; the opponents argue that it is merely different, neither better nor worse than the surrounding white culture.

The problem that concerns us in this chapter is: How much love is there is the lower-class family, black or otherwise? And the answer that comes out, whichever way we turn, is: very little. The scholars who oppose the view that blacks are culturally deprived (Ginsburg, 1972) stress their different values and different backgrounds but do not examine in any detail their psychological state. For example, granted that black English is a language in its own right, why do black children refuse to learn standard English when everyone around them does? The answer must lie in their resentment at being oppressed and downtrodden.

MENTAL HEALTH AND SES

Some information about love also comes out of the mental health statistics. It is well established that serious psychopathology of all kinds is far more prevalent among the lower classes than among the middle and upper, and that these groups are far less amenable to treatment of any kind (see Chapter 14). But after all, psychopathology involves an excess of hatred over love and a high degree of unhappiness; here the psychiatric illusion that somehow mental "illness" is an illness like scarlet fever or tuberculosis must be given up. As has been argued at length before (see Chapter 14), the notion of illness and the medical model are incorrect. They serve a certain purpose in a culture that suddenly finds that large numbers of its members are seriously in need of help. But they do not serve the cause of scientific understanding.

Since mental illness is basically misery and unhappiness, it comes as no surprise that it is much more frequent among the lower classes and that they are much more resistant to any effort to ameliorate their condition by psychological measures. In other terms, there is little love in their lives. It may exist as an ideal, but the realities are different. They would seem to conform more to the Hobbes's dictum that life is nasty, brutish, and short.

The Realities of Lower-Class Living

It is sometimes said that social scientists expend enormous efforts to demonstrate the obvious. And so it is here. In the book cited earlier, Lillian Rubin (1976) found that the affluent and happy worker of whom we have heard so much in recent decades seems not to exist.[39] There were few stories of happy childhoods. Not a single couple was without some problems of sexual adjustment. Work is a complex picture of struggle, of achievements and disappointments, of successes and failures (the median income of her families was $12,300 per year). Leisure often consists of doing nothing. At best a wife could say of her husband: He's a steady worker, he doesn't drink, he doesn't hit me.

Conclusion: Love and the Family Structure

Ideally the family is supposed to be where love and affection find their fullest expression. The reality seems to be quite different. In middle- and upper-class families, a greater modicum of satisfaction seems to be present because of less pressing economic needs, but psychological conflicts are abundant. In lower-class families, by and large, the grinding nature of poverty distorts all human relationships. The sociological evidence indicates that the family rarely provides the love it is supposed to offer its members.

Since the family remains the indispensable core of every culture (cf. the Russian experiment), many attempts have been made to reform it. Almost always these attempts are external: liberate women, provide more leisure time for men, extend the family, make special arrangements for children, and so on. While all of these measures are desirable, they do not hit at the heart of the matter.

In the psychoanalytic vision, love remains a central experience. Any reform of the family should strive to permit more love, regardless of the external arrangements. The most effective way of doing that is through psychotherapy. As has repeatedy been seen, the real goal of psychotherapy is to teach people how to love more effectively. In this way psychotherapy becomes a vehicle for social reform, as vital in its own way as any rearrangement of the marital or economic system.

RELIGION AND LOVE

Of the sociological forces that preach love in modern society, theory at least would attach prime importance to religion. However, we are concerned not merely with theory but with reality. The question is: To what extent in the modern scene does religion promote love, and to what extent does it stand in its way?

In his book on current religions Trevor Ling (1968) distinguishes three kinds of religion in the modern world: (1) the theology of the omnipotent (typically Islam), (2) the anthropology of the awakened (typically Buddhism), and (3) the christology of the new man (typically Christianity). The emphasis on love has come primarily from the latter two. Also, even though an increasing number of Americans have turned to Buddhism, the primary religion in our culture is still Christianity.

The centuries in which Christianity represented a system of delusion, destructiveness, and paranoia have passed. Nevertheless, Catholicism at least, and to a lesser extent many of the Protestant churches as well, have never renounced the theoretical beliefs in witches and demons that led to mass paranoia. When the underlying beliefs remain irrational, they are bound to have some effect on the reality.

In theory, religious love as sanctioned by supernatural forces, as in Christianity, is considered to be humanly impossible without supernatural aid. Further, in general love among humans is thought to be secondary and derivative; primary is the love for God (Hazo, 1967). Love for men must be conscious, and it must include all men. These conditions have repeatedly turned out to be psychologically impossible, which may account in part for modern man's loss of faith. The psychological critique has also exerted a profound influence on contemporary church organizations, which speak over and over of the "manpower crisis" in religious orders because people no longer wish to adhere to the harsh precepts of chastity and total renunciation.

FROM ROMANCE TO RITUAL

The question that always comes up in connection with religion or any other system that preaches love is how much of the love that is practiced is ritualized. In an earlier chapter I mentioned Oskar Pfister, a Swiss minister who was a friend of Freud. Pfister saw the history of Christianity as a caricature of Christian ideals. To achieve true Christianity, he said, believers would have to be psychoanalyzed. In the terms used here, the earlier faith in love had become a ritualized dogma that did more harm than good.

Many men have found that what begins as a divinely inspired form of revelation soon turns into a series of empty forms, the performance of which becomes of the highest importance to the established clergy (Douglas, 1970). Revolts against the dominant theology almost invariably begin by attacking the rituals.

A similar process of ritualization can occur with any theoretical system that urges men to love, including psychoanalysis. As a result alienation from the current social values often takes the form of a denunciation, not only of irrelevant rituals, but of ritualism as such; exaltation of the inner experience and denigration of its standardized expressions; preference for intuitive and instant forms of knowledge; rejection of mediating institutions; and rejection of any tendency to allow habit to provide the basis of a new symbolic system.

In its extreme form antiritualism is an attempt to abolish the old communication by means of complex semantic systems. It is a viable attitude only in the early, unorganized stage of a new movement. After the protest stage, the need for organization is recognized and the negative attitude toward rituals gives way to the need for a coherent system of expression. Then ritualism reasserts itself around the new context of social relations. After a while the demands of inner experience again make themselves felt, and the whole process starts all over again.

As noted before, psychoanalysts have almost unanimously rejected the notion that religion is essential to the good life. Their experience has been that religion is a ritualized dogma, the meaning of which in actual living has to be explored, like that of any other belief system. Statistical data on the degree to which religious people are more loving than nonreligious are obviously lacking. Certainly in some cases religion serves as a brake on the most extreme forms of violence; in others it does not even do that. The contribution of religion to the promotion of love remains an open question.

Patterns of Violence

The assassinations of the two Kennedys and of Martin Luther King in the 1960s together with wholesale crime at the highest levels revealed in the Watergate scandals again brought forcefully to the attention of the American public how endemic crime and violence are in the United States. As usual a presidential commission was appointed to investigate and produced a book edited by H. T. Graham and T. R. Gurr, *Violence in America* (1969), which contains much relevant valuable material.

First of all the authors correct the impression that violence is new. Tilly says:

> Collective violence has flowed regularly out of the central, political processes of western countries. Men seeking to seize, hold, or realign the levers of power have continually engaged in collective violence as part of their struggles. The oppressed have struck in the name of justice, the privileged in the name of order, those in between in the name of fear.[40]

In the distinctively American tradition, Graham and Gurr list six factors that have contributed substantially to the American penchant for violence: (1) The fact that we are a nation of immigrants, (2) the uniquely prolonged experience with the frontier, (3) the Declaration of Independence, which stands as a justification for legitimate violence, (4) the pervasive Jeffersonian–Lockean fear of excessive governmental power, (5) the industrial revolution and the move to the city, and (6) the uneven distribution of affluence, which has given rise to the "revolution of rising expectations."[41]

To discuss violence at greater length would take us too far afield. Sufficient for the present issue is the observation that when violence becomes an integral and approved part of the national scene, there is little room for love. Thus the recurrent recourse to violence is another factor that militates against the transformation of the hate culture into a love culture.

REFLECTIONS ON THE AMERICAN CHARACTER

From the very beginning psychoanalysis has been a powerful critic of the social milieu in which it found itself. When looked at from the vantage point of the analytic ideal, modern man is found to be wanting in many important respects.

Clinical experience (to be discussed more fully in the next chapter) has shown how widespread are the difficulties in loving. Sexual frustration, to the verge of outright psychosis, is endemic. Pleasure is condemned by many official and unofficial doctrines. The feeling life of many Americans is blocked and schizoid. Emotion rather than reason dominates. Family life is seriously disrupted in many areas. Large numbers of persons are thoroughly dissatisfied with the social roles into which they are thrust, and from which they have little chance of escaping; for a considerable percentage of the population social mobility is a myth. Feelings of shame and guilt are so strong that they undermine the self-image drastically. Creative outlets and the creative impulse are soon transformed into commercial products, drowning the creative act and its humanistic roots. Communication occurs more through insipid fantasy products than through direct conversation. Psychiatric symptomatology is extremely widespread. Even in a study of healthy adults, Dorothy Cox (1970) could not find a single one who was completely symptom-free.

Such is the disturbing picture of *homo Americanus* that has emerged from a century of psychoanalytic research and observation. Analysts attribute it to the inner self-image, which in turn derives from the parents, for the strongest influences on development are those emanating from the family. Sociologists have confirmed these observations in almost all respects but tend to place their faith in social rather than personal reconstruction. Either way, however, there seems little doubt that the institutional restraints placed on the average individual seriously interfere with his love life in many ways.

THE BUREAUCRATIC OCTOPUS

Since Max Weber it has been apparent that modern society would suffer from increased bureaucratization. Weber regarded bureaucracy as good in a certain sense, believing that it resulted in an increase in efficiency. But he failed to consider its human consequences.

Otto Sperling (1950) offered some psychoanalytic comments on the bureaucrat. The most frequent charges he leveled against the bureaucrat of his day were indecision; avoidance of responsibility; misleading advice; waste of work hours, manpower, and tools; lack of respect for the citizen's time; infringement on the pursuit of happiness, allegedly for some higher purpose; unnecessary work; disregard of individuality; repression of new ideas in favor of routine and an unwillingness to experiment; and coercion to do things that make no sense.

Robert K. Merton (1962), who has studied the bureaucrat extensively, states that the norm of impersonality is central. Functionaries minimize personal relations and resort to categorization, thereby ignoring the peculiarities of individual cases.

The bureaucrat's official life is planned for him in terms of a graded career through the organizational devices of promotion by seniority, pensions, salary increments, and so forth, all designed to provide incentives for disciplined action and conformity to the official regulations. The official is tacitly expected to and largely does adapt his thoughts, feelings, and actions to the prospect of this career. But the very devices that increase the probability of conformance also lead to an overconcern with strict adherence to regulations, which induces timidity, conservatism, and technicism. Displacement of sentiments from goals to means is fostered by the tremendous symbolic significance of means (rules).

Thus in all essential respects bureaucracy interferes with the love life immeasurably; in fact, love and bureaucracy seem like contradictory terms. Sperling felt that most of the bureaucrats he saw were obsessive-compulsive individuals who vented their sadism on the public they were supposed to serve. Merton does not go quite so far but is in essential agreement.Thus one price paid for the bureaucratic octopus is a diminution of love.

THE HUMANIZATION OF THE LAW

The profound influence that psychoanalysis has exerted on modern thinking has understandably gradually extended to the law as well. Ralph Slovenko (1973) has documented the many ways in which humanization of the law has taken place and indicated directions in which it may go in the future. He stresses that psychiatry has taken over many of the functions of religion. Many legal principles that had their source in religion are now supplied by psychiatry. "Psychiatry is having profound effects on the very meaning of life."[42]

Increased referrals from judges and lawyers to psychotherapists and mental health clinics are a reflection of the fact that the traditional concepts of the law are being questioned because they conflict with psychological observations or principles of psychology. In every area the human factor is being accorded increasing recognition.

Alhough psychoanalysts in general have been reluctant to testify in courts of law because of the large area of incomprehension of psychological thinking that still persists, some analysts have actively attempted to influence judicial decisions in a psychologically meaningful manner. Perhaps best known and most influential in this direction is a book by Joseph Goldstein, Anna Freud, and Albert Solnit, *Beyond the Best Interests of the Child* (1973). With great sophistication they write:

> This volume focusses on the development of guidelines to decision making in law concerned with the selection and manipulation of a child's external environment as a means of improving and nourishing his internal environment. . . . Alert to the limits of law and of our knowledge, we translate what we know from psychoanalysis about growth and development into procedural and substantive guidelines for deciding a child's placement. Finally, we apply our guidelines . . . to drafting provisions for a model child placement statute.[43]

While the goals of these authors seem admirable, it is still surprising that in the question of placement of the child, they make no provision for psychotherapy. In their later work, *For the Best Interests of the Child* (1979) psychotherapeutic considerations are also virtually omitted.

LITERATURE AND ART

We have previously referred to the fact that a man's deepest wishes are often brought out in his literature and art. With regard to love, the study of products of the imagination serves clinically (as in the Rorschach and Thematic Apperception Tests) to uncover the deepest images, which may even be completely unconscious to the subject.

Leslie Fiedler traces the treatment of *Love and Death in the American Novel* (1966) from 1789 to 1959, viewing them as the expression of the American emotional climate. There is a pattern, he argues, imposed both by the writers of our past and by the very conditions of life in the United States from which no novelist can escape, a pattern that is different from that of many other countries. The essential features of this pattern are the failure of the American fictionist to deal with adult heterosexual love and his consequent obsession with death, incest, and innocent homosexuality.

The poetry of love has appeared in every known culture (Petroni, 1968), with themes typical of the mentality of that time and place. In American love poetry one is struck over and over by the tremendous longings for love that are never fulfilled.

SUMMARY COMMENTS: LOVE AND OUR SOCIETY

Our brief review of a number of the institutions in American society that are in theory designed to provide an outlet for love discloses numerous deplorable weaknesses. The family is often the home of conjugal violence; in most cases marriage is at best utilitarian. Violence, in the family and outside, is endemic. Religion preaches love, but what it practices is unknown; psychoanalytic experience indicates that it offers little more than empty rituals. Bureaucracy becomes an oppressive octopus. Economic realities impose unhappiness and misery on millions. Literature is obsessed with death and violence. The poetry of love expresses longing and nostalgia rather than joyful affirmation.

The expert in social forces, when he sees them as disturbing as they are in our society, is often moved to change the social structure. Thus critics of family disturbance suggest extended marriage, multiple marriage, marriage by contract renewable every five years, or even homosexual marriage. Historically and currently many of these alternatives have been tried. Sooner or later they run up against harsh psychological realities, and the same misery recurs.

Without defending the institutions as such, the psychoanalytic approach is rather to try to change the individuals in them. This accords with the revised twentieth-century image of man, while the overemphasis on the institutions stems more from the nineteenth-century image. Once it is recognized that man can change himself and then change the institutions in a constructive way, the solution becomes easier. Because psychotherapy is the principal change agent in psychoanalysis, and psychotherapy is a restructuring of the love life, it becomes a method of social reform.

Child Psychology

It might be thought that the overwhelming need of the young child for love would be an age-old truism. Yet even in psychoanalysis it took many years to discover it. Freud himself was so preoccupied with other questions that he neglected to pay much attention to the mother–child bond. Knowledge of the oral stage began to accumulate in the 1930s, after Freud had finished his major work.

The book that first directed the attention of the world to the infant's hunger for good mothering was Margaret Ribble's *The Rights of Infants* published in 1943. It was she who coined the term "TLC" (tender loving care), which has since become part of the language. She spelled out the infant's indispensable cravings: to feel secure, and above all to derive this security from a warm, gratifying relationship with the mother in the first year of life. "Good mothering" thereafter became the prime concern of enlightened young mothers. Ribble stressed that the relationship was reciprocal, giving as much pleasure to the mother as to the child:

> Our highly impersonal civilization has insidiously damaged woman's instinctual nature and has blinded her to one of her most natural rights—that of teaching the small baby to love, by loving it consistently through the period of helpless infancy. It is for this reason that the

modern woman may need help and guidance in her relationship with her baby. She needs reassurance that the handling and fondling which she gives are by no means casual expressions of sentiment but are biologically necessary for the healthy mental development of the baby.[44]

THE ORGANIZING PRINCIPLES OF INFANCY

In her work Ribble was summarizing what the psychoanalyst René Spitz had demonstrated at a more technical level from 1935 on. When he began, Spitz says, he was a lonely figure; soon many joined him. By comparing children brought up in orphanages with children brought up in normal homes, he was able to prove how vital good mothering is to the young infant. In the extreme, many infants without adequate mothering waste away with the disease of marasmus, and an extraordinarily high percentage of them die in the first year. SIDS (sudden infant death syndrome) still occurs, but much less frequently when the mother gives the infant adequate love and care. Most infants do not die. But when the mothering is deficient, they grow up with a variety of characterological problems, which lay the basis for future neuroses.

Spitz distinguished three organizing principles at different ages: the smiling response, at approximately two months; the eight-month anxiety, when the infant for the first time insists on its own mother exclusively; and the ability to say no, about fifteen months, an ability that initiates the capacity for dialogue.

All these organizing principles are interpersonal. The infant smiles in response to being smiled at and taken care of. The eight-month anxiety is probably the result of ego maturation. Various observers place it at different time points, but in any case it is the earliest indication of the infant's awareness of its tie to the mother and its mother alone, what Margaret Mahler (1975) was later to call the psychological birth of the human infant. The capacity to differentiate yes and no is clearly also the expression of an interpersonal interaction.

In all these cases, while part of the behavior is due to the inherent maturation of the infant, an equal and often more important part is due to the nature of the mother's response. Spitz initiated a long series of inquiries into the concept of good and bad mothering, which are still continuing all over the world. Because of his observations and those of many who followed (See Emde et al., 1976), we can no longer be sure of the effect of genetic endowment or distinguish it precisely from the environmental effect.

About the same time, Hans Selye was developing his concept of the general adaptation syndrome, which lies at the basis of all illness. He divided it into three parts: alarm, resistance, and death (or exhaustion). Spitz was able to show that the emotional deprivation syndrome he had discovered in the infant exposed to bad mothering was in many ways quite similar to the general adaptation syndrome of Selye. The worst shock a human being can experience is the loss of an important person, and the younger the person, the greater the shock, because the capacity to recuperate after the shock is so much weaker.

BOWLBY AND THE WORLD HEALTH ORGANIZATION

In 1948, in the wake of the havoc wrought by World War II, a Special Commission of the United Nations was invited to make a study of the needs of homeless children. The British psychoanalyst John Bowlby, noted for his studies of children separated from their mothers in World War II, was appointed to head the commission. In a report issued in 1951 (Bowlby, 1951), Bowlby first summarized the myriad researches that had shown how desperate the infant is for mother love and how the lack of this love leads to mental illness. What was most significant, however, was that this view, long propounded by psychoanalysis, was adopted as its official position by the prestigious world health body. Bowlby summarized the position as follows:

> For the moment it is sufficient to say that what is believed to be essential for mental health is that the infant and young child should experience a warm, intimate and continuous relationship with his mother (or permanent mother-substitute) in which both find satisfaction and enjoyment. Given this relationship, the emotions of anxiety and guilt, which in excess characterize mental ill-health, will develop in a moderate and organized way. When this happens, the child's characteristic and contradictory demands, on the one hand for unlimited love from his parents and on the other for revenge upon them when he feels that they do not love him enough, will likewise remain of moderate strength and become amenable to the control of his gradually developing personality. It is this complex, rich, and rewarding relationship with the mother in the early years, varied in countless ways by rela-

tions with the father and with siblings, that child psychiatrists and many others now believe to underlie the development of character and of mental health.[45]

In other words, in order to be able to love, a child must be loved in infancy. By now everybody accepts this proposition as a basic fact.

THE COURSE OF CHILD–MOTHER ATTACHMENT: SEPARATION-INDIVIDUATION

The child needs love, but it also needs independence. Accordingly, researchers focused next on the course of the attachment patterns between mother and child. Bowlby (1969, 1973) and Ainsworth et al. (1978) have distinguished four phases: (1) the initial preattachment phase, (2) attachment in the making, (3) clear-cut attachment, and (4) a goal-corrected partnership.

From the earliest period, but especially since 1914, analytic theory has stressed the internalization of the significant figures in the child's environment. Accordingly it seems more fruitful to examine the child's development in the light of first attachment to the mother, then separation, then finally reaching the status of an independent individual. Mahler has reformulated this process as that of separation-individuation, and her terminology has been widely adopted. In the first six months of life she distinguishes the autistic (first two months) and then the symbiotic (next four months) or clinging phase. At roughly six months begins the hatching phase, when the infant can first sit up. Then comes the practicing phase, when the infant practices the experience of separation from the mother. This is followed by what she calls the rapprochement phase, her most signal contribution, in which the infant moves back and forth from the mother. And finally, at approximately three years of age there is the phase of object constancy, in which the infant has internalized the mother and is guided by internal commands as much as by external ones.

The separation-individuation process has reverberations throughout life. In other important interpersonal relationships the same process takes place: attachment, separation, practicing, rapprochement, and object constancy. Thus a pattern is laid down for all human relationships, filling in Freud's own observations that all human relationships are guided by transferences from the earliest attachment figures.

Effects on Later Development

Not all mothers are ideal. While bad mothering may be better than no mothering, the question still remains of the effects on later development of the earliest experiences with the mother. Sylvia Brody, among many others, has shed great light on this question. In her most recent book (with Sidney Axelrad), *Mothers, Fathers and Children* (1978), she tried to correlate experience with the mother in the first year with experience at later years, up to age seven, and also tried to see whether mothers behaved consistently toward their children over this period. In all, a total of 121 cases were followed up with a large battery of tests and interviews.

The results in general were in line with theory. Throughout (except at ages four and five, of which more below), more favorable behaviors were seen among the children who were in general more adequately reared, and less favorable behaviors were in general seen among those who were less adequately reared in the first year of life. Among these more favorable behaviors were higher IQ scores, indicating that the IQ is also a measure of a favorable emotional climate. The lack of significant differences at ages four and five was attributed to the extremely disturbing effects of the Oedipal conflicts at those ages. The main factor leading to inadequate development in the opinion of these authors is neglect:

> Were we to single out a cardinal contribution to unfavorable development in the child we should, with knowing simplification, name *neglect*. We mean neglect, intentional or not, that appears in seemingly benign forms: in *ignorance*—in an inability to recognize uneasiness, distress or age-inappropriate behavior in the child; in *intolerance*—in overhasty judgments of the child's motives, leading to erratic or excessive expectations of behavior, which are incongruent with the child's capacities; in *disinterest*—in a reluctance to respond or to act on behalf of the child's emotional states, curiosities, and other age-adequate needs; in *excessive indulgence*—in a failure to nourish the child's capacity for delay or for frustration tolerance; and in *carelessness*—in a failure to protect the child from excessive stimulations, gratifications, and deprivations, from aggressive acts or libidinal seductions, physical or psychic, or from threats of such experiences.[46]

THE OVERWHELMING SIGNIFICANCE OF THE INTROJECT

The fateful effects of the first year of life derive not only from the inherent weakness of the infant but also, and even more, from the peculiarly human process of introjection. Whatever kind of mothering the infant has is incorporated as part of its expectation of the external world. If the mother is good, kind, warm, and considerate, then the child incorporates or introjects a good mother and approaches the outside world with sureness and confidence. If, however, the mother is bad, cruel, cold, or inconsiderate, then this too is introjected, and the child approaches the outside world with the expectation that it too will be cold, cruel, and inconsiderate.

The introject develops gradually. It is difficult to pin it down to precise time epochs. Brody and Axelrad feel that it begins at three months; others say somewhat later. In any case, whenever it begins, it increasingly assumes a life of its own. By the time of the Oedipal conflicts, at four and five, the formation of the superego to resolve the Oedipus complex sets the personality on certain tracks once and for all. After that, to change in certain essential characterological respects is quite difficult, as a rule impossible.

It was the discovery of the introject that led to the twentieth-century image of man, and it is ignorance of its effects that leads social scientists to hold to the nineteenth-century image, of which so much has been written in these pages. For, once crystallized, the introject dominates more and more of the personality structure. To effect real change the introject must be changed, and that is a long-drawn-out procedure. At later ages the only adequate method is psychotherapy; at earlier ages a transformation of the environment can be telling.

While the early years are important in the lives of all mammals, in the human they are especially important because they are internalized in the form of an introject and continue to influence the person throughout the entire life span. This is particularly important when the mother is bad, for the child soon learns to obey the dictates of this introject, regardless of what the external environment orders him to do. The trouble is that the bad introject is at variance with healthy living, so there is increasing conflict as the person gets older.

Another problem, paradoxical in nature, arises here. The individual cannot free himself from this introject, but he may and often does note its harmful consequences. There then arises what Burnham et al. (1969) call the need–fear dilemma: the child fears the mother but needs her at the same time; later the child fears the introject but needs it too. The result is a state of continual conflict, which eventuates in a variety of pathology. For example, we are puzzled by the frequency of the hate affair, a relationship in which two people hate one another bitterly, yet are unable to separate no matter how bad things become. Many times the hate affair leads to a bad marriage, which the Cubers christened the conflict-habituated. The conflict can be understood only through the realization that each side represents the projected introject of the other. What they are fighting through their constant bickering and quarrels is the introject, which they are unable to escape (Strean, 1979).

Love, Transference, and Introjection

The significance of introjection for love is that it strongly colors the kind of love experienced and the consequences of that love. If the early figures are bad, leaving the person with a damaging introject, then the love feelings will be directed toward persons who do not reciprocate or who are otherwise detrimental to the welfare of the person. Not infrequently, the love affair becomes a hate affair. As will be brought out in more detail in the next chapter, love of this kind is a transference, not a mature, shared pleasurable experience.

These considerations are all-important for the evaluation of nonanalytic prescriptions about love. In religion the love of God, which relegates human beings to a secondary role, may be, and often is, a defense against unhappy relationships in childhood. The ferocity with which Christians have persecuted other Christians, whom they are supposed to love, has struck observers all through the ages. A fuller discussion of this all-important topic of love and transference will be offered in the next chapter.

Child Psychology and the Psychoanalytic Vision

Child psychology is completely confirmatory of the psychoanalytic vision of love. It is beyond dispute that a human being learns to love by being loved. And this love must be extended at the earliest age possible and continued throughout life.

Philosophy

For the most part philosophers have had little to say about love, and what they have said is as a rule not very enlightening. In his attempt to unify the philosophical literature, Hazo (1967) could find little in common. He says:

> The expository literature, however slight a part of the total literature on love, reveals, even on cursory perusal, a very great range of reference. Perhaps every human action has been called—in one way or another—an act of love. The range of the idea encompasses the nonhuman also. Taking the works we have examined in this book as a whole, we find that love has been attributed to everything in the universe either as loving or as being loved—or both.[47]

The wide variety of meanings attached to love derives from the fact that philosophers as a rule have tried to find the essence of love rather than to explore what love does and could mean in human existence. For Plato, for example, the focus is not on love among human beings. For him interpersonal love is decidedly a derivative and not a primary theme.[48] Or else he confuses love with destructive desire, as when Socrates says in the dialogue *Phaedrus*: "Just as the wolf loves the lamb, so the lover adores his beloved."[49]

For Aristotle love was also a kind of cosmic force. He refers to a universal striving to participate in the eternal and the divine.[50] There is hardly any reference to the topic outside of Books VIII and IX of the *Nicomachean Ethics*.

In the Christian period philosophers generally used the religious image of love. But to the philosopher it was of little consequence in the total scheme of things. In most textbooks, such as Randall (1962, 1976), Höffding (1900), and McGill (1967), the topic of love is not even listed in the index.

Some modern philosophers have paid more attention to it. Schopenhauer said that compassion was the basis of all social life. Charles Peirce had a theory of evolution through creative love.[51] William James did not consider it in his philosophy. In his *Principles of Psychology* (1890) he goes along with the nineteenth-century psychiatric condemnation of love: "The passion of love may be called monomania to which all of us are subject, however otherwise sane. It can coexist with contempt and even hatred for the 'object' which inspires it, and whilst it lasts the whole life of the man is altered by its presence."[52]

It is perhaps this failing in traditional philosophy that called forth the revolt of the existentialists, who do refer to more human concerns. Heidegger made *Sorge*, or caring, the center of his philosophy, but his writings were so obscure that he left himself open to innumerable interpretations. Hegel in his earlier years had a concept of the Spirit that had as its point of departure the suspension of differences within the living relationship of love.[53]

Rollo May distinguishes four kinds of love in Western tradition: sex (lust), eros, philia (friendship), and agape or caritas, the love that is devoted to the welfare of the other. "Every human experience of authentic love is a blending, in varying proportions, of these four,"[54]

One point made throughout this work is that the philosophical system of psychoanalysis represents a significant step forward beyond all philosophies of the past. The case of love is an illustration of what is meant.

Summary: Love and the Social Sciences

We have reviewed the positions of a number of the social sciences on love. Historically, Western culture has witnessed a seesaw between the images of the tender and sexual aspects of love; now one has been dominant, now again the other. It is only in our own day that a determined effort to unite the two has been made, in practice and in theory.

The anthropological material on love has been sifted to see how Freud's proposition that love is aim-inhibited sexuality fits in with the evidence. In one direction it does, in that cultures with a free sexual life do not demonstrate the severe torments that are seen in our culture. But in the other direction, the search for a love without sexuality seems fruitless. Thus anthropology indicates that the separation of love from sexuality is harmful and, in the extreme, psychologically impossible.

Sociologically, an examination of our current social institutions to see whether they facilitate the love experience or hinder it reveals little that is consciously designed to further the love life of modern man; as Goode has put it, love is as a rule an enemy to the social order. The humanization of life, to allow more outlets for love, is one of the philosophical goals that comes out of psychoanalysis.

Child psychology demonstrates unequivocally that the child needs love as much as it needs air and food. The child learns to love by being loved. If he is not loved, the psychological fact of introjection virtually guarantees a miserable existence for the rest of his life.

Ethological research has confirmed the need of all the higher mammals for love in infancy. If the young monkey or other mammal does not receive adequate love, it will either die or become seriously deformed.

Philosophers have paid very little attention to the question of love. Mostly they have been concerned to find the true essence of love, instead of exploring what human beings do with love. Because of this neglect and abstract attitude, psychoanalysis represents a distinct philosophical advance.

Chapter 17

Toward an Integrative Theory of Love

THE PRECEDING CHAPTER focused mainly on the cultural-historical factors that explain the origin and functioning of our hate culture. In order to clarify the psychoanalytic position, in this chapter I shall present in some detail the kinds of neurotic distortions found on the contemporary scene and how the analyst tries to handle them.

Transference and Neurotic Distortion

People who come to the attention of the psychotherapist have generally had in their lives some love experiences, which have brought both gratification and frustration. These experiences have by and large been based on an unsatisfactory introject. For that reason they show typical episodes of passion, elation, and then depression and disillusionment. When the introject is pleased, the person feels elated; when it is displeased, he or she feels depressed. At the same time the internalized image of the world is far away from the reality, so that sooner or later the two come into conflict.

On this score a paradox pervades the entire analytic literature from Freud on. Most of what the analyst encounters, not only in his patients but in the world at large, represents a neurotic distortion of love. Technically we call it a transference. At the same time if a person has never had any transferences at all, he is so remote from other human beings that little can be done for him. Thus love on the one hand is a neurotic distortion and on the other is a sign of hope that some happiness may yet come to the person in life.

A further paradox is that analysts, while they spend a lot of time talking about neurotic love, devote little attention to normal love. Various theories exist among analysts about what constitutes normal love, but there is relatively little discussion of the subject. The reason is that before normal love can be reached, all the transferences have to be overcome. That is such a formidable task that most therapists devote almost all their efforts to it. Such over-devotion to technique is unfortunate, for in the process analysts lose sight of the vision that lies at the bottom of the whole procedure.

The difference between goal and technique must always be borne in mind. The goal of analysis and analytic therapy is to teach the person how to love; the technique is to make the unconscious conscious. It is the goal that provides the analytic vision; the technique provides the analytic machinery. To focus on technique and lose sight of the vision is damaging to the therapist and tends to drive him into channels of rigidity and ossification.

Love and Psychotherapy

By giving examples from actual practice of the way in which neurotic distortions of love appear and of how the psychotherapeutic process helps to overcome them and lead the person to normal channels of love, I hope to make the nature of analytic theory much clearer and to avoid the pitfalls of conventional philosophy, which seeks to define the essence of love rather than explore what real people do with it in the real world.

Many of the neurotic distortions of love described below seem like genuine love to the average person.* It is only through the analytic process that one comes to see how this kind of love is a holdover from infancy and does not lead to the real pleasure and satisfaction of mature love. The conflict between the cultural images of love and the harsh truths uncovered in the therapeutic process is one of the chief reasons for resistances to analysis.

HELEN: THE CLINGING VINE

Helen was a thirty-year-old secretary, unmarried. She was the youngest of three children, with a sister eight years older and a brother ten years older. Father and mother both doted on her; when

*One of these cases has been presented in more detail in my book *The Intimate Hour* (1979) and the reader is referred to that book if he wishes to have a fuller discussion.

she first started treatment, she was speaking to her mother on the phone every day, even though they lived in different cities.

In childhood mother had literally spoon-fed her for a long time, especially when she was ill with a respiratory infection. By some "accident" she had lots of respiratory infections. Father continued the infantilization and always referred to her as "my little baby" even after she had moved to a highly responsible position in her firm.

As a child Helen shared a room with her sister. For a period when the sister was entering adolescence Helen was asked to stroke her arms; the sensations were exquisite, but the experience also left Helen with strong unsatisfied homosexual longings. She looked up to her brother but was somewhat ashamed of her father, who had a stutter and a foreign accent.

Helen's first love experiences were ones of uncritical adoration. As far back as she could remember there was always some handsome boy whom she admired and who became the object of her erotic fantasies. With rare exceptions these boys never returned her affections; most of them did not even know she existed.

In early adolescence Helen began to have "crushes" on older boys and men. Her image of love was a matter of clinging to them and having them cling to her. She felt it was unfortunate that this never happened. Once again, the rule was that whenever she had a crush the man would ignore her.

Although brought up with a strict code that required exclusive premarital virginity, Helen rebelled to some extent and began to experiment with sex at a fairly early age. In her early twenties she went on a vacation trip to Puerto Rico, where she met a handsome young man and had a sexual fling with him. For many years thereafter she maintained an on-off correspondence with him, even though in the meantime he married and sired a family. But she "loved" him and kept hoping that someday he would come to New York and marry her. This "love" was obviously the aim-inhibited sexuality discussed earlier (see pp. 36–39).

Thereafter Helen sought out a number of men who were superior to her in status and wealth and would offer herself sexually to them in the hope that this would entice them to pay more attention to her. With one man, a physician, she kept up a relationship for several years, although it was clear that he wanted her only for sexual purposes and was not interested in the marriage she craved.

The other side to her love pattern was an attachment to weak, unsuccessful men who she could mother. These men would spend time with her, thereby gratifying her clinging fantasies, but could never satisfy her fully because they were at such odds with themselves.

A typical relationship was with an alcoholic who lived by his wits. He moved in with Helen and stayed by her side all the time. Only gradually did it become apparent that he was exploiting her financially. Only when it turned out that he was also in rather serious trouble with the law did she find the courage to leave him.

All of this anyone could have uncovered by assiduous interviewing. What came out in the analytic relationship was deeper and more meaningful. Her surface complaint, the one that had brought her to analysis, was that she was unmarried. But a number of other and more profound sources of dissatisfaction soon came to the surface.

First of all was the feeling that her body was inadequate. In her mind men did not reciprocate her feelings because she was not attractive enough. As the analysis progressed, different parts of the body were blamed. Originally, she complained about her breasts, which in her estimation were much too small. Should she have a silicone injection to enlarge them? A gynecologist to whom she was referred confirmed that her breasts were on the small side but also pointed out the dangers of the silicone operation. The analysis brought out repeatedly that the size of her breasts had made no difference in her overall love pattern. But her preoccupation with them persisted for years.

Once convinced that her breasts were adequate, she began to deplore other parts of her body. Her behind was too big; her chin was beginning to show signs of age; her face did not look so young; her thighs were too heavy. It was difficult for her to see that this was all part of a self-deprecation that went back to the infantilization by her parents and to her defiance of their excessively strict sexual code. Since she was having sex without their knowledge, she reasoned that they must think her a "bad" girl, and this feeling was expressed in the comments about her body.

A second preoccupation was with thoughts about being tied up and beaten. A novel about a woman who was captured by sadistic men, beaten, and exposed to all kinds of sadistic sex was a great favorite with her, and she would read it over and over again. Several times she asked lovers to tie her up and beat her, though she never went so far as to allow them to hurt her. When the analyst interpreted this as an infantile wish to be punished by her parents for being "bad," she fought him bitterly, arguing that he was merely old-fashioned about sexual pleasure.

One time during the analysis she visited a club where men went to be beaten by women. The men would bare their behinds, and women would spank them, sometimes quite severely. It was hard for Helen to see that this too was one of her strongest wishes, an unconscious reversal that brought about her anger toward men, which was otherwise concealed.

One significant memory from childhood showed how the anger at men was turned into its opposite, "maternal concern." When she was a little girl of four or five, her father used to come home and go to sleep on the sofa. She fantasized that he was dead and would stealthily crawl up to him and put her head on his chest to see whether his heart was beating. It took years for her to grasp the hostility involved in the death fantasy about her father.

A third source of constant preoccupation in the analysis was her failure to achieve orgasm. She took this as a confirmation that there was something wrong with her body, which made her an inadequate woman. At the same time she was too shy to talk about the details of her sexual experiences, because in the transference the analyst was the father who would not permit her to be sexual. For example, once she said that she never masturbated; then later she revealed that she masturbated a great deal but did not actually insert her finger into her vagina, which to her was the definition of masturbation. What she did was a compromise formation, masturbating but at the same time avoiding full pleasure.

The homosexual conflict became strong at various stages in the analysis. She realized that it was a kind of sublimated homosexuality, expressing itself primarily in strong, clinging friendships with women, such as that with her older sister and mother throughout her life.

At one point, in rebellion at the slow pace of analysis, she went to a behavior therapist, a woman graduate student, who promised her orgasms in six or seven weeks of training in masturbation. At first Helen was excited by the "training"; then the effects began to diminish. After a while she discontinued, but characteristically she blamed herself for not following instructions to the letter. Eventually she could also see that the whole experience was a sublimated homosexual relationship with the therapist, who was, unlike her mother, giving her permission to masturbate.

In the transference, Helen appeared on the surface to be the obedient little girl. She came to her sessions faithfully, free-associated, paid her fees, and quickly fell into an adoring positive transference. The analyst was the greatest, the best, the most competent in the world. In this respect she was again the child who adored her doting parents.

Underneath, however, there was a strong streak of defiance. Its most subtle form was that since the analyst was so all-wise and all-powerful he could decide everything for her. She did not really have to participate in the analytic process; it was enough for her to show up, and he would do the rest. For example, before many sessions she would fall asleep in the waiting room, content just to be there. Thus the analyst was turned into the powerful father-figure and father-substitute who had always been the object of her love.

An event in the life of her analyst served to intensify the transference and bring out her fantasies more forcefully. Indirectly she heard that he had been divorced, which made him available as a marriage partner. She began to offer herself to him, first timidly, then boldly and quite directly. Through analysis of these fantasies she was able to see some of her deepest resistances, particularly the belief that an all-powerful man would come along and rescue her and that she had nothing to do but wait—a variation of the Sleeping Beauty fable.

Another real-life event helped her to clarify her image of love. One of her adored boyfriends ran into personal trouble and went into analysis. It surprised her that a man whom she had put on such a high pedestal should need help in his own right.

The resolution of her love problem came first with an increase in sexual freedom, which for a while allowed her to have sex with a number of men at the same time. The lack of punishment for this defiance of the traditional code highlighted two facts for her. One was that she really was attractive to men, regardless of what she thought of her own body. The second was that merely having a lot of men did not resolve her problems.

The real solution must lie in the achievement of mutuality and pleasure with a man whom she could both admire and enjoy. And this was eventually achieved.

HENRY: THE EXTRAMARITAL AFFAIR

Henry, a forty-year-old physician, came to analysis because of an unhappy marriage and general dissatisfaction with his life, including the fact that his practice was most unsuccessful.

The patient was the younger of two children; his older sister was completely estranged from him. He was born in Poland, where he had finished his medical training, and had barely managed to escape Hitler's armies. His parents' marriage was stormy and unhappy. Father, a minor functionary, was always away, and Henry suspected that he was having extramarital affairs. In fact, in his teens he had once met his father at a dance where men picked up women. Mother was a depressed, shadowy, unhappy figure who served only biological functions.

Henry was a tall, attractive man. In Poland he had joined the equivalent of the Boy Scouts, and this had been one of his greatest pleasures in his teens. He loved to be a guide and mentor to younger children.

In medical school he had hard sledding financially. To support himself he worked as a tutor for some young children. This led to his first serious love affair, with the mother of the children. She was a much older woman but highly attractive to him. She introduced him to sex and took care of him in many other ways. He called her L. At the time of the great emigration, she too managed to leave Poland and went to California. However, because she was married to someone else and so much older than he, the question of marriage between them was never seriously broached.

Once he arrived in the United States Henry had to stay in the East pending his admission to medical practice, which took a number of years. During that time he married and had two children. At first he had some affection for his wife, but then he complained bitterly that she had "dried up" and all affection had disappeared. Yet he could not bring himself to leave her because of the children.

When he left Europe, his mother was already dead. Sister had also left, but father could not get out. Actually, father accompanied Henry as far as Paris, then returned to Poland, confident that nothing would happen. Then Hitler walked in, and father was eventually murdered in the horrors of the gas chambers. Forever after Henry was full of guilt and reproached himself unmercifully for not insisting that father leave Europe.

Shortly after coming to this country, he found out that L. had managed to get to California. Thereafter, for a number of years, he went to visit her for one week a year. His life in that period was full of pressure and misery. He had to work long hours to make a meager living, and his marriage brought him nothing but unhappiness. So he lived for that one week a year when he could see L. Then she developed a cancer of the spine, which eventually led to her death. Once more he reproached himself, feeling that in some way he had been the cause of her cancer, even pulling in questionable medical theories to justify his guilt: If only she had been willing to marry him, or if he had been more insistent, the cancer would never have developed.

Henry was always attractive to women, and he had always had occasional flings even while he was in love with L. These casual sexual affairs continued for a long time without either great satisfaction or much guilt. His sex life with his wife continued to be miserable, especially, he said, because she wanted nothing but anal sex.

After L. died, he started another affair, this time with an analyst. She was described as in every respect the opposite of his wife: vivacious, interesting, well-informed, sexual, and adoring of him. But she too was much older than he, and though this time she wanted to marry him, he felt obligated to preserve his marriage because of his two children. The new sweetheart, unlike the old, appreciated his dilemma and encouraged him to go to analysis to resolve his problems.

The analysis began on a very negative note. Henry would come only once a week, ostensibly for financial reasons, but actually because he had little faith in it. He was doing it only for the sake of his mistress. At the same time he expressed some rivalry, saying that maybe he too would some day became an analyst (which he never did). Besides, he was only trying it out to see what it was like, and he did not know how long he would continue.

In addition to this negativism, two major resistances appeared in the early stages. He would come late to every session because he was so busy with his own practice, though he complained that he lived in a working-class district and that his patients never could pay reasonable fees. On top of that he would not reveal the name of his mistress. The analyst might know her; everybody was human, and to disclose her identity would damage her professionally. When the analyst probed into this fantasy of professional damage, Henry could not be specific. Another resistance, of a minor nature, was that he would pay by the session rather than by the month, as is customary, and would put the check on the analyst's desk at the beginning of every hour. This was interpreted as a bribe so that the analyst would not be angry with him; it also concealed his anger at the analyst for charging him much more than he could charge his own patients.

After about six months of once-a-week therapy, the transference became more positive, and he decided to continue. Later he also increased his sessions to the more usual three times per week, even though his financial situation was no different; it thus became obvious that money had been used to disguise his feelings of suspicion and despair.

What came out above all in the first year of analysis was his strong sense of hopelessness about his life. Nothing had ever done him any good, and nothing would ever do him any good. In a sense he too would go to the gas chambers like his poor father. Since there was nothing to expect in life, the only solution was to experience some momentary pleasure, which he did in his continual sexual flings. By this time he was equally miserable in both the extramarital affair and his marriage but did not feel strong enough to get out of either.

As this sense of despair and hopelessness was brought to the surface and was related to his tragic childhood and life experiences, his first reaction was to put himself in the analyst's hands entirely. Two dreams of this period were revealing:

> I'm in a lecture hall. The lecturer, to make his point, comes behind me and with a penlight flashes it into the back of my head as though to hypnotize me.
>
> A whale is lying down. His brain is being picked by some birds. He lies there passively. After it is done for a while he begins to have hallucinations.

Both dreams bring out his sense of passivity and his wish to submit to the analyst. In the first he wishes to be hypnotized; in the second he brings out the fear that the analysis will drive him "crazy." This fear is a common one and expresses the fear of the impulses that will be released by the analytic process. Around this time, for example, he also had a dream that he had murdered his sister. Being a physically powerful man, he had a strong fear of his own aggression.

There followed a long period of working through his problems. This working through depends on what the patient brings and can scarcely be systematized in any meaningful way. Certain aspects, however, can be highlighted.

Suddenly he began to bring up more memories of his childhood. His sister was strongly preferred by father, and he remembered his overpowering jealousy of her. When he was a year and a half old he developed serious eye trouble, which took a year to treat; this was undoubtedly one of the roots of his interest in medicine. As was customary in his early family milieu he was taken care of by a nursemaid. He had vivid memories of Maria's big, warm body, which was just like the body of his current mistress. From an early age and throughout adolescence, girls and adult women tried to seduce him; since he knew how much they liked him he became passive about his experiences. Thus his love life became divided into the woman he wanted but could not have (mother, L.) and the women who wanted him but whom he did not care for. After a while he began to express almost total indifference to women, concentrating his affections mainly on his older daughter. He recalled that he had been a gifted painter as a child and was forced to give it up when he was fourteen because the school he went to had no art teacher—another of the many disappointments in his life.

But what surprised him most and what probably was most decisive in his growth was the formation of a powerful homosexual transference. This began about the third year of analysis and continued for a long time. Its first direct intimation was a dream:

> I visit a psychiatrist. He says he has a homosexual problem, and wants my help. I say I can help him only as a friend.

This dream brought out his usual defensive meaneuvers: It was not *his* homosexual wish, it was that of the psychiatrist, and all he wanted was friendship. The theme of male friendship then became very important, as he realized that he did not have any close men friends and that his constant chase after women and eternal dissatisfaction came about because at bottom he wanted a man.

Several months later he had another dream that took him unawares:

> I'm sucking on two penises, which belong to two women; I'm doing it just to please them. For my pleasure I go off to a garage where there's a green couch, and there I have sex with R. [the analyst-girlfriend].

The dream of a woman with a penis is not unusual in men who have been brought up with a sexually strict mother; theoretically it is mother's penis, which the boy thinks she has until he learns better. The obvious homosexual wish for the analyst (who had a green couch) did not escape him. Somewhat later he had a dream of self-castration, and thereafter homosexual wishes became fairly conscious.

However, homosexual feelings are so strongly condemned by the culture that it always takes a long time for a man to accept them, and above all to accept the fact that one can have homosexual wishes without being a homosexual. The negativism Henry had so often displayed toward the analyst was seen as a cover-up for the homosexuality. Likewise the lifelong pattern of letting women seduce him as he lay there passively pointed to the wish to be a woman. In the jealousy of his sister, who was preferred by father, the wish to be a woman also came out.

After seven years of analysis Henry terminated treatment. He expressed the feeling that the analysis had been the most rewarding relationship of his life. Although he was still married because of the children, he had given up his mistress, who had become too nagging and demanding. Eventually, after the children were grown, he did leave his wife and move on to another woman, who was more gratifying in the essential ways.

In broad outline, what this case brings out is that the extramarital affair is often the result of a deep-seated homosexual conflict. Once the homosexuality is worked out, the man can move on to a more rewarding kind of love with one woman (Strean, 1980).

LINDA: MARRIAGE ON THE REBOUND

Linda, a twenty-two-year-old schoolteacher, started her analysis in a rather strange way. She called for an appointment a month in advance to make sure an hour would be open. And in the month before she began she made arrangements to get married, which she did shortly thereafter. The presenting problem was a feeling of sadness and unhappiness about life set off by the death of an aunt.

Her life history was full of dramatic excitement. The younger of two girls, as far as back she could remember she fought bitterly with her sister. Her father in fact made them fight like boys, which she did even though she hated to do so. At an early age she contracted polio, which affected one arm slightly. The concern with the sick child was so great that both parents were in a constant fuss about her.

Illness was part of the background. For years before coming to treatment she had suffered from fainting spells, which her physician diagnosed as psychogenic. She did not believe him, but they did clear up in the course of treatment. Migraine, menstrual cramps, and numerous respiratory illnesses also persisted until the analysis disentangled their dynamic meaning, after which they disappeared.

Sexual excitement began very early. She had distinct memories of the odors of father and mother in their bed and of how she would get into bed with them and snuggle up, especially to her father. Many times she saw her mother naked and hated her pendulous breasts. Father was on the one hand seductive and on the other prudish, to such an extent that when he went to the bathroom at night he would get fully dressed before venturing out of his room.

When she was about seven she and a girlfriend used to play girl and soldier, alternating the roles of boy and girl. The next year she began to have fantasies of being tied to the mast of a ship and whipped by all the sailors (a typical disguised sexual fantasy of little girls). Again, some years afterward she had a girlfriend who had made her brother into a slave. Linda was a slave too, and the three of them would play at grooming the girl. When the girlfriend had her brother trim her pubic hair, it became too much for Linda and she quit the relationship.

Once she entered puberty boys became the chief thing on her mind. When she was seventeen, she met a boy who agreed to marry her, and she had her first sexual experience. But then she decided that he was too much of a "jock" and called off the engagement. Thereafter she dated constantly and had a number of sexual affairs. Her mother knew about them but winked at it, apparently out of identification and a wish to recover her own sexual youth. At nineteen Linda went through a period of visiting burlesque shows, where she particularly enjoyed watching the strippers and fantasizing that she too was a stripper on the stage. Once she had an abortion, which was quite traumatic; abortions were then still illegal.

When she was twenty she entered therapy because of her depression and overexcitement. This seemed to yield nothing. All she remembered was that the therapist had told her, "There is nothing in your head." When she left she felt hopeless. It was only with the encouragement of a girlfriend that she was able to resume with another therapist some time thereafter.

With a background of such extraordinary excitement, her marriage seemed most peculiar. Her husband was a rather passive man, a civil servant with marked sexual problems. He suffered from premature ejaculation so severe that he ejaculated as soon as he entered her, sometimes before. Then he would withdraw and not touch her again. There was no petting, no embracing, no fondling. On top of that his mother had been paranoid for years, and Linda was required to visit her every week.

The course of the analysis was completely dominated by two main themes: sex and babies. No sooner had she entered treatment than she went into a strong erotic transference, which persisted more or less undiminished until the end. There were rarely any negative feelings expressed, and little resistance was shown.

The sexual material appeared both directly and indirectly. There were many direct expressions of sexual desire. One persistent fantasy was that both she and the analyst would undress, and she would lie naked on his stomach. While initially there was some hesitancy about bringing out these sexual fantasies, after a while the hesitancy disappeared completely, and she seemed to relish them. To some extent they had a teasing quality, but to a larger extent they were similar to the fantasies she had had about her father as a little girl and about a favorite uncle, a highly sexual man, who had died prematurely.

A fairly typical sexual dream was the following:

You and your wife come to visit us. I take your things. I don't know whether to call your wife Dr. or Mrs. She goes in with Ralph [Linda's husband]. I go into the bathroom; you follow me. I take off my clothes, but not all. I'm totally unselfconscious about it. Finally I step into the shower.

Or again:

I'm in a house with a lot of people. There's an orgy; both sexes.

Concomitant with the sexual fantasies came a constant improvement in her sex life with her husband. Previously she had not been fully aware of any sexual problems but now she did realize that she was not enjoying sex as much as she could. For the first time she was able to perform fellatio on a man and swallow the semen. At times she would experience orgasm, but because of her husband's ineptness such times were rare.

It was not long before she began to wonder why a woman as passionate as she would marry a man as cold and sexually frustrating as Ralph. The analysis of her childhood sexual experiences and the family climate brought out the intense guilt she had felt about her wishes for her father. This guilt had been reinforced by the previous therapy, which was conducted by a man who was a borderline homosexual (though she did not know it) and filled with hatred of women. She took the therapist's negative evaluation of her quite seriously and was left with the feeling that she did not deserve and could never have the love she craved. Besides, in numerous affairs before marriage she had had crushes on the man, had her hopes raised, and then had been disappointed over and over again. It was thus a marriage on the rebound: She felt unworthy of love and married the first man who asked her, sure that she could never get a man she really wanted.

At this point she might very well have left the marriage and gone on to try again; after all, she was only twenty-two. But the other constant theme, of having babies, interfered with this solution. After all, she could be sure of Ralph, and he was willing to start a family. How could she be sure of any other man in view of all her fiascoes? A bird in the hand is worth two in the bush, she reasoned.

A typical dream about babies was this:

I'm pregnant and am looking for work. I think it's wrong to work when you're pregnant. The job is connected with Laura.

Laura was the girl through whom she came into analysis the second time. Thus she wanted the analyst to be the all-powerful father of her childhood, who would give her work and babies, that is, take care of her completely.

It should be mentioned here that originally Linda had made up a curious story about her family. She said that her father had originally been a large-scale contractor worth millions of dollars, who traveled all over the country to take care of his properties. Mother, she said, had had three children, one of whom died. In the Depression her father had lost all his money, and thereafter he had to make do with a small retail store. This story sounded plausible enough, for such ups and downs had happened to large numbers of people in the Depression, but eventually it turned out that the story was a complete fabrication, which she had initially made up while still in school in order to impress her classmates with her wealthy background. The powerful fantasies about babies were still part of this Oedipal fantasy. (The little girl has a strong desire to have the father give her a baby; later she turns to other men whom she regards as strong and powerful to do that. The wish is both intense and unrealistic because of the childhood origin.)

Linda was caught between the desire to leave her husband and the desire to have babies. At one point she dramatically made a big bonfire into which she threw her diaphragm and announced that she was leaving analysis. Shortly thereafter she changed her mind about termination, once she realized that having a child with her present husband was highly ill-advised.

In the meantime she had been making steady progress in her professional career. She was a highly capable young woman and was promoted time and time again. In one of her jobs she met a man, ten years her senior, who took a fancy to her, and they began an affair. He was exactly the opposite of her husband: exciting, interesting, an artist, and highly sexual. Sometimes they would have sex four or five times a day.

She made up her mind to leave her husband and marry her lover. There was little hesitation or guilt about this decision; by this time she had worked out enough of the childhood feeling that she did not deserve anything good. The couple were married and soon had two children. In spite of some stressful times, the marriage seems to have been a happy and loving one.

An epilogue occurred some four years later, when Linda's first daughter was three years old. The child had in many ways repeated the mother's pattern. She was highly excitable, to such an extent that she could not sleep. At night she would crawl into her father's bed and ask her mother to leave. If the sleeping problem had not become so severe, the parents, both sophisticated individuals, would have disregarded the sexual play for father. But the sleep disturbance made this impossible.

The child was brought to the analyst for a consultation. In a play situation with dolls (the type commonly used in play therapy with children) she hit the mother and went for the father's penis. The mother was struck by the similarity with her own childhood. No treatment was attempted, but the child's sleeping arrangements were manipulated by putting her bed near the parents. Once she was close enough, she no longer had to crawl into bed with daddy and managed to go to sleep. After several months of this controlled regression, the child was able to go back to her own room and sleep through the night.

Subsequent contacts have indicated a satisfactory love life. In this case the guilt that had interfered with the gratification of her desires was worked out in the analysis, so that she could enjoy herself in real life.

JOSEPH: THE LOVE FOR PROSTITUTES

Twenty-eight-year-old Joseph came to analysis because his wife had left him for another man. He had been deeply in love with her and felt deeply hurt by her desertion. After she left, he resumed his former pattern of limiting his female contacts to prostitutes, with one of whom he had fallen in love. At the time the analysis began, she had been urging him to "join in with her" by becoming a pimp, and he was giving the idea serious consideration.

The life history that unfolded in the course of treatment sounded in many respects like a living nightmare. Joseph's father had deserted the family before the boy was two. For a while he paid child support erratically, then disappeared almost entirely for about eight years. The mother hauled him into court, where he was ordered to pay alimony regularly. Unable to do so, he was sent to alimony jail for three months. Mother regarded this as the great triumph of her life, repeating over and over: Revenge is sweet.

Father had gone off with another woman, with whom he had a daughter. Mother refused to see any other man and filled her whole mind with vindictive thoughts about father. When father wanted to remarry she refused to consent to a divorce, and under the legal conditions of that day (the 1920s) he could do nothing about it. He lived in a consensual union with the other woman for the rest of his life.

Mother remained extremely bitter. After her husband left, she went to live with her sister and brother-in-law, who had one son. The mother went to work, so Joseph saw her only on weekends. Until he was eight years old Joseph was brought up by this aunt, who took care of him and his sister, two years older. For some reason, his mother and his aunt had a falling out, whereupon the aunt and her family moved away. This was another severe blow to Joseph, as it represented the loss of another mother-substitute and left him to take care of himself. Besides, the quarrel between mother and aunt began over a pair of scissors, which mother alleged her sister had "stolen" from her. Joseph could not understand this argument, typical of his mother's bizarre resentments. Later mother and sister were reconciled, but the scar remained with Joseph.

One of the more serious consequences of the neglect by mother and desertion by father was a deep sense of shame that developed about his body. Joseph was afraid that he was dirty and could not really get himself clean. One day someone jokingly told him that potatoes were growing out of his ears, and for years he remembered this as a severe reproach. Actually, mother paid so little attention to him that his hygenic habits were poor.

Mother herself was so ashamed of being deserted that she told people she was a widow and required Joseph to tell everyone who asked that his father was dead, although he knew that father was not dead.

When Joseph was about eleven, he began to collect stamps, like the other boys in his neighborhood. For some reason that could never be fathomed his mother objected and would not give him any money for the stamps. Defiantly Joseph began to steal money from her and from his uncle, who had a small restaurant. When the thefts were discovered a stormy scene ensued.

Mother blamed his thefts on his "companions" and decided to move to a new neighborhood some distance from where they had been living. There Joseph, who had previously been sleeping on the living room couch, had a room of his own for the first time. But he had no friends and was completely isolated and desperately lonely.

It was around this time that his "bogeyman" episode occurred. Suddenly Joseph could not fall asleep because he thought there was a man in his room. He feared that the man would take him away "somewhere," though what would happen there was not spelled out. Terrified, he would lie awake half the night in his bed, then make a dash for the bed in the next room, where mother slept with his sister. The bogeyman fear persisted for several months until the family moved back to an old neighborhood. In the analysis, of course, it was interpreted as a wish to be rescued by father from mother's anger.

Crawling into bed with his mother at thirteen and being forced to tell the fictitious story that father was dead represent the extremes of the Oedipus complex. Joseph in effect had come close to incest with his mother and close to thinking about murdering his father. It was not surprising that he entered puberty severely traumatized.

In puberty, he was terrified of making any contacts with girls. He had gone to an all-male high school and college so that some additional effort, which he was then not capable of, was required to meet girls. Instead of normal dates he became a very heavy masturbator and frequented burlesque shows.

Although he had been a star student in elementary and high school, by the time Joseph entered college the sexual conflicts were so overpowering that his grades fell off sharply. It was only by sheer luck that he managed to graduate from college, but the natural progression to graduate school was beyond him.

His first sexual experience came at eighteen, with a prostitute who hurried him through the act. Thereafter he would have sex with prostitutes occasionally. With one he did not exercise enough care and contracted gonorrhea.

This was in the 1930s, before antibiotics were discovered. The treatment for gonorrhea at that time was long and painful. Unfortunately the first physician he consulted was incompetent and adopted some antitherapeutic measures, which made matters worse. Joseph was ill for a year. The whole episode left him petrified. He could not go with "good" girls because he could not imagine that they would have sex; he could not go with prostitutes because they might infect him again.

It was only natural that in this dilemma he should make an early marriage. At first things went well, and Joseph experienced a bliss that had never been his before. His wife could not get along with his mother, which was all the better. But then his wife became psychologically ill. She felt more and more depressed, more and more isolated, and finally went off with another man.

This new desertion drove Joseph back to prostitutes again as a last desperate measure. It was at this juncture that he entered analysis.

In the analysis an immediate and powerful positive transference developed. The analyst was the father whom he had longed for all his life and had never been able to find. His progress was rapid.

The first dream in analysis already foreshadowed what was to come in the future. He dreamt:

My wife has a baby. I leave her.

The dream pointed on the one hand to a strong identification with father, indicating that Joseph likewise wished to leave his children, and on the other to an equally strong wish to frustrate the woman, again like father, to give her something she dearly wanted, then disappoint her. He had had no children with his first wife, hence these dynamic factors did not make themselves felt until much later.

What did come out almost immediately was that the positive transference became excessive. After the second session he suddenly had an episode of tachycardia so severe that he immediately called a physician, even though it was the middle of the night. As soon as the physician entered the room the rapid heartbeat came to a halt. The analyst interpreted it as the great excitement attendant upon a new relationship with a father figure.

Joseph began to make the analyst the entire center of his life. He waited eagerly for each session, would come half an hour early, would be unwilling to leave, would avidly gobble up any interpretations the analyst offered him. His physiological reactions were so acute that for the first six months of the analysis he had to get up in the middle of each session to go to the bathroom and urinate.

Still, for quite a while everything seemed to proceed with utmost smoothness. Joseph was able to return to graduate school and resume where he had left off. It was soon apparent to him that he had placed "good" girls on a pedestal and that they were likely to enjoy sex just as much as he. The prostitutes, he realized, were a compromise—women with whom he could have some physical contact but did not have to get involved emotionally. The fantasy of becoming a pimp, which he had almost acted out, was a wish to take revenge on mother, who had always urged on him the duty of supporting her. As a pimp, instead of supporting the woman, he would be supported by her.

When he did begin to go out with ordinary girls again, sexual difficulties appeared: premature ejaculation and occasional temporary impotence. These were readily seen as reactions to the virtually incestuous attachment to the mother, and quickly passed.

However, a deeper problem emerged at this juncture. It was easy enough to talk about the split between the good girl and the bad girl intellectually—by this time Joseph could easily grasp these notions. But it was much harder to work out in practice. Further, there was the anger at women that came out in the first dream and in the homosexual drive toward father, which did not surface until much later.

The compromise that resulted from all these conflicts was a pattern of falling in love at first sight, especially with girls who were not likely to reciprocate. For after the desertions by father, mother, substitute mother (aunt), and wife, the fear of another desertion was tremendous. Falling in love meant that he could fantasize without actually committing himself to a relationship.

With the encouragement of the analyst, Joseph began to have various sexual affairs. He was an attractive young man, bright and well respected, and girls responded to him favorably. But as soon as a girl came to like him, he would have little use for her and eventually drop her. A number of girls wanted to marry him, and some would indeed have made excellent partners. But the urge to get rid of them was too strong.

Instead he went after Sally, who bore a strong physical resemblance to his mother. Sally was some ten years younger than he, just out of college. Her father had died when she was in puberty, which led her to seek out strong father figures. Joseph did not fill the bill, so his love for her went unrequited. Disappointed, he married another girl, who quickly bore him two children.

At this point the analyst moved away to another city. Joseph was in such thralldom to him that he could not even think of going to someone else. The analysis seemed to have succeeded in a number of essential areas, so he stopped treatment. His love for prostitutes had been overcome, but the need for unrequited love remained unresolved. We shall come back to Joseph's later development subsequently (pp. 485–487).

BEATRICE: THE REJECTED WOMAN

Beatrice experienced what many women dread: Her beloved and betrothed broke the engagement and abandoned her. Panic-stricken, she started therapy on an emergency basis, on New Year's Day.

At the time she began Beatrice was twenty-five years old. Her life history was extremely traumatic. She was the older of two siblings, with a sister seven years younger. After years of bitterness and quarreling the parents finally divorced. Mother remarried but father did not.

Father was a European who had emigrated to Cuba before World War II. Because of the unstable political conditions and father's deteriorating health, the whole family had come to America, where father had a wealthy brother who assisted them financially. By the time the analysis began father was suffering from a peptic ulcer and a heart condition, and because his wife had abandoned him he was dependent on Beatrice for assistance. Very attached to him, she cooked, took care of him, and even gave him money at times.

Father acted toward her like a stern parent of the old school. She was to obey him, and if she did not he had the right to beat her. Physical punishment was meted out all through her childhood, once even when she was in her twenties. Still, she was "daddy's girl" in the family structure, so she remained devoted to him.

Mother, who was much younger than father, despised her husband. Frequently she intimated that he was impotent. It was widely rumored that she had taken lovers from an early age, and Beatrice believed these rumors. Mother's conscious attitude to men was: Get what you can out of them. She and Beatrice got along badly. One of Beatrice's strongest fears was that her boyfriends would reject her because her mother was so nasty, so she tried her hardest to keep them away from her.

Beatrice remembered her childhood as an unmitigated horror. One of her earliest memories was of going to the roof all alone, where she would daydream of a nice quiet house in the country, far from all the fighting and screaming. In reality her principal outlet became school, where she did well. As will be seen, this later became the source of constant conflict, but eventually of brilliant success. Feeling herself ugly and skinny, Beatrice cried a lot about her fate when she was a child. The tears continued throughout the analysis.

She was eighteen when the family came to this country. Her life remained quite stormy. She did not know where to live, moved around a lot, changed jobs over and over, and repeatedly dropped out of school with failing grades. Depression and discouragement plagued her. Her one comfort was a car, which she bought and maintained at great sacrifice.

At nineteen she "fell in love" and hastily married an unemployed actor, Herman. But Herman had a severe sexual problem, inability to ejaculate. He was also unwilling to work and eventually began to hit her. The marriage occurred in August, and by the following January it was annulled. It left deep scars.

Her life then centered upon a series of romantic affairs. Little else counted in life than to be loved by a man. The first after Herman was the owner of the restaurant where she worked as a waitress. At first the affair elated her, then when he tired of her she became depressed. Again the unstable pattern of changing jobs, entering school and dropping out, and changing apartments continued.

Then came Juan, a Mexican physician who had a residency in this country. There was an intense love feeling on both sides. Juan turned out to be a good lover, and they found each other agreeable in many other ways. Thoughts of marriage again came to the fore. But Juan, the spoiled darling of a wealthy family, was not ready for marriage; he was also not ready to give her up. Instead he began to go out with other girls, telling her, whenever she tried unsuccessfully to reach him, that he was in surgery. Finally matters came to a head when he refused to invite her to spend New Year's Eve with him. This was the last straw, and they broke up.

In the analysis Beatrice continued her pattern of a series of romances. But underneath, it quickly emerged, lay a deep sense of shame about herself. Men might find out about Herman, about her mother, or about some of her secret fantasies. Two of these, which came out after several years, were particularly important. In one she is in a movie, sitting next to a handsome man. He puts his hand on her thigh, she does not resist, they go to her home and have sex. In the other she is in the subway and smiles at a man, and he takes her off on the spot to have sex. When they are recounted, both of these fantasies seem harmless enough, but her sense of shame was so strong that it took years to get them out.

Initially, the main theme in the analysis was her abandonment by Juan. Why had he left her? They could have had such a wonderful life together. Now everything was hopeless. The reason, she thought, must have been her mother; his mother, who had visited this country and spent some time with Juan, would never let him marry into a family in which there was a woman like her mother. With such a mother she would never be able to marry. Alternately she would decide to cut herself off from mother entirely or, out of guilt and longing, to pay her a visit, which usually ended in more fighting and mutual recrimination.

A fair amount of material also came out about her various roommates. In order to save money Beatrice would take an apartment larger than she needed and rent out part of it to other girls, whom she solicited by newspaper advertisements. No roommate managed to last very long. Very quickly arguments would develop, often set off by some peculiarity on the part of the other girl. For example, one girl insisted on keeping all the food bought by the two separate, which was manifestly impossible in a small three-room apartment. This led to incessant quarrels about whose egg was whose. There were few dreams. One particularly vivid one showed how terrified she was of her aggression:

> I spent the night in the dream killing people with a knife, but they would not die and whatever organ I attacked regenerated before my eyes. The feeling of terror that finally woke me up was either seeing the knife fly through the air coming to cut me in half, or the feeling that I was being cut in half.

This dream was so frightening that she called a friend in the middle of the night, who allowed Beatrice to come and spend the rest of the night with her.

Toward the analyst her feelings initially were quite ambivalent. Wary of all men by now, she did not know what to make of him. Little material appeared in the beginning. She kept her hours punctually, talked freely, and paid her fees regularly, as agreed upon. She seemed grateful for the sympathetic interest shown her by the analyst, yet she kept her distance.

Because she had begun on a New Year's day, the duration of her analysis was easy to time. The next New Year she quipped: "This is our first anniversary." Then unexpectedly she began to come late—

fifteen minutes, twenty minutes. Life was depressing, so what was the point to analysis? One day she did not show up at all; a few hours later she called to say that she had forgotten the hour entirely. The next session a vague dream appeared: "I'm angry at the mechanic fixing my car."

It was easy enough to interpret this as a transference dream. This interpretation brought forth a surprising piece of information. Shortly after the first session she had begun a sexual affair with a man named Clyde who worked as a lathe operator. She felt nothing in common with him except sex. She had picked him up in a singles bar and had gone to bed with him immediately. Thereafter they met regularly to have sex; occasionally they would go to the movies, but nothing else. This had gone on for several months. Then she suddenly dropped him.

The question naturally arose: What was her need to conceal the Clyde affair from the analyst? She wanted him to think well of her, and if he knew how loose she was sexually he would condemn her. Further inquiry along these lines revealed that she had, since coming to this country, on occasion picked up men whom she did not know and had sex with them. Sometimes she would see them again, sometimes not. At this point she was really panicky, certain that the analyst would stop the therapy.

A request for more associations brought out the two repetitive fantasies mentioned above. Much more came out. When she reached puberty she was friendly with another girl, Sylvia, who was quite promiscuous. For hours she would listen to Sylvia's stories, fascinated. Sometimes she would fantasize doing the same thing, but as long as she remained in Cuba she never did. Sylvia had also emigrated to the United States and the two saw each other occasionally.

All of these revelations were used to clarify the nature of her love for Juan and other men. What was bothering her most underneath was her own sexually promiscuous wishes; the battle was really between her id and her superego. She saw the analyst as a superego, similar to the puritianical father. Her jealousy of Juan derived from her wish to be a man like him, one who could seduce many women and abandon them.

The discussion of this first major transference distortion and the image of love led to a new sense of freedom on her part. If the analyst was not going to be the bad father, he must be the good father who would let her have anything she wanted. With an improved sense of self-worth she straightened herself out on her job, where she became quite important to the firm. Then she resumed school on a part-time basis and began to do well for the first time since high school. Finally she entered a stable living arrangement with another girl; she even sold her car.

There followed a long series of affairs with different men, none of whom turned out to be suitable for her. But she no longer blamed herself. When one man who could not get adequate erections told her that she was "built too low," she realized that he was merely covering up his own inadequacy. One man, a gynecologist, was a perfect lover. But he was too perfect for her; she felt that his sexual competence derived from his technical familiarity with the vagina and not from any strong feeling.

The working-through continued to improve her life in all ways. Finally she decided that she wanted to go back to school full time. In order to do that she borrowed money from her father and asked the analyst to defer half the fee, which he agreed to do (it was all repaid after the analysis ended). School was the great dream of her life, and the return aroused a tremendous feeling of accomplishment in her. She was calm enough to study and made excellent grades.

Shortly before she was due to graduate, one of her advisers asked if he could see her at home to discuss her program. This seemed an odd request, but because he was an attractive young professor she readily assented. Thus began the affair with Ethan, which eventually culminated in a most happy love marriage. The two turned out to be ideally suited for each other. Sexually they functioned perfectly. He was as anxious to find love as she. Shortly after they met they decided to get married.

Ethan secured an appointment out of state. Beatrice bore him three children. Occasionally she sends a card, indicating that her life is completely gratifying.

JOHN: PERVERSION AND LOVE*

John, a man in his mid-thirties, sought out analysis because of severe anxiety, which could be relieved only by indulgence in an unusual perversion. This perversion was not fully disclosed until about six months after analysis began. it drove him to such desperation that he had fantasies of living the life of a woman. He had at one

*This case history is abstracted from Freedman (1978).

point considered a transsexual operation, but when the doctors spoke of amputating his penis he became disturbed and ran away.

The perversion, which occurred when he was in a state of anxiety, took the following form: He would look for a barber shop in which there was only one barber. This man could not be lean, could not have long hair, should be of medium height or possibly taller, but not too tall and never short. Other details were important too.

John would enter the barber shop if the barber conformed to his image. He would sit in the chair and ask to be shaved. When the barber was almost finished shaving him, John would rub his hand over his face and complain that it was not smooth enough. The barber would then shave him again. After doing this a few times, John would notice that the barber was becoming annoyed and was breathing heavily. With the barber's increasing annoyance and heavy breathing, John would have an erection and ejaculate in his trousers under the barber's sheet. He would then announce that the shave was finished, pay the barber and hurriedly leave. Following each episode he felt humiliated and resolved never to do it again, but later the anxiety would return, and at some point he would repeat the perversion.

The ritual was his principal means of sexual discharge. For the previous two years he had developed another, this time with a woman, Sally. He would lie on the couch with her, and they would pet for a while. Then he would explore her mouth with his index finger. When he became more forceful, she would generally gag and protest. He would then ejaculate inside his trousers and break off the petting. Apparently though she knew what was going on, she did not object.

In his adolescence John had had a brief idealization of some girl, which had passed. He was essentially a man so caught up in his fears that he had spent almost all his life without any love feeling for a woman. In order to reach love he had to overcome the fear and the compulsion to carry out the perversion.

John was born in the Jewish quarter of a Polish village in the early 1920s. There had been a daughter before him who had died in infancy, and another girl was born when he was about four. Father traveled a good deal. When father was away John usually slept with mother; he also slept in the parents' bed if he was ill, even if the father was home.

The younger sister was a sickly baby with a congenital heart disorder. He wanted to be loved like her. Often he would watch her silently to get a look at her genitals. For a long time he was not sure whether or not she had a penis. She died in her third year, when John was about seven. Mother reacted with depression and wept constantly.

When John was about nine, the family moved to a larger town. The father, in order to become more successful, hired a young female teacher to perfect his Polish. The teacher used a pencil to manipulate his tongue and lips into the correct positions. There was also some sex play between the father and teacher, which John discovered. Occasionally his father would take him on business trips, when he would secretly take a prostitute to bed. John discovered what his father was doing and accused his father, who only laughed.

When John entered puberty a new fantasy appeared: He imaged torturing the Polish officer-teachers by tying them up, shaving their heads, and threatening to cut their throats like pigs. He also imagined sticking pencils down their throats until blood gushed out. In school he comforted himself with these fantasies whenever the teachers were cruel to him.

In adolescence he had many other strange fantasies and fears. He and some close friends sometimes played that they were making love with girls. He felt strange because, while the others always knew that they were boys, he was not so sure about himself.

When the war came he was in his late teens. Somehow he managed to get to Warsaw and took refuge in the ghetto. There he became a hero of the Polish Underground. Because of his education he spoke flawless Polish and passed for a Pole on dangerous missions in enemy territory. He was safe as long as his circumcized penis was not discovered. Once he killed two guards on a dark street as they struggled to take down his pants to see if he was Jewish.

After the war he was evacuated to Belgium, where he drifted around aimlessly, full of despair. One day he happened to go into a barber shop and felt strangely in control of his fate. He gave the barber explicit instructions, suddenly felt an erection and ejaculated. That was the beginning of his perversion. Thereafter he regulated his anxieties by means of the perversion. There was not enough energy left for a love life other than that described.

The patient had had one previous analysis before, which had ended in failure. It began with suspicion and provocativeness on John's part. He was working for his uncle and, feeling unappreciated and underpaid, began to steal from the company. When the analyst took this up, he felt that he too was persecutory like all the men in his life. He was saving the money to go into business for himself when the uncle discovered what he was doing and fired him. The analyst allowed him to run up a debt. This gave John the feeling that he now had the analyst in his power, instead of the reverse. When he broke off without paying his debt he felt that he had taken revenge.

In the second analysis the patient felt desperate yet remained provocative. Although his income was increased, the analysis started at a reduced fee because John kept the increase to himself. Holding back on money was a way of controlling the analyst in his mind.

After the initial resistances were overcome, the genesis of the perversion was traced in considerable detail. His relief from castration anxiety was obtained by the fantasies of making a victim out of the persecutor. In the barber chair he exposed his throat as if he were a victim to be cut in a symbolic castration. But he was still the master who gave the orders. He sadistically controlled the castrator and forced him to submit to ridiculous commands. When the castrator was utterly annoyed, perhaps the game was becoming too dangerous; then John could achieve victory by ejaculating, which made him the dominant male and denied the castration. The helpless barber was the Polish officer who was made into the pig, the victim of the child's early imagery. In the secondary perversion with the woman, John made her into the father and at the same time penetrated her as he had seen the father penetrate many women.

Once the worst of the perversion had come out and the patient was not rejected by the analyst, as he had feared, some change could occur in his love life. At first he began to experiment with prostitutes, whom he could control by use of money. A real-life trauma interfered with his growth. He had become fond of one call girl whose husband disapproved of what she was doing. This man followed John to a restaurant one night and beat him up. Because of this beating he gave up heterosexual activity for a while and returned to the perversion.

In this regression, he attempted constantly to provoke the analyst again in the transference. When the analyst analyzed instead of being provoked, John was eventually able to move on again. The incident with the call girl and her husband seemed to be a miniature version of what had happened to him before in life whenever he had tried to be heterosexual.

When he returned to heterosexual exploration he again resumed activities with prostitutes, this time in massage parlors, where the sheets reminded him of the barber chair. The girls meant nothing to him, and again the money served to give him a sense of control.

Then he went on to re-examine his relationship with Sally. Now that he felt better about himself, he discovered that he really loved her, that she was bright and interesting and more responsive sexually than the prostitutes whom he had been paying. Eventually he married Sally and had a satisfactory sex and love life with her.

A rather striking aspect of this case that does not get much attention in the history is that the patient was a hero during the war. He described the murderous part of his heroic activities with relish. At that time of his life he did not suffer from neurotic anxiety, there were no sadistic masturbatory fantasies, and the perversion had not yet developed. This is one more example of how war and violence can mask deep-seated neurotic conflicts.

Similar observations were made on American soldiers during and after the war. In a number of cases men who were overtly schizophrenic adjusted well under wartime conditions. One flyer who was hallucinating actively explained that he listened to his "voices, who told him exactly what to do." But once demobilized, these men often went to pieces and ended up in veterans' mental hospitals for the rest of their lives.

Dr. Freedman relates that when his patient John had been in treatment for a year and a half, the case was presented to the Philadelphia Psychoanalytic Association. Many of the members there considered him unanalyzable.[1] This again shows that even among experienced analysts the prediction of analyzability is shaky (see Erle, 1979). If the goal is, as it should be, to help the patient move on to a higher stage of gratification in his love life, the rule still holds that no patient should ever be given up completely.

REBECCA: LOVE AND SUICIDE

The lover's suicide has always been a favorite theme of poets and writers. Goethe's novel *The Sorrows of Young Werther*, which deals with this topic, was a best-seller in the Europe of his day. The following case will help to clarify some of the dynamics.

Rebecca was twenty years old when she first came to psychotherapy. She had gone to the George Washington Bridge, intending to jump off and kill herself. A kindly policeman saw her, talked her out of the suicide attempt, and persuaded her to go to Bellevue (the central psychiatric receiving hospital in New York) for treatment. After some time there she felt that the treatment offered was too superficial and applied to a low-cost service for analysis. Once she had started treatment the suicidal impulses ceased to be a pressing problem, although they did come up from time to time.

Her life history was bizarre in the extreme. Rebecca was the older of two daughters of a lower-middle-class Jewish family. Father was a carpenter, some twenty-five years older than mother. The parents' marriage was decidedly miserable. They had little to do with or say to each other as far back as Rebecca could remember. Further, she was clearly daddy's girl, and her sister was mommy's; from earliest childhood she had slept in one bed with father while sister had slept in another bed with mother.

The mother was a strange woman. She dressed the children poorly, although there was enough money in the family. She had a passion for charity bazaars and would visit them all the time. Later, when Rebecca began to work, her mother insisted on taking the girl's entire weekly salary check and donating it to charities. Mother's greatest desire was to sell the house after father died and move to Israel, which she eventually did.

It was not surprising that Rebecca grew up deeply isolated and ashamed of herself. Mother was so peculiar that she would not even supply toilet paper, claiming that it was a "gyp." Instead the family had to cut up pieces of paper from paper bags. When they urinated, they were instructed to wipe themselves with a rag towel, which was washed only once in a while. Sex was a taboo subject, so it was all the more amazing that the most commonly used word in the household was "fuck," which was thrown around on every conceivable occasion—another example of mother's peculiar personality structure.

Rebecca had few clear memories of her childhood; everything then was just fine, which apparently meant that she was left to her own resources to go to school and play with other children. Mostly she could think of how nice it was to sleep with daddy, put her feet up against his, and feel his warmth. At times she intimated that she had felt his penis on several occasions.

As soon as she reached puberty a severe disturbance ensued. Mother would not provide Kotex or Tampax, so Rebecca learned to make do with toilet paper, which she stole from school and folded to make it thicker. She thought the smell was terrible and that the boys knew. One of the most embarrassing incidents of her life was when she was walking along the hall in high school, and the toilet paper fell out of her pants onto the floor. She quickly ran away to another floor. Naturally she dreaded the times when she was "sick" and did not know where to turn.

Rebecca developed rather early and was ashamed of her large breasts. One day her sister told her that her breasts were bouncing too much. Mother did not believe in brassieres, so it was not until her late teens that Rebecca learned what a bra was and bought one for herself. Mother taunted her about her big "tsitses" and told her how vulgar she was. For a long time Rebecca hid her breasts behind large, unattractive sweaters.

The most significant change right after puberty was that she became convinced that father was going to rape her. The analysis could not bring any incident to the surface. It was evidently simply the result of her own fantasies. To avoid being raped, she left her father's bed and went to another part of the house to sleep.

Before puberty she had been a good athlete, the best runner among the girls, and could even beat most of the boys. She could skip rope and was proud of her physical prowess. All of this ended abruptly with sexual maturity.

It was replaced by a deepened sense of shame and a strong sexual obsession. She became fascinated by penises. In school there was one attractive male teacher; she would spend all her time in his classes looking at his crotch and imagining his penis. She was so humiliated by this preoccupation that she dated very little and had few girlfriends. When she did go out with boys, they occasionally asked her to give them a "hand job." She readily complied, closing her eyes and letting the semen come into her hand. Then she or the boy would break off their relationship. She was mortified by these incidents, and they occurred only rarely. Most of the time she spent daydreaming. As a result, although she had been a good student in elementary school, in high school she just barely managed to graduate. Having no skills, eventually she worked as a typist-clerk.

When she graduated from high school, she looked through the papers for available jobs and saw one: "Dancers wanted, no experience." She applied and was accepted for the chorus line of a show in Philadelphia. The hiring agent told her that it was for a burlesque show, but she did not know what that was. She asked her father for permission, and he, equally innocent, gave it.

On the chorus line at the burlesque show, she danced and occasionally bared her breasts. She was "innocent" of what else was going on, even though several of the girls were quite openly prostitutes.

Surprisingly, no men approached her. But she did get into a battle with one of the other girls, who accused her of being a "whore," a word she was not familiar with. The battle with the other girl was typical of her behavior.

When she had been in Philadelphia for some six months, her father suddenly died. He was already in his late seventies, and the death came as no great surprise. When she returned home for the funeral, she left the job in Philadelphia and moved back to her mother's home in New York. At the burial ceremony she behaved in a peculiar way. Instead of crying about the loss, she began to laugh hysterically and uncontrollably. She jumped up and down on the newly dug grave and shouted: "Mother's dead, mother's dead." In a family like hers apprently no one paid any attention to this behavior; and nothing was said about it. For several weeks afterward she would laugh hysterically and shout: "Mother's dead!"

By this time she had acquired some inkling of what a burlesque show really was. She took a job as a typist-clerk. She thought of going back to college but was too upset to attempt it.

It was then that she went to the George Washington Bridge to commit suicide, and shortly thereafter entered therapy. Her therapist was a handsome young psychiatrist who would sit in a chair with his feet up on a desk. She said that he wore tight pants and that she could see his crotch. In the therapy she would not listen to anything that was said, instead spending all her time fantasizing about his penis. This was never verbalized and never interpreted by him.

In the analysis she felt some relief at being allowed to lie on the couch. Although the transference was strong and positive from the very beginning, it did not acquire erotic overtones until much later. She spoke of her crazy mother, her somewhat retarded sister, and her work and produced numerous dreams. The dreams highlighted the intensive paranoia that had been building up since childhood. Two typical ones are these:

> My father comes after us with a broom. My sister and I run into the kitchen, my mother into the pantry. He comes after us, but drops dead of a heart attack.

> My mother and I are in a room waiting to be attacked. All the doors are locked. I have a bread knife in my hand ready to stick anybody who breaks in. The door opens, I lunge and strike the person in the neck, but it only leaves a small mark. It turns out to be P. [a friend of mother's]. We stand guard again for another attacker. Somebody

breaks in. I hide in the closet, underneath a pile of clothes. Deep down there is a passage where I can hide. I walk through it. Soon I come out into the light; I see my next door neighbor's house. It is full of my enemies. I see Fine-Malenkov. I go back into the passage, to the closet. When I get out of the closet I see a short Italian-looking man. I stab him in the neck; it also only leaves a scratch. The Gestapo is there; they have my mother. I run and run and run.

In both of these dreams the sharp Oedipal conflict is accentuated. There is a wish to be alone with mother, with father seen as the intruder. At the same time in real life mother was so strange that being alone with her would certainly have led to a complete psychosis, which seems to have been the fate of her younger sister.

After about two years of analysis Rebecca finally met a man, Joe, who fell in love with her. He was a newspaper man, about the same age as her father when she reached puberty. She began to have her first sexual experience. Mostly she liked his passion: When they were having sex, he would say over and over, "I'm in heaven, I'm in heaven." She felt relatively little. Joe wanted to marry her right away, but she was hesitant. But she did go to live with him and allowed him to support her.

Some time after she had met Joe the transference intensified. She was a big girl, about 5'8", weighing about 165 pounds. Suddenly she decided that she should slim down to 115 pounds. To do this she cut her diet to the bone and began to walk tremendous distances. She was then living about 5 miles from the analyst's office. The transference was so intense that she would walk to the office, go into the bathroom to wash her panties, which were by then full of perspiration, have her session, and than walk home again. Thus she was literally spending five or six hours a day, four days a week, on the analysis.

She managed to slim down to 125 pounds and stopped menstruating for almost a year. Alarmed by what she was doing to herself, the analyst insisted on a medical examination. She refused until he threatened to stop the analysis if she did not have one. The physician reported that her pulse had slowed to about 55 but that she was otherwise in good shape, including a normal EKG. Characteristically, she complained about the extra ten dollars she had to pay for the EKG, because it showed nothing abnormal.

It was clear that she was trying quite directly to reinstate the prepubertal relationship with father in the transference. Eventually the interpretation of this regression got through to her, and she resumed a more normal way of living.

After about five years of analysis, the mother was ready to move to Israel and wanted Rebecca to go along with her. This made no sense to Rebecca, although because of her insecurities she did flirt with the idea for a while. Mother and sister left, and she remained with Joe and a few social contacts.

Her work life was extremely erratic. She could never rise beyond the level of a typist-clerk. Frustrated by her poor performances, she would provoke the boss and be fired over and over again. Once she called up a boss after he had fired her and said, "Drop dead!" This constant provocation on the outside was in marked contrast to her behavior in analysis, where she remained the demure, obedient little girl.

Although she did have the wish to date boys of her age and to go back to school, her life with Joe began to absorb more and more of her attention. Joe was in fact a kind, considerate man who loved her, and the only difficulty with the relationship was the disparity in age. She also had little feeling for him; her libido was still tied up with the analyst. Nevertheless she remained with Joe as the most acceptable compromise.

Unfortunately, after about seven years of analysis the analyst became ill and had to cut his schedule down. She was referred to another analyst but made little progress with him. When last heard from she had resolved her life situation in favor of staying with Joe, although as a final act of rebellion she declined to marry him.

In this case considerable progress was made in Rebecca's self-esteem, general behavior, and overall functioning. The suicidal thoughts were gone. But she had stopped at a compromise relationship with a father-figure.

Alfred: Homosexual Love

Alfred, a forty-year-old bisexual college professor of English literature, began his analysis with two goals in mind: to resolve his problems about life and to become an analyst himself. Eventually, as will be seen, he gave up the wish to become an analyst and went on brilliant career in his professional field.

Alfred's parents had divorced when he was a little boy; he had one brother several years older who was his exact opposite, aggressively heterosexual. In fact, it was known in the family that the brother had had sex in his teens and had contracted syphilis. Rivalry with the brother played a central role in his life.

One of his earliest memories, before the divorce, was of mother and father having a knife fight in the bathroom when he was about two and one-half years old. Although he explored this memory over and over again, he could never establish who was going after whom with the knife or what actually happened in the bathroom.

Both parents were on the stage in the days of vaudeville, the father as a comedian, the mother as a singer. Alfred, a cute little boy, was brought onstage a number of times by his parents. He did not do anything but served to liven up the act. Mother used to sing to him a good deal; he especially remembered the campfire songs dating from the Civil War, which had been important in her background. Alfred became an excellent pianist; in fact he was sufficiently accomplished to have made a career at it, but chose to play only for fun.

Alfred remained very attached to mother all through childhood. She worked downtown and came home by subway. When he was a school child, Alfred would get out at 3 P.M., then would wait around the subway exit for mother to come home. She continued to wash him and to baby him in many ways until a late age.

Father remarried, but mother never did. Alfred recalled that for some time when he was very small, mother used to have rather wild parties in the house; he was put to sleep in the next room. There must have been sex going on at these parties, but he knew nothing about it then. Later, during the analysis, he began to wonder about possible homosexual affairs on mother's part, because she had several very close girlfriends but never established a relationship with a man again. Alfred used to visit his remarried father regularly every weekend with his brother until he reached puberty. Then he suddenly stopped and never again stepped into his father's home. On the surface, however, he felt cordial to father.

In puberty Alfred went off on several wild rampages with other boys, which got him into a good deal of trouble. At one point there was a school conference on him, and he remembered that the idea of putting him in a reformatory was discussed. This terrified him so much that a complete change of personality ensued. Thereafter he never displayed any anger or strong emotion except under extreme provocation.

In adolescence he tentatively dated a few girls but could make no headway. One time he actually went to bed with a girl. But he did not know what to do, and she would not help him, so he never saw her again. Instead he began palling around with other boys, and a few scarcely concealed homosexual incidents took place, such as a "circle jerk," in which the boys gathered around to see who could masturbate first and furthest.

During World War II Alfred was drafted into the Navy, and it was there that his actual homosexual experiences began. One of his buddies enticed him into bed, and he enjoyed the closeness and feeling of great warmth exuding from the other man's body. It reminded him very much of how he used to feel when he slept with his brother as a little boy.

After the war he resumed his studies and went on to graduate school. There he showed great promise and was soon a teaching assistant, eventually to become a full-fledged member of the faculty. It was while he was in graduate school that the first big love of his life occurred, with Karl.

Karl was a lower-class Lithuanian, the son of poverty-stricken parents who beat him mercilessly, and a manual laborer, tall, strong, and powerful. It was this strength and power that were so attractive to Alfred. The two exchanged vows of eternal love and swore that they would live the rest of their lives together as man and wife. For a short time things went well, and Alfred was deliriously happy. Then Karl began to take an interest in other men, as did Alfred. Quarrels ensued, and on a number of occasions the two came to blows. Eventually they separated.

The break-up was such a shock to Alfred that he sought desperately for a psychiatrist. Because he was then living in a small town, he consulted the phone book. He found a rather off-beat analyst who helped him greatly by somewhat unorthodox methods. This analyst, however, also directly encouraged him to became an analyst himself and even referred two patients to him while Alfred was still in treatment.

In the meantime Alfred had also started to lead a double life. On the one hand he was the austere, sedate professor on the college campus, introducing young men and women to the pleasures of literature. On the other hand he found a small town nearby where he would go and enjoy himself at the bars, playing the piano, drinking, and singing. He was so good that one of the bar owners, not knowing who he was, offered him a steady job as a piano player. He might have taken it, but it was known that other professors at the college who had similar talents had done something like that, and the university had fired them for inappropriate conduct. So he declined.

In this period he also began to study Buddhism and eventually became a convert. He memorized the Buddhist tracts, met with Buddhist monks, and thoroughly immersed himself in the whole philosophy. Even though the analysis revealed many of the unconscious motives underlying the Buddhism, he remained attached to it for the rest of his life, though later it served more as a verbal philosophy than anything else.

Once he had decided to become an analyst, Alfred made arrangements to come to New York to study and continue to make a livelihood teaching. But on the way something vital happened. He stopped off in his home town to see mother and brother. Brother had married and divorced, but was on friendly terms with his ex-wife. On one visit to the brother's home, the ex-wife was also there. She knew about Alfred's background and with little ado seduced him. During the first sexual experience his brother was in the next room, giving his full approval.

The affair with his ex-sister-in-law, Betty, was ecstatically happy. They spent all their time together for a while. They swam, walked, talked, and made love a good deal. He had no sexual difficulties, for she was an experienced and able partner. Betty was wild about him and wanted to marry him (by this time the brother was involved with someone else). But a typical intellectual resistance set in. Betty had had a hysterectomy and was unable to have children. He would not marry a woman who could not bear him children. So he went on to his new career in New York alone, with fond memories of Betty but no great longing to return to her. Besides, his Buddhism had taught him that attachment always brings sorrow with it, so he felt justified in leaving her without regrets.

In the analysis the initial resistances were all, as might have been anticipated, highly intellectual. There was an almost total denial of any feelings of anger, and he pooh-poohed explaining the motives of others in terms of their hostility. Just meet anger with love, Buddhism had taught him, and it will wash away.

Shortly after beginning analysis he was driving along Eighth Avenue, in one of the worst sections of the city, when a young man motioned to him asking for a lift. He opened the door and let him in. When the door closed, the man pulled a knife and demanded all his money. There was a policeman on the corner a block away, but the man warned him that if he called the police, he would let Alfred have it. Alfred turned over his money, and the man left. In analysis he stated that he felt no anger toward the thief, merely compassion. He was not used to New York yet and would stay out of bad neighborhoods in the future.

Other intellectualizations abounded. When he recovered memories, he said he would study the neuronal system in order to find out what the recovery process was like physiologically. At one point he burst out: "How long can I live without love?" Then he denied any feelings connected with his outburst. He found women repulsive if they were dirty and smelly, but if a man was dirty he would merely say that he had not washed. When the discrepancy was pointed out to him he denied it.

After some years he had a most striking homosexual-transference dream, which brought out the element of revenge in his homosexuality. It ran:

> We are in a house. We are lying together on a sort of couch. I give you some bread. You are wearing a T-shirt and slacks. Then you throw yourself across the lower part of my body and say fuck me in the ass. I won't do it, and go to the toilet to piss. I think the therapy is over.

He woke up with the feeling that this was very real. To the house he associated the house of his first therapist. To bread he associated mother, since she baked bread, and it was quite a ritual with her. To fucking in the ass he associated an aspect of homosexuality that he disliked. He would not allow a man to do it to him, and on the few occasions he had done it to another man, he washed his penis off afterward. To the toilet he associated the bathroom scene from childhood, when mother and father had a knife fight. The whole dream was clearly a wish to take revenge on the analyst and revealed that an essential aspect of the homosexuality was an identification with mother.

While he at first denied any of the implications of this dream (there were others somewhat similar, too), the next stage in his self-analysis was to deny the analyst's contribution and to incorporate it into his own thinking. A few sessions later he came back to say that he had made a great discovery about his homosexuality: It was an identification with mother. He was quite oblivious to the fact that this interpretation had been given to him only a short while before. But this insight remained intellectual too; his main concern was to defeat the rival brother-analyst.

In the first few years of the analysis he experimented bisexually in various ways. He did get rather close with one girl, but then she went to graduate school in another part of the country and they broke up. None of the contacts in these years had any great meaning for him.

Then after about three years in analysis he "fell in love" again. This time it happened during the analyst's summer vaction. He met a young man, big, burly, and strong, with a terrible childhood, much like Karl. This man, Lester, had lost his mother when he was five. Alfred offered to hypnotize him (at which he had become quite adept) to help him bring back memories of his mother. Lester was about twenty years younger, very poor, and still a part-time college student. When Alfred offered to take him in and further his education, he snapped at the chance. For him it was obviously a way of getting an older man to take care of him; the sex was incidental. For Alfred it was a way of acting out a resistance to analysis: Instead of being analyzed, he would take care of a younger man. Instead of allowing himself to experience the loneliness for the analyst, he reversed roles (as in the dream) and became the analyst to a young man desperately in need of help.

When all of this was interpreted, it made no impression on him. He still regarded himself as a competent therapist, on a par with the analyst.

The relationship with Lester turned out to be one of the most powerful resistances to analysis, and much time had to be spent on it. As before with Karl and later with Betty, he felt deliriously happy. Lester, with his big, powerful body, would hold him in his arms in the morning; sometimes they would have sex, sometimes not. What meant most to Alfred was the warm feeling in being held. He could not see that he was repeating the relationship with mother and brother.

Through it all a number of feelings about women and mother came to the surface. The hostility toward women was strong. In one dream he saw a girl whose ass was too big; he remarked that the problem could be corrected surgically. In another dream he sees some naked women and begins to piss. One girl says, "You're pissing on a book." The book is titled *My Life Story*. More material about the strong incestuous attachment to mother came out. He recalled how as late as eighteen and nineteen he would go out with mother, pretending to be her beau. They had even made plans to live together for the rest of her life. He would take care of her and never marry till she died.

All of this, though clear enough, was accompanied by strong feelings of denial. As far as he was concerned, he would live out the rest of his life in wedded bliss with Lester. The analysis was a countertransference. In fact, he claimed, boys would normally become homosexual if society did not force them into a heterosexual role.

On the one hand he would try to get the analyst involved in an intellectual argument about homosexuality. Then when the analyst would insist on analysis instead of argument, Alfred would say he was dodging truths he did not care to face.

The factor that allowed this resistance to be broken was that Lester proved to be unreliable. Once he had finished college he wanted to go on to graduate school. The pretense faded more and more. Increasingly he made it plain that he provided sex in return for money and support. Alfred denied this vigorously, rationalizing with the idea that after all Lester had lost his mother at five, so he was taking it out on him.

Lester became increasingly nasty and provocative. He would lie passively in sex, indifferent to whatever was done. At first Alfred associated this with his mother's indifference; then he had no choice but to face the fact that Lester did not care for him. Next Lester began to go out with other men, and later with girls. His friends had been urging him to give up the homosexual life, and he was beginning to agree with them. Eventually he made it plain in so many words that he no longer wished to have any sex with Alfred, that all he wanted was money and support. On this note the relationship broke up.

Once he was alone Alfred began to cruise the bars again. One time he went to a bar in the midtown area and picked up some boys, who took him to Queens and robbed him. This was the last straw needed to help him realize what he was doing. Thereafter the analysis gave him enough strength to stay away from cruising.

Increasingly, however, he had been having success and recognition in his field. In fact he became an international authority and was invited to lecture abroad on a number of occasions. This served to reinforce his self-esteem to such an extent that he could do without sex for months at a time. However, he was not strong enough to pursue women. He rationalized that he was "fixated" (he knew the lingo) at homosexuality and that it was too late to do anything about it.

Because of the rivalry with the analyst, which could never be overcome in spite of repeated interpretations, he felt less and less urge to change. On his trips abroad he would occasionally have casual sex; sometimes he would even date women, but never with any sexual intent. In one of his later letters on a vacation he wrote:

> All goes well here . . . still living life with appropriate detachment and am quite happy—many things consolidate.

At another point he reiterated how self-sufficient he was: "I feel a pretty good sense of well-being—However I have learned to analyze myself—and I intend to do it when necessary."

Thus ended some ten years of stormy analysis. He no longer needed a powerful young male body near him to feel adequate, but equally he felt no great urge for a woman. In line with his Buddhistic principles he had reached a stage of narcissistic contentment. At times he even spoke of being in Nirvana. He loved all men equally and did not consciously feel the need for a close love relationship with either man or woman.

PAULINE: LOVE AND RELIGION

Pauline started her therapy in a strange way, by asking for vocational guidance. She was a forty-five-year-old schoolteacher-nurse who had been in the system for many years. There seemed to be no urgent reason for her to leave teaching. When the vocational counselor heard her story he urged her to seek psychotherapy first and decide on a change of career later.

The therapy revealed very quickly that her problem was not vocational at all, even though she felt a great deal of anxiety about her work. Pauline was an extraordinarily determined spinster, still a virgin—so virginal in fact that she had had only two dates in her life, both casual social ones. Her religion did not forbid marriage but did declare premarital or extramarital sex to be a sin. However, even these were not the decisive factors in her virginity; it was rather a kind of *fin de siècle* fixation on her father.

As so often with patients of this type, little information about the early years emerged in the analysis. Pauline was the youngest of four children and the only girl. Father was a prosperous retail merchant in a small town in Pennsylvania, mother a housewife. To all queries about her early life she would say over and over that everything was fine. Her brothers were all married and living in their native city. She would visit them regularly, reporting only that everything was "fine."

Pauline had always felt drawn toward men but was too shy to go out with them unless strongly pushed. Apparently no one pushed her very strongly. Her earliest interest was in nursing, at which she did well, becoming an RN at an early age. She then took a job with a Protestant religious order in a foreign country as a nurse. Her duties involved religious teaching as well as nursing. Throughout she remained a devout churchgoer. Had she been a Catholic, in fact, she might have become a nun at this stage in her life.

In the five-year stint abroad there were no opportunities to meet men of her age. The women were closely guarded by the religious order, and to go out with a man meant marriage. As mentioned, this was not forbidden, but no man came along who wanted to marry her.

After the five years abroad she returned to this country and practiced nursing for a while. Then her mother died, and father developed a terminal illness. He retired to Florida, where Pauline went to take care of him. His illness lasted some seven years, through which she served him faithfully. On a number of occasions, because he was so old and ill, she saw him in a state of nudity or seminudity. She also fulfilled the usual nurse's duties of emptying bedpans.

Toward the end of her stay in Florida a quarrel broke out between her father and the minister of the church they attended. The nature of this quarrel never became very clear; it seemed to be a doctrinal matter on which they could not agree. In a huff father left the church and went to another. Pauline followed. Thus, even though she remained devoutly religious, she had begun to question the particular denomination in which she had been brought up.

When father died, Pauline came back to New York, where she took a job as a teacher of nursing at one of the local schools. In this capacity she was confined almost exclusively to female companionship; she had no direct contacts with the male physicians. Further, she moved to a hotel that catered only to single women, with stringent regulations on any men to be allowed into the building. As a result, hardly anyone in the hotel had any romantic life, or even a casual date. Thus all in all, when Pauline started therapy she was almost entirely surrounded by women, in her social life by women in her age bracket whose lives were devoid of men. While some of them must have been homosexuals, Pauline never reported any direct lesbian activity.

Now Pauline began to become nervous about her work. She would be afraid that she had given the class an assignment that was too difficult or that she had marked the papers incorrectly. Occasionally she would go out into the field because she was particularly interested in new mothers. Part of her job was to advise young black and Hispanic mothers on how to take care of their newborn babies. In this area she was equally nervous, fearful that she had given the wrong advice, that she had not given adequate advice, that the baby would die or become seriously ill, or that the mother was not adequate to take care of the baby and it was Pauline's obligation to take over.

In short, she had broken out in a complete anxiety neurosis. In her dilemma she thought it was because she was unfit for her nursing-teaching career. It was then that she applied for help, thinking that she should undertake a different kind of work.

In the analysis the transference was always distant. She came on time, paid her fees, and associated, but no feeling for the analyst developed. Her associations centered almost exclusively on her fears of having made a mistake, and she was constantly asking for reassurance that she had not. Interpretations about her lack of a love life had little impact.

After about a year she asked for permission to lie down on the couch. When this was granted she promptly revealed extensive masturbation activities, but without sexual fantasies attached. Mostly she would relate, often in medical terminology, how she would play with different parts of her genital apparatus.

In order to offer her more stimulation, after about three years of analysis she was invited to join a group with four other women and five men. All of these had an active sex life. Her main reaction to them was that although they had a great deal of sex, it did not make them happy: They still had problems. She held on to the religious-moral code of her childhood.

There were some tentative moves in the direction of the opposite sex. On her own she found another group situation, with many inhibited men and women, where the group leader had the men go around and kiss the women on the lips and sometimes did so himself. Pauline was aroused by this experience and finally allowed herself to date one of the men in the group. But she was so terrified when he came to call on her she would not allow him to come up to her room but insisted that he meet her downstairs. He did kiss her goodnight, but that was the end of the relationship; she had no response to him, even though he wanted to see more of her.

In the meantime the anxieties about her work continued to diminish and she could accept herself in her lifetime role as a nurse and teacher. After about five years of analysis she decided to terminate. There has been no communication from her since.

In this case the love feelings went as far as love for the father and love for mankind. The anxieties represented some wish to grow beyond that limited range. But while the anxieties did diminish as a result of the analysis, her love life underwent no essential change. It remained fixated at the level of the religious father.

JOSEPH: ROMANTIC LOVE

Joseph was previously discussed (pp. 457–462) as the man whose love relationships were limited for quite a while to prostitutes. In the course of his first analysis he overcame this problem, married, and had two children. It may be recalled that the analysis was terminated prematurely because the analyst moved to another city. On the surface Joseph seemed well adjusted. Underneath, however, a number of conflicts remained, particularly the romantic urge to fall in love. When his children were still very young, Joseph did fall in love with another woman, Maria. This created so much turmoil in his life that he resumed analysis, this time with a woman.

The marriage had been a marriage of convenience. Although everything seemed to be smooth on the surface, closer examination revealed many fantasies about prostitutes and ideal women, in which he did not include his wife. These were added to the depression his wife experienced after the birth of the second child and worries about his professional career. Some five years after the termination of the first analysis Joseph seemed terribly depressed.

It was at this juncture that he met Maria. She was an attractive woman of his age, divorced, without children, sexual, accommodating, and responsive. His wife had in the meantime become frigid and unattractive because of the need to take care of two small children without adequate help. Joseph had to spend a lot of time on household chores, which he resented bitterly.

Maria, on the other hand, symbolized both freedom and lack of pressure. She was always available to him, unlike his wife, who put the children first. She admired him immensely, again unlike his wife, who constantly piled up duties and chores for him and blamed him for her depression and lack of zest for life. After about a year of an extramarital affair Joseph asked his wife for a divorce.

Then problems with the children erupted. Joseph realized that his children were repeating his childhood pattern, which was one reason for resuming analysis. His wife refused to consent to a divorce and made things very difficult with the children, leading to a long and bitter court battle. Since his income was quite insubstantial, the court battle also precipitated intense financial pressures. Eventually they were divorced.

In the second analysis again there was an intense positive transference, though not as strong as in the first. Additionally, there was a great deal of anger, because the second analyst used a technique somewhat different from the first; had Joseph known more about it, he would have realized that no two analysts work in exactly the same way, even if they have had identical training (Glover, 1955). But her differences from the first therapist aroused many stormy reactions, which frequently led him to want to stop abruptly, a feeling that he had never known before.

The first dream in the new analysis brought a tremendous surprise:

> I'm giving birth to a baby. My body is divided into a number of rectangular partitions, all firmly attached to one another. There seems to be no way of finding an opening in these partitions, and there seems to be no way of letting the baby come out. I am afraid that I will die in childbirth (woke up terrified).

The obvious wish to be a woman and give birth to a baby gave him a new insight into his resentment of his wife: Basically he was jealous of her because she could stay home and take care of babies while he had to go out and muscle his way around the world. Much material came out about the bisexual identification in childhood: Part of him wanted to be like mother, part like father. Because of the parental divorce these two wishes had to be kept sharply separated, causing intense inner conflict.

The dream and the anger at the second analyst caused him to focus more squarely on his feelings about her. First he noticed that whenever he went to the toilet in the analyst's office he was acutely conscious that she might walk in on him and discover his odors; this reminded him of many childhood scenes with mother, especially one where he had walked in on her while she was moving her bowels and both were quite embarrassed.

Then he became aware of his intense jealousy of other patients. Like most analysts, this one saw one patient after another. Joseph was annoyed by the one before, and even more so by the one who came after him. Once he even peeked at some papers in the closet to find out more about the patient who followed him, and then built up fantasies that he was really more worthwhile than the other person, so that the analyst would have to prefer him. This was similar to his rivalry with his sister all through childhood.

He also verbalized a large number of sexual fantasies about the analyst. For some time he focused on her underwear, until he realized one day that her underwear did not distinguish her from other women in any respect. Then he propositioned the analyst directly, imagining that she was a single, unattractive spinster with no love in her life. Typically the fantasy was that she should take care of him so that he could spend all his time writing the great American novel he had been contemplating for so many years.

There were constant speculations about the analyst's age. Sometimes he saw her as old and withered, in her seventies, sometimes as relatively young and vibrant, in her forties. After a while he realized that he must be projecting all kinds of fantasies to have such widely discrepant notions of her age and that his speculations must have some meaning. When she looked old she was like mother who always took care of him (and like his present wife, too), and when she was young she was the attractive mistress, Maria.

Eventually the constant analysis of the transference led to a clarification of his romantic falling in love. It was the search for mother that dominated his psychic life. When the woman was giving, permissive, and accepting she was like the mother of early childhood; it was then that he fell in love. When she was demanding, harsh, and rejecting, she was like the mother of later childhood. He would then get angry and fall out of love. Thus his loves were a series of variations on the desire for mother, colored by the relationship with father and other experiences of his childhood.

With these insights, Joseph's resentment of his wife diminished considerably. She was able to make a match with another man, and he was able to go on and marry Maria. Once the romantic idealization was gone he could enjoy Maria on a realistic basis without idealizing or denigrating her. It was then that he could have a really happy, mature love life.

Psychotherapy as a Clarification of Love

The foregoing cases have been presented in detail in order to show how the psychotherapeutic process is intimately related to the love experiences of the patient. For while religious leaders have exhorted love, philosophers have tried to define it, sociologists have focused on the social forces and anthropologists on the surrounding rituals, poets have rhapsodized about it, and lovers have loved, either winning or losing, psychoanalysts for the past eighty years have actually been exploring the details of the love lives of men and women in a manner never tried before. it is here that the difference between psychoanalysis and other approaches to the human being becomes most apparent and most significant. Love is still by far the most essential component of the psychoanalytic vision.

The preoccupation with technique has led many current writers to lose sight of the goal. There has been too strong a tendency within analysis to concentrate on diagnostic (Kernberg, 1975, Kohut, 1977), developmental (Mahler et al., 1975), or psychophysiological (Gedo, 1979) questions, and too little attention to the basic objectives of psychoanalysis. It is understandable that persons who spend their lives helping others should emphasize above all the problems involved in extending such help. Still, such a preoccupation diverts both the professional and the layman from the chief contribution of Freud and his co-workers.

As the case material shows, the structure of intensive long-term psychotherapy with regard to love shows first the clarification and consequent loss of the kinds of love feelings with which the patient came into analysis; then a reconstructive period, centering on the patient's relationship to the analyst (transference); and finally the attainment of a new kind of love, more mature and gratifying than the old kind. The case material also shows that this ideal pattern can by no means be carried out with all patients. The background, desires, and preoccupations of the patient play a decisive role in the ultimate outcome, as decisive as the wishes of the analyst. Human beings cannot be manipulated at will (as religious and political leaders often discover to their dismay), but they can be strongly influenced by the techniques that were discovered by or that derive from Freud.

We have passed in review different aspects of love: dependency, extramarital affair, marriage on the rebound, love for prostitutes, rejection, perversion, suicide, homosexuality, religion, and romance. To the average person brought up in our culture, any or all of these may be identified with love. What the course of the psychoanalytic process shows is that all of them are partial attempts to resolve the dilemmas of life and that all involve overattachment to the parents, in a greater or lesser degree.

Further, and equally important, the final outcome varies from case to case. In some, such as the rejected woman or the extramarital affair, a complete resolution took place. But in many others the success was only partial. The homosexual man became celibate but could not move on to love women. His Buddhism, which served as a powerful intellectual defense, had convinced him that detachment was the best way to live, and even though the analysis demonstrated this to be a rationalization of his childhood disappointments, he was unable to get over it and continued to regard himself as homosexually fixated. The girl who began with a suicidal wish eventually settled for a love relationship with a father-figure, although she dearly wanted one with a man of her own age. Other instances could be cited to show that the analytic ideal of love is rarely reached and that most cases end up with compromises. People move toward the ideal kind of love, but stop part way.

The reasons people stop short of the ultimately gratifying kind of love are many. Prime among them is the influence of the surrounding culture. As we have seen in the discussion of sociology, in the main the social forces in our culture are inimical to love. The analytic patient is, after all, brought up in this culture. Thus he has a great deal to overcome if he wants to go all the way. A substantial part of the outcome in therapy depends on the attitude of the patient. Here, unfortunately, the battles within the professions have done much damage. For, as was seen in Chapter 15, the cultural reaction to Freud's discovery of psychotherapy was to resort to a variety of half-baked techniques devised by charismatic figures who had never had any real training. In addition, these nonanalytic theoreticians have carried on a ceaseless barrage against analysis as "Victorian," "middle-class," and the like. The result is that the patient in analytic therapy must overcome not only the biases of the culture but also the enmity of otherwise highly respected professionals. It is surprising that so much good work has been and is being done in the psychoanalytic field.

Toward a Redefinition of Psychotherapy

It would be far preferable to tie psychotherapy directly to love. Then the redefinition would read: *Psychotherapy is a method of teaching people how to love.* It differs from the visionary (such as the Christian) approach in that it has a technique. It differs from the technicians' approach, like behavior therapy, in that it has a goal. The definition is a restatement of the psychoanalytic vision.

Psychoanalytic Theories of Love

Originally love seemed to need no definition; Freud accepted the normal standards of his day. Then he discovered that neurotic problems stem from peculiarities of the love life in childhood and that one manifestation of these peculiarities was distortion of the love image (the man who loves a prostitute, or the woman in love with an unattainable man). He learned that these inadequate and frustrating love feelings are the result of fixations in psychosexual development. It was then that Freud produced the idea that love is a union of tender and sexual feelings toward a person of the opposite sex, and it is the result of a long developmental process from birth onward, in which any failure to pass through one stage will be reflected in failures at later stages.

However, Freud's image of mature and healthy love proved to be rarely attainable. He himself suffered from certain fixations in his love life, which have been amply documented and discussed (see Jones, 1953–57; Schur, 1972; Anzieu, 1975). Above all, the definition turned out to be not so much a definition as the statement of an ideal. Thus analytic authors continued to discuss the true meaning of love and to put forth various theories.

Freud himself held to the basic significance of sexuality, and rightly so. With the development of ego psychology after Freud's introduction of it in 1923, different points of view appeared, particularly since the earlier emphasis on orgasm as a touchstone of love proved to be exaggerated and often incorrect. Fenichel (1945) took exception to Freud's notion of "tenderness"; instead, he saw love as requiring a higher identification with the other person, but, he said: "the nature of the identification on a higher level which constitutes love is still obscure."[2]

Sullivan (1940) defined love as a state in which the satisfaction and security of the other person are as important as one's own.[3] This seems to be a variation of the Christian image of submission. Balint (1953) stressed a primary object–love, not linked to any of the erogenous zones; thus he was one of the earliest theoreticians to make the mother–infant relationship primary.

In more recent years some French authors have resumed the discussion of love. David (1971) and Chasseguet-Smirgel et al. (1970) assert that in the state of being in love there is an increase in the libidinal investment of the self because of the fulfillment of an ideal state of the self and because the exalted relation of the self to the object at that point reproduces an ideal relation between the self and the ego ideal. Van der Waals (1965) stresses the simultaneous increase of object and libidinal investment in normal love. David

(1971) notes that the quality of longing for the unattainable object energizes sexual relations but also creates guilt, which may affect future love relationships (this is a restatement of Freud's earlier position).

Kernberg (1976) has postulated a series of stages of development of the love relationship, from the earliest falling in love to the mature object-love, but his consideration of mature love remains skimpy. Altman (1977) concludes his discussion of the analytic literature with the Italian saying, *Che cosa e l'amore*? (What is love?).

Fromm sees love as an active force impelling the individual to seek out other people. Thus for him loving is at a higher stage than being loved. However, this too seems like a reformulation of the Christian image of devotion and submissiveness and leaves out of account the sensual and other pleasures derived from being in love.

The existence of so many definitions and the return to the topic in the analytic literature are sufficient proof that much remains to be said about the nature of mature love. This will be attempted in the next section.

Toward a Definition of Mature Love

In formulating an integrative approach, it must first be recognized that psychoanalytic theory has successfully clarified the development toward mature love and the variety of fixation on immature love. But it has failed as yet to offer a wholly satisfactory theory of mature love. Such a theory must consider the problems of jealousy, monogamy, parenthood, homosexuality, and the structure of society, all of which come out in more or less distinct form in every analysis.

JEALOUSY

In his classic 1922 paper on jealousy, paranoia, and homosexuality, Freud distinguished three kinds of jealousy: delusional, projected, and normal or competitive. He comments, "There is not much to be said from the analytic point of view about normal jealousy."[4] Then he devotes the bulk of his paper to the delusional and projected forms, making the important point that such jealousy is often the result of repressed homosexual impulses.

However, it is the normal kind of jealousy that is of concern here. And since Freud, apart from analytic experience, considerable data have accumulated from social experimentation and from anthropological observation to show conclusively that jealousy in the mature adult is culturally determined. Further, the more intense the jealousy, the more disturbed the individual or the culture.

The "normal" feeling of jealousy in our culture relates almost exclusively to the sexual aspect of the relationship. A wife would normally not be jealous if at a party her husband danced with other women (and vice versa for the husband), or if in another social situation the husband interacted with other women (again, vice versa). In many circles it is even obligatory to behave in this way. On the other hand, the taboos in other cultures may be even more extensive in these respects than in the sexual area. For example, a large part of mankind places an absolute taboo on contacts between the husband and his mother-in-law.

In the area of sexuality, it is now known that ours has been among the most repressed of all societies known (Murdock, 1949). In the course of the present century, the sexual taboos have gradually been weakened to the point where at present many couples (an unknown but large number) are openly experimenting with wife-swapping, swinging, and other forms of flouting the traditional moral code. There is really no evidence that "open" marriages are much worse than closed, and Denmark has even gone so far as to remove adultery as grounds for divorce.

We are still in the dark about what man would be like if he were completely free sexually. As the case of Beatrice shows, a deep feeling of rejection is more often the result of repressed promiscuous sexual wishes than of anything else. It seems likely, then, that as people achieve more complete sexual liberation they will experience much less sexual jealousy, or none at all. it is known that in a number of cultures (such as the Eskimo) men even offer their wives to other men and enjoy the experience.

A caveat must be entered here. Whatever is established as the ideal must nevertheless be analyzed in the actual therapeutic situation. In practice many persons are seen nowadays who swing, swap spouses, and so on, and claim to feel no jealousy, only to discover later that they are gratifying voyeuristic wishes, repressing their homosexuality, or fulfilling some other infantile demand. Whatever the theory each individual case must be analytically understood.

The Ideal of Monogamy

The earlier analysts showed more concern with the analytic reconstruction of society than the present generation. And one of the institutions they discussed with much intensity was the monogamous ideal. In 1908 Freud expressed agreement with the proposals for reform of van Ehrenfels, who argued that the glorification of monogamy paralyzes the process of selection.[5] Freud also repeatedly stressed that adherence to a strict code of monogamy has produced a race of sexual cripples.

In 1928 Karen Horney published an interesting paper on "The Problem of the Monogamous Ideal." She began by saying: "For some time past I have asked myself with growing astonishment why there has as yet been no thorough analytical exposition of the problems of marriage."[6] After considering the various neurotic problems connected with the monogamous ideal, she expressed the feeling that man's constitution does not allow of any real solution: "It never has been and never will be possible to find any principle which will solve these conflicts of married life."[7]

Likewise, Ernest Jones summed up the thinking of Freud and his early co-workers: "Every form of marriage relationship so far attempted . . . has been accompanied by serious disadvantages. Polygamy, monogamy, easy divorce; none provides a satisfactory solution."[8]

The inability of analysts to provide a reasonable theory for a happy marriage derives essentially from the confusion of an institution with inner feelings. If the analytic ideal is the guideline, then the emphasis would be not on monogamy as such but on an intense happy relationship, sexual and tender, between two mature adults. In such a relationship, if the mutual experience is highly gratifying, there will be relatively little urge to experiment with someone else. However, once men and women are more liberated sexually than they are even now, under many easily conceivable circumstances, extramarital sexual encounters need do no harm. The test is whether the extramarital contact interferes with the happiness of the marriage or not.

Thus in our theory, instead of talking of the monogamous ideal, it would be better to talk of the ideal of a mutually gratifying relationship. When that is reached the rest will fall into line. If it is not reached, the other questions do not matter.

In this regard some broadening of the analytic horizon is necessary within our own culture. Customarily marital infidelity is seen as a reason for seeking out analysis. Though there is no denying that infidelity may have harmful consequences, it is also frequently the case that marital fidelity has even more harmful consequences. Here too there must be a shift from the institution to the inner feeling to make analysis fully operative as a form of social reform.

PARENTAL LOVE

In spite of its importance, relatively little has been written about normal parental love; here too the emphasis has been on pathology. Still, if Harlow's description of the development of affection in the rhesus monkey (see pp. 406–407) is taken as a biological root of the same development in humans, then parental love is seen to be of vital moment to the individual. Actually, analytic theory has always recognized parenthood as a significant stage in development, though only recently has this been put forth as official doctrine (Benedek, 1959).

The biological element seems to pertain more to the woman than to the man. In the human being the strongest motives derive from identification with the parents, overriding the biological factor considerably; this of course is not true of monkeys.

Normally parental love may be seen as an outgrowth of the active capacity for love. If love is not restricted to a single other person, as it cannot be in a healthy psychological atmosphere, the next available object for the adult is a child. Hence the child should be seen as an outlet for feelings of affection, not as a biological drive. Children lead to a complete family, still the most beneficial social institution available. However, as stressed before, the emphasis should be on the feelings within the family, not on the family itself, as an institution.

HOMOSEXUALITY

If there is such a thing as normal homosexual love, how does it relate to jealousy, monogamy, and the other question under discussion here? Clinically, homosexuality affects marriage like the plague, at best offering a pale simulacrum in the "homosexual marriage." On the other hand, a strong homosexual drive often keeps a marriage together because neither partner has any conscious desire to experiment heterosexually. Usually in such marriages the sex life is dreary, but that can easily be concealed from the outside world.

The vociferousness of the "gay" groups and the puerility of official societies, such as the American Psychiatric Association, have prevented a clear statement on the normal character of homosexuality. What analysts refer to is the *exclusive* attachment to a person of the same sex, which when carefully examined turns out to have strong elements of hatred and revenge mixed up with it (see the case of Alfred). Further, the sex life of the homosexual is markedly bizarre, since after rejecting the idea of the other sex he (or she) then behaves in the manner of that sex.

Theoretically, one could say that in homosexuality everything is normal *except* the sexuality. No one brought up with free sexual expression would ever *prefer* homosexuality, although in adolescence or later he may occasionally experiment with it. The feelings of closeness, intimacy, and companionship that so often prevail between friends of the same sex are valuable components of the human experience. Even the exclusivity of this relationship at certain ages in our culture (as among latency-age children) is a cultural artifact rather than a result of a biological drive. Further, the very violence sometimes displayed by groups of overt homosexuals is an indication that they are sometimes more interested in violence than in sex.

THE STRUCTURE OF SOCIETY

Finally, consideration must be given to the structure of society insofar as it affects sexual and love relationships.

As a working definition of love, I would suggest the following: Love develops as a result of satisfactory fulfillment of the needs of the pregenital stages. It must derive from loving feelings toward the parents. In adulthood, once these earlier stages are satisfactorily negotiated, *love is a feeling of mutual pleasure with another person.* If the other person is of the opposite sex, the mutual pleasure would lead to sexual relations from puberty on, perhaps from childhood on. If the other person is of the same sex, the mutual pleasure could lead to occasional sexual experimentation, but primarily to experiences of friendship, companionship, and social exchange.

It has been a thesis of this book that our society is a hate culture. As such, it offers few outlets for pleasure, and even fewer for the exchange of feelings of mutual pleasure with other people. No one can cross every *t* or dot every *i* to indicate exactly how society should be reorganized to allow love to have its day. But at least it is possible to stress the psychoanalytic vision, with its image of the kind of love society should help to cultivate.

Part IV

A Summing-up

Chapter 18

A Program for Progress and Reform

IN THIS FINAL chapter I wish to sum up the previous argument and to present my main theses in more direct form. In order to avoid any distraction I shall omit documentation and supporting evidence; all this can be found in the body of the text.

First, the growth of the psychoanalytic vision in Freud's own development was traced. He began in the 1890s with the exploration of neurosis, in accordance with the conceptualizations of his day. Nor did he in this period go far beyond his contemporaries.

The revolutionary change in Freud came about with his self-analysis, from about 1895 to 1902. It was here that he discovered the existence of incest, castration anxiety, the Oedipus complex, and other aspects of the psychosexual life of the child. Here too he originated a method of analysis that could be applied to other people. Experience has repeatedly shown that without personal analysis Freud's ideas are extremely difficult or impossible to grasp. Thus the first component of the analytic vision arose: a workable method for analysis and self-analysis.

With this method Freud developed the first system of psychoanalytic psychology, id psychology, in the period from 1900 to 1914. Its three cornerstones, apart from the analysis, were the unconscious, psychosexual development, and the concepts of transference and resistance as the essentials of psychotherapy. In this period Freud's vision deepened to help him realize that the world was very disturbed.

In the final period of his life, from 1914 until his death in 1939, Freud further elaborated the second system of psychoanalysis, that of ego psychology. The structural theory, involving the tripartite structure of id, ego, and superego, comes from this time. While the ego and id are refinements of earlier ideas, the superego was completely novel.

It was in this final stage that he also completed his vision of what the world could look like if it grasped the contributions of psychoanalysis. He saw psychoanalysis scientifically as the basis of psychology and the social sciences, while the technique of psychoanalysis, either pure or modified, could be applied to the broad mass of mankind. In these insights, however, he remained rather ambivalent, confounding his enemies and confusing his friends. Nevertheless the vision is there for all who wish to read it.

When Freud died, in September 1939, the world was in the midst of one of the worst conflagrations ever witnessed. Before it was to end some hundred million people were to die as a direct or indirect result of the actions of mad dictators. For the first time it was widely realized that large numbers of people here and abroad were seriously disturbed emotionally. Modern psychology was born.

During World War II psychoanalysis was perforce confined essentially to the military. It was only when the war was over that its enormous potentialities for good were recognized by political leaders and mental health professionals. Then began an enormous growth and an equally impressive fratricide. The mental health professions, psychiatry, psychology, and social work, expanded to such an extent that for all practical purposes they could be considered an entirely new profession—the fifth profession, as Henry was to call it. At the same time the professionals were involved in unceasing warfare among themselves. While many deplored the spectacle presented to the public, no one could do anything about it. Both the growth and the fratricide must be considered in evaluating subsequent developments.

One of the biggest changes was the expansion of psychotherapy to the entire population. Where before it had been confined to the markedly aberrant, the maladjustment neurosis, now it was embraced by wide sectors of the population, adjusted as well as maladjusted. The creation of a new profession was accompanied by a shift to the normal population, two dramatic leaps into the future.

Scientifically, psychoanalysis came to be seen, with Freud, as a system of psychology. It soon penetrated especially far into psychiatry and psychology, but also into many other fields. Many saw Freud's vision coming to realization; many others still fought it.

Vital to the new image of the sciences of man was a revised image of human nature. Previously social scientists had held to the nineteenth-century image of man as rational, conscious, and subject to external forces over which he had no control. Accordingly science had to concentrate on these external forces; psychology had little or nothing to do with it. Now, following Freud, there was a twentieth-century image holding that man was often unconscious, irrational, and subject to internal forces over which he could gain control through psychotherapy. This changed image of man led to an entirely different approach to the subject matter of psychology and the social sciences. While the academic world in general adhered to the nineteenth-century image, making little progress in its research endeavors, the clinical world was able to assimilate the twentieth-century image and make rapid strides toward understanding and helping suffering mankind.

The fratricidal warfare among psychotherapists revolved around a struggle for power. Many psychiatrists nominally embraced psychoanalysis, but it was an open question whether the embrace was oral-erotic (loving) or oral-sadistic (destructive). There is ample reason to believe that it was and is more destructive than erotic.

After War War II organized medicine made massive efforts to prevent the growth of other helping professions, and in particular to prevent them from offering psychotherapy. It tried to stop training, placed all kinds of legal obstacles in their path, and obstructed them in many other ways. As of 1980 its efforts have been remarkably unsuccessful. The newer professions have gained legal sanction, systematized training, and a wide popular following. Current statistics indicate that the number of nonmedical psychotherapists exceeds the number of medical.

In the battle between medicine and the nonmedical professions, the official psychoanalytic organizations played an ambivalent role. In some ways they seem to have identified with one of Freud's weaknesses, choosing psychiatry as the beloved friend and lay analysis as the hated enemy. But while publicly they condemned the lay analyst, privately they trained him. The training system adopted has always led to such bitter battles that strict control remained impossible.

The fights within the psychoanalytic organizations took on such intensity that more than one authority began to speak of the "crisis" in contemporary psychoanalysis. The political lines were accompanied by the most devious misrepresentations of theory on the part of both Freudians and neo-Freudians.

Yet in the midst of all this growth and fratricide the psychoanalytic vision persisted and made consistent progress. As Freud once said, the voice of reason is weak, but it persists until it gets a hearing. Psychoanalysis and the psychoanalytic vision are increasingly getting more of a hearing.

The essentials of mainstream psychoanalysis center upon the concept of the analytic ideal, which states that man can achieve the greatest happiness if he loves, seeks pleasure, has sexual gratification, feels yet is guided by reason, is part of a family structure, has a role in the social order, has an adequate sense of self, can communicate, has creative outlets, can work, and is free from psychiatric symptomatology. It is around this analytic ideal that both the science of man and the practice of psychotherapy can concentrate.

The vision of experimental psychology, approximately of the same vintage as Freud, was that somehow the secrets of human beings would be revealed through systematic experimentation guided by what were conceived to be the superior methods of the natural sciences, Typically, it has been shown that Wundt, the so-called father of experimental psychology, did not believe that it could unlock the mysteries of the deeper emotions, such as love, social life, and the like. What counted was not the text but the spirit.

Thus eventually within psychology the battle narrowed down to experimental versus clinical psychology. In experimental psychology learning theory became paramount; in clinical, psychoanalysis held sway. Meanwhile, within the larger professional body, experimental psychology allied itself with organic psychiatry and milieu social work. Their common enemy was psychotherapy; their common belief was in the nineteenth-century image of man, which emphatically denied the importance or even the existence of the inner forces of which the psychoanalysts spoke so much.

Experimental psychology prided itself on being "scientific," an honorific term that has supplanted "good" in the professional vocabulary. However, its claims to an exclusive lease on science could not be substantiated. Rather, it appears that experimental psychologists, like many social scientists, have misunderstood what actually happened in the natural sciences and have pursued a path that has not and cannot lead anywhere because it strays too far from the human material under investigation. Surprisingly, it would appear that psychoanalysis comes much closer to a scientific approach to the human being. It deals with relevant material, no matter how imprecise the outcome may be. Nor is the outcome so imprecise as has been supposed, as the Fisher–Greenberg synthesis of 1977 shows. These authors, after reviewing some two thousand studies, were able to conclude that psychoanalysis is by far the most extensively tested and the most completely verified theory of personality currently available. Within the field of psychotherapy, the widely quoted handbook by Garfield and Bergin (1978) grudgingly admitted that the evidence is now in favor of psychotherapy. The formation of a new division of psychoanalysis within the American Psychological Association marks the end of one era and the beginning of another.

In the field of psychotherapy most experimentalists have tended to favor behavior therapy and its variations. Because they were ignorant of the history of psychotherapy, they failed to grasp that behavior therapy is essentially a repetition of Freud's position of the 1890s, in which the therapeutic effect is achieved by making the unconscious (conditioned) conscious (deconditioned). These therapists failed to understand the forward sweep of Freud's work, in which transferences, the ego-id conflict, and philosophical assumptions of living eventually became part and parcel of the analytic enterprise.

The vision of organic psychiatry in 1900 was that mental illness would be shown to be the result of brain damage: Mind disease is brain disease. Two important discoveries seemed to favor this vision: the equation of paresis with the last stages of syphilis and the discovery of the EEG pattern for epilepsy. But in spite of heroic efforts to do more, biological psychiatry has no other striking successes to display. Many claims are made; all are questionable.

Historically, psychiatry may be dated from the French Revolution, thus making it a little less than two hundred years old. At that time doctors took over the care of the mentally ill from the clergy, who had in previous centuries tortured and murdered hundreds of thousands. Medicine gave these unfortunates humane treatment. Acting on the theory of brain damage, it also provided hospitals where they could be isolated and cared for. This attempt at hospitalization, which began on a large scale in the early 1800s, is now being discontinued, thus marking the defeat of a roughly two-hundred-year experiment.

Study of the historical record also indicates that medicine took over the care of the mentally ill because the clergy had been sadistic, indulging in such practices as witchhunts and inquisitions where the accused never had a chance. Toward the latter part of the twentieth century, medicine itself had become more cruel toward its mental patients. As a result their treatment was increasingly being returned to the nonmedical professions.

The paradox was noted that for two hundred years organic psychiatry has always been wrong about the mentally ill: in the nomenclature, in the diagnosis, in the treatment, and in the concepts of etiology and education. More than one expert in the field has called the treatment of the mentally ill a national disgrace. Yet in reaction to all this, psychiatry seeks more power rather than looking for the roots of its errors.

Much praise has been lavished on the drug revolution that began in the mid-1950s with the discovery of various neuroleptics and minor tranquilizers. Yet upon more careful examination, the effects of the drugs turn out to be obscure, uncertain, and in many cases damaging. At best the drugs offer temporary relief. Psychotics on drug treatment are doomed to gloomy lives. The side effects of the drugs may be serious, on rare occasions fatal.

Studies over the past two hundred years, from Jarvis in nineteenth-century Massachusetts, through Sullivan in the 1920s, and down to Bleuler in the 1960s, all show that in the great majority of cases patients labeled schizophrenic will respond to kindly care and understanding; yet this fact is denied over and over by the organically minded psychiatrist.

The vast expansion of psychiatric services raises the question of how well trained today's psychiatrists are to deliver such services. Research indicates that they are not well trained at all, particularly with regard to psychotherapy. An official study published in 1975 presents a deplorable state of affairs within the office practice of psychiatry. Other incidents, such as the acceptance of behavior therapy, the refusal to condemn Russian psychiatric terror, and the reclassification of homosexuality, all indicate that the American Psychiatric Association is as much a political body designed to protect the economic interests of its members as a scientific body established to resolve pressing scientific problems, if not more so.

Thus the vision of organic psychiatry has not been realized. The great advances that have been made come from psychoanalysis and its applications.

A general review of theory in the social sciences shows that by and large they have held to the nineteenth-century image of man. All of them developed *pari passu* with psychoanalysis—roughly in the last hundred years. When they began, psychology in its modern form did not exist, and their founders could not find any useful psychology to incorporate in their studies. Accordingly, and also in order to free themselves from philosophical speculation, they rejected a psychological approach and the newer image of man provided by Freud.

Like experimental psychology, the social sciences overidentified with the natural sciences, overlooking the fact that what is needed to understand man better is the conquest of bias, not the accumulation of special skills. But the mirage of mathematics continued to lure them. Methodologically they bogged down in such a morass that more than one expert half-humorously advised that all social science research should be thrown out the window and a new start undertaken. Surface research based on questionnaires and superficial probing nevertheless continued, even if the results impressed no one.

In the course of time, the social science disciplines became isolated from one another. Each had to have its own separate identity, even though no agreement could ever be reached even on their definitions. In reaction to this isolation came an increasing demand for interdisciplinary cooperation, a tacit admission that the division into a large number of disciplines was arbitrary and unjustified. Examination of the history of each discipline also revealed that the choice of subject matter in many cases resulted from historical accident. The uncertainty of social facts has also been used to bolster skepticism, instead of reinforcing more careful methodology.

It is in the area of methodology that psychoanalysis makes one of its principal contributions to all the social sciences. For with the newer image of man, it can help to unearth facts that were previously obfuscated, and by the careful study of individuals it can provide data that are otherwise inaccessible. Unfortunately, it appears that only persons who have had some personal analysis are able to appreciate the profundity of the psychoanalytic contribution, so the inroads of the newer methodologies have been limited.

Attention was then directed to each of the disciplines that deal with man.

Examination of history began with the observation that a clear-cut definition of the field has yet to be found. Most meaningful seems to be Gay's notion of history as critical reflection on the past, which would equate history with philosophy.

In accordance with the nineteenth-century image of man, for a long time historians have attempted to tease out of their field some inexorable laws that would explain what happened and why. This traditional vision of the historian has had to be abandoned, for every law put forth has sooner or later been disproved. Apart from critical reflection, the most meaningful observation seems to be Jacob Burckhardt's that history is the record of what one age finds of interest in another.

Examination of standard treatises revealed that in traditional history the ideology of victory dominates: History is seen as the account of how one nation or group after another came to conquer part or all of the known world. In such an account the victors became all-important; the vanquished are ignored.

Further, in the chronicle of victories, the brutalities and massacres that have characterized conquest from time immemorial have generally been underplayed. Even for our own age, the mass murders committed by Hitler and Stalin are conveniently omitted.

The role of slavery in the course of civilization has been understated. Had Freud appeared in an earlier century, he could not have seen work as part of normality, for so much of the important work was still being done by slaves.

The attitude of previous centuries toward madness was explored. It seems probable that throughout the years man has been more insane than sane, more irrational than rational. Bleuler's description of the phasic-benign pattern of schizophrenia as the typical one can be applied to the past.

Some subtle changes in the humanitarian ideals that dominate our present lives seem to have occurred around the time of the French Revolution. The change may be best understood in terms of the gradual awareness of the analytic ideal. It culminated in Freud's discovery of psychoanalysis a hundred years later and has progressed steadily ever since. Most likely it is this slight shift in the direction of the analytic ideal that accounts for the disappearance of slavery in the nineteenth century.

Two intriguing theses come out of the material. First, the switch to the analytic ideal around 1800 may have arisen out of a revulsion against the bestiality, barbarism, and cruelty of previous centuries. The shift from the clergy to medicine in the treatment of the mentally ill may have been part of this revulsion. Second, future generations may yet come to see the nineteenth and twentieth centuries as the time when the nature of mental illness was uncovered and effective treatment and preventive measures instituted, in much the same way as the conquest of physical illnesses from 1300 to 1700 eventually resulted in an enormous lengthening of the life span from 1800 on. It may also be that both of these shifts were made possible by the lessening of the hold of Christianity on men's minds, because Christianity, whatever it may have preached, in practice in previous centuries represented a system of delusion, destructiveness, and paranoia.

Two much-disputed recent movements in history, cliometrics and psychohistory, are given consideration. Neither is new. Cliometrics is a refinement of previous tools, but the notion that through such refinement the historical picture will emerge more clearly is another illusion nursed by a misconception of mathematics. Psychohistory has always existed. The difference is that because depth psychology is now available, psychohistory can now be written more intelligently.

Sociology and anthropology confront the individual with the society or culture. The external forces have been sought in the form of social facts à la Durkheim, and a sharp separation from psychology has been undertaken. It has been forgotten that, when Durkheim wrote, this separation may have been necessary because psychology was not yet properly born; it is no longer necessary.

Primarily sociologists study a variety of psychological events and seek out the social forces that will help to explain these events. These forces then are seen as superordinate social facts. Because the sociologist is much more familiar with the social than with the psychological forces, he tends to hold to the nineteenth-century image of man and to see the social as the primary causative factor. This is the result of bias, not of objective evaluation. An example is the labeling theory of social deviance, popular in certain quarters.

Again, there has been a strong tendency to idealize the community. A community or group or class is seen as something inherently "good," isolation or alienation from the community as something "bad." This fails to distinguish between constructive and destructive groups, even though Sumner almost a hundred years ago showed that in-groups maintain themselves by finding and killing enemies. Numerous studies by now have shown that the mental health of the contemporary world is deplorable. If groups, organizations, communities, classes are mentally disturbed, then their cohesiveness may be calamitous rather than desirable. A survey of the important institutions in our own society indicates that we are living in a hate culture rather than a love culture.

Social scientists, especially in the field of sociology, have tended to become social activists. Confronted by large-scale misery, the natural tendency is to move to change the structure of society. Unfortunately, in this process the possibility of changing individuals as well through psychotherapy tends to be overlooked or played down.

In anthropology, the main external force investigated has been the superorganic concept of culture. By now it has become evident that culture is what the individual denizens of any society do, and a "science of culture" cannot be different from a science of psychology. Indeed, anthropology was initially used in the sense in which modern psychology is used; the differences between the two fields represent historical accidents.

In economics, the external force sought has been that which guided "economic man": impersonal and unsocial. The image of economic man is in fact prototypically the nineteenth-century image of man. The search for the forces that control economic man dominated the thought of scholars until roughly 1900, when a number of economists began to see that here too man can become master of his own destiny, and that these forces must be controlled to serve humanitarian purposes.

The Keynesian revolution of the 1930s, although not directly connected with psychoanalysis, was in the spirit of the twentieth-century image of man. Since that time economic analysis has perforce had to take the human factor into account.

In the area of work considerable advances have been made in replacing the Protestant ethic with a rationale that would stimulate modern man to be more productive. By and large the answers have been sought in the numerous pragmatic programs visible all over the market place. In many of these improvements of the work life psychotherapy has played a meaningful role.

Religion is the field *par excellence* in which external forces reign. In the eighteenth century religion came under attack because it was too absurd (Voltaire); in the twentieth it has come under attack because it is too infantile. Analysts in general have found religion to be a series of empty rituals, and few have seen any role for it in human happiness.

Historically, the hold of religion on men's minds can be ascribed to the therapeutic functions it serves: Man, frightened by inner as well as external demons, has sought comfort and solace in the rituals and beliefs of religion. But this has been both rational and irrational, and whether religion has actually served as an adequate psychotherapy remains open to question. Religion should be seen mainly as a step in man's development toward a freer, more conscious humanity.

Philosphers at times have had some inkling of the internal forces that move men, but their psychology before the modern era has been so grossly inadequate that these insights have fallen on barren soil. The critical function of the philosopher is no longer important in the modern scientific world.

Traditionally, many philosophies have offered men ways of living, just as religion has. In so doing they have also performed a psychotherapeutic function. Analytically, this function merely serves to shift the person from one superego system to another; it creates no fundamental intrapsychic change. Psychoanalysis offers a more meaningful philosphy than any other and also serves as a critical basis for evaluating other aspects of man's life. Because of this, psychoanalysis may be seen as a philosophical system that replaces all previous philosophies.

In literature and art an external force has been sought in connection with creativity. Through the ages the creative individual has been seen as either a genius or a madman. Aestheticians and critics concern themselves mainly with the manifestiations of the geniuses and very little with the psychological and social conditions that allow geniuses to flourish. Here psychoanalysis provides a much-needed corrective in two ways. First, it has shown how any work of art is intimately bound up with the personality and inner conflicts of the artist. And second it has shown that every man has some innate artistic ability, so that often what matters is not so much talent as the work performed to put that talent to use.

Much light has been shed on the psychology of creativity by psychoanalysis. The range of human abilities rarely shows any quantum leaps from one person to another; there is rather an orderly progression from the least able to the most able. Hence the creative individual is simply more able than others, not qualitatively different. An essential distinction must also be drawn between inner and outer creativity. Inner creativity is the growth process in which everybody can participate unless hampered by neurotic obstacles. Outer creativity is the ability to produce something new for the world. Such an ability is much rarer; it is also heavily dependent on external circumstances.

The cursory examination of the social sciences and humanities has revealed that psychosocial causation is exceedingly complex. This explains why research in these areas has been so inadequate and inconclusive. In general more research has been done by academically positioned individuals who have placed the greatest stress on external forces (nineteenth-century man). Psychoanalysis can provide a much-needed balance by showing how the dynamics of the internal forces can be elicited and brought into a meaningful context. For a full analysis of any situation, knowledge of both external and internal forces is essential.

Next, attention was directed to psychotherapy, one of the most important inventions arising from psychoanalysis. While psychotherapy in one form or another had always existed prior to Freud it was mainly a method of manipulation; it had relied on magic, religion, philosophy, or more recently medicine. What Freud introduced was the inner world, the heart of psychology. After him psychotherapy became scientific and based on understanding the inner causes of difficulties.

Freud himself went through four stages in the evolution of his technique: (1) making the unconscious conscious, (2) working through transferences and resistances, (3) replacing the id with the ego, and (4) working out a suitable philosphy of living. Only the first of these has been grasped by the other schools, which have usually reformulated it without knowing it (for example, behavior therapy or Ellis's rational-emotive therapy).

When the shift to the entire population as subjects for therapy occurred after World War II, the established professions were not prepared for it. They were inadequately trained and inadequate in their conceptualizations. Still, they were asked to treat, and they could not refuse the power and income offered to them. Thus arose the half-trained professions that have dominated the field ever since. Most of these professionals inveigh mightily against psychoanalysis not because they have studied it and found it wanting but because they are unfamiliar with it, either theoretically or practically.

Perusal of the writings of the nonanalytic therapists discloses that most of them go back to the Freud of the 1890s. Some are visionaries without technique (Rogers, Gestaltists), others are technicians without vision (behavior therapists, rational-emotive, reality therapy). Intellectually their writings are at a shockingly low level.

Analysis teaches that psychotherapy is a method of social reform designed to transform a hate culture into a love culture. In the individual case the person is brought as close to the analytic ideal as possible. Sometimes this is quite close, and in other cases a considerable distance remains. The key concept is love.

In an attempt to clarify love, material is drawn from history, anthropology, sociology, ethology, child psychology, religion, philosophy, literature, and art. All of these point to a number of significant conclusions. First of all, love leads to happiness, hatred to unhappiness. Second, what has been seen so far in the course of history is largely a series of neurotic distortions of love. And third, because

love is the key concept in psychotherapy, the vision of psychoanalysis is that psychotherapy is a way of teaching others how to love.

Finally the connection between psychotherapy and love is explored more fully. A number of case histories are presented in which
the patients initially thought that they were in love: submissiveness
(the clinging vine), extramarital affairs, promiscuity, rescue fantasies (love for prostitutes), rejection (unrequited love), perversion,
marriage on the rebound, love and suicide, homosexual love, religious love, and romantic love. In all of these the kind of love with
which the patient comes into therapy is first seen as a neurotic distortion of love. This distortion derives from a variety of inner conflicts,
which come to the fore in the analysis. When they are cleared up the
initial love then disappears or recedes into the background. A new
self-image, confident and self-loving, is formed. Then a mature,
gratifying love can be reached.

The developmental obstacles to love have been well researched
by analysts from Freud on; less clear is the definition of normal mature love. Such a definition is offered, after the successful passage of
the earlier stages: Love is mutual pleasure. Jealousy is seen as a cultural restriction. Monogamy, for which the basis is mutual love, is a
new attempt in human history; it is full of difficulties. Sexuality
without love is possible, but love without sexuality is not. Parenthood is a different kind of love, though there too the physical element must remain strong. And finally the society must be reorganized to facilitate more love experiences and inhibit the more usual
hate experiences.

Where Do We Go from Here?

The previous chapters have offered many suggestions for progress and reform. These can now be summarized and systematized.

TOWARD A NEW PROFESSION

From an early date Freud saw that a new profession was indispensable to the psychoanalytic vision. He wished to set up such a
profession, whose practitioners "need not be doctors and should not
be priests." The creation of this profession has run up against such
enormous obstacles that much rethinking is needed.

At present most professionals come from one of the three major health professions. First they must get a degree, then they get special postdoctoral training to acquire the skills needed to do psychotherapy. In general, their previous academic training is largely irrelevant. The situation, besides being intellectually unsatisfactory, is extremely burdensome to the new therapist.

Ideally, it has been argued, all therapists should be analysts or at least thoroughly trained analytically (the difference is trivial). Analytic training has four phases: personal analysis with a specially qualified training analyst; a curriculum of theoretical studies; control analyses; and society control of training. On the score of the personal analysis, the curriculum, and control analyses there is no argument: All are indispensable to the well-trained clinician. Questions arise about the choice of training analysts, where the curriculum should be taught, and the society control.

Originally anyone could be a training analyst if he had more knowledge and experience than his patient. Gradually the societies weeded out those whom they considered less competent and promoted those whom they considered more competent to be the sole training analysts. This system has led to such bitter disputes that it is of questionable value. It would seem to be just as effective to let any qualified member of an analytic society analyze the prospective analyst. Some societies do work that way, and it has yet to be shown that they are worse off than the others.

The curriculum for the prospective analyst actually covers the entire range of psychology and psychiatry. Inasmuch as it involves theoretical instruction, it could more profitably be taught in academic institutions, where such theoretical instruction is well organized. Actually, much of this already goes on in academic institutions, so that by the time a person comes to an analytic institute, he is frequently confronted with an enormous amount of needless repetition. If it were better focused in academic departments of psychology, this repetion could be avoided.*

Considerable acrimony has also resulted from the attempt of the societies to control training. Here too a unique situation has arisen, with no real parallel in any other field. Because the analytic society is a transitional object historically, created because of the hostility of both the medical and the academic schools, it may be expected to serve less and less of a function as this hostility diminishes.

*This reasoning lies behind the program headed by the present writer at Mercy College and the New York School of Professional Psychology.

Viewed in terms of the larger picture, society control does not exist for the total body of psychotherapists, only for those interested in joining a particular society. There are literally thousands of analysts who have received "unofficial" training with the same essential components: personal analysis, curriculum, control analyses. There is little reason to believe that these persons are far inferior to those who have been through the standard procedures. In one large analytic institute the physicians who were dropped because of incompetence formed their own society, and the public never knew the difference. Society control creates more problems than it solves.

Thus ideally new professionals would receive personal analysis from an analyst of their choice, would study the curriculum in an academic setting, and would find control analyses on their own. Whatever deficiencies would result from this system would be far less damaging than what is going on now.

The question of whether medical training is essential for the practice of psychotherapy can by now be answered quite easily: It is not. In spite of determined medical opposition, the bulk of psychotherapy today is carried on by nonmedical therapists, largely psychologists and social workers, with a fourth group, mental health counselors, coming up strong.

While some have even argued that medical training per se is harmful to the future psychotherapist, this seems to be an exaggeration in the other direction. However, it is true that in the present cultural climate when a practitioner does have an M.D. degree, there is a strong temptation to prescribe drugs to excess, especially with the more refractory patients. Even a cursory glance at the pages of the *American Journal of Psychiatry* reveals that almost all of the advertising comes from drug companies. That this advertising and propaganda influence the scientific opinions of psychiatrists in favor of drugs has been suggested by a number of authorities.

This should not be understood as an argument against drug therapy as such. Where drugs are used for rational purposes, with knowledge of their effects and lack of effects, they may be and often are of great value. What is undesirable is the widespread practice of prescribing drugs *instead of psychotherapy* for any and all emotional disturbances. Unfortunately, the evidence is that the bulk of the psychiatric profession's members would resort to drugs because they know them better rather than to psychotherapy, where they are inadequately trained and where the personal involvement is so much greater.

Nor is this to be taken as any argument against properly conducted research in psychopharmacology. Here too what is essential is that the established facts should be separated from the speculative theories.

The other degrees generally considered to be preliminary to psychoanalytic training are likewise thoroughly disorganized. Organic psychiatry, experimental psychology, and milieu social work are all united in their antagonism to psychotherapy. Once a person takes the degree, further training in psychotherapy is fraught with perils and obstacles.

Because the degree programs are artifacts of history, it would be far more sensible to change them to prepare the practitioner to do psychotherapy properly. In spite of the surface hullabaloo, many changes along these lines are being introduced all over the country. However, the official party lines of the professions are opposed to psychotherapy (and do not understand it), so the actual situation looks like confusion worse confounded.

A consistent appreciation of the psychoanalytic vision would do much to undo this confusion. It should be recognized that we are in the process of creating an entirely new profession, psychotherapist, which, though it may have some of the same titles as the older ones, still represents something entirely different. The most essential requirement for this profession is the capacity for warmth, empathy, and love on the part of the therapist, whose job it is to teach these qualities to other people. Given the present social structure, warmth, empathy, and love can be acquired only through a long personal analysis, which should begin as early as possible. Other aspects of the training should be centered on this vital personal experience.

TOWARD ONE UNIFIED SCIENCE OF MAN

Entrenched interests are so powerful in each of the "disciplines" that it will no doubt prove harder to reach one science of man than to reach one unified group of psychotherapists. Nevertheless, it can and should be done.

All of the social sciences began with the pre-Freudian image of man as rational, conscious, and subject to control by powerful external forces. All came to maturity somewhere around the turn of the century. At the time there was no psychology worth mentioning, so all adopted the commonsense psychology of the day. In accordance with this commonsense psychology and the older image of man, they sought to identify the powerful external forces that were directing man's destiny: social facts in sociology, superorganic culture in anthropology, the "inexorable" laws of history, the "iron" law of wages, the "brain damage" of the psychotic, the "laws" of learning in psychology, and the like. Because the academic world lives by the force of tradition, the followers of the founders, without realizing it, held on to their unverbalized assumptions about human beings. This is still the case today.

By contrast, the Freudian image of man stresses the internal forces, seeing man as often irrational, unconscious, and subject to internal forces over which he can acquire control through psychotherapy or psychoanalysis. Man thus becomes to a much greater extent free and independent. There is no assumption here that man is subject only to these internal forces—a balance between the internal and external must always be struck.

The notion that man can have greater control over his fate has caught on among many thinkers, quite independent of psychoanalysis. Thus in economics Keynes in particular freed man from the shackles of the classical assumptions. Galbraith today is the most eminent economist who is continuing in his spirit.

Human affairs are so complex that it is understandable that efforts at simplification will always be proposed. The history of the field is not encouraging to these simplifications. It will always be necessary to consider both internal and external factors in any psychosocial situation. From Freud on, the better analysts have always stressed this complexity, but they have rarely been heard.

Any investigation of a human problem inevitably brings in a large number of different disciplines. It it does not, it is so woefully incomplete that it becomes worthless.

Consider, for example, the plight of the blacks in this country. Recently a number of historians have tried to show that the black family was and is more stable than had been "supposed." Various inferences are then drawn from this stability. Left out of consideration are the inner dynamics of the family, the culture of poverty, the economic situation, the linguistic factor, even questions of health and longevity. The isolation of stability from everything else proves nothing. If the current life of blacks is to be fully understood, there must be an examination of their history, economic well-being (or ill-being), language, schooling, health, socioeconomic status, culture patterns, art forms (often a reaction to extreme poverty and misery), religion, and philosophical outlook, among many other matters.

Thus if the focus is on the problem, the barriers between the disciplines disappear. If the focus is on the discipline, the barriers return. If a full understanding is the desideratum, it is clearly better to focus on the problem.

What problems should be investigated? No conflict need arise here: the same problems under investigation now. Only it would be better, since the core is the human being, to organize the problems around the analytic ideal. In the past this has not been done, and as a result an enormous amount of motion has been wasted. It is only recently that such vital questions as love, sexuality, the self-image, communication, and the like have been made the subject of scientific inquiry. Nor can it be argued that the data are not available; wherever competent scholars look they find huge banks of material.

The avoidance of human topics is the consequence of bias rather than of lack of skill. Once this bias is overcome, new and more pressing questions come to the fore.

But how is the bias to be overcome? There are only two ways known: education and psychotherapy. Since education is still in the hands of people affected by the bias, psychotherapy is left alone with the task. Thus it would make sense to analyze not only future therapists but also future social scientists. The same biases that interfere with adequate therapy interfere with competent social science.

Once this bias is overcome, the pressing issues in human life can be pursued more vigorously. It is not only the treatment of the mentally ill that is a national disgrace; the lack of understanding of mental illness is a national disgrace as well. As noted earlier, the meticulous work of Manfred Bleuler, certainly the most meaningful study of schizophrenia to appear in the past quarter of a century, has shown that the old catastrophic schizophrenia has virtually disappeared. This disappearance can only be ascribed to vastly improved public education and knowledge, for the profession itself has by and large lagged far behind.

If mental illness is poorly understood, mental health is also. With the decline of religion, the public has increasingly turned to psychiatry and psychology for advice, guidance, and assistance in leading a happier life. So many popularizers are at work that self-help literature has become a genre all to itself. The profession should support this kind of literature when it is well done.

One consequence of this approach is that a new division suggests itself to replace the older compartmentalization into different disciplines. The skills required for gathering data are quite different from those involved in interpreting data. For the former, mathematical and statistical knowledge is essential; for the latter humanitarian and psychological skills. Hence it would be desirable to separate the two tasks. Let the statistically minded gather the data, and let the psychologically minded interpret them. Then the confusion apparent in such developments as cliometrics or mathematical economics would be avoided.

In this way one majestic profession would emerge: the social scientist. Trained in the data of all the areas in which the human being functions, he would be able to offer a synthesis of viewpoints far more meaningful than the fractionalized material currently displayed. His essential training would be in the fields of human concern to gather his background, and in psychotherapy to overcome his biases.

Toward Social Reform

Social scientists almost automatically become social critics, developing as a result of their observations of human misery a natural desire to reform society. To make such reform most meaningful the analysis of the situations must be made as adequate as possible.

Here once more the biases of the investigators immediately come into play. It has been seen how there are two entirely different kinds of social science in the world today, one dominant in the Western democratic countries, the other in the totalitarian groups. Within Western culture there are also two kinds of social science, one dominated by the nineteenth-century image of man, the other by the Freudian twentieth-century image. Obviously from the very beginning bias enters the picture and plays a most significant role.

For effective social reform problems beyond the control of the individual must be separated from those within his control. In this separation the existence of control through psychotherapy must be explicitly recognized.

If any lesson is to be learned from the revolutions of the twentieth century it is that the economic system as such is less important than how power is exercised. Many scholars have shown that "capitalist" and "socialist" economies are much closer than had been thought. What is most relevant is the degree of coercion and violence adopted for the maintenance of power.

The psychoanalytic vision from the very beginning has turned against violence. By contrast many social reformers have been indifferent to violence or have even welcomed it, with the argument that no ruling class in history has ever turned over its power peacefully. With this rationalization, the violence that has erupted from the revolutions designed to put an end to violence has multiplied beyond measure. A basic feature of the social reform envisioned by psychoanalysis is the removal of hatred and violence.

There is a strong tendency to isolate certain segments or groups in society and to focus heavily on them: women, blacks, the poor, and the like. Combined with this is the notion, unfortunately all too widespread, that psychoanalysts do not concern themselves with minority groups. This antagonism derives from a misunderstanding. The psychoanalyst is just as much concerned with social injustice as anyone else. But in his professional capacity he must limit himself to those who can benefit from his services, agreeing that the others require a reordering of their socioeconomic circumstances.

On the other hand, in practice the demand for a social reordering is often used as a resistance to inner change; the patient argues that the only thing that counts is external change. Whatever the merits of the argument may be from a theoretical point of view, in the actual situation such an attitude all too often prevents the individual from seeing that beneficial changes may still occur within the given conditions. Again a flexible attitude is essential.

Allied to this question is the observation that many liberals have made in the present century that many of the most violent upheavals have yielded bitter fruit, with the revolution beginning to eat its own children before it has even digested the original enemy. Both external and internal change have to be evaluated carefully; extreme attitudes in either direction are apt to be misleading. As a rule totalitarian governments try to deny any social problems; but when the veil is lifted, they seem to have many of the same problems that exist elsewhere.

The psychoanalytic vision stresses two tools as methods of social reform: education and psychotherapy. In education psychoanalysis has served as a guide; in therapy, as a leader. In both cases a restructuring of the existing environment has been attempted in many different ways. In the family, for example, there have been attempts to introduce extended families, multiple families, wife-swapping, communal families, and even the destruction of the family altogether. None of these ideas has proved to be of lasting value, and mankind always seems to come back to a family built around the nuclear core. Thus again the inner change is the decisive component that psychoanalysis can contribute.

The Essence of the Psychoanalytic Vision: From a Hate Culture to a Love Culture

Like all the social sciences, psychoanalysis also seeks to transform society. It sees our society as one in which a hate culture predominates. Scientifically, it is essential to see how all the components of the hate culture interact, so that alteration of one part will not materially affect the whole structure. Nevertheless, a consistent attack on all the undesirable aspects of the culture should eventually produce beneficial results. Such a reform effort must be guided above all by the conviction that the hate culture should be transformed into a love culture.

Toward a Psychoanalytic Utopia

Modern man is in an eternal quandary. Every step forward seems to be marked by the emergence of new and less controllable problems. Christianity has become a useless relic. Sex is now easy but unsatisfying. The American dream looks impossible. The Marxist hope has turned into a threatening Russian juggernaut. Drugs are at best band aids. The Eastern religions look like a kind of suicide.

The psychoanalytic vision offers a way out. At present it remains a Utopian solution. Yet at least it indicates a direction in which man can move.

Necessarily the psychoanalytic Utopia works by way of education and persuasion. In some respects its effects have been noticeable; in others it has scarcely made a ripple. To push it further, different approaches to different groups of the society must be distinguished: for the mental health profession, for the social scientist, and for society at large.

For the *profession* the principal need is more adequate training. Of the approximately 200,000 psychiatrists, psychologists, and social workers in the country, perhaps 5 percent have some clear idea of what they are doing. The rest bumble along as technicians without vision.

This situation has arisen because of what we have referred to as the "diploma disease." From the very beginning Freud stressed the need for personal analysis, first as self-analysis, later as analysis by a more experienced person. Instead the emphasis was shifted to the degree—M.D., Ph.D., or M.S.W. The result has been referred to as the half-trained professions.

Paradoxically, the leaders of analysis have sought power rather than the expansion of training. It is startling, in fact, to discover what strenuous efforts have been made to *prevent* adequate training. The euphemism for this prevention is "society control," an aspect of training that has never even been seriously discussed.

The alliance of official analysis with psychiatry and medicine has helped to turn the United States into a drug-ridden country. At present (Cummings, 1979) one of every six teenagers suffers from a severe addictive problem. At any given time one out of every seven Americans is regularly taking a psychotropic drug prescribed by a physician.

Thus for the profession the Utopian pathway lies first in returning to psychoanalysis and psychotherapy as the preferred modes of treatment, and second in a vast expansion of all training facilities.

For the *social sciences* a number of changes are indicated. First of all the older nineteenth-century image of man must be replaced by the newer Freudian image if any profound observations of the social scene are to be made. Yet such a change is by no means easy to achieve. It is easily demonstrable that few leading social scientists are sufficiently conversant with the doctrines of psychoanalysis to present them correctly to their students. E.g., Manuel and Manuel in their recently published *Utopian Thought* (1979) offer a completely distorted account of the Freudian position. In particular they are blissfully unaware that the essence of the Freudian Utopia lies in analysis, not in one or another doctrine, and that analysis is an essentially novel idea.

It was shown earlier that psychoanalysis has penetrated most deeply in those fields where its practitioners have had some personal analysis. Thus the most feasible way to transform the social sciences is to insist that personal analysis be part of the training of every social scientist. Only in this way will one valid unified science of man be fully established.

Again one finds that without sufficient psychological under-standing the most elementary errors are projected all over, with pro-found effects on large sectors of society. Thus in education in the last twenty years the concept of "minimal brain dysfunction" or MBD has gained wide currency. Essentially it means that children who do not do well in school have something wrong with their brains, even though this brain damage is undetectable by any avail-able techniques. In their most recent review of the topic Rie and Rie (1980) conclude that the entire concept of MBD is a myth, and a to-tally unnecessary one. Nevertheless this myth persists, to the serious detriment of the entire educational system

For *the public at large* the greatest need is for education in the components of the analytic ideal. In some respects this task is easier than that of transforming the professions, because the public has less dry rot to unlearn. Nevertheless, its difficulties should not be under-estimated, It should be emphasized that the heart of the psychoana-lytic philosophy lies in the transformation of a hate culture into a love culture by means of universal analysis.

So for all groups the essential path to Utopia lies through analy-sis or self-understanding. This is the heart of the psychoanalytic vi-sion. Will the profession take hold of this vision and pursue it, or will it go down in the books as another futile effort to rescue man-kind? What will happen to the psychoanalytic vision?

Notes

For fuller data on the publications cited in the Notes, see the Bibliography following this section.

Abbreviations Used in the Notes and Bibliography

CP   Collected works of authors other than Freud
IJP   *International Journal of Psychoanalysis*
JAPA   *Journal of the American Psychoanalytic Association*
PQ   *Psychoanalytic Quarterly*
PSC   *Psychoanalytic Study of the Child*
PSM   *Psychosomatic Medicine*
SE   Standard Edition of Freud's works
           The Standard Edition is arranged chronologically, in 24 volumes. For individual books and papers cited, the reader should consult the appropriate volume in the Standard Edition.

Chapter 1. The Central Argument

1. J. H. Randall, one of the most brilliant American philosophers of the twentieth century, in his book *The Making of the Modern Mind* (1976) presents a completely distorted account of psychoanalysis (pp. 516–517). Many other examples could be cited.
2. *Partisan Review,* XLVI (1979): 515.

Chapter 2. The Expansion of Horizons

1. H. Nunberg and E. Federn, eds., *Minutes of the Vienna Psychoanalytic Society,* I: 396.
2. *Ibid.,* II: 27.

3. *Ibid.,* II: 561.
4. *Ibid.,* II: 564.
5. D. Anzieu, *L'Auto-Analyse de Freud.* An English translation has been announced by International Universities Press but has not yet appeared.
6. *Ibid.,* p. 685.
7. SE, V: 636–37.
8. E. Erikson, "The Dream Specimen of Psychoanalysis," *JAPA,* 2 (1954) 5–56.
9. SE, XII; 169–70.
10. Cf. M. Burr, *History of Autobiography,* and P. Delany, *British Autobiography in the 17th Century.*
11. Attempts by revisionist historians such as Hannah Decker (1977), claiming that the Freudian story of isolation is a "myth," are wholly incorrect. See Fine, 1979a.
12. Peter Gay and R. N. Webb, *History of Modern Europe,* p. 929.
13. O. Hale, *The Great Illusion: 1900–1914.*
14. *Ibid.,* p. xiii.
15. E. Jones, *The Life and Work of Sigmund Freud,* 2: 170.
16. *Ibid.,* 1: 304.
17. P. Roche de Coppens, *The Ideal Man in Classical Sociology.*
18. E. Durkheim, *Suicide,* p. 67.
19. *Ibid.,* Editor's Introduction by George Simpson, p. 17.
20. M. Weber, *The Protestant Ethic,* p. 244.
21. SE, XIV: 16.
22. E. Jones, *The Life and Work of Sigmund Freud,* vol. 2, chap. 6.
23. M. Harris, *The Rise of Modern Anthropological Theory,* p. 291.
24. M. Fortes, "Custom and Coercion," *International Review of Psychoanalysis,* 1977, pp. 133–34.
25. SE, XX: 70.
26. E. Jones, *The Life and Work of Sigmund Freud,* 2: 347.
27. H. Nunberg and E. Federn, eds., *Minutes of the Vienna Psychoanalytic Society,* II: 236.
28. *Psychoanalysis and Faith,* p. 126.
29. SE, XX: 230.
30. W. Henry, *The Fifth Profession,* p. 2.

Chapter 3. Mainstream Psychoanalysis: A Statement of Essentials

1. A. L. Kroeber and C. Kluckhohn, *Culture,* p. 357.
2. "Myths and Reality," U.S. Department of Labor, April, 1971. Cited in *Work in America,* p. 57.

Chapter 4. The Vision of Experimental Psychology

1. G. Murphy, *Historical Introduction to Modern Psychology*, p. 169.
2. In D. Rapaport, *Influence of Freud on American Psychology*, p. 34.
3. E. Nagel, *The Structure of Science*, p. 480.
4. In D. Rapaport, *Influence of Freud on American Psychology*, p. 60.
5. E. Nagel, "Psychology and The Philosophy of Science," in B. Wolman and E. Nagel, eds., *Scientific Psychology*, pp. 25–26.
6. For example, H. Hartman, Review of Sears, *PQ*, 13 (1944): 101–2.
7. B. F. Skinner, *Beyond Freedom and Dignity*, p. 12.
8. A. Bandura, "Behavior Theory and the Models of Man," *American Psychologist*, 29 (1974): 859–69.
9. Skinner, *Beyond Freedom and Dignity*, p. 182.
10. W. Reich, "Diagnosing Soviet Dissidents," *Harper's*, 251, no. 1539, (August 1978): 31–37.
11. E. Nagel, *The Structure of Science*, p. 15.
12. E. Boring in *Psychoanalysis as Seen by Psychoanalyzed Psychologists*, p. 10.
13. In N. Hanson, *Patterns of Discovery*, p. 119.
14. Skinner, *Beyond Freedom and Dignity*, p. 8.
15. Mackenzie, "Behaviorism and the Limits of Scientific Method," *Contemporary Psychology*, July 1978.
16. G. S. Klein, "The Role of Consciousness in Psychoanalytic Theory," *JAPA*, 7, (1959): 15–34.
17. Quoted in Murphy, *Historical Introduction* p. 176.
18. A. D. Baddeley, *Psychology of Memory*, p. 270.
19. S. S. Stevens, *Handbook of Experimental Psychology*, p. 811.
20. F. M. Andrews and S. B. Withey, *Social Indicators of Well-Being*, p. 21.
21. N. Bradburn, *The Structure of Psychological Well-Being*, p. 226.
22. *Ibid.*, p. 40.
23. A. Kinsey et al., *Sexuality in the Human Male*, p. 80.
24. A. Kinsey et al., *Sexuality in the Human Female*, p. 584.
25. A. Leighton, *The Character of Danger*, p. 131.
26. E. Chinoy, *Automobile Workers and the American Dream*, p. xiv.
27. F. Herzberg, *Work and the Nature of Man*, Ch. 8.
28. *Ibid.*, p. 165.
29. *Ibid.*, p. 167.
30. G. Murphy, *Historical Introduction*, pp. 430–31.

Chapter 5. The Vision of Organic Psychiatry

1. D. Musto, *The American Disease*, pp. 253–54.
2. E. Jones, *Free Associations*, pp. 145–48.

3. E. Jones, *Life and Work of Freud*, 2: 98.

4. *Ibid.*, 2: 109.

5. L. Srole and A. N. Fisher, *Mental Health in the Metropolis*, 1978, p. 205 (revised edition of Rennie, 1962).

6. W. Henry, *The Fifth Profession*, p. 168.

7. *Ibid.*, p. 42.

8. D. Musto, *The American Disease*, p. 64.

9. D. L. Rosenhan, "On Being Sane in Insane Places," *Science*, 179 (1973): 250–58.

10. J. Talbot, *The Death of the Asylum*, p. 35.

11. *Ibid.*

12. *Ibid.*, p. 38.

13. In V. M. Rakoff et al., *Psychiatric Diagnosis*, p. 5.

14. *Ibid.*, p. 193.

15. E. Kraepelin, *One Hundred Years of Psychiatry*, pp. 150–56.

16. *Ibid.*, p. 136.

17. In C. Chiland, ed., *Long-Term Treatments of Psychotic States*, p. 108.

18. In *Ibid.*, p. 635.

19. J. M. Davis and J. O. Cole, "Antipsychotic Drugs," Ch. 22 in *American Handbook of Psychiatry*, V: 442.

20. In Chiland, ed., *Long-Term Treatments*, p. 126.

21. *American Journal of Psychiatry*, April 1978.

22. Kraepelin, *One Hundred Years*, pp. 148–49.

23. Ahmed and Plog, *State Mental Hospitals*, p. 212.

24. E. Jones, "Psychoanalysis and Psychiatry," *Collected Papers*, 5th ed. p. 373.

25. H. S. Sullivan, *Schizophrenia as a Human Process*, pp. 219–20.

26. F. Fromm-Reichmann, *Psychoanalysis and Psychotherapy*, pp. 163–64.

27. Quoted in T. Lidz et al., *Schizophrenia and the Family*, p. 15.

28. L. Wynne et al., *The Nature of Schizophrenia*, p. 22.

29. A. Hollingshead and F. Redlich, *Social Class and Mental Illness*, p. 13.

30. *American Handbook of Psychiatry*, II: 436.

31. A. Green, "The Middle-Class Male Child and Neurosis," *American Sociological Review*, 1946, pp. 31–41.

32. A. Leighton, "Social Disintegration and Mental Disorder," in S. Arieti, ed., *American Handbook of Psychiatry*, II: 411.

33. H. S. Sullivan, *Schizophrenia as a Human Process*, pp. 236–44.

34. *Ibid.*, p. 236.

35. *Ibid.*, p. 238.

36. *American Handbook of Psychiatry*, V: 121.

37. P. May et al., *Treatment of Schizophrenia*, p. 136.

38. *Ibid.*, p. 77

39. *Ibid.*, p. 84.

40. *Ibid.*, p. 84.

41. *Ibid.*, p. 297.

42. E. Jarvis, *Insanity and Idiocy in Massachusetts*, p. 69.
43. *New York Times*, Dec. 11, 1978, p. D14.
44. *DSM III*, Draft Criteria, 1/15/78, p. 125.
45. V. Rakoff et al., *Psychiatric Diagnosis*, p. 207.
46. L. Wynne et al., *Nature of Schizophrenia*, p. 87.
47. M. Bleuler, *The Schizophrenic Disorders*, pp. 634–35.
48. L. Wynne et al., *Nature of Schizophrenia*, p. 260. Italics added.
49. E. Hartmann, *The Sleeping Pill*, jacket.
50. J. Marmor, *Psychiatrists and Their Patients*, p. 172.
51. W. Henry et al., *The Fifth Profession*, p. 160.
52. *American Handbook of Psychiatry*, I: 77–78.
53. In D. Schuster, *Clinical Supervision of the Psychiatric Resident*, p. 54.
54. *American Handbook of Psychiatry*, I: 117.
55. G. Rosen, *Madness in Society*, p. 282.
56. E. Jones, *Collected Papers*, p. 365. Italics added.

Chapter 6. Toward Clarification of the Social Sciences

1. F. Boas, "The History of Anthropology," *Science*, 20 (1908): 513–24.
2. R. Nisbet, "History of Social Science," *Encyclopaedia Britannica*, 16: 981–990.
3. A. Simirenko, *Social Thought in the Soviet Union*, p. 12.
4. R. Nisbet, "History of Social Science," p. 990.
5. M. Cohen, *Reason and Nature*, p. 350.
6. T. Kuhn, *The Structure of Scientific Revolutions*, p. x.
7. M. Cohen, *Reason and Nature*, p. 351.
8. *Annual Review of Psychology*, 1979, p. 20.
9. *American Psychoanalytic Association, By-Laws*, 1976, p. 1.
10. In G. H. Weber and G. J. McCall, *Social Scientists as Advocates*, pp. 172–73.
11. *Ibid.*, p. 56.
12. *Ibid.*, p. 139.
13. M. Harris, *The Rise of Anthropological Theory*, p. 261.
14. R. W. Fogel and S. L. Engerman, *Time on the Cross*.
15. *International Review of Psychoanalysis*, 1979, p. 15.
16. N. Bohr, *Atomic Physics and Human Knowledge*, p. 11.
17. SE, XIV: 77.
18. SE, XIV: 117.
19. F. Boas, *The Mind of Primitive Man*, p. 209.
20. SE, XIII: 100.
21. *Science*, June 22, 1979.
22. *New York Times*, December 20, 1978. Obituary of Harold Lasswell.

23. Cohen, *Reason and Nature*, p. 351.
24. S. Reinharz, *On Becoming a Social Scientist*, p. xii.
25. *Ibid.*, p. 240. Italics added.

Chapter 7. The Dilemmas of History

1. E. B. Fryde, "Historiography and Historical Methodology," *Encyclopaedia Britannica*, 8: 945– 61.
2. *Ibid.*, p. 962.
3. W. McNeill, *A World History*, p. 404.
4 *Encyclopaedia Britannica*, 7: 630.
5. L. R. Ladurie, *Montaillou*, pp. 20–21.
6. *Ibid.*, p. 23.
7. W. McNeill, *A World History*, p. 261.
8. *Encyclopaedia Britannica*, 2: 586.
9. *Encyclopaedia Britannica*, 7: 1010.
10. *Encyclopaedia Britannica*, 5: 300.
11. Encyclopaedia Britannica, 5: 306.
12. P. L. Gay and R. K. Webb, *History of Modern Europe*, p. 254.
13. W. McNeill, *A World History*, p. 441.
14. *Ibid.*, p. 439.
15. *Encyclopaedia Britannica*, 18: 1043–44.
16. M.. Weber, *The Protestant Ethic and the Spirit of Capitalism*, p. 244.
17. Gay and Webb, *History of Modern Europe*, p. 842.
18. J. Hemming, *Red Gold*, p. 492.
19. As this is being written the *New York Times* (August 4, 1979) reports that the monument at Babi Yar in the Soviet Union, where 70,000 Jews were murdered by the Nazis over a ten-day period in 1941, does not mention Jews.
20. R. W. Fogel and S. L. Engerman, *Time on the Cross*, Ch. 1.
21. *Ibid.*, p. 31.
22. *Ibid.*, p. 32.
23. *Encyclopaedia Britannica*, 16: 856.
24. *Exodus*, 21: 20.
25. *Encyclopaedia Britannica*, 16: 857.
26. G. Vaillant, *The Aztecs of Mexico*.
27. SE, XIX: 72.
28. It is impossible to be precise about the numbers of "witches" murdered in what is usually referred to as the "witchcraft craze." Gay and Webb (p. 127) merely state that "witches" were "burned by the thousands."
29. F. Goodman, *Speak in Tongues*.
30. G. Rosen, *Madness and Society*, p. 83.
31. *Ibid.*, p. 84.

32. F. Nietzsche "Twilight of the Idols," *The Portable Nietzsche*, p. 475.

33. *Encyclopaedia Britannica*, 15: 612.

34. T. K. Rabb, "The New Jerusalem," *New York Times*, December 20, 1978.

35. L. Deschner, *Das Kreuz mit der Kirche*, p. 120.

36. *Ibid.*, pp. 120–21.

37. L. Saul and I. Wenar, "Early Influences on Development and Disorders of Personality," *PQ*, 34 (1965): 327–89.

38. R. Fortune, *The Sorcerers of Dobu.*

39. *Encyclopaedia Britannica*, 19: 895–96.

40. B. Rosen, *Witchcraft*, p. 43.

41. J. Russell, *Witchcraft in the Middle Ages*, p. 265.

42. *Ibid.*, p. 260.

43. *Ibid.*, p. 270.

44. *Ibid.*, p. 278.

45. *Ibid.*, p. 285.

46. *Ibid.*, pp. 288–289.

47. *Ibid.*, p. 273.

48. J. Dean, *Blind Ambition*, flyleaf.

49. B. Tuchman, *A Distant Mirror*, p. 258.

50. P. Gay and R. K. Webb, *History of Modern Europe*, p. 523.

51. W. McNeill, *A World History*, p. 195.

52. *Encyclopaedia Britannica*, 8: 961.

53. *Ibid.*, p. 964.

54. *Ibid.*

55. *Ibid.*, p. 965. See also G. Grob and G. Billias, *Interpretations in American History.*

56. R. Collingwood, *The Idea of History*, p. 18.

57. M. Cohen, *The Meaning of Human History*, p. 296.

58. *Ibid.*, p. 132.

59. R. W. Fogel and S. L. Engerman, *Time on the Cross*, p. 4.

60. *Ibid.*, p. 262.

61. *Ibid.*, p. 9. Emphasis added.

Chapter 8. Society Versus the Individual: Sociology and Anthropology

1. *Webster's New International Dictionary*, p. 2163.

2. E. Durkheim, *The Rules of Sociological Method*, p. 10.

3. *Encyclopaedia Britannica* (1978), 16: 999.

4. E. Durkheim et al., *Essays on Sociology and Philosophy*, p. 363.

5. E. Durkheim, *The Rules of Sociological Method*, Introduction.

6. E. Faris, in *Encyclopaedia Britannica*, 16: 995.

7. B. Barry, *Sociologists, Economists and Democracy*, p. vi.
8. R. Tucker, ed. *The Marx–Engels Reader*, pp. 115–16. Emphasis in original.
9. A. Mitzman, *The Iron Cage*, p. 3.
10. R. Nisbet, *The Sociological Tradition*, p. 47.
11. *Ibid.*, p. 75.
12. Tucker, ed., *Marx-Engels Reader*, p. 144.
13. *Ibid.*, p. 97. Emphasis added.
14. In M. Rosenbaum and A. Snadowsky, *The Intensive Group Experience*, p. 179.
15. W. Sumner, *Folkways*, pp. 12–13.
16. K. Wolf, ed. *The Sociology of George Simmel*, p. 379.
17. T. Rennie et al., *Mental Health in the Metropolis*, p. 197; revised ed., 1978.
18. *Ibid.*, p. 199.
19. *Ibid.*, p. 463.
20. *Ibid.*, p. 469.
21. Tucker, ed., *Marx–Engels Reader*, p. 510.
22. R. Lowry and R. Rankin, *Sociology*, p. 15.
23. E. Durkheim, *Suicide*, p. 50.
24. *Ibid.*, pp. 51–52. Emphasis added.
25. M. Harris, *The Rise of Anthropological Theory*, p. 397.
26. *Ibid.*, p. 425.
27. *Ibid.*, p. 430.
28. *Ibid.*, p. 431.
29. *Ibid.*, p. 448.
30. *Ibid.*, p. 449.
31. O. Fenichel, *The Psychoanalytic Theory of Neurosis*, p. 588.

Chapter 9. The Myth of "Economic Man"

1. B. Ward, *The Ideal Worlds of Economics*, p. 467.
2. Knight, quoted in A. Lowe, *On Economic Knowledge*, p. 105.
3. S. Weintraub, ed. *Handbook of Modern Economic Thought*, p. 23.
4. R. Heilbroner, *The Worldly Philosophers*, p. 23.
5. *Ibid.*, p. 121.
6. Quoted in *Ibid.*, p. 271.
7. J. K. Galbraith, *The New Industrial State*, p. 129.
8. *Ibid.*, p. 128.
9. *Ibid.*, p. 143.
10. Quoted in J. K. Galbraith, *Economics and the Public Purpose*, p. 4.
11. *Ibid.*, p. 324.
12. *Ibid.*, p. 233.

13. W. Weisskopf, *Alienation and Economics*, p. 192.
14. S. Nosow and W. H. Form, *Man, Work and Society*, p. 11.
15. Postgraduate Center, New York City, personal communication.

Chapter 10. Believers and Skeptics: Religion and Philosophy

1. SE, XXI: 54.
2. *Psychoanalysis and Faith*, p. 126.
3. In *Encyclopaedia Britannica*, 15: 613.
4. G. Roheim, *Magic and Schizophrenia*, p. 221.
5. O. Pfister, *Christianity and Fear*, p. 22.
6. In *Encyclopaedia Britannica*, 14: 248.
7. W. Durant, *The Story of Philosphy*, p. xxiii.
8. B. Russell, *The Basic Writings*, p. 268.
9. J. Randall, *The Career of Philosphy*, p. 556.
10. M. Cohen, *The Meaning of Human History*, p. 7.
11. P. Ricoeur, "The Question of Proof in Freud's Psychoanalytic Writings," p. 835.
12. In C. Hanly and M. Lazerowitz, *Psychoanalysis and Philosophy*, pp. 14–15.
13. V. J. McGill, *The Idea of Happiness*, p. 322.
14. P. Radin, *Primitive Man as Philosopher*, p. 98.
15. In P. L. Entralgo, *Therapy of the Word in Classical Antiquity*, p. 13.
16. N. Hale, *Freud and the Americans*, p. 228.
17. *Ibid.*, p. 230.
18. *Encyclopaedia Britannica*, 14: 274.
19. R. May et al., *Existence*, p. 10.
20. *Ibid.*, p. 33.
21. *JAPA*, 10 (1962): 166–215.
22. R. Fine, *A History of Psychoanalysis*, Ch. 16.

Chapter 11. Creativity and Communication: Art and Language

1. *Encyclopaedia Britannica*, 2: 40.
2. W. Niederland, *PQ*, 45 (1976): 189.
3. *Ibid.*, p. 185.
4. *IJP*, 53 (1972): 25.
5. F. Barron, *Creative Artists in the Making*, p. 49.
6. J. W. Getzels and M. Csikszentmihalyi, *The Creative Vision*, p. vi.
7. In F. Barron, *Creative Artists in the Making*, p. xiv.
8. E. Wilson, *The Twenties*, p. xlviii.
9. *Ibid.*, p. xix.

10. D. C. Rich, ed., *Essays and Criticisms of Henry McBride,* flyleaf.
11. *Ibid.*
12. N. Balakian, *Critical Encounters,* p. 49.
13. C. M. Otten, *Anthropology and Art,* p. 25.
14. SE, IX: 146.
15. S. Thompson, *The Folktale,* p. 367.
16. In C. F. Jopling, *Art and Aesthetics in Primitive Societies,* pp. 374–81.
17. Quoted in A. Hauser, *The Social History of Art,* p. 119.
18. In J. H. Anderson and G. R. Bower, *Human Associative Memory,* p. 120.
19. In H. Greenberg, *The Movies on Your Mind,* p. 7.

Chapter 12. The Complexities of Causation

1. Quoted in *New York Times Book Review,* July 29, 1979.
2. E. Nagel, *The Structure of Science,* p. 322.
3. *Ibid.,* pp. 508 ff.
4. J. Tedeschi, ed., *The Social Influence Processes,* p. vii.
5. *Ibid.,* p. ix.
6. *Ibid.,* p. 13.
7. *Ibid.,* p. 234.
8. *Ibid.,* p. 404. Emphasis added.
9. *Ibid.,* p. 403.
10. M. S. Weinberg and C. J. Williams, *Male Homosexuals,* p. 274.
11. M. S. Weinberg and A. P. Bell, *Homosexualities,* pp. 22–23.
12. *Ibid.,* p. 25.
13. V. Rakoff et al., *Psychiatric Diagnosis,* p. 207.
14. C. Socarides, "The Sexual Unreason," *Book Forum,* 1 (1974): 172–85.
15. W. Masters and V. Johnson, *Homosexuality in Perspective,* book jacket.
16. *Ibid.*

Chapter 13. The Emergence of a New Profession

1. W. Bromberg, *The Mind of Man,* p. 45.
2. *Ibid.*
3. *Ibid.,* p. 46.
4. A. Boisen, *The Exploration of the Inner World,* p. 5.
5. *IJP,* 1 (1920): 211.
6. A. Kardiner, *Diary of My Analysis with Freud,* p. 15.
7. R. Langs, *The Technique of Psychoanalytic Psychotherapy,* 1: 40.
8. P. Chodoff, "The Question of Lay Analysis revisited," *Journal of the American Academy of Psychoanalysis,* 5 (1977): 440.
9. *Newsletter of the New York Psychoanalytic Institute,* 16, no. 3: 14–25.

10. *Ibid.*, p. 16.
11. R. Knight, "The Present Status of Organized Psychoanalysis in the United States," *JAPA*, 1 (1953): 219.
12. N. E. Zinberg, "Psychoanalytic Training and Psychoanalytic Values," *IJP*, 48 (1967): 88–96.
13. S. Firestein, *Termination in Psychoanalysis.* A number of the patients in the course of their treatment expressed the desire to become analysts, but this wish was ignored.
14. G. Maetze, ed., *Zehn Jahre Berliner Psychoanalytisches Institut*, p. 51.
15. B. Lewin and H. Ross, *Psychoanalytic Education in the United States*, p. 169.
16. *Ibid.*, p. 175.
17. Bulletin, *New York Psychoanalytic Society*, 1979–1980. Emphasis added.
18. G. Maetze, ed., *Zehn Jahre Berliner Psychoanalytisches Institut*, p. 51.
19. Freud, *Psychoanalysis and Faith*, p. 126.
20. Lewin and Ross, *Psychoanalytic Education* p. 174, and Goodman, *Psychoanalytic Education and Research*, p. 342.
21. *Ibid.*
22. S. Goodman, *Psychoanalytic Education and Research*, p. 123.
23. *Ibid.*, p. 3.
24. *Ibid.*, p. 171.
25. *JAPA*, 23, (1975): 876.
26. *JAPA*, 9 (1961): 340–41.
27. *JAPA*, 21 (1973): 445. Emphasis added.
28. G. Maetze, ed., *Zehn Jahre Berliner Psychoanalytisches Institut*, pp. 50–52.
29. Goodman, *Psychoanalytic Education and Research*, p. 343.
30. R. Shapiro, "Ego Psychology," in J. M. Quen and E. T. Carlson, *American Psychoanalysis*, p. 164.
31. R. Schafer, *A New Language for Psychoanalysis.*
32. Goodman, *Psychoanalytic Education and Research*, p. 141.
33. *JAPA*, 23 (1975): 433. For details of the Kubie plan, see L. S. Kubie, "The Overall Manpower Problem and the Creation of a New Discipline."
34. Goodman, *Psychoanalytic Education and Research*, p. 332.
35. G. Maetze, ed., *Zehn Jahre Berliner Psychoanalytisches Institut*, p. 48.
36. Lewin and Ross, *Psychoanalytic Education*, p. 45.
37. Goodman, *Psychoanalytic Education and Research*, p. 40.
38. G. Maetze, *Zehn Jahre Berliner Psychoanalitisches Institut*, p. 53.
39. R. Fine, *A History of Psychoanalysis*, pp. 137–38.
40. *JAPA*, 27, (1979): 931.
41. *JAPA*, 24 (1976): 911.
42. *JAPA*, 26 (1978): 430.

43. D. S. Jaffe and S. E. Pulver, "Survey of Psychoanalytic Practice 1976", *JAPA*, 26 (1978): 615–31.
44. M. Eckhart in Quen and Carlsson, eds., *American Psychoanalysis*, pp. 150–51.
45. *IJP*, 1978, p. 72.
46. L. Rangell, Similarities and Differences between Psychoanalysis and Dynamic Psychotherapy," *JAPA*, 2 (1954) 152–66.
47. *JAPA*, 8 (1960): 699.
48. *Ibid*.
49. *IJP*, 37 (1957): 118–20.
50. SE, XIV: 16.
51. E. Glover, *The Technique of Psychoanalysis*, Part II.
52. C. Kadushin, *Why People Go to Psychiatrists*, p. 307.
53. C. P. Oberndorf, *A History of Psychoanalysis in America*, p. 169.
54. *Ibid.*, p. 168.
55. V. Calef and E. Weinshel, "The New Psychoanalysis," *PQ*, 48 (1979): 479–91.
56. *Ibid*.

Chapter 14. Vision Versus Technique: Psychotherapy and Social Reform

1. J. J. Putnam, *Letters*, p. 118.
2. *Ibid.*, p. 121. Emphasis added.
3. *Ibid.*, p. 170.
4. SE, XX: 250.
5. SE, XXI: 83.
6. J. Meltzoff and M. Kornreich, *Research in Psychotherapy*, p. 74.
7. G. Maetze, ed., *Zehn Jahre Berliner Psychoanalytisches Institut*, p. 19.
8. S. Garfield and A. Bergin, *Handbook of Psychotherapy*, pp. 179–80.

Chapter 15. The Half-trained Professions: Diplomas Instead of Analysis

1. B. Lewin and H. Ross, *Psychoanalytic Education in the United States*, p. 443.
2. *Ibid.*, p. 448.
3. H. Levin, "War Between the Shrinks," *New York*, May 21, 1979, pp. 52–54.
4. E. Jones, *The Life and Work of Sigmund Freud*, 3: 298.

5. R. Fine, *A History of Psychoanalysis*, p. 144.
6. *JAPA*, 24 (1976): 274.
7. *PQ*, 48 (1979): 470–91.
8. *Ibid.*, p. 489.
9. R. Corsini, ed., *Current Psychotherapies*, p. 231.
10. *Ibid.*, p. 233.
11. *Ibid.*, p. 254.
12. *Ibid.*, p. 232.
13. *Ibid.*, p. 267.
14. *Ibid.*, p. 263.
15. *Annual Review of Behavior Therapy*, 6 (1978): 19–22.
16. B. F. Skinner, *Beyond Freedom and Dignity*, p. 182.
17. *Ibid.*, p. 170.
18. *Annual Review of Behavior Therapy*, 6 (1978): 21.
19. J. Wolpe, *Theme and Variations*, p. 130.
20. *Annual Review*, 6: 1.
21. *Annual Review of Behavior Therapy*, 4 (1976): 37.
22. Wolpe, *Theme and Variations*, p. 26.
23. R. Corsini, *Current Psychotherapies*, p. 131.
24. *Ibid.*, p. 142.
25. *Ibid.*
26. *Ibid.*, p. 134.
27. *Ibid.*, p. 135.
28. *Ibid.*, p. 151.
29. *Ibid.*, p. 185.
30. SE, XIII: 159.
31. Corsini, *Current Psychotherapies*, p. 191.
32. *Ibid.*, p. 250. Emphasis in original.
33. *Ibid.*, p. 205.
34. *Ibid.*, p. 206.
35. R. Corsini, *Current Psychotherapies* (1973 ed.) p. 251.
36. *Current Psychotherapies* (1979 ed.), Ch. 7.
37. *Ibid.*, p. 273.
38. *Ibid.*, p. 274.
39. *Ibid.*, p. 278.
40. Corsini, *Current Psychotherapies* (1973 ed.), p. 251.
41. *Ibid.*, p. 253.
42. *Ibid.*
43. Corsini (1979 ed.), p. 290.
44. Corsini (1973 ed.), p. 287.
45. Corsini (1979 ed.), p. 311.
46. Corsini (1973 ed.), p. 293.
47. M. A. Lieberman et al., *Encounter Groups: First Facts*, p. 3.

Chapter 16. The Meaning of Love
in Human Experience

1. SE, VII: 149.
2. Andreas Cappellanus, *Courtly Love*, p. 2.
3. *Malleus Maleficarum*, Part I, Quest. 6.
4. M. Hunt, *The Natural History of Love*, p. 218.
5. L. De Mause, *The History of Childhood*, p. 1.
6. *Ibid.*, p. 428.
7. *Ibid.*, p. 25.
8. M. F. Ashley Montagu, "Aggression and the Evolution of Man." In R. E. Whalen, ed., *The Neuropsychology of Aggression*, pp. 1–33.
9. In D. S. Marshall and R. C. Suggs, *Human Sexual Behavior*, p. 34.
10. G. Murdock, *Social Structure*, p. 263.
11. *Ibid.*, pp. 278 ff.
12. C. Levi-Strauss, *The Savage Mind*, p. 95.
13. C. Levi-Strauss, *The Elementary Structures of Kinship*, p. xxiii.
14. M. Fortes, *Kinship and the Social Order*, p. 237.
15. M. Mauss, *The Gift*, p. xiv.
16. B. Malinowski in *Encyclopaedia Britannica*, 1963 edition, 14: 950.
17. G. Schaller, *The Year of the Gorilla*, p. 50.
18. H. Harlow, *Learning to Love*, p. vii.
19. *Encyclopaedia Britannica*, 10: 479.
20. M. F. Ashley Montagu, *The Nature of Human Aggression*, p. 325.
21. G. Simpson, *People in Families*, p. 219.
22. J. Cuber and P. Harroff, *The Significant Americans*, p. 9.
23. *Ibid.*, p. 9.
24. *Ibid.*, p. 204.
25. R. Gelles, *The Violent Home*, p. 20.
26. R. Beavers, *Psychotherapy and Growth*, p. 127.
27. C. Jencks et al., *Who Gets Ahead?*, p. 311.
28. SE, XXI: 99–100.
29. H. Nunberg and E. Federn, eds., *Minutes of the Vienna Psychoanalytic Society*, II: 100.
30. J. Flugel, *The Psychoanalytic Study of the Family*, p. 11.
31. O. Fenichel, *The Psychoanalytic Theory of Neurosis*, p. 585.
32. R. Faris, *Handbook of Sociology*, p. 684.
33. M. Komarovsky, *Blue-Collar Marriage*, pp. 330–331.
34. O. Lewis, *The Children of Sanchez*, p. xxvi.
35. D. Moynihan, *The Negro Family*, pp. 47–48.
36. L. Rainwater and W. L. Yancey, *The Moynihan Report and the Politics of Controversy*, p. 475.
37. H. G. Gutman, *The Black Family in Slavery and Freedom*, jacket.
38. *Ibid.*, p. 284. Emphasis added.

39. L. Rubin, *Worlds of Pain*, p. 204.
40. H. D. Graham and T. R. Burr, eds. *Violence in America*, p. 788.
41. *Ibid.*, pp. 793–98.
42. R. Slovenko, *Psychiatry and the Law*, p. vii.
43. A. Freud et al., *Beyond the Best Interests of the Child*, p. 7.
44. M. Ribble, *The Rights of Infants*, p. 14.
45. J. Bowlby et al., *Maternal Care and Mental Health*, p. 11.
46. S. Brody and S. Axelrod, *Mothers, Fathers and Children*, p. 553.
47. R. G. Hazo, *The Idea of Love*, p. 4.
48. *Ibid.*, p. 183.
49. *Ibid.*, p. 189.
50. *Ibid.*, p. 204.
51. J. E. Smith et al., *The Spirit of American Philosophy*, p. 34.
52. W. James, *Principles of Psychology*, p. 543.
53. K. Lowith, *From Hegel to Nietzsche*, p. 78.
54. R. May, *Love and Will*, p. 38.

Chapter 17. Toward an Integrative Theory of Love

1. A. Freedman, "Psychoanalytic Study of an Unusual Perversion," *JAPA*, 26 (1978): 772.
2. O. Fenichel, *The Psychoanalytic Theory of Neurosis*, p. 86.
3. H. S. Sullivan, *Conceptions of Modern Psychiatry*, p. 42.
4. SE, XVII: 223.
5. E. Jones, *Life and Work of Sigmund Freud*, 2: 293.
6. *IJP*, 9 (1928): 318.
7. *Ibid.*, p. 330.
8. E. Jones, *Life and Work of Sigmund Freud*, 3: 440.

Bibliography

ACHTE, K. A. AND NISKANEN, D. P. 1972. *The Course and Prognosis of Psychosis in Helsinki.* Monographs from the psychiatric clinic of the Helsinki University Central Hospital, Helsinki.

ACKERMAN, N. W. 1951. " 'Social Role' and Total Personality." *American Journal of Orthopsychiatry,* 21: 1–17.

ACKERMAN, N. W. 1958. *The Psychodynamics of Family Life.* New York: Basic Books.

ADLER, S. 1979. *Poverty Children and Their Language.* New York: Grune and Stratton.

ADORNO, T. et al. 1950. *The Authoritarian Personality.* New York: Harper.

AHMED, P. I. AND PLOG, S. Z., eds. 1976. *State Mental Hospitals: What Happens When They Close.* New York: Plenum.

AICHHORN, A. 1925. *Wayward Youth.* New York: Viking Press, 1935.

AINSWORTH, M. D. S. et al. 1978. *Patterns of Attachment.* New York: Lawrence Erlbaum Associates.

ALEXANDER, F. 1950. *Psychosomatic Medicine.* New York: Norton.

ALEXANDER, F., FRENCH, T. M. AND POLLOCK, G. H. 1968. *Psychosomatic Specificity.* Chicago: University of Chicago Press.

ALMOND, R. 1974. *The Healing Community.* New York: Jason Aronson.

ALTER, R. 1979. *A Lion for Love.* New York: Basic Books.

ALTMAN, L. L. 1977. "Some Vicissitudes of Love." *JAPA,* 25: 35–52.

American Association for the Advancement of Science. 1979. *Science,* June 22, 1979. Washington, D.C.

American Psychiatric Association. 1978. *DSM-III: Diagnostic Criteria Draft.* New York.

American Psychoanalytic Association. 1976. *By-Laws.* New York: APA.

ANDERSON, J. H. AND BOWER, G. R. 1973. *Human Associative Memory.* New York: Wiley.

ANDRESKI, S. 1972. *Social Sciences as Sorcery.* New York: St. Martin's Press.

ANDREWS, E. D. AND ANDREWS, F. 1974. *Work and Worship: The Economic Order of the Shakers.* Greenwich, Conn.: New York Graphic Society.

538

ANDREWS, F. M. AND WITHEY, S. B. 1976. *Social Indicators of Well-Being.* New York: Plenum.

Annual Review of Behavior Therapy. Vol. 4, 1976. New York: Brunner/Mazel.

Annual Review of Behavior Therapy. Vol. 6, 1978. New York: Brunner/Mazel.

Annual Review of Psychology. Vol. 30, 1979. Palo Alto, Calif.: Annual Reviews.

ANZIEU, D. 1975. *L'Auto-Analyse de Freud et la Decouverte de la Psychoanalyse.* Rev., enlarged ed. Paris: Presses Universitaires de France (1st ed., 1959).

APTHEKER, H. 1943. *American Negro Slave Revolts.* New York: Citadel Press.

APTHEKER, H. 1971. *Afro-American History: The Modern Era.* New York: Citadel Press.

ARIETI, S. 1974. *Interpretation of Schizophrenia.* New York: Basic Books.

ARIETI, S., ed. 1974–1975. *The American Handbook of Psychiatry.* 6 vols. New York: Basic Books.

ARIETI, S. 1976. *Creativity: The Magic Synthesis.* New York: Basic Books.

ARKIN, A. M. et al. 1978. *The Mind in Sleep.* New York: Lawrence Erlbaum Associates.

ARLOW, J. AND BRENNER, C. 1964. *Psychoanalytic Concepts and the Structural Theory.* New York: International Universities Press.

ARNHEIM, R. 1974. *Art and Visual Perception.* Berkeley: University of California Press.

ASHLEY MONTAGU, M. F. 1974. "Aggression and the Evolution of Man." In R. E. Whalen, ed., *The Neuropsychology of Aggression,* pp. 1 33.

ASHLEY MONTAGU, M. F. 1976. *The Nature of Human Aggression.* New York: Oxford University Press.

ASHLEY MONTAGU, M. F. AND MATSON, F. 1979. *The Human Connection.* New York: McGraw-Hill.

BADDELEY, A. D. 1976. *The Psychology of Memory.* New York: Basic Books.

BALAKIAN, N. 1978. *Critical Encounters.* New York: Bobbs-Merrill.

BALINT, M. 1953. *Primary Love and Psychoanalytic Technique.* New York: Liveright.

BALINT, M. 1954. "Analytic Training and Training Analysis." *IJP,* 35: 157–62.

BANDURA, A. 1974. "Behavior Therapy and Models of Man." *American Psychologist,* 29: 859–69.

BARANDE, I. AND BARANDE, R. 1975. *Histoire de la Psychoanalyse en France.* Paris: Privat.

BARDWICK, J. 1979. *In Transition.* New York: Holt, Rinehart and Winston.

BARRON, F. 1963. *Creativity and Psychological Health.* New York: Van Nostrand.

BARRON, F. 1972. *Creative Artists in the Making.* New York: Seminar Press.

BARRY, B. 1978. *Sociologists, Economists and Democracy.* Chicago: University of Chicago Press.

BATESON, G. et al. 1956. "Toward a Theory of Schizophrenia." *Behavioral Science,* 1: 251–64.

BAZAR, J. 1979. "Psychology Making a Comeback." *APA Monitor,* 10: 17–23.

BEAVERS, R. W. 1977. *Psychotherapy and Growth.* New York: Brunner/Mazel.

BECKER, E. 1968. *The Structure of Evil.* New York: Free Press.

BELL, M. 1979. *Marquand: An American Life.* Boston: Atlantic–Little, Brown.

BELLAK, L. AND LOEB, L. 1968. *The Schizophrenic Syndrome.* New York: Grune and Stratton.

BELLAK, L. et al. 1973. *Ego Functions in Schizophrenics, Neurotics and Normals.* New York: Wiley.

BELMONTE, T. 1979. *The Broken Fountain.* New York: Columbia University Press.

BENEDEK, T. 1959. "Parenthood as a Development Phase." *JAPA,* 7: 389–417.

BENEDICT, R. 1934. *Patterns of Culture.* Boston: Houghton Mifflin.

BERG, I. A. 1967. *Response Set in Personality Assessment.* Chicago: Aldine.

BERKMAN, T. 1972. *To Seize the Passing Dream.* New York: Doubleday.

BETEILLE, A. 1971. *Caste, Class and Power.* Berkeley: University of California Press.

BIEBER, I., et al. 1962. *Homosexuality.* New York: Basic Books.

BIEBUYK, D. 1973. *Tradition and Creativity in Tribal Art.* Berkeley: University of California Press.

BIRKET-SMITH, K. 1959. *The Eskimos.* London: Methuen.

BLANTON, M. G. 1939. *Bernadette of Lourdes.* New York: Longmans, Green.

BLANTON, S. 1940. "Analytical Study of a Cure at Lourdes." *PQ,* 9: 348–62.

BLEULER, M. 1970. "Some Results of Research in Schizophrenia." In R. Cancro, ed., *The Schizophrenic Syndrome,* I: 3–16. New York: Brunner/Mazel.

BLEULER, M. 1978. *The Schizophrenic Disorders.* New Haven: Yale University Press.

BLUCH, S. AND REDDAWAY, P. 1977. *Psychiatric Terror.* New York: Basic Books.

BOAS, F. 1908. "The History of Anthropology." *Science,* 20: 513–24.

BOAS, F. 1911. *The Mind of Primitive Man.* New York: Macmillan.

BOHR, N. 1958. *Atomic Physics and Human Knowledge.* New York: Wiley.

BOISEN, A. T. 1936. *The Exploration of the Inner World.* New York: Harper.

BORING, E. 1957. *A History of Experimental Psychology.* New York: Appleton-Century-Crofts.

BOWLBY, J. 1951. *Maternal Care and Mental Health.* New York: Schocken Books.

BOWLBY, J. 1961. "Processes of Mourning." *IJP,* 42: 317–40.

BOWLBY, J. 1973. *Attachment and Loss.* Vol. II: Separation. New York: Basic Books.

BOWLBY, J. 1980. *Attachment and Loss.* Vol. III: Loss. New York: Basic Books.

BOYER, L. V. 1979. *Childhood and Folklore.* New York: Library of Psychological Anthropology.

BRADBURN, N. 1969. *The Structure of Psychological Well-Being.* Chicago: Aldine.

BRAGINSKY, B. M. AND BRAGINSKY, D. D. 1974. *Mainstream Psychology: A Critique.* New York: Holt, Rinehart, and Winston.

BRELAND, K. AND BRELAND, M. 1961. "The Misbehavior of Organisms." *American Psychologist,* 16, 681–684.

BRENNER, C. 1971. "The Psychoanalytic Concept of Aggression." *IJP,* 52, 137–44.

BRENNER, C. 1976. *Psychoanalytic Technique and Psychic Conflict.* New York: International Universities Press.

BRIERLEY, M. 1947. "Psychoanalysis and Integrative Living." *IJP,* 28: 57–105.

BRODY, S. AND AXELRAD, S. 1978. *Mothers, Fathers, and Children.* New York: International Universities Press.

BROMBERG, W. 1954. *The Mind of Man: A History of Psychotherapy and Psychoanalysis.* New York: Harper.

BURNHAM, D. L. et al. 1969. *Schizophrenia and the Need-Fear Dilemma.* New York: International Universities Press.

BURR, M. 1909. *The History of Autobiography.* Boston: Houghton Mifflin.

BUTTERFIELD, F. 1980. "Love and Sex in China." *New York Times Magazine,* January 13, 1980, pp. 15–49.

CALEF, V. AND WEINSHEL, E. M. 1979. "The New Psychoanalysis and Psychoanalytic Revisionism: Book Review Essay on Borderline Conditions and Pathological Narcissism." *PQ,* 48: 470–91.

CANNING, J. W. 1966. "A Logical Analysis of Criticisms Directed at Freudian Psychoanalytic Theory." *Dissertation Abstracts,* 27: 1078.

CANTRIL, H. 1965. *The Pattern of Human Concerns.* New Brunswick, N.J.: Rutgers University Press.

CAPPELLANUS, A. 1180. *The Art of Courtly Love.* New York: Norton, 1969.

Carnegie Commission on the Future of Public Broadcasting. 1979. *A Public Trust.* New York: Bantam Books.

CAROTHERS, J. C. 1970. *The African Mind in Health and Disease*. New York: Negro Universities Press.

CARTWRIGHT, F. F. 1972. *Disease and History: The Influence of Disease in Shaping the Great Events of History*. New York: Thomas Y. Crowell.

CATTELL, R. B. 1971. *Abilities: Their Structure, Growth and Action*. Boston: Houghton Mifflin.

CHASSEGUET-SMIRGEL, J. et al. 1970. *Female Sexuality*. Ann Arbor: University of Michigan Press.

CHILAND, C., ed. 1977. *Long-Term Treatment of Psychotic States*. New York: Human Sciences Press.

CHINOY, E. 1955. *Automobile Workers and the American Dream*. Boston: Beacon Press.

CHISHOLM, G. B. 1946. "The Psychiatry of Enduring Peace and Social Progress." *Psychiatry*, 9: 3–20.

CHODOFF, P. 1977. "The Question of Lay Analysis Revisited." *Journal of American Academy of Psychoanalysis*, 5: 431–46.

CHOMSKY, N. 1968. *Language and Mind*. New York: Harcourt Brace Jovanovich.

CLARK, M. 1970. *Health in the Mexican-American Culture*. Berkeley: University of California Press.

COHEN, J. 1962. "Statistical Power of Abnormal Social Psychological Research: A Review." *Journal of Abnormal and Social Psychology*, 65: 145–53.

COHEN, M. R. 1933. *Reason and Nature*. New York: Dover, 1978.

COHEN, M. R. 1961. *The Meaning of Human History*. LaSalle, Ill.: Open Court.

COHEN, N. 1975. *Europe's Inner Demons: An Inquiry Inspired by the Great Witch-Hunt*. New York: Basic Books.

COLE, R. E. 1979. *Work, Mobility and Participation*. Berkeley: University of California Press.

COLLINGWOOD, R. G. 1946. *The Idea of History*. New York: Oxford University Press.

CORSINI, R. J., ed. 1973. Current Psychotherapies. Itasca, Ill.: F. J. Peacock Co.

CORSINI, R. J., ed. 1979. *Current Psychotherapies*. 2nd ed. Itasca, Ill.: F. J. Peacock Co.

COX, D. 1970. *Youth into Maturity*. New York: Mental Health Materials Center.

CUBER, J. AND HARROFF, P. 1965. *The Significant Americans*. New York: Appleton.

CUMMINGS, D. A. 1979. "Turning Bread into Stones: Our Modern Antimiracle." *American Psychologist*, 34: 1119–29.

DAVID, Z. 1971. *L'Etat Amoureux*. Paris: Payot.

DAVIDSON, P. O. AND DAVIDSON, S. M., eds. 1980. *Behavioral Medicine: Changing Health Life Styles*. New York: Brunner/Mazel.

DAVIDSON, T. 1978. *Conjugal Crime.* New York: Hawthorn.

DAVIS, A. AND HAVIGHURST, R. J. 1946. "Social Class and Color Differences in Child-Rearing." *American Sociological Review,* 698–710.

DAVIS, B. D. 1966. *The Problem of Slavery in Western Culture.* Ithaca: Cornell University Press.

DAVIS, J. M. AND COLE, J. O. 1975. "Anti-Psychotic Drugs." Ch. 22 in S. Arieti, ed., *American Handbook of Psychiatry,* Vol. V.

DEAN, J. 1976. *Blind Ambition.* New York: Simon and Shuster.

DECKER, H. S. 1978. *Freud in Germany.* Psychological Issues Monograph 41. New York: International Universities Press.

DEGROOT, A. D. 1949. *Sint Nicolaas: Patroon Van Liefde.* Amsterdam Noord-Hollandsche Witgevers Maatschappij.

DELANY, P. 1919. *British Autobiography in the 17th Century.* New York: Columbia University Press.

DE LOME, R. H. 1979. *Children, Inequality and the Limits of Liberal Reform.* New York: Harcourt Brace Jovanovich.

DE MAUSE, L. 1974. *The History of Childhood.* New York: Psychohistory Press.

DERRIDA, J. 1978. *Writing and Difference.* Chicago: University of Chicago Press.

DESCHNER, K. 1974. *Das Kreuz mit der Kirche.* Dusseldorf: Ezon Verlag.

DEUTSCH, A. 1949. *The Mentally Ill in America.* New York: Columbia University Press.

DE ZULUETA, T. 1980. "Abolishing Mental Hospitals." *Atlas,* February, 1980, pp. 57–59.

DIAMOND, S. 1974. *In Search of the Primitive.* New Brunswick, N.J.: Transaction.

DIENER, E. AND CRANDALL, R. 1978. *Ethics in Social and Behavioral Research.* Chicago: University of Chicago Press.

DILLARD, J. L. 1972. *Black English.* New York: Random House.

DIXON, N. S. 1976. *On the Psychology of Military Incompetence.* New York: Basic Books.

DOBZHANSKY, T. 1973. *Genetic Diversity and Human Equality.* New York: Basic Books.

DOHRENWEND, B. P. AND DOHRENWEND, B. S. 1969. *Social Stress and Psychological Disorder.* New York: Wiley.

DORE, R. 1976. *The Diploma Disease.* Berkeley: University of California Press.

DOUGLAS, M. 1970. *Natural Symbols.* New York: Random House.

DRABKIN, I. E. 1954. "Remarks on Ancient Psychopathology." Mimeographed paper read at a meeting of the History of Science Society, City College of New York, December 29, 1954.

DURANT, W. 1961. *The Story of Philosophy.* New York: Simon and Schuster.

DURKHEIM, E. 1895. *The Rules of Sociological Method.* Reprint ed. New York: Free Press, 1966.

DURKHEIM, E. 1897. *Suicide: A Study in Sociology.* New York: Free Press, 1951.

DURKHEIM, E. et al. 1960. *Essays on Sociology and Philosophy.* New York: Harper and Row, 1964.

EAGLETON, T. 1976. *Marxism and Literary Criticism.* Berkeley: University of California Press.

EATON, J. W. AND NEIL, R. J. 1955. *Culture and Mental Disorders: A Comparative Study of the Hutterites and Other Populations.* Glencoe, Ill.: Free Press.

EBBINGHAUS, H. 1913. *Memory.* New York: Teachers College.

EGBERT, D. 1970. *Social Radicalism, and the Arts.* New York: Knopf.

ELLEN, R. F. AND REASON, D. 1979. *Classifications in Their Social Context.* New York: Academic Press.

ELLENBERGER, H. F. 1970. *The Discovery of the Unconscious.* New York: Basic Books.

EMDE, R. N. et al. 1976. *Emotional Exprssion in Infancy.* Psychological Issues Monograph 37. New York: International Universities Press.

Encyclopaedia Britannica. 15th Edition. 1978.

ENGEL, G. L. 1977. "The Need for a New Medical Model: A Challenge for Biomedicine." *Science,* 196, No. 4286: 129–36.

ENTRALGO, P. L. 1970. *The Therapy of the Word in Classical Antiquity.* New Haven: Yale University Press.

ERICKSON, E. 1950. *Childhood and Society.* New York: Norton.

ERICKSON, E. 1954. "The Dream Specimen of Psychoanaysis." *JAPA,* 2, 5–56.

ERICKSON, E. 1959. *Identity and the Life Cycle.* Psychological Issues Monograph 1. New York: International Universities Press.

ERLE, J. B. 1979. "An Approach to the Study of Analyzability and Analyses: The Course of Forty Consecutive Cases Selected for Supervised Analysis." *PQ,* 48: 198–228.

ESMAN, A. 1977. "Changing Values: Their Implications for Adolescent Development and Psychoanalytic Ideas." In S. Feinstein et al., eds. *Adolescent Psychiatry,* 5: 18–34. New York: Basic Books.

FARIS, R. E. L. AND DUNHAM, H. W. 1939. *Mental Disorder in Urban Areas.* Chicago: University of Chicago Press.

FARIS, R. E. L., ed. 1964. *Handbook of Modern Sociology.* Chicago: Rand McNally.

FEDERN, P. 1928. "Narcissism in the Structure of the Ego." *IJP,* 9, 410–19.

FEDERN, P. 1929. "The Ego as Subject and Object in Narcissism." *Internationale Zeitschrift Fuer Psychoanalyse,* 15: 393–425. Reprinted in P. Federn, *Ego Psychology and the Psychoses,* 283–322. New York: Basic Books.

FENICHEL, O. 1930. "Statistischer Bericht ueber die therapeutische Taetig-keit." In G. Maetze, ed. *Zehn Jahre Berliner Psychoanalytisches Institut*, pp. 13–19. Verlag Anton Hahn, Meisen Heim, 1970.

FENICHEL, O. 1945. *The Psychoanalytic Theory of Neurosis*. New York: Norton.

FIEDLER, L. 1966. *Love and Death in the American Novel*. New York: Dell.

FINE, R. 1969. "On the Nature of Scientific Method in Psychology." *Psychological Reports*, 24: 519–40.

FINE, R. 1972. "The Age of Awareness," *Psychoanalytic Review*, 59: 55–71.

FINE, R. 1973 "Review of Hooker's Papers on Homosexuality." *International Journal of Psychiatry*, 11: 471–75.

FINE, R. 1975. *Psychoanalytic Psychology*. New York: Jason Aronson.

FINE, R. 1975. "The Bankruptcy of Behaviorism." *Psychoanalytic Review*, 63: 437–51.

FINE, R. AND FINE, B. 1977. "The Mathematician as a Healthy Narcissist." In M. Colemen, ed. *The Narcissistic Condition*, pp. 213–47. New York: Behavioral Sciences Press.

FINE, R. 1977. "Psychoanalysis as a Philosophical System." *Journal of Psychohistory*, 4: 1–66.

FINE, R. 1979a. *A History of Psychoanalysis*. New York: Columbia University Press.

FINE, R. 1979b. *The Intimate Hour*. New York: Avery Publishing Co.

FINE, R. 1980. "Freudian Misconceptions of Freud: A Review of J. Gedo, *Beyond Interpretation*." *Contemporary Psychology*, 25.

FISHER, S. AND GREENBERG, R. P. 1977. *The Scientific Credibility of Freud's Theories and Therapy*. New York: Basic Books.

FITZGERALD, F. 1979. *America Revised*. Boston: Atlantic-Little, Brown.

FLUGEL, J. 1921. *The Psychoanalytic Study of the Family*. London: Hogarth Press.

FOGEL, R. W. AND ENGERMAN S. L. 1974. *Time on the Cross*. Boston: Little, Brown.

FORTES, M. 1969. *Kinship and the Social Order*. Chicago: Aldine.

FORTES, M. 1977. "Custom and Conscience in Anthropological Perspective." *International Review of Psychoanalysis*, 4, 127–54.

FORTUNE, R. 1932. *The Sorcerers of Dobu*. New York: Dutton.

FREEDMAN, A. 1978. "Psychoanalytic Study of an Unusual Perversion." *JAPA*, 26: 749–77.

FREEDMAN, N. AND GRAND, S. 1977. *Communicative Structures and Psychic Structures: A Psychoanalytic Interpretation of Communication*. New York: Plenum.

FREEDMAN, N. AND STEINGART, I. 1976. "Kinesic Internalization and Language Construction." In D. F. Spence, ed. *Psychoanalysis and Contemporary Science*. New York: International Universities Press, IV: 355–404.

FREIMAN, G. 1979. "A Soviet Teacher's J'accuse." *New York Times Magazine*, 121–27.

FREUD, A. 1936. *The Ego and the Mechanisms of Defense.* New York: International Universities Press.

FREUD, A. 1965. *Normality and Puthology in Childhood.* New York: International Universities Press.

FREUD, A. et al. 1973. *Beyond the Best Interests of the Child.* New York: Free Press.

FREUD, A. et al. 1979. *For the Best Interests of the Child..* New York: Free Press.

FREUD, S. 1974. *The Standard Edition of the Complete Psychological Works of Sigmund Freud.* Edited by J. Strachey. London: Hogarth Press and Institute of Psychoanalysis. 24 vols. All references, unless otherwise noted, are to the Standard Edition, abbreviated SE.

FRIED, E. et al. 1964. *Artistic Productivity and Mental Health.* Springfield, Ill.: C. C. Thomas.

FRIEDMAN, P. R. 1976. "Legal Regulation of Applied Behavioral Analysis in Mental Institutions and Prisons." In *Annual Review of Behavior Therapy*, Ch. 4, pp. 73–105.

FRIEDRICH, D. 1976. *Going Crazy: An Inquiry into Madness in Our Time.* New York: Simon and Schuster.

FROMM, E. 1939. "Selfishness and Self-Love." *Psychiatry*, 2: 507–23.

FROMM, E. 1941. *Escape from Freedom.* New York: Farrar and Rinehart.

FROMM, E. 1956. *The Art of Loving.* New York: Harper and Row.

FROMM, E. AND MACCOBY, M. 1970. *Social Character in a Mexican Village.* Englewood Cliffs, N.J.: Prentice-Hall.

FROMM-REICHMANN, F. 1959. *Psychoanalysis and Psychotherapy.* Chicago: University of Chicago Press.

FRYDE, E. B. "Historiography and Historical Methodology." *Encyclopaedia Britannica*, 8: 945–61.

GAGLIARDO, J. G. 1969. *From Pariah to Patriot: The Changing Image of the German Peasant, 1770–1840.* Lexington: The University Press of Kentucky.

GALBRAITH, J. K. 1973. *The New Industrial State.* Boston: Houghton Mifflin Co.

GALBRAITH, J. K. 1978. *Economics and the Public Purpose.* Boston: Houghton Mifflin Co.

GARFIELD, S. L. AND BERGIN, A. E. 1978. *Handbook of Psychotherapy and Behavior Change.* 2d ed. New York: Wiley.

GAY, P. L. AND CAVANAGH, G. 1972. *Historians at Work.* 4 Vols. New York: Harper.

GAY, P. L. AND WEBB, R. K. 1973. *A History of Modern Europe.* New York: Harper.

GAY, P. L. 1978. "Philosophy of History." *Encyclopaedia Britannica*, 8: 961–965.

GEDO, J. AND GOLDBERG, A. 1973. *Models of the Mind: A Psychoanalytic Theory.* Chicago: University of Chicago Press.

GEDO, J. 1979. *Beyond Interpretation.* New York: International Universities Press.

GEDO, J. AND POLLOCK, G. H., eds. 1976. *The Fusion of Science and Humanism.* New York: International Universities Press.

GELLES, R. J. 1972. *The Violent Home.* Beverley Hills, Calif.: Sage Foundation.

GETZELS, J. W. AND CSIKSZENTMIHALYI, M. 1976. *The Creative Vision.* New York: Wiley.

GINSBURG, H. 1972. *The Myth of the Deprived Child.* Englewood Cliffs, N.J.: Prentice-Hall.

GLASER, R., ed. 1971. *The Nature of Reinforcement.* New York: Academic Press.

GLOVER, E. 1955. *The Technique of Psychoanalysis.* New York: International Universities Press.

GOLDBERG, A., ed. 1978. *The Psychology of the Self: A Casebook.* New York: International Universities Press.

GOLDFREID, M. R. 1971. "Homosexual Signs." In M. R. Goldfreid et al., eds. *Rorschach Handbook of Clinical and Research Applications.* Englewood Cliffs, N.J.: Prentice-Hall.

GOLDHAMMER, H. AND MARSHALL, A. 1953. *Psychosis and Civilization.* Glencoe, Ill.: Free Press.

GOODE, W. L. 1951. *Religion Among the Primitives.* Glencoe, Ill.: Free Press.

GOODE, W. 1959. "The Sociology of the Family." In *Sociology Today,* ed. R. Merton et al., pp. 178–96. New York: Basic Books.

GOODE, W. J. 1970. *World Revolution and Family Patterns.* New York: Free Press.

GOODENOUGH, F. L. 1926. *Measurement of Intelligence by Drawings.* Yonkers, N.Y. World Book Co.

GOODMAN, J., ed. 1977. *Psychoanalytic Education and Research.* New York: International Universities Press.

GORER, G. AND RICHMAN, J. 1949. *The People of Great Russia.* London: Cresset Press.

GRAHAM, H. T. AND BURR, T. R. eds. 1969. *Violence in America.* New York: Bantam Books.

GREEN, A. W. 1946. "The Middle-Class Male Child and Neurosis." *American Sociological Review,* 11: 31–41.

GREEN, P. AND LEVINSON, S. 1970. *Power and Community: Dissenting Essays in Political Science.* New York: Vintage Books.

GREY, A. L. ed. 1970. *Man, Woman and Marriage.* New York: Atherton.

GREY, L. 1979. *Stalin: Man of History.* New York: Doubleday.

GRIESINGER, W. 1867. *Mental Pathology and Therapeutics.* London: New Sydenham Society.

GRINKER, R. R. AND SPIEGEL, J. P. 1963. *Men Under Stress.* New York: McGraw-Hill.

GRINKER, R. R. et al. 1968. *The Borderline Syndrome.* New York: Basic Books.

GROB, G. N. AND BILLIAS, G. A. eds. 1978. *Interpretations in American History.* 2 Vols. New York: Free Press.

Group for the Advancement of Psychiatry. 1978. *The Chronic Mental Patient in the Community.* New York: Mental Health Materials Center.

GUILFORD, J. P. 1950. "Creativity." *American Psychologist,* 14: 469–79.

GUTMAN, H. 1976. *The Black Family in Slavery and Freedom. 1750–1925.* New York: Pantheon Books.

HALE, N. G. 1971. *Freud and the Americans.* New York: Oxford University Press.

HALE, O. J. 1971. *The Great Illusion: 1900–1914.* New York: Harper and Row.

HAMBURG, D. et al. 1967. "Report of Ad Hoc Committee on Central Fact-Gathering Data of the American Psychoanalytic Association." *JAPA,* 15: 841–61.

HANLY, C. AND LAZEROWITZ, M., eds. 1970. *Psychoanalysis and Philosophy.* New York: International Universities Press.

HANSON, N. R. 1958. *Patterns of Discovery.* Cambridge: Cambridge University Press.

HARLOW, H. 1974. *Learning to Love.* New York: Jason Aronson.

HARRIS, M. 1956. *Town and Country in Brazil.* New York: Norton.

HARRIS, M. 1968. *The Rise of Anthropological Theory.* New York: Thomas Y. Crowell.

HARRIS, M. 1979. *Cultural Materialism: The Struggle for a Science of Culture.* New York: Random House.

HARTMANN, E. 1978. *The Sleeping Pill.* New Haven: Yale University Press.

HARTMANN, E. von. 1870. *Philosophy of the Unconscious.*

HARTMANN, H. 1933. "Psychoanalyse und Weltanschauung." *Psychoanalytische Bewegung,* 5: 416–29.

HARTMANN, H. 1939. *Ego Psychology and the Problem of Adaptation.* New York: International Universities Press.

HARTMANN, H. 1944. "Review of Sears: Survey of Objective Studies of Psychoanalytic Concepts." *PQ,* 13: 101–102.

HARTMANN, H. 1956. "Presidental Address." *IJP,* 37: 118–20.

HARTMANN, H. 1960. *Psychoanalysis and Moral Values.* New York: International Universities Press.

HARTMANN, H. 1964. *Essays in Ego Psychology.* New York: International Universities Press.

HAUSER, A. 1951. *The Social History of Art.* 4 Vols. New York: Vintage Books.

Hayek, F. A. 1944. *The Road to Serfdom.* Chicago: University of Chicago Press.

Hazo, R. G. 1967. *The Idea of Love.* New York: Praeger.

HEILBRONER, R. 1973. *The Worldly Philosphers*. New York: Simon and Schuster.

HELFAER, P. M. 1972. *The Psychology of Religious Doubt*. Boston: Beacon Press.

HEMMING, J. 1978. *Red Gold: The Conquest of the Brazilian Indians 1500–1760*. Cambridge, Mass.: Harvard University Press.

HENDIN, H. 1975. *The Age of Sensation: A Psychoanalytic Exploration*. New York: Norton.

HENRY, W. E. et al. 1971. *The Fifth Profession*. San Francisco: Jossey-Bass.

HENRY, W. E. et al. 1973. *Public and Private Lives of Psychotherapists*. San Francisco: Jossey-Bass.

HERZBERG, F. 1966. *Work and the Nature of Man*. New York: World.

HERZBERG, F. 1974. "Work Satisfaction and Motivation–Hygiene Theory." *Book Forum, I*, 213–21.

HILLEL, M. AND HENRY, C. 1976. *Of Pure Blood*. New York: McGraw-Hill.

HINGLEY, R. 1979. *Russian Writers and Soviet Society*. New York: Random House.

HITE, S. 1976. *The Hite Report*. New York: Macmillan.

HOFFDING, H. 1900. *A History of Modern Philosophy*. 2 Vols. New York: Dover, 1955.

HOLLINGSHEAD, A. B. AND REDLICH, F. C. 1958. *Social Class and Mental Illness*. New York: Wiley.

HOOK, S. ed. 1959. *Psychoanalysis, Scientific Method and Philosphy*. New York: Grove Press.

HOOKER, E. 1957. "The Adjustment of Male Homosexuals." *Journal of Projective Techniques*, 21 · 17–31.

HOOKER, E. 1958. "Male Homosexuality in the Rorschach." *Journal of Projective Techniques*, 22: 33–54.

HOROWITZ, I. L., ed. 1967. *The Rise and Fall of Project Camelot*. Cambridge, Mass.: MIT Press.

HUGHES, R. AND BREWIN, R. 1979. *The Tranquilizing of America*. New York: Harcourt Brace Jovanovich.

HULL, C. 1943. *Principles of Behavior*. New York: Appleton-Century.

HUNT, M. 1959. *The Natural History of Love*. New York: Knopf.

HUXLEY, A. 1932. *Brave New World*.

HYMES, D., ed. 1972. *Reinventing Anthropology*. New York: Pantheon.

JACOBSON, E. 1955. "Sullivan's Interpersonal Theory of Psychiatry." *JAPA*, 3: 149–56.

JAFFE, D. S. AND PULVER, S. E. 1978. "Survey of Psychoanalytic Practice 1976: Some Trends and Applications." *JAPA*, 26: 615–29.

JAMES, W. 1890. *The Principles of Psychology*. Reprinted 1950. New York: H. Holt.

JAMES, W. 1902. *The Varieties of Religious Experience*. Modern Library Edition. New York: Random House.

JARVIS, E. 1855. *Report on Insanity and Idiocy in Massachusetts by the Commission on Lunacy.* Reprinted 1971. Cambridge, Mass: Harvard University Press.

JELLINEK, M. AND LAZARE, A. 1979. "Relations Between Academic Departments of Psychiatry and Pharmaceutical Companies." *American Journal of Psychiatry.* 136: 827–29.

JENCKS, C. 1972. *Inequality: A Reassessment of the Effect of Family and Schooling in America.* New York: Basic Books.

JENCKS, C. 1979. *Who Gets Ahead? The Determinants of Economic Success in America.* New York: Basic Books.

JONES, E. 1912. *On the Nightmare.* Reprinted. London: Hogarth Press, 1931.

JONES, E. 1948. *Collected Papers on Psychoanalysis.* 5th ed. London: Bailliere, Tindall and Zox.

JONES, E. 1953–57. *The Life and Work of Sigmund Freud.* 3 Vols. New York: Basic Books.

JONES, E. 1959. *Free Associations.* New York: Basic Books.

JOPLING, C. F., ed. 1971. *Art and Aesthetics in Primitive Societies.* New York: Dutton.

KADUSHIN, C. 1969. *Why People Go to Psychiatrists.* New York: Atherton Press.

KANTER, R. M. 1976. "The Romance of Community." In M. Rosenbaum and A. Snadowsky, eds. *The Intensive Group Experience,* 146–185.

KANTER, R. M. 1977. *Men and Women of the Corporation.* New York: Basic Books.

KANTER, R. M. AND STEIN, B. A. eds. 1979. *Life in Organizations.* New York: Basic Books.

KARDINER, A. 1939. *The Individual and His Society.* New York: Columbia University Press.

KARDINER, A. 1945. *The Psychological Frontiers of Society.* New York: Columbia University Press.

KARDINER, A. 1977. *Diary of My Analysis with Freud.* New York: Norton.

KATONA, F. 1951. *Psychological Analysis of Economic Behavior.* New York: McGraw-Hill.

KERNBERG, O. 1975. *Borderline Conditions and Pathological Narcissism.* New York: Jason Aronson.

KERNBERG, O. 1976. *Object Relations Theory and Clinical Psychoanalysis.* New York: Jason Aronson.

KEYNES, J. M. 1935. *The General Theory of Employment, Interest and Money.* New York: Harcourt.

KHRUSCHEV, N. 1970. *Khrushchev Remembers.* Boston: Little, Brown.

KIEV, A. 1964. *Magic, Faith and Healing.* New York: Free Press.

KINSEY, A. C. et al. 1948. *Sexual Behavior in the Human Male.* Philadelphia: Saunders.

KINSEY, A. C. et al. 1953. *Sexual Behavior in the Human Female.* Philadelphia: Saunders.

KIRKPATRICK, C. 1955. *The Family as Process and Institution.* New York: Ronald Press.

KLEIN, G. S. 1959. "The Role of Consciousness in Psychoanalytic Theory." *JAPA,* 7: 5–34.

KLEIN, G. S. 1976. *Psychoanalytic Theory: An Explanation of the Essentials.* New York: International Universities Press.

KNAPP, P. et al. 1960. "Suitability for Psychoanalysis: A Review of One Hundred Supervised Cases." *PQ,* 29: 457–477.

KNIGHT, R. P. 1953. "The Present Status of Organized Psychoanalysis in the United States." *JAPA,* 1: 197–221.

KOHUT, H. 1977. *The Restoration of the Self.* New York: International Universities Press.

KOLLONTAI, A. 1971. *The Autobiography of a Sexually Emancipated Communist Woman.* New York: Herder and Herder.

KOMAROVSKY, M. 1967. *Blue-Collar Marriage.* New York: Vintage Books.

KRAEPELIN, E. 1906. *Lectures on Clinical Psychiatry.* London: Bailliere, Tindall and Cox.

KRAEPELIN, E. 1917. *One Hundred Years of Psychiatry.* New York: Citadel Press.

KREN, G. 1977. "Psychohistory in the University." *Journal of Psychohistory,* 4: 339–50.

KRIS, E. 1952. *Psychoanalytic Explorations in Art.* New York: International Universities Press.

KROEBER, A. L. AND KLUCKHOHN, 1952. *Culture: A Critical Review of Concepts and Definitions.* New York: Vintage Books.

KUBIE, L. S. 1967. "The Overall Manpower Problem and the Creation of a New Discipline: The Nonmedical Psychotherapist." In M. Klutch. *Mental Health Manpower.* California Medical Education and Research Foundation, II: 112–20.

KUBIE, L. S. AND ISRAEL, H. A. 1955. "Say You're Sorry." *Psychoanalytic Study of the Child,* 10: 289–99.

KUHN, T. S. 1962. *The Structure of Scientific Revolutions.* Chicago: University of Chicago Press.

KUSMER, K. L. 1979. "The Concept of 'Community' in American History." *Reviews in American History,* 7: 380–87.

LABARRE, W. 1961. "Psychoanalysis in Anthropology." In J. Masserman, Ed., *Science and Psychoanalysis,* 4: 10–20.

LABOV, W. et al. 1968. *A Study of the Non-standard English of Negro and Puerto Rican Speakers in New York City.* New York: Columbia University Department of Linguistics.

LADNER, J. A. ed., 1973. *The Death of White Sociology,* New York: Vintage Books.

LAPIDUS, G. W. 1979. *Women in Soviet Society*. Berkeley: University of California Press.

LACAN, J. 1977. *Ecrits*. New York: Norton.

LACHENMEYER, C. W. 1973. *The Essence of Social Research*. New York: Free Press.

LADURIE, L. R. 1978. *Montaillou: Promised Land of Error*. New York: Braziller.

LAING, R. D. AND ESTERSON, 1964. *Sanity, Madness and the Family*. New York: Basic Books.

LAMB, H. R. 1976. *Community Survival for Long-Term Patients*. San Francisco: Jossey-Bass.

LAMB, H. R. 1979. "Roots of Neglect of the Long-Term Mentally Ill." *Psychiatry*, 42: 201–7.

LAMB, M. E. 1976. *The Role of the Father in Child Development*. New York: Wiley.

LANGER, W. 1972. *The Mind of Adolf Hitler*. New York: Basic Books.

LANGS, R. 1974. *The Technique of Psychoanalytic Psychotherapy*, 2 Vols. New York: Jason Aronson.

LASSWELL, H. D. 1930. *Psychopathology and Politics*. New York: Viking.

LASSWELL, H. D., LEITES, N. et al. 1949. *Language of Politics. Studies in Quantitative Semantics*. Cambridge, Mass.

LEIGHTON, A. H. 1963. *The Character of Danger*. New York: Basic Books.

LEIGHTON, A. 1975. "Social Disintegration and Mental Disorder." In S. Arieti, ed. *American Handbook of Psychiatry*, Vol. II, Ch. 28.

LE PLAY, F. 1855 (expanded and revised 1877–1879). *The European Working Classes*.

LEVINE, F. 1976. *The Culture Barons: An Analysis of Power and Money in the Arts*. New York: Thomas Y. Crowell.

LEVINE, R. A. 1973. *Culture, Behavior and Personality*. Chicago: Aldine.

LÉVI-STRAUSS, 1966. *The Savage Mind*. Chicago: University of Chicago Press.

LÉVI-STRAUSS, C. 1969. *The Elementary Structures of Kinship*. Boston: Beacon Press.

LEVISON, A. 1974. *The Working Class Majority*. New York: Coward, McCann, and Geoghegan.

LEWIN, B. AND ROSS, H. 1960. *Psychoanalytic Education in the United States*. New York: Norton.

LEWIS, O. 1961. *The Children of Sanchez*. New York: Vintage Books.

LEWIS, O. 1966. *Anthropological Essays*. New York: Random House.

LICHTENBERG, J. 1978. "The Testing of Reality from the Standpoint of the Body Self." *JAPA*, 26: 357–85.

LICHTENBERG, J. D. 1979. "Factors in the Development of the Sense of the Object." *JAPA*, 27: 375–86.

LIDZ, T. et al. 1965. *Schizophrenia and the Family*. New York: International Universities Press.

LIEBERMAN, M. A. et al. 1973. *Encounter Groups: First Facts.* New York: Basic Books.

LIFTON, R. 1969. *Thought Reform and the Psychology of Totalism.* New York: Norton.

LINDBLOM, C. E. AND COHEN, D. K. 1979. *Social Science and Social Problem Solving.* New Haven: Yale University Press.

LINDSEY, D. 1978. *The Scientific Publication System in Social Science.* San Francisco: Jossey-Bass.

LING, T. 1968. *A History of Religion East and West.* New York: Harper and Row.

LIN YUTANG. 1937. *The Importance of Living.* New York: Reynal and Hitchcock.

LOEWENSTEIN, R. M. 1951. *Christians and Jews: A Psychoanalytic Study.* New York: International Universities Press.

LONDON, P. 1972. "The End of Ideology in Behavior Modification." *American Psychologist,* 27: 913–20.

LOWE, A. 1965. *On Economic Knowledge.* New York: Harper and Row.

LOWITH, K. 1967. *From Hegel to Nietzsche: The Revolution in 19th Century Thought.* New York: Anchor Books.

LOWRY, R. AND RANKIN, A. 1970. *Sociology.* New York: Scribner's.

LUBART, J. 1976. "The Mackenzie Delta Eskimos." In W. Muensterberger, A. H. Esman and L. B. Boyer, eds. *The Psychoanalytic Study of Society.* New Haven: Yale University Press, 7: 331–58.

LUDWIG, A. 1965. *The Importance of Lying.* Springfield, Ill.: C. C. Thomas.

LYNCH, W. H. 1977. *The Broken Heart.* New York: Basic Books.

LYONS, J. O. 1978. *The Invention of the Self: The Hinge of Consciousness in the 18th Century.* Carbondale: University of Southern Illinois Press.

LYONS, R. E. 1979. "Beneficial Valium Can Also Prove to Be Bad Medicine." *New York Times,* September 16, 1979, p. 20E.

McBRIDE, H. 1975. *Essays and Criticisms.* Ed. D. C. Rich. New York: Atheneum Publishers.

McCLELLAND, D. C. 1961. *The Achieving Society.* Princeton: Van Nostrand.

McGILL, V. 1967. *The Idea of Happiness.* New York: Praeger.

MACKENZIE, B. D. 1977. *Behaviorism and the Limits of Scientific Method.* Atlantic Highlands, N.J.: Humanities Press.

McNEILL, W. H. 1967. *A World History.* New York: Oxford University Press.

McNEILL, W. H. 1976. *Plagues and Peoples.* New York: Anchor Press.

MADAULE, J. 1967. *The Albigensian Crusade.* New York: Fordham University Press.

MAETZE, G., ed. 1970. *Zehn Jahre Berliner Psychoanalytisches Institut.* Meisenheim, West Germany: Verlag Anton Hain.

MAGARO, P. A. et al. 1978. *The Mental Health Industry: A Cultural Phenomenon.* New York: Wiley.

MAHLER, M. et al. 1975. *The Psychological Birth of the Human Infant.* New York: Basic Books.

MANUEL, F. E. AND MANUEL, F. P. 1979. *Utopian Thought in the Western World.* Cambridge, Mass.: Harvard University Press.

MARLOW, H. C. AND DAVIS, H. M. eds. 1976. *The American Search for Woman.* Santa Barbara, Calif.: Clio Books.

MARMOR, J. *Psychiatrists and their Patients.* Washington, D.C.: American Psychiatric Association.

MARSHALL, D. S. 1971. "Sexual Behavior on Mangaia." in Marshall and Suggs, *Human Sexual Behavior,* Ch. 5.

MARSHALL, D. S. AND SUGGS, R. W. 1971. *Human Sexual Behavior.* New York: Basic Books.

MARX, K. 1841–1883. *The Marx-Engels Reader.* Edited by R. Tucker 1978. New York: Norton.

MASER, W. 1971. *Hitler: Legend, Myth, and Reality.* New York: Harper and Row.

MASSERMAN, J. ed. 1958–. *Science and Psychoanalysis.* Vols. I–XXI. Ongoing Series. New York: Grune and Stratton.

MASTERS, W. AND JOHNSON, V. 1966. *Human Sexual Response.* Boston: Little, Brown.

MASTERS, W. AND JOHNSON, V. E. 1979. *Homosexuality in Perspective.* Boston: Little, Brown.

MAUSS, M. 1925. *The Gift.* New York: Norton, 1967.

MAY, P. R. et al. 1968. *Treatment of Schizophrenia.* New York: Science House.

MAY, R. et al., eds. 1958. *Existence.* New York: Simon and Schuster.

MAY, R. 1969. *Love and Will.* New York: Norton.

MEHTA, D. et al. 1978. "Mortality of Patients with Tardive Dyskinesia." *American Journal of Psychiatry,* 134, March.

MEISELMAN, K. C. 1972. *Incest.* San Francisco: Jossey-Bass.

MEISSNER, W. W. 1978. "Theoretical Assumptions of Concepts of the Borderline Personality." *JAPA,* 26: 559–98.

MELTZOFF, D. AND KORNREICH, M. 1970. *Research in Psychotherapy.* New York: Atherton.

MERKLE, L. AND LITTLE, R. B. 1967. "Beginning Psychiatry Training Syndrome." *American Journal of Psychiatry,* 124: 193–97.

MERTON, R. K. 1962. "Bureaucratic Structure and Personality." In *Work, Man and Modern Society,* ed. S. Nosow and W. Form, pp. 457–60. New York: Basic Books.

MESSENGER, J. C. 1971. "Sex and Repression in an Irish Folk Community." In D. S. Marshall and R. C. Suggs, *Human Sexual Behavior,* Ch. 1.

MILAN, M. A. AND MCKEE, J. M. 1977. "The Cellblock Token Economy." *Annual Review of Behavior Therapy,* Ch. 20, pp. 535–70.

MILLER, A. G. 1972. *The Social Psychology of Psychological Research.* New York: Free Press.

MITROFF, I. T. AND KILMAN, R. H. 1978. *Methodological Approaches to Social Science.* San Francisco: Jossey-Bass.

MITZMAN, A. 1970. *The Iron Cage: An Historical Interpretation of Max Weber.* New York: Knopf.

MITZMAN, A. 1973. *Sociology and Estrangement: Three Sociologists of Imperial Germany.* New York: Knopf.

MODELL, J. et al. 1979. "Colloquium on Herbert Gutman's *The Black Family." Social Science History,* 3: 45–85.

MOYNIHAN, D. 1965. *The Negro Family: The Case for Nationalization.* Washington, D.C.: U.S. Department of Labor.

MURDOCK, G. P. 1949. *Social Structure.* New York: Macmillan.

MURPHY, G. 1972. *Historical Introduction to Modern Psychology.* New York: Harcourt.

MUSTO, D. F. 1973. *The American Disease: Origins of Narcotic Control.* New Haven: Yale University Press.

MYERS, J. K. AND BEAN, L. L. 1968. *A Decade Later.* New York: Wiley.

NAGEL, E. 1961. *The Structure of Science.* New York: Harcourt, Brace and World.

NEILL, A. S. 1960. *Summerhill.* New York: Hart Publishers.

New York Psychoanalytical Society. 1979. *Newsletter.* New York.

New York Times. 1978a. "Mental Patients See Liberation in Rising Challenge to Therapies." December 11, 1978.

New York Times. 1978b. December 20, 1978. Obituary of Harold Lasswell.

New York Times, 1979. "Mental Patients and the Community." November 20, 1979, p. B4.

NIEDERLAND, W. 1976. "Psychoanalytic Approaches to Artistic Creativity." *PQ,* 45: 185–212.

NIETZSCHE, F. *The Portable Nietzsche.* New York: Viking.

NISBET, R. A. 1966. *The Sociological Tradition.* New York: Basic Books.

NISBET, R. A. 1978. "History of the Social Sciences." *Encyclopaedia Brittanica,* 16: 980–90.

NOSOW, S. AND FORM, W. H., eds. 1962. *Man, Work and Society.* New York: Basic Books.

NUNBERG, H. AND FEDERN, E., eds. 1962–75. *Minutes of the Vienna Psychoanalytic Society.* 4 Vols. New York: International Universities Press.

OBERNDORF, C. P. 1953. *A History of Psychoanalysis in America.* New York: Grune and Stratton.

ODIER, C. 1956. *Anxiety and Magical Thinking.* New York: International Universities Press.

O'FAOLAIN, J. AND MARTINES, L., eds. 1973. *Not in God's Image: Woman in History from the Greeks to the Victorians.* New York: Harper Torchbooks.

OFFER, D. AND SABSHIN, M. 1974. *Normality.* New York: Basic Books.

OLLENDORF, R. 1966. *The Juvenile Homosexual Experience and Its Effect on Adult Sexuality.* New York: Julian Press.

OLNEY, J. 1979. "The Value of Autobiography for Comparative Studies." *Comparative Civilizations Review*, 8: 52 64.

OTTEN C. M. 1971. *Anthropology and Art: Readings in Cross-Cultural Aesthetics*. Garden City, N.Y.: The Natural History Press.

PAGE, C. H. 1969. *Class and American Sociology*. New York: Schocken Books.

PALMORE, E. 1969. "Predicting Longevity: A Follow-up Controlling for Age." *Gerontology*, Vol. 9.

PARSONS, T. 1953. "The Superego and the Theory of Social Systems." In T. Parsons et al. *Working Papers in the Theory of Action*. pp. 13–28. Chicago: Free Press

PARSONS, T. AND BALES, R. 1955. *Family: Socialization and Interaction Process*. Glencoe, Ill.: Free Press.

PARSONS, T. AND CLARK, K. B. 1966. *The Negro American*. Boston: Beacon Press.

PATAI, R. 1973. *The Arab Mind*. New York: Scribner's.

PENFIELD, W. et al. 1975. *The Mystery of the Mind*. Princeton, N.J.: Princeton University Press.

PETERFREUND, E. 1971. *Information Systems and Psychoanalysis*. Psychological Issues Monograph 25/26. New York: International Universities Press.

PETRONI, G., 1968. *Poesia d'Amore*. Bologna: Gherardo Casini Editor.

PFISTER, O. 1944. *Christianity and Fear*. London: Allen and Unwin.

PFISTER, O. 1963. *Psychoanalaysis and Faith*. New York: Basic Books.

PIAGET, J. 1977. *The Essential Piaget*. Ed. H. E. Gruber and J. J. Voneche. New York: Basic Books.

PIOTROWSKI, C. S. 1979. *Work and the Family System*. New York: Free Press.

PLAIDY, J. 1969. *The Spanish Inquisition: Its Rise, Growth and End*. New York: Citadel Press.

POLLOCK, G. H. 1974. *Remarks Concerning Chicago Proposal to Executive Council American Psychoanalytic Association*. Xeroxed Copy. Chicago: Chicago Institute of Psychoanalysis.

PRIBRAM, K. H. AND GILL, M. M. 1976. *Freud's "Project" Reassessed*. New York: Basic Books.

Psychoanalysis as Seen by Psychoanalyzed Psychologists. 1953. Washington, D.C.: American Psychological Association.

PUTNAM, J. J. 1971. *Letters: James Jackson Putnam on Psychoanalysis*. Cambridge, Mass.: Harvard University Press.

QUEN, J. M. AND CARLSSON, E. T., eds. 1979. *American Psychoanalysis: Origins and Development*. New York: Brunner/Mazel.

RADIN, P. 1927. *Primitive Man as Philosopher*. New York: Dover Books.

RAINWATER, L. 1965. "Crucible Of Identity: The Negro Lower-Class Family." In T. Parsons and K. B. Clark, eds, *The Negro American*.

RAINWATER, L. AND YANCEY, W. L. 1967. *The Moynihan Report and the Politics of Controversy.* Cambridge, Mass.: MIT Press.

RABB, T. K. 1978. "The New Jerusalem." *New York Times,* December 20, 1978, p. A27.

RAKOFF, V. M. et al. 1977. *Psychiatric Diagnosis.* New York: Brunner/Mazel.

RANDALL, J. H. 1962. *The Career of Philosophy.* 3 Vols. New York: Columbia University Press.

RANDALL, J. H. 1976. *The Making of the Modern Mind: 50th Anniversary Edition.* New York: Columbia University Press.

RANGELL, L. 1954. "Similiarities and Differences between Psychoanalysis and Dynamic Psychotherapy." *JAPA,* 2: 734–44.

RANK, O. 1932. *Art and the Artist: Creative Urge and Personality Development.* New York: Tudor.

RAPAPORT, D. 1960. *The Structure of Psychoanalytic Theory.* Psychological Issues Monograph 6. New York: International Universities Press.

READ, H. 1936. *Art and Society.* New York: Schocken Books. 1966.

REGIN, D. 1968. *Culture and the Crowd: A Cultural History of the Proletarian Era.* New York: Chilton.

REICH, W. 1978. "Diagnosing Soviet Dissidents." *Harper's,* 251: 31–37.

REICH, W. 1927. *The Function of the Orgasm.* New York: Orgone Institute Press.

REIDER, N. 1955. "The Demonology of Modern Psychiatry." *American Journal of Psychiatry,* 11: 851–56.

REINHARZ, S. 1979. *On Becoming a Social Scientist.* San Francisco: Jossey-Bass.

RENNIE, T. et al. 1962. *Mental Health in the Metropolis.* New York: McGraw-Hill.

RIBBLE, M. A. 1943. *The Rights of Infants: Early Psychological Needs and Their Satisfactions.* New York: Columbia University Press.

RICOEUR, P. 1967. *The Symbolism of Evil.* Boston: Beacon Press.

RICOEUR, P. 1970. *Freud and Philosophy.* New Haven: Yale University Press.

RICOEUR, P. 1977. "The Question of Proof in Freud's Psychoanalytic Writings." *JAPA,* 25: 835–71.

RIE, H. E. AND RIE, E. D. 1980. *Handbook of Minimal Brain Dysfunctions.* New York: John Wiley.

RIESMAN, D. et al. 1950. *The Lonely Crowd.* New Haven: Yale University Press.

RIESSMAN, F. 1967. "In Defense of the Negro Family." In L. Rainwater and W. L. Yancey, eds. *The Moynihan Report and the Politics of Controversy,* 474–78.

ROCHE DE COPPENS, P. 1976. *Ideal Man in Classical Sociology: The Views of Comte, Durkheim, Pareto and Weber.* University Park: Pennsylvania State University.

ROHEIM, G. 1932. "Psycho-Analysis of Primitive Cultural Types." *IJP*, 13: 1–224.

ROHEIM, G. 1950. *Psychoanalysis and Anthropology*. New York: International Universities Press.

ROHEIM, G. 1955. *Magic and Schizophrenia*. New York: International Universities Press.

ROOSENS, E. 1979. *Mental Patients in Town Life: Geel—Europe's First Therapeutic Community*. Beverly Hills, Calif: Sage.

ROSE, P. E. ed. 1970. *Slavery and Its Aftermath*. New York: Atherton.

ROSEN, B. 1972. *Witchcraft*. New York: Taplinger.

ROSEN, G. 1968. *Madness in Society: Chapters in the Historical Sociology of Mental Illness*. New York: Harper Torchbooks.

ROSENBAUM, M. AND SNADOWSKY, A., eds. 1976. *The Intensive Group Experience*. New York: Free Press.

ROSENHAN, D. L. 1973. "On Being Sane in Insane Places." *Science*, 179 (4070): 250–58.

ROSENTHAL, R. R. 1976. *Experimenter Effects in Behavioral Research*. New York: Wiley.

ROSTOW, W. W. 1966. *The Stages of Economic Growth*. Cambridge, Mass.: Harvard University Press.

ROTHENBERG, A. AND HAUSMAN, C. R., eds. 1976. *The Creativity Question*. Durham, N.C.: Duke University Press.

RUBIN, L. B. 1976. *Worlds of Pain: Life in the Working-Class Family*. New York: Basic Books.

RUBINS, J. 1978. *Karen Horney: The Gentle Rebel*. New York: Dial Press.

RUESCH, J. AND BATESON, G. 1951. *Communication: The Social Matrix of Psychiatry*. New York: Norton.

RUESCH, J. 1957. *Disturbed Communication*. New York: Norton.

RUESCH, J. 1961. *Therapeutic Communication*. New York: Norton.

RUHLE, J. 1969. *Literature and Revolution*. New York: Praeger.

RUSSELL, B. 1948. *Human Knowledge: Its Scope and Limits*. New York: Simon and Schuster.

RUSSELL, B. 1961. *The Basic Writings*. New York: Simon and Schuster.

RUSSELL, J. F. 1972. *Witchcraft in the Middle Ages*. Ithaca, N.Y.: Cornell University Press.

RYLE, G. 1949. *The Concept of Mind*. London: Hutchinson's University Library.

SACHS, W. 1947, *Black Anger*. Boston: Little, Brown.

SANCHES, M. AND BLOUNT, B. G., eds. 1975. *Sociocultural Dimensions of Language Use*. New York: Academic Press.

SANDLER, J. AND JOFFE, W. 1969. "Towards a Basic Psychoanalytic Model." *IJP*, 50: 79–90.

SAPIR, E. 1921. *Language*. New York: Harcourt, Brace and World.

SAUL, L. AND WENAR, I. 1965. "Early Influences on Development and Disorders of Personality." *PQ*, 34: 327–89.

SAUNDERS, E. 1940. *Lourdes.* New York: Oxford University Press.

SCHAFER, R. 1968. *Aspects of Internalization.* New York: International Universities Press.

SCHAFER, R. 1976. *A New Language for Psychoanalysis.* New Haven: Yale University Press.

SCHALLER, G. B. 1965. *The Year of the Gorilla.* New York: Ballantine Books.

SCHARFSTEIN, B. AND OSTOW, M. 1970. "The Need to Philosophize." In C. Hanly and M. Lazerowitz, *Psychoanalysis and Philosophy.* New York: International Universities Press. 258–79.

SCHECTER, D. E. 1979. "Problems of Training Analysis: A Critical Review of Current Concepts." *Journal of the American Academy of Psychoanalysis,* 7: 359–74.

SCHILDER, P. 1935. *The Image and Appearance of the Human Body.* Reprint ed., New York: International Universities Press, 1950.

SCHMIDT, V. 1924. *Psychoanalytische Erziehung in Sowjetrussland.* Vienna: Internationaler Psychoanalytischer Verlag.

SCHNEIDER, D. E. 1950. *The Psychoanalyst and the Artist.* New York: Mentor Books.

SCHUMPETER, J. 1942. *Capitalism, Socialism and Democracy.* New York: Harper.

SCHUR, M. 1972. *Freud: Living and Dying.* New York: International Universities Press.

SCHUSTER, D. B. et al. 1972. *Clinical Supervision of the Psychiatric Resident.* New York: Brunner/Mazel.

SCHWAB, J. J. 1979. *Social Order and Mental Health: The Florida Health Study.* New York: Brunner/Mazel.

SCOTT, J. P. AND SENAY, E. C. 1973. *Separation and Depression.* Washington, D.C.: AAAS.

SCRIVEN, M. 1965. "An Essential Unpredictability in Human Behavior." In Wolman, B. B. and Nagel E., eds. *Scientific Psychology,* Ch. 22, pp. 411–25.

SEARS, R. R. 1943. *Survey of Objective Studies of Psychoanalytic Concepts.* Bulletin 51. New York: Social Science Research Council.

SEBALD, H. 1978. *Witchcraft: The Heritage of a Heresy.* New York: Elsevier.

SELLIN, J. T. 1976. *Slavery and the Penal System.* New York: Elsevier.

SEWARD, R. R. 1978. *The American Family.* Beverly Hills, Calif.: Sage.

SHACKLE, G. L. S. 1977. "New Tracks for Economic Theory 1926–1939." In S. Weintraub, ed. *Modern Economic Thought,* pp. 23–40.

SHAPIRO, R. L. 1978. "Ego Psychology: Its Relation to Sullivan, Erikson and Object Relations Theory." In J. M. Quen and E. T. Carlsson, eds., *American Psychoanalysis.* Ch. 9, pp. 141–61.

SHORTER, E. 1975. *The Making of the Modern Family.* New York: Basic Books.

SHYE, S., ed. 1978. *Theory Construction and Data Analysis in the Behavioral Sciences.* San Francisco: Jossey-Bass.

SILK, L. 1976. *The Economists*. New York: Basic Books.

SILVERMAN, I. 1977. *The Human Subject in the Psychological Laboratory*. New York: Pergamon.

SIMIRENKO, A. 1969. *Social Thought in the Soviet Union*. Chicago: Quadrangle Books.

SIMMEL, G. 1950. *The Sociology of Georg Simmel*. New York: Free Press.

SIMON, B. 1978. *Mind and Madness in Ancient Greece*. Ithaca, N.Y.: Cornell University Press.

SIMON, H. A. 1957. *Administrative Behavior*. New York: Free Press.

SIMPSON, G. 1966. *People in Families: Sociology, Psychoanalysis and the American Family*. Cleveland: World.

SKINNER, B. F. 1971. *Beyond Freedom and Dignity*. New York: Knopf.

SLOVENKO, R. 1973. *Psychiatry and Law*. Boston: Little, Brown.

SMITH, J. E. 1963. *The Spirit of American Philosphy*. New York: Oxford University Press.

SMITH, J. M. et al. 1979. "A Systematic Investigation of Tardive Dyskinesia in Inpatients." *American Journal of Psychiatry*, 131: 918–22.

SOCARIDES, C. 1974. "The Sexual Unreason." *Book Forum*, I: 172–85.

SOCARIDES, C. 1978. *Homosexuality*. New York: Jason Aronson.

SPERLING, O. 1950. "Psychoanalytic Aspects of Bureaucracy." *PQ*, 19: 88–180.

SPIEGEL, L. 1954. "Acting Out and Defensive Instinctual Gratification," *JAPA*, 2: 107–19.

SPIEGEL, R. 1959. "Specific Problems of Communication." In S. Arieti, ed., *American Handbook of Psychiatry*, pp. 909–49.

SPIRO, M. 1963. *Kibbutz*. New York: Schocken Books.

SPIRO, M. AND BURROWS, E. G. 1953. *An Atoll Culture*. Human Relations Files, New Haven, Conn.

SPIRO, N. E. 1970. *Buddhism and Society*. New York: Harper and Row.

SPITZ, R. 1965. *The First Year of Life*. New York: International Universities Press.

STAFFORD, P. 1967. *Sexual Behavior in the Communist World*. New York: Julian Press.

STERN, F., ed. 1956. *The Varieties of History from Voltaire to the Present*. Cleveland: World.

STEVENS, S. S. 1951. *Handbook of Experimental Psychology*. New York: Wiley.

STEWARD, P. L., AND CANTOR, M. G., eds. 1974. *Varieties of Work Experience*. New York: Wiley.

STONE, N. M. AND SCHNEIDER, R. M. 1975. "Concurrent Validity of the Wheeler Signs of Homosexuality in the Rorschach." *Journal of Personality Assessment*, 39: 573–79.

STRAUSS, R., ed. 1979. "Clinical Sociology." *American Behavioral Scientist*, Vol. 22, No. 4.

STREAN, H. S. 1974. *The Social Worker as Psychotherapist*. Metuchen, N.J.: Scarecrow Press.

STREAN, H. 1979. *Psychoanalytic Theory and Social Work Practice*. New York: Free Press.

STREAN, H. 1980. *The Extramarital Affair*. New York: Free Press.

STRUPP, H. H. 1973. *Psychotherapy: Clinical, Research, and Theoretical Issues*. New York: Jason Aronson.

SULLIVAN, H. S. 1940. *Conceptions of Modern Psychiatry*. New York: Norton.

SULLIVAN, H. S. 1962. *Schizophrenia as a Human Process*. New York: Norton.

SUMNER, W. G. 1906. *Folkways*. New York: Dover, 1959.

TALBOT, J. A. 1978. *The Death of the Asylum*. New York: Grune and Stratton.

TAR, Z. 1977. *The Frankfurt School: The Critical Theories of Max Horkheimer and Theodor W. Adorno*. New York: Wiley.

TAX, S. et al., eds. 1953. *An Appraisal of Anthropology Today*. Chicago: University of Chicago Press.

TEDESCHI, J. T. ed. 1973. *The Social Influence Processes*. New York: Aldine-Atherton.

TEMERLIN, M. K. 1975. *Lucy: Growing Up Human*. Palo Alto, Calif.: Science and Behavior Books.

THOMPSON, S. 1977. *The Folktale*. Berkeley, Calif.: University of California Press.

THORNBERRY, T. P. AND JACOBY, J. E. 1979. *The Criminally Insane*. Chicago: University of Chicago Press.

THORNTON, A. AND FREEDMAN, D. S. 1979. "Changes in the Sex Role Attitudes of Women, 1962–1977." *American Sociological Review*, 44: 832–42.

TISCHLER, G. L. 1968. "The Beginning Resident and Supervisor." *Archives of General Psychiatry*, 19: 418–22.

TINGSTEN, H. 1973. *The Swedish Social Democrats: Their Ideological Development*. Totowa, N.J.: Bedminster Press.

TISSOT, R. 1977. "Long-Term Drug Therapy in Psychoses." In C. Chiland, ed., *Long-Term Treatments of Psychotic States*, pp. 89–171.

TOMASSON, R. F. 1970. *Sweden: Prototype of Modern Society*. New York: Random House.

TOWLE, C. 1969. *Helping*. Chicago: University of Chicago Press.

TOWNSEND, J. M. 1978. *Cultural Conceptions and Mental Illness*. Chicago: University of Chicago Press.

TOYNBEE, A. 1947. *A Study of History*. New York: Oxford University Press.

TRAFFORD, A. 1979. "Mental Patients." *U.S. News & World Report*, November 19, 1979, pp. 49–52.

TROTTER, S. AND WARREN, J. 1974. "Behavior Modification Under Fire." *APA Monitor*, 5: 1, 4 (a).

TRUAX, C. B. AND MITCHELL, K. M. 1971. "Research on Certain Therapist Interpersonal Skills in Relation to Process and Outcome." In A. E. Bergin and S. L. Garfield, eds. *Handbook of Psychotherapy and Behavior Change.* 1st Ed. New York: Wiley.

TUCHMAN, B. W. 1978. *A Distant Mirror.* New York: Knopf.

TUCKER, R. C. 1978. *The Marx-Engels Reader.* New York: Norton.

TURNBULL, C. M. 1972. *The Mountain People.* New York: Simon and Schuster.

TWEEDIE, J. 1979. *In the Name of Love.* New York: Pantheon.

VAILLANT, G. C. 1955. *The Aztecs of Mexico.* New York: Gannon.

VAN BERGEN, A. 1968. *Task Interruption.* Amsterdam: North Holland Publishing Co.

VAN DER WAALS, H. G. 1965. "Problems of Narcissism." *Bulletin of the Menninger Clinic,* 29: 293–311.

VAN LAWICK-GOODALL, J. 1971. *In the Shadow of Man.* Boston: Houghton Mifflin.

VAN MAANEN, J., ed. 1977. *Organizational Careers: Some New Perspectives.* New York: Wiley.

VEBLEN, T. 1899. *The Theory of the Leisure Class.* Modern Library Edition.

VOLKOV, S., ed. 1979. *Testimony: The Memoirs of Dmitri Shostakovich.* New York: Harper and Row.

WARD, B. 1979. *The Ideal Worlds of Economics.* New York: Basic Books.

WARNER, W. L. 1963. *Yankee City.* New Haven: Yale University Press.

WEBER, G. H. AND McCALL, G. J., eds. 1978. *Social Scientists as Advocates.* Beverly Hills, Calif.: Sage Publications.

WEBER, M. 1905. *The Protestant Ethnic and the Spirit of Capitalism.* New York: Scribner's, 1958.

WEINBERG, M. S. AND BELL, A. P. 1978. *Homosexualities: A Study of Diversity Among Men and Women.* New York: Simon and Schuster.

WEINBERG, M. S. AND WILLIAMS, C. J. 1974. *Male Homosexuals.* New York: Oxford University Press.

WEINER, D. B. 1979. "The Apprenticeship of Philippe Pinel." *American Journal of Psychiatry,* 136: 1128–34.

WEINTRAUB, S., ed. 1977. *Modern Economic Thought.* Philadelphia: University of Pennsylvania Press.

WEISSKOPF, W. A. 1955. *The Psychology of Economics.* Chicago: University of Chicago Press.

WEISSKOPF, W. A. 1971. *Alienation and Economics.* New York: E. P. Dutton.

WHALEN, R. E., ed. 1974. *The Neuropsychology of Aggression.* New York: Plenum Press.

WHITEHORN, J. C. AND Betz, B. J. 1954. "A Study of Psychotherapeutic Relationships Between Physicians and Schizophrenic Patients." *American Journal of Psychiatry,* 111: 321–31.

WHITEHORN, J. C. AND BETZ, B. J. 1960. "Further Studies of the Doctor as a Crucial Variable in the Outcome of Treatment with Schizophrenic Patients." *American Journal of Psychiatry*, 117: 215–23.

WICKLER, W. 1972. *The Sexual Code.* New York: Doubleday.

WILLIAMS, F., ed. 1970. *Language and Poverty.* Chicago: Markham.

WILSON, E. 1975. *The Twenties.* New York: Farrar, Straus and Giroux.

WILSON, E. O. 1975. *Sociobiology: The New Synthesis.* Cambridge: Harvard University Press.

WILSON, E. O. 1978. *On Human Nature.* Cambridge, Mass.: Harvard University Press.

WILSON, E. W. 1976. *The Loyal Blacks.* New York: G. P. Putnam.

WINN, R. B., ed. 1961. *Psychotherapy in the Soviet Union.* New York: Grove Press.

WINNICOTT, D. W. 1953. "Transitional Objects and Transitional Phenomena." *IJP*, 34: 89–97.

WINOGRAD, T. 1972. "Understanding Natural Language." *Cognitive Psychology*, 3: 1–191.

WOLF MAN. 1971. *The Wolf Man.* New York: Basic Books.

WOLFF, K., ed. 1950. *The Sociology of Georg Simmel.* New York: Free Press.

WOLLHEIM, R., ed. 1974. *Philosophers on Freud.* New York: Jason Aronson.

WOLMAN, B. B. AND NAGEL, E., eds. 1965. *Scientific Psychology: Principles and Approaches.* New York: Basic Books.

WOLPE, J. 1976. *Theme and Variations: A Behavior Therapy Case Book.* New York: Pergamon.

WOLPERT, E. A. 1972. "Two Classes of Factors Affecting Dream Recall." *JAPA*, 20: 45–58.

WOODWORTH, R. W. AND SCHLOSBERG, H. L. 1954. *Experimental Psychology.* Rev. Ed. New York: Holt, Rinehart and Winston.

Work In America. 1972 Report of a Special Task Force to the Secretary of Health, Education, and Welfare. Cambridge, Mass.: MIT Press.

WUNDT, W. 1873–1874. *Principles of Physiological Psychology.* New York: Macmillan.

WYNNE, L. C. 1970. "Communication Disorders and the Quest for Relatedness in Families of Schizophenics." In R. Cancro, ed., *Annual Review of the Schizophrenic Syndrome*, 2 (1972) 395–414. New York: Brunner/Mazel.

WYNNE, L. C. et al. 1978. *The Nature of Schizophrenia: New Approaches to Research and Treatment.* New York: Wiley.

ZELDITCH, M. 1964. "Family, Marriage and Kinship." In R. E. L. Faris, ed. *Handbook of Modern Sociology*, Ch. 18, pp. 680–733.

ZINBERG, N. 1967. "Psychoanalytic Training and Psychoanalytic Values." *IJP* 48: 88–96.

Index

Abraham, Karl, 25, 310
Abrahams, D., 296
Achte, K. A., 136, 149, 150
Ackerman, Nathan W., 52, 141, 252, 420
Acting-out, 44, 48
Actual neurosis, 11
Adams, John, 207
"Adaptive," 35
Adjustment neuroses, 132, 152-153
Adler, Alfred, 24, 327, 332, 340, 364
Adorno, T., 334
Aesthetic attitudes, 64
Aggression, 46, 396-398, 411-412
Ahmed, P. I., 127, 137
Ainsworth, M. D. S., 436
Alexander, Franz, 126, 310, 348
Alexander I, Czar of Russia, 203, 204
Alienation, 55, 63, 224, 250-251
Alienation and Economics (Weisskopf), 250
Alienists, 133-134
Altman, L. L., 491
American Academy of Psychoanalysis, 323, 324
American Anthropological Association, 333
American culture, critiques of, 60
American Handbook of Psychiatry, The, 115, 118, 158
American Medical Association, 316
American Psychiatric Association, 86, 128, 131, 135, 156, 159, 299, 336, 353, 367
American Psychoanalysis, 324
American Psychoanalytic Association, 7, 104, 158, 174, 311, 313-316, 318, 321-323, 325, 326, 333, 336, 362
American Psychological Association, 5, 78-79, 333
American Sociological Association, 333
Amin, Idi, 307, 371
"Analysis Terminable and Interminable" (Freud), 197, 365, 383
Analytic ideal, 271, 329

components of, 33, 36-71
history and, 211-212
Andrews, F. M., 101, 106
Angel in the House, The (Patmore), 391
Annual Review of Behavior Therapy, 370, 371
Annual Review of Psychology, 169
Anthropology, 5, 236-240, 395-406
Anxiety, 42-46, 124
Anzieu, Didier, 13, 16, 363, 490
A-P psychiatrists, 146
Aptheker, H., 209
Arieti, Silvano, 140, 158, 276
Aristotle, 66, 387, 440
Arkin, A. M., 176
Arlow, Jacob, 4, 71, 34
Arnheim, R., 278
Art, 5, 66, 273-285, 432
Artistic attitude, 64
Ashley Montagu, M. F., 38, 59, 114, 396-398, 410, 411, 412
Atomic Physics and Human Knowledge (Bohr), 175
Auden, W. H., 16
Augustine, St., 16, 389
Autobiographical writing, 16
Autobiography (Freud), 340
Autonomous ego, 35
Axelrad, S., 52, 114, 437, 438

Balakian, Nona, 277-278
Bales, R., 52
Balint, M., 490
Baltimore study, 229
Bandura, A., 81, 371
Barande, I., 324
Barande, R., 324
Barron, F., 276
Barry, B., 216
Bateson, G., 63, 141
Beag, Inis, 400

565

Bean, L. L., 146
Beard, Charles, 207
Beavers, R. W., 39, 416–417
Becker, E., 89
Behavior therapy (and behavior modification), 83–85, 96–98, 367–372
Behaviorism, 5, 75–76, 80–90, 96–98, 111, 175, 334, 367–372
Bell, A. P., 298
Bellak, L., 70, 132, 149, 326
Benedek, T., 494
Benedict, Ruth, 225, 238
Berg, I. A., 175, 177
Bergin, A. E., 348, 349–350, 503
Bergler, Edmund, 344
Berkman, T., 64
Berlin Institute, 311
Betz, B. J., 145, 146
Beyond the Best Interests of the Child (Goldstein, A. Freud, and Solnit), 431
Beyond Freedom and Dignity (Skinner), 80, 370
Bias, observer, 89–90, 94–95, 103, 111–112, 168–170, 174
Bieber, I., 300
Biebuyk, D., 278
Biochemical factors in organic psychiatry, 154–156
Biographical writing, 16
Bion, W., 332
Birket-Smith, Kaj, 396
Black families, 422–424
Blanton, Smiley, 259
Bleuler, Manfred, 135, 136, 138, 140, 148–150, 155, 195, 220, 309, 504, 516
Blind Ambition (Dean), 202–203
Bloch, Iwan, 11
Boas, Franz, 25, 164, 173, 174, 177, 178
Body image, 54
Body-mind problem, 12, 109–110
Bohr, Niels, 175
Book of Baby Care (Spock), 383
Boring, Edwin, 91
Bossuet, Bénigne Jacques, 185
Boulding, K., 251
Bourne, Peter, 126
Bowlby, J., 45, 57, 410, 435–436
Boyer, L. J., 334
Bradburn, N., 106
Braginsky, B. M., 182
Braginsky, D. D., 182
Brave New World (Huxley), 129, 161
Breland, K., 293
Breland, M., 293
Brenner, C., 34, 46, 71, 153
Breuer, Josef, 9, 10, 62, 121, 288
Brewin, R., 138
Brill, Abraham, 123, 331
Brody, Sylvia, 52, 114, 437, 438

Broken Heart, The (Lynch), 345
Bromberg, W., 267, 306
Burckhardt, Jakob, 188, 202, 206, 506
Bureaucracy, 430–431
Burnham, D. L., 438, 439
Burr, M., 16
Burrows, E. G., 225

Calef, V., 332–333, 363, 364
Canning, J. W., 179, 263
Cantril, Hadley, 101
Capellanus, Andreas, 389
Capitalism, Socialism and Democracy (Schumpeter), 250
Cardano, G., 16
Carothers, J. C., 142
Casanova, Giovanni, 391
Casriel, Daniel, 379
Catlin, G., 216
Causation, 291–302
Chambless, D. L., 367, 368
Charcot, Jean Martin, 259
Charismatic figures, 330–333, 361, 363
Chasseguet-Smirgel, J., 490
Chiland, C., 137, 150
Child psychology, 38–39, 433–439
Childhood, history of, 392–394
Chinoy, Eli, 103
Chomsky, Noam, 286
Christian demonology, 119–120, 122, 198–200, 306, 390
Christianity, 6, 165, 185, 188–189, 199, 202, 208, 257, 259–260, 267, 305–308, 388–389, 406, 426–427
Civilization and Its Discontents (Freud), 341
"Civilized Sexual Morality" (Freud), 104
Class struggle, psychology of, 233–234
Class structure (SES), 231–232
Clinical psychology, 79–80, 90–94; see also Experimental psychology; Psychoanalysis; Psychological testing
Cliometrics, illusions of, 208–210
Cognition and emotion, 112–114
Cognitive psychology, 34, 49, 98–100, 108
Cohen, D. K., 291
Cohen, Morris, 166, 167, 173, 181, 206, 207, 262, 270
Cole, J. O., 136
Collingwood, R. G., 205, 206, 262
Commercialism vs. art, 66
Communication, 33, 61–63, 285–290
Community, 220–228
Comte, Auguste, 20, 173, 217
Conceptual framework of psychology, 34–35, 93, 100, 178–180
Conditioning, 81–82
Conolly, John, 134, 160
Consciousness, 110–112
    altered state of, 39

Contemporary Psychology, 83
Control analysis, 319–320, 337
Cooley, C. 216
Corporate system, work in, 67
Corsini, R. J., 367
Counterwill, 24
Cox, Dorothy, 429
Creativity, 33, 64–66, 273–285
Croce, Benedetto, 205, 206
Cromwell, R. L. 141
Csikszentmihalyi, M., 276
Cuber, John, 414, 422
"Cultural," 35
Cultural models for identification, 57
Cultural reaction to redefinition of psycho-
    therapy, 352–366
Cultural universals, 59
Culture
    art and, 281–282
    critiques of American, 60
    the individual and, 238–239
    nature of, 58–59, 237
    organic psychiatry and, 127
    rsonality and, 59–60
    schizophrenia and, 141–144
    social sciences and, 164–166
Culture and the Crowd (Regin), 282
Cummings, D. A., 520
"Cure," redefinition of, 351
Current Psychotherapies, 367

Darrow, Clarence, 172
Darwin, Charles, 186, 257
David, Z., 490
Davidson, T., 416
Davis, A., 143
Davis, B. D., 210
Davis, J. M., 136
de Mause, Lloyd, 211, 392–393, 395
Dean, John, 202–203
Defense, concept of, 11
Defense mechanisms, 26, 35, 45
Degree vs. training, 353–360, 362, 364
Dpression, 284
Depressive anxiety, 45
Deschner, K., 196
Despert, Louise, 393
Deutsch, A., 134
Developmental lines, 70
Dewey, J., 216
Diagnostic system, psychiatric, 129–132,
    150–152
Diamond, Bernard, 144
Dillard, J. L., 424
Discharge, need for, 42–43
Displaceability of instinctual feelings, 44
Distler, Luther, 147
Dix, Dorothea, 134
D-O psychiatrists, 146

Dobzhansky, T., 412
"Doctor," redefinition of, 350–351
Dohrenwend, B. P., 90
Dohrenwend, B. S., 90
Don Juanism, 37
Dopamine theory, 154–155
Dore, R., 359
Douglas, M., 61, 427
Drabkin, I. E., 266
Dreams, 13–18, 26, 49, 60, 62, 104, 288
Drive strength, 44
Drugs, in organic psychiatry, 119, 123–124,
    129, 135–138, 152, 154–156, 161
Du Bois-Raymond, Emil, 76
Dunham, H. W., 142
Dunlap, Knight, 357, 364
Durant, Will, 261
Dürer, Albrecht, 278
Durgnat, Raymond, 290
Durkheim, Emile, 20, 173, 213, 215–217,
    220, 221, 228, 234–235, 237, 507
"Dynamic," 34

Eaton, J. W., 55, 142, 225
Ebbinghaus, H., 98–100
Eckhardt, Marianne, 324
"Economic," 34
*Economic Interpretation of the Constitu-
    tion, The* (Beard), 207
Economic and Philosophic Manuscripts
    (Marx), 218
Economics, 5, 241–255
Economics and the Public Purpose (Gal-
    braith), 248
Egbert, D., 281
Ego, 26, 35, 49, 280
Ego-assessment profiles, 70, 132
Ego autonomy, 49–50
Ego and the Id, The (Freud), 32, 49
Ego and the Mechanism of Defense, The
    (A. Freud), 26, 35
Ego psychology, 26–30, 32
Einstein, Albert, 93, 179, 331
Eissler, K. 173–174
Eitingon, Max, 25, 311, 324, 331
Ellenberger, H. F., 195, 288
Ellis, Albert, 96, 357, 375–377, 382
Ellis, Havelock, 11
Emde, R. N., 434
Emmanuel Movement, 268
Emotion: *see also* Instinctual feelings
    cognition and, 112–114
Emotionally Troubled Child, The (Despert),
    393
Empiricism, 174
Encounter groups, 383–385
Encyclopaedia Britannica, 198, 273
Engel, G. L., 118, 159
Engels, Friedrich, 418

Engerman, S. L., 208–210, 423
Entralgo, P. L., 266
Epicureanism, 267
Erikson, Erik, 15, 56, 259, 379
Essais (Montaigne), 267
Essay on Population (Malthus), 245
Esterson, A., 141
Ethics
    behavior therapy and, 370–372
    psychology and, 263–264
    religious, 260–261
Ethological data on love, 38, 406–412
European Working Classes, The (Le Play), 222–223
Existentialism, 268–270
Experimental psychology, 5, 76–86, 91–94, 169, 170
Experimental Psychology (Woodworth), 77, 82
Exploration of the Inner World, The (Boisen), 308
Expressive communication, 63, 289
Eysenck, Hans, 147, 348, 349, 358, 368

Factor analysis, 368–369
Family, 51–53
    functions of, 51–52
    love and, 413–426
    nuclear, 394–395
    schizophrenia and, 139–140
    suppression of pleasure by, 40, 51
    transference and, 52–53
Family pathology, 53
Family role, 33
Fantasy, 279, 290
Faris, R. E. L., 142, 215, 216
Fear: *see* Anxiety
Federn, P., 57
Feelings, 33, 41–49
Feinstein, S., 130
Fenichel, Otto, 120, 240, 310, 326, 348, 349, 412, 419, 490
Ferenczi, Sandor, 25
Fiedler, Leslie, 432
Fight-flight syndrome, 43–44
Fine, B., 195
Fine, R., 105, 145, 195, 197, 219, 227, 230, 292, 293, 299, 319, 350, 365, 366, 380, 419, 420
Fisher, S., 91, 106, 170, 263, 348, 503
Fitzgerald, F., 186
Fleming, Joan, 323, 324
Fliess, W., 20
Flugel, J., 51, 419
Fogel, R. W., 208–210, 423
Folkways (Sumner), 221, 223
Fortes, Meyer, 25, 238, 399, 404
Frank, Jerome, 146
Frankfurt school of sociology, 106

Frankl, V., 269
Franklin, Benjamin, 207
Franks, C. 370, 371
Frederick II, King, 286
Free associations, 110
Free will, 114–115
Freedman, N., 63, 288
Freid, Edrita, 283
Freud, Anna, 26, 34, 35, 70, 132, 326, 336, 342, 361, 431
Freud, Sigmund, 3, 4, 9–32, 60, 70, 71, 89, 93, 97, 104–106, 115, 164, 168, 172, 179, 191, 193, 200, 202, 210, 216, 217, 228, 235, 238, 239, 305, 311, 319, 327–328, 352, 357, 359, 387, 441, 488, 499–503, 506, 510, 511, 515, 520
    analysis and social reform and, 339–342
    on art, 274, 275
    on body-mind problem, 109–110
    on causation, 294–295
    as charismatic figure, 330–332
    on communication, 62, 285, 288
    on community, 223–224
    conception of analysis, phases of, 347
    on consciousness, 110–111
    contributions of, 18
    on controls, 349
    on creation of new profession, 309, 314
    death instinct theory of, 412
    on determinism, 292
    early work of, 10–12
    ego psychology of, 26–30
    errors of, 20
    on the family, 52, 418–419
    on fantasy, 279
    holopsychological scheme of, 33–35
    id psychology of, 22–26
    on image of man, 219–220
    on instinctual feelings, 42, 44, 45, 47–49, 51
    on jealousy, 491
    on love, 36, 38, 489–493
    on measurement problem, 176
    on neuroses, 130
    on normality, 197
    objectivity of, 170
    on pleasure, 40, 41
    on religion, 256
    on resistance to lay analysis, 361, 365–366
    self-analysis of, 12–18, 26, 346
    on sexuality, 47–48, 387–388, 392, 399, 402
    on technique, 365, 383
    on transference, 23, 52, 327, 348, 380, 436–437
Freudian slips, 99
Friedman, Milton, 251
Friedman, P. R., 84, 85

Fromm, Erich, 58, 59, 106, 172, 334, 491
Fromm-Reichmann, Frieda, 139
Frustration, 43, 47
Future of an Illusion, The (Freud), 256

Gagliardo, J. G., 252
Galbraith, John Kenneth, 67, 242, 243, 247–249, 251, 252, 515
Galileo, 168, 180
Garfield, S. L., 348, 503
Gay, Peter L., 19, 172, 189, 191, 193, 203, 204, 206, 209, 306, 505
Gedo, J., 105, 263, 267, 488
Gelles, R. J., 415
Gender identity, 54
General Theory of Employment, Interest and Money, The (Keynes), 246–247
"Genetic," 34
Genius, madness and, 273–274
German Ideology, The (Marx), 221–222
Gesell, Arnold L., 174
Gestalt psychotherapy, 328, 377–378
Getzels, J. W., 276
Gift, The (Mauss), 404
Gill, M. M., 105
Ginsburg, H., 424
Glaser, R., 293
Glasser, William, 379, 380, 381
Glover, Edward, 313, 328
Goethe, Johann Wolfgang von, 470
Goldberg, A., 105, 328
Goldhammer, H., 193
Goldstein, Joseph, 367, 368, 431
Goode, W. J., 420
Goode, W. L., 257, 258
Goode, William, 225–226, 404, 411
Goodenough, F. L., 113
Goodman, J., 314, 315, 320, 321, 354
Gorer, G., 168
Gorgias, 266
Graham, H. T., 428–429
Grand, S., 63, 288
Gratification, 33, 41, 43–44
Great Illusion, The (Hale), 19
Greeks, ancient, 387–388
Green, A. W., 143
Greenberg, R. P., 91, 106, 170, 263, 348, 503
Gregory XI, Pope, 191
Grey, A. L., 413
Grey, Ian, 201
Griesinger, Wilhelm, 17, 118, 119, 140
Grinberg, Leon, 324
Gross, Chaim, 283
Group behavior, 61, 220–228
Group fantasies, 224, 289
Group Psychology and the Analysis of the Ego (Freud), 223
Guilford, J. P., 276

Gurr, T. R., 428–429
Gutman, Herbert, 423, 424

Halbwachs, Maurice, 20
Hale, N., 268
Hale, Owen, 19
Half-trained professions, 352-360
Hall, Stanley, 112
Hamburg, D., 7, 325
Hanson, Norwood R., 93, 178
Happiness, 30, 33, 47–49, 100–103, 211–212, 271
Harlow, H., 38, 48, 406–409, 494
Harp, Howie, 150
Harris, M., 59, 237–239, 401
Harroff, Peggy, 414, 422
Hartmann, E. von, 23
Hartmann, Ernest, 155–156
Hartmann, H., 32, 35, 49–50, 104, 170, 272, 326, 332, 342–343, 412
Hate: see Hostility
Hate cultures, 38, 224–227, 395, 519
Hauser, Arnold, 282–283
Hausman, C. R., 281
Havighurst, R. J., 143
Hayek, F. A., 247
Hazo, R. G., 427, 440
Hegel, Georg, 186, 206, 211, 237, 441
Heidegger, Martin, 269, 441
Heilbroner, R., 242–246, 250
Helmholtz program, 76
Hemming, J., 191
Hending, H., 102, 106
Hendrick, Ives, 325
Henry, W. E., 30, 80, 124, 125, 156, 157, 159, 351, 354
Herodotus, 187
Herzberg, Frederick, 67, 103, 252
Historical Introduction to Modern Psychology (Murphy), 75
History, 5, 185–212
    analytic ideal and, 211–212
    cliometrics, illusions of, 208–210
    ideology of victory, 187-204
    of love, 37–38, 386–395
    philosophy of, 204–208
    psychohistory, 210–211
    psychology and, 203–204, 212
History of Childhood, The (de Mause), 211, 392–393
History of Experimental Psychology, The (Boring), 91
History of Psychoanalysis, A (Fine), 105
History of the Psychoanalytic Movement (Freud), 340
Hite, Shere, 299
Hitler, Adolf, 122, 123, 188–190, 200–202, 289, 307, 506
Höffding, H., 262, 263, 440

Hollingshead, A. B., 142
Holopsychological scheme, 33–35
Homosexuality, 37, 298–301, 347, 387, 388, 494–495
Hook, S., 262
Hooker, E., 299, 301
Horney, Karen, 310, 313, 314, 320, 332, 493
Hostility, 42–44, 46–47, 113
Hughes, R., 138
Hull, C., 77
Human functioning, 100–103
    alteration of, 107–108
Hunt, Morton, 38, 392, 395
Huxley, Aldous, 129, 161
Hygiene factors, 67
Hymes, Dell, 182
Hyperactivity, 124
Hysteria, 3, 285

Id, 26, 35, 279–280
Id psychology, 22–26
Ideas of Happiness, The (McGill), 264–265
Identification, 56–57
Identity, 33, 53–54, 56–61
Identity crises, 56
Ideology, 164–166
Illness, redefinition of, 344–346
Image of man, 216–220, 308–309
Importance of Living, The (Lin), 41
Increst taboo, 398–402, 410
Inequality (Jencks), 417
Infantile sexuality, 17, 23
Inner creativity, 65–66, 280–281
Inner life of man, 308
Inner self, 55
Inner world, 110–112
Institutional feelings, 41–49
Integrative theory of love, 39, 443–496
Interchangeability of instinctual feelings, 44
Internalization, 47, 48, 54
International Psychoanalytic Association, 25, 104, 377
International Psychoanalytisher Verlag, 27
"Interpersonal," 35
Interpretation of Dreams, The (Freud), 15–16, 60, 104, 288
Introjection, 438–439
Israel, H. A., 285–286

James, William, 60, 76, 257, 440
James-Lange theory of emotion, 43
Janet, Pierre, 3
Jarvis, E., 148, 504
Jealousy, 491–492
Jefferson, Thomas, 207
Jencks, Christopher, 417–418
Joffe, W., 42
Johnson, V., 102, 300

Jokes (Freud), 402
Jones, Ernest, 24–25, 113, 122, 130, 138, 160, 162, 193, 328, 331, 348, 352, 361, 490, 493
Jones, James, 195–196
Jopling, C. F., 278
Journal of the American Psychoanalytic Association, 323, 362
Journal of Marriage and the Family, 415
Jung, Carl, 24, 172, 327, 332, 364

Kadushin, C., 329
Kant, Immanuel, 119, 206, 264
Kanter, Rosabeth Moss, 61, 222
Kardiner, A., 57, 59
Kedward, H. B., 129
Kempler, W. 377–378
Kernberg, Otto, 48, 332–333, 363–364, 488, 491
Keynes, John Maynard, 242, 246–247, 515
Khayyam, Omar, 216
Khomeini, Ayatollah, 194
Kiev, A., 144
Kilman, R. H., 167
Kinsey, A., 101–102, 106
Kinsey Institute for Sex Research, 298
Kinship, love and, 402–404
Kirkpatrick, C., 413
Klein, George, 98, 105
Klein, Melanie, 327, 332, 422
Kluckhohn, C., 58, 237
Knapp, P., 253
Knight, R. P., 157
Knight, Robert, 312
Kohut, Heinz, 48, 151, 330, 332, 343, 488
Komarovsky, Mirra, 421–422
Kornreich, M., 348
Kraepelin, Emil, 18, 69, 118–121, 130, 133–135, 137–139, 144, 145, 149, 160–162, 195, 197, 308
Kraepelinian system, 6, 121
Kramer, Heinrich, 390
Kren, G., 210
Kringlen, E., 141
Kris, E., 65, 158, 341
Kroeber, A. L., 58, 237
Krudener, Baroness Julie de, 203
Kubie, Lawrence, 285–286, 318, 336
Kubie plan, 319
Kuhn, Thomas, 24, 85, 166–167

Labov, W., 424
Lacan, Jacques, 105, 331, 332, 363, 364
Laing, R. D., 141
Lamb, H., 137
Lamb, M. E., 53
Lambert, M. J. 349–350
Langer, W., 212
Langsley, Donald, 355–356

Language, 285–290
Lasswell, Harold, 181, 289
Law, humanization of, 431–432
Lay analysis, 361–366
Lay Analysis (Freud), 319
Lazarus, Arnold, 96, 371
Le Play, F., 222–223
Learning to Love (Harlow), 406–409
Learning theory, 79, 357
Lebensohn, Z. 156
Leighton, A. H., 50, 88, 102, 106, 144
Leites, N., 289
Leontief, Wassily, 251
Leopold, King of Belgium, 190–191
Levi, 261, 268
Levin, Hillel, 355–356
Levine, Faye, 283
Levine, R. A., 59
Lévi-Strauss, C., 240, 403–405
Lewin, B., 313, 314, 320–321, 353, 354
Lewin, Kurt, 99
Lewis, Oscar, 53, 142, 143, 422
Libido theory, 20, 23, 47
Lichtenberg, J. D., 35n., 54
Lidz, T., 140
Lieberman, M. A., 384
Lifton, R., 63, 84, 231
Lin Yutang, 41
Lindbolm, C. E., 291
Ling, Trevor, 426
Linguistics, 286–289
Linton, R. 59
Literature, 5, 432
Little, R. B., 346
Locke, John, 191–192
Loeb, L., 149
Loewenstein, R. M., 168
London, P., 96
Long-term studies of schizophrenia, 148–150
Lorenz, Konrad, 411–412
Love, 7–8, 33, 36–39, 48, 386–442; see also
    Sexuality
    anthropological data on, 38, 395–406
    child psychology and, 38–39, 433–439
    clinical observations on, 36–37
    ethological data on, 38, 406–412
    historical data on, 37–38, 386–395
    integrative theory of, 39, 443–496
    mature, definition of, 491–496
    philosophy and, 440–441
    psychoanalytic theories of, 489–491
    psychotherapy and, 444–489
    sociological forces and, 413–433
    stages of, 39
Love cultures, 38, 224–227, 395–398, 519
Love and Death in the American Novel
    (Fiedler), 432
Love of the pure woman, 37
Lowe, A., 242

Lowry, R., 234
Lubart, J., 396
Ludwig, A., 289
Luther, Martin, 251, 259
Lying, 288–290
Lynch, W. H., 345
Lyons, J. O., 251

Maccoby, M., 334
Mackenzie, B. D., 96
MacLean, M., 371
Madness
    genius and, 273–274
    in history, 193–200
Madness and Society (Rosen), 194
Maetze, G., 319, 321, 336, 349
Magaro, P. A., 136
Magic, 256, 258, 265, 305
Magic and Schizophrenia (Roheim), 258
Mahler, Margaret, 48, 53, 434, 436, 488
Mainstream psychoanalysis, 4, 32–71
    analytic ideal, components of, 33, 36–71
    conceptual framework of, 34–35
    conceptual unity and, 326–328
Making of the Modern Family, The
    (Shorter), 394–395
Maladjustment neurosis, 132, 152–153
Malinowski, Bronislaw, 238, 239
Malleus Maleficarum (Kramer and
    Springer), 306, 390
Malthus, Thomas, 245
Manic-depressive psychosis, 121–122, 124
Manipulative communication, 63, 289
Mann, Thomas, 4, 27
Manuel, F. E., 520
Manuel, F. P., 520
Marcuse, Herbert, 106
Marmor, Judd, 71, 118, 125, 156, 162, 351,
    354, 364
Marriage, 405, 413–426, 493–494
Marshall, Alfred, 241, 246
Marshall, D. S., 400
Marx, Karl, 164, 173, 179, 187, 190, 214,
    217, 218, 220–221, 224, 232, 233, 237,
    245, 246, 252, 294
Marxism, 165, 207, 208
Maser, W., 201
Masters, W., 102, 300
Maternal loss, 45, 46, 57
Matson, F., 410, 411
Maugham, Somerset, 36
Mauss, M., 404
May, Philip, 146–148, 152
May, Rollo, 268, 269, 441
McBride, Henry, 277
McCall, G. J., 171, 172
McClelland, David C., 67, 252
McGill, V. J., 30, 264–265, 440
McKee, J. M., 84

McLuhan, M., 62, 282
McNeill, William H., 187–189, 201, 203
Mead, Margaret, 216, 238
Meador, B. D., 372
Measurement problem, 175–177
Medical model, 353–356
Medicine, 342, 345, 351; *see also* Organic psychiatry
Medium is the Message, The (McLuhan), 282
Mehta, D., 137
Meiselman, K. C., 398
Meltzoff, D., 348
Mental Health in the Creative Individual (Gross), 283
Mental health profession, 7
Mental health studies, 228–230
Mental hospitals, dismantling of, 127–128
Mental illness, concept of, 344–346
Mentalization, 43
Merkle, L., 346
Merton, Robert K., 293, 430, 431
Mesmerism, 267
Messenger, J. C., 400
Metapsychological scheme, 33–35
Methodology, 166–168
Meyer, Bernard, 275
Michelangelo, 280, 283
Midtown Study, 229–230
Milan, M. A., 84
Milieu social work, 83–84
Mill, John Stuart, 20, 245, 292
Mind of Primitive Man, The (Boas), 25, 177
Mitchell, K. M., 146
Mitroff, I. T., 167
Mitzman, A., 219
Modell, J., 423
Modern Economic Thought (Weintraub), 241
Monogamy, 405, 411, 493–494
Montaigne, Michel, 267
Moore, Burness, 362
Mora, George, 120, 157
Most Holy Foreskin of Jesus, The (Muller), 196
Mother-child bond, 45, 48, 410–411, 433–439
Mothers, Fathers and Children (Brody and Axelrad), 437
Moynihan, Daniel P., 422, 423, 424
Mueller, Conrad, 169
Murdock, G. P., 51, 399, 401, 492
Murphy, Gardner, 75, 111, 115, 401
Myers, J. K., 146

Nagel, Ernest, 77, 78, 87, 175, 292–294, 302
Narcissism, 57–58, 65, 280, 283, 330
Natural History of Love (Hunt), 38
Need, disturbances in, 40–41

Need-gratification-rest-need cycle, 40–41
Need-reduction theory, 40
Neill, A. S., 51, 419
"Neuropsychoses of Defense, The" (Freud), 11
Neurosis, 28, 63, 70–71, 130, 132, 152–153, 160, 193, 284, 285, 288
redefinition of, 344–346
Neurotic distortion, 443
New Industrial State, The (Galbraith), 67, 247–248
New York Psychoanalytic Institute, 312, 313
New York Psychoanalytic Society, 331, 362–363
Newton, Isaac, 331
1984 (Orwell), 63
Niederland, W., 274
Nietzsche, Friedrich Wilhelm, 194, 269
Nisbet, R. A., 165, 220–221
Niskanen, D. P., 136, 149, 150
Nixon, Richard, 127, 203
Normality, 17–18, 28, 197
Nymphomania, 37

Oberndorf, Clarence, 123, 331
Object loss, 45, 46
Object relations, 35
"Observations on Transference Love" (Freud), 15
Odier, C., 258
Oedipal crisis, 51, 52
Of Human Bondage (Maugham), 36
Offer, D., 198
O'Hara, John, 414
Ollendorf, R., 299–300
One Hundred Years of Psychiatry (Kraepelin), 69
Organic psychiatry, 5, 18, 19, 29, 83–84, 118–163, 307–308, 309
biochemical factors in, 154–156
diagnostic system of, 129–132, 150–152
drugs in, 119, 123–124, 129, 135–138, 152, 154–156, 161
as half-trained profession, 353–356
historical background of, 119–128, 200–201
incorporation of psychoanalysis into, 125
maladjustment neurosis and, 152–153
personality and training of psychiatrists, 156–158
vs. psychoanalysis, 125, 139–153, 161–163
re-evaluation of, 158–159
schizophrenia problem, 132–152, 154–155
Origen, 306
Origin of the Family, The (Engels), 418
Orwell, George, 63
Ostow, N., 265

Our Dreams (Freud), 14–15
Outer creativity, 66, 280–281
Outline of Psychoanalysis, The (Freud), 104

Parent-child love, 392–394
Pareto, Vilfredo, 20, 217
Parsons, Talcott, 232
Passages (Sheehy), 335
Patient, redefinition of, 343–344
Patient population, shift in, 328–330
Patmore, Coventry, 391
Peirce, Charles, 440
Perls, Fritz, 377, 378
Personality theory, 95–96, 369, 379
Person-centered therapy, 372–375
Peterfreund, E., 105, 168
Petroni, G., 432
Pfister, O., 256, 259, 427
Phasic-benign psychosis, 195
Philosophy, 6, 261–272, 440–441
Philosophy of the Unconscious, The (Hartmann), 23
Piaget, Jean, 49, 112
Picasso, Pablo, 283
Pinel, Philippe, 119, 193
Plagues and Peoples (McNeill), 201
Plato, 194
Pleasure, 33, 39–41
Pleasure gain, 41
Plog, S. Z., 127, 137
Poincaré, Henri, 166
Political myth, 289
Pollock, George H., 105, 267, 319, 365
Preconscious, 34
Pribram, K. H., 105
Primitive Man as Philosopher (Radin), 265–266
Prince, Morton, 122
Principles of Physiological Psychology (Wundt), 76
Principles of Political Economy (Mill), 245
Principles of Political Economy (Ricardo), 245
Principles of Psychology (James), 440
Problem of Anxiety, The (Freud), 26, 35
Propaganda, 63, 289
Protestant ethic, 66–67, 190–191, 252
Protestant Ethic and the Spirit of Capitalism, The (Weber), 21
Psychiatric symptomatology, 33, 68–71
Psychiatry: *see* Organic psychiatry
Psychic energy, 44
Psychoanalysis
    alternatives to, 366–392
    vs. anthropology, 238–240
    attempts to define, 325–326
    vs. behaviorism, 75–76, 80–90, 96–98, 111
    bias and, 170

body-mind problem and, 109–110
causation and, 294–295, 301–302
centrality to social sciences, 333–335
child psychology and, 439
Christian-psychiatric tradition and, 305–308
cognition and emotion and, 112–114
cognitive psychology and, 98–100, 108
communication and, 287–290
community and, 222–228
conceptual framework of, 34–35, 93, 100, 178–180
creation of, 309–310
creativity and, 274–275, 284–285
defined, 3–4
vs. economics, 243, 254–255
expansion of psychiatry through, 69
vs. experimental psychology, 76–86, 169, 170
free will and, 114–115
Freudian revolution and, 308–309
growth of, 79–80
historical and philosophical perspective on, 9–31; *see also* Freud, Sigmund
human functioning and, 100–103
incorporation into psychiatry, 125
lay analysis, 361–366
love and, 443–496
mainstream: *see* Mainstream psychoanalysis
measurement problem and, 176–177
methodology, 167–168
vs. organic psychiatry, 125, 139–153, 161–163
philosophy and, 261–272
psychological factor and, 184
redefinition of psychotherapy and, 343–351
reformulations of, 104–106
religion and, 256, 261
reorganization of, 104–105
schizophrenia and, 139–152
shift in patient population, 328–330
social inquiry and, 294–295
social reform and, 338–351, 517–519
splits in, 323–325
technique vs. vision, 172–174, 339–343, 383–385
training in, 7, 310–322, 332, 335–337, 342, 350–366
unconscious and, 110–112
"Psychoanalysis and Moral Values" (Hartmann), 104
Psychoanalytic Movement, The (Hartmann), 27, 104
Psychoanalytic Psychology (Fine), 105
Psychoanalytic Quarterly, 363
Psychoanalytic Study of the Family, The (Flugel), 51, 419

Psychoanalytic Theory: An Exploration of Essentials (Klein), 105
Psychoanalytic utopia, 519–521
Psychodynamics of Family Life, The (Ackerman), 52, 420
Psychoeconomic disorders, 253–254
Psychohistory, 210–211
Psychological factor, 177–178, 183–184, 244–247
Psychological testing, 79
Psychology, 125–126, 351
    anthropology and, 240
    as clinical science, 90–92
    cognitive, 34, 49, 98–100, 108
    conceptual framework of, 34–35, 93, 100, 178–180
    ethics and, 263–264
    experimental, 5, 76–86, 91–94, 169, 170
    growth of, 78–80
    as half-trained profession, 356–358
    history and, 203–204, 212
    as integrative discipline, 115–116
    normal, transition to, 16–18
    psychoanalytic: *see* Psychoanalysis
    psychosocial change vs. psychosocial understanding, 108–109
    sociology and, 215–216
    theory vs. therapy, 92–93
    therapy training and, 106–107
Psychology of Economics, The (Weisskopf), 250
Psychopathology of Everyday, The (Freud), 22
Psychosexual development, 23
Psychosis, 17, 18, 70–71, 112, 133, 160, 193–200, 288, 368
Psychosocial change vs. psychosocial understanding, 108–109
Psychosomatic medicine, development of, 126
Psychotherapy, 5, 6
    analytic: *see* Psychoanalysis
    economic situation and, 254
    emergence as profession, 305–337
    half-trained professions and, 352–360
    love and, 444–489
    as means of social reform, 230–231
    nonanalytic, 76–86, 91–98, 366–382
    philosophy and, 266–270
    program for progress and reform, 511–521
    redefinition of, 343–351, 489
    redefinition of, cultural reaction to, 352–366
    religion as stage in development of, 258–260
    social reform and, 338–351
    vs. sociology, 229–231
    stages of, 305

Psychotic identifications, 56–57
Publication system, 180–181
Puritanism, 391
Putnam, James, 339, 340

Question of Lay Analysis, The (Freud), 29, 341

Rabb, Theodore K., 196
Radin, Paul, 265–266
Rado, Sandor, 224, 310
Rakoff, V. M., 129
Randall, J. H., 261, 270, 440
Rank, Otto, 25, 65, 276, 280, 374
Ranke, L. 172
Rankin, A., 234
Rapaport, D., 71
Rasmussen, K., 225
Rational-emotive therapy, 375–377
Rationalization, reason and, 50
Reality therapy, 379–380
Reason, 33, 49–51
Reciprocity, principle of, 404
Redlich, F. C., 142
Reductionistic system, 110
Referral situation, redefinition of, 346–347
Regin, Deric, 282
Reich, Wilhelm, 44, 102, 106, 377, 419
Reider, N., 122, 307
Reinharz, Shulamit, 182
Release, 47
Religion, 6, 61, 194, 251–252, 256–261, 265, 305–308, 426–428
"Remembering, Repeating and Working Through" (Freud), 24
Rennie, T., 50, 88, 102, 106, 179, 198, 334
Reproducibility of data, 89, 103
Rescue fantasy, 36–37
Resistance, 23, 24, 327
Rest, disturbances in, 41
Ribble, Margaret, 433–434
Ricardo, David, 245
Richman, J., 168
Ricoeur, P., 262, 264
Rie, E. D., 521
Rie, H. E., 521
Riesman, D., 60, 220
Riessman, Frank, 423
Rifkin, Alfred, 158–159
Rights of Infants, The (Ribble), 433–434
Rise of Anthropological Theory, The (Harris), 238
Ritual, 61, 427–428
Road to Serfdom, The (Hayek), 247
Roche de Coppens, Peter, 20, 216, 217
Roger, Daniel, 391
Rogerian therapy, 98
Rogers, Carl, 357, 372–375, 381, 510
Roheim, G., 55, 61–62, 179, 258

"Role of Consciousness in Psychological Theory, The" (Klein), 98
Role theory, 55
Romans, ancient, 388
Romantic ideal, 389–390
Roosens, E., 137
Rose, P. E., 210
Rosen, B., 199
Rosen, G., 70, 159, 194
Rosenhan, D. L., 127, 157, 308
Rosenthal, R. R., 82, 175
Ross, H., 313, 314, 320–321, 353, 354
Rothenberg, A., 281
Rousseau, J.-J., 16, 153, 393
Rubin, Lillian, 421, 425
Rubins, J., 105
Rubinstein, Artur, 283–284
Ruesch, S., 63
Russell, Bertrand, 20, 77, 261, 262
Russell, J. F., 199
Ryle, G., 262

Sabshin, M., 198
Sachs, Hanns, 25, 310, 321
Salimbene, 286
Salmeron, 196
Samuels, Warren J., 242–243
Samuelson, Paul A., 248–249, 251
Sandler, J., 42
Santayana, George, 364
Sapir, E., 286
Sartre, Jean Paul, 269
Saul, L., 197
Saunders, E., 259
Scapegoats, psychotherapy and need for, 364–365
Schafer, R., 47, 168, 318
Schaller, G. B., 38, 406
Scharfstein, B., 265
Schilder, P., 54
Schizophrenia, 63, 121, 124, 132–152, 154–155, 258, 287, 349
Schizophrenic Disorders, The (Bleuler), 149–150
Schizophrenic panic, 45–46
Schneider, D. E., 64
Schneider, R. M., 299
"Schools," myth of, 366–367
Schultz-Hencke, H., 332
Schumpeter, Joseph, 250
Schur, M., 490
Schuster, D. B., 157
Science, 180
Science, psychological, 79–95, 100–117
Scientific Credibility of Freud's Theories, The (Fisher and Greenberg), 91
Scientific Revolution, The (Kuhn), 85
Scott, J. P., 410
Scriver, Michael, 293

Searles, H., 83
Sears, R. R., 76, 167, 170
Self-aggrandizement, 54–55
Self-awareness, 54
Self-criticism, 349
Self-effacement, 54–55
Self-fulfilling prophecy, 293
Self-image, 49, 54–55
Selfishness, 58
Self-love, 57–58
Self-object, 55
Selye, Hans, 435
Senay, E. C., 410
Seneca, Lucius Annaeus, 283
Separation anxiety, 45, 410–411
Separation-individuation, 48
Sexual gratification, 33
Sexual repression, 60
Sexuality, 11, 15, 17, 36–38, 42, 47–49; see also Love
   changed emphasis on, 48
   ego structure and, 49
   ethological data on, 409
   Freud on, 47–48, 387–388, 392, 399, 402
   historical data on, 387–392
   incest taboo, 398–402, 410
   Kinsey studies of, 101–102, 106
   psychoanalysis and, 443–496
   relation to love, 406
   self-image and, 49
Shackle, G. L. S., 246
Shakespeare, William, 280, 282, 389, 390
Shapiro, Roger, 318, 366
Sheehy, Gail, 335, 383
Shorter, Edward, 192, 394–395
Shye, S., 167
Sibling influence, 53
Significant Americans, The (Cuber and Harroff), 414
Silk, Leonard, 251
Silverberg, William, 321
Silverman, I., 82
Silverman, Julian, 195
Simirenko, A., 165
Simkin, J. S., 377, 378
Simmel, G., 226
Simon, B., 266
Simpson, George, 235, 413
Skepticism, 267
Skill vs. bias, 168–170
Skinner, B. F., 80–84, 87, 88, 93, 239, 293, 367, 370, 371
Slavery, 191–192, 209–210
Sleep difficulties, 41
Sleeping Pill, The (Hartmann), 155–156
Slovenko, Ralph, 431
Smith, Adam, 243, 244, 245
Snyder, S. H., 154
Socarides, C., 37, 151, 299, 300

Social class, 53
Social facts, 181-182, 214
Social History of Art, The (Hauser), 282-283
Social Influence Processes, The, 295-297
Social order, 33, 55, 58
Social reform, 28-29, 338-351, 517-519
Social research, 295-301
Social Science and Social Problem Solving (Lindblom and Cohen), 291
Social sciences, 333-335; *see also* Behaviorism; Experimental psychology; Organic psychiatry; Psychoanalysis
    anthropology, 5, 236-240, 395-406
    art, 5, 66, 273-285, 432
    bias, theory, and empiricism, 174
    causation, 291-302
    conceptual framework, 178-180
    cultural context, 164-166
    economics, 5, 241-255
    history: *see* History
    language, 285-290
    lesser certainty of social facts, 181-182
    love and, 386-442
    measurement problem, 175-177
    methodology, 166-168
    philosophy, 6, 261-272, 440-441
    psychological factor, 177-178, 183-184
    publication system, 180-181
    religion, 6, 61, 194, 251-252, 256-261, 265, 305-308, 426-428
    skill vs. bias, 168-170
    social consequences of, 170-171
    sociology: *see* Sociology
    vision vs. technique, 172-174
Social structure, insanity and, 70-71
Social work, 29, 83-84, 125-126, 351, 358-359
Socialization, 43
Society control of training, 320-322, 337
Sociology, 5, 213-236
    class structure (SES), 231-232
    class struggle, psychology of, 233-234
    community, 220-228
    Durkheim on suicide, 234-235
    image of man, 216-220
    love and, 413-433
    love cultures and hate cultures, 38, 224-227, 395-398, 519
    mental health of contemporary world, 227-228
    mental health studies, 228-230
    psychology and, 215-216
    vs. psychotherapy, 229-231
Socrates, 194, 266
Solnit, Albert, 431
Sophists, 266
Sorcerers of Dobu, The (Fortune), 50

Sorrows of Young Werther, The (Goethe), 470
Soviet Union, 418-420
Spengler, Oswald, 186, 205
Sperling, Otto, 430
Spiegel, L., 48
Spiegel, Rose, 289
Spinoza, B., 267
Spiro, M., 225
Sprio, N. E., 61, 142
Spitz, René, 38-39, 52, 288, 434, 435
Spitzer, R., 129, 130, 151
Spock, Benjamin, 335, 383
Springer, James, 390
Srole, Leo, 230
Stalin, Joseph, 188, 190, 200, 201, 307, 506
Stancer, H. C., 129
Steingart, I., 288
Stoicism, 267
Stoller, R., 151
Stone, Leo, 312
Stone, N. M., 299
Strean, H. S., 126, 416, 439, 453
Strindberg, August, 283
"Structural," 35
Structure of Science, The (Nagel), 77, 87
Structure of Scientific Revolutions, The (Kuhn), 166-167
Strupp, H. H., 96
Studies in Hysteria (Freud), 10
Suicide, Durkheim's work on, 234-235
Sullivan, Harry Stack, 26, 54, 120, 122, 123, 136, 138, 139, 145, 147, 161, 258, 332, 490, 504
Sumner, W. G., 221, 223, 507
Superego, 26, 27, 35, 53-55
Surface-statistical interview, 101
Sutton, S., 155
Swift, Dean, 391
Swift, Jonathan, 391
Szondi, L., 44

Talbot, J. A., 128
Tax, Sol, 172
Technique vs. vision, 172-174, 339-343, 383-385
Tedeschi, James, 295, 296
Temerlin, M. K., 410
Terman, L., 275
Tertullian, 306
Theme and Variations (Wolpe), 96
Theoretical courses, 317-319, 336-337
Theory, 92-93, 174
Theory of the Leisure Class, The (Veblen), 246
Thompson, Clara, 321
Thompson, Robert, 282
Thompson, S., 279

Thorndike, E., 293
Three Essays on Sex (Freud), 22, 25, 35*n.*, 109, 111
Thucydides, 187
Tilly, C., 428
Time on the Cross (Fogel and Engerman), 208–210
Tischler, G. L., 157
Tissot, R., 136
Titchener, Edward, 99
Tomasson, R. F., 261
Tönnies, Ferdinand, 220, 221
Topography, 34
Totem and Taboo (Freud), 22, 25, 223, 238, 256, 294–295, 375, 399
Toynbee, Arnold Joseph, 186, 205
Training
  psychiatric, 124–125, 156–158
  psychoanalytic, 7, 310–322, 332, 335–337, 342, 350–366
  social work, 126
Training analysis, 310–317, 332
Transference, 23–24, 52–53, 177, 327, 348, 369–370, 437, 439, 443
Transference love, 37
Treatment, redefinition of, 347–350
Trotter, S., 85
Truax, C. B., 146
Tuchman, Barbara, 203
Tuma, A. H., 147
Turnbull, C. M., 401
Turner, Nat, 209

Unconscious, 22–23, 81, 110–112
Unconscious anxiety, 44–45
Unpalatable findings, 88–89, 103

Values, science and, 94–95
Van Bergen, A., 99
Van der Walls, H. G., 490
Van Gogh, Vincent, 65
Van Lawick-Goodall, Jane, 410
Varieties of Religious Experience, The (James), 257
Veblen, Thorstein, 246
Victorianism, 391–392
Victory, ideology of, 187–204
Vienna Psychoanalytic Society, 22
Violence, 415–416, 428–429, 518
Violence in America (Graham and Gurr), 428
Voltaire, 508
Von Ehrenfels, Christian, 28, 493

Wagner-Jauregg, Julius, 123
Wallerstein, Robert, 319
Walster, E., 296
Ward, Benjamin, 241, 242, 418

Warner, W. L., 228
Warren, J., 85
Washington Psychoanalytic Society, 323
Wealth of Nations, The (Smith), 244
Webb, R. K., 189, 191, 193, 203, 306
Weber, G. H., 171, 172
Weber, Max, 20, 21, 66, 173, 190, 216, 217, 246, 252
Weil, R. J., 55, 142, 225
Weinberg, M. S., 298
Weinshel, E. M., 332–333, 363, 364
Weinstock, Harry, 324
Weintraub, Sidney, 241, 242
Weisskopf, Walter A., 242, 244, 250, 252
Wenar, I., 197
Weygandt, Wilhelm, 122
Whalen, R. E., 412
Wheeler, W. M., 77
Whitehorn, J. C., 145
Who Gets Ahead? (Jencks), 417
Wickler, W., 411
Williams, C. J., 299
Williams, F., 424
Wilson, E. W., 209, 237
Wilson, Edmund, 277
Wilson, G. T., 370, 371
Winnicott, D. W., 53
Winograd, T., 286
Witchcraft, 198–200, 306, 390
Withey, S. B., 101, 106
Wittgenstein, Ludwig Josef Johann, 79, 169, 262
Wolff, Harold, 345
Wolheim, R., 262
Wolpe, Joseph, 96, 367, 371–372
Wolpert, E. A., 49
Women's liberation, 420, 421
Woodhull, Victoria, 11
Woodworth, R. W., 77, 82
Woolf, Virginia, 277
Worcester, Elwood, 268
Work, 33, 66–68, 251–254, 283–284
Work in America, 68, 252
Working-class families, 421–422
World History, A (McNeill), 187–189
Worlds of Pain (Rubin), 421
Wright, Richard, 372
Wulff, M., 122
Wundt, W., 76, 80, 82, 88, 169, 502
Wynne, L. C., 141, 287

Yale studies, 146
YAVIS patients, 329
Young Man Luther (Erikson), 259

"Zeigarnik effect," 99
Zelditch, M., 419
Zinberg, N., 313
Zwerling, I., 136